COLUMBUS

"Columbus' Enterprises" by Peter D. Franklin

Produced in cooperation with
the Columbus Area Chamber of Commerce

Windsor Publications, Inc.
Chatsworth, California

COLUMBUS
The Discovery City

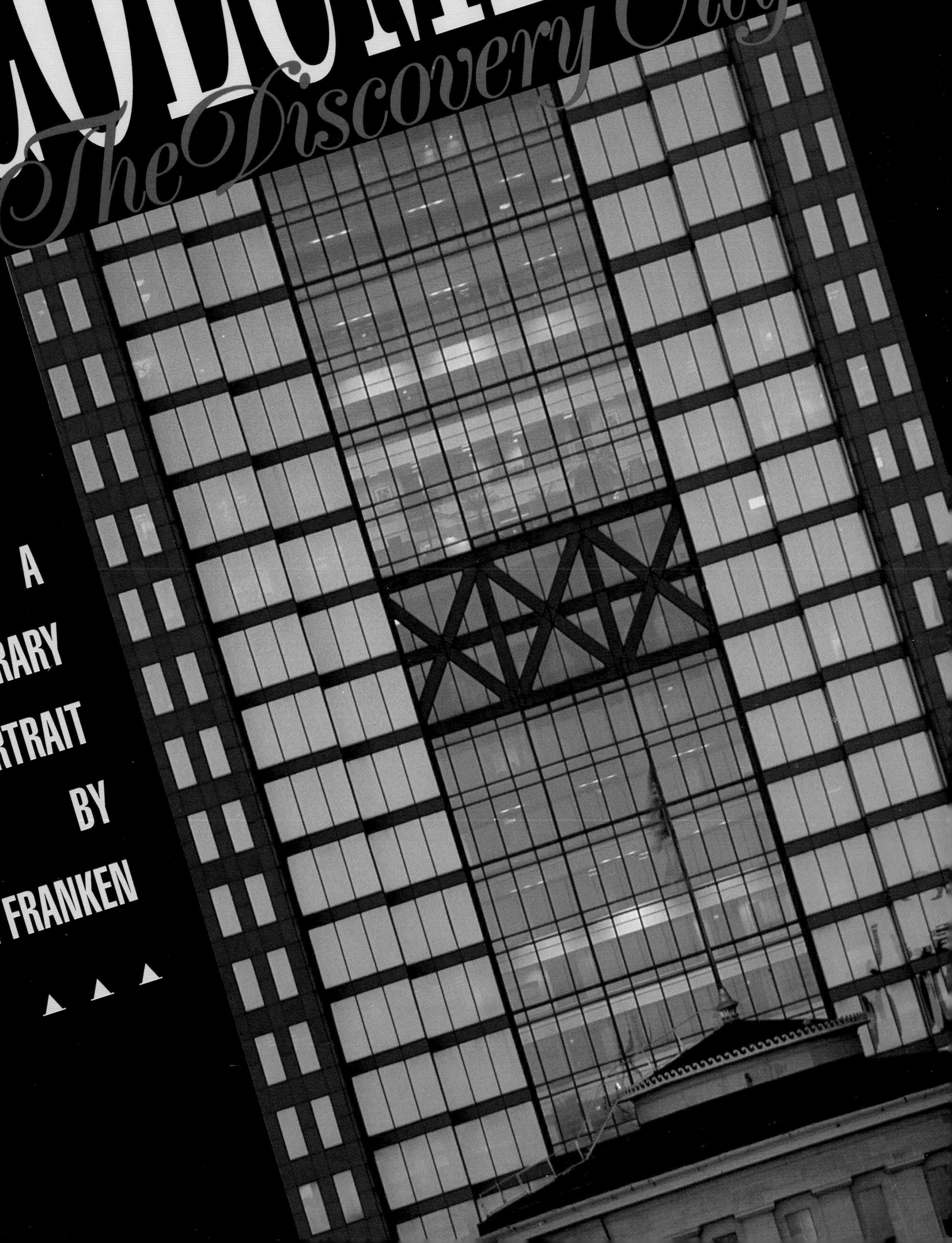

A
CONTEMPORARY
PORTRAIT
BY

HARRY B. FRANKEN

For Mark, Paul,
Greg, Dave, Julie,
and Angela

Windsor Publications, Inc.—Book Division
Managing Editor: **Karen Story**
Design Director: **Alexander D'Anca**
Photo Director: **Susan L. Wells**
Executive Editor: **Pamela Schroeder**

Staff for *Columbus: The Discovery City*
Manuscript Editor: **Douglas P. Lathrop**
Photo Editor: **Robin Sterling**
Copy Editor: **Teri Davis Greenberg**
Senior Editor, Corporate Profiles: **Jeffrey Reeves**
Production Editor, Corporate Profiles: **Justin Scupine**
Editorial Assistants: **Elizabeth Anderson, Alex Arredondo,
Kate Coombs, Lori Erbaugh, Wilma Huckabey**
Proofreader: **Annette Nibblett Arrieta**
Customer Service Manager: **Phyllis Feldman-Schroeder**
Publisher's Representatives, Corporate Profiles: **Merle Gratton,
Kelly Lance, Jennifer Olevitch**
Layout Artist, Corporate Profiles: **Lisa Barrett, Trish Meyer**

Designer: **Christina L. Rosepapa**

Windsor Publications, Inc.
Elliot Martin, Chairman of the Board
James L. Fish III, Chief Operating Officer
Mac Buhler, Vice President/Acquisitions

©1991 Windsor Publications, Inc.
All rights reserved
Published 1991
Printed in the United States of America
First Edition

Library of Congress Cataloging-in-Publication Data
Franken, Harry.
Columbus, the discovery city : a contemporary portrait / by
Harry B. Franken. Columbus enterprises / by Peter D. Franklin.--
1st ed.
p. 504 cm. 23x31
"Produced in cooperation with the Columbus Area Chamber of
Commerce.
Includes bibliographical references and index.
ISBN 0-89781-397-9
1. Columbus (Ohio)--Civilization. 2. Columbus (Ohio)--
Description--Views. 3. Columbus (Ohio)--Economic conditions.
4. Columbus (Ohio)--Industries. I. Franklin, Peter D. Columbus
enterprises. 1991. II. Columbus Area Chamber of Commerce
(Ohio) III. Title.
F499.C75F73 1991
977.1'57--dc20   91-21886
CIP

**THIS PAGE: Sharon Woods Metro Park awakens to a new day.
Photo by Robert E. Schwerzel**

**TITLE PAGE: Aglow with the rays of the setting sun, the glass-
adorned Huntington Center rises 37 stories into the Columbus
sky, towering over Ohio's historic State House in the heart of
downtown Columbus. Photo by Larry Hamill**

**FOLLOWING PAGE: The sparkling lights of Columbus' skyline are re-
flected in the waters of the Scioto River. Photo by William A.
Holmes/Image Finders**

CONTENTS

▲ ▲ ▲

FOREWORD 11

PART 1 ▲ THE DISCOVERY CITY

1 ▲ A LOOK BACK

As five centuries pass since Columbus' discovery of America,
the city bearing the Great Navigator's name looks back on
a history full of triumph and change. 17

2 ▲ THE DISCOVERY CITY

As befits a city named after the discoverer of the New World,
Columbus today is a world center of research,
development, and information. 45

3 ▲ DOING BUSINESS

Well-known as a center of government and of the insurance business,
Columbus also nurtures a diverse and thriving marketplace. 67

4 ▲ CENTER OF LEARNING AND HEALING

Home to one of the world's largest, most diverse state universities,
the city's outstanding educational roster also boasts medical, law,
and business schools. A comprehensive and innovative health care community
ensures the well-being of all Columbus residents. 105

5 ▲ CULTURAL SCENE

Columbus' artistic and cultural opportunities appeal to residents of all tastes,
from connoisseurs of classical music to fans of experimental theater. 141

6 ▲ WINGS AND WHEELS

With rail freight lines, two interstate highways, and four public airports,
Columbus serves as a hub around which the wheels of Ohio commerce turn. 173

7 ▲ THE GOOD LIFE

The multicultural diversity of Columbus' many neighborhoods continues to
enrich the city. Opportunities for sports and recreation appeal to all interests. 207

PART 2 ▲ COLUMBUS' ENTERPRISES

8 ▲ NETWORKS

Columbus' role as a modern, thriving metropolitan center is made possible by its network of energy, communication, and transportation providers. 277

Ohio Bell, 278; Access Energy, 282; American Electric Power/ Columbus Southern Power Company, 284; WSNY/WVKO, 286; Columbus Gas Co., 288; Central Ohio Transit Authority (COTA), 290; American Telephone & Telegraph, 292; WBNS-TV, 294; Business First of Columbus, 296

9 ▲ MANUFACTURING

Producing and distributing goods for individuals and industry, manufacturing firms provide employment for Columbus area residents. 299

Kal Kan Foods Incorporated, 300; Superior Die, Tool & Machine Company, 304; EBCO® Manufacturing Company, 306; Lake Shore Cryotronics, Incorporated, 308; Karlshamns USA Inc., 310; Adria Laboratories, 312; TOMASCO mulciber, Inc., 314; Daifuku U.S.A. Inc., 315; Jeffrey Division, Dresser Industries Incorporated, 316; Rage Corporation, 318; Crane Plastics, 320; Lennox Industries, 321; ARC Industries, Incorporated, 322; Ranco Incorporated, 324; Liebert Corporation, 326; Columbus Col-Weld Corporation, 328; ASC Colamco, 329; Inland Products Incorporated, 330; Columbus Steel Drum Company, 332; Medex, Inc., 334; Technology Alliance of Central Ohio, 336; Betlin Manufacturing, 338; Liqui-Box Corporation, 339; GE Superabrasives, 340; Flxible Corporation, 342; Schuler Incorporated, 344; Electric Power Equipment Company, 345; Toledo Scale, 346; TS Trim Industries Incorporated, 348; Worthington Industries, 349; Honda of America Manufacturing Incorporated, 350; Epro Incorporated, 352; MTM Americas, Incorporated/ Pharmaceutical Intermediates Division, 354; Worthington Foods, 355; Borden, Inc., 356; Akzo Coatings, Incorporated, 358; Photonic Integration Research, Incorporated, 360; Edison Welding Institute, 361; Anheuser-Busch, Incorporated, 362; Combibloc, Inc., 364; Eaton IDT Incorporated, 365

10 ▲ BUSINESS AND FINANCE

Columbus' solid financial base has provided a dynamic environment for the economic growth and opportunity of both individuals and businesses in the community. 367

The Huntington National Bank, 368; Columbus Area Chamber of Commerce, 372; Household Bank, 373; BancOhio National Bank, 374; Online Computer Library Center (OCLC), 376; Grange Insurance Companies, 378; U.S. Check, 379; Battelle Memorial Institute, 380; Society Bank, 382; Nationwide Insurance, 384; Central Benefits Mutual Insurance Company, 388; Industrial Association of Central Ohio, 390; The Midland, 391; Banc One Corporation, 392; Chemical Abstracts Service, 394

11 ▲ Professions

Columbus' professional community brings a wealth of ability and insight to the area. 397

Brubaker/Brandt Incorporated, 398; Myers-NBD Incorporated, 400; Jones, Day, Reavis & Pogue, 401; R.D. Zande & Associates, Limited, 402; Zande Environmental Service, Inc., 403; Burgess & Niple, Limited, 404; Ernst & Young, 406; Emens, Hurd, Kegler & Ritter Co.,L.P.A., 408; Moody/Nolan Ltd.,Incorporated, 410; M-E Engineering, Inc., 411; Squire, Sanders & Dempsey, 412; Porter, Wright, Morris & Arthur, 414; KPMG Peat Marwick, 415; Arthur Andersen, 416

12 ▲ Building Greater Columbus

Developers, contractors, and real estate professionals work to shape the Columbus of tommorrow. 419

Borror Corporation, 420; Turner Construction Company, 424; HER Realtors, 426; Continental Real Estate, 428; King, Thompson/Holzer-Wollam, Realtors, 430; Gioffre Construction Incorporated, 431; Capital Fire Protection Co., 432; The Galbreath Company, 433

13 ▲ Quality of Life

Medical, educational, and recreational facilities draw people to Columbus and contribute to the quality of life of Columbus area residents. 435

The Ohio State University Hospitals, 436; Arthur G. James Cancer Hospital, 438; Riverside Methodist Hospitals, 440; Grant Medical Center, 442; Otterbein College, 444; Capital University, 445; Ohio's Center of Science and Industry (COSI), 446; Saint Anthony Medical Center, 447; Ohio Dominican College, 448; Ohio Wesleyan University, 449; Mount Carmel Health, 450; Children's Hospital, 452; Franklin University, 454; Columbus Zoo, 456; Columbus College of Art and Design, 457; Columbus State Community College, 458; Greater Columbus Convention Center, 460

14 ▲ Marketplace

Columbus' retail establishments, service industries, and accommodations are enjoyed by both residents and visitors. 463

Ricart Ford Incorporated, 464; White Castle System,Incorporated, 466; McGlaughlin Oil Company, 468; Stouffer Dublin Hotel, 470; The Limited Incorporated, 472; Wendy's International, Inc., 473; Executive Office Place, 474; Temporary Corporate Housing, Inc., 476; Kroger Company, 478; Continental Office Furniture & Supply Corporation, 480; Chemlawn Inc., 482; Columbus Marriott North, 484; Mid-American Waste Systems, 485; The Butler Company, 486; Frigidaire Company, 488; Columbus City Center, 489; Big Bear Stores Company, 490; Headquarters Companies, 492; Long's College Book Store, 494; Fiesta Salons Incorporated, 496

Bibliography 499

Index 500

FOREWORD

▲ ▲ ▲

During the past two decades Columbus has opened its doors to the world, never to be closed again. But a funny thing happened while the world was discovering Columbus—we somehow rediscovered ourselves. Our neighbors, once transferred with their companies from Des Moines or Denver, are now also arriving with their household goods from Oslo or Osaka. Our colleagues and coworkers are of many different cultures and colors, and our friends invite us to their homes to celebrate holidays and traditions we did not even know existed 20 or 30 years ago. The arrival of a New World happened over a century and overnight, and we have embraced that New World and the people who have become a part of it.

So, when Central Ohio celebrates the 500th anniversary of the discovery of the New World, we will not only reaffirm what we have become and what we do as a region, but will also celebrate who we are as a people.

As you thumb through the pages of this book, sure—you'll find the traditional verbiage about everything from the Columbus area's humble beginnings to the Central Ohio businesses whose steel and glass reflect the progress of the present day. But in this publication you will also find a tribute to the people of this region who, for some inexplicable reason, have had the courage, spirit, and sometimes just plain old spunk to defy convention and successfully settle a wilderness, establish a capital city, create a new ballet, and discover a breakthrough in aviation, a turning point in technology, or a better way to educate our children.

While the Christopher Columbus Quincentennial Commission and AmeriFlora '92 will virtually be out of business at the end of 1992, the people who have been a part of this massive quincentennial endeavor will leave us with a legacy that our community can celebrate for decades to come.

AmeriFlora '92 has changed the shape of Franklin, Wolfe, and Academy parks with permanent improvements that would have taken decades, if ever, to make possible without the support of government, business, and individual investors.

The beautiful and historic Franklin Park Conservatory is not only more beautiful with its expansion, but has become one of the finest horticultural conservatories in the world. Nearby is a new open-air international amphitheater where our children—and their children—will be able to enjoy the arts and entertainment of the day in a 3,000-seat artscape theater with space for an additional 2,000 fans seated alfresco on blankets.

The former athletic facility at Franklin Park has become a permanent exhibit and social hall for use by neighbors for many years to come. And, a new athletic complex will remain at Nelson Road and Franklin Park South.

The Ohio State University is now home to a $2.5-million biological quarantine facility, which will be used for horticultural research by future graduates of the

institution. The center served as the quarantine site where AmeriFlora's plants and foliage from around the globe were inspected before becoming a part of the AmeriFlora exhibition.

The Christopher Columbus Quincentennial Commission and its many contributing organizations have brought us the *Santa Maria,* a replica of Christopher Columbus' flagship especially crafted for the anniversary observance as a permanent legacy on the Scioto River in downtown Columbus.

Through the generosity of Community Quest, a fund established by the commission through donations by business members of the Columbus Area Chamber of Commerce—and the contributions and support of thousands of individuals, government agencies, and others—hundreds of community arts, education, athletic, and cultural events and projects have been staged or constructed to help us rediscover the excellence of our people, our neighbors, our heritage, our future.

The quincentennial has encouraged our people to muster their best—to band together and present to the world the talent, skills, and products that many of us didn't even know existed in our souls. Whether it is a new opera, a special exhibit at the Columbus Zoo, the completion of the Greater Columbus Convention Center, a special African-American program at the King Center, an original musical to salute Columbus the adventurer, or the dedication of a children's fountain or a renovated neighborhood historic site, it is the spirit of discovery in our people that made it happen.

The quality of our past heritage is what has made us a sturdy, spirited region ready to take on the future. As we welcome the people of the world to our doorstep in 1992, remember, Columbus—it is also you we celebrate.

—The Columbus Area Chamber of Commerce

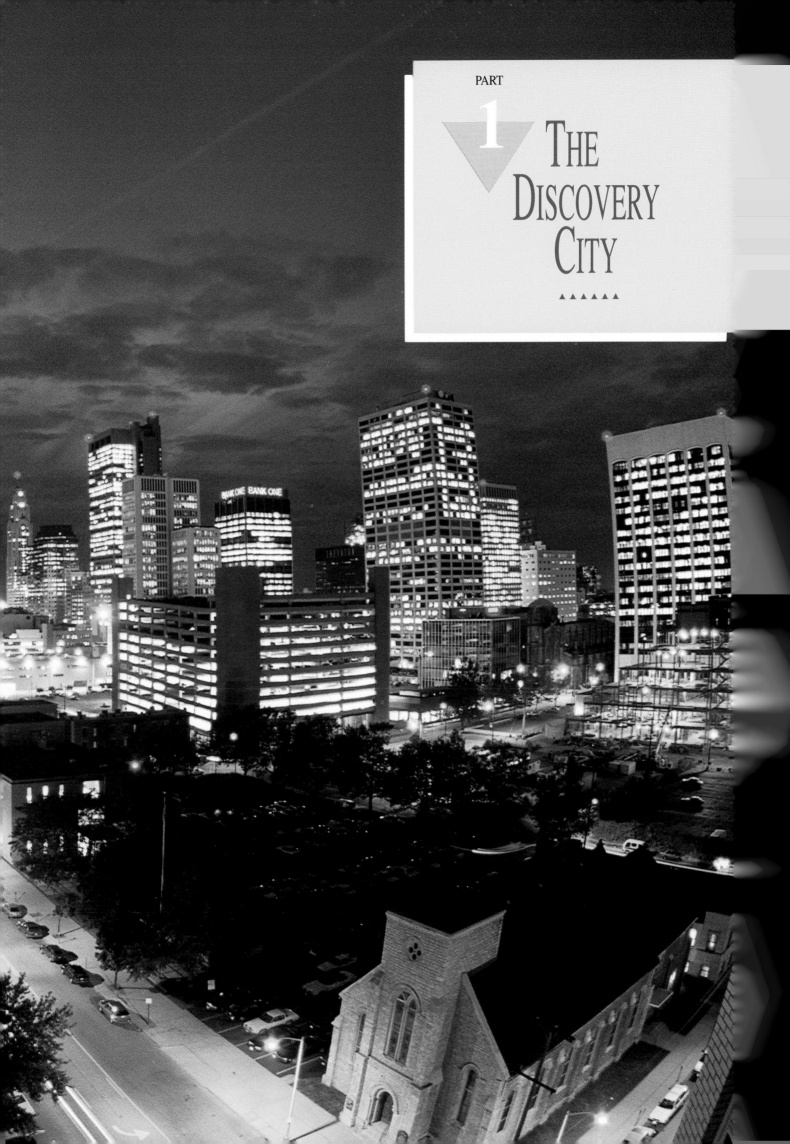

PART

1

THE
DISCOVERY
CITY

▲▲▲▲▲▲

The earliest human inhabitants of the Ohio country were hunters and gatherers who roamed the area from about 6000 until 1000 B.C.

These ancient people were followed by the Mound Builders—the Adena, Hopewell, Fort Ancient, and Cole peoples—who left thousands of earthen mounds throughout what is now Ohio. A burial mound some 40 feet long near Mound and High streets in Columbus gave Mound Street its name. The mound's earth, and the remains it covered, were used to make bricks for the first statehouse in Columbus, while the flat land that remained after the earth removal became the site of the Franklin County Courthouse. The best remaining example of Franklin County's 50 mounds is the Campbell Mound on McKinley Avenue.

The next people to settle the Ohio country were members of the Erie nation, whose presence has been traced back to about 1300. A continuing migration of other tribes, forced out by white settlers in the east and Canada, brought the Shawnees from the Carolinas, the Delawares from Pennsylvania, and the Wyandots from the Great Lakes.

The Iroquois, who defeated the Eries in gaining control of the land, came from New York. They defended the land as long as they could, but the great migration of Indian peoples displaced them. By the time the first whites arrived in Ohio, mostly French and English explorers, they found villages of Wyandots, Shawnees, Miamis, Delawares, and Mingoes.

While some of the Indians were friendly to the whites, most did not relinquish their land easily. They often killed settlers, sometimes kidnapping and adopting their children.

John Brickell, who lived along the Allegheny River two miles from Pittsburgh, was kidnapped by an Indian in 1791 while clearing out a fence row. At the Auglaize River, three months later, an Indian named Whingway Pooshies ("Big Cat") took Brickell into his family. After four years, Brickell was released, and two years later he came to Columbus to live. He died July 20, 1842.

In 1794 Jeremiah Armstrong, his brother, and his sister were taken captive by Wyandot Indians, who earlier had killed their mother and two of their older siblings. The three were taken to Upper Sandusky, where each was

The Indian Mound Builders (1000 B.C.-A.D. 1700) of the eastern United States left countless burial mounds throughout the region, which has helped us to learn about the society and technology of these early dwellers. Thousands of mounds have been found in Ohio, and of the 50 mounds in Franklin County, the Campbell Mound pictured here on McKinley Avenue is the main one remaining today. Courtesy, Ohio Historical Society

adopted by a different family. They did not see each other for about four years. Then Jeremiah and his brother John, with the help of their brother William, gained their freedom at about the same time. Since Jeremiah and John had grown so attached to the Indians, they refused to go with William and had to be taken away by force. Their sister, meanwhile, had spent only a few months with the Indians before being liberated by a man in search of his sister. She went to Detroit and later to Canada.

Leatherlips, a Wyandot Chief, was friendly to the white settlers and remembered as "a peaceable and harmless old Indian." He was executed by members of his own tribe for witchcraft. A pile of stones was placed atop his shallow grave, which is now marked with a monument along the Scioto River Road. A huge limestone sculpture of Leatherlips has been dedicated in the Scioto Park at Dublin. The Dublin Arts Council's first public artwork, it was designed by Boston artist Robert Helmick.

FOUNDERS AND SETTLERS

Lucas Sullivant, a surveyor from Kentucky, brought a surveying crew to the area to locate warrants in the Virginia Military District west of the Scioto River. In 1797 he laid out the town of Franklinton and, to attract settlers, offered free lots on a street he named Gift Street, which still bears that name.

Sullivant was a founding father in every sense. After settling in the area, he married Sarah Starling and fathered three children, became active in government, served as county clerk of courts for many years, and died in 1823 at the age of 58 in the town he founded. He was followed by a number of settlers who built log cabins on the free plots he offered.

Among the area's early settlers were Sarah's sister, Lucy McDowell, and her husband, James. Sarah's brother, Lyne Starling, arrived in 1805 and became a successful merchant and trader. He purchased land on the east (or high) bank of the Scioto,

Early settler Lyne Starling was instrumental in lobbying the state legislature to locate Ohio's new state capital on the east side of the Scioto River. The seat of government was established at this new town site of Columbus in February 1812. Courtesy, Ohio Historical Society

where Columbus was eventually established. Starling was six feet, six inches tall, had red hair, and "an aristocratic manner," according to the historians of the day.

Among the other early arrivals were Dr. Lincoln Goodale and Dr. James Hoge. Goodale was a physician who later donated the land for Goodale Park to the community. Hoge was a Presbyterian minister who operated free schools at his home, lobbied for public education, and became a respected member of the community. Hoge Memorial Presbyterian Church on West Broad Street is named in his honor.

A Tradition of Service

▲▲▲▲▲▲▲▲

Though Columbus is seldom thought of as a military city, the nation's armed forces have long had a presence in the Ohio capital, ranging from makeshift camps hastily erected during the Spanish-American War to one of the world's largest military supply bases.

Columbus' history as a federal military installation seems to start in earnest with the Civil War. Among the early bases was Camp Jackson, located on the site of what is today Goodale Park.

Camp Jackson seems to have been a wartime-only facility, because there are no accounts of it after the Civil War. In fact, some of Camp Jackson's barracks were taken down in 1861 and relocated to the site of a new installation, Camp Chase, which was being built four miles west of the city, near what is now Sullivant and Hague avenues.

Camp Chase quickly became a Confederate prisoner of war camp. On 100 acres lived 8,000 Southern soldiers at the camp's peak in 1863, wrote William H. Knauss in his 1906 book, *The Story of Camp Chase*. Though Knauss was one of the camp's commanders, he acknowledged that conditions were not pleasant.

In fact, more than one-fourth of the 8,000 prisoners never left. The graves of 2,260 Confederates remain at Camp Chase today. They are still cared for by the Daughters of the Confederacy.

Two years after Camp Chase was established, another base was being planned northeast of the city. Land for what was to become Fort Hayes (named after President Rutherford B. Hayes) was purchased from the family of Robert and Jeanette Neal for $16,000 on February 17, 1863. The site, near what is now Cleveland Avenue and I-670, was half a mile from the city limits at the time.

The new fort originally was established as an arsenal, but it eventually became a recruit depot—a function it served through two world wars. By 1905 it had become known as the Columbus Barracks Recruit Depot. In 1922 it was named headquarters for the Fifth Corps Military. That same year it was offically named Fort Hayes.

After World War II Fort Hayes faced an uncertain future. It remained a recruit induction center through the Vietnam era, but by the mid 1960s Army officials made it clear they had no long-range plans for the 70-acre base, which by then was in the heart of a deteriorating part of the city. The Columbus Board of Education purchased most of the land in 1971 and turned it into the Fort Hayes Career Center, a vocational education facility.

The nation's next conflict, the Spanish-American War, saw yet another camp formed in Columbus, though of a much less permanent nature. The call to arms in 1898 led to the formation of Camp Bushnell on April 27 of that year on 500 acres east of Columbus in what is now the heart of Bexley. In a matter of weeks it was teeming with 10,000 men who were assembled to head south. By May 20 the last regiment had departed and the camp was disbanded, but not before it had provided weekend diversions for thousands of families who packed up picnic baskets and took trolleys to see the boys off.

Just as the Spanish-American War spawned Camp Bushnell, it was the World War II which led to the birth of Lockbourne Air Force Base, near Groveport, southeast of Columbus.

The base, now an Air National Guard Base and industrial park, got its start as a glider school on June 15, 1942, according to a base history. Shortly afterward it became a B-17 instructor training base, and by the end of the war it had trained 3,808 combat pilots and 2,956 instructors.

Lockbourne was deactivated in 1949, but was returned to active status during the Korean conflict. In the 1950s it became a Strategic Air Command base and home of the 301st Bombardment Wing, which later became a refueling wing. On May 18, 1974, it was renamed Rickenbacker Air Force Base after World War I flying ace and Columbus native Captain Eddie Rickenbacker.

But even the base's association with one of the nation's most famous war heroes could not save it from budget cuts. In September 1979 the 301st was moved and the base lost its SAC status. Air Force functions ceased shortly after and it was deactivated in 1980. The base is still home to several Air National Guard units, several of which served in Operation Desert Storm. Today, the military's presence consists primarily of the Defense Construction Supply Center, part of the Defense Logistics Agency.

DCSC, which has had no fewer than a dozen other monikers since it was started in 1918, is one of the largest military supply bases in the world. It buys $1 billion of supplies a year and warehouses and supplies parts for vehicles, weapons systems, tanks, ships, construction material, and material handling equipment.

The center, at 3990 East Broad Street, was established as the Columbus Quartermaster Reserve Depot to help route material overseas during World War I. Between the world wars activity slowed, but World War II saw employment grow to more than 10,000 civilians on 575 acres.

More than 5,000 people work at the one-square-mile reservation today. Besides acting as a supply center, it also houses the Defense Logistics Agency's Information Processing Center and is headquarters for the 83rd Army Reserve Command of Ohio.

—Christopher A. Amatos

The Great Navigator Immortalized

▲▲▲▲▲▲▲▲▲▲▲▲▲

No one knows how Christopher Columbus looked, how tall he was, how much he weighed, on which side (if either) he parted his hair, or any of his mannerisms.

While it is unlikely that he ever sat for a portrait, we do have the description of him written by his son, Ferdinand. He described his father as a well-built man of more than medium stature, "long visaged with cheeks somewhat high, but neither fat nor thin." He was described as having red hair that had turned white by the time he was 30 (long before he set sail for the New World). Others said he had a light complexion and a trace of freckles.

In spite of this meager description, there are literally hundreds of portraits and heroic statues of Columbus depicting him at the time of his voyages, as a small child, and as an old man. Three of the statues occupy places of honor in the largest city named for Columbus.

The oldest stands in a plaza on the southwest quadrant of the statehouse yard. Another stands on the south side of City Hall. The third is on the campus of Columbus State Community College, a 40-foot portrayal of the admiral holding a scroll in his right hand and pointing with his left hand toward the buildings of downtown Columbus.

The statue on the statehouse grounds was a gift of the Pontifical College Josephinum. It shows Columbus holding a glove in his left hand, standing next to another glove on which is perched a bird with its wings spread, presumably the land bird that landed on Columbus' ship, an indication that land was nearby. The statue was commissioned by the founder of the Josephinum, Monsignor Joseph Jessing, and was carried through the streets of Columbus in the Columbus Day Parade of 1892. At that time the Josephinum was located at Eighteenth and Main streets.

It was believed for many years that the sculptors were the Pelzer Brothers, who worked for Mullins, but recent research has led historians to believe that the sculptress of the statue was Mary Lawrence, a student of Augustus Saint-Gaudens, the renowned Irish-born American sculptor. The statue, of the beaten copper type, was done by the W.H. Mullins Company of Salem, Ohio.

When the Josephinum moved from the east side of Columbus to its present location in Worthington, Oreste Paul Gallo, an Italian-born tailor who had come to Columbus in 1908, arranged for the statue to be made a gift to the state.

The statue once again took to the streets, and on Columbus Day in 1932, it was unveiled on the statehouse grounds by Governor George White.

Monsignor Gerald Durst, archivist at the Josephinum, says at least four of the Columbus statues were made by Mullins. One was displayed at Chicago's World Columbian Exposition in 1893.

Vandals and thieves have victimized the statue on the statehouse grounds over the years. The bird on the present statue is not the original, and missing are a pair of calipers that Columbus held in his right hand and a dagger that hung from his waist.

The 16-foot statue in front of City Hall was a gift to the city from the schoolchildren and people of Genoa, who collected $20,000 for the bronze work by sculptor Edoardo Alfieri. The statue crossed the Atlantic on the Italian liner *Cristoforo Colombo*. Passengers included the sculptor and Genoa's deputy mayor, Giuseppe de Andre.

The unveiling occurred on Columbus Day in 1955. The principal speaker was Harold Stassen, then special assistant to President Dwight D. Eisenhower. More than 200,000 people crowded the sidewalks and street on West Broad Street as Metropolitan Opera singer Salvatore

Baccaloni led the singing of "The Star Spangled Banner."

Governor Frank Lausche, U.S. Senator John Bricker, U. S. Representative John Vorys, and Mayor M.E. Sensenbrenner pulled the rope that lifted the linen cover that had been placed over the statue. (The linen was loaned by O.P. Gallo, who took it back to his tailor shop and incorporated it into a number of shirts.)

Mayor Gianeario Piambino of Genoa visited the statue in 1973.

The newest arrival is the huge statue at Columbus State Community College. Sculptor Alfred Solani used nearly three tons of Carrara marble to fashion the statue of Columbus on the deck of the *Santa Maria* pointing toward whatever might lie beyond the horizon. The statue is a gift of the citizens of Barrington, Illinois, where it arrived in 1959. An Italian immigrant named DeTomasi gave it to his adopted city of Barrington, having it shipped to Columbus from Milan.

The impressive statue was somewhat the worse for wear when it reached Columbus on April 4, 1986. As a matter of fact, it lacked the forefinger that Columbus used to point the way. So it was taken to a Columbus Recreation and Parks Department warehouse for cleaning and repairs while city fathers wondered about a final home for it. There was consideration given to having it put at the Port Columbus International Airport on the median of the road to the main terminal, and there were thoughts of putting Christopher Columbus near water again, somewhere along the Scioto River downtown.

The ideal location turned out to be the rapidly growing campus of Columbus State, where the statue is admired daily by young students on their way to and from classes.

Columbus is also at the location of the old Aquinas High School and just a few feet from the location of the first Catholic cemetery in the city. Some people have compared this statue with the one in the colonial section of Santo Domingo in the Dominican Republic.

Christopher Columbus has been called one of the great American trinity— Columbus, the discoverer; Washington, the founder; and Lincoln, the savior. He has also been called a metaphor for the spirit of adventure and discovery.

When Columbus astronaut Donn Eisele flew on *Apollo 7,* much was made of the fact that the mission was in orbit on Columbus Day and that Eisele, an expert in navigation, was following in the way of the great navigator.

Columbus has been used in countless newspaper cartoons to depict the people of the city. But perhaps the most unusual Columbus was on the Chamber of Commerce float in the 1955 Columbus Day Parade. An actor had been hired to ride the float, dressed as Columbus. It is said that too much preholiday celebrating caused him to cancel out. Bob Zimmer of the chamber staff agreed to fill in, but some concessions he refused. And perhaps for the first time anywhere, any time, Christopher Columbus appeared with a mustache!

—H.B.F.

CAPITAL CITY

By the time Ohio became a state in 1803, log and wood structures, as well as some brick homes, stood in Franklinton. While most of these original buildings have disappeared, it is believed that a house in what is now referred to as "the bottoms" may have been the headquarters of General William Henry Harrison during the War of 1812.

While temporary capitals of the new state were established in both Zanesville and Chillicothe, in 1800 the legislature decided that Ohio should have a permanent capital near the geographic center of the state. Several settled locations, including Franklinton and Worthington, were candidates for the designation. Franklinton was bypassed as the state capital because its location on the lower side of the river subjected it to frequent flooding.

Lyne Starling, James Johnston, Alexander McLaughlin, and John Kerr formed a proprietorship and successfully lobbied the legislature to locate the new capital on the high ground on the east side of the Scioto River, just across from Franklinton. General Joseph Foos, who operated a ferry across the Scioto and became a member of the legislature, is credited with suggesting the name Columbus for the proposed settlement, though historians give little reason for naming the town in honor of Christopher Columbus.

The proprietorship of Starling, Johnston, McLaughlin, and Kerr, which had successfully lobbied the legislature to establish the capital in Columbus, proposed to lay out the new town, to donate 10 acres to the state for a public square with a state capitol, and to provide an additional 10 acres for a penitentiary. The four proprietors agreed to spend some $50,000 on the new town and to have the penitentiary completed by January 1815 and the state capitol and offices by December 1817. If

This sweeping bird's-eye view of Columbus depicts the thriving city as it appeared in 1872. Note the state capitol (center) and the meandering Scioto River on the left. Courtesy, Ohio Historical Society

The two-story United States Courthouse in Columbus was established in the early part of the nineteenth century to help serve the legal needs of the state. Pictured here after the advent of electricity, this courthouse interior shows the fine skill and craft that went into the construction of this landmark structure. Courtesy, Ohio Historical Society

the buildings were appraised at less than $50,000, the proprietors would make up the deficiency. If they were appraised at more than $50,000, the legislature would "remunerate us in such way as they may think just and equitable."

Though the legislature sought to establish a permanent capital, because of some objection to the Columbus location, the agreement called for the capital to remain there only until 1840, at which time the location might be reconsidered.

The law establishing the seat of state government at Columbus was passed the same day that war broke out between the United States and Britain. Franklinton soon became headquarters for the northwestern army, and 1,000 to 3,000 troops at a time would occupy that town for short periods.

Columbus' streets were laid out to cross at right angles, with the main north-south street (actually 12 degrees west of north) to be named High Street, which was to be 100 feet wide. The main east-west street, Broad Street, was 120 feet wide. The public square would be the 10 acres at the southeast intersection of Broad and High, with Third Street as its eastern border and State Street as its southern border. All other streets in the city were to be 82 feet six inches wide and the alleys were to be 33 feet wide.

The sale of lots began June 18, 1812. Prices ranged from $200 to $1,000, with one-fifth of the price to be paid at the time of the sale and the remainder to be paid in four equal annual installments.

By 1815 there were stores, taverns, a post office, a market house, and about 700 people in Columbus. A school was started in a log cabin on the public square. On February 10, 1816, the town was incorporated as the "Borough of Columbus."

The Ohio State House was built at the southwest corner of the public square, a square-roofed, brick building 75 feet long, 50 feet deep, and two stories high. It had cornices at both sides and ends and a steeple in the center with a "first-rate, well-toned bell." The top of the spire was 106 feet above the ground. Representatives Hall was on the first floor and the Senate Chamber was on the second. The state offices were in a separate, two-story, brick building just north of the statehouse. Just north of this was the United States Courthouse, another two-story brick building.

The statehouse was completed in 1815, and the following year Governor Thomas Worthington invited a number of women to a social sewing party to put together the first carpet for the building.

The legislature met in the old statehouse for 35 years before the building was destroyed by fire on February 1, 1852. The blaze was discovered in the center of the Senate Chamber when the alarm was given at about 4 a.m. on a Sunday. The *Ohio State Journal* reported: "The belfry, after burning brilliantly for a few minutes, came down with a crash upon the floor of the Senate Chamber. The roof then gradually fell in and the upper story of the building was a mass of flames."

Construction of a new statehouse at the center of the public square had started with the laying of a cornerstone on July 4, 1839. The law authorizing the building's construction had been passed January 26, 1838, and candles were arranged in the windows of the National Hotel to spell "NEW STATE HOUSE." (The site of the National Hotel was later the Neil House hotel and now the Huntington Center.)

By the end of the construction season in 1839, the building had been completed up to ground level. It was expected that work would be resumed the following spring. But politics interfered.

During the 1839-1840 session of the legislature there had been an investigation of William B. Lloyd, a member from Cuyahoga County. He had been censured for forgery in altering certain accounts and papers. A friend of Lloyd's had drawn up a statement of confidence in the legislator, which was signed by 63 persons, mainly young men of Columbus. Without their knowledge, it was printed in the *Ohio State Journal*. Members of the legislature were incensed, and the representative from Licking County introduced a bill repealing the act authorizing the new statehouse. It was passed and became law March 10, 1840.

Noting that $41,585.22 had already been spent on the new structure, William Martin said, "This amount of the public money, a majority of the savants were willing to throw to the wind, in order to gratify a spirit of personal resentment towards a few citizens of Columbus."

The legislature then took under consideration moving the state capital from Columbus to a permanent location. It was suggested that "all portions of the state have an opportunity of offering such inducements as they may deem proper for its permanent location at such point as may be designated." The resolution was passed by the senate on March 6, 1843, by a vote of 18-16. It was defeated the following day in the House of Representatives by a vote of 36-29.

The bill authorizing completion of the new statehouse was passed in the session of 1847-1848. The building was not completed until 1856, however, and the legislature met briefly in it on January 5, 1857. A great public festival was held to dedicate the building on January 7, 1857.

More than 20,000 tickets were issued to the dedication ball, which was to be opened with a speech by Governor Salmon P. Chase. The speech was never delivered because it took the governor an hour and a half to make his way through the crowd to get in. Tickets were sold at $5 each to local men, while ladies and out-of-towners were admitted free. Because all the city's hotels were full, many people stayed and danced all night.

The statehouse was built in the Doric style, with eight stone columns on the east and west sides and four each on the north and south sides. The gray limestone build-

LEFT: Ohio Governor Salmon P. Chase (1808-1873) was on hand for the dedication of the new State House in January 1857. Educated at Cincinnati and Dartmouth colleges, Chase was an active political leader, serving as secretary of the treasury in President Lincoln's cabinet during the Civil War and as chief justice of the United States during the Reconstruction years. Courtesy, Ohio Historical Society

ing measures 304 feet long and 184 feet wide. The measurement from the rotunda floor to the dome, with its stained-glass seal of the state, is 136 feet. The dome is truncated rather than round. This has led to speculation through the years that the dome was not rounded because there were no funds.

The building, which was constructed at a total cost of $1.35 million, is one of the largest and most impressive state capitols in the country. While it once towered over surrounding structures, now towering skyscrapers surround it. The statehouse remains, however, the impressive center of the city and may still be considered, as authorities considered it at the time, "the greatest state capitol building in the United States."

CIVIL WAR

On September 16, 1859, Abraham Lincoln delivered a major address from the east side of the Ohio State House. (A plaque now marks the point where he stood.) The nation would soon be divided by a bitter war, and Columbus would be a center of Union Army activities and the location of a major camp for Confederate prisoners of war.

Governor Chase would depart to serve as Lincoln's Secretary of Treasury and be succeeded by Governor William Dennison, Jr., by the time of the Civil War.

The other Ohioan in the President's cabinet was Secretary of War Edwin Stanton, a former reporter of the Supreme Court of Ohio. Ohio generals in the Union Army included William T. Sherman, James A. Garfield, Rutherford B. Hayes, Philip P. Sheridan, and Ulysses S. Grant. Mother Ohio now embraces them all in a statue called "These Are My Jewels" on the northwest portion of the statehouse grounds.

The general assembly had been asked by the Ohio militia in 1859 to appropriate funds for a military organization, and volunteers began to pour into the city after the declaration of insurrection on April 15, 1861.

Goodale Park, used to bivouac the soldiers before they could be outfitted, was re-named Camp Jackson. It became the gathering place for all troops north of Hamilton County and south of the Western Reserve.

Columbus was a center of Union Army activity during the Civil War. Pictured here around that time is the Camp Chase prison facility on the west side of town, where Confederate prisoners of war were held after being captured by the Union forces. Courtesy, Ohio Historical Society

Construction started on an arsenal north of the city. The arsenal included a tall shot tower, from which molten iron, dropped from the top of the structure, would solidify into round shot by the time it reached the ground. This military installation was later designated Fort Hayes and remained an Army installation until after World War II.

Confederate General John Hunt Morgan led 2,500 troops on a cavalry raid into Ohio in the spring of 1863. Most of his force was captured in Columbiana County and taken to the Camp Chase prison camp on the west side. Morgan and some of his officers, however, were put in the Ohio Penitentiary on West Spring Street. After only two months in the "escape proof" prison, Morgan and his men, digging with tablespoons, managed to escape. They were eventually recaptured.

At times there were as many as 3,500 Confederate prisoners at Camp Chase, many of whom died and are buried there. At the end of the nineteenth century the Daughters of the Confederacy erected a stone monument among the 2,260 grave markers. It is topped by the statue of a Confederate soldier and the word "Americans."

Franklin County lost more than 500 men in the War Between the States, and many of them are buried in Greenlawn Cemetery.

Abraham Lincoln made his final visit to Columbus on May 4, 1865, when the train carrying his body from Washington, D.C., to Illinois stopped at Union Station. The body was placed on a long horse-drawn hearse and taken to the statehouse, which was draped in solemn black. Thousands passed through the rotunda to pay their last respects to the fallen President. In a service that began at 3 p.m., the Reverend B.F. Foster read from the Scriptures and the Reverend F.C. Holliday delivered the funeral address. A choir, accompanied by a band, sang "Before Jehovah's Awful Throne."

Abraham Lincoln's funeral train stopped in Columbus en route from Washington, D.C., to Illinois on May 4, 1865. The body was taken to the State House on a long horse-drawn hearse, where thousands came to pay their last respects to the late president. Notice that the columns and windows of the State House were draped in black for the occasion. Courtesy, Ohio Historical Society

Making History Come Alive

▲▲▲▲▲▲▲▲▲▲▲▲

Seen from the freeway, the Ohio Historical Society appears as little more than a funny-looking building next to a quaint old-time village.

But the view from Interstate 71 is but a glimpse of what the society is, what it stands for, and what it has to offer.

The Ohio Historical Society was formed in 1895, when a group of Ohio citizens realized there was no central organization to preserve the state's artifacts. The realization hit them when a group of British scientists acquired some prehistoric remains found in the state, said Maggie Sanese, the society's communications director. The group wanted to make sure that Ohio's history remained in Ohio.

To that end, the society enlisted the Ohio General Assembly's help and now receives about three-fourths of its financial support from the state. In return, the society maintains the state archives, which include records from all state agencies. Records dating to 1789 concerning land sales, canal, railroad, and road construction, vital statistics, census data, military service, minutes of board and commission meetings, and the state's constitutions are among those.

The society's headquarters are located at 1982 Velma Avenue, adjacent to the state fairgrounds in a building constructed in 1970. *Architectural Record* described the pedestal-shaped building as "no doubt the most architecturally significant public structure built in Ohio since the State Capitol of 1841."

Inside the structure, exhibits tracing Ohio history from prehistoric times through today make up the lower level. Upstairs are the society's archives and research center, which contain more than 130,000 books and pamphlets, 3,000 newspapers, 6,000 separate manuscript collections, one million audiovisual materials, and 20,000 cubic feet of state and local government historical records.

The center's reading room is available to the public and the archives can be used by serious historians. One historian who made use of the archives was film maker Ken Burns, who did some research for his award-winning documentary, "The Civil War," in Columbus.

Behind the society's headquarters is

tains almost 60 other historical sites throughout Ohio, ranging from the Neil Armstrong Air & Space Museum in Wapakoneta to forts used in the French and Indian War to a glacial bog that is home to rare wildlife.

The society also operates the Ohio Historic Preservation Office, which it formed in 1967 to identify historic places and archaeological sites, nominate properties to the National Register of Historic Places, review rehabilitation work on income-producing National Register sites for federal investment tax credits, and consult on the preservation of buildings. The office is funded in part by the U.S. Department of the Interior.

Ohio ranks second in the country in the number of sites listed on the National Register of Historic Places. Ohio's preservation program receives one of the largest federal grants awarded to the states because of the program's strength.

Among the society's publications are two magazines, *Ohio History,* a scholarly historical journal, and *Timeline,* a bimonthly magazine that goes out to the society's 10,000 members.

Throughout the year the society conducts workshops, seminars, lectures, tours, and special presentations at its many sites. Topics range from murder mysteries to scholarly speakers on anthropology. The functions are just part of the society's efforts to make history come alive. As Sanese said, "We have an overriding purpose to preserve and interpret Ohio history."

—Christopher A. Amatos

Ohio Village, a reconstructed mid-nineteenth-century town. The village depicts life as it was in the mid-1800s and includes a schoolhouse, blacksmith shop, hotel, town hall, general store, Masonic Lodge, and the Colonel Crawford Inn, a restaurant that serves traditional meals of the period. Throughout the year the society hosts special events in the village to highlight a period of time. One of the more popular is during Christmas, when the village stays open in the evenings, shops are decorated, and carolers in period dress stroll the boardwalks.

Beyond the Columbus headquarters and the Ohio Village, the society main-

The intersection of Broad and High streets shows the diverse assortment of businesses in operation in 1867, just a few years after the close of the Civil War. The Young Men's Christian Association, Griswold's Photograph Rooms, and an early American Express office shown here are but some of Columbus' thriving concerns of the time. Courtesy, Ohio Historical Society

BUILDING THE CITY

By the time of the Civil War, nearly a third of the city's residents were German and lived just south of the downtown area. There was also a large Irish population, centered mostly on the north side of the city. The South Side was marked by Schiller Park and the brewery district along South Front Street. Around St. Patrick's Church to the north, Naghten Street was called "Irish Broadway."

To promote the establishment of agricultural colleges, Abraham Lincoln had sponsored the Morrill Act to grant each state in the union 30,000 acres for each senator and representative it had in Congress. The result in Columbus was the opening on September 17, 1873, of the Ohio Agriculture and Mechanical College in a building on Neil Avenue north of the city. It is now The Ohio State University.

The city grew, and the advent of the horse-drawn streetcar after the Civil War meant that people no longer had to live within walking distance of where they worked. This led to the separation of industrial and residential areas into neighborhoods. After 1893 the streetcars would be powered with electricity.

The Spanish-American War in 1898 lasted only three months. Again Columbus volunteers flocked to the colors, although most did not see action. Camp Bushnell, east of town, was established as a mobilization center. The suburb of Bexley is now at that location.

Notable local births in this period included Eddie Rickenbacker in 1889 and James Thurber in 1894.

Also of note at the close of the nineteenth century was the incarceration in the

ABOVE: Now known as The Ohio State University, the Ohio Agriculture and Mechanical College opened on September 17, 1893, to meet the exciting challenge of Columbus' growing educational needs. Courtesy, Ohio Historical Society

LEFT: The S. Lazarus' Sons & Company store in Columbus was a thriving turn-of-the-century business. Courtesy, Ohio Historical Society

FACING PAGE: Still standing on West Broad Street today, the landmark Wyandotte Building was constructed in 1897 in the Chicago style of architectural design. Its 11 floors once towered over the Columbus skyline, as seen here in this turn-of-the-century photograph. Courtesy, Ohio Historical Society

Electric lights came to the unique arches of Columbus' High Street in 1905, and the city prided itself as the "Arch City" from that time until the lights were removed in 1914. Courtesy, Ohio Historical Society

Ohio Penitentiary on April 25, 1898, of an alcoholic bookkeeper named William Sydney Porter, who had been sentenced to serve five years for embezzlement from a Texas bank. Some of his writings were smuggled out by a friendly guard and were published under the pseudonym O. Henry.

The Wyandotte Building, an 11-story "skyscraper" in the Chicago style of architecture, was built in 1897. It now houses The Ohio Hospital Association on West Broad Street and is dwarfed by more recent buildings.

As the twentieth century began Columbus was linked to surrounding communities by interurban cars, and the automobile began to appear on city streets. Sixteen owners of horseless carriages formed the Columbus Automobile Club in 1908. Two years later gasoline-powered racers were hitting 60 miles an hour at the Columbus Driving Park.

Memorial Hall (now the Center of Science and Industry) opened on East Broad Street in 1908, and citizens flocked there to hear the likes of opera star Enrico Caruso and orator William Jennings Bryan.

Arches that had been erected over High Street in the downtown area in 1888 were illuminated with gaslights. These were replaced with bright electric lights in 1905, and from then until 1914 Columbus called itself the "Arch City."

It was the golden era of amusement parks for the city, with Olentangy, Minerva, and Indianola parks locally and Buckeye Lake for those who preferred to travel farther away.

The Ohio Constitution was amended in 1912 and among the most important changes was one allowing cities to adopt home rule. Columbus was the second city in the state, after Cleveland, to adopt home rule. In 1913 a commission was chosen to write a city charter.

TROUBLED TIMES

The year 1913 brought a disastrous flood that wiped out much of what had been Franklinton. Power and water were cut off to the west side for weeks. Four bridges across the Scioto River were destroyed, and parts of the Bottoms between downtown and the Hilltop district were under from three to 22 feet of water. Damage was estimated at $6 million.

The war that would be called the World War and the War to End All Wars started in Europe in 1914, and the United States became a participant in 1917. With much public sentiment against the local German community, its members were urged to be "100 percent American." There was a move to get rid of German place names, and stores began to sell sauerkraut as "victory cabbage" and schmeercase as cottage cheese.

How ironic that the flying "ace of aces" of World War I was Captain Eddie Rickenbacker, the son of a Swiss-German family. He shot down 26 German airplanes during the war and was given a hero's welcome when he returned home in 1919.

On the home front, Columbus industry worked overtime to meet war production quotas. The citizens at home did without many so-called necessities to support the boys in the trenches.

Columbus-born Elsie Janis was the first woman entertainer allowed to go to Europe and entertain the troops "at the very threshold of danger."

There was more celebrating when the troops came back from "Over There" following the armistice in 1918. There were also more fresh graves in Greenlawn and the city's other cemeteries. The men are remembered by the doughboy statue in front of the statehouse and another at the Ohio Historical Society Museum on Seventeenth Avenue.

Prohibition came after the war. This led to bathtub gin, home brew, and speakeasies. Women got the right to vote in 1920, but the Roaring Twenties are best remembered as the jazz age and the age of the flapper. In Columbus there was Valley Dale on Sunbury Road for dancing, and Hennicks across from The Ohio State University campus was a favorite hangout.

Born in Columbus on October 8, 1890, Edward Vernon Rickenbacker (right) became the most decorated United States flying ace of World War I. Upon his reentry into civilian life, Rickenbacker pursued a career in the automobile industry. He later returned to aviation in the 1930s, joined Eastern Airlines in 1935, and eventually became company president and later chairman of the board. Rickenbacker is seen here in the full glory of his World War I career. Courtesy, Ohio Historical Society

Patriotic fervor swept
through the city of Columbus
when the United States
joined in World War I in
1917. These proud Ohio soldiers posed for their group
portrait while training for
the battle overseas.
Courtesy, Ohio Historical
Society

Columbus was a bustling city
of growth and prosperity in
this view along High Street in
the 1920s. Courtesy, Ohio
Historical Society

The busy intersection of Broad and High streets belies the fact that this photograph was taken during the harsh years of the Great Depression. Courtesy, Ohio Historical Society

The people got around to building levees to prevent a recurrence of the 1913 flood, and the results were the new Columbus Civic Center, City Hall on Marconi Boulevard, and Central High School across the river.

Though the economy crashed in 1929, Columbus was not as badly hit by the Great Depression as other locations because of the diversity of the local economy.

The American Insurance Union Citadel was completed at Broad and Front streets in 1926 and, partly because of the Depression, was the tallest building in the city and virtually the only skyscraper until the construction of the State Office Tower on East Broad Street in 1974. Many consider it the grand building of downtown Columbus. Now called the LeVeque Tower, its upper floors are bathed in a mantle of bright lights at night.

Nevertheless the Depression was felt deeply by the city, with men selling apples on street corners and itinerants going door-to-door, offering to do odd jobs in exchange for a meal.

Citizens arising early in the morning could move the dials of their radios and pick up, by short wave, speeches made in German by a man named Adolf Hitler. His threat was made most evident to the citizens of Central Ohio when he refused to acknowledge Jesse Owens of The Ohio State University after his victories in the 1936 Olympics in Berlin.

Public buildings that went up at the time were likely to be WPA projects, and many homes had NRA signs (blue eagles) in their windows, showing their support of the New Deal and National Recovery Act.

Real recovery was not to come until World War II. Citizens who are old enough still remember where they were when they heard the news of a place called Pearl Harbor.

Columbus industry and people went to work to win the war. Fort Hayes, the installation dating back to the Civil War, became a reception center for newly inducted troops. The Columbus General Depot (now the Columbus Defense Construction Supply Center), which had opened during World War I, was a major supply center.

Curtiss-Wright built a major factory at Port Columbus to produce warplanes for the Navy. The Port Columbus Naval Air Station was opened on the opposite side of the field to provide pilots with the capability to ferry planes to their wartime destinations. "Rosie the riveter" worked on the assembly lines.

Lockbourne Army Air Base, later Rickenbacker Air Force Base and now Rickenbacker Air National Guard Base, was built south of the city. It was first used to train glider pilots and then converted to the training of B-17 crews.

Once again a local warrior would become a major hero of the war. Curtis Emerson LeMay was born in Columbus, graduated from South High School, and commissioned into the Army Air Corps from The Ohio State University ROTC. He would develop the strategic bombing that brought victory in Europe and the Pacific and after the war would become commander of the Strategic Air Command and Chief of Staff of the Air Force. At the time of his retirement, he had served longer as a general than any other person in uniform.

A MODERN CITY

During World War II Columbus came of age as a modern city. It had large industry and would play a great part in government, education, a growing insurance industry, and the development of high technology.

M.E. "Jack" Sensenbrenner, who was elected mayor in 1953, is credited by many with the slogan, "Come to Columbus and Discover America." Residents were aware that their city was well named. It is the Discovery City.

Fort Hayes served as the reception center for newly inducted troops during World War II. Pictured here in 1942, this facility dated back to the Civil War. Courtesy, Ohio Historical Society

Amusement Parks—The Golden Era

▲▲▲▲▲▲▲▲▲▲▲

The turn of the century has been called the golden era of amusement parks. It is estimated that there were 2,000 such parks in the country, few of which survived beyond 1950.

The growth of the parks has been attributed to electric streetcars and interurbans. The owners of these transportation companies encouraged the parks, and even invested in them, to provide riders on weekends and off-peak hours.

Two of the Columbus parks—Olentangy and Minerva—were built by the Columbus Street Railway Company, which later evolved into the Columbus Railway Power and Light Company and then into the Columbus and Southern Ohio Electric Company and Columbus Southern Power Company.

Indianola Park, near The Ohio State University campus on Indianola Avenue, was not as large as these, consisting mainly of a dance pavilion and a swimming pool. The park has evolved into a small shopping area.

Robert M. Turner opened Olentangy Villa in 1893, a restaurant and picnic grounds that also offered boating and swimming in the Olentangy River. He sold out to the Columbus Street Railway Company in 1896, and on June 12 of that year the park opened, stressing the natural beauty of the area, with hiking trails, seats along the river, double swings for adults, and swings and playgrounds for children. An Olde Mill still operated along the river. The park was at the north end of the High Street car line and across from the streetcar barns. The tracks entered the park through a "castellated gate."

The park was sold in 1899 to brothers Joseph and Will Dusenbury, who formed the Olentangy Park Company. They built the huge Olentangy Park Theatre, which seated 2,248 patrons—1200 on the main floor, 600 in the balcony, 400 in the gallery, and 48 in eight boxes. They advertised that "all the leading vaudeville artists as well as comic opera and minstrel stars, will appear upon this stage, an entire change of program being given each week." Since downtown theaters had no air conditioning, the park theater drew huge crowds in the summer.

The park zoo opened in 1903 with buffalo, camels, elk, deer, lions, leopards, bear, wild hogs, wildcats, foxes, fowl, "and a large variety of other rare and interesting specimens of wild animals, together with the finest taxidermist collection of birds to be found in the country."

A Japanese Garden and Tea House were brought to the park from the St. Louis Exposition in 1905. Two years later the transition was speeded from a nature park to an amusement park.

A steel dance pavilion, built in 1909, featured a huge mirrored rotating ball above the dance floor. During the moonlight waltz, the regular lights were turned out and spotlights of various colors were turned on the ball, causing moving reflections throughout the hall.

The beginning of the thrill rides came in 1909 with such things as the Circle Ride, Chute the Shoots, Loop-the-Loop, Whirlwind, Temple of Mirth, Love's Voyage, and a twisting, winding roller coaster called the Red Devil.

Between 1910 and 1920 as many as 40,000 persons a day paid admission to the park. In the later part of that decade, a huge swimming pool was added. It had a waterfall at the deep end and a beach of white sand and seashells. (Sunbathers were warned to wash off the sand before entering the pool.)

The Joy Mill, one of the later additions, blew air jets from the floor to raise the skirts of blushing ladies and had a huge polished wooden wheel in the floor. Patrons would sit on the wheel (as near the entrance as possible) and see how long they could keep from being thrown off as the wheel spun faster and faster.

The *Columbus Dispatch* had its annual picnic at the park and also sponsored popular "Nickel Days." Special outings were also sponsored by such groups as the Grocers Association and the North Side Business Association.

The Dusenbury Brothers had run into financial problems in 1923, and the park went into receivership and was sold to another pair of brothers, Leo and Elmer Haenlein. They leased the park to Max Stearn's Parkview Amusement Company in 1929.

The end came in 1938, when it was announced the park would not open for the season. It was sold to L.L. LeVeque's Olentangy Village Housing Corporation, which developed the 400-unit residential housing project known as Olentangy Village.

Minerva Amusement Park had a much shorter life than Olentangy Park. It was opened in 1895 along the line operated by the Columbus Railway Company from Columbus to Westerville. The park was named for Minerva Shepard, the wife of the first president of the railway system. It was in a wooded hollow nine and a half miles north of the city and had 150 acres surrounding a large lake. The Railway Company built bowling alleys, a merry-go-round, baseball diamonds, target range, tennis courts, monkey and bear cages, deer pens, and boating facilities for the lake.

The main attraction at Minerva was a magnificent casino that seated 2,500. The Rosenthal Stock Company, a large dramatic troupe, appeared at the park through the summer. Light opera, vaudeville shows, band concerts, and a variety of dramatic productions made the park a major Central Ohio resort during the summer.

Although the park was served by the "Green Line" of the streetcar company, and the round-trip from Columbus was 15 cents, it was difficult to reach by any other means. The inadequacy of transportation

and the competition from Olentangy Park caused its closing in 1902. It remained inactive until the development of the present-day village of Minerva Park began in 1926. The beautiful lake remains one of the village's major attractions.

Much longer lived was the park at Buckeye Lake. The lake, a half-hour's drive east of Columbus, remains a favorite summer place for people from Columbus. Many have cottages along the banks of the lake or on its islands. Others go for the swimming, fishing, boating, and waterskiing in the summer and for ice fishing, skating, sledding, and even motorcycle races on the ice in the winter.

Best remembered are the two ballrooms—the Crystal and the Pier. Generally there was a set admission price for the Crystal, which overlooked the huge swimming pool at the lake, and patrons were charged a "dime a dance" at the Pier.

The best known bands of the Big Band era played at Buckeye Lake, and often the performances were broadcast nationally on radio. The park had the usual thrill rides and also had one of the nation's first miniature golf courses, right across from the Crystal Ballroom. There was lodging for those who wanted to spend a week or a weekend. A huge structure, called Leppert's Lodge, rented small apartments at one end of the park, and at the other end, just past the Gypsy fortune teller's tent, was the Lake Breeze Hotel with the popular Hideaway Bar in the basement.

A little further along that stretch of beach was the Buckeye Lake Yacht Club, still the social center of the lake.

It would be hard to date the death of the amusement park. One night, as the roller coaster car neared the top of the first hill, a cog broke and the car slid backwards down the stretch of track it should have been climbing before its first steep plunge toward the waters of

the lake. It never ran again, and sometime later part of the structure rotted and collapsed into the small lake that was connected to the main lake.

The different attractions went the same way—used until they wore out, never repaired, and eventually bulldozed away. Soon all that was left of the Pier Ballroom were the pilings on which the pier had been built. The same happened to a nearby pier, the one that held the shooting gallery and a little stand where a grandmotherly lady fixed the best fish sandwiches imaginable.

The interurban train first took people from Columbus to Buckeye Lake. Later they could take the Greyhound bus out Route 40 to Hebron and then change to a local bus that ran down to the lake from Newark. The lake maintained its popularity with the boom in automobile ownership following World War II.

It was once said that anyone running for elective office in Columbus or Franklin County wasn't really serious unless there were campaign signs posted around Buckeye Lake.

Since the disappearance of the park, any attempts to rebuild it have been opposed by the residents of the area. Some say the parks have been killed by changing interests and the coming of television. They also point out that not every community can have a huge theme park such as Disney World or Kings Island.

But the amusement park does live in Central Ohio. When Olentangy Park closed, some of its rides and amusements were moved to the Zoo Park, operated for many years by the late Floyd Gooding.

The park has been revived in the Wyandot Lake Amusement and Water Park, next to the Columbus Zoo. Its giant waterslides and man-made waves carry on a spirit of fun that is nearly a century old.

—H.B.F.

2 ▼ THE DISCOVERY CITY

▲▲▲▲▲▲
45

Columbus has earned the sobriquet of "Discovery City" by being the home of major institutions developing the technology that will take the nation and the world into the twenty-first century.

The nation's first gas station opened in Columbus on June 1, 1912. The horseless carriage entered, had its tank filled with gasoline, and drove out the other side. Prior to this innovative "service station," owners of cars had to purchase their fuel in cans and other containers and pour their own.

Among Columbus' other firsts was the first banana split, concocted by Letty Lally at Foeller's Drug Store for a customer who wanted "something different."

Today Central Ohio is home to some 150 technology and research companies, and nearly $150 million a year is spent for sponsored research at The Ohio State University alone. Other local leaders in research include the Battelle Memorial Institute, the world's largest private research facility, Chemical Abstracts Service, CompuServe, the Online Computer Library Center, Inc., and the Honda of America Transportation Research Center.

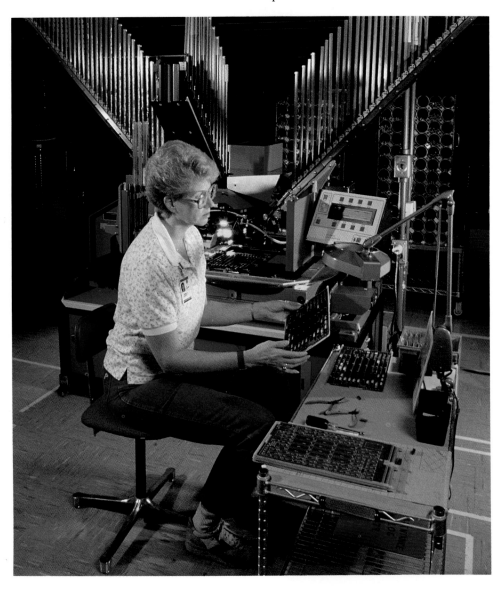

Columbus is part of a tri-city corridor (along with Dayton and Cincinnati) believed to have more research and development professionals than anywhere in the world.

AT&T opened its Bell Laboratories in Columbus in 1959. It is one of six major Bell Lab locations in the country and about 80 percent of its research and development is for software and related applications. In addition, the technology for the 800-number services for nationwide toll-free calling was developed in Columbus.

Other local developments include ComCare, software packages to provide information to doctors' offices, clinics, pharmacies, and hospitals; and AT&T Conversant 1 Voice System, a system to help turn a caller's voice into a computer keyboard.

Columbus has also become one of the world centers for the development of software. Goal Systems International and Information Dimensions market their products throughout the world

FACING PAGE: AT&T's Bell Laboratories in Columbus has developed programmed insertion of microchips and other components for telecommunications equipment. Photo by Larry Hamill/AT&T Network Systems

Columbus plays an important role in the development and management of information technology products. Photo by Jim Baron/Image Finders

and also offer training and consulting services. Data center management and information technology products of Goal Systems have been installed at more than 10,000 sites around the world, mostly for users of IBM computers. Though based in Columbus, Goal has 20 sales offices throughout the world. Information Dimensions sells a text-information management system called BASISplus, used by the publishing, financial, insurance, chemical, and pharmaceutical industries and by government offices.

In addition to these firms dealing entirely in software development, many local firms have thousands of workers developing programs for their own use. These include AT&T's Bell Laboratories and the OnLine Computer Library Center, a nonprofit computer library service and research organization that links nearly 10,000 libraries around the world by computer.

More than 1,000 computer programmers work for the Defense Logistics Agency, which develops systems used by the military for a diverse number of things, including the purchase of food for nine million military personnel.

"PUTTING TECHNOLOGY TO WORK"

Millions of people throughout the world are touched every day by some of the products resulting from the research of Battelle. The golfer gets fewer gouges in his golf ball because of the urethane coating developed at Battelle. U.S. quarters, dimes, and half dollars are made of a sandwich-like combination of copper and nickel alloys developed at Battelle for the United States Treasury Department. If you make a purchase at the supermarket, it is most likely rung up on the cash register by the Universal Product Code lines, which Battelle helped develop. Typewriter correction fluid, too, is a product of Battelle, developed there in 1955.

The technology giant, whose motto is "Putting Technology to Work," was established through the will of Gordon Battelle, an Ohio industrialist.

In his will, Gordon Battelle directed that Battelle Memorial Institute be for the encouragement of creative research and the making of discoveries and inventions.

LEFT: Battelle headquarters in Columbus serves nearly 2,000 industrial and government clients throughout some 30 countries. A Battelle scientist is pictured here conducting a metallurgic test at one of the institute's high-tech facilities. Photo by Larry Hamill

FACING PAGE: Battelle electronics experts are working on leading edge fiber-optic devices for industry-wide applications. Courtesy, Battelle

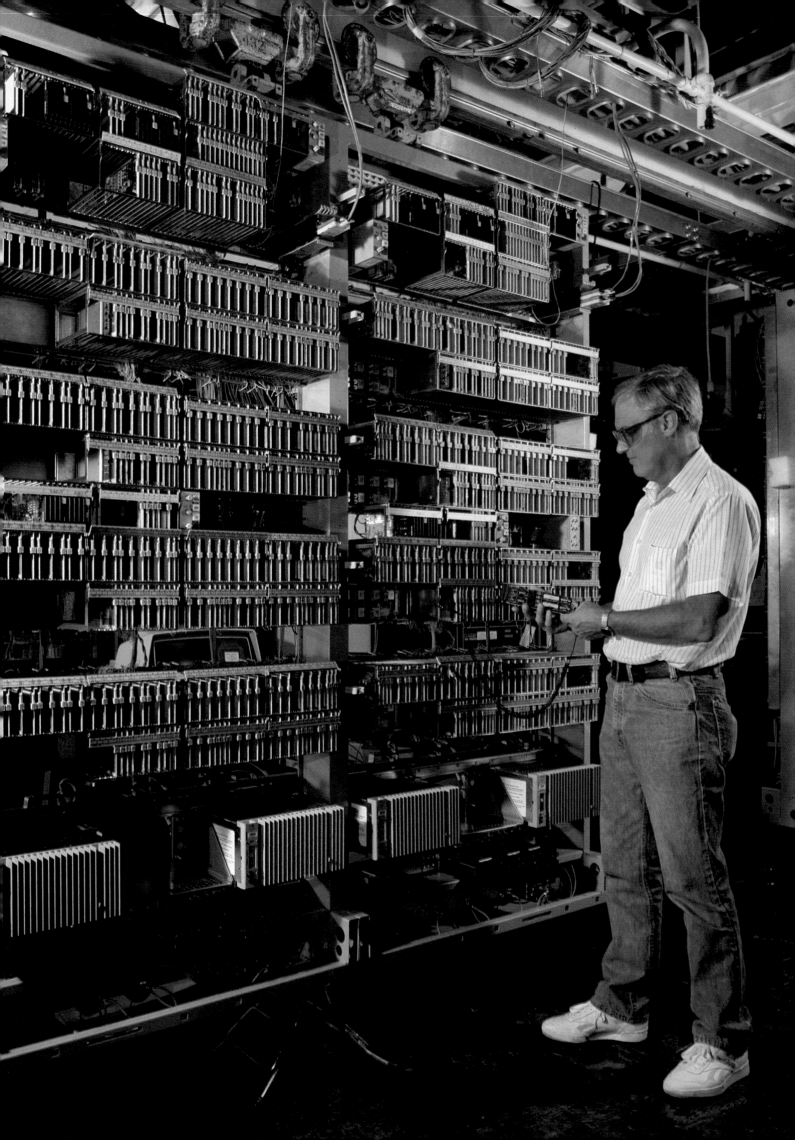

The institute's first board of trustees purchased 10 acres along King Avenue just south of The Ohio State University. The building housing the first laboratory was opened for use in October 1929.

The trustees chose Dr. Horace W. Gillette, known as the "Dean of American Metallurgy," as the institute's first director. The first sponsored project at Battelle was the preparation of a number of volumes, known as *The Alloys of Iron Research* monograph series.

Although Battelle started at the beginning of the Great Depression, it grew in size and research and development expenditures every year. During the 1930s Gillette asked to be relieved of his administrative duties, and Clyde E. Williams was named director. Williams' goal was diversity, so the staff was expanded to include chemists, physicists, engineers, and economists.

Battelle developed capabilities in nuclear technology and became involved in the World War II Manhattan Project, in which it studied the fabrication of uranium. At one time more than 400 Battelle scientists were engaged in nuclear technology, and in the early 1950s the company built the first privately owned nuclear technology center in the world at nearby West Jefferson. (Also in the early 1950s Battelle founded major technology centers at Frankfurt, Germany, and Geneva, Switzerland.)

Clyde Williams retired in 1957 and Dr. B.D. Thomas became president of Battelle. This was about the time that the Soviet Union launched *Sputnik,* the first man-made satellite, and Battelle found itself in the space age and the space race.

In 1965, with the stroke of a pen, Battelle's staff grew by 1,959 when the U.S. Atomic Energy Commission selected it to operate the former Hanford Laboratory in Richland, Washington (now known as Battelle's Pacific Northwest Laboratories).

Also in this period, Battelle began the management and operation of the William E. Clapp Laboratories in Duxbury, Massachusetts, a world-renowned center for marine research. Battelle had established a Florida Marine Research Facility near Dayton several years earlier.

The 1960s were also years of expansion during which Battelle built its Seattle Research Center on 18 wooded acres near the University of Washington.

Chester Carlson, who held the original patent on xerography, approached Battelle in 1944 for help in advancing the invention. More than 20 companies had declined to help develop and market the invention before Carlson took it to Battelle.

In December 1946 Battelle signed the first of a series of agreements with the Haloid Company for commercialization of the xerography process.

Haloid later became the Xerox Corporation, and in the early 1960s Battelle sold its patents on xerography to Xerox in exchange for equity in the corporation. By skillful management of this stock and other holdings, Battelle had an investment portfolio valued at $225 million in the early 1970s. (This dollar figure was partially offset by an interpretation in the courts of Gordon Battelle's will that required Battelle to distribute $80 million to charitable endeavors.)

Dr. Sherwood Fawcett was president of Battelle from the late 1960s to 1984—a period of considerable diversification in Battelle research. He was succeeded as president in 1984 by Dr. Ronald S. Paul. He, in turn, was succeeded by the present president, Dr. Douglas E. Olesen, who came from the Pacific Northwest Laboratories to serve as executive vice president and chief operating officer during Paul's tenure.

The Columbus headquarters of Battelle today serves nearly 2,000 industrial and

FACING PAGE: Just one of many revolutionary high-technology firms located in the Columbus area that have made a significant impact in the field of communications, AT&T of Central Ohio developed the technology for the nationwide 800-number, toll-free calling service. Here, circuit verification at AT&T's Bell Laboratories ensures built-in quality. Photo by Larry Hamill/AT&T Network Systems

government clients in some 30 countries. It is a leader in advanced materials, defense systems and technology, design and manufacturing engineering, electronic systems, health and environment, information systems, manufacturing systems, energy systems, and technical services.

On a typical day recently, Battelle technologists were working on the problems of factory automation. Tests were being run on improved shock absorbency in sports shoes and the development of inflatable front and rear foot soles to meet wearer needs. In addition, an ultrasonic inspection system was developed to detect flaws in glass bottles. Means were being sought to inspect the nation's 300,000 miles of high-pressure natural gas pipelines.

In the military field there were studies of enhanced fighter maneuverability, automatic mission planning for the U.S. Air Force in Europe, the battery system of F-16 aircraft, and a next-generation armored wheeled vehicle with a combat weight of more than 30 tons. Furthermore, a computer-controlled robot that simulates breathing, skin temperature, and sweating was being used to test protective clothing for the U.S. Army, and large numbers of chemical substances were being screened in the hope of finding drugs to treat senile dementia and Alzheimer's disease. Also, a technique was being perfected to produce cell-cultured skin in the laboratory to use as skin grafts for burn victims, and a study was under way to use microorganisms to

RIGHT: The Arthur G. James Cancer Hospital and Research Institute is one of the country's four medical institutions that specialize exclusively in cancer treatment and research. The hospital features a 160-bed capacity and is able to handle 100,000 outpatient visits a year. Courtesy, The Ohio State University

FACING PAGE TOP: One of the fastest and most powerful computers in the world can be found at The Ohio State University in Columbus. The Cray Y-MP8/864 is operated out of the school's supercomputer center, linking some 20 Ohio colleges and universities and providing leading edge research facilities. Courtesy, The Ohio State University

remove pollutants from deep, subsurface aquifers, a major source of fresh water in the United States.

During 1990 Battelle made charitable distributions of more than $1.3 million to a wide range of organizations and programs dedicated to educational activities and community services.

The main purpose of Battelle continues to be the development, commercialization, and management of technology.

As Battelle president Douglas Olesen said recently, "We firmly believe that our most important innovations are still before us because the demand for new technology will continue at an increasing rate. Our rewards come from seeing innovations improve the quality of life as they are applied in the marketplace."

FOUNDATION FOR RESEARCH

In addition to Battelle's numerous technological projects, the list of research projects at The Ohio State University is lengthy as well.

The Byrd Polar Research Center at Ohio State is world renowned for studies conducted in the polar regions. For instance, studies of Antarctic microfossils show that ice has covered the continent and receded many times in the past 38 million years, contrary to the belief that Antarctica has always been covered with ice. Scientists report that every few million years the glaciers have receded and seaways have stretched across Antarctica, mountain chains have emerged, and migration routes have opened for animals and plants.

The $6.5-million Cray X-MP/24 supercomputer, funded by the Ohio General Assembly, is operated from the Ohio Supercomputer Center of the university and links 20 Ohio colleges and universities. It gives researchers on all the campuses an unsurpassed tool for research and is running at full capacity.

The Columbus Project is a cooperative effort with the University of Arizona and a consortium of Italian universities to design and build the world's largest and most powerful optical telescope. The Italian astronomical community is represented by the Arcetri Observatory in Florence. The telescope will have two eight-meter mirrors side by side, forming an equivalent 11-meter instrument. Plans call for it to be inaugurated in Arizona in 1992, the 500th anniversary of Columbus' discovery of the New World.

Research in the College of Veterinary Medicine has produced a vaccine against feline leukemia. A number of other veterinary projects has also led to advances in human medicine.

The Arthur G. James Cancer Hospital and Research Institute was opened recently on campus with the declaration that "The Ohio State University is determined to find a cure for cancer." As the university has stated:

These new resources will help the 500 physicians, biologists, and pharmacologists—scientists from eleven disciplines in all—who draw on the resources of The Ohio State University as well as University Hospitals, to seek new answers, test new drugs, perfect new therapies, and then share what they learn with all the world, advancing hope for millions.

The idea for the hospital and research institute was first put forth by Dr. Arthur G. James in the late 1940s. He was president of the American Cancer Society in 1972-1973 and is professor emeritus of surgical oncology at Ohio State.

The hospital has 160 patient beds and the capability of handling 100,000 outpatient visits a year. The top two floors contain research laboratories and are the focal point of 177 cancer research projects being conducted in 10 colleges.

Most research spending at the university is through the Ohio State University Research Foundation, but other programs are funded through the Engineering Experiment Station, the Ohio Agricultural Research and Development Center, and the Children's Hospital Research Foundation.

Research at Ohio State is linked with graduate studies, and Jack M. Hollander is vice president for research and graduate studies. Graduate courses were first available at Ohio State in 1878, and the first Ph.D. degree was awarded in 1894 to Lucy Adelaid Booth, in history.

Dr. Hollander has stated:

The university's unique role is to educate students to be intellectually adaptable, to meet the changing future confidently and capably. At Ohio State this role remains our foundation, and research remains integral to it. The more we excel in our research, the richer will be the educational environment that we offer our students, and the stronger our many services to society.

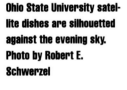

Ohio State University satellite dishes are silhouetted against the evening sky. Photo by Robert E. Schwerzel

Columbus Discoveries

▲▲▲▲▲▲▲▲▲▲▲▲

Although few people know it, just about every man and woman in the United States carries a little bit of Columbus technology in his pocket or purse.

In the 1960s, when the U.S. Treasury was looking for ways to reduce the cost of minting coins, it turned to Battelle Memorial Institute in Columbus, one of the world's largest private research organizations, for a solution. Armed with the government contract, Battelle developed the copper-nickel "sandwich" coin to replace silver quarters, dimes, half-dollars and dollars minted by the government.

The coin technology is just one of many to come out of Battelle—and out of Columbus—that people use everyday, not only in the United States but throughout the world.

Perhaps the most ubiquitous is the process of xerography. Although New York patent attorney Chester Carlson developed the idea and a rough process elsewhere, he came to Battelle in 1944 to move the process toward commercial development. Battelle research showed that the invention could be brought to the market in a workable fashion, research that eventually attracted the attention of the Haloid Corp., a Rochester, N.Y., photo image company. Haloid in 1959 produced the first commercially successful office copier and went on to change its name to Xerox.

Kenneth E. Jackson was a young chemist in Battelle's coatings department in 1952 and was wondering why a report he had submitted for printing was taking so long to complete. Upon investigation he found that Battelle went through an arduous correction process on typed reports because they were ultimately photographed to be printed for mass distribution.

Jackson went back to his lab and in a day's time developed a fluid that typists could use to paint over errors and then type over.

The research giant quickly realized it had a product that not only greatly increased its own efficiency, but was marketable as well. Though Jackson left Battelle the following year, he followed the product's development. Battelle contracted with an office supply distributor to make and market the product, called SnoPake, and a new business was born. "It sold like wildfire," Jackson recalls.

Though Battelle did not do the original research, the Universal Product Code now used by the grocery industry was refined in Columbus by the research lab in the early 1970s, says project manager Rick Thatcher.

Battelle was approached by McKinsey & Co., the management consulting firm, on behalf of the grocery industry to test different product coding systems. The car codes were developed by IBM, but their use on consumer goods was refined by Battelle, according to Thatcher. "At the time there were about 30 codes on the market," he says.

Tests included setting up a prototype grocery checkout line and bringing in employees from Kroger and Big Bear to man the registers, Thatcher said.

Like many modern inventions, the bowling pin spotter was an invention of war. In 1944 Columbus businessman and bowling alley owner Leslie LeVeque had a difficult time finding enough young men to work on his North High Street lanes. He hired Michael O'Leary, an aircraft factory worker with an inventive mind, to study the problem and devise a machine to spot the pins. O'Leary developed the device, whose rights were sold after LeVeque's death to a Buffalo company called American Machine & Foundry, which later changed its name to AMF and became a giant in the recreation industry.

One Columbus invention has saved countless lives among airline and general aviation passengers since the 1970s. In 1977 Paul Ryan, whose navigation devices had earlier helped place a man on the moon, introduced the Ryan Stormscope. By using a computer coupled to delicate receiving equipment, the Stormscope can detect and plot bolts of lighting up to 260 miles away in any direction from an aircraft. Knowing the location of lightning helps pilots stay away from dangerous turbulence. The device was named one of the most significant inventions of the year in 1977 by the scientific community.

One widely held belief, almost impossible to prove today, is that the first drive-in gasoline station was started here at Young and Oak streets. Newspaper stories from the 1930s and 1960s make the claim that a station opened by H.S. Hollingsworth, a Standard Oil employee, opened the station at the corner on June 1, 1912. However, other accounts put the opening as early as 1901. Before the gasoline station was developed the flammable fluid was sold by grocers and hardware stores, according to one account.

Less in dispute is that the first independent auto repair shop and auto dealership was opened in Columbus in 1899 by F.E. Avery at 1199 Franklin Ave. Avery, who had been a bicycle dealer, became a Winton auto dealer and opened a repair facility at the same time. In 1926 Avery took on a new line of cars known as Pontiac and, though it had changed locations, until the 1980s continued to call itself the oldest and first car dealership in the nation. That distinction ended when new owners took control in 1982.

—Christopher A. Amatos

Programmers and systems analysts at Chemical Abstracts Service are responsible for the development of computer software required for its large-scale information processing and retrieval system. Courtesy, Chemical Abstracts Service

"BREVITY COMMENDS ITSELF"

Most citizens of Central Ohio are familiar with Chemical Abstracts Service as the providor of the rolling lawn for the Columbus Symphony Orchestra's "Picnic with the Pops" series. North of The Ohio State University campus, however, stand two large buildings that house a service where more than 1,500 people work to make the world's knowledge of chemistry accessible worldwide to those who need it.

More than 500 document analysts, nomenclature specialists, and supporting personnel read about 10,000 scientific and technical journals and patent documents issued by 27 nations and two international patenting bodies. Their index of more than 10 million substances is accessible through the CAS ONLINE Registry File.

The purpose of the editorial operation is not to add to scientific knowledge, but rather to make new chemical information available to scientists, engineers, students, government officials, and others around the world. The documents searched are printed in such languages as Afrikaans and Vietnamese, in addition to English, Russian, Japanese, German, and French.

The document analysts have degrees from the universities of Paris, Leeds, Edinburgh, and Cairo, the Tokyo Institute of Technology, Bahr Dar Polytechnical Institute of Ethiopia, and the Technical University of Poland. Their work is distributed in published form and also through computers. In addition to the people who write and distribute the abstracts, there is a staff to train and assist users of CAS services.

Chemical Abstracts Service is a nonprofit division of the American Chemical Society. *Chemical Abstracts* was first published January 1, 1907, by the Bureau of Standards

Chemical Abstracts Service project managers use state-of-the-art technology to research and develop new approaches to making chemical information accessible to users around the world. Courtesy, Chemical Abstracts Service

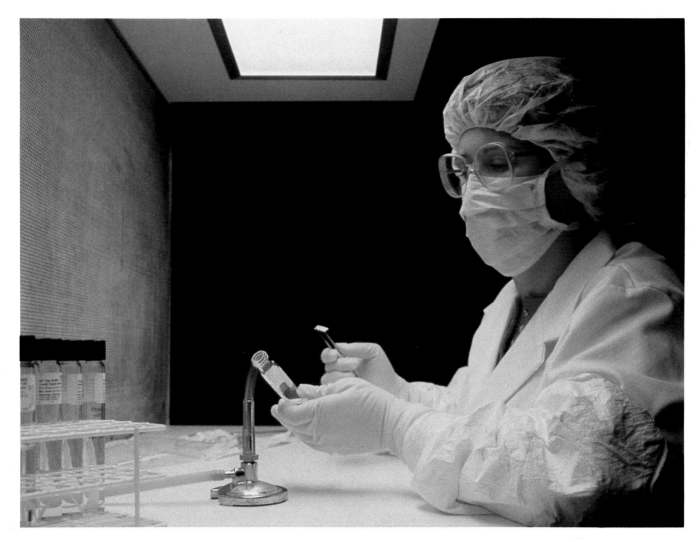

ABOVE: A Medex technician conducts a test in the facility's sterile room. Photo by Jeffrey A. Rycus/Rycus Associates Photography

FACING PAGE: Columbus is home to about 150 technology and research companies. Photo by Jim Baron/Image Finders

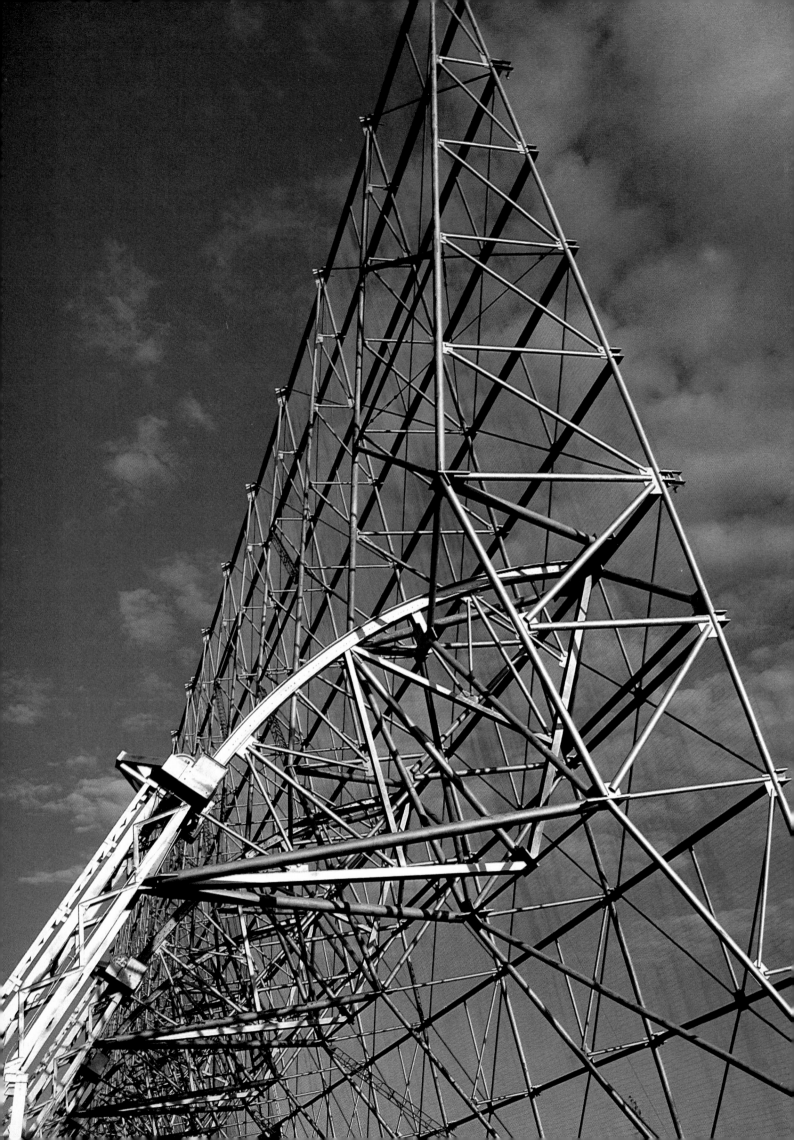

in Washington. The first editor was William A. Noyes, Sr., chief chemist at the bureau. He was succeeded in 1909 by Austin M. Patterson, who, at the invitation of William McPherson, head of the chemistry department, moved the editorial offices to The Ohio State University campus.

Chemical Abstracts grew tremendously under the editorship of Evan J. Crane from 1915 through 1958. Crane had started work at CAS in 1911, at the age of 22, as an associate editor. The mission of the service was to abstract the complete world's literature of chemistry, a task it performed through the two world wars and the Great Depression.

When World War II closed many channels of communication, European publishers sent journals through Italy, whose shores were not then blockaded. When Mussolini took Italy into the war, journals were sent by way of Siberia. When Hitler violated the nonaggression pact with Russia, that venue of distribution was closed. To continue publishing, Chemical Abstracts organized a staff of 75 in Switzerland who typed abstracts in German and French on thin paper and then sent them by clipper plane mail to Columbus.

German scientific material, including patents, was brought to the United States through the Office of Strategic Services. Though Japanese material was inaccessible during the war, postwar efforts resulted in 120 bags of Japanese scientific material arriving in Columbus within a few weeks in 1946.

Judgment on the quality of the papers abstracted has always been left to the readers. Abstracts are printed without critical comment. The abstracts reflect what is printed in the primary literature whether or not it is correct. The purpose is not to report all that it said, but rather to permit access to the original papers.

Editor Evan J. Crane believed abstracts should be concise and frequently passed on this opinion to the staff members in terse verse. One example of his poetic prescription for abstracts follows:

BREVITY COMMENDS ITSELF

In speeches, yes,
In skirts, I guess,
In hair, perhaps,
In office naps,
And now, anew,
In abstracts, too.

CAS soon outgrew the offices in McPherson Chemical Laboratory and occupied an entire building of its own on campus by the 1960s. The physical growth of CAS in Columbus has been from a 15-foot by 30-foot room in 1909 to the two large buildings on Olentangy River Road, where the service is now housed. A company publication tells in a few words the accomplishments of the people who work in those buildings: "They help ensure that information which could spark new research—or prevent the duplication of costly experiments—comes to the hands of the scientist or engineer seeking it, no matter where in the world that scientist lives."

Dale B. Baker became director in 1958 and began exploring computer technology for the processing of chemical information. The automated processing system emerged in the late 1960s and 1970s.

FACING PAGE: This state-of-the-art radio telescope at Ohio Wesleyan transmits and receives radio signals, enabling the continuing study of advanced communications needs. Photo by Dennis Barnes

George Barclay Foster

▲ ▲ ▲ ▲ ▲ ▲ ▲

George Barclay Foster, now president of Foster Technology in Columbus, may be proof that necessity is the mother of invention. He seems to have been at the right place at the right time to solve a number of perplexing problems. For the most part he has solved them and moved on. While there are a limited number of inventions and inventors, there seems to be no limit to problems.

"It just seems that when a company's business passes $4 million a year, it's too big to keep my interest," Foster said recently. "That's when it's time to move on."

Foster founded Foster AirData Systems in 1972. The company has developed RNAV equipment (which has allowed the country's thousands of small airports to electronically access navigation equipment belonging to modern international airports), as well as collision warning systems for aircraft and navigation sensors. Foster says he started the company because he was a pilot and, at the time, "The advent of integrated circuits promised practical applications of computing to many aspects of air navigation, communication and safety systems at moderate cost with increased safety and efficiency."

The company manufactured commercial and military RNAV systems and developed innovative multichannel scanning TACAN for precision position data for civil and military applications. Foster AirData Systems also entered into a contract with the Navy to demonstrate a radical Airborne Collision Warning System.

As Foster put it, "the company's rate of growth outgrew its financial base." In 1989 he sold the company to B.F. Goodrich Co., and it is undergoing major expansion in Columbus operations.

While he operated the company, Foster received the Small Business Innovator Award from President Ronald Reagan at the White House in 1984. That same year the Instrument Society of America awarded him the Albert F. Sperry Award for distinguished achievement in instrumentation in the fields of nuclear radiation, industrial control systems, laser optics, air navigation, and communications systems. In 1985 he won the local Christopher Columbus Award for distinguished service in community economic development.

As a Harvard undergraduate, George Foster studied history. In 1941 he was commissioned in the Navy and spent two years at Underwater Sound Laboratories doing research on antisubmarine warfare. In 1944 Foster was named the navy's military port commander at Brest, France, and two years later he was discharged as a lieutenant commander.

Soon enrolled in the University of Illinois, Foster received a degree in electrical engineering in 1949.

His first job was as a founder and technical director of Columbus' former Accu-Ray Corporation, a company that pioneered the city's "Technology Corridor." It manufactured process control systems based on interaction of nuclear radiations with matter. Foster directed technical operations during the first 10 years of the company, during which it achieved a commanding lead in industrial applications of radioactive emissions. These developments led to major advances in continuous sheet and extrusion manufacturing, resulting in improved quality, productivity, and profitability in the paper, plastics, tobacco, and metallurgical industries.

When Foster left the company, it had $8.5 million in annual revenues, eventually growing to more than 2,000 employees with worldwide operations.

Next, Foster founded Raydata Corporation, which manufactured mechanical malfunction instrumentation with applications to gas turbine compressors, jet engines, reciprocators, and machine tools. The company was sold to Reliance Electric Company five years after its founding, and Foster worked five years for Reliance as Director of Instrument Technology.

Foster next founded Autech Corporation, which made systems utilizing laser-based measurements, and two years later he founded Foster AirData Systems. During the years Foster worked with these companies, he was issued 44 United States and foreign patents.

Since 1986 he has headed Foster Technology Corporation, a consulting business for planning, organization, operations, and finance for various businesses.

He joined Three R Technologies, Inc., in 1990 as treasurer, director, and chief financial officer. The company is in the business of designing and licensing municipal solid waste separation systems for recovery of marketable materials and reduction of waste flow to landfills.

The three R's in the company name stand for "resource, recovery, recycling." The methods of recovery are based on the technology and experimental experience of Walter Roman, an aeronautical engineer who received a master's degree in natural resources from The Ohio State University in 1971. Working for the Ohio Department of Natural Resources, he felt that composted municipal solid waste could be used in reclaiming the state's stripmined land.

George Foster is certainly no laboratory recluse. He lists his hobbies as baroque music, economics, political science, computers, ham radio, flying, history, and French.

He has been a visiting lecturer in the Graduate School of Business and the College of Engineering at The Ohio State University and is on the advisory board of the College of Engineering of Franklin University. Among his many public service activities, Foster lists his work for the Jefferson Academy of Music, in which he promotes excellence in music education.

—H.B.F.

U.S. PATENTS HELD BY GEORGE B. FOSTER

2,884,530 Standardizing Means
2,933,606 Electromagnetic Radiation Device
2,951,161 Cascade Standardization
2,964,631 Measuring System
2,999,935 Convertible Radiation Source
3,013,721 Automatic Control System
3,092,724 Mass Distribution Analysis System
3,100,843 Radiation Dosage Limiter
3,154,685 Measuring System
3,160,745 Measuring System
3,180,136 Transducer
3,187,256 Run-out Monitor
3,219,909 Transducer
3,257,652 Operation Monitor
3,263,163 Inspection System
3,263,167 Inspection System
3,281,665 Inspection System
3,348,234 Operation Monitor
3,353,098 Transducer System
3,379,972 Non-contact Displacement Gauge
3,390,849 Identifying Flying Craft
3,416,040 Frequency Relay
3,447,419 Non-contact Tool Postioner
3,452,273 Non-contact Displacement Gauge
3,451,148 Acceleration Monitor
3,455,149 Vibration Amplitude Monitor
3,486,113 Standardization of Measuring
3,488,543 Sequential Switcher
3,488,581 Surface Instrument Calibrated
3,504,279 Non-contact Dimension
3,632,285 Gas Igniter System
3,858,983 Shaped Product Measurement
3,918,816 Tire Inspection Apparatus
4,037,086 Area Navigational System
4,061,297 Approach Range Monitor
4,069,412 Area Navigational System
4,335,468 Simultaneous Transmission
4,366,578 Transmit/Receive Mode
D 270901 Controls for Navigation
4,413,322 Automatic Waypoint Navigation
RE25353 Radioactive Thickness Gauge

3 ▼ DOING BUSINESS
▲▲▲▲▲▲▲▲▲▲▲▲
67

C olumbus' ever-changing skyline makes the most persuasive graph showing that the city is a good place to do business.

To commuters from the suburbs, it sometimes seems that each week brings a new location in which structural steel is reaching skyward. The billions of dollars in the growth of commercial property is the success story of the city. From the top of one of those impressive new buildings you can see how much undeveloped land remains. That is the story of the potential of Columbus.

At the center of it all is the magnificent domed Ohio State House, the newly renovated seat of state government. In the summer workers from the surrounding skyscrapers sit on the grass, eat their lunches, and listen to noontime concerts.

The newest of the buildings surrounding Capitol Square will be Capitol Tower at 50 South Third Street. It is 42 stories of steel, glass, and granite topped by two octagonal towers. The building is a joint venture of the Dispatch Printing Company and the Galbreath Company. (The *Columbus Dispatch* newspaper remains in the six-story building just to the north.)

North of the Dispatch is the 23-story BancOhio National Plaza, which was built in 1977.

North of the State House, at 30 East Broad Street, is the 40-story James A. Rhodes State Office Tower, constructed in 1974. Although it has two fewer stories than Capitol Tower, it remains the tallest building in the city, rising 629 feet above street level. It is one of the largest granite structures in the world, and each carnelian red granite block weighs 450 pounds.

Looking down on State House Square from the west are the Huntington Center—37 stories high and completed in 1984—and the Riffe Center for Govern-

ment and the Arts, sometimes referred to as State Office Tower II. It is 31 stories high with an art gallery and theaters on the lower floors and a restaurant on the top floor.

On the south side of Capitol Square are the 26-story Capitol Square Office Tower and the 22-story Hyatt Regency at Capitol Square, both completed in 1984. Also on the south is the newly renovated Beggs Building, which has had its height increased to 15 stories from the original 12. This downtown landmark was built in 1928.

Ask most Columbus residents to name the first skyscraper in the city and they will say the LeVeque Tower on Broad and

Front streets. The ornate 44-story building was finished in 1927 and purposely constructed to be just a bit taller than the Washington Monument. Columbus' first building designated as a skyscraper, however, is the Wyandotte Building, located just across the street at 21 West Broad Street. When its 11 stories were completed in 1897, it was the city's first steel-frame building. Constructed by the Wyandotte Office Building Company and Wyandotte Savings & Loan Company, the structure was called one of the most pure examples of the Chicago School-style office buildings.

The LeVeque Tower, built as the American Insurance Union Citadel (some old-timers still refer to it as the AIU Building), is now connected to One Columbus, a gleaming 26-story building completed in 1986. The structure occupies the "Deshler Corner" of Broad and High, the site for many years of the Deshler Hotel. Mrs. LeVeque also restored the Palace Theatre, which is on the ground floor of the Le-Veque Tower.

The north end of downtown is marked by a group of buildings known as the Nationwide Complex and built around the Hyatt Regency at the Ohio Center.

Nationwide Insurance had outgrown its longtime headquarters at 246 North High Street and faced the choice of building a new headquarters in the area or moving to land it owned in Delaware County near the old Green Meadows Country Inn and WRFD, the company's radio station. Dean Jeffers, president at the time, decided to remain downtown. Ground was broken for One Nationwide Plaza, the new 40-story international headquarters of the company, in 1974. A year later plans were announced for the new Hyatt and the Ohio Center just across the street on the east side of High Street. Nationwide became an investor in those projects.

LEFT: The gleaming 26-story One Columbus Tower is conveniently situated in the heart of downtown Columbus. Photo by Larry Hamill

FACING PAGE: Originally constructed as the American Insurance Union Citadel in 1926, today's LeVeque Tower is pictured here silhouetted against the early evening sky. Photo by Larry Hamill

Nationwide II was also built on the east side of High Street. This was followed by Nationwide III, a 27-story office building just south of Nationwide Plaza's original building. That complex has been completed with the 31-story William Green building for the Ohio Bureau of Workers Compensation and the Ohio Industrial Commission. Nationwide III and the BWC building were the largest coordinated government and private office developments in the United States.

The showpiece of the project is the 40,000-square-foot atrium that links the two buildings. The atrium, which has been called a winter version of the outdoor plaza that was such a popular part of the first Nationwide skyscraper, features 8,000 plants and flowers, including ferns, cacti, banana trees, and more than 80 varieties of palms. It has a waterfall, pools, serene places to sit, and two fast-service restaurants.

Completing this northern anchor to downtown is One Riverside Plaza, the 37-story building at West Spring Street and Marconi Boulevard that is the headquarters of American Electric Power. It was built in Columbus in 1983 for the company, which had relocated from New York City. An impressive, though smaller building nearby is the Columbus Safety Building.

The southern anchor of downtown was somewhat slower in developing. It began with the 10-story Franklin County Hall of Justice at Mound and High streets and was followed by the connecting 18-story Municipal Court Building just to the south at Fulton and High streets. The newest addition to this complex is the 27-story Franklin County Tower at Fulton and Front streets, which houses county offices and courts. Just across the street is the new Juvenile Detention Center and a parking garage.

ABOVE: Two Nationwide Plaza is an outstanding achievement of modern architecture. Photo by Larry Hamill

RIGHT: Emphasis on insurance as a major industry has established Columbus as one of the big three insurance centers in the nation alongside Hartford and Boston. Photo by Jim Baron/Image Finders

The south end of downtown is also marked by the Waterford Tower condominiums overlooking the Scioto River and various condominiums and businesses in the brewery district just south of downtown. The Columbia Gas of Ohio Building is at 101 West Town Street.

The other growth of tall buildings has been east along Broad Street with the 88 East Broad Street Building (21 stories), Capitol Square Office Tower (26 stories) at 100 East Broad Street, and farther east, the Midland and Motorist buildings. There's also the Borden Building.

For many years Columbus was known as a "one tower" city, with the LeVeque Tower poking into the air like a finger as one approached Columbus from just about any direction. Most of the change has occurred in recent years, and the diversity of the buildings reflects the diversity of the city's economy.

INTERNATIONAL BUSINESS

As global perestroika opens markets and boundaries once closed to would-be immigrants and traders, the Central Ohio area has become more than a tourist destination to people from other nations . . . it has become their home.

Columbus has more residents who have lived in the city 10 years or less than any other city in Ohio, and many of those new residents have come from outside the United States. Through international business expansion and investment, colleges and universities, and research and development institutions, citizens of the world have done what their American counterparts have—they've moved to Central Ohio, and they've stayed.

Business interests from 12 nations representing almost 120 foreign-owned firms are located in the Central Ohio area. Approximately 3.5 percent of the region's workforce is employed in foreign-owned enterprises.

Companies from four nations—Japan, the United Kingdom, Germany, and Switzerland—account for 82.9 percent of foreign businesses in the area, with about three-fourths of the employment in foreign-owned firms concentrated in manufacturing.

Companies such as Combibloc, Inc., of Germany; the Farmers Insurance Group of the United Kingdom; Hagglunds Denison Corporation of Sweden; Nestlé Dairy Systems of Switzerland; Wagons-Lit Travel USA of France; and Himont USA, Inc., of Italy, are just a few of the diverse enterprises international firms have brought to the region.

The greatest impact on the region has been made by Honda of America, which opened in Marysville just a little more than a decade ago. The company now has two auto manufacturing facilities, a $27-million research center, a motorcycle plant, and a facility that manufactures engines and drive trains—all employing almost 9,500 people in Ohio and doing business with almost 200 domestic suppliers.

While the economic impact of Honda and other international investors in Central Ohio has been significant, the social impact has been equally exciting.

The families of Cleavers and Nelsons who once transferred with their companies to live next door are now the families of Nishidas, Petrakovs, or Pejathayas. Columbus' steak and potatoes restaurants and supermarket selection have been expanded to include sushi, borscht, falafels, and a wide variety of international foods unheard of in the city just a decade or two ago. The business representatives we deal with now need to know how to exchange kopecks into dollars or where to purchase an all-vegetarian lunch.

In fact, the population of Franklin County residents born outside of the United States has grown steadily since 1980.

But Central Ohio is also making its mark on the worlds outside of its boundaries. Ohio ranks third among states in the nation in volume of exported goods, and Central Ohio has made a significant contribution to that ranking. Companies as diverse and/or small as T-shirt manufacturers, cattle sperm producers, and footwear manufacturers are shipping Columbus-made products to markets around the world.

Who benefits from internationalization? All of Central Ohio. Through the rich cultural heritage and diversity of its neighbors and the economic impact on the region as a whole, Central Ohio rediscovers itself while the world continues to discover Columbus.

STRENGTH IN DIVERSITY

Columbus is truly a diverse city, and observers have said this diversity has made the city virtually recession proof. Columbus is the only major city in the northeastern quadrant of the United States that has experienced consistent growth since 1970.

To really know Columbus, you must look beyond the city limits to what is called the Metropolitan Statistical Area (MSA). This includes Delaware, Fairfield, Franklin, Licking, Madison, Pickaway, and Union counties.

While the percentages vary even from month to month, a recent survey showed that 25.7 percent of the workers in Columbus were engaged in trade, 21.3 percent in services, 19.2 percent in manufacturing, 16.5 percent in government, and 17.3 percent in miscellaneous occupations. The strength in services available has been a drawing card for outside industry. So has the availability of research and technology.

Columbus is one of the big three insurance centers in the nation, alongside Hartford and Boston. It all started in 1926 when a group of Ohio farmers rebelled against their auto insurance rates. They were angry because they paid as much for insurance as city drivers, but had considerably fewer accidents.

The Ohio Farm Bureau Federation put up $10,000 in capital, and the farmers went looking for 100 persons who would pledge to buy a policy. The first car insured was a 1924 Ford with a list price of $1,580.

Murray D. Lincoln was chosen to head the company, which was named Farm Bureau Mutual Automobile Insurance Company and sold only to rural Ohioans. But before long the company branched out into other states, and policies were offered to city dwellers in the early 1930s.

By the 1950s Lincoln felt the company had outgrown its name, and it was changed to Nationwide in 1955. The company had acquired the American Insurance Union in 1935, including the AIU tower in downtown Columbus.

The major Nationwide companies today are Nationwide Mutual, Nationwide Mutual Fire, Nationwide Life, Nationwide General, and Nationwide Property and Casualty. The organization has more than 45 companies and has expanded into radio and television communications, real estate development, consumer finance, mutual funds, and a financial services holding company. Today the company operates in a number of foreign countries.

LEFT: Enthusiastic Columbus residents have helped to build a city of which they can be proud. Photo by Larry Hamill

FOLLOWING PAGE: The growing need for office space and services to support local industry has resulted in a recent flourish of construction activity and employment opportunities for the Columbus area. Photo by Larry Hamill

More than 60 home-based insurance companies have helped to catapult Columbus in the forefront of the nation's growing insurance community. Photo by T. Williams/Image Finders

The Downtown Skyline

▲▲▲▲▲▲▲

Approaching the city from any direction, day or night, you are treated to a breathtaking view of the Columbus skyline. This table shows the buildings that are outstanding in the downtown area—that part of the city inside the innerbelt.

Photo by Robert E. Schwurzel

BUILDING/ADDRESS/YEAR COMPLETED OR OCCUPIED/HEIGHT

LeVeque Tower   44 stories
50 West Broad Street (1927)

Capitol Tower   41 stories
Dispatch/Galbreath Building
40 South Third Street (under construction)

James A. Rhodes State Office Tower
40 stories
30 East Broad Street (1974)

One Nationwide Plaza (1977)
40 stories

Huntington Center   37 stories
41 South High Street (1984)

Borden Building   34 stories
180 East Broad Street (1974)

William Green Building   34 stories
30 West Spring Street (1991)

Vern Riffe Center for Government and
the Arts 32 stories
77 South High Street (1988)

One Riverside Plaza   31 stories
1 Riverside Drive (1982)

Ohio Bell Building   29 stories
150 East Gay Street (1970)

Three Nationwide Plaza (1989)
27 stories

Franklin County Office Tower
27 stories
Front and Fulton streets (1990)

Capitol Square Office Building
26 stories
85 East State Street (1984)

One Columbus   26 stories
10 West Broad Street (1988)

Columbus Center   24 stories
100 East Broad Street (1966)

BancOhio Plaza   23 stories
155 East Broad Street (1977)

Motorists Mutual   21 stories
471 East Broad Street (1975)

88 East Broad Street Building
21 stories
88 East Broad Street (1964)

Midland Building   21 stories
250 East Broad Street (1970)

Columbia Gas   18 stories
200 Civic Center Drive (1983)

Two Nationwide Plaza   17 stories
280 North High Street (1981)

Waterford Tower   17 stories
155 West Main Street (1989)

Beggs Building   15 stories
Fifth Third Center (1928) (increased
from 12 stories in 1991)

Wyandotte Building   11 stories
21 West Broad Street (1897; renovated
1979)
(city's first steel-frame "skyscraper")

—H.B.F.

Murray D. Lincoln headed Nationwide until 1964. The present president, John E. Fisher, took office in 1981. The company has assets of more than $22 billion and yearly revenues of around $10 billion.

Columbus now has more than 60 home-based insurance companies, while national insurance companies with their headquarters in the Columbus MSA include Buckeye Union Insurance, Central Benefits Mutual Insurance, Columbus Mutual Life Insurance, Fidelity & Guaranty Underwriters, Grange Mutual Casualty Company, Midland Mutual Life Insurance Company, Motorists Mutual Insurance Company, Physicians Insurance Company of Ohio, State Auto Mutual Insurance, Universal Guaranty Life, and J.C. Penney Casualty Insurance.

From banking and insurance to manufacturing and retailing, Metropolitan Columbus offers a wide selection of careers and professions for the area's skilled work force. Photo by Trufield Enterprises/Image Finders

Manufacturing has always been an important part of the Columbus economy, but the city has never had its well-being linked to just one industry, such as Detroit's has been to automobiles, Akron's to rubber, or Pittsburgh's to steel. Because of the ready availability of coal in southeastern Ohio and iron ore from the Great Lakes region, Columbus has had its share of smokestack industries, but they never dominated the work force.

Columbus could never be considered part of the "rust belt," although it is very near to cities that are. The nearest Columbus came to such a fate was in the 1880s when it was known as the "buggy capital of the world." There were 20 companies in the city making buggies, and by 1890 the Columbus Buggy Company employed

LEFT: The Columbus area work force is relatively equally divided among the fields of government, education, manufacturing, retail, insurance, finance, and real estate, illustrating the spirited diversity of Columbus' economy. Courtesy, McDonnell Douglas Corporation

A center for the manufacture of military aircraft since World War II, Columbus now has a McDonnell Douglas facility at the Port Columbus International Airport, where parts for the giant C-17A cargo plane are manufactured for the Air Force. Courtesy, McDonnell Douglas Corporation

1,100 workers and turned out a buggy every eight minutes. It was a successful business, but one doomed by the coming of the automobile.

Large-scale manufacturing came to Columbus during World War II when Curtiss-Wright built an airplane factory at Port Columbus. At its peak the factory employed 25,000 workers. The huge factory is still an asset to the city and is now part of McDonnell-Douglas, turning out parts for the huge C-17A cargo plane. It was operated for years by North American Aviation (later Rockwell International) and was home to the Lustron Corporation, a company that made prefabricated houses for the postwar market.

Currently Honda is the largest manufacturer in the Columbus MSA. Honda of America came to Ohio in 1982 to build a plant at Marysville. Honda now makes its engines in a plant at Anna and has a second automobile plant at East Liberty. This adds up to more than 10,000 workers in Ohio and the capability of manufacturing 500,000 cars and 60,000 motorcycles a year. When the Marysville Honda plant

Located 30 miles northwest of Columbus in Marysville, Honda of America is the largest manufacturer in Central Ohio with more than 6,000 employees. The company's two factories have the capability of assembling some 500,000 cars and 60,000 motorcycles each year. Photo by Larry Hamill

Worthington Industries' energy efficient annealing furnaces feature the first computerized, high convection, carbon steel annealing bases in the United States. This expansion has reduced overall energy costs while improving quality and productivity with more uniform heating and rapid cooling of various steel products. Courtesy, Worthington Industries

LEFT: Brewing beer has been a vital Columbus industry ever since the city's first German immigrants arrived in the mid-1800s. Anheuser-Busch, whose aging room is pictured here, brews the popular Budweiser beer at its northern Columbus plant. Photo by Dennis Barnes

FACING PAGE TOP: Although well-diversified in service industries, Columbus remains a strong manufacturing center in such areas as steel and plastics. Photo by Jim Baron/Image Finders

FACING PAGE BOTTOM: Founded by Leslie Wexner in the late 1960s, The Limited has evolved into a nationwide fashion conglomerate. The company's distribution center in the Columbus suburb of Reynoldsburg is pictured here in full operation. Photo by Jeffrey A. Rycus/Rycus Associates Photography

assembled 363,668 cars in 1988, that was more cars than any other single auto plant in the United States.

John McConnell's Worthington Industries is a local manufacturing success story. The company operates 27 processed steel, custom plastics, and steel casting facilities in a dozen states, mostly in the Midwest and South. Fourteen of these are in Ohio, including five in Columbus.

McConnell worked in the steel mills of Weirton, West Virginia, in his younger years. He started his own business in 1955 with $1,800 in savings and $600 borrowed on the family car. The money was used to buy his first load of steel for processing. Today sales of Worthington Industries, Inc., tops $1 billion a year.

Worthington Industries pays 17 percent of its pre-tax profits to employees in quarterly bonuses. This has brought about productivity figures higher than any others in the industry. For instance, sales per employee in a recent fiscal year were $431,000. This is compared to $135,000 in the metal manufacturing industry and $111,000 for all manufacturing in the United States.

Worthington makes flat-rolled steel products for the automobile, appliance, office equipment, and machinery industries. Plastics are made largely for the automobile industry, but also include microwave oven doors and lawn mower engine covers. Steel castings are for mass-transit car undercarriages and the defense industry. The company got into the pressure cylinder field in 1971, making cylinders to be used in outdoor barbecue grills and camping equipment.

The company's biggest expansion came on its 25th anniversary in 1980, when it acquired Buckeye International, Inc., one of the largest steel castings firms in the country.

McConnell started a Japanese connection when Worthington Industries teamed with Nissen Chemical Industry Company Ltd. and Sumitomo Corporation of America to form London Industries in London, Ohio, a firm that produces plastics for the computer, automobile, and appliance industries.

All manufacturing in Columbus isn't big. For example, Custom Coach Corporation is not a large concern, but it is known around the world for transforming buses into luxurious custom homes on wheels. They're ideal for people who don't like to fly, like former NFL coach John Madden, and for entertainers who spend long stretches of time on the road. They are also great for people who take short journeys when flying is not practical.

Columbus has been called the "fast-food capital of the world." It all started here with White Castle Systems, Inc., in 1926. Columbus' original white, castle-shaped building, in which the small, square hamburgers were grilled in a bed of chopped

onions, has been moved to the Ohio Expositions Center.

The distinctive taste of a "Castle" is unique to Central Ohio, and people who have moved away from the area often have them air expressed thousands of miles for parties and special occasions. A politician recently had a sellout fund raiser by offering supporters White Castle burgers and champagne.

There is an annual contest at the restaurant at Greenlawn Avenue and South High Street to see who can eat the most Castles in an allotted period of time. Those who thrive on the little hamburgers in white boxes refer to them as "sliders" or "groaners." Be advised, the only way they come is "with onions."

In addition to White Castle, Wendy's International, Inc., Rax Restaurants, Inc., G.D. Ritzy's, Bob Evans Farms Restaurants, Sisters Chicken & Biscuits, and Snapps all call Columbus home.

R. David Thomas was 37 years old, a high school dropout, and a former Army cook when he opened the first Wendy's in 1969. The restaurant, located in a former automobile showroom at 257 East Broad Street, was named for Thomas' eight-year-old daughter. The original is still there, but it is joined now by nearly 4,000 others throughout the world. There is more than one way to get a Wendy's. Counting singles, doubles, with or without cheese, and with a variety of condiments, there are more than 400 ways to order a hamburger at Wendy's.

Thomas has built the company into one of the top four burger giants in the country, but still says he nurtures the business, "one customer at a time."

Retailing has been big in the city since Columbus' founding. Simon Lazarus opened a one-room men's clothing store at Town and High streets in 1851, and it grew into the city's major department store.

The whole pattern of urban shopping was changed by Don M. Casto, Sr., in 1949 when he opened the country's first shopping mall. Town & Country Shopping Center, also known as the "Miracle Mile," opened along East Broad Street in a sparsely populated suburb beyond the end of the city's bus line. While other retailers thought it was folly, Casto believed that people would drive for miles to find a shopping center with ample parking and a variety of stores to meet their shopping needs.

J.C. Penney was one of the people who believed in Casto's dream. The retailer

The quaint German Village is a great place for walking, sightseeing, and shopping in the restored neighborhood just south of downtown Columbus. Photo by Larry Hamill

Offering a traditional atmosphere of quality and style, Worthington Square is a fine example of the malls that have sprung up in the Columbus suburbs in recent years. Photo by Larry Hamill

When Don M. Casto, Sr., opened the country's first shopping center in 1949 he forever changed the face of the nation's shopping districts. Casto's Town & Country Shopping Center, also known as the "Miracle Mile," is pictured here along East Broad Street in the area that has now developed into the Columbus suburb of Whitehall. Photo by Jeanne Conte

The long-awaited Columbus City Center opened in 1989 to record-breaking crowds. This $200-million shopping center features more than 160 stores and some 1.3 million square feet of retail space. Photo by Jeanne Conte

leased 40,000 feet in the new center for a department store. Soon Casto attracted other stores that had never previously located outside the downtown area of a major city.

Another innovation in retailing, the supermarket, was introduced to Columbus in 1934 when Wayne E. Brown opened the first of his Big Bear stores just across Lane Avenue from Ohio State in a building that had been a dance hall and a roller rink. One of the store's attractions was a live big bear in a large cage in the parking lot. Brown selected the name for the store because it was catchy and easy to remember, particularly for children.

More than 200,000 people passed through Big Bear the first three days it was open, and they were amazed, they said, at the grocery carts and self-serve shelves. Opening specials included coffee at 18 cents a pound and ham at 10 cents a pound.

The trained bear, which learned to do tricks for the kids, was eventually donated to the Columbus Zoo. The building is no longer there, but the Big Bear chain thrives and has also added Harts Family Centers.

There are now more than a dozen retail centers in and around Columbus as well as a renewal of the downtown shopping scene.

The big boost to downtown shopping came with the opening of the City Center in 1989. The mall, just south of State Street and east of High Street, has 160 stores in 1.3 million square feet of leasable space. It opened after more than 17 years of planning and a $30-million investment by the city. The $200-million center brought two large department stores to the city, Marshall Field's and Jacobson's. In addition, a major occupant of the mall is The Limited Inc., the domain of Ohio State graduate Leslie H. Wexner, the vast company's founder and chairman.

The Limited employs nearly 10,000 people locally, including those in the company headquarters near Morse Road and I-270 and those in the Lane Bryant Division near Reynoldsburg. The Reynoldsburg complex also has the office and distribution center for Victoria's Secret stores and catalogue. Other divisions of The Limited are based in New York City.

Columbus Center, the office building at 100 East Broad Street, is one of the many structures built and operated by the Galbreath Company. John Galbreath, who came to Columbus from Mount Sterling, was 32 years old and broke in 1929. He went into the real estate business with the idea that people felt a sense of pride and worth by owning their own homes. Following this hypothesis, he purchased the town of McDonald, Ohio, in 1941 and converted the company town into one owned by the workers.

This led to developing, arranging financing of, managing, and leasing high-rise office buildings. The Galbreath developments include New York's Mobil Building, Chicago's Montgomery Ward Plaza, and Cleveland's Erieview Tower. Galbreath also built Mei Foo Sun Chuen in Kowloon, Hong Kong. With 80,000 residents, it is the world's largest privately financed residential complex.

Galbreath also raised thoroughbred racehorses at his Darby Dan Farm west of Columbus and owned the Pittsburgh Pirates. the Galbreath Company is now operated by John's son, Daniel M. Galbreath.

John Galbreath hosted Presidents and royalty at Darby Dan, but he never forgot making someone a homeowner with the first house he sold.

The success of any city depends on finances, and banking has been a major industry in Columbus. Following World War II the city had three major local banks, City National, Ohio National, and Huntington.

ABOVE: More than 45 banking institutions serve the growing needs of Metropolitan Columbus. Photo by Jim Baron/Image Finders

FACING PAGE: Capitol Square is one of the many commercial structures built and operated by the Galbreath Company. Photo by Larry Hamill

RIGHT: With combined total assets of about $30 billion, Bank One is a leading force in Columbus' financial community. Photo by Gregory M. Franken

Bank One, the former City National Bank, had its beginning in Columbus in 1868 as Sessions and Company. A year later the name changed to Commercial Bank, and it moved to offices at 9 East Long Street. Bank One of Columbus, NA, now has more than 4,000 employees.

BancOhio Corporation had its beginnings in 1907 when Harry P. Wolfe and Robert F. Wolfe invested in the Ohio Trust Company. They operated it as Citizens Trust and Savings Bank until purchasing controlling shares of Ohio National Bank in 1928. BancOhio Corp., the state's first bank holding company, was formed in 1929 and two years later the two banks were merged into Ohio National Bank. BancOhio National Bank came into being in 1979 as the largest in the state and the 31st-largest in the United States. The bank has more than 3,000 employees locally.

Peletiah Webster Huntington opened his own bank in 1865 when the Market Exchange Branch of the State Bank of Ohio, where he had worked, closed its doors. P.W. Huntington and Company opened at the northwest corner of Broad and High streets, where it stayed until 1878, when a five-story brick "skyscraper" was built for the bank across the street on the south side of Broad Street. As the tallest building in town at the time, it also housed the weather bureau. In 1924 it moved to its present location at 17 South High Street, and now has more than 100 offices throughout the state and employs more than 2,500 people in Columbus.

A number of banks now serve the financial needs of the city including Society Bank, which was founded in Cleveland, and Fifth-Third, which originated in Cincinnati.

Founded as the Citizens Trust and Savings Bank by Harry P. Wolfe and Robert F. Wolfe in 1907, the BancOhio Corporation has developed into one of the state's largest banking institutions. BancOhio offices are housed in this tower at Broad and Fourth streets. Photo by Larry Hamill

Nerve Center for the State

▲▲▲▲▲▲▲▲▲

When Columbus was picked as the name for the state capital of Ohio, the only other name seriously considered was Ohio City.

Although that name wasn't chosen, the city at the confluence of the Olentangy and Scioto rivers might still be referred to as Ohio City. There is no doubt that it is the center of government for the state of Ohio, and Columbusites are also Buckeyes.

Many say the fact that this is the capital, plus the diversity of business and industry here, almost makes Central Ohio recession proof. Take out the buildings that are state property and those that house many state offices, and the city would look like it had been ravaged by a bombing attack.

The Ohio Department of Administrative Services reported on one recent payday that there were 21,865 state workers in Franklin County. That does not include employees of The Ohio State University. Both the state and the university publish telephone directories that are larger than some of those in Ohio cities outside Central Ohio.

In addition to the workers the state has in Franklin County, there are a number of state employees in the surrounding counties. There are 771 in Delaware County, which has a major headquarters of the Ohio Department of Transportation; 454 in Fairfield County, with a state prison; 188 in Licking County, mostly employees of the Department of Transportation; 952 in Madison County, with two state prisons; and 1,453 in Pickaway County, with a state prison and a state park.

County auditors file a report with the state tax commissioner every year listing the value of state-owned property in the county. Franklin County leads all the rest with state-owned property valued at $2,224,323,690. (This total does include The Ohio State University.)

The state occupies seven major buildings downtown—the Ohio State House, the James A. Rhodes State Office Tower, the Riffe Center for Government and the Arts, the William Green Building, and the three buildings of the old State Office Building complex on the east bank of the Scioto River.

In addition to occupying the building at 25 South Front Street, the Department of Transportation has several offices at 1600 West Broad Street, including the testing laboratory and the bureau of rail planning. The bureau of aviation is in a building at the north side of Don Scott Field, the Ohio State University Airport. The building also houses the air arm of the State Highway Patrol. Just north of it is Beightler Armory, the home of the office of the Adjutant General.

The Ohio Expositions Center, home of the State Fair, is on Seventeenth Avenue. Just across the street is the Highway Patrol Academy, the building where all of the state's highway patrol troopers and many of the local police officers receive their training.

The Department of Highway Safety and the Highway Patrol are in buildings that were once part of the Old Blind School at Parsons Avenue and East Main Street. The laboratories of the Ohio Department of Agriculture are on East Main Street in Reynoldsburg.

The governor's mansion is located in Bexley.

On the part of the West Side called the Hilltop, you will find the Central Ohio Psychiatric Hospital and the Developmental Center for the mentally retarded.

In addition to these, there are state offices in rented quarters in all parts of the city.

The lives of thousands of people are affected by the boards that sit in Columbus and license such professionals as accountants, barbers, dentists, physicians, nurses, occupational and physical therapists, attorneys, optical dispensers, optometrists, pharmacists, professional engineers and surveyors, sanitarians, speech pathologists, and veterinarians.

—H.B.F.

The historic Ohio State House is a center of government for the state of Ohio. Photo by William A. Holmes/Image Finders

Established by Peletiah Webster Huntington in 1865, P.W. Huntington now has more than 100 branch offices throughout the state and employs more than 2,500 people in the Columbus area. Photo by Dennis Barnes

Among the banks from other cities that have expanded into Columbus' growing financial community is Fifth Third from nearby Cincinnati. The bank now boasts more than $350 million in local assets. Photo by Jeanne Conte

A WINNING PERSPECTIVE

Tom Matthews, Jr., operated a hot-dog stand on the sidewalk outside the State Office Tower at 30 East Broad Street. Though there were other hot-dog vendors, he likes to explain that he was the one who showed up even when it was cold and rainy.

When Huntington Plaza was looking for someone to operate a 112-seat restaurant inside, the Minority Business Development Center of the Columbus Area Chamber of Commerce came to the rescue. They helped Tom Matthews, Jr., develop a business plan and got him together with the people from Bank One and the City of Columbus to arrange a loan for equipment. In January 1990 Matthews opened his Big City Diner. So Huntington, one of the largest businesses downtown, plays host to one of the smallest. That's part of the story of Columbus' success as a place to do business.

It is this sort of cooperation between the private sector, the government, and the Chamber of Commerce that caused *Newsweek* magazine to designate Columbus as one of the nation's "Hot Cities."

The Columbus Board of Trade was founded in 1884 as a central office to address business problems and recommend solutions. The board actively encouraged new firms to locate in Columbus and worked to provide a healthy economic climate in which business could grow. It changed its name to the Columbus Chamber of Commerce in 1910 and became the Columbus Area Chamber of Commerce in 1956 to offer the entire Central Ohio area a winning perspective.

Government continues to be big business in Columbus. The State of Ohio has more than 26,000 employees, not counting the nearly 30,000 who work for The Ohio State University. The City of Columbus has more than 7,000 on its payrolls, and Franklin County has more than 5,000. The Columbus Public Schools employ more than 7,000.

In the Columbus MSA there are more than 60 establishments that employ more than 1,000 persons. In their diversity these businesses represent a cross section of America and make the region a good place to do business.

LEFT: The need for new construction has continued to meet the challenging demands of Columbus' ever-growing economy. Photo by Jim Baron/Image Finders

FOLLOWING PAGE: This workman tackles the arduous task of constructing a Columbus high rise. The substantial increase in the number of people involved in local construction reflects the rapid growth of the city. Photo by Larry Hamill

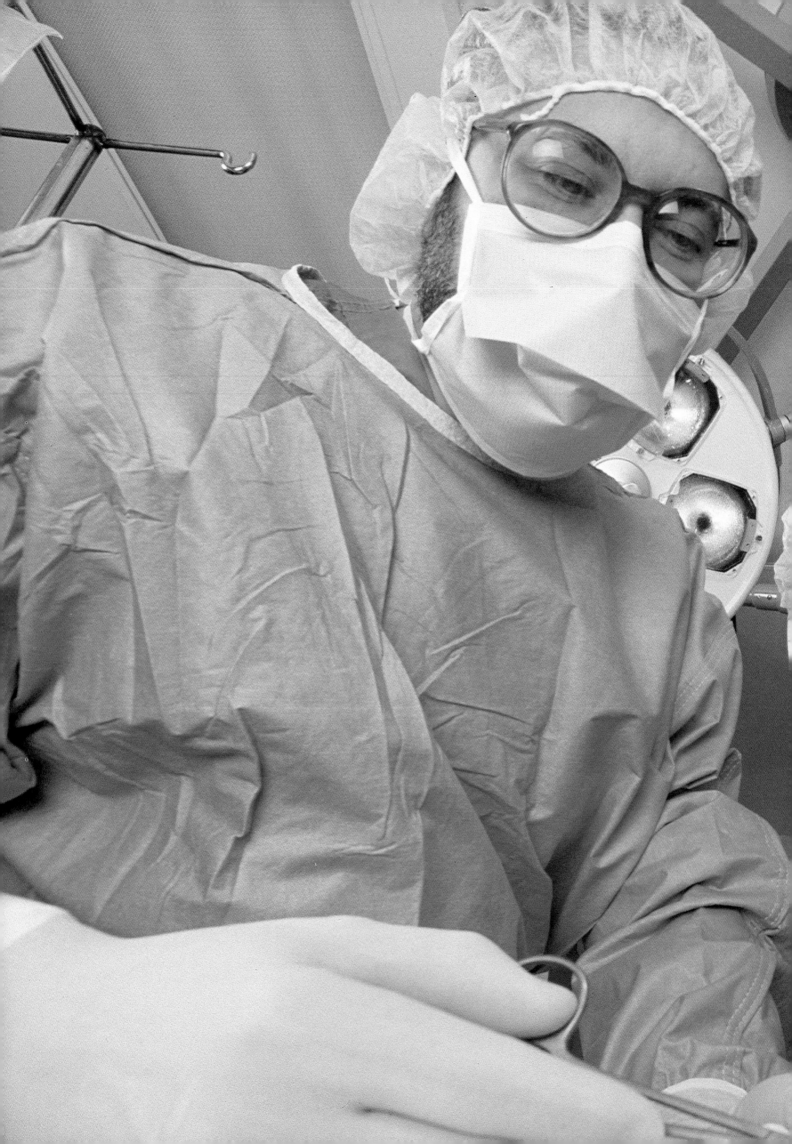

Center of
Learning and
Healing

▲▲▲▲▲▲▲▲▲▲▲

I n 1976 a portion of Fort Hayes, a military installation that had been training soldiers since the days of muskets, was converted into the Fort Hayes Career Center of the Columbus Public School system. One of the most innovative programs of the new center was the Department of Theater of the School of Performing Arts, which was headed by Dr. Phillip Wilson.

A student in the first graduating class of the department recently had this to say about Wilson and the program:

His message in the classroom was simply to be the best. There could be no text because this was the first class of its kind in the country. We sat through college-type lectures and went straight to putting the lessons into practical use. In that first year we built the scenery, hung the lighting, wired the sound, and literally watched a room with a hole in the cement floor transformed into a theater complete with a state of the art hydraulic thrust stage.

The student also remembers such diverse visitors to this educational experiment as President Gerald Ford and comedian Red Skelton.

The former Third Street School in Columbus has inscribed above its door the quotation: "Learning Softens Poverty and Adorns Riches." It is symbolic of the importance placed on education in Central Ohio.

Beginning in the 1990s the "Columbus Discovery" award will be given each year to individuals and institutions that have made outstanding contributions to the field of education. The project targets the international educational community and seeks to make Columbus recognized as a major educational center.

Another project, "Right From The Start," promotes the idea that every child is entitled to a good beginning regardless of family situation or socioeconomic background.

In Franklin County nearly eight out of 10 people over the age of 25 have a high school diploma and about a quarter of them are college graduates.

There are 17 public school districts in Franklin County, and excellence is the goal of each. The diversity makes them competitive. Superintendents closely monitor the amount each district spends per pupil, the number of scholarships won by students, and the number of students who go on to college.

In addition to the public schools, there are a number of private and parochial schools. The Roman Catholic Diocese of Columbus, which includes several Central and Southern Ohio

counties, operates 11 high schools, 52 elementary schools, 23 kindergartens, and 3 special preschools. This makes the Diocese of Columbus one of the community's biggest employers.

There are 35 high schools in Franklin County, 16 of which are operated by the Columbus Public School System. The system is the largest in the county and the second-largest in the state.

ABOVE: Bright yellow school buses signal the opening of another school year in Columbus. Photo by Larry Hamill

LEFT: The 17 public school districts in Franklin County and a host of private and parochial schools strive for excellence in the field of education. Photo by Larry Hamill

The district operates some 136 schools, including 85 elementary schools, of which 22 are alternative schools. The elementary schools offer grades kindergarten through fifth.

Since July of 1990 attendance at kindergarten is a prerequisite for admission to the first grade in Ohio. There are 26 middle schools (grades 6-8), including eight alternative schools. The 16 high schools (grades 9-12) include one alternative. There are four career centers and four special schools for the physically and emotionally handicapped.

The elementary alternative schools differ from conventional schools either in how subjects are taught or in the focus of instruction. Recently four of the alternative schools stressed science, mathematics, and environmental studies. One was a Montessori school. Douglas, a downtown school, was an "open space" school with many city institutions and activities incorporated into the instructional program. Cedarwood and Devonshire were "project adventure" schools, which give students opportunities to learn from firsthand experience in the natural environment. Two of the schools stressed the performing and visual arts. Two offered individually guided education programs to meet the specific needs, abilities, talents, and learning styles of each individual. Two termed schools of academic and physical excellence were geared toward educating the total child—intellectually, physically, and

emotionally. Two schools advocated traditional instruction and homework. These schools emphasized patriotism and respect for authority. One school stressed international studies. Two stressed literature-based language arts in which students were exposed to many forms of literature and urged to create literature of their own. Gladstone, a Spanish immersion school, and Kenwood, a French immersion school, conducted all classroom instruction and conversation in either Spanish or French. Students learned the foreign language by hearing it and using it in daily activities. After five or six years in this program students are expected to speak, read, and write fluently in Spanish and French as well as English.

Five regional middle schools offered a program that utilizes double time blocks for reading/language arts and math/science. Of the other alternative middle schools, one specialized in traditional education, one in foreign language and international studies, and the third was termed Success IMPACT, a program to give students the opportunity to achieve some measure of success daily. This program offered six foreign languages, computer-supported instruction, and additional courses in math, science, social studies, and vocational programs.

The alternative high school was designed for the needs of the academically oriented and college-bound student. Foreign language offerings included French, Spanish, Latin, Russian, German, and Chinese. In addition, the school offered the Community Internship Program, which allowed students to participate in a full-day cooperative program with a business, university, research, or service organization in the community.

Another outreach program is the "Adopt-A-School" partnership cosponsored by the Columbus Area Chamber of Commerce and Columbus Public Schools. In a recent year this program linked more than 300 organizations with every Columbus public school, with the organizations providing services, goods, and money to the

Columbus-area students literally have the world at their fingertips. Photo by Jim Baron/Image Finders

Sometimes education steps outside of the traditional classroom and into a divergent environment in an effort to introduce children to all facets of the learning process. Here, children get a change to learn about nature during a field trip to Black-lick Woods. Photo by Jeffrey A. Rycus/Rycus Associates Photography

FACING PAGE: Higher educational opportunities abound in Central Ohio, offering a fine selection of colleges and universities from which to choose a major field of study. The eight members of the Higher Education Council of Columbus employ more than 18,000 people, and nearly $2.3 billion in revenue is generated by these institutions of higher learning. Photo by Dennis Barnes

schools they "adopt." The value of these in one year totaled more than $1.2 million. Organizations in the partnerships allow their employees to work directly with students, giving tours and sharing equipment with the schools, providing the students with "hands on" learning opportunities.

Beginning in 1990 the school district instituted tougher and tighter course work in high schools. This includes urging all students to take algebra and advanced math courses, stressing reading and English, and having physical education classes that emphasize lifetime fitness activities.

Those who complete their high school education do not have to look far for a multitude of higher educational opportunities in Central Ohio.

There are eight members of the Higher Education Council of Columbus. In addition there is the Pontifical College Josephinum, which trains young men for the priesthood. There are also universities in two adjoining counties.

The Higher Education Council reports that the annual budget of its eight members surpasses $1 billion a year. Nearly $2.3 billion comes to the county by way of higher education. The campuses are visited by 6.3 million people a year, who spend nearly $700 million. More than $100 million a year is spent in the county on university research. The 477 buildings of the eight member institutions (on campuses total
ing 3,479 acres) account for $2.7 billion in assets. The libraries house over 4.9 million volumes. The schools employ 18,724 persons full- and part-time.

Capital University, the grandmother of the area's institutions of higher learning, is now located in Bexley. Since its founding in 1830 by the Lutheran Church, Capital has grown to three undergraduate colleges—the College of Arts and Sciences, the Conservatory of Music, and the School of Nursing. All 3,000 students at the university take the 12-course University Core Curriculum. There are two graduate schools—the Law School and Graduate Center (located in downtown Columbus) and the Graduate School of Administration (MBA Program).

Located on 50 acres in the suburban community of Bexley, Capital University is a coeducational, liberal arts institution with a history that dates back to its founding in 1830. It is the oldest institution of higher learning in Central Ohio. Photo by Jeffrey A. Rycus/Rycus Associates Photography

Dispute resolution procedures developed by the Capital Law School are used by the Columbus City Attorney's office to settle more than 40,000 cases a year, resulting in an estimated savings of $10 million a year to the city. The school has recently received a $150,000 grant from the Ford Foundation to provide training in dispute resolution to Jamaican court and social service personnel, police, and lay magistrates.

The Conservatory of Music offers such unique programs as Jazz Studies and the Music Industry. Capital is the only school in the country that offers a semester of undergraduate study at the Zoltan Kodaly Pedagogical Institute of Music in Kecskemet, Hungary.

Established by the state legislature in 1870 as the Ohio Agricultural and Mechanical College, The Ohio State University got its present name in 1878. It is said that when the school opened, the president set up a table in front of the unfinished University Hall and enrolled 21 men and 3 women. Since then the university has awarded about 400,000 degrees. Additionally, Ohio State's 53,000-person student body makes the Columbus campus the nation's biggest single campus. An additional 6,000 students attend branch campuses.

Ohio State appears to be a city within a city. While the Columbus campus is 1,629 acres, its other holdings bring the total to 15,672 acres. These include a 1,376-acre airport, 295 acres for its golf courses, 5,935 acres for the Ohio Agricultural Research and Development Center and Agricultural Technical Institute at Wooster, and an additional 6.437 acres in various places, including a research facility on an island in Lake Erie.

Established as the Ohio Agriculture and Mechanical College in 1893, today's Ohio State University offers a vast selection of nearly 8,000 courses leading to more than 400 degrees in bachelor's, master's, and doctoral programs. Photo by Jeanne Conte

The university includes 14 undergraduate colleges, 5 professional colleges, 7 schools, a graduate school, and 109 departments and academic faculties. Approximately 8,000 different courses are taught.

The university employs almost 30,000 people, with a full-time equivalent of more than 20,000. Recently the annual payroll of these workers amounted to $550 million.

One person has said the mission of the university is to "teach everything to everybody," and a former president says the future belongs to the large public institutions because "they alone will have the resources for greatness."

That statement does not impress Sister Mary Andrew Matesich, O.P., the president of Ohio Dominican College, who goes along with the motto of the Council of Independent Colleges that "Small Colleges Can Help You Make It Big."

Chartered as the College of St. Mary of the Springs in the fall of 1911, Ohio Dominican did not open its doors to full-time students until 1924. It first admitted male students in 1964 and took its present name four years later.

The school is guided by the 700-year-old educational theology and philosophy of St. Dominic and his followers. It offers four different degrees and 28 majors.

Smallness hasn't stifled innovation at Ohio Dominican. Its Weekend College was the first of its kind in the area, bringing 275 adult students to Saturday classes to work on college degrees. English as a Second Language (ESL) classes at Ohio Dominican have attracted students from all over the world, boosting international enrollment to nearly 15 percent of the student body.

Otterbein College in Westerville was founded in 1842 and is affiliated with the United Methodist Church. Its theater program, which is internationally famous, has been in existence for more than 80 years and currently presents no fewer than 11 major productions a year.

Otterbein also has a 150-piece marching band, a concert band, wind ensemble, and jazz-lab band. In addition, its students participate in the Westerville Civic Symphony, and the campus has been the site of more than 175 exhibits of the Westerville Music and Arts Festival.

Otterbein's 2,400 students attend classes in 25 buildings on a 70-acre wooded campus. There are more than 35 majors from which to choose, and the college offers the following degrees: bachelor of arts, bachelor of science, bachelor of music education, bachelor of fine arts in theater, bachelor of science in education, bachelor of science in nursing, master of arts in education, and master of arts in teaching.

Columbus State Community College's 11 buildings sit on a 45-acre campus bordered by East Spring Street, Cleveland Avenue, I-670, and I-71. The campus features a large statue of Christopher Columbus standing on a pedestal and pointing toward the skyline of downtown Columbus. The citizens of Barrington, Illinois, presented the statue to the citizens of Columbus as a gift.

Columbus State had its beginning as the Columbus Area Technician School, created by the Columbus Board of Education at Central High School in 1963. It moved to the site of the old Aquinas High School in 1965. It was chartered, with approval of the Ohio Board of Regents, as the Columbus Technical Institute on July 1, 1967. The Board of Regents rechartered it as Columbus State Community College in 1987 as a result of a survey of the educational needs of the community. More than 14,000 students have earned associate degrees in 30 technical fields since 1965. These programs prepare students for immediate employment in fields such as business, public service, health, and engineering.

FACING PAGE TOP: The grassy tree-lined oval is considered to be the traditional heart of Ohio State's campus, where students make their way to and from daily classes. Photo by Larry Hamill

FACING PAGE BOTTOM: More than 50,000 students attend the sprawling 3,250-acre Ohio State University campus in Columbus. Photo by Robert E. Schwerzel

ABOVE: Ohio Dominican College was founded in 1911 as the College of Saint Mary of the Springs, catering to the liberal arts education of women. Now a coeducational institution, Ohio Dominican awards bachelor's degrees in 30 majors. Photo by Dennis Barnes

LEFT: Otterbein College currently enrolls about 2,400 students. The school is a private liberal arts institution and is located on 70 acres in the town of Westerville just 15 miles northeast of Columbus. These recent graduates of Otterbein radiate with pride and accomplishment. Photo by Jeanne Conte

Created as the Columbus Area Technician School in 1963, Columbus State Community College now features an enrollment of more than 11,000 students in 35 degree programs. Photo by Jeanne Conte

Two new transfer programs at Columbus State, associate of arts and associate of science degrees, meet the majority of freshman and sophomore requirements toward bachelor's degrees offered by four-year colleges and universities in Central Ohio and throughout the state. Specific transfer programs with area colleges and universities have been developed.

In addition to its home campus, Columbus State operates five off-campus centers, including an aviation maintenance facility at Bolton Field Airport, where aviation maintenance technology is taught.

Franklin University at 201 South Grant Avenue is one of Columbus' downtown universities that is also aimed at working people. Eighty-six percent of its 4,200 students hold jobs while attending school, and 86 percent of the alumni work in positions relevant to their studies at Franklin.

Franklin's College of Arts and Sciences has divisions of developmental education, humanities, nursing and health science, and social and behavioral

In addition to its main 45-acre campus in downtown Columbus, the Columbus State Community College operates five satellite centers, which includes the Eastland Career Center near Groveport and an aviation maintenance technology facility at Bolton Field Airport. Photo by Jeffrey A. Rycus/Rycus Associates Photography

A Columbus College of Art
and Design student sketches
a still life at the Franklin
Park Conservatory. Photo by
Jeanne Conte

sciences. The College of Business and Technology has divisions of accounting, computer and information science, management, engineering technology, and economics, finance, and quantitative methods.

The school of commerce and the first evening law school, forerunners of Franklin University, were established under the sponsorship of the YMCA in 1902. (The night law school is now part of Capital University.) Technical classes were instituted in 1903, and the first auto mechanics school was added in 1909. The institution became coeducational in 1917. The name Franklin University was adopted in 1933, and the university separated from YMCA sponsorship to become an independent nonprofit university in 1964. It moved to its present location in 1969 and named this building Frasch Hall in 1981 in honor of Dr. Joseph F. Frasch, who served as president from 1951 until his death in 1977.

Franklin offers the following degrees: bachelor of science, bachelor of public administration, and bachelor of science in nursing. The Franklin University library, open to the public, contains the most extensive tax information center in Central Ohio.

The DeVry Institute of Technology might be called the city's "chain college." DeVry has 11 campuses throughout the United States and Canada and offers undergraduate degree programs in electronics technology, computer information systems, telecommunications management, business operations, and accounting. The curricula of the school are designed to bring education, technology, and business together.

DeVry was founded in Chicago in 1931 by Herman DeVry, an inventor and manufacturer of motion picture projectors. Columbus' DeVry is at 1350 Alum Creek

Drive. It opened in 1952 as the Ohio Technical College, offering courses in radio and television servicing. Within two decades the school outgrew three facilities, was allowed to issue bachelor and associate degrees, and became one of the DeVry Institutes under the name of Ohio Institute of Technology. The institute took its present name in 1983 and expanded its curricula to include business operations in 1987 and accounting in 1989.

The school expanded in 1973 by adding a one-story, 52,000-square-foot structure. The glass-and-aluminum-sheathed building features a sunken commons area in its center, which is the focal point of the campus. The commons includes dining areas, a comfortable student lounge, and meeting rooms.

The Columbus College of Art and Design began as the Columbus Art School in January 1879 with three students and a teacher. By the end of that school year attendance had grown to 118.

One of the school's early students was George Bellows, born in Columbus in 1882. Bellows' artwork was exhibited in the New York Armory Show in 1913, a show that startled the art world and moved it away from post-Impressionism. At the age of 27, he became the youngest man ever elected to the National Academy of Art.

In the early 1960s, after making a name for himself with depictions of World War II air combat, another of the college's students, Robert T. McCall, turned his talents to subjects relating to space. One of his works is a 58-foot-high mural at the Smithsonian Institution's National Air and Space Museum. His work for *Life* magazine led him to doing advertising promotions for such films as *2001: A Space Odyssey, Tora! Tora! Tora!,* and *Meteor.*

Columbus College of Art and Design has about 1,700 students, including 900 who attend full time. There are three schools—the professional day school for full-time students, the evening school for professional and continuing cultural education, and the Saturday school for young people from elementary through high school.

The college consists of seven divisions: advertising design, retail advertising, industrial design, interior design, illustration, fine arts, and photography. The bachelor of fine arts degree is offered in each of these disciplines.

The tall steeple of the Pontifical College Josephinum is visible when approaching Columbus from the north on Route 23 or when driving along the I-270 outerbelt just south of the 100-acre campus. The college's mission is to prepare young men for the priesthood. Founded in 1888 and four years later named a Pontifical Institution (the only such college outside of Italy), the college has a School of Theology and a College of Liberal Arts.

Joseph Jessing, a German immigrant to the United States, who was ordained a priest in 1870, founded a home for orphan boys and appealed for support through the *Ohio Waisenfreund,* a newspaper. Through the pages of the paper, Monsignor

LEFT: With an average enrollment of 130 students, the Pontifical College Josephinum is the only pontifical seminary located outside of Italy. The primary focus of the school is to train students for the Roman Catholic priesthood. Photo by Larry Hamill

BELOW: Students at the Columbus College of Art and Design work toward their Bachelor of Fine Arts degrees in this life-drawing class. Founded in 1879, the school now features a 16-building campus for its more than 2,500 students. Photo by Jeffrey A. Rycus/Rycus Associates Photography

The landmark Pontifical College Josephinum tower is visible to travelers along Interstate 270 and Route 23.
Photo by Larry Hamill

Jessing offered to sponsor two boys who wanted to become priests. There were applicants from 11 states, and Jessing accepted 23 of them. Then, on September 1, 1888, Father Jessing began the College Josephinum. In 1894 it was incorporated under the laws of Ohio and chartered as a degree-issuing institution.

Six of the college's original students were ordained in 1899. Though for many years the college trained priests to serve German-speaking immigrants, most recently it has trained priests to minister to Hispanic Americans. To date, nearly 1,100 priests have received their training at the college.

Half an hour east of Columbus is Denison University at Granville, a town founded in 1805 by a group of settlers from Granville, Massachusetts. A group of Baptist laymen purchased 200 acres of farmland in 1831 and founded the Granville Literary and Theological Institution to provide teachers and preachers for their frontier country. It was outside the village on a road known as an "unmeasured mile of unmeasured mud."

In 1850 residents voted to move Granville College into the village on 250 acres now known as College Hill. The name of the college was changed to honor William W. Denison, a Muskingum County farmer who had pledged $10,000 toward the school's endowment.

The first young women to attend classes at Denison came up the hill in 1870 from the Young Ladies Institute. The Institute was renamed Shepardson College in 1886, became a part of Denison in 1900, and, in 1927, was consolidated under one board of trustees.

Today Denison offers bachelor of arts, bachelor of science, bachelor of fine arts, and bachelor of music degrees. A student may choose from more than 30 majors.

The university operates on an unusual 4-1-4 academic year, with two four-month terms and the month of January set aside as a term for students to concentrate on a single subject not normally covered in any academic course.

Ohio Wesleyan University, north of Columbus in Delaware, was founded by the Methodist Church in 1842 "on the most liberal principles of higher education." The school opened its doors two years later to 29 male students taught by three professors in Elliott Hall, formerly the Mansion House Hotel.

What is now Ohio Wesleyan's east campus was originally a health resort with a sulphur spring known for its "health-giving although odoriferous waters." It was at this spring that Rutherford B. Hayes, a Delaware native who was to become the 19th President of the United States, wooed and won Lucy Webb, one of Ohio Wesleyan's first coeds and the woman for whom the present Hayes Hall is named.

Another famous Ohio Wesleyan graduate is Branch Rickey, class of 1904. The university's new athletic facility is named in his honor. The Ohio Wesleyan Branch Rickey Award was established in 1988 to honor outstanding contributions to the cause of equal opportunity and reinforce the university's commitment to values and ethics. Rickey integrated professional baseball when, as manager of the Brooklyn Dodgers, he brought Jackie Robinson into the major leagues.

Arthur Flemming, a 1927 graduate, became the first non-clergyman to be president of the university and later served as Secretary of Health, Education, and Welfare under President Dwight D. Eisenhower. Later Flemming served as the nation's civil rights chief.

The university still maintains the liberal principles on which it was founded. Its

Notable Alumni

▲ ▲ ▲ ▲ ▲ ▲ ▲ ▲ ▲ ▲ ▲ ▲ ▲

The colleges and universities of Central Ohio have enriched the life of the nation and the world through the talents of their graduates in such diverse fields as the military, politics, the visual and performing arts, and industry.

Ohio Wesleyan produced two graduates close to the presidency of the United States. Lucy Webb, one of the first coeds at the school, married Rutherford B. Hayes, who became the 19th President of the United States. Charles Fairbanks, vice president under Theodore Roosevelt from 1905 to 1909, was an OWU graduate. Although he was born in Indiana, tiny Unionville Center in Union County prides itself as his hometown. It is likely the village has changed little since Fairbanks lived there.

Dr. Norman Vincent Peale, the religious leader and author of *The Power of Positive Thinking,* is a graduate of OWU. Branch Rickey graduated from the school in 1904 and is credited with integrating major league baseball when, as manager of the Brooklyn Dodgers, he hired Jackie Robinson. The physical education center on the campus is named for Rickey and an award is given in his honor.

Reportedly the first coed at OWU to wear knickers was Mildred Elizabeth Gillars, who went to Germany and became infamous as "Axis Sally" during World War II. After the war she returned to Central Ohio to live out her life, completing her education at Ohio Wesleyan, attending plays and concerts, and trying to forget a part of her life that began with a tragic love affair with a young German officer.

Frank Stanton, president emeritus of CBS, Inc., graduated in medicine at OWU and then went on to get a master's degree and doctorate in psychology at Ohio State.

Denison University at Granville gave the world of entertainment Hal Holbrook, known among other things for his stage characterizations of Mark Twain. John Davidson, singer, actor, and television personality, graduated from Denison in 1963. John Shuck, who graduated a year earlier, played Captain Waldowski in the movie *M*A*S*H*. It was apparently a golden era for Denison. Michael Eisner (class of 1964) became president of Paramount Pictures before moving on to his current powerful post at Disney.

Earlier Denison graduates excelled in other fields. Dr. Herbert G. Dorsey (class of 1894) invented sonar. Judson Harmon (class of 1866) became governor of Ohio and attorney general of the United States. Dr. Leonard Heaton (class of 1923) became head of the Walter Reed Army Medical Center and personal physician of President Dwight D. Eisenhower.

An early graduate of Otterbein College was Benjamin R. Hanby, composer of "Darling Nelly Gray" and "Up on a Housetop."

Also out of Otterbein are A. Gordon Jump of the TV series "WKRP in Cincinnati"; Dr. Frances M. Pottenger, pioneer in the prevention and cure of tuberculosis; and Ernest S. Barnhard, president of the Cleveland Indians and second president of the American Baseball League.

Capital University lists Armin H. Meyer (class of 1935) as one of its most distinguished graduates. He served as U.S. Ambassador to Lebanon, Iran, and Japan before becoming a member of the Georgetown University faculty and a consultant to the State Department. His ambassadorial appointments were by presidents Kennedy, Johnson, and Nixon. He's now president of the Washington Institute of Foreign Affairs.

Former Columbus Mayor Tom Moody is a product of Capital's law school. Two distinguished historians from Capital are Harold Grimm (class of 1924), an authority on the reformation, and Ernest Schweibert (class of 1921), a

FACING PAGE: Notable Ohio State University alumnus Jesse Owens is pictured here during the 1936 Olympic Games in Germany. Courtesy, The Bettmann Archive

Luther scholar.

Probably the best-known graduates of The Ohio State University are Curtis E. LeMay and Milton Caniff, both products of the university in the 1930s. LeMay headed bomber forces in Europe and the Pacific in World War II, became head of the Strategic Air Command, and was Air Force Chief of Staff. He was a general on active duty in the military longer than any other American.

Milt Caniff was the creator of well-known comic strips "Terry and the Pirates" and "Steve Canyon." Much of his original work is in the School of Journalism at the university. He did the official portraits of inductees in the Aviation Hall of Fame of his native Dayton. His tribute to the OSU stadium on its 50th anniversary is a classic.

Mention should also be given to Jesse Owens, the track star who won four gold medals in the 1936 Olympic Games in Hitler's Berlin. The track at the university is named in his honor and is marked by a plaque that says, in part, "As long as athletes compete in sports, or people strive for success in any undertaking, the life and accomplishments of Jesse Owens will remain an enduring inspiration."

The Columbus College of Art and Design points with pride to George Bellows, who was a student there in the 1920s and continued a long association with the school after gaining fame as a painter in New York. The school also cites Robert T. McCall, an aviation artist whose works go from air combat of World War II to the space age. One of his largest murals was done for the National Air and Space Museum in Washington.

With such a past, there is little wonder that most local schools feel a president, the author of world peace, or the conqueror of cancer is sitting right now in one of their classrooms.

—H.B.F.

Although the road from kindergarten to cap and gown may seem long at times, education is the pathway to a bright and prosperous future. Photo by Larry Hamill

academic programs lead to the bachelor of arts degree or to one of three professional degrees—bachelor of fine arts, bachelor of music, and bachelor of science in nursing.

The road from kindergarten to cap and gown is a long one, and the story of education in Central Ohio would not be complete without mentioning the work of a group of women who help make the journey possible for many.

The Childhood League, formed in Columbus in 1945, is composed of 100 women who make a five-year commitment to raise more than half a million dollars annually to operate a nonprofit preschool for developmentally disabled children. The disabilities of the children attending the Childhood League Center range from autism, severe behavior disorders, and mental retardation to multiple developmental delays.

In addition to raising money, Childhood League members must also work in the classrooms and handle administrative duties. Children receive a specialized education to meet their individual learning needs. These special programs include speech and language therapy, occupational therapy, and a unique therapy called Theraplay to meet their psychological needs.

This early-childhood comprehensive education and therapy program has had remarkable results—more than half the students are able to attend regular public school kindergarten or first grade classes upon graduation from the center.

HERE'S TO YOUR HEALTH

There are 11 hospitals in Franklin County and five hospitals in adjacent counties. Franklin County has more than 5,000 hospital beds and a physician for every two beds. In addition to these there are many clinics, urgent care facilities, and publicly funded agencies. Because there are adequate and available health-care facilities offering a variety of specialized services, Columbus is a healthy community.

The largest hospitals are Riverside Methodist, a complex along West North Broadway and Olentangy River Road, and University Hospitals, a teaching and research center associated with The Ohio State University. Each of these complexes has more than 1,000 beds.

Riverside Methodist offers an array of services for women in its Elizabeth Blackwell Center and Elizabeth Blackwell Hospital. These specialize in women's health problems and maternity services. Other specialized services of the hospital include microsurgery for the reattachment of limbs and other procedures, open-heart surgery, neurology, and orthopedic surgery. The Riverside Regional Cancer Institute treats cancer patients. There is inpatient and outpatient treatment of psychiatric problems, including alcohol and drug dependency. Kobacker House is a hospice for terminally ill patients.

Nearby are the Riverside Neurological Rehabilitation Center and the Ohio Kidney and Gall Stone Center. The 24-hour emergency room has a quick care area for minor injuries. Riverside also operates an outpatient surgery facility at 4971 Arlington Centre Boulevard.

University Hospitals are teaching and research centers as well as treatment facilities. The newest building in the complex is the Arthur G. James Cancer Hospital. The hospital has the nation's seventh-largest kidney transplant program and also has transplant programs for the heart, pancreas, liver, cornea, and bone marrow. Dodd Hall is a 72-bed rehabilitation center. Upham Hall provides psychiatric treatment on inpatient and outpatient bases including treatment of sleep and eating disorders. The emergency room has a Level 1 trauma center for life-threatening injuries.

Mount Carmel Medical Center at 793 West State Street is a 479-bed teaching hospital that opened the first Alzheimer's Disease center in the country. The hospital provides care for medical, surgical, obstetric, gerontology, and psychiatric patients.

The center also operates Mount Carmel East, a hospital on the far east side of Columbus along East Broad Street. It is a 292-bed general hospital with an extensive emergency services department, including an EmUrgent Care Center for minor injuries and illnesses.

Mount Carmel also operates a Family Practice Center at 1300 Dublin Road.

Grant Medical Center, a downtown facility with 640 beds, specializes in high-risk obstetrics, laser surgery, cardiac

The Heart Institute of Ohio at the 1,092-bed Riverside Methodist Hospitals complex specializes in the prevention and treatment of heart disease. A Riverside Methodist patient is shown here undergoing the lifesaving balloon angioplasty operation. Photo by Jeffrey A. Rycus/Rycus Associates Photography

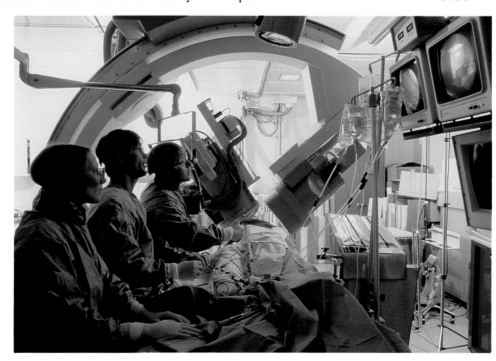

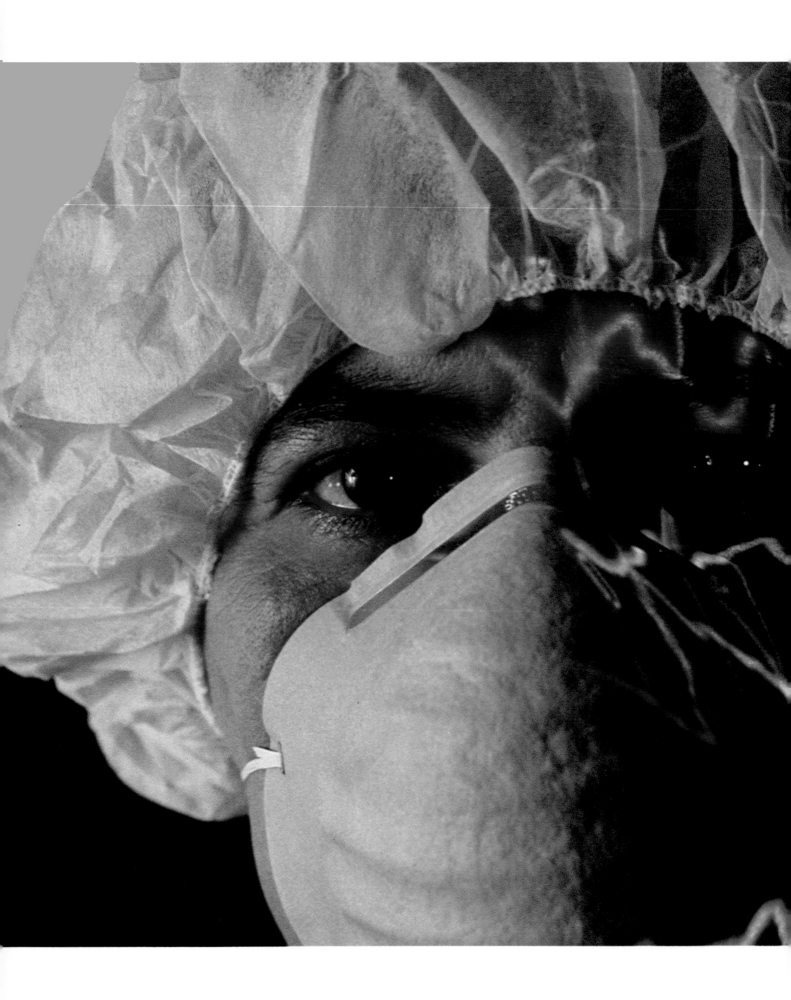

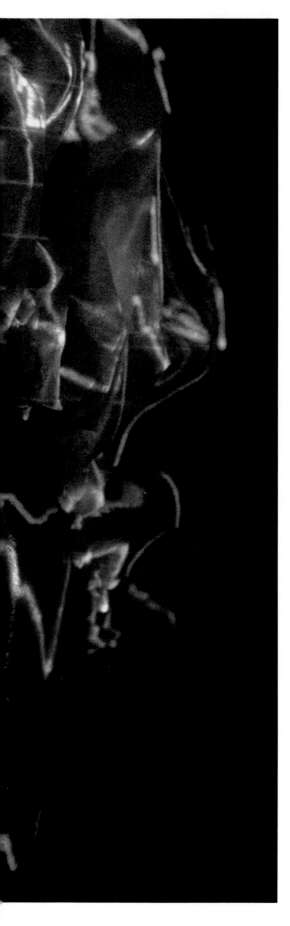

LEFT: A wide spectrum of medical services help to maintain the health of Columbus' population. Photo by Larry Hamill

ABOVE: Proud, new parents enjoy the benefits of Columbus' state-of-the-art obstetrical care and can choose from a large number of delivery options throughout the city's health care facilities. Photo by Larry Hamill

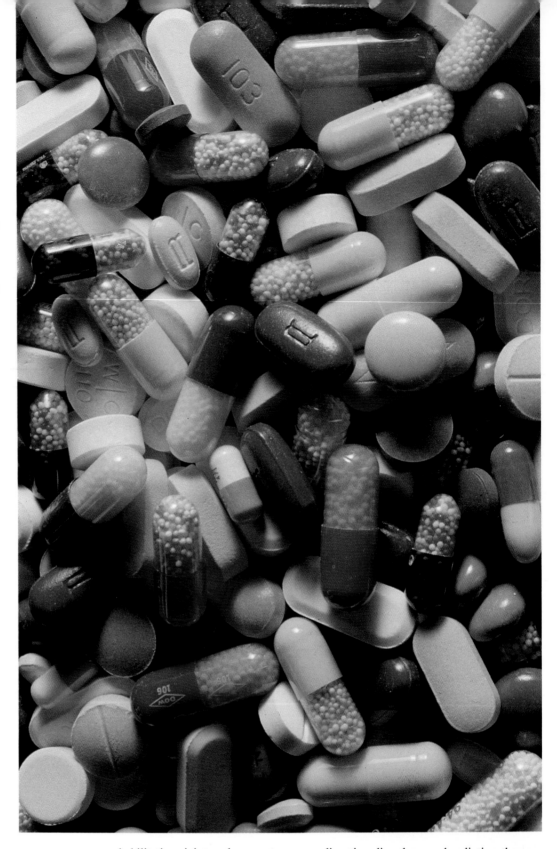

rehabilitation, joint replacement surgery, digestive disorders, and radiation therapy. There is an eye and ear center and a psychiatric unit across Town Street from the main facility.

Grant also features a fitness center with a 1/15th-mile cushioned jogging track and exercise equipment. This is used for a cardiac rehabilitation program and is also available to the public on a membership basis.

Grant's Life Flight helicopter serves a 125-mile radius around Columbus.

Saint Anthony Medical Center is a 404-bed hospital primarily for adults on the near east side. While it specializes in hip and knee-joint implant surgery, it also has a reproductive sciences institute that diagnoses and treats infertility problems. The hospital has an alcohol-treatment program for adults and adolescents and a pain-

RIGHT: Eleven hospital systems and a vast selection of clinics and urgent-care facilities in Columbus provide comprehensive health care for the more than 900,000 residents of Franklin County. Photo by Larry Hamill

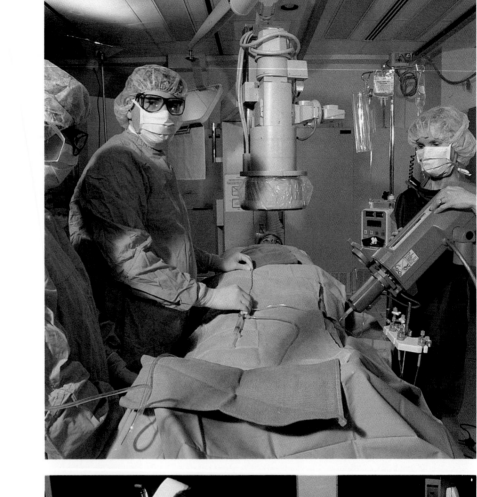

A private, nonprofit hospital sponsored by the Franciscan Sisters of the Poor, St. Anthony's Medical Center features the city's only headache clinic along with services in the fields of reproductive sciences, sleep disorders, oncology, and surgery. These young Columbus residents are introduced to the exciting field of health care at St. Anthony's. Photo by Larry Hamill

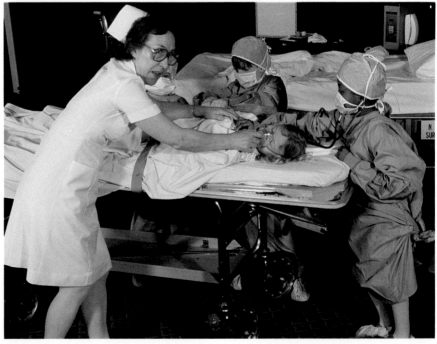

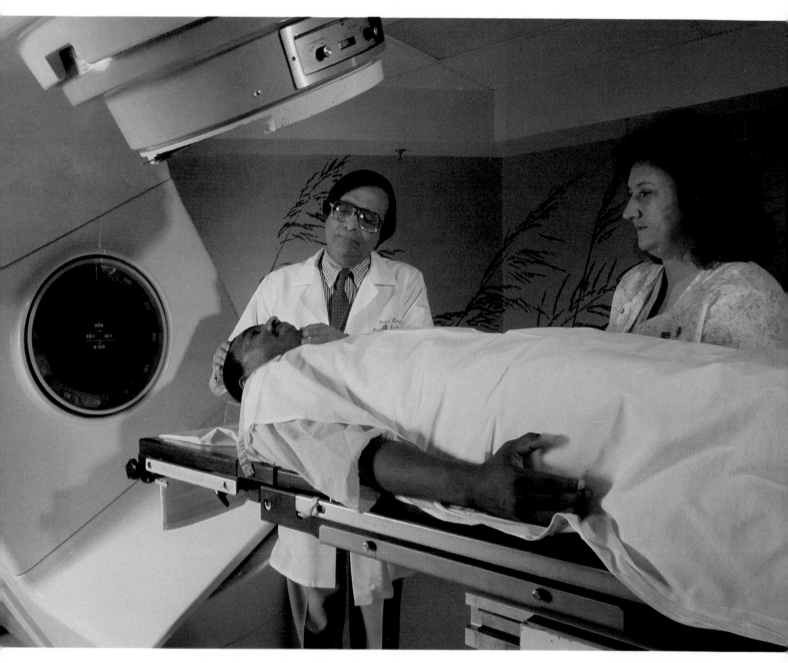

control center and a laboratory for sleep disorders. It also has the city's only headache clinic.

Columbus Community Hospital now operates at 1430 South High Street. The building formerly operated as Mercy Hospital and Saint Anthony Mercy Hospital. The new hospital is operated by American HealthMark as a partnership with a group of Columbus-area physicians. The 56-bed hospital is the only for-profit in the Columbus area.

Saint Ann's, a 180-bed community hospital in Westerville, formerly operated on Bryden Road in Columbus as a maternity hospital. In its new location it has a sports medicine treatment center, a family-centered maternity unit, an obstetrics and gynecology clinic, a coronary care unit, and a full range of medical and surgical care for men and women.

Children's Hospital is a comprehensive pediatric hospital near Parsons and Livingston avenues, providing care for patients up to the age of 21, although it has no

State-of-the-art diagnostic equipment help to make Columbus-area hospitals among the best in the nation. Photo by Larry Hamill

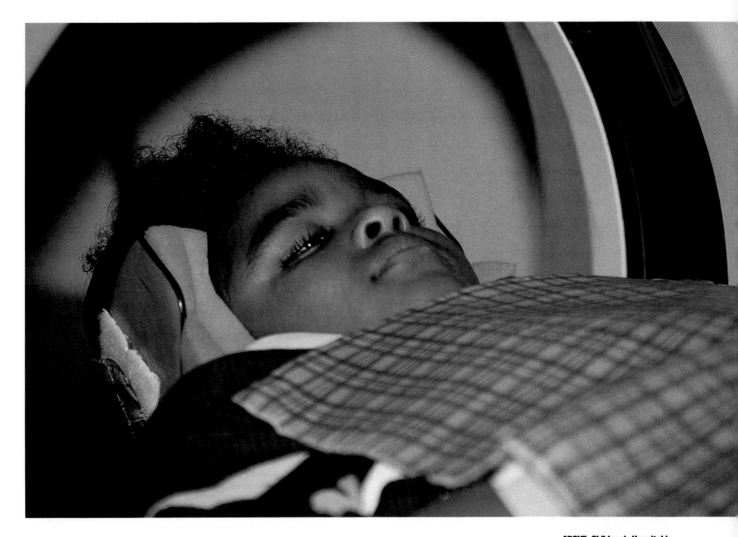

ABOVE: Children's Hospital in Columbus is a comprehensive pediatric facility, which provides care for patients from birth until age 21, and features the Wexner Institute for Pediatric Research. This young patient receives a painless CAT scan at Children's Hospital. Photo by Jeanne

FACING PAGE: Specialized services in trauma and emergency care are provided by the 640-bed facility of Grant Medical Center. The hospital's Life Flight Helicopter shown here reaches patients within a 125-mile radius. Photo by Larry Hamill

A Doctors Hospital medical
student looks on as Dr. Carol
Hostetter confers with a patient in this teaching situation at the Westerville Family
Practice Center. Photo by
Jeanne Conte

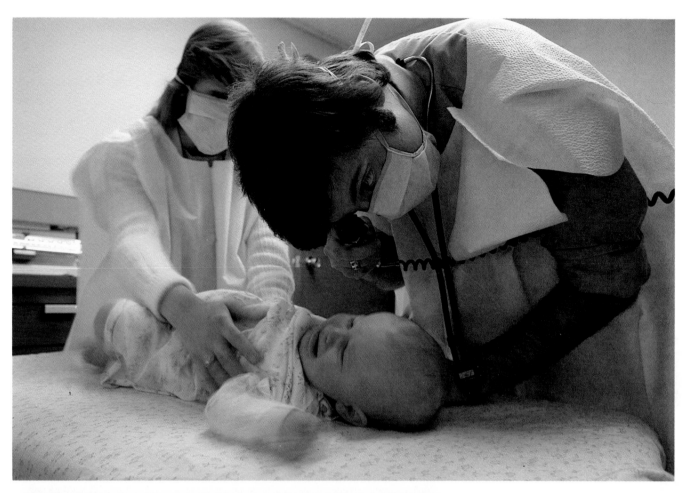

ABOVE: Even the youngest patients benefit from the quality care provided by Columbus health professionals. Photo by Trufield Enterprises/Image Finders

LEFT: Technologically-advanced facilities will carry the Columbus medical community well into the next century. Photo by Jeffrey A. Rycus/Rycus Associates Photography

maternity services. Connected to the hospital is the 122,000-square-foot Wexner Institute for Pediatric Research. There is also the six-story, $18.3-million Children's Hospital Education Building.

Inpatient and outpatient services cover pediatric medicine, surgery, and dentistry, diagnostic treatment, rehabilitation, and preventive health care. The adjacent Ronald McDonald House provides accommodations for parents and other family members of hospitalized children. The emergency room is open 24 hours a day.

Doctors Hospital North and Doctors Hospital West are general and acute-care osteopathic teaching hospitals. They are especially important as teaching hospitals with the completion of the Osteopathic Medical College at Ohio University at Athens.

Recently opened is the Doctors Hospital Center for Operative Laparoscopy and the Institute for Advanced Pelviscopic Surgery. The treatment for gall bladder disease includes preoperative education, surgery, and postoperative education. Much of the operative laparoscopy is done on an outpatient basis.

New Horizons at Doctors Hospital North provides birthing rooms for family-type obstetric services. There are also childbirth preparation, sibling, early pregnancy, and breast-feeding classes. The hospital's specialty services include open-heart and vascular surgery, pediatrics, outpatient services, and rehabilitation. Doctors North is at 1087 Dennison Avenue and Doctors West is at 5100 West Broad Street. There is also a general practice center at 4120 Indianola Avenue.

The two psychiatric hospitals in the county are Harding Hospital in Worthington and the Central Ohio Psychiatric Hospital at 1960 West Broad Street.

Harding, a private, nonprofit hospital with 120 beds, offers inpatient and outpatient services for children, adolescents, and adults. Chemical dependency and eating disorder programs are available in addition to a full range of psychiatric services and counseling. The hospital also includes the North Area Mental Health Emergency Services, a 24-hour emergency mental health facility.

The Central Ohio Psychiatric Hospital is a state-operated mental hospital with 420 beds. It provides psychiatric care for adults, and most of its patients are referred by 17 mental health centers in 12 counties. No outpatient services are offered.

Columbus Health Department and the Franklin County Health Department offer other health services in the community. These include home health services by visiting nurses. The Franklin County Board of Alcohol, Drug Abuse, and Mental Health Services offers publicly supported programs and services for persons with mental health and substance abuse disorders.

For minor illnesses and accidents, there are urgent care centers throughout the community.

In the area surrounding Franklin County, there are hospitals in Newark, Lancaster, Delaware, London and Circleville.

Along the south side of Clime Road is the Heinzerling Foundation, where full-time care is provided to severely mentally retarded children and adults. The foundation is named in honor of the late Otto Carl Heinzerling, who saw the need for such care after retiring from a career in the Navy. He originally started providing the care in a home he called the "Peck O' Wee Ones." The home grew with Heinzerling's feeling that there is something of value and something to be loved in every human life.

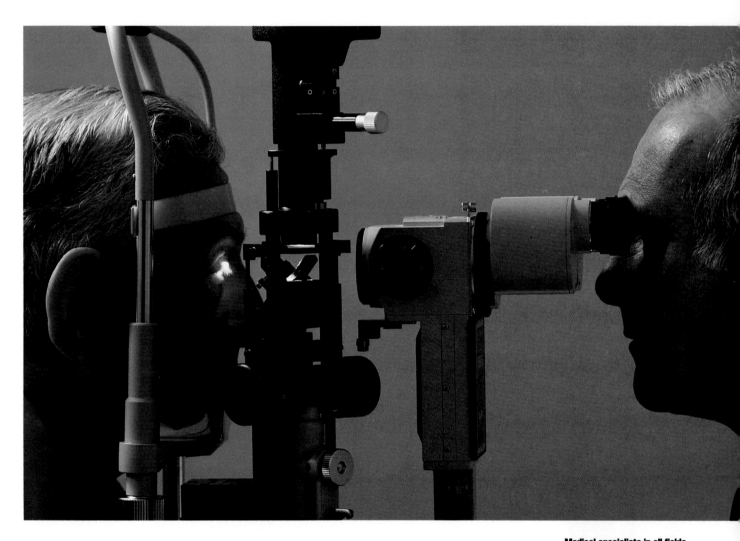

Medical specialists in all fields of modern health care can be found in Columbus. Photo by Mike Steinberg/Image Finders

5 ▼ CULTURAL
SCENE

▲▲▲▲▲▲▲▲▲▲▲▲▲▲▲

141

Much of the explosive growth in Columbus' performing and visual arts scene has been credited to the Columbus Association for the Performing Arts (CAPA), the Vern Riffe Center for Government and the Arts, the Martin Luther King, Jr., Center, and the Wexner Center for the Arts.

CAPA was formed in 1969 to save the Ohio Theatre from the wrecking ball. Construction of the theater on the site of the old Columbus City Hall, which had burned down in 1927, began the same year, and the theater opened on St. Patrick's Day in 1928 as Loews and United Artists Ohio Theatre. After spending $865,000 to build the theater, Loews spent more than $1 million to furnish it. Designed by Scottish-born Thomas White Lamb, who had also done the original Madison Square Garden and theaters in England, North Africa, and India, the theater was intended to be a palace for the average man. According to its designer, the Ohio had "probably as rich an interior as will be found in the country."

Though some of the great names of show business appeared on the Ohio stage and many of the great movies were shown there, attendance fell off in the 1950s and 1960s, and the theater was closed in 1969 when Loews sold it to a local real estate firm. The announcement that it would be closed devastated local theater and organ buffs, who formed the Save the Ohio Theatre Committee. This group failed to raise enough money to buy the theater, but it joined forces a year later with the newly organized CAPA, and a new fund-raising campaign netted $2.5 million to buy the theater, restore it, and convert it into a performing arts hall.

In 1978 the Ohio Theatre was declared a National Historic Landmark, was placed on the National Register of Historic Places, and was named "Official Theater for the State of Ohio." As the official theater, it has been used for a number of functions. New attorneys are sworn in at the Ohio by the state supreme court twice a year.

In 1984 the theater's seven-story John and Dorothy Galbreath Pavilion was unveiled, as was an expanded stage and orchestra pit with a 30-ton orchestra shell to enhance acoustics on stage and in the audience.

In 1988 CAPA acquired the Southern Theatre in the Great Southern Hotel on the southern boundary of the downtown area. CAPA calls this theater a "Victorian gem."

CAPA acquired the Palace Theatre on April 1, 1989. This theater, in the LeVeque Tower on West Broad Street, was also designed by Lamb. It was built in 1926 as a vaudeville/movie theater after the style of the Palais de Versailles and had been

preserved and improved through the efforts of Katherine S. LeVeque.

CAPA uses the Ohio and Palace to screen a number of films and for live performances throughout the year. The Summer Movie Series at the Ohio is the nation's most successful classic film series. Other regular presentations include the Family Series, the Steps Ahead Series, Signature Series, and American Popular Song Series.

MUSIC AND DANCE

The Columbus Symphony Orchestra, which has grown faster than any other orchestra in America and boasts ticket sales of nearly 200,000 a season, begins a new era with Italian conductor Alessandro Siciliani.

Maestro Siciliani was named music advisor for the 1991-92 season and will become artistic director and conductor beginning with the 1992-93 season.

He plans, he says, to help the orchestra develop its own distinctive sound, one that will increase the national recognition the orchestra has won.

Siciliani was chosen as the sixth director of the orchestra after a search committee considered more than 80 candidates. He is a composer and pianist as well as conductor.

A native of Florence, Siciliani is the son of Francesco Siciliani, longtime director of La Scala Opera in Milan. The younger Siciliani studied conducting with Franco Ferrara in Rome.

Siciliani made his American debut in 1980 in Philadelphia. He was a guest conductor with the Columbus Symphony Orchestra in 1986 and 1989.

The Columbus Symphony Orchestra makes its home at the Ohio Theatre. Its regular season runs from October to May, and it often draws internationally known visiting artists for guest appearances.

In the summer the orchestra plays a very popular "Picnic with the Pops" series on the lawn of the Chemical Abstracts Service grounds on Olentangy River Road. Patrons dine on gourmet food and sip wine as they listen to favorite tunes. There is also a pops series as part of the regular season.

The orchestra also leaves the Ohio to play the Amadeus Series of chamber music at Weigel Hall on The Ohio State University campus.

The orchestra's typical season includes a Symphonic Series of the classic symphonic repertoire mixed with lesser-known contemporary pieces, a Favorite Series of classical works known to the casual listener, and the Masterworks program, which allows the orchestra to tackle the great classical masterpieces.

Opera/Columbus stages its productions at the Palace. Its first season was in 1980, and many of the current productions are sellouts. The season, which usually opens in October, includes seven programs.

The tenth season of Opera Columbus was almost its last.

But when it appeared in February of 1991 that the opera would not have the economic resources to continue, the city's music lovers rallied to save it.

Now Opera Columbus is looking to a brighter future under its new general director, William E. Russell.

Before coming to Columbus, Bill Russell spent two and a half years as general director of the Anchorage, Alaska, opera. A native of Denver, he was a piano major at the University of Colorado and has a master's degree in vocal performance from the University of Illinois and a master's in business administration from the University of California.

Among Russell's visions are putting together weekend packages that would bring people from all over the country to Columbus to listen to opera. He sees opera, first and foremost, as drama, and he told the *Columbus Dispatch*, "I'm all for breaking down all the barriers to opera. I think people should be able to wear anything they want to the opera. Going to an opera is an event, but it is not just for people with tuxedos and jewelry."

BalletMet has blossomed under the artistic hand of director John McFall, who came to the city in 1986. Before starting his career as a choreographer, McFall was a principal dancer with the San Francisco Ballet for 18 years. The company has presented a number of world premieres, including works by McFall done specifically for the group.

After joining the company, McFall engaged 24 talented dancers from prominent companies across the country, added new works to the repertoire, and began featuring works by some of the nation's brightest choreographers. As a result, BalletMet has become one of the fastest growing and most innovative companies in America.

The Pro Musica Chamber Orchestra has sometimes been called the city's "other" orchestra. It is known for its innovative programs and for premiering new works. The group, directed by Timothy Russell, has a Sunday series in Weigel Hall at Ohio State and schedules a "Saturday Plus" series, which has been staged in the downtown Riffe Center.

The Jazz Arts Group of Columbus (JAG), under artistic director Ray Eubanks, is a jazz repertory orchestra with a mission of preserving, promoting, and encouraging the appreciation of jazz as an art form in Central Ohio. In its annual series at the Battelle Auditorium, the group has showcased local talent and also brought in such jazz notables as Maynard Ferguson and Joe Williams.

FACING PAGE: Downtown Columbus is the site for many of the city's musical events. Photo by Larry Hamill

BELOW: Local colleges and universities help to introduce new generations of artists and performers into the Columbus arts community, some of whom have achieved national recognition in their respective fields. Here, students at Ohio State University's school of dance practice their art. Photo by Jim Baron/Image Finders

Armando Luna and Liz
Zengara perform in the BalletMet production *Across
the Boards*. Photo by Will
Shively

ABOVE: A crowd enjoys fresh air, food, and good music during a recent Picnic with the Pops concert. Photo by Larry Hamill

LEFT: Artistic Director Ray Eubanks and the Jazz Arts Group of Columbus perform at the Riverfront Amphitheatre during a "Music in the Air" concert, sponsored by the Columbus Recreation and Parks Department. Photo by Jeffrey A. Rycus/Rycus Associates Photography

ABOVE: Local musician Arnett Howard plays to a captivated audience. Photo by Pamela J. Willits

LEFT: Whether your taste runs to classical or the avant-garde, there is something for everyone within Columbus' musical community. Early Music in Columbus concerts feature Renaissance and Baroque music played on period instruments. Photo by Jeffrey A. Rycus/Rycus Associates Photography

These jazz concerts normally fill the hall to capacity, and so JAG has been looking for larger accommodations. Eubanks is a trumpet player who received bachelor's and master's degrees from Ohio State, and while there, worked with Ladd McIntosh to transform the OSU jazz band into the "Live New Breed."

Dr. Paul Droste, Professor of Music at The Ohio State University, formed the Brass Band of Columbus after serving 13 years as director of the university's marching band.

Whereas Ohio State's marching band is the world's largest all-brass marching band, the BBC only has 39 players. The instrumentation of the Brass Band of Columbus is brass and percussion only, following the tradition of British brass bands. Averaging 31 rehearsals and about 25 performances per year, many of them in local churches, the band includes five college band directors, a dozen high school band directors, a few college students, and others, such as a dentist, a pathologist, an author, a student minister, and an instrument repairman.

The band has won first place in the Championship Section of the North American Brass Band Association in three successive years, and it appeared before more than 1,000 band directors in the Mid-West International Band and Orchestra Clinic in Chicago and received five standing ovations.

In 1986 the BBC hosted a national competition and will do so again in 1992.

CURTAIN CALLS

The recent completion of the Riffe Center for Government and the Arts provided a new home for Players Theatre Columbus. The 32-story center is named for Vern Riffe, Jr., longtime speaker of the Ohio House of Representatives. Producing Director is Ed Graczyk, who is also a playwright. His "Come Back to the Five and Dime, Jimmy Dean, Jimmy Dean" played on Broadway.

The modern Riffe Center offers "theater as you've never seen it before" with a

thrust stage surrounded on three sides by the audience. A typical season at Players includes comedy, music, and drama. The two Studio Theatres in the building house the Players Theatre Youth Theatre Columbus.

Players Theatre started nearly 70 years ago as a small private club committed to producing quality theater. It has grown into a professional regional theater company.

Center Stage Theatre, a black community theater, has moved into the Garfield Annex of the Martin Luther King, Jr., Center for the Performing and Cultural Arts. The group performs in the Center's 444-seat theater and also conducts a children's theater workshop.

LEFT: The new 32-story Riffe Center for Government and the Arts in downtown Columbus is home to Players Theatre Columbus. Photo by Jeanne Conte

FACING PAGE: The only professional company in the nation that presents the traditional music and dance of Yugoslavia, the Zivili dance troupe of Columbus performs its unique repertoire to delighted audiences throughout Central Ohio. Photo by Jeffrey A. Rycus/Rycus Associates Photography

ABOVE: Under the leadership of director Ed Graczyk, Players Theatre Columbus has evolved into a successful troupe and is the city's only Equity theater company. Its recent production of *Babes in Arms* is pictured here. Photo by Will Shively

The Martin Luther King Jr. Center for Performing and Cultural Arts opened its doors in March 1987 in what had been the old Pythian Theatre, at 867 Mt. Vernon Avenue.

The building has some 27,000 square feet of usable space, including a 444-seat theatre on the ground floor with great acoustics and dressing rooms. There are offices on the second floor, and on the top floor a large ballroom with full kitchen facilities.

Since that opening the center has also expanded into the adjacent Garfield School, which has been renovated to include classrooms, a multipurpose room/gymnasium, and the Elijah Pierce Gallery of Fine Art.

The center is Central Ohio's largest provider of children's programs that focus on African-American Art and Culture. More than 10,000 schoolchildren attend programs at the complex annually, and there is a broad spectrum of classes in the arts for people of all ages.

The complex also houses the Martin Luther King Jr. Institute for the Arts, a joint project with the Ohio State University College of Arts that provides exceptional instruction in the arts to selected students in the Columbus Public Schools.

Major traveling art exhibits are shown in the Pierce gallery, named in honor of the wood carving artist, who was a barber and resident of the East Side community.

Although the center is relatively new, its genesis dates back to 1969, when the Columbus Metropolitan Area Community Action Organization (CMACAO) established the Cultural Arts Center (later renamed the Paul Laurence Dunbar Cultural Arts Center), which featured nationally recognized touring groups and provided classes for young people in creative writing, dance, drama, music, and the visual arts.

The center was located in the old Lincoln Theatre on East Long Street and the old Columbus Boys' Academy on Nelson Road. The center found itself without a home after the Boys' Academy burned to the ground and consultants recommended against going to the expense of restoring the Lincoln Theatre.

The King Center project was the result of community-wide discussions held in early 1984 regarding an appropriate honor to Dr. King and was the recommendation of a Martin Luther King Jr. Memorial Tribute Committee appointed by the president of the Columbus City Council.

That committee and the restoration committee joined forces and chose the grand old brick-and-masonry Pythian Theatre as the site for the new center. The governing body is the Community Arts Project Board of Trustees.

"The King Center builds on a long standing heritage," say the trustees. "It is not only the revival of an African-American cultural arts center in Columbus, nor is it only a memorial for the late Dr. Martin Luther King, Jr. Today the King Center also stands tribute to all the artists, educators, and leaders—the dreamers of our city and our state—whose foresight and fortitude have brought identity and purpose to the black community once again."

Community theater thrives in Central Ohio. Among those offering regular productions are the Gallery Players of the Leo Yassenoff Jewish Center, the Contemporary American Theatre Company, The Little Theatre Off Broadway in Grove City, the Gahanna Community Theatre, the Worthington Community Theatre, the Buckeye Dinner Theatre at the Villa Milano Party Center, and the Reality Theatre in the Short North neighborhood.

There are also active performing arts groups at Ohio State, Capital University, Denison University, Ohio Wesleyan University, and Otterbein College.

The Columbus Recreation and Parks Department and the Columbus Federation of Musicians present a summer series at the Riverfront Amphitheatre downtown and in the city's parks. The free performances include big band music, rock, bluegrass, classical, country and western, and others.

Fun After Dark

▲▲▲▲▲▲▲▲▲▲▲▲▲▲▲

And the night shall be filled with music,
And the cares, that infest the day,
Shall fold their tents, like the Arabs,
And as silently steal away.

—"The Day is Done"
Henry Wadsworth Longfellow

When the office lights go out, when the drive-time traffic has thinned, when the streetlights come on and the stars become visible in the sky—that is when the people of Columbus seek to shed "the cares that infest the day."

The possibilities are endless.

Two of the major contributors to those possibilities have been brothers Dave and Jed Pallone, who have been in the nightclub business in Columbus for nearly a quarter century.

Their current offerings in "theme" nightclubs are Rosie O'Grady's, on Morse Road in the north end, and The Lost City of Atlantis, on Channingway Drive on the far east side just off Brice and Livingston Roads. The goal of the Pallones is to provide fun after dark and to keep one jump ahead of the public choice in entertainment.

Entering Atlantis, a customer passes downward through a tunnel whose walls are lined with aquariums set in crevasses that simulate the ocean's deeps. The fun seeker then emerges into a large room with brightly flashing beams of multicolored light surrounding what is called the largest dance floor in Ohio. But Atlantis, half an acre of entertainment under one roof, is more than just this huge nightclub. Off to one side is the cozy Hard Shot Cafe, a bar surrounded by comfortable seating, blackjack tables, and a pool table.

To the other side, a door leads to Bourbon Street, where the floor is Louisiana brick and the tables give a feel of New Orleans. There is even a seafood bar with a real oyster shucker.

At one end of Bourbon Street, doors lead to the Bijou Theatre, a theater where motion pictures are shown two or three times a night and one where the brothers hope to have showings of locally made films. At the other end of Bourbon Street is Guidos Pizzeria. The counter on one side opens on the nightclub for use by the patrons. On the other side, customers come in from the outside for takeout orders.

Also just off Bourbon Street is the Preservation Pool Hall, eight regulation tables for tournament or friendly play.

"A nightclub is no longer just a place to sit and drink," says Jed Pallone. "We are seeing people who drink in moderation, those who are interested in fitness and health. They come here for something interesting to do."

Dave Pallone also points out that with the variety of rooms at Atlantis, it is possible to open only part of the complex during the slower midweek nights and then have the entire facility jumping on weekends. When that happens, the population of Atlantis includes 1,500 fun seekers.

The Pallones got into the nightclub business in 1968 when they opened Cabaret on East Twelfth Avenue in The Ohio State University district. The popular student hangout was a bar in front and a nightclub with live entertainment in the rear. They ran it until 1974.

In 1974 came King Tut's, a nightclub with an Egyptian theme. It was decorated to resemble the Pharoahs' Valley of the Nile, complete with a 15-foot statue of King Tutankhamen. (The Valley of the Nile is now Rosie O'Grady's.)

In May 1980 the Pallones opened the first Screamin' Willies on Morse Road. One of the attractions was a mechanical bull. A short time later the movie *Urban Cowboy* was released, starring John Travolta.

"We went around to all the theaters

The Plaza Restaurant in the Hyatt on Capitol Square is a favorite Columbus eatery. Photo by Jeffrey A. Rycus/Rycus Associates Photography

where it was playing and put up posters advertising the mechanical bull. For weeks we had people standing in line from 7 p.m. until 2 a.m.," Dave Pallone recalls.

Eventually the Pallones had three Screamin' Willies. Screamin' Willies East was where Atlantis now thrives. Screamin' Willies Saloon and Steakhouse was downtown in the Ohio Center.

Screamin' Willies was followed by Dallas and East Dallas, cashing in on the popularity of both the television series and the professional football team. Waitresses at the Dallas nightclubs dressed like the Dallas Cowboys Cheerleaders.

Not all of the Pallone ideas have been successful. The Haunted House lasted less than five months. Sir Laffalot's, an early try at a comedy club, was not a financial success.

A number of attractions have been tried over the years. The Pallone clubs have had a shooting gallery, bumper cars, and dunk tanks to attract and entertain customers. They've had professional wrestling in the clubs and are considering boxing matches.

While the Pallones use mostly local bands and entertainers, they have featured such nationally known personalities as Boxcar Willie, Ricky Scaggs, and Ricky Nelson.

There are Sunday parties and concerts for teenagers at which no alcohol is served or allowed. These were formerly booked as Sarsaparilla Rock Concerts.

The Pallones won't predict what might come next. They travel the country to see what's new and different in night life. They would like one day to have a place downtown again.

Their business is providing fun for the people of Columbus when the business day ends and the sun sets. They say they have fun doing it.

—H.B.F.

RIGHT: Mural artist George Monaghan composes a new work of art at the Continent shopping center. Strictly Columbus in content, the mural is complete with Buckeye fans and Ohio State football players. Photo by Jeanne Conte

FACING PAGE: Designed by architects Peter Eisenman and Dick Trott, the Wexner Center for the Arts has more than 100,000 square feet of exhibition and performance space. Located on the campus of The Ohio State University, the center is devoted to the contemporary arts and offers programs and concerts in the fields of dance, music, film, and visual arts. Photo by Dennis Barnes

GALLERIES AND MUSEUMS

The Wexner Center for the Arts is the newest—and perhaps the most spectacular—showplace for the arts in Columbus. The center was the dream of Leslie H. Wexner, chairman of The Limited and an Ohio State graduate who donated $25 million to the university for an arts center. It is on The Ohio State University campus between Mershon Auditorium and Weigel Hall.

The center's main hall is a long, wavy ramp that connects four unusually stacked galleries. Its architect was Peter Eisenman. The building has unfinished-looking scaffolding and grids as a theme. Red brick used in the construction has the appearance of the ROTC armory that once occupied the spot.

With 108,750 square feet of space, the center serves as an exhibition hall and a performance venue and research facility for painting, sculpture, graphic arts, design, dance, theater, music, film, video, and sound. In addition to its four galleries, it has a film and video theater that seats 278 and a performing theater with accommodations for up to 250 people.

The Columbus Museum of Art on East Broad Street is the traditional center for visual arts in Columbus. It is located close to the downtown section and is known for its sculpture gardens. The museum features a permanent collection of the masters, particularly nineteenth- and twentieth-century European and American paintings. The collection also

LEFT: The traditional center for visual arts in the city, the Columbus Museum of Art maintains a diverse collection that ranges from the old masters to American contemporary works. Traveling exhibitions, year-round activities, children's workshops, and a renowned sculpture garden add to the fun and attraction of the museum. Photo by William A. Holmes/Image Finders

ABOVE: A young visitor browses through the exhibits at the Columbus Museum of Art. Photo by Jeffrey A. Rycus/Rycus Associates Photography

The Gallery Hop through Columbus' Short North district takes place the first Saturday evening of each month. Art lovers can wander through the various galleries, which feature everything from glass creations to experimental art. Photo by Larry Hamill

FACING PAGE: Columbus sculptor Chris Mohler, who has been active in the arts community for more than 10 years, poses with one of his recent projects. Photo by Dennis Barnes

includes paintings by the old masters and a representation of Asian art, and special exhibits are held regularly.

The Short North, the area of North High Street just north of downtown, has become the city's art district, with monthly "Gallery Hops" a popular attraction.

The Schumacher Gallery at Capital University is also noted for its permanent art collection and traveling exhibits.

Columbus has given the world three noted artists—George Bellows, Emerson Burkhart, and Elijah Pierce.

Bellows, who was born in Columbus in 1892, went to New York in 1904. His work, marked by use of vivid colors to portray social realism, first startled the art world when it was exhibited in the New York Armory Show in 1913. A copy of one of his prizefighting paintings may be seen at the Ringside Cafe in downtown Columbus.

Burkhart moved to Columbus in 1931 at the age of 26 and stayed there the remainder of his life. He showed his work annually in his large house on Woodland Avenue, and if a number of his paintings had a price such as $76.54, you knew that was the amount of his current car payment.

Elijah Pierce lived most of his life on East Long Street, where he worked as a barber. Between haircuts he used a pocket knife to make wood carvings. He would

Housed in a renovated building that was once an arsenal, the Cultural Arts Center on Main Street is now the site for art classes and exhibitions run by the Columbus Recreation and Parks Department. Photo by Larry Hamill

sandpaper the finished carving and use bright lacquers to paint them. Many of his works had a religious motif. He did 33 carved pictures that he called the "Book of Wood," which were his view of the New Testament, representing highlights from the 33 years of Jesus' life.

Pierce is honored by the Elijah Pierce Gallery in the renovated Garfield School at the Martin Luther King, Jr., Center, where many of his works are featured. Pierce was born on a Mississippi Delta cotton farm in 1892 and died in Columbus at the age of 92.

The restored home at 77 Jefferson Avenue where James Grover Thurber grew up, is a center for the literary arts in Columbus. "Jamie" was actually born at 147 Parsons Avenue, but the restored brick house on Jefferson is the one featured in many of his stories set in Columbus.

The home's furnishings are typical of those that were there when the Thurber family occupied it. Each room has a Thurber drawing, and the upper floor is often used by an author in residence.

Offered for sale at the house are copies of Thurber's works, as well as those of several other authors. The house sponsors a number of "Evenings with Authors" during its season, and in July and August there are literary picnics featuring readings by Ohio and Midwestern authors.

The Ohio Historical Center and Ohio Village are located just off I-71 at Seventeenth Avenue, just north of the Ohio Expositions Center. The museum has exhibits featuring the state's natural, social, and political history.

Ohio Village recreates a small Ohio town of the mid-1800s, including shops, a

A local Columbus artisan practices her craft at the city's Cultural Arts Center. Photo by Pamela J. Willits

school, a general store, and a restaurant—the Colonel Crawford Inn. At the inn you can dine on the typical fare of the period, and during the Christmas Season, the Fourth of July, and some weekends, the village hosts special events.

From astronomy to zoology, from pre-history to the future. That is the scope of the Center of Science and Industry (COSI,) where having fun is down to a science.

The building, at 280 East Broad Street, is known to old timers as Memorial Hall, which was built to honor military veterans, but since March of 1964 it has been one of only 22 science-technology centers in the world and the only one in Ohio.

The building is crammed with four floors of hands-on science exhibits, which attract schoolchildren from all over the state during the school year. In the summer the center features a number of two-hour workshops for children from the age of four through the sixth grade. There are also workshops that involve the entire family.

After the new Veterans Memorial building was erected on West Broad Street, there arose the problem of what to do with the old building. Much of the credit for establishing a Center of Science and Industry goes to the late S.N. Hallock II, an advertising executive who became the first executive director of COSI after interesting civic leaders in the concept and taking them to such places as the Center of Science and Industry in Chicago to see similar facilities.

The Thurber House on Jefferson Avenue is a central focus for literary arts in Columbus. Once the home of renowned writer James Grover Thurber, the house features a museum of Thurber memorabilia, sponsors writing workshops, and holds the special Evenings with Authors Series. Photo by Jeanne Conte

A "solar front" was put on the building, giving it a modern look and allowing passersby to see an example of some of the exhibits inside.

The ground floor has a coal mine as well as the food service operation and a workshop center.

The first floor has a number of scientific exhibits, including at least one—the electrostatic generator—that will make your hair stand on end. Here visitors can also watch the mysterious swinging of the Foucault pendulum.

The Columbus street of yesteryear on the second floor is a re-creation of the downtown Columbus of 1790 to 1935. The "street" is partially unpaved, for when wagons rolled on dirt roads; has the cobblestones that paved the streets in 1885; and finally is made of the brick laid around 1917.

The visitor can see the shops and trades of Columbus' past, including the Dreamland Nickelodeon, featuring the silent movies of 1915-1935. It is modelled after the Dreamland Theatre, which stood in downtown Columbus in the 1920s.

The third floor exhibits are built around the Life Science Theater. Exhibits include the story of birth, the transparent woman, and a special area on veterinary medicine.

A new addition to COSI is the "Limited space" structure next door. An extraordinary array of traveling exhibits have been seen there, including Mission to Mars, Dinosaurs, and Bionics and Transplants.

The Ohio History of Flight Museum at Port Columbus International Airport is still in the development stage. One day it may house an example of each of the airplanes built in Ohio. Several are already there. Foster A. Lane, an aviation pioneer and founder of Lane Aviation Corporation at the airport, has been responsible for much of the development of the museum, which is operated by a number of volunteer aviation buffs, including many who helped make Ohio aviation history.

Life in mid-nineteenth century Ohio is recreated at the Ohio Village in Columbus. This living museum includes a general store, schoolhouse, shops, and other historical structures that help bring history alive for visitors of all ages. Photo by Mark E. Gibson

Ohio's Center of Science and Industry (COSI) features four floors of hands-on science and technology exhibits. A favorite destination for the entire family, some highlights include a planetarium, an old-time movie theater, and the AnimaLab exhibit. Here, a youngster experiences the electrifying Van de Graaff display. Photo by Larry Hamill

Grandparents Living Theatre

▲▲▲▲▲▲▲▲▲▲▲▲▲▲

Grandparents Living Theatre qualifies as both one of the newest and one of the oldest theater groups in Columbus.

"Forget your preconceptions, these talented seniors are vibrant, energetic, highly professional and alive!!!" That's the way one reviewer characterized this troupe's presentation of theater, song and dance.

"Above all we aim for exciting theater that is joyous, sometimes provocative, but always truthful and unafraid," says Joy Reilly, Ph.D., founder and artistic director of GLT, now an independent and nonprofit theater group, with headquarters at 65 Jefferson Avenue, in an historic carriage house that has been converted to the Jefferson Center for Learning and the Arts.

The group was founded in 1984 as the Columbus Living Theatre, a program within the Columbus Recreation and Parks Department. It took its present name in 1988. Reilly directed its development into a multimedia group, one of only a couple dozen independent senior theater groups in the country and one of the forerunners.

Voting membership in the theater group is open to any person over 60. Honorary memberships are available to some who have not reached that age. The mission of GLT is to provide an opportunity for older actors to create and perform theater works in an atmosphere that promotes a striving for excellence, theatrical discipline, honesty, and a sense of humanity.

The first theatrical production of the company was *Sacred Hearts,* an original, full-length romantic comedy written by Margo Haas of Cleveland. It was about a golden-age affair in a Catholic nursing home and the difficulties of budding romance under the watchful, unapproving eye of Sister Damien.

Revues presented by the seniors have included *Spring Fling, Fall Frolic, I Was Young . . . But Now I'm Wonderful,* and *Golden Age is All the Rage.*

The touring season of the troupe is from mid-September to early December and from mid-March to early June. They have taken their performance throughout Ohio and neighboring states and say they are willing to travel the world.

GLT performs in schools, clubs, libraries, churches, hospitals, nursing homes, recreation and retirement centers, prisons, and other shut-in communities.

Sacred Hearts had its premiere in the Davis Discovery Center Shedd Theatre at 549 Franklin Avenue, the former home of Players Theatre. The group is also well known at the Riffe Center downtown, the present home of Players Theatre.

Older actors, singers, dancers, and offstage supporters are welcome. No experience is necessary, but performers are expected to learn new skills and to rehearse and perform at a high level of professionalism.

"The company strives to be a friendly and socially active family that is representative of seniors in the entire community," says Reilly. "Above all, GLT hopes to present theater which speaks to audiences of all ages with vision, humor and lasting impact."

One audience member attested to its success with a letter stating, "The presentation didn't just strike a chord, it pounded my entire soul." And a member who helped present that show said, "GLT gives me the pleasure of living, not merely existing."

National attention was drawn to GLT when members were taped in Columbus for appearances on the "Art Linkletter Show." Company members frequently appear on local radio and television programs, participate in fund-raising events, and act in educational films and videos.

Members make a number of public appearances before various groups to "promote a positive image of the older adult as a vibrant, enthusiastic and talented participant in the new area of Senior Adult Theater."

Reilly, an assistant professor of theater at The Ohio State University, is assisted by Managing Director Jane Celehar, a secretary, and a group of volunteers.

The image they have projected to the community is that of "A highly professional troup for which age is merely an asset."

—H.B.F.

6 ▼ WINGS AND WHEELS

▲▲▲▲▲▲▲▲▲▲▲▲▲▲▲▲▲▲▲

Past and present are the same at the southeast corner of Port Columbus International Airport thanks to test pilot E.A. Gillespie.

Ed Gillespie, a native of Ann Arbor, Michigan, completed U.S. Navy Flight School in 1950 and the U.S. Navy Test Pilot School in 1954. Two years later he became an engineering test pilot at North American Aviation at Port Columbus. He was named senior engineering test pilot in 1963 and chief test pilot in April 1964, a position he held until his retirement in 1987.

He has described his nearly 10,000 hours in the air—in everything from propellor-driven, single-engine planes to rocket jets—as "actual test time flown during extensively briefed, relatively short, very busy flights. Aircraft damage has occurred during combat and due to structural failure caused by test conditions, but (I) have never scratched an airplane because of pilot error during (my) military or civilian flight career."

After Ed Gillespie's retirement, his special project became restoring the original terminal at Port Columbus, which had been scheduled for demolition. It took him 14 months and cost him $600,000. When the job was finished, Ed invited some friends over, tapped a keg of beer, and roasted hot dogs over charcoal.

He says the building is the last terminal in America dating from the 1920s with the original control tower intact. In restoring the building, which is subleased as office space, Gillespie located the plaque that was on the original and found the rotating beacon that was on the top of the original tower.

The building served as the airport terminal for nearly 30 years and during the period had nearly tripled in size. A mail and freight facility was built onto the east side of the building and a restaurant was added to the west.

After signing a 40-year lease with the city, Gillespie tore away all the additions that had been built. He was left with a building that had been poorly maintained for many years. The basement was flooded, the interior was rotting, the utilities were unusable, and the roof had been patched so often that tons of material had to be removed before it could be rebuilt. Much of the work was done by retired test-flight mechanics who had cared for the planes Gillespie flew during his career as a test pilot.

The result was a beautiful building that is a tribute to city fathers who brought Columbus into the air age in 1929. It was not an easy fight, but it was one that has given the city a facility that has survived into the jet age and has been a major part of the nation's airport system.

In 1927 the voters of Columbus were asked to provide a "first-class airport" for the city, but the issue failed to pass, probably because the city's voters thought the area's existing unpaved runways were sufficient. With the formation of Transcontinental Air Transport, Inc., in 1928, this collective attitude changed. The company, which has since evolved into Trans World Airlines, was formed by executives of Curtiss Aero Industries and the Pennsylvania Railroad. An airport commission was named to get public support for a bond issue and to convince TAT President C.M. Keys to make Columbus the eastern terminus of the airway.

The route between New York and Los Angeles was surveyed by Colonel Charles A. Lindbergh, and Columbus was chosen as one of the stops. The site chosen for the new airport was just north of the Pennslyvania and B&O Railroad right of way and west of Poth Road (now Hamilton Road), just east of Columbus.

Airplanes of USAir take on passengers at the new concourse of Port Columbus International Airport. Photo by Gregory M. Franken

The three local newspapers promoted the bond issue in stories, editorials, and cartoons. Don M. Casto, a member of the airport commission, demonstrated that the air age had arrived by booking a passage from Germany to New York aboard a dirigible. The bond issue passed handily.

The city fathers noted that other major cities, if on major rivers or with harbors, had grown. Following this logic, they named the airport Port Columbus, reasoning that the ocean of air surrounding the globe gives any city a chance for greatness if it has an adequate airport. Their wisdom has survived a number of misguided attempts to change the name of the airport.

The nation's first transcontinental service was to be a combination of rail and air transportation, with passengers sleeping in Pullman cars by night and switching to airplanes—the Ford Tri-Motor— by day. To initiate this notable event, Colonel Lindbergh pressed a button in the California governor's office that caused a gong to ring in Pennsylvania Station in

City fathers named their new air facility Port Columbus in the late 1920s, because of the great sea of air that surrounds the globe. Columbus was soon destined to become a major port in the nation's transportation network. Photo by Larry Hamill

New York City. This signalled the conductor of the *Airway Limited* to wave his lantern at the engineer and start the trip to Columbus. The train carried more than 200 passengers, including 20 who would continue the trip to the West Coast. Among these was Amelia Earhart.

The train arrived at Port Columbus at 7:55 a.m., and the passengers hurried across the street and through the terminal to board two airplanes that were to depart at 8:15 a.m. The Secretary of Commerce pressed a button in Washington, D.C., that telegraphically sounded a gong at the airport in Columbus, the signal to start the plane engines. The airplnes would fly all day to reach Waynoka, Oklahoma. The second night aboard the train took passengers to Clovis, New Mexico, and the final flight to Los Angeles included stops at Albuquerque, Winslow, and Kingman. Traveling the breadth of the nation, from coast to coast, had been reduced to 48 hours.

The air-rail service continued for three years. Then the airline (by then Transcontinental and Western Airways) started flying at night and introduced the new and reliable DC-3 to the route.

Columbus became the first city with regular passenger service at two airports

when an airline started north-south service with a landing at Sullivant Avenue Airport on the city's west side.

In 1940 Curtiss-Wright Corporation leased 83 acres from the city and built a factory at the southwest corner of the airport. During World War II the facility employed 25,000 industrial workers and turned out the SO3C-1 Seagull observation planes and the SB2C Helldiver for the Navy. One of the Navy pilots in the group that delivered the airplanes was Francis A. "Jack" Bolton, who remained after the war as superintendent of the airport. He was at the helm when the operation moved into its present terminal and when the jet age arrived in Port Columbus.

After the war Curtiss-Wright stopped production, and the factory was converted into a plant in which prefabricated homes were constructed. Later North American Aviation (which became Rockwell International) took over the plant and produced jet fighters and bombers for the Korean and Vietnam conflicts. Parts for Rockwell's B-1 bomber were built there, and now McDonnell-Douglas operates the plant, making parts for the giant C-17 transport plane for the military.

With the test flying of military jets at the airport, the main east-west runway was extended to more than two miles in length. In addition to the 10,700-foot main runway, a new east-west runway was also built on the north side of the airport. The present terminal, occupied in 1958, is between these two runways.

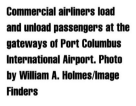

Commercial airliners load and unload passengers at the gateways of Port Columbus International Airport. Photo by William A. Holmes/Image Finders

ABOVE: Ground crews move quickly and efficiently to service a jetliner as it prepares for departure at Port Columbus International Airport. Photo by Jeanne Conte

LEFT: PDQ Aviation operates its cancelled check delivery service from its facility along International Gateway at Port Columbus International Airport. Photo by Dennis Barnes

Ed Gillespie's Work of Love

▲ ▲ ▲ ▲ ▲ ▲ ▲ ▲ ▲ ▲ ▲ ▲ ▲

Past and present come together at 4920 East Fifth Avenue.

That is the address of the original passenger terminal at Port Columbus International Airport—the same building that greeted air and rail passengers traveling between New York and Los Angeles in July 1929.

This bit of history is still standing and functional thanks to Edward A. Gillespie, a man of about the same age as the terminal and one who took part in his share of aviation history.

When the city planned to raze the old terminal building, Gillespie arranged a 40-year lease with the city and set about the task of returning it to its original condition and renting its rooms as offices.

The outstanding feature of the building is its glass-enclosed octagonal control tower, the most modern of its kind when the Pennsylvania Railroad carried passengers overnight from Penn Station to Columbus, where they boarded TAT Ford Tri-Motor airplanes for the flight to Waynoka, Oklahoma, where they again climbed aboard a train for the night. By the time another Ford Tri-Motor landed at the Los Angeles Airport in downtown Burbank, they had been traveling 48 hours.

When the Columbus chapter of the American Institute of Architects surveyed Columbus architecture in 1975, it said of the old terminal, "The whole facility is strictly functional in design, with very little architectural embellishment, though the design of the control tower makes it very distinctive. It certainly is one of the earliest air facilities remaining in the country, and in that it is unique."

Despite the lack of architectural embellishment, the building was a thing of beauty to Ed Gillespie, and it also represented an important piece of aviation history.

The Ford Tri-Motors that started passenger service in Columbus were replaced by DC-3's, DC-7's, and Constellations before the tower's service was ended. Four-engine giants lined up along the ramp on the south side of the airport and passengers walked out to board them. More than one found himself walking down that line of aircraft and climbing aboard the wrong airplane.

The aviation giants of the era landed there. Amelia Earhart was on that first airline flight and would return to the terminal often. Others who would land there included Charles Lindbergh, Roscoe Turner, Howard Hughes, and Douglas "Wrong Way" Corrigan.

Gillespie was a native of Ann Arbor who entered the Navy as an officer candidate in 1946. He started pre-engineering studies that same year at Syracuse University and later was transferred to Western Michigan University at Kalamazoo. He graduated from Navy Flight School in 1950 and graduated from the Navy Test Pilot School in February 1954.

He was based aboard several aircraft carriers during his Navy career in oceans and seas around the world. He flew 80 missions from the flight deck of the USS *Kearsarge* as a fighter-bomber pilot in the Korean conflict. (The *Kearsarge* was later known for its mission in recovering astronauts who splashed down at sea during the early part of the space age.)

Gillespie flew tests on a number of Navy aircraft before becoming an engineering test pilot for North American Aviation at Columbus in 1956. Many of his early flights were controlled from the original tower at the airport. He recalls that test flights used the name of the pilot in communicating with the tower. In one instance where "Flight Ed" was cleared for an early landing because of a shortage of fuel, a TWA pilot asked the tower, "If I tell you my first name, can I land early too?"

Gillespie was appointed chief test pilot for the Columbus Aircraft Division of Rockwell International Corporation (formerly North American Aviation) in March 1964. He retired from Rockwell in 1987 but still does free-lance airplane testing. He has retired from the Naval Reserve with the rank of captain.

His job of restoring the old terminal was one of destruction before work began. The original building had been haphazardly expanded as time passed. A mail and freight facility had to be torn down on the east side of the building. On the west side a restaurant, with offices on a second floor, had been built.

When Gillespie razed these structures, he was left with a brick building with a flooded basement, unusable utilities, the a rotting interior, and a roof patched so often that it sagged under tons of material.

Much of the work was done by retired test-flight mechanics Gillespie had trusted with his own safety when he was a test pilot.

Gillespie, meanwhile, located and obtained the plaque that had been on the building when it was dedicated (he says he had to ransom it) and the original rotating beacon that had been on the tower.

It was a work of love for Gillespie, after nearly 10,000 hours flying everything from single-engine propellor aircraft to rockets and jets.

When the building was completed, Gillespie found he had invested 14 months and $600,000. He invited some friends over, tapped a keg of beer, and had a wiener roast.

They all admired a beautiful building that is a tribute to the city fathers who brought Columbus into the air age in 1929.

—H.B.F.

Thanks to the dedication of Edward A. Gillespie, the original passenger terminal of the Port Columbus International Airport still stands today. Photo by Gregory M. Franken

The jet passenger age came to Columbus on September 1, 1961, with the Convair 880 jetliner. A little more than a month later Captain Lawrence Wolf took off from Port Columbus in one of the new Convairs, setting a record of 52 minutes to New York City.

Port Columbus has always had a mix of military, general, and commercial aviation. All of these have contributed to the success of the airport. Foster A. Lane, a barnstormer in the 1920s, started Lane Aviation Corporation at Port Columbus in 1935. He originally operated out of the 1929 hangar, but his was the first business to move to the new terminal area. There he has expanded into a number of large hangars that offer corporate storage, fuel, jet and piston maintenance, meeting rooms, office space, a pilots' lounge, and an aviation store.

A mix of commercial airliners, general aviation, and military traffic is handled by the four airports located within Metropolitan Columbus. Photo by David S. Wadsworth/Image Finders

Lane also deserves credit for the Ohio History of Flight Museum just west of the terminal, where he hopes eventually to have a model of every airplane manufactured in Ohio on display.

West of Lane Aviation, along International Gateway, is PDQ Aviation, an operator that first specialized in the aerial delivery of cancelled checks. At the south side of the airport, along Fifth Avenue and west of the old terminal, is Central Skyport, a company providing flight training and aircraft rental in addition to other general aviation services.

Future general aviation development on the field is expected along the north east-west runway.

The first hangar on the field is controlled by Executive Jet Aviation (EJA), which was formed by the late Brigadier General O.F. "Dick" Lassiter, who first came to Columbus as commander of an Air Division and decided to return after retiring from the military.

Believing that people wanting to go places not served by major airlines should be able to have the advantages of jet speeds and jet comfort, Lassiter started a company that sold jet service by the mile in Lear business jets. After Lassiter left the company, Brigadier General Paul W. Tibbets served as its president for a number of years. Tibbets became famous as the pilot of the *Enola Gay,* the B-29 superfortress that dropped the atomic bomb on Hiroshima, bringing an end to World War II.

EJA now flys Cessna Citation jets and is the the largest jet air charter operator and aircraft management company in the United States.

Over the years, history has had a way of touching Port Columbus. In 1946 a Navy twin-engine bomber, the *Truculent Turtle,* touched down at Port Columbus after flying nonstop 11,236 miles from Perth, Australia. It set a distance record that was to last for many years.

Columbus was the first city in the country to provide regular passenger service at two airports when an airline started north-south service with a landing at Sullivant Avenue Airport on the city's west side in the 1930s. Photo by David S. Wadsworth/Image Finders

The crew had planned to land in Washington, D.C., but encountered headwinds along the way and decided to touch down in Columbus rather than venture over the Allegheny Mountains while low on fuel. Joey, a nine-month-old kangaroo that was en route to the National Zoo in Washington, was greeted on his arrival in this country by Jack Bolton, not Harry Truman.

Another notable moment in the airport's history came when Captain Eddie Rickenbacker returned to his hometown to start service with Eastern Air Lines. He led a group of city leaders on a fun-filled trip to Miami aboard an Eastern Constellation.

On March 19, 1964, Jerrie Mock, a 38-year-old pilot and housewife strapped herself into the seat of a single-engine Cessna 182 and took off from Port Columbus headed east. On April 17 the airplane appeared out of the southwest, and Mock made a perfect landing. She entered the aviation history books as the first woman to fly solo around the world. The airplane she flew, the *Spirit of Columbus,* is now in the National Air and Space Museum of the Smithsonian Institution in Washington.

Columbus is unusual for a city of its size in that it is served by four publicly owned airports: Port Columbus International Airport, Bolton Field, Rickenbacker Air/Industrial Park, and Don Scott Field (The Ohio State University Airport).

Rickenbacker Port Authority and Rickenbacker Air National Guard Base south of Columbus is a joint-use airport that was originally Lockbourne Air Force Base but was renamed in honor of Columbus native Captain Eddie Rickenbacker on May 18, 1974. The base was constructed in 1942 as part of the nationwide expansion of military facilities made necessary by America's entry into World War II. First used for the training of glider pilots and then for training B-17 crews, the base served the

Tactical Air Command and the Strategic Air Command after the war. While the base was part of SAC, it was headed by General Curtis E. LeMay, a Columbus native and graduate of South High School and Ohio State.

The base's runways were expanded when it was part of SAC. Now the airport has parallel northeast-southwest runways capable of handling the largest transport planes built. One runway is 12,100 feet long and the other is 10,000 feet. Both, according to military specifications, have paved 1,000-foot overruns at each end.

In response to the Carter administration's plan to cut military spending in 1979, the Department of Defense decided to turn the base into a joint civil and military facility. The military section is used by the Air Force Reserve for its C-130 cargo planes, the Navy Reserve, and the Ohio Air National Guard and its KC-135 jet tankers and A-7 jet fighters. A number of Army National Guard helicopters have also moved to the field. (The Department of Defense announced in 1990 that the Air National Guard and Military Reserve functions of Rickenbacker will be phased out.)

Rickenbacker has the potential to become an air cargo hub facility, but the release of former military buildings for civilian use has created a number of other possibilities. Housing units built and used for the military have been converted for civilian family living.

One of the former military buildings houses Designs of Wood, which is literally a mom-and-pop business. Ron Bendele started the business in his garage in Grove City after a career as a salesman. When the business outgrew the garage, Ron and his wife, Pat, moved to Rickenbacker. They found it an ideal place to make their sandblasted wood signs.

That's the small business side.

The modern air cargo facility at the airport is a pre-engineered, high-quality structure with eight-inch reinforced concrete floors. The facility is a one- and two-story steel-frame structure with insulated metal panel exterior. It is 1,100 feet long and 181 feet wide with 274,280 square feet on the ground level and 15,720 square feet on the second-floor mezzanine. The space includes 67,560 square feet used for offices, lounges, lunch rooms, and other employee-related uses.

A mezzanine-level sort system handles packages of up to 70 pounds at a rate of 10,000 pieces per hour. The heavy freight equipment is designed for nonconveyable packages averaging 150 pounds. The heavy freight system uses forklifts and heavy-duty transfer vehicles. The entire cargo sort area has a total capacity of 7 million pounds of freight per day.

A foreign trade zone, or FTZ, has been established at Rickenbacker to allow reduction of certain operating costs normally encountered in foreign trade. This is one of the advantages that makes Rickenbacker a good place to do business.

During the Vietnam era, from 1964 through 1972, Rickenbacker had a military population of 18,000 people, the most ever stationed there. Today the military presence remains a major one. It contributes significantly to the economy of the area. The 45 military aircraft assigned to the base have a total value of $547,700,000. The annual military payroll is more than $16 million, and the civilian payroll is more than $29 million.

The military aircraft use more than 10 million gallons of fuel a year. Airmen perform a number of services for the military establishment and the groups maintain operational readiness through their training.

The 160th Air Refueling Group of the Ohio Air National Guard was sent to an airbase on the Arabian Peninsula during Operation Desert Storm and participated in refueling all types of aircraft during and following that operation. The KC-135 stratotankers served in the Persian Gulf as part of the 1712th air refueling wing.

While Columbus is many miles from the nearest seaport, Naval Reservists training at Rickenbacker support two nuclear carriers, the USS *Enterprise* and the USS *Vinson*; a major Naval Air Station, Oceana; the naval hospital at Patuxent River, Maryland; and several intelligence commands. They are ready to augment regular forces in time of national emergency. The SeaBees trained there (Reserve Naval Mobile Construction Battalion Twenty) are specialists in the delivery of supplies and in the recovery of vehicles from snowed-in areas.

The growth of Port Columbus pointed up the need for a secondary airport to handle noncommercial airline traffic, and Columbus' secondary airport, on the southwest side, filled the vacuum.

Much of the planning for Columbus' secondary noncommercial airport was accomplished by Jack Bolton, and after his death the airport was named in his honor. Although a center for flight training and general aviation, it is also used by local hot-air balloonists and by rugby leagues.

Bolton has also been the base for blimps visiting the city to photograph sporting events. The basement of the terminal is a police substation, and there is a new city firehouse on the north side of the airport along Alkire Road.

Columbus State Community College has constructed a major facility at Bolton for the training of aircraft mechanics and others seeking a future in aviation.

Named in honor of famed Columbus aviation director Francis A. "Jack" Bolton, non-commercial Bolton Field is a center for general aviation and flight training. In addition, Columbus State Community College operates a facility for the training of those interested in a career of aviation mechanics and other aviation fields. Photo by Larry Hamill

Danger as a Day Job

▲ ▲ ▲ ▲ ▲ ▲ ▲ ▲ ▲

When the aeronautical engineers have finished their work and the men and women in the factory have put all the pieces together, there comes a time to see if the wind tunnel tests and the computer models have been accurate. That is the time when one person—the test pilot—straps on a parachute, climbs aboard, and bets his life that a complicated piece of machinery that has never been off the ground will one day safely bring fighter and bomber pilots back from combat, or will haul tons of freight to places where they are needed, or will provide safe and comfortable transportation for millions of people.

Test pilots have been glorified in movies and in books. If you're old enough, you think of Spencer Tracy or stars of his era in the flying movies. If you follow aviation, the names are familiar—Chuck Yeager, Bill Bridgman, Tony Levier, and Ivan Kincheloe.

As a nest for warplanes since World War II, Port Columbus International Airport has been home base to a number of test pilots.

B. Lee Miller is probably the best-known local test pilot. That is partly because he was the "Mr. Aviation" of Columbus before Curtis-Wright decided to build an airplane factory in the city during World War II.

Lee Miller was born in Franklin County, a couple of miles north of New Albany, and spent his early childhood in the Linden area of Columbus. He sold newspapers for five years to save enough money to attend barber college at the age of 16 and, at 17, to buy a barbershop. A short time later he was bitten by the flying bug, and he sold the barbershop to get money for flying lessons.

He continued to work as a barber on Saturdays until he had accumulated the 200 flying hours needed to be a commercial pilot and flight instructor. The year was 1934, and he started training students at the old Sullivant Avenue Airport. He later moved to Port Columbus, where from 1937 to 1942 he operated Miller's Flying School. Among the hundreds of graduates were 200 pilots who learned to fly under the federal Civilian Pilot Training Program. Miller himself could not have passed the physical to learn to fly in the program. He had worn glasses since he was 10 years old.

He joined Curtis-Wright in June 1942, testing such planes as the Navy Helldiver. Curtis-Wright built two jet airplanes in Columbus after the war, and Miller was the first to fly the XF-87, which did not go into production.

Staying on when North American Aviation (later Rockwell) took over the local plant in November 1950, Miller flew the FJ-2 Fury jet, the F-86 Sabrejet, the F-100 Supersabre, and the mach two A3J Vigilante bomber, among other airplanes, during that period.

By the end of his flying career, he had flown more than 150 different types and models of airplanes, all the way from the Curtiss Robin, which he soloed in 1928, to jets that traveled twice the speed of sound. Indeed, Miller had logged hours of supersonic time during his more than 12,000 hours in the air.

Although he was certainly one of the leading production test pilots in the country, he never forgot his beginnings. He'd often get out the scissors and clippers to give a trim to someone in the hospital or confined at home. And he never stopped flying for fun. One of his favorite "off duty" pastimes was piloting the Super Ventura, which was owned by Louis Benua and the Ebco Manufacturing Company.

Miller's first wife, Marge, was an accomplished pilot who lost her life in an international race to Cuba. Miller later married Bonnie, who was Marge's copilot on her final flight.

Miller was chairman and a founder of

FACING PAGE: Known as "Mr. Aviation" to the community, local test pilot B. Lee Miller flew more than 150 different types of airplanes and logged some 12,000 hours in the air by the end of his flying career. Miller is pictured here in 1948. Courtesy, Harry B. Franken

the Columbus Technical Committee for Flight Operations, a group made up of test pilots, airline pilots, military pilots, commercial pilots, flight instructors, and air traffic controllers. The group met regularly to promote flying safety in the Port Columbus control zone and to reduce noise over residential areas in the zone.

Miller is remembered as a quiet gentleman and a master aviator.

Richard M. Wenzell, Sr., was one of five test pilots inducted into the Hall of Honor of the Patriots Point Naval and Maritime Museum aboard the USS *Yorktown* in Charleston, South Carolina, in 1990.

Dick Wenzell entered the University of Michigan in 1940 to study architecture. The war interrupted his studies, and he enlisted in the Navy in 1942. He flew torpedo bombers and fighters during World War II and Korea.

He attended the first class at the Naval Air Test Center in Patuxent River, Mary-

land, in 1948, finishing first in the class. He came to Columbus in 1953 and eventually became chief test pilot of North American, flying the FJ Fury series of fighters and the Vigilante, an airplane that proved to be far ahead of its time.

In 1968 a jet being tested by Wenzell disintegrated in the air south of Columbus near Circleville. Wenzell managed to eject, but his parachute only partially opened. He suffered a broken back and severe lacerations of one leg. Recovering, he returned to test flying, but complications from those earlier injuries caused his death in 1986. He passed his love for airplanes on to his sons, two of whom are pilots.

At the ceremony in which Wenzell was inducted into the Hall of Honor, his wife, Mary Ellen, recalled, "He was an avid admirer of Charles Lindbergh. His biggest thrill was when he got to meet Lindbergh in the 1960s. He always loved flying. The happiest times of his

life were when he was in an airplane."

George W. Hoskins was a Navy Blue Angel before his test pilot career in Columbus. He flew the chase plane when Wenzell made the first flight in the Vigilante. Later he was chief test pilot on the YAT-28E project, an effort to make a close support fighter out of the T-28 trainer.

Hoskins was making a sharp turn out of a dive at between 315 and 320 knots. The plane had experienced the same speed and stresses before, but never in this maneuver. The tail separated from the airplane, and Hoskins was killed. After the investigation and after more static tests on the ground, test pilot Donald W. McCracken went out and flew the maneuver successfully.

Not all test pilot careers end in tragedy, of course. James Pearce had downed more than five enemy planes and was an ace by the time he started his test pilot career in Columbus. He left the city to become number-one man on the Apollo space program in Florida and remains there now as a specialist in oil spills.

Don McCusker served as a test pilot successfully and then barely survived the airline crash that took the life of the son of Aristotle Onassis. It was learned that the ailerons had been wired backwards in the plane before young Onassis took off with McCusker in the right seat.

A number of pilots probably owe their lives to Alan R. "Bud" Holcombe. He wrote the book on deadstick landings in jet aircraft. It was once thought that a jet that lost power had to be abandoned. Holcome proved that a jet losing power at 40,000 feet could safely get to the ground in airports as much as 75 miles away.

Danger may be the daily job of the test pilot, but safety is always the goal.

—H.B.F.

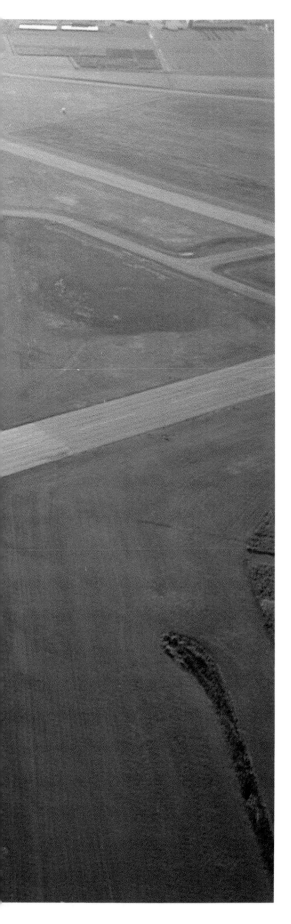

ABOVE: Convenient business travel is available for Columbus area residents. Photo by Jim Baron/Image Finders

LEFT: The approach to Don Scott Field's main runway lends a bird's-eye view of this important Columbus transportation facility. Photo by Larry Hamill

Don Scott Field, the Ohio State airport, is located in the northwest part of the county along Case Road. Although aviation training was offered by the university as early as 1916, the present airport is a product of World War II. Foster Lane first operated the airport for flight training of military cadets assigned to the university.

The university airport began operation after the war, mostly training GI Bill veterans in a number of military surplus airplanes. A B-25 bomber sat unused at the airport for a number of years, and a German V-1 "buzz bomb" was used as a wind tee. The field is named in honor of Captain Don Scott from Canton, a former All-American football player at Ohio State who, while stationed in England during the war, was killed in a training accident.

The Department of Aviation at OSU, which operates from Don Scott Field, has developed into one of the leading facilities in the country in the fields of aviation training and research. Its flight teams have won national honors in competition.

Because of its location between Upper Arlington and Dublin, the airport also serves a fast-growing and wealthy segment of the community. Business jets from all over the nation land there for the Memorial Golf competition at Muirfield. Once, when an intercollegiate flying competition and the Muirfield tournament were occurring simultaneously, the FAA control tower at OSU was the busiest in the country.

The airport is also home base for airplanes belonging to local companies. Worthington Industries has even constructed its own hangar for its fleet of business jets.

In addition, the airport houses the aviation section of the Ohio Department of Transportation and the air arm of the State Highway Patrol.

With all of its activity, the airport works at being a good neighbor. When the university let it be known that it was considering closing the airport and selling the land to developers, there was an immediate outcry not only from those who use the airport, but also from the communities and neighborhoods near it.

LEFT: Interstate highways, such as I-70, link Columbus with the rest of the nation in all directions. Photo by Larry Hamill

FACING PAGE BOTTOM: Central Ohio's major north-south artery, Interstate 71, connects Cleveland with Cincinnati and intersects the state's main east-west route of Interstate 70 on the city's east side. This vital interchange is shown here looking north. Photo by Jeffrey A. Rycus/Rycus Associates Photography

ON THE ROAD

I-270, known locally as the Outerbelt, makes a ring around Columbus. Whether you are trying to avoid downtown traffic or transporting hazardous materials, using the Outerbelt is a must.

Driving toward Columbus from Cleveland, you come to I-270 in Sharon Township just south of Sharon Woods Metropolitan Park and just north of the Anheuser Busch Brewery. Because it is shorter to go around the Outerbelt in a clockwise direction, head east. The highway runs along the south side of Westerville and then turns south to cross Route 161, the road to New Albany and Granville. Passing just west of Gahanna, you then swing east again to make a loop around Port Columbus International Airport. You cross Route 16, the road to Newark, and then Route 40, the road to Zanesville and Wheeling. Next there is I-70, the east-west interstate through the city.

After traveling across I-70, you swing west to cross Route 33, the road to Lancaster. Continuing around the southern part of the city, you pass the exit for Rickenbacker Airport and then cross Route 23, the road to Circleville and the exit for Scioto Downs race track.

By the time you reach I-71 again, you are halfway around the city. I-71 goes south to Cincinnati. Route 62, the road to Washington, is reached between Columbus and Grove City. Then the Outerbelt goes north. The next exit is for Bolton Field. Continuing north you cross West Broad Street and its major shopping area. I-70 is next, going west to Dayton and Indianapolis. Then there are exits for Hilliard on the west or Upper Arlington on the east. You cross Route 33 again. This time it goes off to the northwest toward Marysville and the Honda plant. The Outerbelt turns east and crosses the Scioto River. You can exit at Sawmill Road for Ohio State University Airport. Route 315 will take you south into Columbus along the Olentangy River. The road has been named in honor of former Mayor Tom Moody and former Columbus service director Richard Jackson. The exits at Route 23 will take you north to Delaware or south to Worthington. In a few miles, you are back where you started.

The amazing thing about a journey around the I-270 Outerbelt is that it takes

nearly as long to tell about it as it does to make it. You have passed within a few minutes of all four public airports in the county. Most of the highways you cross are four-lane routes to the major cities in Central Ohio.

If you do not choose to use the Outerbelt, during most times of the day you will have no problem staying on I-70 or I-71 going through the city, and both

will give you a great look at the downtown skyline. In fact, you can circle the downtown area on what we call the Innerbelt. It is made up of parts of I-70, I-71, and I-670, the freeway to Port Columbus.

The Columbus area is home to 130 firms offering trucking service of all types. The city's larger public distribution and warehousing facilities occupy a total of 55 million square feet. Larry R. Scott, head of Consolidated Freightways, Inc., of Menlo Park, California, has called Columbus the "gateway to the rest of the world." He employs 5,000 Ohioans in 56 terminals and chose Columbus for a 212-door "super terminal" at Alum Creek Drive and Watkins Road.

Columbus is the freight consolidation hub for 40 terminals in Ohio and adjoining states and handles 5 million pounds of freight a day. It all started with the National Road, or Route 40, which goes from Baltimore, Maryland, to the Pacific Ocean. It developed from an Indian footpath to a wagon trail to a paved highway, and it goes through Columbus on Main and Broad streets. The canal from the south reached Columbus first, but explosive development did not begin until the pioneer wagon trains rolled along the National Road. Some of the early milestones are still to be found in the county.

ABOVE: The 212-door super terminal of Consolidated Freightways, Inc., helps make Columbus a hub for the trucking industry. Consolidated's Larry R. Scott has called Columbus the "gateway to the rest of the world." Photo by Dennis Barnes

FACING PAGE: Known locally as the Outerbelt, Interstate 270 forms a 55-mile loop around Columbus and its surrounding suburbs and connects travelers to other freeways around the city. I-270 is pictured here where it crosses Broad Street on the west side. Photo by Larry Hamill

Columbus is home to nearly 130 trucking companies and more than a dozen major public distribution and warehouse facilities. Photo by Jim Baron/Image Finders

A Piece of History

▲▲▲▲▲▲▲▲▲▲▲▲▲▲▲▲▲▲▲

The main arch of the third and final Union Station in Columbus was saved from the wrecking ball in 1976 and now stands as a reminder of the city's glorious past in Sensenbrenner Park. Photo by Dennis Barnes

A last-minute reprieve saved the arch of the third, and final, Columbus Union Station, giving the city Sensenbrenner Park, a small, quiet island at Marconi Boulevard and West Hickory Street.

In the early evening of October 22, 1976, an 82-ton crane started taking bites out of the abandoned station as the first part of the construction of a new hotel and convention center.

It was Friday, and preservationists would later charge that the building was to be destroyed over the weekend in hopes that they would have no time to take steps to save it. Those wanting to build the hotel would claim that the

work in the evening and on the weekend would be less disruptive to the traffic on North High Street.

Those interested in preserving the Union Depot Arcade first learned of the crane moving into place with its 130-foot boom when they saw it on the evening television news.

One who heard about it at the last minute was George C. Smith, then prosecuting attorney and now a federal judge in Columbus. He contacted attorney C. William Brownfield, who, working for the Historical Society, went to the home of Judge Myron B. Gessaman on Saturday and obtained a temporary restraining order against destroying the main arch. He served it on the wreckers just as they were about ready to rip it out.

The Arcade, designed by Daniel Burnham of Chicago, was on the National Register of Historic Places of the U.S. Department of the Interior. It is the second of his works to be preserved in Columbus, the first being the Wyandotte Building on West Broad Street.

The arch that came so close to being reduced to rubble had been completed in 1897. Soon after that a writer for the Columbus Board of Trade (forerunner of the Columbus Area Chamber of Commerce) had written about the new Union Station:

As the train rolls majestically into Columbus, one sees what is admitted by all to be architecturally the finest, most ornate, and most commodious depot in the Middle West.

The traveller alighting passes up the easy flight of stairs that carries him to an immense elevated platform safely above the score of trains that are discharging and receiving simultaneously, the multitude of passengers who daily come and go. As he glances down at the busy arena, where many throbbing locomotives eagerly await the moment when the throttle valve shall be drawn and send them flying with their burden of precious lives across the fair face of Ohio, he cannot fail to notice the absolute order and safety in which each embarking or disembarking passenger goes his way without necessity of crossing a track or passing a locomotive.

The first passenger station in Columbus was built by the Columbus & Xenia and the Cleveland, Columbus, & Cincinnati railroads, which started serving here in 1850 and 1851, respectively.

They located at the northeast corner of North High Street and Naghten Street because that was as close as they could get to downtown on land that had not already been developed.

The first depot was a barnlike building 90 feet wide and 175 feet long. An octagonal cupola was located on each end of the building as an escape hatch for locomotive smoke. Three tracks ran through the building for its full length, each allowing five coaches to be loaded or unloaded under the roof. Passengers stepped out onto a floor of heavy wooden planks. By 1854 the station, still with only three tracks, was handing the passenger trains of four railroads.

The industrial growth of the city and the increased traffic resulting from the Civil War quickly made the station obsolete. The Union Depot Company, incorporated in 1868, finally became active in 1871. A new station was planned just north of the original one. The new station was opened in February 1875. It was a three-story, dark red brick building some 800 feet northeast of High and Naghten. It had two square towers on the front corners, extending a story and a half above the roof.

Trains entered the station through six round-arched portals, each accomdating one track. Passenger trains of eight divisions used the facility when it opened.

The city was growing and extending to the north and a constant complaint was the blocking of High Street by the trains entering and leaving the station. A traffic study done in 1891 said that during one 24-hour period, High Street was closed a total of seven hours and 25 minutes because of 233 passenger and freight trains and 211 switch movements over the crossing. The report said this delayed 15,000 of the 45,000 pedestrians on High Street and delayed 3,500 of the 7310 vehicles moving along the street.

By 1893 the official railway guide listed 118 scheduled trains of 14 divisions serving Columbus each day.

Plans were drawn for a new building in 1895. They called for a viaduct to be built over the tracks on High Street, eliminating the problems of the street crossing. Overhead structures had already been built over the tracks on Front Street and North Fourth Street.

The new building was opened in 1897 with eight tracks. The Board of Trade writer, cited above, said of the interior: "In addition to a perfectly conducted information bureau there are elaborate toilet rooms, a private smoking room, barber shop, bathrooms, dining room, lunch counter and buffet . . . in fact, all comforts and conveniences of the first class hotel . . . all save the sleeping apartment."

For nearly half a century the station handled most of the traffic of travellers in and out of the city. It was particularly busy during World Wars I and II, with the movement of servicemen between duty stations, on leave, and on furlough. The station was extensively remodeled during 1928 and 1929.

At its peak early in the twentieth century, the station handled 124 passenger trains a day. By 1956 that number had dropped to 42 daily trains, the same number which moved to the second depot in 1875.

Some passenger service remained in Columbus after the station was demolished. That came to an end on October 1, 1979, with the last run through Columbus of the National Limited, the train that ran from New York to Kansas City. The last passenger was Mike Leyshon, a local train buff who rode the final trip between Columbus and Dayton, a one-hour-and-35-minute trip over rails that were no longer smooth and fast.

Sylvester Stanley, the conductor on the train that pulled out of Columbus at 7:25 a.m., recalled on the way to Dayton that regular passengers on the train, when it was called the Spirit of St. Louis, were Harry and Bess Truman, travelling from Washington D.C. to their home in Independence, Missouri.

"The president always took a walk around the train at 6 a.m. and after that he was ready to relax with his wife," Stanley recalled. "Every morning at 6:30 their bedroom compartment door would open and they would sit and talk to people who passed by. Every member of the crew knew them and they, in turn, were sociable and interested in us.

"I know if old Harry were around, he wouldn't let this happen."

Arch Park, as it was known before being named in honor of former Mayor M. E. Sensenbrenner, was dedicated in June of 1980. The land was donated by the Columbus & Southern Ohio Electric Company.

The tracks the arch stood over carried Abraham Lincoln through Columbus on his way to the White House and brought back his body after he had been martyred. They very likely carried every president since then through the presidency of Harry S Truman.

Some say you can look at the arch at night and almost hear a distant train whistle and the conductor's cry of "All aboooard."

—H.B.F.

HITTING THE RAILS

A look at the county map not only shows freeway coverage, but also demonstrates
that Columbus is the center of a railroad network.

Rail transporation began in the city in 1858 with the opening of the Columbus
and Xenia Railroad. Within a short time the Central Ohio and the Columbus, Cincinnati, and Cleveland railroads were also operating.

Between 1870 and 1900 rails and the ready availability of coal from southeastern
Ohio had made Columbus a major manufacturing center as well as a center of government.

Soon many major rail lines, including the Pennsylvania, the Baltimore and Ohio,
the Chesapeake and Ohio, the Norfolk and Western, and others, were serving the
city.

Union Station on North High Street was packed with travelers going to and com-
ing from points all over the country. It was especially a bustling center during World
War II. Union Station is now gone, its beautiful arched gateway the centerpiece of
Sensenbrenner Park.

An equally busy area today is the Conrail Buckeye Yards, 640 acres just south of
Hilliard and extending nearly to West Broad Street. This computerized classification
yard handles 2,000 freight cars a day. Almost 7.5 million tons of freight pass through the

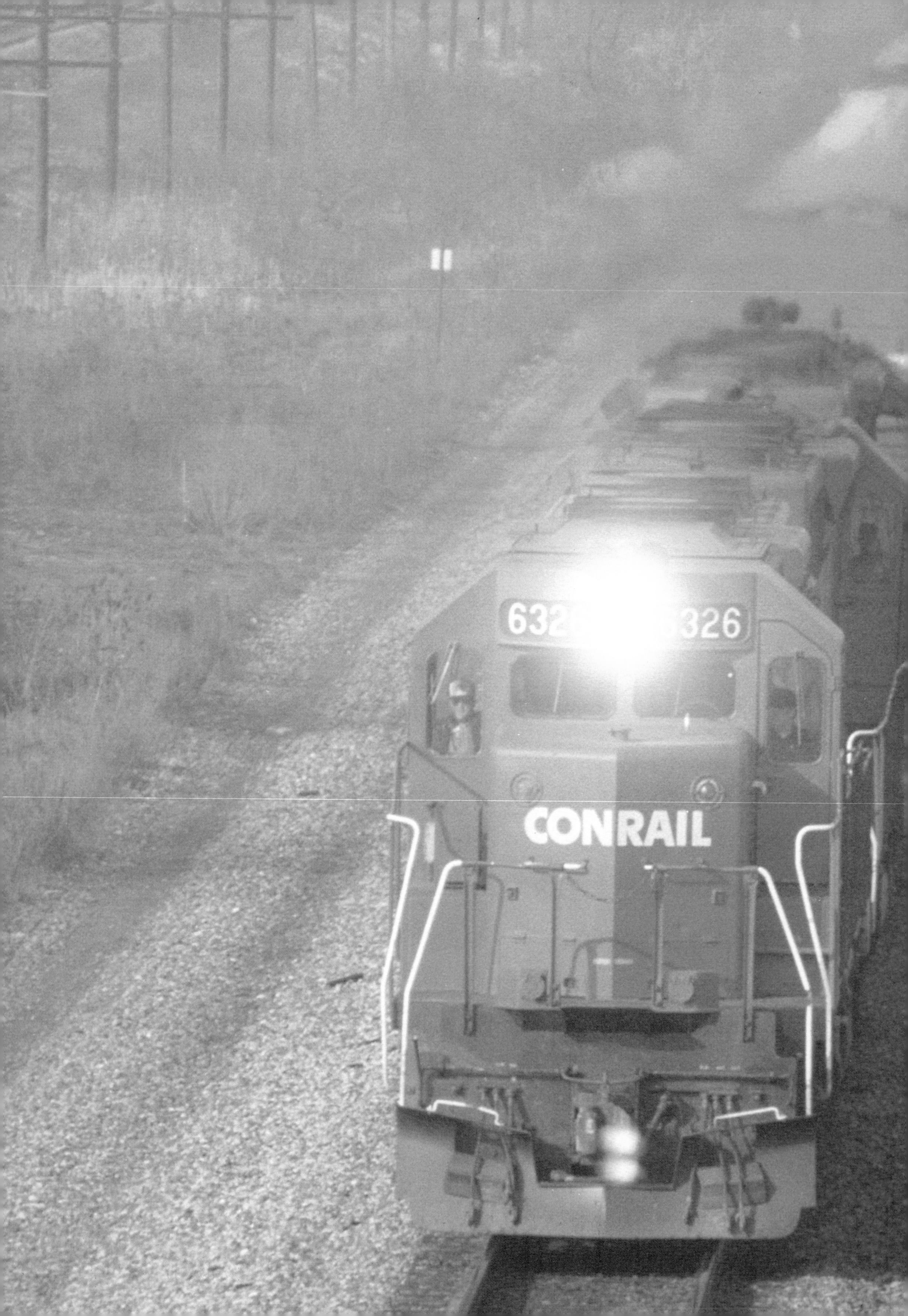
6326
CONRAIL

yard every month. Trains enter the 40 classification tracks, and the cars are sorted to be sent to 87 different destinations. Some trains are made up for dropping off cars at as many as nine different destinations.

The enormity of the Conrail Buckeye Yards is not readily visible from the highways in the area, but from the air it is easy to see that this is a major operation. Trains assembled here average about 100 cars. They may depart north to Cleveland and Toledo, east to Granville and points beyond, south to West Virginia, southwest to Dayton and Cincinnati, and west to Indianapolis, St. Louis, and coastal ports such as San Diego in only 72 hours.

The huge yard is somewhat bowl-shaped, and gravity does much of the sorting work. A car rolls downhill along the track as a computer switches it to the proper rail, and retarder brakes on the rail slow it to the proper speed. The cars going "off the hump" join together as trains that may exceed a mile in length.

The yard has a trailvan facility that provides a parking area for 800 trailers, which are loaded onto the railroad cars. Stacked two high, 10 of these are placed on one railroad car. Steamship lines link with overland double-stack trains, combining rail, motor freight, and cargo ships to move products to the Pacific Rim from Central Ohio in just 14 days.

The yard also has repair shops, inspection facilities, and a diesel facility. Fueling locomotives takes up to one million gallons of diesel fuel a month.

In addition, the yard handles shipments for 250 local industries. A car entering the yard may contain freight for business a few miles away, or it may be destined for a port from which it may be shipped anywhere in the world.

7

THE GOOD LIFE

▲▲▲▲▲▲▲▲▲▲▲▲

207

One measure of a city's quality of life is the quality of the individual lives lived there. To learn something of the lives of Columbus, visit the Columbus Hall of Fame in the first floor hallway at Columbus City Hall. Those honored there either were born in Columbus or have chosen Columbus as their home. Their lives have brought credit to the city and have enriched the world.

Those enshrined in the Hall of Fame come from the fields of sports, business, arts, military, government, and entertainment. Many of these people have excelled in more than one field.

The large number from the world of sports reflects the interest Columbus and Central Ohio have in sports competition. Football has given the list W.W. "Woody" Hayes, Charles "Chic" Harley, Jack Cannon, Bill Willis, Howard "Hopalong" Cassady, and Archie Griffin.

Woody Hayes was one of the winningest college coaches in football history. Under his coaching, Ohio State won 3 national championships and 10 "Big 10" titles, and appeared 7 times in the Rose Bowl. He coached two Heisman Trophy winners and 45 first-team All Americans.

Chic Harley began Columbus' reputation as football capital of the world. This East High graduate played before and after his service in World War I. Ohio Stadium has been called the "house that Harley built." He played only two losing games in Columbus, one at East High School and his final game at Ohio State.

Bill Willis, also a product of East High School, was an All-American tackle at Ohio State. Following his college career, he played for the Cleveland Browns from 1946 through 1953 and has been enshrined in the Professional Football Hall of Fame. He later served as director of the Ohio Youth Commission.

Jack Cannon played college ball at Notre Dame, where he was an All-American guard in 1929. He returned to Columbus as the head of one of the largest florist establishments in the city.

Hop Cassady and Archie Griffin both won the Heisman Trophy. Cassady, from Central High School, was a halfback at Ohio State and later played for the Detroit Lions, Cleveland Browns, and Philadelphia Eagles. The next "Big 10" athlete to win the Heisman was Griffin, the only football player to have won it twice. He is a product of Eastmoor High School and returned to the athletic department at Ohio State after his professional football career.

The world of boxing has seen Columbus' Jerry Page, national Golden Gloves champion, make great contributions to the sport. Page was also a three-time Ohio State Fair Champion and Gold Medal winner in the 1984 Olympics.

Columbus' Horace "Hank" Gowdy, baseball player and coach, was the hero in the Boston Braves' win of the 1914 World Series and later coached that team. He returned to Columbus to manage the former Columbus Jets and to be the organization's youth activity director.

The city's contribution to the world of golf is Jack Nicklaus. The "Golden Bear," a product of Upper Arlington High School and The Ohio State University, became the world's winningest professional golfer at the age of 34. He hosts the annual PGA Memorial Tournament at his Muirfield golf course in Dublin.

From the military are heroes Captain Eddie Rickenbacker, the "Ace of Aces" of World War I, and General Curtis E. LeMay, the bombing leader of World War II

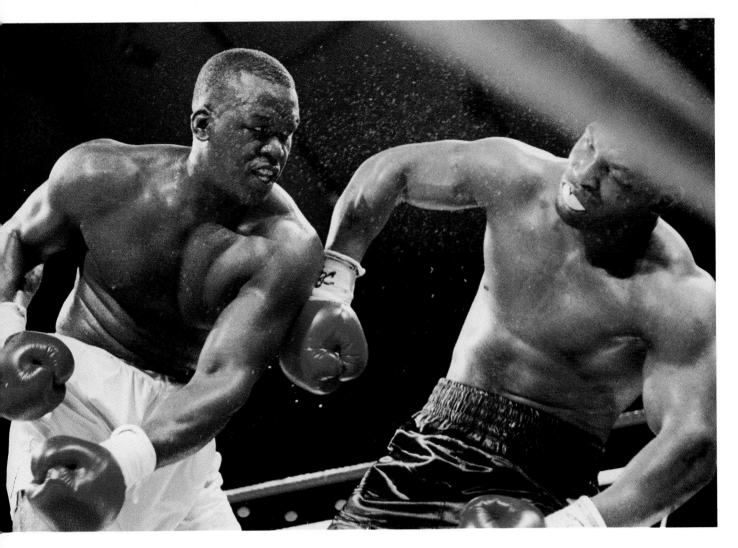

ABOVE: Columbus native
James "Buster" Douglas
knocks out champion Mike
Tyson during the 10th round
of their world heavyweight
title bout in Tokyo, Japan, on
February 11, 1990.
Courtesy, Reuters/Bettmann

FACING PAGE: Graduate of
Upper Arlington High School
and The Ohio State University, "Golden Bear" Jack Nicklaus became the world's
winningest professional
golfer at the age of 34. Nicklaus hosts the PGA Memorial
Tournament at his Muirfield
course in Dublin each year.
Courtesy, UPI/Bettmann
Newsphotos

who later became Commander of the Strategic Air Command and Air Force Chief of Staff. LeMay served actively as a general officer longer than any other American military man.

Rickenbacker might also be termed a business leader. After his military duty, he made a name for himself as the operator of the Indianapolis Motor Speedway and as head of Eastern Air Lines. He also served with distinction in a civilian capacity during World War II.

Captain Phil H. Bucklew may be the least-known person on the military list because his job with the Navy in World War II was highly classified. He organized the first psychological warfare unit of the Navy. In addition, he won two Navy Crosses, the award for valor second only to the Medal of Honor.

Phil Bucklew might also be included in the sports category. In 1961 he was nominated to the *Sports Illustrated* Silver Anniversary All-American football team, and prior to World War II he coached a professional football team in Columbus.

Ronald E. Rosser, who won the Medal of Honor in Korea for acts of bravery on January 12, 1952, became the 34th member of the Hall of Fame in 1990.

Show business names in the Columbus Hall of Fame include Howard Thurston, Elsie Bierbower Janis, Warner Baxter, and Nancy Wilson. Thurston, born in 1869, was known as the "World's Greatest Magician."

Elsie Janis wrote songs and books and earned an international reputation as a singer. She appeared on the London stage, sang in the White House during the presidency of William McKinley, and became the "Sweetheart of the American Expeditionary Forces" for her appearances before troops in France during World War I.

Warner Baxter was a handsome and urbane star in the early days of talking pictures in Hollywood. One of his biggest box office hits was as the *Cisco Kid.*

Nancy Wilson graduated from West High School and attended Wilberforce College before starting her singing and acting career. Before becoming a national star with Capitol Records, she hosted her own Columbus televison show.

James Thurber's writings personified Columbus, and through him much of the world was introduced to the city. His story "The Day the Dam Broke" is about the flood of 1913, while his play *Male Animal,* supposedly fictional, presents an accurate portrait of the football craziness at Ohio State during the flapper era. There is a neighborhood named for Thurber, and the house where he grew up is a location for literary and other events throughout the year.

Visual artists honored in Columbus City Hall include George Wesley Bellows, Robert Osborne Chadeayne, and Elijah Pierce. Though Bellows made his name in New York City, many of his fine works are displayed in Columbus. Chadeayne

began his artistic career in Columbus, but became nationally acclaimed as an artist and illustrator after leaving the city. Mississippi-born Elijah Pierce, the son of a former slave, worked in Columbus as a barber and used pocket knives and chisels to make internationally acclaimed wood carvings.

Among Columbus' humanitarians were Dr. Nimrod Booker Allen and Dr. Benjamin B. Caplan. Allen devoted his life to creating better interracial understanding in Columbus and the nation. He developed Frontiers International in 1936 to unearth, mobilize, and develop black leadership, and organized the Columbus Urban League and served as its executive secretary for 23 years. Caplan, a physician-philanthropist, served as a medical missionary for more than 50 years, visiting 114 countries, including serving three tours of duty as a voluntary psychiatrist in Vietnam. In 1970 he personally immunized 22,500 children in Bolivia against polio, subsidizing the cost with his own money.

Real estate developer John W. Galbreath is listed here as a business leader, but his interest in sports—particularly horseracing and baseball—certainly qualifies him for that category.

Brothers Robert Frederick Wolfe and Harry Preston Wolfe started the Wolfe Brothers

RIGHT, FACING PAGE & FOLLOWING PAGE: Downtown Columbus comes to life each year with the summertime Columbus Arts Festival street fair. Artists, craftspeople, and musicians gather along the Scioto riverfront to display their wares and entertain the crowds. Children's activities, a Gourmet Fare food area, and other captivating attractions help to round out this favorite event. Photos by Larry Hamill

LEFT: Crowds that gathered for the Columbus Arts Festival street fair are captivated by sculptures such as this. Photo by Larry Hamill

Shoe Company in 1895 and expanded the family interest into newspapers, broadcasting, and banking. Robert Wolfe explained their philosophy: "I was born to circumstances which I refused to accept. I changed them."

James R. Trueman, who founded the Red Roof Inns, Inc. (the largest privately owned and operated motel chain in the country) in 1972, is also known for his True-Sports auto racing team, winner of the 1986 Indianapolis 500.

Frank Fetch was instrumental in the development of the German Village Commission, which was a pioneer in historic neighborhood preservation and protection.

Then there are the politicians: John W. Bricker, James A. Rhodes, and Maynard E. "Jack" Sensenbrenner. Bricker, from a small Ohio town, made his name in Columbus. He served as governor and United States senator and was a candidate for vice president of the United States in 1944. He was also a founder of the law firm of Bricker & Eckler, which restored and now occupies the historic old Post Office building at State and Third streets. Rhodes came to Columbus from the coal-mining

area of Appalachia. Starting his career as Columbus' city auditor, he advanced to mayor, then to state auditor, and finally served four terms as governor of Ohio. Sensenbrenner, who came up Route 23 from Circleville, served as Columbus' mayor for 14 years. During his time in office Columbus experienced unprecedented growth, both through business expansion and annexation. Sensenbrenner said the dynamic growth resulted from something he called "spizzerinctum."

There are three Miss Americas from Columbus: Mary Catherine Campbell Townley, Laurel Lea Schafer, and Susan Yvonne Perkins. Mary Catherine Campbell Townley won the crown in 1922 after her boyfriend submitted a picture of the East High School student. She also won the pageant in 1923, making her the only two-time winner in history. She is likely to retain that distinction unless the rules of the pageant are changed. Laurel Lea Schafer reigned in 1972 after graduation from Bexley High School and Ohio University, and Susan Yvonne Perkins reigned in 1978. At the time she won the pageant, she was employed as a legislative assistant in the Ohio General Assembly. She's a graduate of Miami University at Oxford, Ohio.

COLUMBUS' NEIGHBORHOODS

The Columbus neighborhood of German Village provides a bit of "Old World" charm within sight of downtown's skyscrapers. While the restaurants and shops of the village are tourist attractions, this is not just a place to visit. It is a working neighborhood of families, people who have lovingly restored the neat, small, brick homes built in the early 1800s by German immigrants who settled in what was then called South Columbus. There are hand-laid brick streets, brick sidewalks, and houses with slate roofs, carved stone lintels, and clay chimney pots.

As previously noted, the acknowledged father of German Village is the late

Frank Fetch. In the 1950s the rundown area was slated for urban renewal. Then Fetch, a city employee in the Urban Renewal Department, bought a house for $3,500 and restored it. Convinced that restoration was better than tearing down the old homes and starting over, he recruited some 80 people to join him in forming the German Village Society. Fetch served as president of the society for 10 years, during which time he and his wife were involved in more than two dozen village rehabs. German Village became the largest restoration area of its type in the United States.

In 1975 the village was put on the National Register of Historic Places. The city council set the boundaries of German Village. They are Livingston Avenue on the north, Pearl Alley on the west, Nursery Lane on the south, and an uneven eastern boundary varies from as far west as Jaeger Street and as far east as Lathrop Street. Within these boundaries are some 1,600 residential and 100 commercial buildings on 233 acres of land.

The society sponsors several events to raise money for restoration, and the restoration has been accomplished entirely with private funds. The Haus und Garten Tour is held the last Sunday in June and the Backyards-by-Candlelight tour is the second weekend in August. In addition private tours of the village may be arranged at any time through the German Village Society at 624 South Third Street.

The German Village Oktoberfest, held the second weekend in September, has outgrown a number of locations. It was once held in Schiller Park, the beautiful park in the village named for the German poet, Johann Christoph Friedrich von Schiller. Concerts and theater presentations attract many to the park in the summer, and it is an ideal place to take a lunch to get away from the hustle of business on a work day.

The success of German Village has spawned other restoration projects in Columbus. The Short North, once a rundown area along High Street between downtown and the University District, offers a number of art galleries, theaters, and restaurants. The Short North Gallery Hop takes place from 6 p.m. to 10 p.m. on the first Saturday of the month. You can stroll from gallery to gallery or buy a

Renovated in the 1960s and 1970s and considered to be the largest restoration project of its kind in the nation, German Village was originally settled by nineteenth-century German immigrants, many of whom found work in the city's nearby breweries. Hand-laid brick streets, lovingly-restored homes, and scenic Schiller Park continue to attract tourists to this unique residential neighborhood. Photo by Larry Hamill

ticket on the Gallery Hop Shuttle.

An annual event in the Short North is the Doo Dah parade on the Fourth of July. The participants in this zany march call it the greatest unplanned happening of the holiday. The Short North has been called the artistic haven of Columbus.

Adjacent to the Short North area are the Victorian Village and Italian Village restoration areas.

Traveling in just about any direction from downtown, you will find restoration. Bryden Road, called an "arrogant street" by James Thurber, was once the location of the homes of the leading families of the city. Then it fell on hard times, and the stately old homes were carved into rooming houses. Now the trend has reversed as the city council has declared the 1.6 miles of Bryden Road between Parsons Avenue and Nelson Road a Columbus Historic District.

South of I-70 on Front Street, the Brewery District has undergone amazing growth with new buildings and the restoration of older buildings. To remind people of the many breweries that the German population built in the area, there is even a mini-brewery. At the south end of the district there is a statue of King Gambrinus, his foot on a keg and his mug held high. The statue once stood over the gateway of the August Wagner Brewery, where Gambrinus beer was one of the products.

The brewery district now is a collection of restaurants, offices, condominiums, and apartments for those who like living within walking distance of downtown.

An Immigrant's Story

▲ ▲ ▲ ▲ ▲

Be not forgetful to entertain strangers: for thereby some have entertained angels unawares.

—Hebrews 13:2

When the fall of Saigon was imminent in 1975, Chuy Van Nguyen was able to get his family—a wife and 10 small children—onto a decrepit Vietnamese naval vessel that had no pilot and was only marginally seaworthy.

Chuy, who had worked several years in the traffic bureau of the Saigon Police Force, supervised more than 5,000 civilians in a district defense force in the closing days of the war.

Soon after his family boarded their floating escape to freedom, word came that they would have to throw all of their belongings overboard so that more refugees could be accomodated on the boat.

So, when the boat finally reached the Philippines, the family possessed only the clothes that they wore. The boat, with a capacity of 200 people, had brought 500 refugees out of Saigon.

Since the fall of South Vietnam in 1975, more than 5,000 refugees have come to Columbus from Southeast Asia, many of them in the past 10 or 15 years. The largest number, more than 2,000, are from Vietnam, while the remainder are from Laos and Cambodia.

Throughout its history, Columbus has been enriched by the immigrants who have found freedom and opportunity in the city. The Germans and the Irish who arrived early in the 1800s virtually built Columbus. Some years later came an influx of Italian immigrants. The Migration and Refugees Service of the United States Catholic Conference has referred to the current influx from Southeast Asia as "entertaining the angels of today."

After a stop in a refugee camp in the Philippines, the Chuy family was sent to Guam. When all of the paperwork had been done to allow them to enter the United States, they were sent to another refugee camp, this one at Indiantown Gap, Pennsylvania. It appeared that they would be hard to place. There was no question of the family remaining together. The difficulty of finding affordable living space for a family of 12 was considerable.

A former sailor from Columbus went to Indiantown Gap to sponsor a refugee after receiving a letter from the man, who had known him when the refugee was a member of the Vietnamese military. The former American sailor learned of the Chuys and a search was started in Columbus for a suitable home. Unfortunately, many prospective landlords who were willing to help just didn't have the space required.

There was a large, abandoned farmhouse on property owned by the Pontifical College Josephinum, just across Route 23 from the college. It was agreed that the family could move here temporarily, although the the old brick house was drafty and in poor repair and a bitter winter was coming on. The family and a number of volunteers went to work, and soon the ramshackle house had its first occupants in a number of years. Chuy got a custodial job at Saint Michael School in Worthington to support his wife, six daughters, and four sons.

Fast forward to the Tet celebration for the most recent Year of the Goat, the year we call 1991. The program, to which American friends have been invited, opens with the national anthems of the United States and Vietnam. Then there is a moment of silence "for those who have died for freedom."

Fruit and candles are placed on an altar on the stage, and Chuy Van Nguyen, still working at Saint Michael and very active in community affairs, especially the Buddhist group, leads the tribute to ancestors and a prayer for peace.

The Chuys now have three American-born grandchildren and are buying a house in suburban Powell.

Guests and friends are welcomed to the celebration by Minh Quang Nguyen, current president of the Vietnam Mutual Assistance Association and one of those children who fled Vietnam by boat nearly 16 years earlier.

The variety show begins with a dragon dance and reflects the affection these new Americans have for the land they left. The songs include "My Village in the Sunset," "The Sound from the Three Great Rivers of Vietnam," "Flower Petals on Your Doorsteps," and "Love at the Harvest Time."

There is the reading of a poem, "The Sad Eyes of a Young Girl from SonTay."

There are humorous skits and a humorous duet, one that reflects the reason this celebration is being held in Heartland America, "Homesick Song From A Communist Reeducation Camp." Healing years have passed, and the song brings laughter from the audience.

After cast members are introduced, everyone joins in the singing of "Vietnam, My Fatherland." Much has happened since they last sang that on their native soil.

Minh, the president of VMAA, works full-time for the data processing department of Franklin County. He graduated in 1990 from Ohio State with a bachelor of science degree in engineering. Huy is an accountant with the Department of Human Services of the state of Ohio and a part-time student at Franklin University. Dao is a full-time student at Ohio State and works part-time for the Franklin County data processing department. Thuy Mai graduated in 1990 from Ohio State with a bachelor of arts degree in business and economics. She works for an insurance company. Phuong Mai is a full-time student at Ohio State, a senior majoring in business and working part-time. Nzoc Mai is also majoring in business, a second year student at Ohio State. She also has a part-time job. Dung is a full-time student at Ohio State, completing his first year in engineering.

Three of the daughters have married and no longer live at home.

Tuyet Mai, who has one daughter, Kim Mai, works for the Ohio Department of Taxation. Her husband, Hai Nguyen, is a supervisor for shipping and receiving for The Limited.

Hoang Mai also works for the tax department. Her husband works as a mechanic for the Schuller Company. They have two daughters, Hoang Tam Pham and Hoang Thy Pham.

Thanh Mai has worked for 13 years for the Catholic Migration and Refugee Resettlement office. Her husband, Hiep Thanh Vo, is a self-employed, licensed general contractor doing commercial and residential remodeling.

Thanh Mai, working with today's immigrants, knows the battle they face and knows the fight that begins with starvation can end with success. She likes playing the role of guardian angel.

—H.B.F.

Held the second weekend in September, the annual German Village Oktoberfest features a festive atmosphere of music, dancing, rides, and authentic German fare.
Photo by Larry Hamill

ABOVE: The first Saturday evening of every month finds the Short North teeming with people for the popular "Gallery Hop." Whether for shopping, browsing, or socializing, the monthly event attracts a big crowd to the galleries, antique shops, boutiques, and restaurants of this High Street area. Photo by Larry Hamill

RIGHT: An extensive choice of housing is available throughout Columbus' more than 50 communities and neighborhoods. Photo by Larry Hamill

LEFT: The historic Brewery District blends past and present with delightful restorations and contemporary structures. Once the site of Columbus breweries, this unique district features a fine collection of eateries, offices, and apartments within walking distance of downtown. Photo by Larry Hamill

FACING PAGE: Colorful tulips add a splash of springtime to the charming brick streets and homes of Columbus' German Village. Photo by Larry Hamill

There is a feeling of pride in all of Columbus' neighborhoods, and more than a dozen area commissions, established under the guidance of the city's Human Services Department, meet regularly to discuss such topics as traffic, zoning, and crime. There are commissions for, among others, the Franklinton, Clintonville, North Linden, and University areas.

Many of the neighborhoods sponsor events that attract thousands each year. The Historic Hilltop Bean Dinner has been held each summer since 1929 in Westgate Park. Former residents of Flytown, an area torn down in an urban renewal project, gather for reunions in Goodale Park. A section of Mount Vernon Avenue between Saint Clair Avenue and North Twentieth Street is blocked off for a weekend each summer for the Comin' Home African American Community Festival.

Lincoln Village, a middle-class neighborhood in Prairie Township, was built by Murray Lincoln's Peoples Development Company as an experiment in providing better and lower cost housing. Lincoln said the homes had hidden values such as thicker concrete, the quality of plumbing fixtures, the size of electric wiring, the weight

From brand-new townhomes to sprawling suburban estates, Columbus offers a vast selection of housing for gracious living. Photo by Larry Hamill

Feelings of community pride pervade Columbus' neighborhoods. Established under the guidance of the city's Human Services Department, more than a dozen area commissions meet regularly to discuss topics such as traffic, zoning, and other concerns that affect daily life within their communities. Photo by Larry Hamill

of roof shingles, and the amount of insulation.

In his autobiography, *Vice President In Charge of Revolution*, Lincoln said that he "had not found a way of demonstrating the value in the houses." Forty years later the value is apparent in the well-cared-for houses. There is seldom a "For Sale" sign seen in Lincoln Village.

The cities and villages of Franklin County offer a diversity of life-styles. These suburbs have their own governments and often their own school systems. Some are growing rapidly, while others have changed little over the years and almost have a rural nature.

The fast-growing area across the northern part of the county includes Dublin with its Muirfield Village, the homes around Muirfield Golf Course, Worthington, Westerville, and New Albany.

The Villages at Rocky Fork are being developed in the New Albany area, a group of large and stately homes on big lots. To the south is Gahanna, a comfortable community adjacent to Port Columbus International Airport. Persons entering Columbus from the east first pass through Reynoldsburg and Whitehall.

Groveport and Canal Winchester in the southeast portion of the county maintain a small-town flavor, as do Lockbourne and Obetz farther west. Grove City is a middle-class community known mostly as the home of Beulah Park, which, as Capital Music Center, features concerts under the stars in the summer.

New Rome is the westernmost city in the county, just east of Galbreath's Darby Dan Farm with its miles of neat white board fences. Hilliard in the northwest part of the county is the home of the Franklin County Fair.

Local developers take great pride in the quality and affordability of their finished homes. Distinctive touches and artistic landscaping enhance many of Columbus' fine dwellings. Photo by Larry Hamill

The closer-in bedroom communities, some of them surrounded by Columbus now, include Bexley, Upper Arlington, Grandview Heights, and Marble Cliff. All in all the county has 23 suburban communities. A few even predate Columbus. And certainly new neighborhoods will become part of the community in the future.

The Polaris Centers of Commerce, along I-71 in Delaware County, is expected to make a large addition to the city. The 1,268-acre development from NP Limited is expected to exceed $2 billion in value over the next 20 years. Projections indicate that it will generate 60,000 construction jobs and employ 27,000 people by the year 2010.

A spokesperson for the Columbus Recreation and Parks Department says, "We have an electrifying energy that has no equal anywhere else because we bring the spark of life to Columbus."

Columbus residents are likely to have a lifelong happy relationship with the department, since it offers something for everyone of every age.

ABOVE: These neighborhood youngsters take a bicycle ride through the recently incorporated development of Shawnee Hills, located to the north of Dublin in nearby Delaware County. Photo by Jim Baron/Image Finders

FACING PAGE: Located east of downtown Columbus, the bedroom community of Bexley houses a population of more than 13,000 residents. Photo by Jeanne Conte

ABOVE: As the population of Metropolitan Columbus continues to expand, so does the demand for new housing. Photo by Jim Baron/Image Finders

LEFT: This Upper Arlington resident takes a moment to enjoy the colorful surroundings of her garden. Photo by Jeanne Conte

Just listing the locations where the fun and games reign takes nearly two columns in the telephone directory. Mothers push babies through the parks in prams and strollers. When the babies grow older, they play there and take part in special events. Many people get married there and soon they're pushing their children through the parks. And after the children have grown and married, the parents attend senior citizen events in the parks.

There are 25 community recreation centers, 8 senior centers, more than 7,000 acres of parkland, and 5,000 acres of waterways, 6 golf courses, 2 campsites, an adult sports program, 5 athletic complexes, 7 shelterhouses, 9 outdoor pools, one indoor swim center, the Cultural Arts Center, the S.S. Davis Youth Complex for the Performing Arts, the Central Ohio Area Agency on Aging, the Golden Hobby Shop, the Garfield School Artists Co-Op at the Martin Luther King, Jr., Center for Performing and Cultural Arts, and probably a number of things that have been added since this book was written.

The people who have run the department have been local heroes and legends. Names such as Nick Barack and Mel Dodge immediately come to mind. Many have been recognized by having facilities named in their honor. There's an athletic complex named for Lou Berliner, the sports writer who covered amateur athletics for years for the *Columbus Dispatch*. There's one called Anheuser-Busch, more for its benefactor than for the after-game recreation of the adult softball teams.

Those adult sports projects involve more than 50,000 persons a year. You can do

FACING PAGE, ABOVE AND LEFT:
The spirited imagination of
youth was unlocked during a
recent Kids Fest celebration.
Photos by Pamela J. Willits
and Larry Hamill

FACING PAGE: Nine outdoor pools and one indoor swim center are operated by the city, providing ample recreational opportunities for the avid swimmer. A host of private pools and country club facilities are also available. Photo by Larry Hamill

LEFT: Named in honor of Lou Berliner, local sportswriter for *The Columbus Dispatch*, the Berliner athletic complex shown here is just one of the many locations in which the popular citywide sport of softball is played. More than 33,000 people participate in the 222 leagues run by the Columbus Recreation and Parks Department. Photo by Jeffrey A. Rycus/Rycus Associates Photography

your own job of translating that into happiness, health, pulled muscles, and trophies. Activities offered include softball, volleyball, basketball, tennis, football, soccer, walking, and jogging.

The golf courses are open to the public 365 days a year and annual revenues amount to around $2 million. Nearly 10,000 people take advantage of free learn-to-swim classes in the summer and winter months. Visits by children to the 75 playgrounds and 25 recreation centers in a year totals about 700,000. In a recent year there were 83 weddings and rehearsals at the Franklin Park Conservatory.

By the way, it is necessary to get permits for boat docks and stakes, garden plots, shelterhouses, recreation meeting rooms and gyms, athletic complexes, the showmobile, and weddings in the parks. The fees are modest, but they total about $400,000 a year.

The "Music in the Air" programs run mostly from May to the beginning of September and bring outdoor music, dance, and theater to parks throughout the city. There are lunchtime programs downtown in front of the statehouse and at Franklin Commons in the county government complex. In the neighborhood parks, programs are generally given on weekend afternoons and evenings. They add up to more than 200 free performances each summer.

The maintenance division of the department manicures the greens and cuts the fairways on hundreds of acres of golf courses, rakes leaves, removes snow, cleans restrooms, paints pools, clears skating ponds, and maintains a combined total of 386 playing fields, bike paths, and horseshoe courts.

The forestry division is responsible not only for the trees in 12,000 acres of city parks, but also looks after more than 2 million trees throughout 1,800 miles of city streets and alleys.

The nursery and landscape crew also plants and maintains 115 flower beds and 21 planters containing more than 75,000 flowers. The Columbus Park of Roses is a 13-acre facility with more than 9,000 roses and 300 varieties of flowers.

Service to senior citizens is a growing responsibility of the department. Each of the eight senior centers has more than 1,000 members. The "Golden Age Hobby Show" has been the Central Ohio showcase for senior citizen crafts and talents for nearly half a century. The Golden Hobby Shop is the nonprofit consignment store that sells handcrafts made by residents of Franklin County who are 60 and older. It is supported by volunteers who donate nearly 30,000 hours of service a year and take in more than $300,000 in sales.

The Central Ohio Area Agency on Aging was created by the Ohio Department of Aging to plan, implement, and administer various federal and state programs for elderly persons in an eight-county area. The Elderly Nutrition Program provides home-delivered meals for 13,000 persons. Other programs help the elderly receive other in-home services as an alternative to nursing home admission. The agency also sponsors the United States Department of Agriculture's program to provide nutritionally balanced breakfasts and lunches to children in summer months, when schools are closed.

A shining star in the Columbus Recreation and Parks Department's crown is the Columbus Zoo, which is open 365 days a year. The zoo made worldwide headlines in 1956 when Colo (the name is a contraction of Columbus, Ohio) became the first lowland gorilla born in captivity. Since then a number of zoos have been able to breed gorillas. The beginning in Columbus has given new hope for the preservation of this gentle giant on the endangered species list. (The zoo has also been successful in the breeding of many other species, particularly the cheetah and the giraffe.)

ABOVE: Members of the Central Ohio Rowing Association have access to the shells and facilities of the club's docks on Griggs Reservoir in Columbus. A haven for sculling enthusiasts, Griggs Reservoir offers the opportunity to partake in what is considered to be one of the best all-around exercises available. Photo by Larry Hamill

FACING PAGE: The Franklin Park Conservatory, located east of downtown Columbus, is a favorite site for weddings. Photo by Larry Hamill

PREVIOUS PAGE: The Scioto River is an ideal place for a leisurely day of fishing. Photo by Robert E. Schwerzel

PREVIOUS PAGE INSET: Walleyes, bass, crappies, catfish, and more can be caught by Columbus anglers throughout the area's lakes, rivers, and reservoirs. Photo by Jim Baron/Image Finders

ABOVE: Young and old alike enjoy the many scenic and recreational attributes of the Columbus area. Here, a young girl feeds the ducks along the banks of the meandering Scioto River. Photo by Robert E. Schwerzel

ABOVE: Eight senior centers cater to the recreational needs of Columbus' growing senior citizens community. Each center boasts a membership of more than 1,000 people. Photo by Larry Hamill

LEFT: Some 9,000 rose bushes of more than 300 varieties adorn the landscape of the Columbus Park of Roses within the city's Whetstone Park. It is a favorite place in which to hold summer weddings. Photo by Pamela J. Willits

Jack Hanna, who became director of the Columbus Zoo in 1978, has literally taken the zoo's story to the world through appearances on national television, through the publication of a book, and by leading expeditions to such places as Africa, Alaska, the Caribbean and the Galapagos Islands.

Hanna has also taken the zoo into the community. He is likely to show up at a meeting downtown accompanied by a monkey, an exotic bird, a snake, or a giant cockroach. Aware that zoos are the best hope for survival of the earth's wildlife, Jack Hanna views education and research as an important part of the zoo's mission. This belief was stressed in the recent opening of a $2-million animal hospital and research facility. Hanna says, "the Columbus Zoo actively cooperates with other zoos in SSP Programs (Species Survival Plans) to accomplish objectives for the captive propagation of endangered and threatened species." Today the zoo's education department offers classes, lectures, camp-ins, and outreach programs for children and adults, and more than 100,000 people visit the Columbus Zoo each year.

When the zoo was established in Delaware County more than 60 years ago, there was some criticism that it was too far from Columbus. Such complaints are never heard now. While some city zoos are hemmed in and have no room for expansion, the Columbus Zoo recently acquired an adjoining golf course that will be used for expansion and new exhibits.

A recent census showed that more than 7,000 animals are kept at the zoo. They included 305 breeds of mammals, 228 types of birds, 5,619 species of fish, 963 varieties of reptiles, and 145 species of amphibians.

ABOVE: A dromedary camel talks to visitors at the exciting Columbus Zoo. Photo by Barbara Durham

LEFT: Open 365 days a year, the Columbus Zoo features more than 7,000 animals. Director Jack Hanna has led the zoo to worldwide fame. Photo by Jeffrey A. Rycus/ Rycus Associates Photography

NATURE AT ITS BEST

A natural complement to the Columbus Recreation and Parks Department is the Columbus and Franklin County Metropolitan Park District, a special government agency created in 1945 by the Franklin County Probate Court.

The Metro Parks, as they are called, are all outside the I-270 Outerbelt, but are easily accessible from all parts of the city. They are the quiet places, the places where nature is preserved.

There are playgrounds and picnic areas in the Metro Parks, but their chief attractions are their nature trails, the wildflowers in bloom, the deer at Sharon Park, and the spring and autumn migrations of waterfowl. For more active parkgoers there is skiing, fishing, canoeing, and even golfing. But the attraction of the parks is to see Central Ohio as it once was.

Highbanks Metro Park is four miles north of Worthington between Route 23 and the Olentangy River. It is just over 1,000 acres with more than six miles of nature trails and a bicycle/jogging trail. It gets its name from the high banks overlooking the river. A naturalist's description of it would be intermixed till plain and Appalachian forest communities, pre-Indian cultural sites, and outstanding geological features.

The "ravine ramble" programs at Highbanks include visiting a breeding pool of the Jefferson salamander at night and taking a two-mile hike covering time from the Devonian period 350 million years ago to the present. Going backwards in time not

Also part of this park are two golf courses, a challenging par-72, 6,686-yard championship course and a par-59, 3,946-yard executive course. Tee times may be reserved on the larger course on weekends and holidays.

Programs in Blacklick Woods include walks to look at the "swamp critters" and an evening wildlife watch in which red "night vision" lights are used to help find the night prowlers of the forest.

Pickerington Ponds are south of Blacklick Woods along Wright Road, east of Gender Road. Its more than 350 acres feature nature trails and viewing shelters. The glacial relic ponds, marshes, and uplands are well known for attracting many species of shorebirds, waterfowl, passerines, and raptors. (In case you're not a bird-watcher, those last two are songbirds and birds of prey.)

Bird-watching is the principal activity at Pickerington Ponds, and there are no picnic facilities as of this time. Future plans call for a mile and a half of nature trails, a nature center, and parking for 160 cars.

Chestnut Ridge is 486 acres in the triangle formed by Slough Road and Lancaster-Winchester Pike in Fairfield County. It is at the eastern limit of Wisconsin glaciation and has a recovering Appalachian forest community.

American chestnuts were once the dominant tree species on the ridge. A favorite program here is "The American Chestnut's Last Stand." Those attending learn the plight of the trees and the efforts to save them and walk to look at the endangered saplings. They are also given literature and information on ordering native seedlings.

For the bird-watchers, bluebirds abound in the nest boxes in the meadows along the ridge.

Slate Run Metro Park and Historical Farm is just southwest of Chestnut Ridge, but is in Pickaway County. It is on State Route 674 N just north of Marcy Road. It can be reached from Route 23 south of Columbus by going east on Duvall Road. The park and farm cover more than 1,600 acres. The park has recovering Appalachian oak-hickory forest association and interface of Devonian-Mississippian geology. It is a fine place to observe tree flowers.

At the farm, at 9130 Marcy Road, the 1880s agricultural life-style is reenacted. The year-round operation is open to visitors who can see the daily life of a family farm during a period of major technological change. Programs include helping with the animals and barnyard chores, observing the shearing of sheep, and the celebration of various holidays on the farm. There is an admission fee.

Battelle-Darby Creek Metro Park is the largest in the system. Located in

LEFT: Visitors can assist costumed park workers with daily chores at the Slate Run Living Historical Farm, a living museum that depicts life on a Central Ohio family farm in the 1880s. Photo by Jeanne Conte

FACING PAGE: Deer and other wild animals can be seen at Blacklick Woods, situated on the far east side of Columbus. An evening wildlife watch in which special night vision lights are used is just one of many programs offered at the park. Photo by Larry Hamill

southwestern Franklin County at 1775 Darby Creek Drive, it covers more than 3,000 acres along both sides of Big Darby Creek and will eventually be expanded to 3,375 acres. It has till plain, upland, and floodplain forest communities and tall-grass prairie remnants. Along the banks of the creek are places to see fish and launch canoes. A favorite program is birding by canoe, but you must bring your own canoe.

There are streamside strolls to look for herons, wood ducks, and other creekside life, as well as to scan the swift waters for colorful fish. The "Geology Ramble" features studies of the landforms in the park, including ravines, stream valleys, and terraces.

Most of the parks have picnic areas available at no cost on a first-come, first-served basis. There are also separate picnic/recreation areas that may be rented at Battelle-Darby Creek, Blacklick Woods, Blendon Woods, and Highbanks. Each has its own shelter, tables, benches, cooking, and meal-serving facilities.

Metro Parks also conducts upper-level science and outdoor skills educational programs in conjunction with The Ohio State University's School of Natural Resources and Otterbein College's Life Sciences Department. These are held at the Spring Hollow Outdoor Education Center at 1069 West Main Street in Westerville. This is also the administrative office of the district.

Five of the Metro Parks feature winter sports. Blacklick Woods Metro Golf Courses offer ice skating, sledding, and cross-country skiing with rentals available at the pro shop. Battelle-Darby Creek and Highbanks have skiing and sledding. Blendon Woods offers skiing. Sharon Woods has sledding and ice skating.

While the parks make up less than two percent of Franklin County's area, they contain thriving examples of most native Central Ohio ecosystems. And whenever city living gets Columbus residents down, they can always go take a hike.

SPECTATOR SPORTS

Perhaps the greatest compliment you can give a typical Central Ohioan is to call him or her a sports nut.

It would be impossible to list all of the places where the appetite for watching athletes is satisfied—dozens of high school football fields, Little League baseball diamonds in churchyards, soccer fields at small colleges.

Surprisingly enough the largest single spectator sports event in Ohio is the Columbus Marathon, the fastest-growing marathon in the United States. It attracts more than 4,000 runners from 37 states and 11 foreign countries. ESPN rates it as one of the top four marathons in the country.

Ohio State Football fills the giant horseshoe stadium with more than 85,000 spectators for every home game. Large as the stadium is, and narrow as the seats are, it is unusual for a game not to be a sellout. Tickets to the Michigan game often bring a premium price.

You won't find anyone at Broad and High who can't tell you about Woody Hayes. And a good percentage of the locals would reply, "Les Horvath, Howard Cassady,

ABOVE: Scarlet and gray Ohio State football players take to the field amid the roar of the crowd and the pounding of The Best Damn Band in the Land. Photo by Larry Hamill

LEFT: Athletics play a major role in the daily lives of Columbus residents, and fans turn out en masse for their favorite sporting events. Photo by Larry Hamill

FACING PAGE BOTTOM: The largest single spectator sport event in Ohio, the Columbus Marathon attracts more than 4,000 runners from 37 states and 11 foreign countries to tackle the 26-plus mile course that winds its way through Bexley, Upper Arlington, German Village, Victorian Village, the Short North, and the Ohio State campus. Photo by Larry Hamill

Vic Janowicz, and Archie Griffin" if you asked them to name the Heisman Trophy winners from Ohio State.

OSU football has been called a way of life rather than an athletic event. It begins with the tailgate party on the polo field, moves to the opening appearance of "The Best Damn Band in the Land," and wraps up with the traditional ringing of the victory bell.

All told, 31 men's and women's teams play varsity sports at Ohio State, and the Scarlet and Gray has contributed champions in most of them.

Tickets are also at a premium for the basketball games in 13,000-seat St. John Arena. The arena was named in honor of Lynn W. St. John, athletic director at Ohio State from 1912 until 1947.

St. John was an innovative administrator. The Ohio Stadium, dedicated in 1922, was paid off in 1928. St. John then immediately chose a site for the OSU golf course. In 1931 he hired Mike Peppe as swimming coach, and the university started winning NCAA titles.

Larry Snyder also came to the university in 1931 as track coach. One of his runners was the great Jesse Owens. Owens set three world records and tied a fourth in little more than two hours in Ann Arbor at a track meet and then went on to the 1936 Olympics in Berlin and won four gold medals, a slap in the face to Hitler's theory of Aryan supremacy.

The Jesse Owens Track & Field Classic now held at Ohio State is one of the top races in the country and a good place to get a glimpse of Olympic champions.

The OSU women's basketball team is a consistent powerhouse, as is the

Fans pack the 13,000-seat St. John Arena to watch the Ohio State Buckeyes battle rival Purdue. Photo by Larry Hamill

ABOVE: A showcase for past and future Olympic champions, the one-day Jesse Owens Track & Field Classic now held at Ohio State attracts top competitors from around the country. Photo by Jeffrey A. Rycus/Rycus Associates Photography

LEFT: Jack Nicklaus' Muirfield Village Golf Club in Dublin is the site for the annual Memorial Tournament, where the best of the PGA golfers compete for cash prizes on the par 72 championship course. Photo by Larry Hamill

RIGHT: Minor-league professional baseball in Columbus is represented by the Clippers. The AAA farm team for the New York Yankees, the Clippers lead the International League in attendance and have sent many of its players up to the major leagues since the team was established in 1977. Photo by William A. Holmes/Image Finders

FACING PAGE TOP: Scioto Downs is considered to be the fastest five-eighths-mile harness racing track in the nation and can boast an average annual attendance of nearly 500,000 racing fans. Photo by William A. Holmes/Image Finders

synchronized swimming team. And the men's hockey team draws enough fans to fill the 1,700-seat OSU Ice Rink.

A list of university golf greats is like a who's who of the PGA tour. Included are such names as Nicklaus, Weiskopf, Sneed, Cook, and Sindelar.

If golf is your sport, you will most likely want to attend the Memorial Tournament at Nicklaus' MuirfieldVillage Golf Club in Dublin. A different golfing great is honored each year at the tournament as big-name golfers compete on the par-72, 7,104-yard course. Here again, each May the demand for tickets is greater than the supply, even though Muirfield has been described as a "spectator friendly" course with many of its greens surrounded by high ground that provides good viewing areas for thousands.

The King of Sports has the thoroughbreds running at Beulah Park in Grove City and the pacers and trotters on the track at Scioto Downs on Route 23 just south of the Outerbelt.

Beulah has a winter/spring meet and a fall meet each year with racing every day except Tuesday during most of the season. All seating areas, including the grandstand, are enclosed and heated during the cold periods.

Scioto Downs is said to be the country's fastest five-eighths-mile track for harness racing. The typical season runs from May through September, with races held Monday through Saturday evenings with matinees on certain holidays. Clubhouse dining is available at Scioto Downs as well as at Beulah.

The real harness-racing fan will also want to attend the Little Brown Jug, a triple crown of that sport. The best three-year-old pacers compete in this race, held on Thursday of fair week at the Delaware County Fairgrounds. The purse is nearly a half million dollars. To watch this September event from box or grandstand seats, it is wise to buy tickets at the beginning of the year. The track is located on Pennsylvania Avenue in Delaware, north of Columbus.

Minor-league professional baseball is one of the oldest sports in the city. Columbus has fielded teams with such names as the Senators, the Red Birds, and the Jets. The current Columbus baseball team is the Clippers, and the home field is Cooper Stadium on West Mound Street. The stadium is named in honor of Harold M. Cooper, who started as a batboy while a student at Central High School and went on to

A favorite recreational pastime in Columbus, golfing is enjoyed on the greens of more than 35 public and private courses in the city and surrounding communities. Photo by Larry Hamill

become general manager of the Red Birds and head of the International League.

The teams play more than 70 home games each season, and good seats are almost always available in the 15,000-seat stadium. As of this writing the Clippers were the AAA farm team of the New York Yankees. The team has top attendance marks for minor-league franchises and many of its players have made it to the big leagues.

The Columbus Horizon, a professional basketball team in the 16-team Continental Basketball Association, plays its home games at the Fairgrounds Coliseum.

Those who like speed and the roar of engines travel 60 miles north of Columbus to the Mid-Ohio Sports Car Course at Lexington, near Mansfield. The 2.4-mile winding track attracts the nation's leading racers, including Bobby Rahal of Dublin. One of the three-day racing weekends during the summer is usually set aside for motorcycle racing. The most popular weekend is usually the one in which the nationally known drivers appear in the Indy car competition.

The Olentangy-Lower Scioto Bikeway, which runs north and south through the length of the city, is just one of the many fine pathways provided for avid cyclists in Columbus. A pivotal event for the city's bicycling community is the annual Tour of the Scioto River Valley, which attracts an average of 5,000 riders each spring. Photo by Pamela J. Willits

RECREATIONAL SPORTS

Columbus is the youngest large city in America, with nearly four out of 10 residents in the metropolitan area between the ages of 25 and 49. They stay fit on 70 golf courses, try for trophies in 1,738 organized softball leagues, and roll for 4,500 bowling teams.

The number 70 for golf courses is subject to change. New clubs are being built all the time. One of the newest is the Jack Nicklaus-designed club in Jefferson and Plain townships northeast of Columbus.

Boating enthusiasts zip along the scenic waters of the Scioto River. Photo by Jim Baron/Image Finders

Most golfers say the big four of the private clubs are Muirfield Village Golf Club, Scioto Country Club, Columbus Country Club, and the Golf Club. Also ranking right up there with them are the two courses of The Ohio State University Golf Club.

The number of events for runners and walkers is also variable and growing. There are also a score or more of places to keep fit, including some downtown such as the Athletic Club, the Capital Club, the Businessmen's Athletic Club, the YMCA, the YWCA, and the Grant Hospital Fitness Center. There are at least five places to play tennis year-round and courts are easily accessible for summer players.

There is a bikeway that runs the length of the city from north to south, and for the real serious cyclist there is TOSRV. Each spring the annual Tour of the Scioto River Valley attracts 5,000 riders, who follow the Scioto River to Portsmouth on a Saturday and return on Sunday.

Boaters have the reservoirs behind Griggs, O'Shaughnessy, Hoover, and Alum Creek dams for recreation. The part of the Scioto River above O'Shaughnessy Dam is strictly for sailing, as are parts of the other reservoirs. Water skiing is popular on the Scioto above Griggs Dam and on Buckeye Lake east of Columbus.

Smaller lakes and creeks are popular for canoeing. Most of the bodies of water also are used for fishing. You are likely to net bluegills, sunfish, crappies, large and smallmouth bass, catfish, walleyes, and rock bass in the waters of Central Ohio.

Thanks to snowmaking machines, there are several places to ski in Central Ohio. Some of the courses are fast and challenging, although there are no mountains in this part of the country. For those who want to try their luck on the slopes, there's Clear Fork in Richland County, and Mad River Mountain and Snow Trails northwest in the Bellefontaine area.

THE STATE FAIR

The Ohio State Fair is a great state fair and the largest in the country. Although the fair is statewide in participation, it is a part of Columbus not to be missed.

The fair is held each summer at the Ohio Expositions Center on Seventeenth Avenue at Interstate 71. It is primarily an agricultural affair with the emphasis on crops and animals, but there are also art and industrial exhibits, including a new museum of organized labor, a midway full of rides, and grandstand shows that attract the top entertainers in the nation. In addition there are dozens of types of food to feast upon.

The largest event of its kind in the country, the Ohio State Fair is held each summer at the Ohio Expositions Center in Columbus. Agricultural exhibits, grandstand shows, thrilling rides, and tempting food are just a few highlights of this perennial favorite. Photos by Larry Hamill and William A. Holmes/Image Finders

PART

2 Columbus' Enterprises

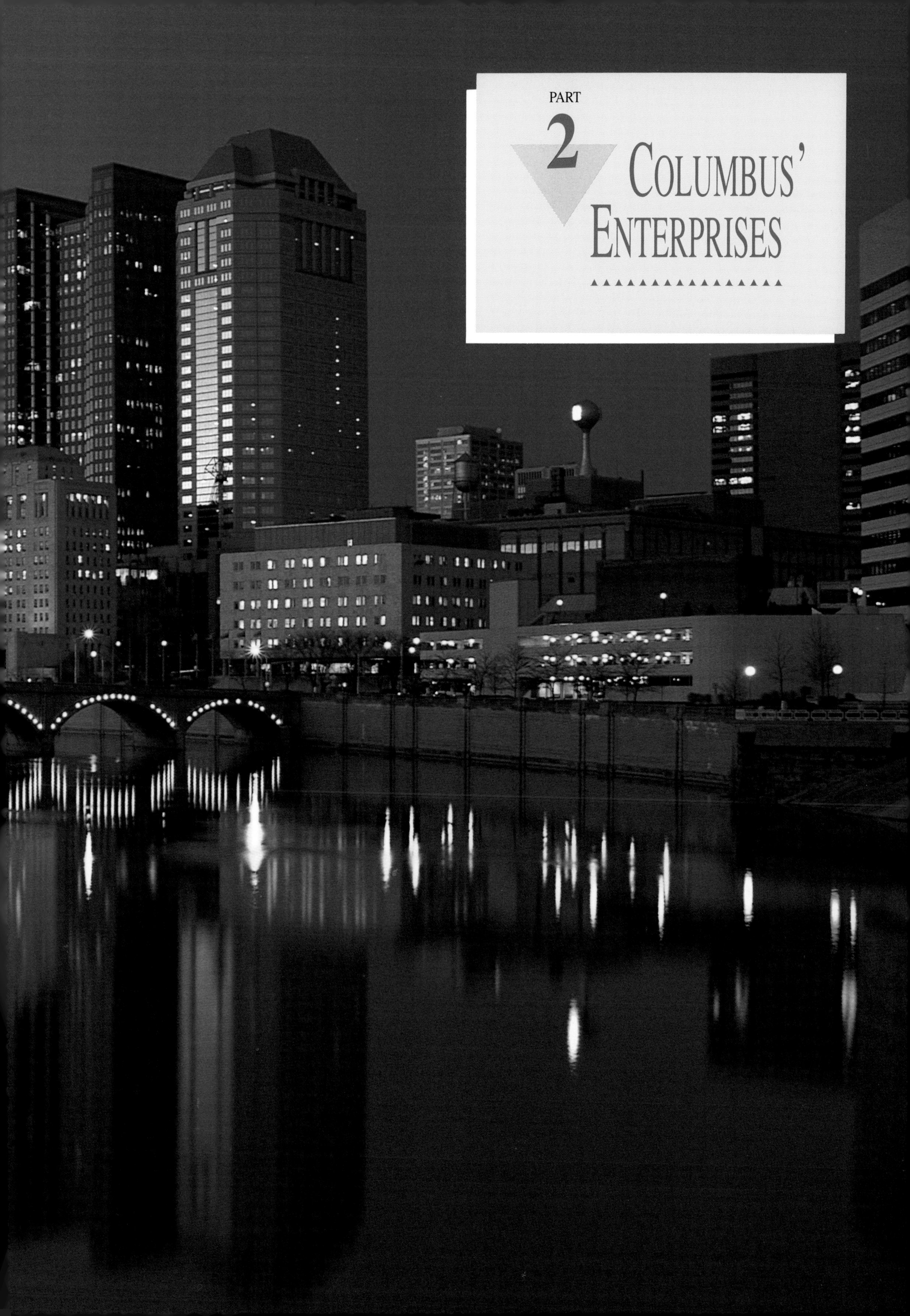

8 NETWORKS

▲▲▲▲▲▲▲▲▲▲▲

277

Columbus' role as a modern, thriving metropolitan center is made possible by its network of energy, communication, and transportation providers.

Ohio Bell, 278;
Access Energy, 282; American Electric Power/
Columbus Southern Power Company, 284;
WSNY/WVKO, 286; Columbus Gas Co., 288;
Central Ohio Transit Authority (COTA), 290;
American Telephone & Telegraph, 292;
WBNS-TV, 294;
Business First of Columbus, 296

Photo by Jim Baron

OHIO BELL

In today's local, national, and international marketplaces, the ability to transport vast volumes of information at lightning speed is a key to economic competitiveness and success. In the Columbus area, three major subsidiaries of Ameritech are helping business and residence customers to meet the challenges this entails.

These subsidiaries are Ohio Bell, the state's premier information technology company; Ameritech Publishing Incorporated, which is at the forefront of directory publishing and related marketing services; and Ameritech Mobile Communications, a leader in such areas of wireless communications as cellular telephones and paging systems. They work together to provide Columbus with a telecommunications infrastructure that helps people send, receive, use, and retrieve information in any form, at any time, from any place in the world.

Ohio Bell, with more than one million customer access lines in the Columbus area, is a crucial partner in the economic development and growth of the community and its environs. Ohio's largest city is at the heart of one of the nation's most information-intensive regions. As a center of government, business, education, medicine, and the arts, Columbus demands a sophisticated communications network to keep pace with the new global information environment.

By employing systems from its parent, Ameritech, and advanced fiber-optic transmission systems and electronic digital technology, Ohio Bell is providing the crucial facilities necessary to meet Columbus' fast-growing communications and information needs. Those needs are as diverse as the interests of the thousands of students from around the world who attend The Ohio State University.

A vital strategy of Ohio Bell involves anticipating the telecommunications requirements of tomorrow by investing in new technologies and state-of-the-art systems to provide its customers with one of the most modern and reliable communications networks in the world. For example, the deployment of electronic digital switching and fiber-optic

transmission systems represents important advancements that help Ohio Bell meet the complex telecommunications needs of Columbus with cost-effective technology.

Fiber-optic systems are capable of rapidly transporting vast volumes of data on a tiny glass filament. With fiber-optic systems, 1.7 billion bits, or flashes of light, can travel on a single fiber each second. That means a pair of fibers— one going in each direction—can transmit 24,000 simultaneous phone calls. In comparison, two pairs of conventional copper telephone wires typically can accommodate no more than 24 calls.

The key to fiber optics is the transmission of laser light pulses along a fiber strand the thickness of a human hair. The edges of the fiber are made of highly refractive glass that nudges wayward light beams toward the center of the fiber, keeping them on course. Because light waves have far more capacity than copper wires for carrying telecommunications signals, they make possible new communications solutions,

Mobile microwave communications from Ohio Bell mean that in the event of a disaster, telephone service can still be provided in any area where an outage may have occurred. This specially equipped truck may be dispatched quickly to any area in the state served by Ohio Bell.

and do so in a transmission medium that requires far less space than previous generations of cable.

Thus the optical-fiber system is the high-speed expressway of the Information Age, which assures virtually instantaneous movement of information along Ohio Bell's telecommunications network.

Columbus is the third-largest data processing center in the world. In the 1980s more than 100,000 new jobs were created here, many of them based on the city's growing information services industry. Protecting the communications network with backup transmission paths is a vital Ohio Bell investment, one that lays the foundation for the next century.

To enhance network security and reliability, Ohio Bell constructed a fiber ring in Columbus. It configures the flow of telecommunications traffic in such a way that even if the fiber should be cut or damaged, fiber ring customer traffic can be rerouted in the opposite direction with no service disruption. In Columbus, the fiber ring originates at the downtown Ohio Bell central switching office at 111 N. Fourth Street and runs through the downtown area, linking buildings along the way.

It then returns to the point of origin, forming a complete circle. In the event that information traveling along the ring is interrupted, it is automatically rerouted in the opposite direction to avoid the problem at the point of interruption. Without the ring, two separate circuits would be necessary for this line of protection.

In addition to the benefit of greater reliability in the local network, the fiber ring project brings to Ohio Bell increased flexibility for customer growth.

Another important advancement in Ohio's telecommunications is the conversion of Ohio Bell switching centers to digital technology. This technology provides greater network capacity, error-free transmission, and more efficient delivery of data and video. As a result, customers have more variety in the communications options available to them.

By providing innovative solutions to meet the demands of the information services industry, such as the building of an "intelligent" network to introduce

BELOW: Students around the state use the Ameritech PagesPlus® in a wide variety of studies, ranging from business classes and research projects to telephone training.

voice and data communications services more quickly, Ohio Bell is striving to take full advantage of its telecommunications system's remarkable capabilities to serve the residents and businesses of Columbus.

Anticipating continued growth in small businesses throughout the state, Ohio Bell has developed special service packages to help smaller firms succeed and prosper. Four packages are available: the single line package, expanded single line package, multiple line package, and fax package. Intended to help businesses with up to six lines and 49 telephones, the packages include resource materials on marketing, business management, and support available from government agencies.

RIGHT: As a major banking center, Columbus relies on Ohio Bell's speedy data transmission. Banc One branches and data centers throughout the region are linked by a telecommunications system that provides instantaneous financial information to hundreds of thousands of area customers.

BELOW: Columbus is Ohio's first test site for a major new technological advance, fiber-optic lines to the home. The project evaluates the most effective means to bring telephone and other information services into the homes of Columbus customers.

Ohio Bell also transports long-distance calls for the Columbus area and connects customers to the long-distance carrier of their choice. Through its Carrier Access organization, Ohio Bell provides the link between local customers and some 30 long-distance companies doing business in Columbus.

As Ohio Bell continues to modernize and expand its capabilities to make new services more widely available, the focus of investment is on ways to apply technologies to help meet every customer's needs. Signaling System 7 (SS7) technology, for example, the

TOP: Columbus is served by countywide enhanced 9-1-1 emergency services from Ohio Bell. Any Columbus citizen may call for help and be connected with emergency services within seconds.

BOTTOM: The expansion of the Columbus Public Library nearly doubled its space—and its telecommunications needs. With an Ameritech® Centrex communications system and the services of Ohio Bell, the library is able to meet the increased demand.

backbone of the "intelligent" network, is a form of digital computer technology that makes it possible to introduce many new telecommunications services.

This new technology offers dramatic improvements in network performance, generating more efficient use of network time and providing faster connections and additional capacity for customers. These enhancements reflect the fact that the signaling network is separate from the voice network. However, the implementation of Signaling System 7 does not require new facilities. Instead, the technology makes use of existing spare facilities, thus providing another bonus in terms of cost efficiency for users of the Ohio Bell network.

Equally important, Signaling System 7 makes possible various new services such as automatic callback, which automatically dials back the last caller; repeat dialing, an automatic dialback service; distinctive ringing, which allows the customer to identify incoming calls from predesignated numbers; call screening, which routes certain incoming calls to a recorded message; and caller ID, which displays the originating number of the incoming call.

Another far-reaching development for business customers is Ameritech® ISDN Centrex service. It allows voice, data, and video messages to be sent simultaneously over an ordinary telephone line.

A significant advantage of Ameritech ISDN Centrex is that it makes possible video teleconferences in which both the voice signals and full-color video are transmitted from one conference room to another site over a single dedicated ISDN line. The system also enables customers to receive clearer, crisper voice communications and cleaner data transmissions with less noise and faster speeds.

Several additional and new telecommunications advances are expected to find widespread application in Columbus in the years ahead.

In fact, Columbus was chosen as a test site by Ameritech to evaluate the most effective and efficient ways to bring the benefits of fiber optics to the home.

Another innovation tested in Columbus involves pay telephones. It permits

Ohio Bell, with more than one million customer access lines in the Columbus area, is a crucial partner in the economic development and growth of the community.

callers to leave a message, in their own voice, when a number is unanswered or busy. The system then automatically tries to complete the call for several hours.

Columbus-area customers also are finding enhanced service and faster connections through the use of computer-based voice recognition systems. One application of this advanced concept is to speed collect, credit card, and person-to-person long-distance calls.

Ohio Bell is the market leader in the provision of public telephone service throughout the state. The company provides approximately 12,000 pay phones in greater Columbus, assuring 24-hour-a-day access to the public telecommunications network. Portable pay phones are also available for special events and to provide emergency services in the event of disasters.

Bringing communications services to people takes different forms, and demands innovative technologies. The mobile telephone is an example. Ameritech created Ameritech Mobile Communications to serve the wire-free communications needs of mobile customers. In 1983 Ameritech Mobile Communications offered the first commercial mobile telephone service to customers in the United States. It was also first to demonstrate digital cellular service in North America.

One of the innovations introduced by Ameritech Mobile makes it possible for customers to be contacted on their mobile telephones in more than 250 American and Canadian cities by merely dialing their local mobile numbers. Voice messaging, newstip hotlines, sports updates, and stock and weather information are more of the innovative services offered through Ameritech Mobile. Ameritech Mobile also provides paging services, and is the largest paging provider in the Midwest.

Ameritech Mobile now has about 250 cell sites in its service region and continues to add them in response to the demand for mobile service.

Directory and marketing services are a natural extension of the communications solutions provided in Columbus by Ohio Bell. A sister Ameritech company, Ameritech Publishing, Inc., is one of the largest directory publishers in the nation. Its 45,000-square-foot, computerized graphics center at Troy, Michigan, uses advanced technology to prepare directories and to provide better service to Columbus advertisers.

API provides the Ameritech Pages-Plus® white and yellow pages directories for Ohio Bell. In addition, Ameritech Publishing offers a variety of specialized marketing services and products that help small and medium-sized

businesses to more effectively reach customers.

For instance it provides Columbus with CASH OFFers™, a direct mail coupon and advertising distribution service. API also operates an audiotex gateway service, Touch Four®, which

LEFT: Ameritech Mobile Communications provides Columbus with anytime, anyplace telecommunications convenience. The largest paging provider in the Midwest, Ameritech Mobile also offers a service which enables its customers to be contacted on their mobile phones in more than 250 North American cities.

BELOW: Ameritech Publishing and Ohio Bell team up to offer the thousands of small businesses in Columbus telecommunications systems and services which are tailored to their individual needs.

Columbus was the first Ohio site for the trial of a new service which enables callers to leave recorded messages via area pay telephones. The message may be delivered up to four hours after the caller records it, enabling communications even when the two parties do not speak directly.

connects callers with timely recorded information such as news, weather, and sports.

For buyers and sellers of industrial products and services, Ameritech Industrial InfoSource Inc. has specialized directories called the Ameritech Industrial Purchasing Guide. Overseas, API-International produces English-language directories in Tokyo and Osaka, Japan. Published jointly with Nippon Telegraph and Telephone of Japan, the CitySource directories list various categories of local businesses.

Another API subsidiary, Old Heritage Advertising and Publishers Incorporated, furnishes more than 80 directories in 14 states.

Together Ohio Bell, Ameritech Mobile, and API are a significant part of Columbus' burgeoning information services industry. They are key elements in the delivery of advanced communications and information products and services to hundreds of thousands of business and residential customers.

In the Age of Information and a highly competitive global environment, Columbus demands a technologically advanced telecommunications infrastructure. The investments Ohio Bell and Ameritech have made not only help keep Ohio's information infrastructure competitive, but also are a powerful driver of economic development.

Ohio Bell understands that access to information is critical to success in today's global, information-based economy. By investing to keep the Columbus telecommunications infrastructure flexible and innovative, the Ameritech companies and their employees are working to bring quality service more quickly to more people.

As both Columbus and Ohio Bell approach the twenty-first century, the delivery of new telecommunications technology is essential to the prosperity of Ohio's capital city.

ACCESS ENERGY

Access Energy, an innovative natural gas marketing firm committed to total customer service, thrives in the volatile world created by the deregulation of natural gas in the early 1980s.

What began as Yankee Resources, Inc., in 1982 became Access Energy Corporation in 1988. Along the way it set the industry standard for creative approaches to natural gas purchasing, transportation, and sales. The result: Access Energy is North America's leading marketer of reliable, cost-effective natural gas, serving more than 10,000 commercial, industrial, utility, and institutional customers throughout the United States and Canada.

Access Energy is the industry leader not because of the commodity the company provides, but because the company develops innovative solutions to customer and supplier needs.

Today Access Energy fulfills the natural gas needs of those who pioneered fast food—Kentucky Fried Chicken, Taco Bell, and Pizza Hut; those who build fast cars and fly fast planes—Honda of America and the United States Air Force; and those who educate fast thinkers and fast running backs—The Ohio State University.

Founded and led by Chief Executive Officer Lance W. Schneier, a pioneer in natural gas marketing and a pacesetter in early legal and regulatory efforts, the

RIGHT: (From left) Access Energy's Steven B. Jaffee, executive vice president; Lance W. Schneier, president, chairman, and chief executive officer; and Scott W. Gebhardt, chief operating officer.

BELOW: Access Energy's team of natural gas marketers, buyers, and administrators in the Dublin office.

company built a reputation for developing partnerships that benefit customers and suppliers alike. Access Energy and the gas marketing industry grew out of the deregulation of natural gas, which began in the late 1970s.

Until that time both large and small end-users were restricted to purchasing

ABOVE: The corporate headquarters of Access Energy in Dublin. The company also maintains offices in Chicago, Houston, San Francisco, and Irvine, California.

RIGHT: Gas supply and marketing professionals arrange for the purchase, transportation, and sale of natural gas from coast to coast.

natural gas from one supplier: their local utility. Local utilities, or LDCs, in turn were limited to buying their natural gas from interstate pipelines.

Not unlike the deregulation of the telephone industry, the deregulation of natural gas opened the door for suppliers, including Access Energy, to sell directly to all types of natural gas users. Hence the term "direct purchase gas."

Today end-users have choices: to buy natural gas from the local utility, or buy it directly from a marketer and pay the utility only to transport the gas to a facility.

Access Energy was the first marketer to own the gas it ships via pipelines, a unique strategy in the days after deregulation, a strategy which quickly became standard procedure. Now the industry's number one independent marketer Access Energy has not lost the edge it acquired in its days as the industry's trailblazer. The basis of Access Energy's success is simple: attract, hire, and retain the best people— men and

women who combine original thinking with attention to detail.

In a relatively young industry, the Dublin company has assembled a team of skilled and seasoned professionals who have demonstrated the capabilities required to maintain industry leadership. Access associates are recognized as experts across the spectrum of disciplines needed for success: marketing, supply and transportation, gas administration, customer service, energy law, regulatory issues, and finance.

In an ever-changing marketplace, Access Energy's

bonds with customers and suppliers are unmatched and long-standing. The company becomes a partner in the natural gas supply process, providing not just the commodity, but also informed counsel and straight talk about a complex industry.

The Access Energy tradition of innovation is best illustrated by the company's lead role in the development of the natural gas futures contract.

In 1984 Access Energy began working in concert with the New York Mercantile Exchange (NYMEX) on the introduction of the contract. Six years

later, on April 3, 1990, the company participated in the first trade of the new futures contract—a method by which savvy natural gas buyers and suppliers can avoid the sharp price fluctuations that can break operating budgets.

The contract is now the fastest-growing contract in the history of NYMEX. Access Energy remains an active participant in the market, offering customized products and services to producers, utilities, and end-users who want to take advantage of futures market hedging without actually trading themselves.

In addition to its suburban Columbus corporate offices, convenient to vast supplies of Appalachian gas, Access Energy has sales offices in Chicago, Illinois; and San Francisco and Irvine, California. Gas supply and transportation operations are located in Houston, Texas.

From Houston, gas buyers, and transportation experts maintain relationships with more than 300 major producers, independent operators, and pipelines. After locating the best gas supply package, they match it with the most effective delivery mechanism.

At headquarters in Dublin, detail-oriented specialists provide backroom support for the marketing team. Skilled gas administrators provide timely, accurate nominations, dispatches, invoices, and other reports integral to managing a natural gas supply program.

The company has become the nation's leading independent natural gas marketer because of its diversified supply base and long-term sales commitments with service-oriented customers of all sizes. It serves natural gas consumers ranging from utilities and *Fortune* 500 companies to individual schools, churches, restaurants, and laundromats.

The name, Access Energy, reflects its mission: securing access to supplies and transportation, so customers have reliable, competitively priced energy.

Access Energy, the nation's first natural gas marketer in the 1980s and the leader in the 1990s, is positioned to continue its tradition of innovation and service into the next century.

AMERICAN ELECTRIC POWER/ COLUMBUS SOUTHERN POWER COMPANY

American Electric Power is a relative newcomer to Columbus. Yet AEP and its local operating subsidiary, Columbus Southern Power Company, together have been serving local customers for more than 100 years.

Commercial electric service was first offered in Columbus in 1883 by Columbus Southern Power predecessor companies. The histories and traditions of Columbus Southern and AEP merged nearly a century later when AEP acquired the local company in 1980. After this acquisition, AEP relocated its corporate headquarters from New York City to Columbus.

The AEP Service Corporation, a subsidiary of the parent American Electric Power Company, is located at One Riverside Plaza where it has 2,200 employees. The Service Corporation is the management and technology arm which provides professional services to the AEP Systems operating electric utility companies and their coal-mining subsidiaries.

Now Columbus plays a central role in the daily activities of the AEP System. It is the hub of the system as well as the largest community served by the system's eight operating companies. AEP System companies serve 2.7 million customers across seven states.

AEP System companies, besides

Columbus Southern Power line crews perform routine maintenance to assure reliable service to commercial and residential customers.

Columbus Southern, are Appalachian Power Company, Indiana Michigan Power Company, Kentucky Power Company, Kingsport Power Company, Michigan Power Company, Ohio Power Company, and Wheeling Power Company.

AEP's downtown office tower houses the nerve center of the seven-state system—a fully automated, computer-directed system control center. The control center continuously rates system conditions, unit efficiencies and operating costs, and customer requirements to deliver the most efficient and economical kilowatt-hour of electricity possible.

Columbus Southern has 2,400 employees working to provide reliable electric service to nearly 550,000 customers in 26 central and southern Ohio counties. Columbus Southern has nine business offices (three of them in Columbus) and 13 service centers (four in Columbus).

CREATING THE FUTURE IS NOTHING NEW

The American Electric Power System has a history of innovations to improve the efficiency and reliability of the electricity production and delivery systems.

AEP primarily uses coal as fuel for its electricity production. Concern for the environment and dedication to local coal production has caused the AEP System to take a leadership role in developing cleaner ways to burn coal.

Pressurized fluidized bed combustion (PFBC) is a clean coal technology being refined by AEP. PFBC promises to increase power plant efficiency, help plants meet environmental standards, and reduce costs.

Another AEP achievement is the Zimmer Plant conversion. Initially designed and begun as a nuclear power plant, Zimmer was redesigned and completed as a coal-burning power plant—the world's first nuclear-to-coal conversion. The AEP Service Corporation was project manager, and Columbus Southern is a part owner of the plant.

Nearer to Columbus, many of the AEP System's efforts to im-

The AEP office building's location at One Riverside Plaza reflects AEP's commitment to downtown Columbus.

prove the electricity production and delivery systems are pursued at the John E. Dolan Engineering Laboratory in Groveport. This modern facility began operation in 1987 and houses three major laboratories—electrical research, environmental sciences, and civil engineering.

PROVIDING CUSTOMERS A BETTER WAY

AEP System companies, including Columbus Southern, help customers find ways to better manage electricity use. This helps customers save initially in the form of lower bills. The companies save even more by delaying the need to build additional power plants.

Because of Columbus' extraordinary housing market, AEP/Columbus Southern chose to locate the nation's first prototype total-electric Smart House here. The Smart House's new cabling system makes electricity, telephone, cable television, audiovisual, and data signals available to all convenience outlets in the house. Its computerized, integrated circuits provide new levels of security, safety, flexibility, and control.

The Smart House demonstrates the latest in home heating, cooling, water heating, insulation, and construction. Featured in the house are new products, including an unpressurized, lightweight hot water tank and a heat recovery system which provides bonus hot water in summer.

TRANSTEXT DESIGNED TO LOWER BILLS

Imagine being able to select the price you pay for electricity. Would you

The control center in Columbus is the nerve center of the seven-state AEP system.

change your electricity use habits to take advantage of lower rates?

That's what the TranstexT® Home Energy Management program is studying. TranstexT offers four rate levels related to the company's costs of providing electricity at various times throughout the day. Approximately 170 Columbus Southern customers in the Dublin area, along with customers of two other AEP companies, have been helping evaluate the program to determine whether it will be offered on a large scale.

One of the most important aspects of AEP's commitment to its customers lies in its research and development of energy conservation equipment and techniques, an enduring discipline that is well-rooted across the AEP System.

For example, AEP has been the leader in the development of heat pumps since the 1930s, a record of some 60 years of study. AEP also insisted on proper insulation in new structures when many

considered it an unnecessary expense.

From the beginning, AEP has worked with its customers to encourage efficient use of energy. It has committed itself to intensify these initiatives as world population increases, energy supplies become more restricted, and as people strive to improve their standard of living.

The nation's first total-electric Smart House, located in downtown Columbus, provides insights for future home automation.

WSNY/WVKO

It's always sunny and 95 in Columbus, says Alan M. Fetch, president and general manager of Franklin Communications, Inc.

Ninety-six percent of Americans listen to radio every week and 79 percent listen every day. Local ratings show substantial numbers of them are tuned to the light rock of WSNY-FM or the urban contemporary format of WVKO-AM, "The Rhythm of the City."

"Ours has been a success story with growth every year," says Fetch. "The big reasons are providing the type of listening people want and being involved in the community."

The building that houses Franklin Communications at 4401 Carriage Hill Lane in Upper Arlington has been expanded twice and the property beneath the three radio towers has room for future growth.

While the broadcasts originate from that building, the presence of the two

radio stations is evident everywhere in the community. In addition to the music provided by the stations, there are traffic reports, up-to-the-minute news, and weather advisories.

Fetch is particularly proud of Sunny 95's "Triple the Traffic" reports during morning and evening rush hours.

Heartbeat of the traffic reporting system is the Bell Jet Ranger Jet Helicopter, *Yellow Thunder*, which is in the air reporting traffic conditions on the roads and freeways below on days when the weather keeps conventional aircraft on the ground.

Traffic eyes on the ground are two Courtesy Crew trucks known as Triple-A Good Samaritan Units One and Two.

The trucks are on the lookout for the things that cause traffic tie-ups and for motorists in trouble. The Ohio Auto Club mechanics on board take care of such emergencies as flat tires and dead batteries on the scene and at no cost.

If the driver is out of gas, he gets

Good morning from Mike and Jane on Sunny 95, WSNY. Photo by Prime Time Cafe, Walt Disney World

fuel enough to get him to a service station, provided at no cost. If the trouble is more serious, they radio the appropriate place for a tow or other help.

The third source of traffic news is the motorists themselves. Any driver with a Cellular One telephone in his car can contact the station by striking *95. If necessary, the driver is put in direct contact with the helicopter above.

The system not only informs drivers of traffic problems, it provides a means of actually clearing blockages and getting traffic moving again.

As 1992 approaches, Sunny 95 is planning to play a major role in AmeriFlora. It will call on the experience the station has built in sponsoring, promoting, and participating in a number of community activities.

Through various promotions the station has raised more than $250,000 for Children's Hospital. A drive to provide 12 monitors to give the hospital state-of-the-art neonatal care was expected to take three years, but was completed in two.

On summer evenings on the riverfront downtown, WSNY has provided laser concerts on

Sunny 95 at the Greater Columbus Arts Festival and Street Fair. Photo by Eric Shinn

Jet helicopter Yellow Thunder, *the Sunrunner van, the WSNY AAA Good Samaritan vehicles, and the Sunny 95 Sundome and Skyball in front of the station. Photo by D.R. Goff*

the state office building, along with other local sponsors. In winter during the holiday season, *Yellow Thunder* gently touches down on the statehouse lawn and Santa emerges.

On summer days when there are rib burnouts, chili contests, and pizza parties, Sunny 95 is there. On winter days the station puts its efforts into the Christmas Wish program. Providing such things as parent and child reunions, new bikes, and Christmas dinners brings out the pleasure of giving.

The station has also given listeners the chance to find summer in the winter with contests offering trips to such places as Hawaii, Jamaica, Aruba, the Bahamas, Montego, Barbados, Cancun, and the Virgin Islands. It also has sponsored tours in which, for a reasonable rate, planeloads of listeners can get away from winter for a day on a sunny beach.

Wherever you happen to be in central Ohio, you're likely to see the smiling sun logo of Sunny 95, and those stylish sunglasses can't conceal the good that is being done.

WVKO has been broadcasting on the Columbus scene since 1948 and Fetch says the station, at 1580 on the AM dial, will continue doing what it does best.

The urban contemporary format offers a diverse musical menu to suit the life-styles of black adults from 25-49. It is a blend of music featuring rhythm and blues, jazz, and classic oldies. Interspersed is local, national, and international news, traffic reports, and weather.

Community involvement has long been a tradition at WVKO. Some of its public service involvement includes sponsoring annual fundraisers for the Martin Luther King, Jr., Center for the Performing and Cultural Arts; raising $25,000 in a 17-hour radiothon for the American Red Cross African Famine Relief Fund; sponsoring annual events to collect canned goods for area food pantries and homeless shelters; coordi-

nating a 100-member team that raised thousands of dollars in the annual United Negro College Fund Walk-a-thon; sponsoring a toy drive benefiting children under the care of Franklin County Children's Services; helping local charities by running daily public service announcements; sponsoring the annual Martin Luther King, Jr., Citywide Birthday Celebration march and program; holding fundraisers for the mayor's Anti-Drug Fund; broadcasting live from the annual Mt. Vernon Avenue Comin' Home Celebration and arranging an impromptu dance at Valley Dale one year when the celebration was rained out; sponsoring Family Fest, a community festival regularly attended by more than 15,000 people; and sponsoring an annual Christmas party attended by more than 1,000 underprivileged children.

Indeed, so much happens at WSNY and WVKO that the staffers have their own newsletters to keep up. "AirCheck" tells the Sunny 95 people news and infor-

Sunny 95's Sgt. Bill Taylor in Yellow Thunder, *Columbus' first choice for traffic information. Photo by D.R. Goff*

mation about Columbus' only light rock station and "Rhythm Report" chronicles what is happening with WVKO.

If Christopher sailed today, they are the two locations on the dial where he would discover Columbus.

COLUMBIA GAS CO.

In the late 1800s natural gas was considered merely a by-product of oil drilling. These "gasser" wells, as they were called, were first discovered in Ohio in 1814 in Noble County during brine drilling in the salt manufacturing process. Some years later, natural gas was a source of aggravation for the early oil explorations in Ohio, and it was merely burned off or was allowed to escape into the air.

No one knew yet the amazing capabilities of this colorless gas. Although it has been recorded that the first natural gas was introduced to Columbus at the Columbus Club on December 31, 1889, it was still very much a misunderstood energy source at the turn of the century. Little knowledge existed about how to transport it effectively, how to store it, or how to market it.

Even in the early 1900s, when some of the advantages of using natural gas for such things as industrial processing and residential cooking became known, what was used then was artificially produced manufactured gas.

It wasn't until companies such as

Ohio Fuel Supply began delivering natural gas in the 1920s from rich fields in Ohio, West Virginia, and Kentucky to many central Ohio towns that natural gas started to become an important mainstay in central Ohio's energy supply mix.

It also was a time that Ohio Fuel Supply moved to the forefront of central Ohio natural gas suppliers, acquired several other smaller gas companies through the 1940s and 1950s, and grew to what now is Columbia Gas of Ohio. Today it serves more than 500 communities and 62 counties with nearly 16,000 miles of pipeline.

In central Ohio alone Columbia Gas has more than 350,000 residential, commercial, and industrial customers, each served by an efficient underground delivery system.

Major industries that depend on natural gas in central Ohio include the Honda of America automotive complex at Marysville and the Anheuser-Busch brewery in Columbus. The number of industries, commercial establishments, and residences utilizing natural gas as the fuel of choice continues to grow.

A common assumption among energy experts is that every energy resource has or will have its day of prominence. In America's infancy, wood was the primary energy source for heating, cooking, and steam production for industrial and rail purposes.

As the nation became more industrialized, coal came to the forefront as the energy source of choice with its variety of uses. Over the past few decades, the emergence and utilization of oil and petroleum have become an important part of the American way of life.

But again today, many energy experts agree that as we proceed further into the 1990s and to the forefront of the twenty-first century—with environmental concerns a high priority and energy supply and access increasingly vital to U.S. security and survival—the prime fuel, the fuel of the future, is clean, efficient,

Columbia Gas invested more than $500 million during the 1980s in its vast natural gas system, assuring that its quality gas service will remain one of Ohio's major energy benefits into the 1990s and beyond.

and domestically abundant natural gas.

Columbia Gas is not only prepared to meet the new demands of the expected era of natural gas prominence prompted by an environmentally conscious global market but has taken the lead in heading the new energy awareness. Gas users benefit from Columbia's leadership in research and support technology which continuously seeks more applications for natural gas and more efficient operation of existing applications.

In 1989 at its headquarters in Colum-

ABOVE: The "Columbia," shown here near the Columbia Gas headquarters, is the first American-built transit bus designed to run solely on clean-burning natural gas.

LEFT: A commitment to providing the very best in customer service at the best possible cost is a Columbia Gas priority.

bus, Columbia Gas introduced a revolutionary new development in the fight for clean air: Aptly named the "Columbia," it was the first American-built transit bus designed solely to run on clean-burning natural gas.

The "Columbia" was hailed by national, state, and regional leaders—and was given extensive national attention—as a true example of what the private sector can accomplish for the betterment of all Americans.

The "Columbia" has continued to receive tremendous interest and support, leading to numerous orders for natural gas-burning buses by transit systems throughout the nation.

Since vehicles powered by natural gas have shown to release up to 90 percent fewer harmful exhaust emissions, which are a leading cause of urban smog, Columbia has become a national leader in natural gas vehicle technology. With more than 150 natural gas vehicles on

the road daily in central Ohio, Columbia Gas continues to demonstrate that the technology works, that natural gas is a superior alternative motor fuel.

Columbia Gas also takes pride in being very active in the areas of economic development and corporate citizenship in central Ohio.

The company is a major role player on efforts to attract business to the area and throughout the state. Columbia officials work closely with city and state economic groups, local and state chambers of commerce, and other entities to aggressively pursue new business for the region.

Columbia Gas recognizes the importance of reliable energy supplies and service to prospective businesses and has proven experience and success in fulfilling the energy requirement of new industry.

During the 1980s, Columbia Gas invested more than $500 million into its integrated natural gas system in Ohio,

upgrading and expanding to keep quality natural gas service in the 1990s one of Ohio's major energy benefits.

Columbia Gas also understands the importance of being active and participatory as a corporate citizen. Company representatives play a key role in many area civic efforts and campaigns, such as the United Way, Operation Feed, the United Negro College Fund, March of Dimes, and the many locally based service organizations, chambers of commerce, the arts, education, and other organizations.

What separates Columbia Gas from virtually every other service-providing business is its high priority commitment to providing the very best in customer service—reliably, economically, and safely.

Providing that service is the responsibility of Columbia's more than 1,500 central Ohio area employees, employees dedicated, competent, caring, and involved with the customers they serve, the service they provide, and the communities where they live.

It is the mission of Columbia Gas to ensure that natural gas assumes its natural position as the clean-burning fuel of choice, and the natural solution for today's and tomorrow's energy needs.

CENTRAL OHIO TRANSIT AUTHORITY (COTA)

As Columbus has grown, so has its need for transportation services. Today the Central Ohio Transit Authority provides Columbus and Franklin County with bus service totaling more than 18 million passenger trips per year and more than 9 million miles traveled.

The demand for public transportation in Columbus has been met by a variety of services throughout the years, including horse-drawn buggies, streetcars, trolleys, and buses. During the early years of the twentieth century automobile use increased, roads were expanded, and downtown areas became transportation hubs.

In 1949 the Columbus Transit Company privately owned and operated a fleet of motor buses and trolley cars. As competition increased many privately owned transit authorities found it nearly impossible to maintain a profit.

The federal government recognized the need for tax support and development and as a result in 1964 passed the Urban Mass Transportation Act, pro-

From horse-drawn buggies to streetcars to buses, public transportation has long been a Columbus institution. Columbus has seen a wide array of transit mechanisms.

COTA offers riders the convenience of Park & Ride areas located throughout Franklin County.

viding funding to develop and operate transit authorities. For three years in the early 1970s community leaders worked together to form a transit authority. Success was achieved January 1, 1974, when ownership of the bus system was transferred officially from the Columbus Transit Company to the Central Ohio Transit Authority.

COTA, established by Franklin County and the municipalities of Bexley, Columbus, Gahanna, Grandview Heights, Grove City, Hilliard, Reynoldsburg, Upper Arlington, Westerville, Whitehall, and Worthington, is now one of more than 1,400 public transit systems serving communities across the United States.

A 13-member board of trustees was named by the mayors of the 11 member cities and approved by the city councils. Two members were appointed by the county commissioners. The board, whose members serve without compensation, set the policies and direction for COTA. COTA's mission is to provide safe, clean, reliable, efficient, and courteous transportation services to the citizens of central Ohio.

COTA's goals for the 1990s are:
• Providing cost-effective service while continually refining routes to balance resources with the growing demand for public transit service.
• Introducing accessible new fixed-route services; increasing services for those who depend on public transportation as their only transportation option; and expanding specialized service for the physically disabled.
• Becoming more involved with the citizens of Franklin County through public meetings and outreach programs designed to gain community input.
• Making the public more aware of

the benefits public transit brings to a growing city, particularly as an alternative means of transportation as the community addresses the problems of increasing traffic and massive highway reconstruction.

• Developing new marketing programs designed to bring new riders to the system and to work with downtown business to encourage their employees to use public transit to avoid growing traffic and parking hassles.

With a total of 56 routes throughout Franklin County, the Central Ohio Transit Authority provides 28 express bus routes, 18 local bus routes, and 10 crosstown routes. Passengers age 65 and older and disabled riders may obtain a Good-As-Gold and Key Card. These special identification cards allow passengers to ride for reduced fares.

Project Mainstream provides special transportation services for physically disabled riders who might otherwise be unable to hold jobs, participate in social activities, receive medical treatment, or conduct the business of everyday living.

The Senior Citizens on the Town (SCOT) program provides round trip travel for senior citizens to restaurants, shopping centers, recreational facilities, and special events all over Franklin County.

COTA has been recognized as a leader in the Columbus Public School's Adopt-A-School program. COTA employees volunteer for activities such as pen pal letters, tutoring, and career day to help students improve their skills in reading, math, and communication.

The Transit On Watch program allows bus operators to report emergency situations directly to the Columbus Division of Police through the use of two-way radios on all buses. This program, the first of its kind in the country, assists the city and surrounding suburbs in crime prevention, safety, and accident reporting.

Special transportation services are offered to and from Columbus' largest outdoor event, Red, White & BOOM!

Passengers board one of COTA's many local downtown buses.

Annually more than 40,000 riders choose the convenience and safety of COTA as their means of transportation for this event.

Since COTA first began providing service, bus routes have nearly doubled and annual ridership has increased by 5 million. Good business and a strong economy have accelerated central

Ohio's growth and increased opportunity for public transportation.

COTA has grown and will continue to grow with the community in response to its changing needs.

COTA's four hand-painted Christmas coaches provide free tours of downtown Columbus' "White Lights of Christmas" displays.

AMERICAN TELEPHONE & TELEGRAPH

AT&T is an integral part of the Columbus community, with a world-class manufacturing facility and development laboratory on the city's east side, a technical training center in Dublin, sales offices downtown, and several other entities in and around the city.

Columbus has been a focal point in AT&T's drive to balance its research and development, manufacturing, marketing, training, and installation efforts to provide its customers with the best possible products, services, and support.

AT&T became part of the Columbus community in 1957, when construction of the Columbus Works was completed. During the late 1950s and 1960s, the Columbus Works primarily manufactured crossbar switches and other electromagnetic equipment to meet the nation's growing telephone service needs. When electronic switching technology emerged in the late 1960s, the Columbus Works helped to pass along this new technology to customers by incorporating electronic switches into its already diversified product line.

During the 1980s the Columbus Works began to manufacture data networking equipment to help link computer and communications systems around the globe. By the early 1990s, the Columbus Works had become AT&T's sole manufacturer of cell site equipment for its cellular product line.

The Columbus Works houses more than 10 separate AT&T resident organizations. One such organization is the AT&T Bell Laboratories, which consists of approximately 1,000 scientists and engineers. These highly skilled people provide the research and development that goes into the products, both hardware and software, and services that are produced at the Columbus Works. Over the past three decades, Columbus Bell Laboratories employees have filed an average of 10 patents each year, and are responsible for 50 to 100 new products or technical advances a year, most of them in software.

At the heart of AT&T's customer focus are hundreds of talented individuals who comprise the national marketing force. This force interacts daily with the end-users of AT&T's wide range of products and services, helping each customer, whether residential, commercial, or business, to obtain the maximum value from their communication and data systems.

Because of Columbus' blend of industry, commerce, and services, local businesses are generally very successful. This success translates to the desire and need of these businesses to stay on the leading edge of technology in the products and services they offer to their customers. Therefore, it is not surprising that many businesses rely heavily on AT&T as their communication company of choice—the source for all of their long-distance voice, data, and imaging needs.

AT&T offers a range of products and services to meet a broad spectrum of communication needs. From cordless telephones, answering machines, and facsimile equipment to personal computers and sophisticated voice recognition systems, AT&T has the experience and technology to build the most effec-

The Columbus Works, at 6200 East Broad Street, brought AT&T manufacturing and development to Columbus in 1957.

TOP: The AT&T National Product Training Center, at 5151 Blazer Memorial Parkway, develops and implements training programs for AT&T employees and customers throughout the world.

ABOVE: A dime provides a reference of scale for some of the tiny components used in AT&T's surface mount technology.

RIGHT: AT&T's Columbus Works uses talented people and the latest technologies to produce a wide range of products.

tive communication tools and applications for each customer.

An example of such an application is The Ohio State University's use of AT&T technology to ease class registration for its more than 55,000 students. Through the BRUTUS system, or Better Registration Using Touch-tone phones for University Students, students can use touch-tone telephone pads anywhere in the world to register for classes at OSU. The BRUTUS system, an application of AT&T Conversant® Voice Information Systems, was

first installed at OSU in 1987.

A skilled workforce is committed to testing AT&T equipment before it is shipped to the customer to ensure that it is working properly. At the customer sites, crews of specialists install the equipment and provide technical support for the life of the product.

To train these specialists and customers, the AT&T National Product Training Center, in Dublin, has provided hands-on instruction for the daily maintenance of technical systems since 1975.

Driving all of these efforts is the theme of quality as part of every product and process at AT&T, from research, development, and manufacturing through

marketing, training, and installation. The ultimate goal is pleasing the customer.

AT&T is committed not only to customer support, but to community support as well, giving millions of dollars to promote the arts, family and social services, health, and education. During the 1980s AT&T employees pledged more than $750,000 per year to United Way, and were instrumental in organizing and expanding the United Negro College Fund solicitation programs and annual Walk-A-Thon. AT&T has also been actively involved with the Minority Purchasing Council and the Center of Science and Industry (COSI).

AT&T's support of area colleges and universities is visible through direct financial grants, matching gifts, equipment donations, teachers in-residence programs, campus curriculum planning, and recruitment. Schools that have benefited from this kind of support include Denison University, Franklin University, and The Ohio State University.

Flexibility has enabled AT&T to stay in step with technological advances and to respond to the changing needs of its customers. Several different product lines are housed within the Columbus Works' 2 million square feet of factory space, where manufacturing employees represented by multiple unions keep operations running smoothly.

AT&T has been one of Columbus' leading employers for more than 35 years. Drawing from graduates of central Ohio's colleges and universities, as well as bringing together people from throughout the world, AT&T provides a work environment rich in talent, knowledge, and culture.

In the technical and fast-paced voice, data, and image markets of the information industry, it is a challenge to stay ahead of worldwide competition. Employees at AT&T have the skill, determination, and customer commitment necessary to achieve excellence in providing products and services to the many different customer segments in the Columbus area.

AT&T employees congratulate Columbus for being a city where broad business success and quality of living go hand in hand.

WBNS-TV

As Casey Stengel's New York Yankees battled it out with Burt Shotton's Brooklyn Dodgers, WBNS-TV (Channel 10) inaugurated its regular programming with coverage of that World Series. The date was October 5, 1949. Central Ohio had a television station that was destined to make local and national history many times over.

WBNS-TV was the first television station in central Ohio to broadcast in color with the Saturday afternoon football games from CBS, beginning in October 1950. In March 1962 came the first color film origination from 10TV. The first color picture to air live from a WBNS-TV studio featured Flippo The Clown in 1967 as host of his early afternoon movie.

10TV Eyewitness News has enjoyed a long tradition as central Ohio's news leader. The 6 p.m. and 11 p.m. newscasts, with their experienced news anchors and professional staffs, have been multiple winners of the prestigious Emmy award given by the National Academy of Television Arts and Sciences. Award-winning performance is what's expected of the local news leader, and it's why more people turn to 10TV Eyewitness News every day to get the news that's important to them.

WBNS-TV has been central Ohio's

news leader since its start more than 40 years ago. The station's newscaster, Chet Long, became synonymous with news in Columbus from his first few years on the air. His credibility was built on strength of personality and character, and he established 10TV as a major source of news for local citizens. That leadership has also been reflected in several innovative moves by 10TV Eyewitness News.

In 1990 WBNS-TV was the only area station with a satellite (SNG) truck in its news-gathering arsenal. WBNS-TV was the first locally owned station in the nation to introduce a fully computerized newsroom. More broadcasting history was written when it became one of the nation's first stations to introduce MiniCam coverage, live news reports from helicopters, and computerized weather graphics.

10TV Eyewitness News has launched a number of news reporters and anchors to network careers, including Faith

RIGHT: Like to be at the center of things? Then Master Control at WBNS-TV is the place to be. All of the station's video and audio sources are monitored here before going out to the public.

BELOW: WBNS-TV has been central Ohio's news and broadcasting leader since it signed on more than 40 years ago.

Daniels and Dana Tyler.

Much of the station's success can be credited to these and other very talented people who have worked at 10TV since its founding. Several national and local celebrities have passed through WBNS-TV on their way to fame and fortune. Popular star and comedian Jonathan Winters worked at the station in the early 1950s as a staff announcer. Rod Serling put in a three-year stint working with movies at the station.

Other 10TV personalities who dominated the airwaves in central Ohio include Roy Briscoe, Joe Holbrook, Irwin Johnson, Pat Wilson, Ray Rose, Edwina Zanes, Aunt Fran, and Lucy and her toyshop.

The initiatives of the station and the professionalism of its people have taken

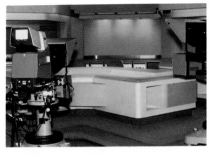

10TV Eyewitness News to the top of its field. In fact, the station literally hit the top during 1983 when local newscasts on WBNS-TV ranked number one in the nation based on May 1983 Nielsen ratings.

WBNS-TV has also been a leader in a central Ohio passion—Ohio State football. The first station to air an OSU football coach's show was 10TV. The popular show began in 1949 with Coach Wes Fesler, moved through 28 magnificent years with the legendary Woody Hayes, and continued through the early seasons of Earle Bruce when the show won a local Emmy and was ranked as the third-highest-rated college coach's show in the nation (1981). The tradition continues today with head football coach John Cooper and head basketball coach Randy Ayers.

WBNS-TV also values its position as a leader in community involvement. As the only locally owned commercial television station in the city, the owners and top management of the station consider that involvement to be one of the station's strengths.

In the area of community responsibility, WBNS-TV again has been a station of firsts. WBNS-TV was the first station in town to have a televised community forum with "Columbus Town Meeting," which dates back to 1949, the station's first year. WBNS-TV was the first to take cameras and on-air personalities into the community to make it possible for citizens to hear, firsthand, from city leaders through "Ask The Mayor." WBNS was the first station in town to find parents for homeless children through "The Adop-

ABOVE: WBNS-TV was the first locally owned station in the nation to have a fully computerized newsroom.

Before the news anchors go on the news set (RIGHT TOP), engineers in the tape room (RIGHT BOTTOM) are busy preparing the video-tapes and video feeds that allow viewers to see the news as it happened.

tion Show" (1965). And WBNS-TV was the first station to offer a televised employment service to help find jobs for unemployed central Ohioans through "The Job Show."

When a 1977 gas shortage closed down the school system in Columbus, WBNS-TV created the "School Without Schools" program. The program hit the air less than a day after the schools closed and lasted for about a month. The station broadcast class lessons from 9 a.m. to 3 p.m. each weekday to fill the educational void in the community. This program earned the station an Ohio State Award and quite a bit of national publicity.

Today the station's community work includes:

• The Children's Miracle Network Telethon to benefit Children's Hospital—the only local telethon to raise a million dollars in a single year. The telethon topped the one-million-dollar mark in 1988, 1989, 1990, and 1991.

• The Food Parade, to benefit Operation Feed, has raised record amounts of food. It is believed to be the world's largest community food drive.

• The Time to Care Family Fund, which collects money to feed needy families during the holidays.

• The Time to Care Human Race

brings together more than 70 community charities in a fundraiser in which people collect pledges for running a 10K race.

• The WBNS-TV/American Red Cross Learn To Swim program.

• The WBNS-TV/League of Women Voters voter information phone services.

Each of these events enjoys a tremendous reputation and feeling of goodwill by the viewing public and the business community in central Ohio.

A recent WBNS-TV community contribution was a two-year community-action campaign entitled Time to Care. The program, started in October 1989, was the largest television public service campaign ever undertaken in central Ohio. The program put the spotlight on the need for, and the benefits of, volunteerism in the community. The WBNS-TV commitment involved eight prime-time programs each year, a major obligation to Time to Care in 10TV Eyewitness News, and more than 1,700 Time to Care messages each year that were featured on the air every day.

WBNS-TV truly understands the meaning of local community projects to the economic and emotional well-being of its community and is committed to do its part to protect and preserve the high quality of life in Columbus and central Ohio.

BUSINESS FIRST OF COLUMBUS

Business First of Columbus was born in 1984 when American City Business Journals was aggressively expanding and carrying its concept of regional business newspapers to cities across the country. By 1990 the company had weekly business journals in 27 cities.

Shaw Communications bought controlling interest in the company and moved the headquarters to Charlotte, North Carolina. That brought the company under the control of Ray Shaw,

ABOVE: In addition to the weekly newspaper, Business First *publishes a number of special publications throughout the year.*

LEFT: Columbus Metro Publishing, a division of Business First, *provides a variety of publications that serve community interests.*

chairman of the board and former president of Dow Jones & Company, publishers of the *Wall Street Journal.* *Business First* and the other ACBJ newspapers provide in-depth coverage of local business news often neglected by other news media outlets.

Business First is an award-winning newspaper that aims to be the leader in providing fair, accurate, and timely local news and business information. Behind the editorial philosophy is the belief that the entire business community prospers when the newspaper makes information available to everyone that previously had been available to only a few.

To do this, *Business First* goes where the news is. Its reporters scan the public record each week for information about new businesses formed, property transfers, mortgages filed, securities filings, bankruptcies, liens, and foreign business opportunities, among others, to give its readers the inside story and

a jump on the competition.

Its readership includes the top business professionals in central Ohio. In fact, 80 percent of its subscribers are corporate decision-makers. To an advertiser its audience represents nothing less than the prime demographic group in the city: affluent, influential executives and professionals who make business and personal purchasing decisions regularly.

In addition to the weekly business report, *Business First* publishes a number of special publications. Quarterly *Office and Commercial Leasing Guide*s highlight the availability of office, warehouse, and commercial space throughout the community. The annual *Top 25 Book of Lists* compiles in one place the weekly lists of the largest businesses in various fields: automobile dealers, stockbrokers, apartment complexes, travel agencies, and many others. *Taking Stock: The Columbus Stock Portfolio* provides detailed financial information that

investors need to know about publicly held local companies.

Columbus Metro Publishing is the specialty publishing division of *Business First*. Its products include *Apartment Tour*; 15 chamber of commerce directories and community guides; and two unique annual publications, the *Women's Directory of Columbus*, and the Lancaster Festival program.

Apartment Tour, the company's full-color flagship publication, is a free monthly magazine serving the Columbus apartment dweller with a circulation of 30,000 via distribution in more than 300 locations. The Lancaster Festival program and the *Women's Directory of Columbus* are two market-specific publications illustrative of Columbus Metro Publishing's diversity and skill in working with a variety of organizations.

The company's special area of expertise is publishing chamber of commerce directories and buyers' guides. Services include verification of member listings, sale of display ads, and consultation on how to make the directory more effective.

Columbus Metro Publishing is looking forward to continued growth as central Ohio's leading publisher of specialty publications and provider of publishing services from advertising sales to consultation on production technicalities.

Photo by Larry Hamill

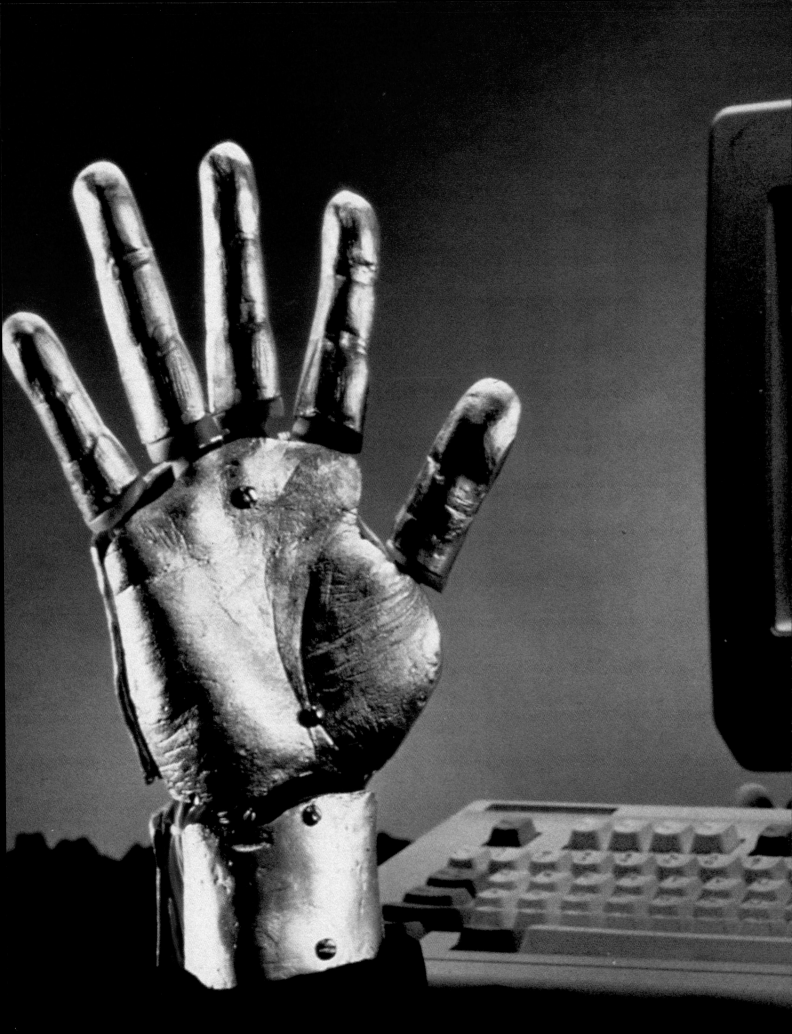

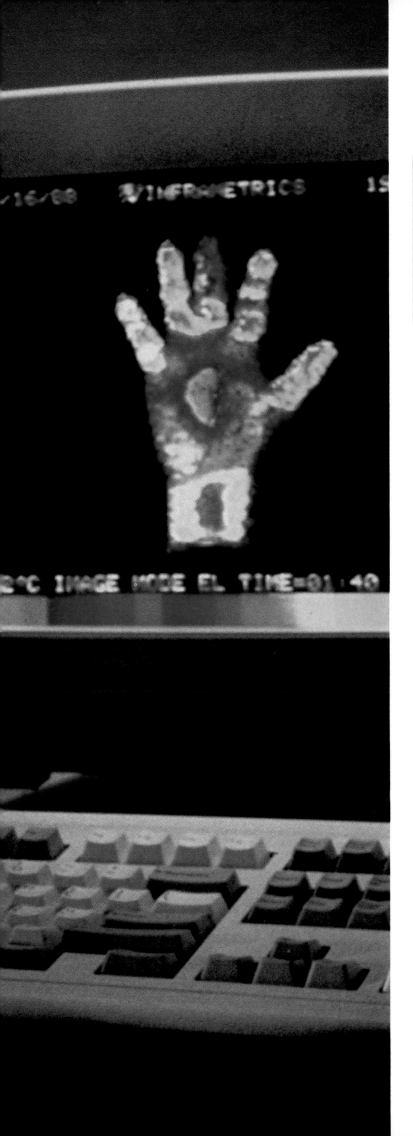

9 MANUFACTURING

Producing and distributing goods for individuals and industry, manufacturing firms provide employment for Columbus area residents.

Kal Kan Foods Incorporated, 300; Superior Die, Tool & Machine Company, 304; EBCO® Manufacturing Company, 306; Lake Shore Cryotronics, Incorporated, 308; Karlshamns USA Inc., 310; Adria Laboratories, 312; TOMASCO mulciber, Inc., 314; Daifuku U.S.A. Inc., 315; Jeffrey Division, Dresser Industries Incorporated 316; Rage Corporation, 318; Crane Plastics, 320; Lennox Industries, 321; ARC Industries, Incorporated, 322; Ranco Incorporated, 324; Liebert Corporation, 326; Columbus Col-Weld Corporation, 328; ASC Colamco, 329; Inland Products Incorporated, 330; Columbus Steel Drum Company, 332; Medex, Inc., 334; Technology Alliance of Central Ohio, 336; Betlin Manufacturing, 338; Liqui-Box Corporation, 339; GE Superabrasives, 340; Flxible Corporation, 342; Schuler Incorporated, 344; Electric Power Equipment Company, 345; Toledo Scale, 346; TS Trim Industries Incorporated, 348; Worthington Industries, 349; Honda of America Manufacturing Incorporated, 350; Epro Incorporated, 352; MTM Americas, Incorporated/ Pharmaceutical Intermediates Division, 354; Worthington Foods, 355; Borden, Inc., 356; Akzo Coatings, Incorporated, 358; Photonic Integration Research, Incorporated, 360; Edison Welding Institute, 361; Anheuser-Busch, Incorporated, 362; Combibloc, Inc., 364; Eaton IDT Incorporated, 365

KAL KAN FOODS INCORPORATED

As millions of American pet owners know, Kal Kan Foods Incorporated has a batch of unbeatable recipes, but the company's recipe for success isn't merely a balanced mix of superior products.

Among the other essential ingredients are a corporate culture that encourages individual creativity, an uncommon concern for the world's pets, a commitment to use the most advanced technology, and a lively sense of partnership with a variety of institutions and the community at large.

Kal Kan's success formula also incorporates the business principles that have powered its parent company, Mars Incorporated, to stellar achievements worldwide.

It is fitting that the 20th anniversary of Kal Kan's start-up of operations in Columbus coincides with the city's quincentennial celebration. The company has both contributed to and shared in the progress that, particularly over the past two decades, has impelled the city's outward expansion, transformed its core, and dramatically redrawn its skyline.

But the Columbus chapter of the corporate story is a relatively recent one, for the roots of Kal Kan Foods are far deeper, reaching back more than half a century and spanning more than 2,000 miles—to Los Angeles in 1936 and greyhound breeder Clement Hirsch.

Determined to give his racing dogs only the finest nutritional care, Hirsch became keenly interested in the nutritive values of various foods. His research eventually convinced him of the need for better, more nutritious formulations. He purchased a small meat packing facility in the stockyard district of Los Angeles, known as Vernon, and began producing canned pet food, a product virtually unknown at the time.

Dog Town Packing, as Hirsch called his enterprise, was thus born of innovation and committed to establishing new standards of excellence—factors that have indelibly marked the company's character and spirit. At the Vernon site, still the company's headquarters, Hirsch laid the foundations for today's vast, complex, and dynamic pet food industry.

With the advent of World War II, Dog Town Packing changed its name to Victory Packing and converted a substantial amount of its capacity to wartime production. The company supplied food for

The state-of-the-art Kal Kan Foods Incorporated plant includes a high-speed packaging area and a 7-million-pound meat freezer. Photo by Chenoweth/Lee Group, Inc.

dollar price tag. Mars realized that in order to assure the success of this large-scale capital investment, the facility would have to be strategically located among potential sources of supply as well as key markets. Columbus, with its excellent transportation facilities, is within 500 miles of half the nation's industry and three-fourths of its population.

Along with these logistical advantages, Columbus offered an unusually stable economy and a skilled labor force with a strong work ethic. Mars found that Columbus people highly value the rewards of enterprise and the quality of life.

But there was one thing more. Mars planners saw Columbus' boundless potential: its enormous energy and eagerness to grow. That powerful, positive thrust matched Kal Kan's own drive for a greater market share.

On August 1, 1971, on a 40-acre tract along Fisher Road on the city's far west side, ground was broken for the new Kal Kan cannery. Viewing downtown Columbus from the construction site, one saw a skyline radically different from today's.

There was no Huntington Center. No Nationwide complex. There was no Rhodes or Riffe state office structures and no Hyatt hotel. In retrospect, perhaps, the magnificently restored Ohio Theatre was symbolic of the renaissance that would soon erupt in the community. At the time the venerable theater had just withstood attempts to be torn down.

The growth of Kal Kan/Columbus has been no less remarkable than the city's. Operations at the new plant began September 8, 1972, with a startup team of 80 associates working one shift. The 240,000-square-foot, state-of-the-art facility had a 500,000-case warehouse, a meat freezer with a 7 million-pound capacity, highly sophisticated meat processing and canning machinery, and a completely automated palletizing system.

Two more shifts were added and more than 7 million cases of finished product were produced by the end of the first year. An expansion project the

ABOVE: Kal Kan Foods markets more than 75 varieties of quality dog and cat foods. Photo by Chenoweth/Lee Group, Inc.

LEFT: After the cans leave the labeling area, they are automatically placed on cardboard trays and shrink-wrapped for shipping throughout the United States. Photo by Chenoweth/Lee Group, Inc.

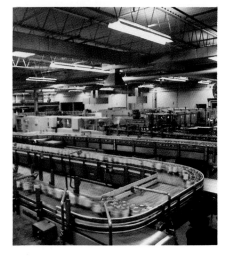

America's K-9 Corps of dogs used by the military in World War II. On the home front, Victory expanded distribution throughout California and established markets in other western states.

Strong consumer acceptance kept the company hustling to meet demand throughout the late 1940s and the 1950s. Victory Packing became Kal Kan Foods in 1957 and embarked on a period of vigorous growth in the early 1960s, introducing many new products, including dry varieties, while steadily increasing market share for existing brands.

Impressive as the company's strides

had been up to that time, they were only a prelude to the major developments that would occur after 1968, when Kal Kan was acquired by Mars Incorporated. With subsidiaries in the United States, Europe, South America, and Australia, Mars is the world's leading manufacturer of pet-care products.

Resources provided by Mars accelerated Kal Kan's move into midwestern and eastern U.S. markets. At the same time, it was apparent that if Kal Kan was to achieve a competitive position in these markets, new manufacturing facilities would be needed east of the Rockies. Accordingly, the search for the ideal location of a second canned pet food plant led to Columbus.

Many factors gave Columbus the edge. The plant and adjoining distribution center would carry a multimillion-

The 240,000-square-foot Columbus headquarters building is on the far west side of Columbus. Photo by Chenoweth/Lee Group, Inc.

following year doubled the plant's production capacity. Today nearly 500 associates keep an unrivaled assortment of products flowing to market to meet an ever-growing demand.

In all, Kal Kan markets more than 75 varieties of foods for dogs and cats. These include such popular brands as WHISKAS canned cat food, WHISKAS™ CRAVE™ dry cat food, SHEBA cat food, PEDIGREE Brand canned dog food, PEDIGREE MEALTIME dry dog food, PEDIGREE Select Dinners dog food, and PEDIGREE Choice Cuts dog food.

The business principles mentioned earlier as underlying the success of Mars Incorporated are integral to Kal Kan's as well. These principles are quality, responsibility, mutuality, efficiency, and freedom.

The Quality Principle emphasizes the need to offer consumers the very best products with the best value. At Kal Kan, adherence to this principle starts with a quality work environment and quality associates—talented, self-

critical men and women who take special pride in their workmanship and the products that reflect it.

Since its inception, Kal Kan has been firmly committed to pet nutrition and product quality second to none. Taste appeal is likewise important. Working with veterinarians and breeders, Kal Kan constantly improves the palatability and nutritional value of its products, and reaffirms its preeminence as the pet food pioneer.

In 1965 the Waltham Centre for Pet Nutrition was established in Waltham, England, to serve as the principal technical adviser to Kal Kan. Staffed by pet nutritionists and veterinarians who are specialists in applied nutritional management, this research facility generates information enabling Kal Kan to discover specific pet nutrition needs. These findings are incorporated into new food formulations.

The success of Kal Kan's brands and the growth of its operations are tangible proof of the company's dedication to quality. They are proof, too, of the appropriateness of Kal Kan's corporate symbol: a protective hand over a pair of pets.

The Responsibility Principle is evident in the decentralized manage-

ment structure of Mars Incorporated, which maximizes the autonomy of the Columbus Kal Kan operation and the decision-making authority of individual associates.

No pet food company in the world more readily embraces its responsibility to promote and support industry organizations and pet-related endeavors than Kal Kan. The company provides food products to animal shelters, underwrites humane society programs, and supports the training of dogs for rescue work and for assisting the blind and hearing impaired.

Kal Kan sponsorship of a veterinarian symposium at The Ohio State University each year brings scholars and clinicians to Columbus from across the United States and around the world. In addition, each spring the company presents a scholarship to a student in the The Ohio State University School of Veterinary Medicine.

Promoting responsible pet ownership is a high priority at Kal Kan. To this end the company created "Pedigree Selectadog," a computerized service offered free to consumers. The service helps the prospective dog owner make an informed breed selection.

Kal Kan maintains close relationships with breeders around the country and plays an active supporting role with pet shows in cooperation with the principal kennel clubs in the United States and other leading organizations.

Closely akin to corporate responsibility is the Mutuality Principle, which focuses on the many reciprocal benefits derived from unselfish relationships with associates, consumers, suppliers, and local and national communities.

Kal Kan enriches Columbus by providing a stimulating and progressive workplace with equal employment opportunities; by boosting the local economy with business generated through area suppliers and distributors; and by continuously supporting local entities such as Pilot Dogs Incorporated, the Columbus Zoo, the Capital Area Humane Society, Children's Hospital, the Easter Seal Rehabilitation Center, and a host of others. In return, Kal Kan and its associates enjoy the hospitality of a more prosperous, more attractive, and more livable community.

The Efficiency Principle is at work throughout Kal Kan—in associates continually looking for ways to reduce costs and increase productivity; in friendly, open office layouts permitting easy interaction and speeding communication; and in an ongoing search for more energy-efficient storage and production methods. Efficiency keeps Kal Kan's products extremely price competitive.

At the heart of the Freedom Principle is the company's need to earn a fair profit. Mars, one of the world's largest privately owned corporations, is the epitome of freedom and a forthright exponent of earning and reinvesting profits.

Like its parent, Kal Kan knows that a reasonable profit keeps a company clear

of burdensome obligations and gives it flexibility—freedom—to pursue new products, implement new technologies, and explore new opportunities.

Kal Kan is committed to profitable growth, to freedom, to the future. The company's future holds incredible promise. Nearly half of all U.S. households have dogs and more than 25 percent have cats. No pet food company is better positioned to win the lion's share of these households than Kal Kan.

The strength of Mars, the loyalty of outstanding associates, the proven reliability of suppliers, and a solid base of distributors—these are assets of incalculable value. No less important, a look at Kal Kan's colorful history reveals a company bred for innovation and entrepreneurship.

With these elements in the background, Kal Kan's view of the future—particularly from a city as visionary as Columbus—is spectacular.

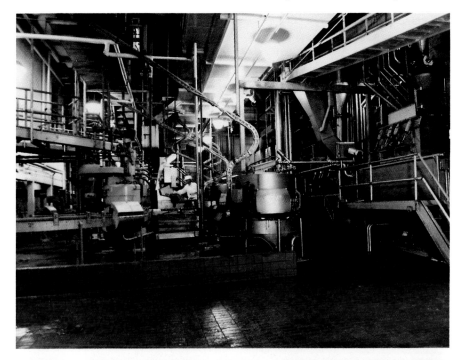

ABOVE: Here the cans of Kal Kan products are filled and sealed. Photo by Chenoweth/Lee Group, Inc.

RIGHT: Some 500 employees work at the Kal Kan Foods plant. This is the manufacturing area for SHEBA, WHISKAS Select, and PEDIGREE Select products. Photo by Chenoweth/Lee Group, Inc.

SUPERIOR DIE, TOOL & MACHINE COMPANY

Superior Die, Tool & Machine Company, a firm with more than 75 years of quality service to its customers, its employees, and the community of Columbus, is perhaps best described by the word "interaction."

At Superior, interaction is the combining of ideas, the working together of all departments, and the juxtaposition of man and machine to accomplish the goals and meet the needs of diverse industries.

Conceived at the company's outset by its founder and continued by his son and grandsons, the Superior concept demands interaction to ensure the desired result: trouble-free dies, correct specifications, and finished parts that are perfectly aligned.

Everything begins with an idea. About half of the time the customer rolls out plans for Superior's engineers to execute. The other 50 percent of the

Superior, which has its headquarters at 2301 Fairwood Avenue, has long been a part of the south side of Columbus.

time, customers turn over the task of total design to Superior's highly qualified and well-equipped engineering department. A project engineer is assigned to the undertaking to follow it from the design phase to construction, testing, and final shipping.

Interaction between the project team and the customer is what it takes, and that's what Superior delivers. The business and work ethic found at Superior was formulated in 1914, when Charles Field and Bruno W. Holstein founded the company. Then it was only a small machine shop of 2,000 square feet at Frankfort and Front streets. Inside were less than a dozen pieces of equipment.

Modest though it was, the enterprise got off to a promising start. The Depression slowed the company down, as industry stopped ordering from suppliers like Superior. But fortunately an investor saw the opportunity and the potential in the company and in Bruno Holstein's son, Paul J. "Bud" Holstein. Holding an option to purchase the company from the investor, Bud Holstein

set out to put Superior back on its feet.

Through hard work, perseverance, and a shrewd knowledge of the tool and die trade, Bud Holstein was able to do just that. In 1948 he exercised his option and gained control of Superior. Two years later he expanded the company in a move to 1432 Parsons Avenue.

The Parsons Avenue plant, Superior's headquarters for the next 37 years, was 10 times larger than the original site. The nation's post-World War II boom was underway and the company was positioned to take advantage of it.

When Bud Holstein died in 1966, his three sons were there to continue the family tradition. Roger Holstein was named president, Richard Holstein became vice president and general plant manager, and Gary Holstein assumed the job of secretary/treasurer.

In a move to become more diversified, the Holsteins added a stamping facility for automobile and truck fenders at 1405 Marion Road. This expansion marked a significant new chapter in the company history. Since its debut in 1971, the

plant's original 10,000 square feet has been increased to 56,000 square feet. About two-thirds of Superior's 200 employees work at the stamping plant. What they produce represents about three-quarters of the company's business annually.

The size and variety of the machines and equipment Superior uses today in the stamping plant would stagger founder Bruno Holstein. The extensive list includes 1,000-ton stamping presses, as well as smaller machines, at 100 tons or less. The company is able to manufacture in excess of 60,000 small to medium-sized metal parts each month with machinery capable of progressive die work and coiled steel blanking operations.

Quality control equipment determines hardness, drawability, and other values to ensure Superior's superb standards are met.

The company has also introduced a Computer Aided Design (CAD) system, one of the few in the industry that is capable of designing electronic models digitally from drawings. The system is often used in tandem with Computer Numerical Control (CNC) equipment that can control the actual die-making process, supplying pertinent data at every stage for extreme accuracy and cost efficiency. The most important result of this marriage of technology is the ability to consistently meet or exceed customer specifications in terms of quality and delivery.

Steady growth under competent leadership necessitated the most recent expansion in 1986. The company had outgrown the Parsons Avenue facility, so

a new home office was built at 2301 Fairwood Avenue, continuing the family traditions on the south side of the city. The 148,000-square-foot building also houses tool and die building equipment, warehouse space, and a die tryout press line.

Three work bays are served by 25-ton overhead cranes. One bay is for machining, another for die construction, and the third for tryout and buyoff. In the machine bay are Makino CNC mill working tables that allow for both horizontal and vertical feeds.

The die construction area is similarly well equipped for all types of die manufacture. In the third area the ultimate test of die effectiveness is performed on a collection of seven presses that complete the buyoff process.

ABOVE LEFT: Computer Numerical Control (CNC) equipment can control the actual die construction process, resulting in extreme accuracy and cost efficiency.

ABOVE: The dedicated press line, with capacities of up to 1,000 tons, facilitates the coordination of dies for tryout purposes. This is critical proving ground for Superior's products.

LEFT: Superior's quality-assurance program is constantly striving for continuous improvement.

Die construction is overseen by six die teams, each with a team leader who works with the project engineer from the inception of the project. Weekly meetings are conducted to make certain quoted hours, specifications, and deadlines are being met. The team involved in making the die also sees it through the tryout and buyoff stage.

In March 1991 the Holsteins sold the tool and die division of the company to independent investors, but the family retained the stamping division and renamed it Superior Stamped Metal Products, Inc. Richard Holstein remained at the die shop as vice president and general manager.

This attention to detail and to quality is, in large measure, responsible for Superior's success over its first 75 years, celebrated in 1989. That has always been a part of the company's mission, and it continues to be so. As Superior strides toward the next century, it renews its commitment to customer satisfaction and industry leadership.

EBCO® MANUFACTURING COMPANY

EBCO Manufacturing Company, makers of OASIS® water coolers and dehumidifiers, draws international attention to Columbus as "The Water Cooler Capital of the World." It is the industry's worldwide leader and is consistently recognized for its innovative product designs and quality.

EBCO products, marketed under the trade names OASIS® and AQUARIUS®, are distributed to more than 50 countries through its worldwide sales network and 11 warehouses located across the United States, Australia, Europe, and Canada. In addition, EBCO, under a licensing agreement, manufactures and markets pressure and bottled water coolers for Kelvinator® and White-Westinghouse®. EBCO products are maintained by approximately 450 authorized service centers internationally.

EBCO, a family-owned business, employs over 400 people, most of whom are in the Columbus area. EBCO believes its employees are the best in the industry because they take great pride in themselves, the company, and the products they manufacture. In return the company provides equal employment and advancement opportunities, a

23C OASIS® and AQUARIUS® brands of pressure water coolers and fountains are manufactured in Columbus by EBCO®. They are distributed to more than 50 countries.

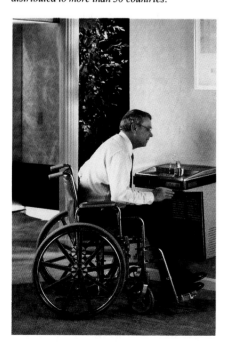

safe, pleasant work environment, competitive wages, and a profit-sharing plan.

EBCO's roots trace back to the D.A. Ebinger Sanitary Manufacturing Company. Founded in Columbus in 1910, the company made ice water and beer coolers, metal toilet partitions, washroom fixtures, and other plumbing supplies. Ebinger played an important role in the development of the first electric water coolers, which were later manufactured for the big-name marketers of those days: Frigidaire, General Electric, Kelvinator®, Norge, Copeland, and others.

At the height of the Depression in 1935, the D.A. Ebinger Company was in receivership. An investor group, headed by A.R. Benua, found itself bidding against another group for the purchase of the plumbing supply company. The opposing group wanted to close the plant and use the assets in another venture. Benua, on the other hand, proposed to continue the business. The courts decided in Benua's favor. In 1935 the company was purchased by Benua's group and renamed EBCO Manufacturing Company.

Louis P. Benua, A.R.'s son and vice president, successfully positioned the company for its dominance in the water cooler industry between 1963 and 1987. His great interest in chemistry and engineering paved the way for EBCO to be an innovator, as well as a leader, in the industry.

A third generation of Benuas now guides EBCO: Thomas R. Benua, Jr., president; Peter L. Benua, executive vice president; and George P. Benua, vice president. They adhere to the management styles and philosophies that have guided the family-owned business through more than 80 years of continued success.

EBCO's early product mix featured washroom fixtures and plumbing supplies, but it soon began to concentrate on the manufacture of drinking fountains and electric pressure water coolers. Eventually it added dehumidifiers and bottled water coolers to its product line.

In 1941 the company introduced

the now famous OASIS® brand water cooler. World War II then broke out and the company turned its production to supplying military installations and defense plants. But once the war ended, EBCO took off and the OASIS® brand soon gained worldwide name recognition and respect for its high quality.

Louis Benua's brother, Tom, got the company unexpectedly moving in a new direction in 1947. Tom had a damp basement in the clothing store he operated and asked his brother if he could find a cure. Louis' answer, the company's first dehumidifier, is in EBCO's museum and still works.

Like many of the other EBCO products in the museum, located within the corporate headquarters, the first dehumidifier represents a tremendous design breakthrough. Also depicted in the museum are the numerous corporate milestones, the proud heritage of the Benua family, and recognition of the many remarkable employees who helped make EBCO the industry leader.

EBCO's corporate headquarters, manufacturing plant, and main warehouse occupy more than 800,000 square feet.

LEFT: EBCO is recognized as a worldwide leader in the design and manufacture of bottled water coolers and nonrefrigerated dispensers.

RIGHT TOP: Point-of-use water coolers that use combinations of filtration, carbonation, and reverse osmosis methods of water purification were added to the EBCO product line in the 1990s.

RIGHT BOTTOM: EBCO is the world's oldest continuous manufacturer of dehumidifiers.

To accommodate increasing sales and an expanding product line, including the Hot 'N Cold unit introduced in 1954, the company moved from the original Town Street location to a new facility in Whitehall, a Columbus suburb. A.R. Benua had the tremendous foresight to select a location that had railroad access, would eventually nestle up to the Columbus airport, and be within a mile of Interstate 270. Then, as today, raw materials and finished products were received and shipped with remarkable ease and efficiency.

EBCO's corporate headquarters/ manufacturing plant, located at 265 N. Hamilton Road, was dedicated in 1955. It was named "Plant of the Year" by *Factory Magazine* because it featured innovative designs for production efficiencies and special amenities for the comfort and safety of employees. For example, at that time, it was one of the few plants in the country that was air conditioned throughout the entire factory production area as well as in the offices.

EBCO's facility occupies more than 800,000 square feet of offices, factory, and warehousing. Contemporary manufacturing techniques and strict quality control, coupled with state-of-the-art equipment and chemistry and engineering labs, help ensure a product that is second to none. The facility has been expanded four times. The latest addition, dedicated in 1990, is a 250,000-square-foot warehouse with 14 dock doors for shipping.

Today a major portion of the manufacturing facility is dedicated to the production of bottled water coolers. In 1987 EBCO introduced a new contemporary look to the traditional bottled cooler lines with the innovative blow-molded cabinet. The cabinets are lightweight, withstand stress and shock, and are stronger by weight than metal panels. Color is molded into the cabinets, which are scratch- and mar-resistant. They can be cleaned or refurbished using household or commercial cleaners, eliminating the costly need to strip and repaint.

With steadily controlled growth, the company has begun to branch out into new areas that deal with the treatment and quality of water. By utilizing its design and manufacturing expertise, coupled with the latest available technologies, EBCO lists among its current achievements such point-of-use water conditioning processes as filtration, carbonation, and reverse osmosis.

Through teamwork, EBCO manufactures more water coolers than any other company in the world. It is also the oldest continuous manufacturer of dehumidifiers. Every EBCO product is made of top-grade materials, is assembled with strict quality control, and is 100 percent tested. It considers its employees the best in the industry. And the company constantly improves upon existing products and the way they are manufactured, as well as designing new ones.

EBCO is the lifetime sponsor of the United Nations flags displayed at Port Columbus International Airport and is actively involved in the Industrial Association of Central Ohio. The company is recognized by the city for its stable employment base and its contributions to numerous civic and charitable organizations.

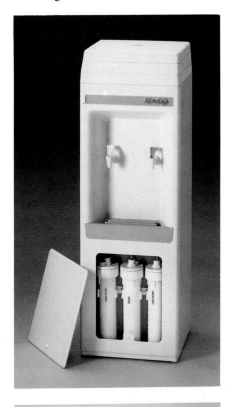

LAKE SHORE CRYOTRONICS, INCORPORATED

In the esoteric world of cryogenics—the branch of physics dealing with very low temperatures—Westerville-based Lake Shore Cryotronics is an international leader. Designers and manufacturers of specialized sensors, monitors and thermometers, control instrumentation, test systems, and the accessories to support these products, Lake Shore delivers high performance in low temperature technology.

The company was founded in 1968 by John M. Swartz, a former professor of electrical engineering at The Ohio State University. From humble beginnings in Swartz's basement, Lake Shore has grown steadily by supplying the needs of scientists and researchers studying the physical properties of metals and ceramics at very low temperatures.

Precise temperature measurement of these materials is critical to the development of such projects as the Na-

tional AeroSpace Plane, a hypersonic (17,500 mph) aircraft capable of flying from Columbus to Tokyo in less than four hours, and Magnetic Resonance Imaging (MRI), which already has had a significant impact in medical diagnostics.

In addition, basic materials research has yielded exciting results in the field of high temperature superconductivity—results that would have been impossible without the rigorous temperature analysis afforded by Lake Shore products.

Company scientists have been involved at the experimental level with those building Texas' superconducting supercollider to create components that will test segments of the dipole magnets and correction coils in the collider. The collider will require sensors to monitor temperature in segments of the magnet coils. Lake Shore also has developed a power supply system that has an application for controlling the current in the superconducting magnets.

Lake Shore's technological contributions have been recognized by *Research and Development* magazine, which each year selects from several thousand applications the 100 most significant technical developments in the United States. Honeywell, General Electric, Minnesota Mining and Manufacturing, and Hewlett-Packard are among the competitors for this recognition. Much smaller than these industrial giants, Lake Shore has nonetheless received five R&D 100 Awards for its sensors, thermometers, and superconductor screening systems.

In 1987 two International Business Machines scientists, using Lake Shore instrumentation, were awarded the Nobel Prize in physics for their research in superconductivity.

Lake Shore is constantly seeking new markets for present technology and acquiring new ideas and patents by license, purchase, or informal associations, although it also holds a number of

An engineer designs an ultra-high density, multi-layer circuit board for electromagnet and superconducting magnet power supplies.

its own patents. Dominant in most market niches it has selected for penetration, Lake Shore plans to diversify its operations to include not only the scientific community but also the commercial, industrial, and biomedical arenas.

The company has entered the field of magnetic property measurement with a new instrument system that measures the ac magnetic susceptibility and dc-magnetization of organic metals as well as ferromagnetic and superconducting materials. Possible applications for other Lake Shore technologies include power generation, transportation, robotics, and motor diagnostics. Through this expansion, Lake Shore expects to continue its present high rate of revenue growth, which for the past 10 years was in excess of 20 percent per year.

Also essential to Lake Shore's con-

Sputter deposited thin film temperature sensors.

tinued success is a supply of highly trained personnel. Though physicists, engineers, and chemists constitute the bulk of the company's employees, even production and sales and marketing staffs must be conversant with science and engineering. Those involved in product assembly must be highly attentive to detail; accuracy is paramount.

Because of the company's high dollar commitment to research and development—which reflects Lake Shore's "long view" outlook—and its collaboration with such institutions as the National Institute for Standards and Technology, the Los Alamos National Laboratory, and the Argonne National Laboratory, senior management anticipates little difficulty in recruiting and retaining the work force the company requires.

A research and development budget that is 100 percent higher than the national average for instrumentation companies; significant research grants from the National Science Foundation and the U.S. Department of Energy; and clients that include academic researchers, international research companies, government agencies, and industrial customers all work synergistically to make Lake Shore an attractive employer for those interested in creating and commercializing technology.

Lake Shore's influence extends far beyond the borders of the United States. For example, the company has been honored by Ohio with the state's Excellence in Exporting Award for successfully meeting the challenges of developing overseas markets. Already marketing its products throughout North and South America, the United Kingdom, Europe, India, Japan, China, Taiwan, and Korea, Lake Shore is continually investigating collaborative relationships with scientists in other lands, such as the Soviet Union.

In the early 1990s the company unveiled the nation's first commercial application of a high temperature superconductor for use in biomedical

technology. This product was developed in conjunction with scientists at the University of Basel, Switzerland.

The relaxed management style within the independent, privately held company belies its intensely competitive, yet practical, nature. Despite more comprehensive industrial policies by other nations, Lake Shore is more than able to hold its own because of its focus on its clients and its understanding of their needs.

Its close relationships with research institutions make it easier for the company to develop new products based on the emerging and constantly changing requirements of its primary customers. Its movement toward diversification is carefully planned, usually involving the application of its existing products to new uses; thus diversification efforts remain congruent with the company's stated business objectives. Lake Shore's management philosophy and close-to-the-customer orientation have allowed the company to grow without the need for external capital sources.

The company is on the move. As the nation grapples with cre-

ating an energy policy, Lake Shore's products, particularly in the area of superconductivity, will become even more attractive. Indeed, Lake Shore Cryotronics, begun in a basement, may just go through the roof.

This susceptometer-magnetometer employs temperature, frequency, and magnetic field to characterize a broad range of materials to be used in computers, communications, aerospace, and medicine.

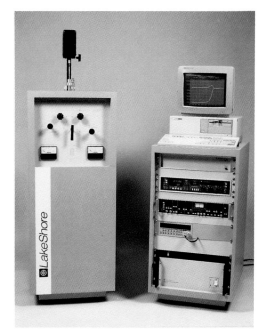

Lake Shore Cryotronics' company headquarters is located in Westerville, Ohio.

KARLSHAMNS USA INC.

The company is one of Columbus' oldest but the name is relatively new.

The Karlshamns USA Inc. sign went up on the former Capital City Products Company in June 1990, inaugurating a new era for an enterprise that already was 107 years old. It also reflected the change of ownership that took place in 1988 when Karlshamns AB, a diverse international company based in Sweden, acquired Capital City.

What Karlshamns also acquired was a slice of Columbus history that began in 1883, the same year the Brooklyn Bridge spanning the East River in New York was completed. Wholesale grocer Dennis Kelly and his partner, H.C. Pirrung, began manufacturing margarine— also known as butterine—in a small building on Front Street. The immediate success of the Capital City Dairy Company required relocation to a five-story structure at First Avenue and Perry Street in 1901. Although expanded many times under several managements, the company hasn't moved since. Kelly's fledgling venture succeeded because he produced a

In 1991 construction was completed on a state-of-the-art processing plant.

quality product. The same is true today as evidenced by the company's leadership position in the industry.

Karlshamns USA manufactures and distributes specialty fats and oils made from a wide variety of vegetable oils. Its standard and custom products serve a range of industries: food service, baking, and vegetable-dairy, confectionery, pharmaceutical and personal care, and textile.

Such diversity developed over many years, but it began almost from the start. Kelly added cold storage and briefly became a distributor of eggs, fruits, fish, nuts, and cheese. The focus soon narrowed once again to the manufacture of margarine and other oil- and fat-based products.

To reflect the changing nature of its business, Capital City Dairy became Capital City Products in 1919. Two years later a vegetable oil refinery was built to ensure the production of finished oil of constant value and quality. Capital City also became the first company in the United States to produce an all-vegetable oil margarine, the first of many firsts for this industry pioneer.

The large, red, neon sign that went up over the plant—"Home of Dixie Margarine and Kingtaste Foods"—

touted the company's product line. For nearly four decades the sign was a familiar landmark to motorists on Route 315. The Kingtaste consumer products line of mayonnaise and salad dressings—and even pickles and jams—was discontinued in 1957, and Dixie Margarine and other oil and shortening products bearing that label were phased out in 1980.

In the years before and after World War II, Capital City modernized and expanded over and over again: Hydrogenation, sterotex, modification, and bottled oil departments were added, for instance, and distillation and hydrogen gas plants were built.

With its advanced technology and research capabilities, the company spearheaded the development of pressed hard butters, a highly specialized product that is made from selected fractions of palm kernel oil and is specially processed to allow year-round confectionery manufacture. Hard butters also are used in the manufacture of nondairy coffee whiteners, whipped toppings, and for other specialized purposes.

Sterotex, a powdered, hydrogenated vegetable oil product, is another specialty product that is widely used in the pharmaceutical and chemical industries as a tablet lubricant and die-release agent. Sterotex compounds also are used in production processes involving ceramics, powdered metallurgy, generator brushes, radio resistors, frozen food coatings, and donut sugars.

The various early expansions were financed by public stock offerings, although control of the company was maintained by Edmund P. Kelly, son of the founder, until his death in 1937.

Twenty years later controlling interest was acquired from the Kelly estate by Stokely-Van Camp, Inc., a highly respected name in the food industry. William B. Stokely, Jr., president of the company bearing his name, served as chairman of Capital City. It became a Stokely division in 1964 after Stokely

LEFT: The Capital City Dairy Company's immediate success led to expansion into this five-story facility located at First Avenue and Perry Street in 1901.

ABOVE: For a time, Capital City Dairy Company distributed eggs, fruits, fish, nuts, and cheese in addition to the company's wide variety of vegetable oil products.

acquired all the Capital City stock.

Under Stokely, Capital City continued its growth, acquiring an edible oil refinery and storage facility in West New York, New Jersey, in 1972, and the Armstrong Chemical Company in Janesville, Wisconsin, seven years later. In that same year the assets of the Theobold Industries plant in Kearny, New Jersey, were acquired to expand Capital City's capacity for confectionery

fats, a product niche in which the company has clearly established itself as the dominant market leader in the U.S.

Another owner came on the scene in 1983 when the Quaker Oats Company acquired Stokely. By the end of the following year, however, the senior management of the Industrial Products Division—as Capital City was then known—purchased it in a leveraged buyout.

The arrival of Karlshamns AB as the new owner of Capital City in 1988 launched what has been the company's most aggressive and progressive period yet. Using Swedish expertise, for ex-

ample, the company instituted a persuasive program to market confectionery fats in Central and South America through a new export division, Karlshamns America.

Furthermore, Karlshamns constructed a 15,000-square-foot technical center for advanced research into new formulations and modifications of existing product lines. The facility includes a research library and conference center for customer seminars and technical presentations.

Another new division, Karlshamns Lipid Specialties USA, was the Specialty Chemicals Division of Capital City. Its oil-based chemical products are sold primarily to the personal care, pharmaceutical, and synthetic fiber industries.

The two other profit centers are Karlshamns Food Ingredients USA, a supplier of custom-formulated specialty fats and oils to the food processor industry, and the Capital City Products Division, providing margarines, oils, and shortenings to restaurants, bakeries, and institutional food services.

In 1991 construction was completed on a state-of-the-art processing plant that replaced an aging facility on Perry Street. With increased flexibility and process control, the plant ensures that Karlshamns USA remains a vibrant and flourishing member of the Columbus community.

Karlshamns' 15,000-square-foot technical center is the site of research into new formulations and modifications of existing product lines.

ADRIA LABORATORIES

The establishment of the North American headquarters of Adria Laboratories in Columbus has been of benefit to the pharmaceutical company for a number of significant reasons.

For instance, Adria has nearby the considerable research resources of Ohio State University and the Battelle Memorial Institute, and it is utilizing several of the local hospitals for clinical investigation of its new compounds.

In addition, Columbus provides a central location for its distribution center, enabling Adria to provide effective and prompt customer service through the many air freight and ground transportation facilities serving the Columbus metropolitan area. The city, through its educational institutions and industry, is also an ideal resource for scientific, research, and administrative employment candidates. High community standards and attention to education makes Columbus attractive to prospective employees as well.

Adria Laboratories began in 1974 as a joint venture between Hercules Incorporated of Wilmington, Delaware, and Montedison S.p.A. of Milan, Italy. These two chemical manufacturers established a corporate alliance and founded a specialty pharmaceutical company using ADRIAMYCIN®(doxorubicin hydrochloride), a newly approved anticancer drug, as their initial product entry. In 1984 Montedison consolidated its ownership of Adria with Farmitalia and formed a health care holding company, Erbamont N.V. ADRIAMYCIN had been discovered by a subsidiary of Montedison–Farmitalia Carlo Erba–and studied extensively by the National Cancer Institute in the United States. It was a "breakthrough compound," which became the largest-selling drug of its type in the world, principally because of its application to many different types of cancer.

Adria became the distributor for ADRIAMYCIN in North America following the completion of many clinical studies monitored by the National Cancer Institute and approval of the Food and Drug Administration.

Following its approval in October 1974, ADRIAMYCIN was rapidly accepted by all leading oncology hospitals and clinics and soon became the most widely used cancer drug in the world.

Adria has quickly developed a unique and much-copied marketing program and an Oncology Advisory Board, consisting of a group of research and clinical oncologists, to assist them in planning clinical investigation for ongoing research in cancer and immunology. ADRIAMYCIN is also distributed in Canada following Adria's establishment of its Canadian company in Mississauga, Ontario.

Adria's field force now numbers approximately 100 medical specialists and is considered by the oncology community and the pharmaceutical industry

The headquarters and administrative/research facilities of Adria Laboratories are located in Dublin, Ohio.

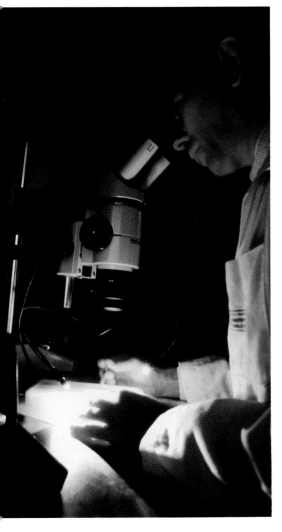

LEFT: Research at Adria and Farmitalia Carlo Erba continues to focus on the areas of cancer, immunology, and AIDS.

ABOVE: Workers perform a sterile filling operation at Adria's state-of-the-art plant in Albuquerque, New Mexico.

to be the most effective and technically competent group of its type in the United States. Training includes months of classroom instruction and field training. Salesmen are constantly monitored for product knowledge to be certain that the company is providing useful and up-to-date information to its hospital and physician customers.

Adria has developed a research communication network with oncologists and hematologists. For example, research is now being conducted in the area of AIDS treatment as well as in the field of immunology.

After several years of expanding its research, manufacturing, and distribution activities, it was obvious that further expansion was necessary if Adria was to keep up with its fast-moving industry. Using land that was acquired with its initial facilities, in 1986 Adria erected two research/administration

buildings in the northwest corner of Franklin County at 7001 Post Road. These facilities provide approximately 170,000 square feet and house all of its research and administrative personnel.

To accommodate the ever-growing need for sterile manufacturing facilities, Adria also acquired a state-of-the-art parenteral manufacturing business in Albuquerque, New Mexico.

In consolidating the efforts of Adria as well as its sister company, Farmitalia Carlo Erba in Milan, Erbamont draws on local as well as international research capabilities and utilizes the talents of some 1,500 research workers throughout the world. Research is global in nature and Adria's operating group parent, Erbamont, has established a presence in every free nation in the world. Cooperative research activities are also conducted in the Soviet Union.

A recent review of worldwide research lists Farmitalia Carlo Erba/Adria as the 12th-largest pharmaceutical research concern in the world. Adria alone posted sales of approximately $200 million in 1989.

Adria has recently won regulatory approval to supply its new anti-leukemia drug, IDAMYCIN®(idarubicin hydrochloride for injection). This compound for the treatment of acute myeloid leukemia was developed as an Orphan Drug. IDAMYCIN is a unique molecule and is the first in a series of new oncological drugs now being studied at Adria's Medical Research Center.

With Farmitalia Carlo Erba, Adria is able to consolidate its research efforts and develop clinical studies on a global basis. All of these studies are conducted in keeping with the Food and Drug Administration standards, and in this way the company can accelerate its patient accruals and increase its treatment resources.

As one might expect, Adria is an active community participant in activities involving the American Cancer Society and the Leukemia Society of America. The firm also continues to be a contributor to cancer research efforts, and several of Adria's medical personnel work with the local hospitals on a consulting basis, particularly in the area of cancer management.

After more than a decade of operations in Columbus, Adria is convinced that both scientifically and geographically Columbus is truly an ideal location. The company eagerly looks forward to continue growth in partnership with Columbus, the Discovery City.

TOMASCO mulciber, INC.

In 1986, on the east side of Columbus, a new company was created not only to manufacture superior automotive products but to establish an entirely new corporate culture based on human harmony, the pioneer spirit, and excellence achieved through a careful balance of personal skill and technology.

That company is called TOMASCO—an acronym comprising the first syllables of Tokyo, Masuda, and Columbus. The company's logo is a two-chambered heart, reflecting the merger of the very finest in Japanese and American management and manufacturing traditions.

TOMASCO's rapidly expanding site just off Courtright Road is enhanced by more than 200 cherry trees, each dedicated to a full-time associate. The trees are a living symbol of TOMASCO's growing presence, its nurturing attitude toward its associates, and the growing together of two different cultures into one family bound by a special team spirit.

TOMASCO mulciber, Inc., was established in 1986 by Masuda Manufacturing Company Ltd. of Japan. Based in Tokyo, Masuda is a leader in design, development, and manufacture of parts for automobiles, trucks, and motorcycles, and a major supplier of parts to Honda Corporation. To create a worldwide presence in the dramatically changing automotive industry, Masuda founded TOMASCO as a wholly owned subsidiary.

In 1987, in order to strengthen and di-

The spirit of teamwork and the power of people are two of the main ingredients in TOMASCO's corporate philosophy.

versify the new subsidiary's technical capabilities, Masuda shared ownership of TOMASCO with three partners: American Honda Motor Company, Inc., Kyoei Metal Industries Company, Ltd., and Marjun Seiki Industries Company, Ltd.

At TOMASCO, ideas and ideals are constantly evolving. Newly emerging concepts concern not only the development of actual products but also the evolution of the development process.

TOMASCO's production operations include four main processes: metal stamping, welding, assembly, and painting. A well-staffed and fully equipped quality assurance lab is the scene of extensive ongoing product and materials testing. Nevertheless, the company believes that quality must be built into a product—not merely tested for after production.

Quality assurance is thus the task of everyone, and departments critically review not only their own work but the performance of other departments as well. As products move through the various process, each department treats the next as if it were the customer—a customer that expects and deserves TOMASCO's superior quality.

TOMASCO uses some of the industry's most advanced stamping presses and robotic welders to produce a variety of automotive parts such as trunk hinges, jack holders, engine mounting brackets, fuel filler lids, and hand-brake assemblies. And by balancing the insights and ingenuity of associates with the time savings of technology, TOMASCO produces high-quality parts at low cost.

Contrary to conventional thinking,

At the heart of TOMASCO's new corporate culture is a highly dedicated and people-oriented management team.

TOMASCO does not believe that total automation necessarily guarantees total quality, superior products, or efficiency. The company firmly believes in the human element, and seeks to involve associates individually and collectively in the challenges of achieving excellence in the production process.

This appreciation for excellence, TOMASCO officials believe, is all the more easily gained in an atmosphere combining Eastern and Western perspectives. TOMASCO associates learn from the very beginning that excellence is an attitude, a matter of personal integrity.

Like the cherry trees growing on the company's site, TOMASCO is continuously rising to new heights and expanding its place in the sun—branching out to meet new technical challenges and embrace new opportunities for superior product development and greater self-sufficiency.

Supporting this growth is TOMASCO's remarkable root structure, deeply embedded in a philosophy that has drawn two great legacies, two widely separated cultures, two very different worlds…into one.

DAIFUKU U.S.A. INC.

When Daifuku Company Ltd. established its U.S. subsidiary in 1983, the corporate headquarters was in Chicago but the largest customer was a few hundred miles south, near Marysville, Ohio. Now the conveyor and materials handling systems manufacturer has moved its U.S. offices to Reynoldsburg, Ohio, since it is more centrally located between their major customers.

Daifuku, an Osaka, Japan-based company whose products are primarily used in the automotive and electronics industries, is a prime supplier of conveyor and related systems to Honda, Ford, Nissan, Mazda, and Toyota plants in the United States.

United States operations were established initially to serve the automotive and motorcycle complex that Honda was building near Marysville, says Natsuo Makino, vice president and secretary-treasurer of Daifuku U.S.A. Inc. Through the years the company has installed an estimated $40-million to $50-million worth of conveyor systems to move automobiles along Honda's assembly lines and to automatically

The headquarters of Daifuku U.S.A. Inc. in Reynoldsburg is centrally located to serve its automotive customers.

store and retrieve parts, Makino says. Most recently Daifuku put in conveyor systems for Honda's second automobile assembly plant, near East Liberty, Ohio.

However, Toyota's assembly plant at Georgetown, Kentucky, has replaced Honda as Daifuku's largest customer, once again shifting Daifuku's business further south. Daifuku moved its Chicago-area headquarters to 6700 Tussing Road in Reynoldsburg to be in the heart of the automotive industry. "The location of Columbus is halfway between Detroit and Kentucky," Makino says. "Columbus is a very good location for this industry."

At the Columbus headquarters, which were established here in 1987, the company maintains its sales and administrative staff as well as a manufacturing operation, says Stephen W. Bennison, vice president of administration.

About 30 percent of the 100-person staff is involved in manufacturing while 40 percent are in service, and another 30 percent are in sales, engineering, and administration. The company produces and assembles conveyor systems with both U.S. and Japanese made parts, Bennison says.

Besides the automobile assembly plants, Daifuku provides material handling systems for automotive suppliers

At the heart of Daifuku's success is American-Japanese cooperation. Here Russell Flax, senior manager, and Steve Tsuruoko, manufacturing manager, map out planning.

such as Tomasco Mulciber and Bellemar, Honda suppliers, also located in central Ohio.

Like many Japanese-based companies, Daifuku is expanding to serve companies other than those also based in its homeland. It created and expanded a system for Ford in Detroit and also installed systems for the jointly run General Motors-Toyota plant in Fremont, California, Makino says.

Outside the automobile industry the company has installed systems for semiconductor and electronics components manufacturers, including Motorola, Intel, and Konica. It recently opened a sales office in Utah—its fifth in the United States—to serve that industry.

Overseas sales account for about 10 percent of the parent company's revenues, which have been growing at about 30 percent annually. With that kind of growth rate and the success of overseas operations, Makino and Bennison expect Daifuku Company Ltd. to soon be generating sales of one billion dollars a year.

JEFFREY DIVISION, DRESSER INDUSTRIES INCORPORATED

The 115-year history of the Jeffrey Division of Dresser Industries has been marked by innovation, expansion, high times, hard times, downsizing, and, most recently, a new concern for quality and employee input.

In 1876 the post-Civil War economy was based on coal, primarily because of its use in the rapidly growing steel industry. In Columbus, Joseph Andrew Jeffrey became intrigued with a coal cutting machine displayed by Francis Lechner in the window of a local hardware store. Acting on his fascination with the machine, Jeffrey gathered a group of investors to form the Lechner Mining Machine Company. Within a year, the first machine was shipped for use in New Straitsville, Ohio.

Though the early on-site experiments with the machine were unsuccessful, Jeffrey began to make changes and refinements, and by 1888, he had bought out his original investors, renamed the firm the Jeffrey Manufacturing Company, and begun to produce the nation's first electrically-powered cutting ma-

A Jeffrey mine electric-powered locomotive— the world's first—shown at an Ohio coal mine portal in 1888.

chines and underground electric locomotives. By the end of the century, the company also was supplying the heavy chains required by this new machinery; Jeffrey himself received a patent on the steel-thimble roller drive chain.

In addition, the company manufactured and sold coal crushers and conveyors. This was indeed a golden era for Jeffrey and his company. By 1900 the firm was preeminent in the coal mining industry, with operations in North America, Europe, Africa, and Australia.

Until the World War II era, Jeffrey maintained its position and acquired other companies, such as British Jeffrey Diamond and the Galion Iron Works. After the war, however, because the company continued to rely on "on track" equipment rather than making the switch to rubber-tired machines, Jeffrey lost its market domination.

By 1963 the company was reorganized to improve profitability, and the strategy was highly successful. Sales improved, profits rose more than $10 million over a three-year period, and expansion occurred once again through decentralizing to the Woodruff Processing, Belton Conveyors, and Morristown Chain plants in the south.

The introduction of Jeffrey's new

Heliminer in the mid-1960s set the industry standard for fixed drum continuous mining machines. This machine combined all four mining steps—undercutting, drilling blast holes, blasting, and loading the coal—into one process, exponentially increasing productivity. By 1972, however, four other corporations were producing similar machines, and market forces dictated the sale of the company.

After 97 years of private ownership, the assets of Jeffrey and its subsidiaries were acquired in 1974 by Dresser Industries Incorporated, a major manufacturing corporation supplying high-tech products and services to the world's energy industry.

In the early 1980s, a major restructuring consistent with a shrinking market reduced the Columbus plant work force by approximately 85 percent and set the stage for a leaner, more efficient Jeffrey Division.

As the company looks to its future, the emphasis is on the quality of existing products, such as high, medium, and low seam continuous miners and haulage systems, ventilating fans, and mine locomotives. The objective is to be the high quality, low cost provider of mining machinery. Company man-

agement believes the way to accomplish this goal is to recruit, train, and retain the finest possible work force and to listen to their suggestions for improving quality.

To that end, the Jeffrey Division instituted an ambitious companywide training program, not only in such technical areas as welding, gauging, and shop management, but also in total quality awareness. With top management heavily involved and clearly signaling its support of this new direction, the company uses its own inside trainers

A Jeffrey 1026HPS continuous miner at work in West Virginia, in the difficult conditions typical of underground coal mines.

A Jeffrey employee operates a multiple-head, flame-cutting machine to begin the initial stage of equipment manufacture.

Welding operations on a continuous miner cutting drum.

to educate all its employees in quality principles, goal setting, team building and problem solving, and analysis. Employees learn to set and measure quality standards.

After quality goals are established across the company, departments and work groups determine their own objectives, based on overall company expectations. Within an established framework, employees are freed to do their jobs as efficiently and creatively as possible. Feedback is frequent; continual measurement against expected outcomes results in the employees taking greater responsibility for the quality of their output. This increases awareness of the needs of the internal customer, bringing about greater cooperation between departments.

More than simply a one-shot "quality fix," the employee focus is an ongoing feature of the company agenda. Jeffrey Division executives believe that many companies are capable of making adequate mining machinery; Jeffrey's mission is to create superior "self-selling" products, designed and built by employees who, because they are valued and consulted, are heavily invested in the company's future and willing to

make the effort necessary to achieve the highest quality. Though most companies say that their greatest asset is their work force, at Jeffrey they're acting on that premise.

In the 1990s the coal mining industry once again finds itself at a critical juncture. Environmental concerns such as high sulfur emissions will either spur greater research in clean-burning technology and low seam mining or sound the death knell for coal consumption.

Increased competition among the remaining mining machine corporations means that companies must manufacture increasingly sophisticated products. Ironically, the very efficiency and durability of today's mining machines, coupled with less demand for coal, has resulted in a diminished call for replacement machinery.

Nonetheless, the Jeffrey Division looks ahead with confidence. Relying on the ingenuity and empowerment of its people, Jeffrey is seeking new market possibilities and researching the needs for innovative new machines. Dresser Industries itself constantly explores opportunities for diversification and complementary business acquisition.

By concentrating on quality and efficient business practices, the Jeffrey Division expects to recapture the excitement that fired Joseph Andrew Jeffrey's imagination when he first peered into that hardware store window so many years ago.

RAGE CORPORATION

The senior management of the Rage Corporation says loud and clear that there are still opportunities for small businesses to grow and thrive if the new business owners find their niche, exploit it fully, work very hard, and deliver a superior product or service.

Rage, a custom plastic injection molder, and its affiliate, Thermoplastic Accessories Corporation, are indeed examples of growth through hard work and exceptional products. Based on a highly successful engineering/prototype business, Rage incorporated in 1968 with four employees. Since then its story has been one of expansion of both its physical plant and its employee force.

In 1990 the company made its third move to larger facilities. The work force had increased by more than 1,000 percent since incorporation. Rage expects to stay in its present location until at least the end of the century, as its property can support a two-fold increase in personnel and construction.

Want a plastic, left-handed, triple threaded, revolving widget? Take the idea to Rage and the company engineers, designers, and operations staff will make it a reality, from designing, building, and maintaining the molds to manufacturing, assembling, and packaging the final product.

Rage, which produces a staggering array of plastic components for a widening circle of diverse businesses, makes items that require molds. Thermoplastic Accessories, the blow-molding arm of the business, fabricates the "skin" into which other products, such as milk, are put.

Rage, for example, makes 100,000 EKG patches each day for the medical market. In addition, the company has produced an intravenous clip that found its way from its original purpose into the space program. The medical clip now is used also by the astronauts to regulate the flow of juices and other liquids during meals in orbit. The company also fabricated a medical instrument component that has helped to reduce operating room time in intestinal surgeries by approximately 2 1/2 hours; another surgical device monitored blood flow during operations.

Late in 1990 the company developed and produced a highly accurate, low-cost height gauge that measures the leg from knee to heel. Such calibrations can help determine the extent of bone loss in those with calcium deficiencies and other medical conditions.

But Rage doesn't restrict itself to medical applications. It has manufactured plastic products for the toy and automotive industries, computer and cash register parts, rollers for dishwasher racks, baby bottles, door parts, kitchen timers, seed spreaders, rakes, and decorative items, to name only a few.

More important than the products Rage manufactures is the company's concern with the quality of those products. Displayed prominently in the company headquarters are testimonials from satisfied customers, praising Rage's quality control process that, in almost all cases, approaches 100 percent client satisfaction with quality of materials, timeliness of performance, shipment of the correct quantity of products, and delivery at the contracted price. Many of the letters and plaques lining the walls are announcements that Rage has been named a client's outstanding vendor.

It's heady approbation, but not surprising considering the fact that the company stresses quality at the opera-

Rage Corporation can turn a concept into a reality, from designing, building, and maintaining molds to manufacturing, assembling, and packaging the final product.

tor level. This has been so successful that some of Rage's customers have suspended their incoming quality-control checks.

Company officials believe that superior, cost-effective products will continue to make Rage successful, even though 300 to 400 other Ohio corporations compete for the same plastic molding business. While management credits its work force for the high quality of its products, quality control is closely monitored. Inspection is a constant, as is a concern with price.

Management has proven the wisdom of this strategy. The majority of Rage's customers represent repeat business, many of them having been with the company since its inception. In fact, the only customers lost to the business are those who have moved their fabrication operations in-house or those who have relocated their operations so far away that shipping is no long feasible.

Innovation is also part of the Rage story. In late 1990 the company was one of the first to use a way to transform polypropylene, usually a semi-opaque substance, into a nearly clear product. By using a technique called "stretch-blow," this less expensive plastic can be used for applications formerly reserved for materials that might cost twice as much. An immediate utilization is in infant formula bottles, for instance, but other uses are on the horizon.

Rage's senior management expects that the company will continue to grow, as will the entire plastics industry. Plastics will be made stronger, tougher, and more resilient, and the ways in which they can be employed will proliferate. Given the ability of the industry to create new and better products, more environmentally friendly plastics should be in the offing.

Management cautions, however, that many of the solid waste stream problems involving plastics are the result of consumers' irresponsible use of the products. They wholeheartedly support recycling efforts and believe that in the future almost all plastics will be reusable.

As one might expect, Rage sees a bright future for the company with the advent of increasingly durable plastics. The automotive market is one example of a fertile territory for its marketing efforts.

The Rage Corporation's guiding vision is to be large enough to provide the equipment, capacity, and technical support required by their customers while staying small enough to be flexible and responsive to their needs. Whether the clients need products made of polypropylene, polycarbonates, polyester, polyethylene, or more exotic materials, Rage intends to fulfill their requirements.

A highly automated company that hasn't lost its human touch, Rage promises to continue to offer superior quality, competitively priced plastic products. The company has banked its future success on the premise that plastic is here to stay—and so is the Rage Corporation.

CRANE PLASTICS

Crane Plastics is a family-owned business that was born and raised in the Discovery City of Columbus.

Founded in 1947 by Robert S. Crane, the company has flourished as a manufacturer of high-quality, custom plastic profile extrusions for such diverse markets as building products, transportation, appliances, electrical equipment, and office machines and furniture. The founder's two sons, Robert S. Crane, Jr., and Jameson Crane, still guide the company as chairman and president, respectively.

Throughout its history Crane Plastics has been an innovator in using the plastics profile extrusion process to form plastic materials into long continuous shapes. When cut to length and finished, the materials end up in the marketplace as such familiar products as vinyl siding and door and window weatherstripping for the home. In addition Crane Plastics has pioneered in the

Using computer-aided design, Crane employees can help customers design extruded parts with careful attention to such factors as the part's function, the type of material used, the tooling and postextrusion fabrication required, and the cost.

manufacture of specialty-engineered products such as office-wiring raceways and cooling-tower splash bars for business and industry.

From a modest beginning with two hand-built extrusion machines, Crane has grown to two large plants and a warehouse, with 115 extrusion machines and more than 600 employees. Its pioneering efforts in extruding tough, rigid-vinyl plastic helped bring about today's high-quality, maintenance-free vinyl siding industry. And Crane is a leader in manufacturing vinyl-clad window products.

The Crane brothers attribute the company's success to their philosophy of "doing more for our customers, adding value to their products, and sharing the rewards with our employees."

Over the years, "doing more" has meant being creative and innovative in helping each customer get a better product. "Adding value" has been most evident in the host of new materials and products brought about through aggressive research and development, and through the design and manufacturing-engineering expertise found in all

Crane Plastics is an innovator in designing and developing its own state-of-the-art tooling to form plastics profile extrusions into a wide variety of intricate shapes.

phases of the company's business.

Crane has been "sharing the rewards" with its employees since 1969 through a Working/Sharing Partnership in which they all participate in a unique cash profit-sharing plan.

Since the inception of the plan, Crane employees have earned more than $18 million as a direct reward for their outstanding efforts. The program benefits not only them but also the greater Columbus area in which they work and live. In addition, it has brought significant and documented savings to Crane's customers through higher productivity, quality, and service.

Crane also is very proud of its employees' consistent growth through their outreach to the community. Their substantial contributions to the Columbus-area United Way effort, for instance, have consistently ranked Crane as one of the top per-capita contributors among the major area employers — adding an important and well-rounded dimension to the company's Working/Sharing Partnership.

Advancing toward the twenty-first century, Crane Plastics remains dedicated to another long-held principle: To best serve the interests of its employees, customers, and community, the company will continue to work at being not necessarily the biggest in its industry, but the best.

Crane Plastics is proud of its heritage and confident of its future.

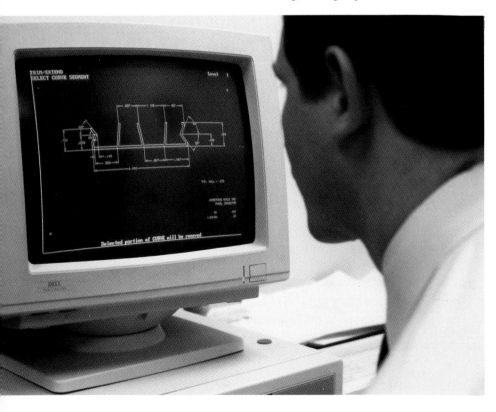

LENNOX INDUSTRIES

Although a world-class corporation in stature and size, Lennox remains a privately held company that still honors the values of D.W. Norris, its founder and first president. In 1904 Norris and other investors purchased a small furnace company started by Dave Lennox 10 years earlier and set it on a course that would make it an industry giant.

Since its founding, Lennox has established itself time and again as a leader and innovator in the heating and air conditioning industry. The long and impressive list of Lennox "firsts" includes:

• Development of a fully hermetic air conditioner suitable for home use.

• Introduction of the revolutionary Pulse combustion gas furnace.

• Development of the first forced-air furnaces.

When Lennox began construction of its Columbus manufacturing facility in 1940, it was to produce gas, oil, and coal furnaces. By the time construction was complete in 1941, however, the country

Lennox is a leader in the heating and air conditioning industry, developing and manufacturing technologically advanced equipment that operates with increased efficiency and reduced energy consumption.

had been plunged into World War II. Instead of furnaces, the factory turned out a variety of military and defense items for the duration of the war.

Today it's not war supplies but heat pumps, condensing units, and coils that come off the assembly lines of the Columbus facility. The plant manufactures Lennox's full line of residential heat pumps and central air conditioning systems, commercial rooftop air conditioning systems, and cooling coils used in other Lennox products.

One of only three Lennox Industries plants that supply the entire world market, the Columbus facility is among the company's largest. With more than 800,000 square feet of production, warehouse, and office space, the facility covers 38 acres.

On the average the facility produces 2,500 units a day. Each month this requires 750 million kilowatts of electricity, 8.8 million cubic feet of natural gas, 1.3 million gallons of water, 1,300 tons of steel, and 124 tons of copper tubing.

TOP: Heating and air conditioning units from Lennox Industries' Eastern Division manufacturing facility reflect "Made in the U.S.A." quality craftsmanship.

BOTTOM: Quality Lennox products begin with quality materials, such as these coils of steel used in manufacturing air conditioning and heating units.

Although Lennox's Columbus facility is nearing its 50th anniversary, constant modernization and the addition of the latest advances in technology keep it young in terms of productivity and performance.

Along the production lines, state-of-the-art machinery and computerized equipment are combined with traditional craftsmanship and attention to detail. This enables the plant to turn out products that meet increasing standards of quality with increasing efficiency.

Whatever their position, on the line, in the office, or in the field, the men and women of Lennox's Eastern Division are committed to quality and to doing the very best job possible to ensure that Lennox remains the industry leader.

ARC INDUSTRIES, INCORPORATED

"ARC Industries, Incorporated, provides the business and industrial community with a broad range of contract services at a competitive cost and strives for the highest standards of quality and excellence in customer service."

These are laudable goals, but they could be the objectives of almost any central Ohio business. What sets ARC Industries apart? What makes them a unique employer? It is that its client-employees are adults with mental retardation and/or developmental disabilities.

An affiliate of the Franklin County Board of Mental Retardation and Developmental Disabilities, ARC Industries assists those adults who are eligible and desire services to increase their independence, self-sufficiency, and productivity; to minimize the effects of their disabilities; and to attain a better quality of life.

A nonprofit corporation chartered by the State of Ohio, ARC Industries employs persons enrolled in the Adult Services Programs and subcontracts with industry to provide work for client-employees.

But ARC Industries is more than a community agency. It is a thriving, competitive business with more than 1,200 client-employees. By 1990 its operations were generating nearly $3 million in annual sales.

As a subcontractor, ARC Industries operates four production facilities—one in each quadrant of the city—and its labor force serves the needs of customers both in and outside of central Ohio. Accredited by the Commission on Accreditation of Rehabilitation Facilities (CARF) and certified by the State Use Committee of Ohio and the U.S. Department of Labor, ARC Industries offers widely diverse services, providing both the labor and equipment necessary for assembly, fabrication, laundry, packaging, salvage, woodworking, mail preparation, collating, and janitorial services. Many of these activities are performed in the more than 200,000 square feet of production and warehouse space in the agency's facilities. Other work is contracted through the industrial enclave program, which offers groups of trained, supervised client-employees

Collating and inserting tab separators for catalog binders at ARC Industries.

who are sent to the customer's site.

Customers seeking a wide variety of packaging options, for instance, need look no further than ARC Industries. Four workshops are able to provide shrink-wrap, poly bagging, blister packaging, boxing, and prepackage assembly services. Its skin packaging capabilities include a rotomatic die cutter with an annual processing capacity of 1.3 million pieces.

Hand assembly work, including automotive and electronic assembly, is a highlight of ARC Industries' services. Its varied projects have ranged from all of the cutting, sorting, coding, packag-

ing, and shipping of samples required to create a customer's new sample distribution system to extensive collating and labeling programs, rejuvenating used telephone equipment, and cleaning, sorting, and packaging truck parts for resale.

Woodworking and fabrication projects are handled by ARC Industries South. In this workshop, client-employees build products for direct sale. Such products range from a popular foot rest for computer users to picnic tables purchased by the Ohio Department of Natural Resources. In addition, client-employees use cutting, drilling, sanding, and shaping equipment to complete work subcontracted from other manufacturers.

To offer the engineering and production management skills required to remain competitive, ARC Industries employs industrial engineers who furnish accurate estimating and bidding systems and timely quotes for potential and repeat customers. These engineers are knowledgeable not only regarding required federal labor guidelines, but also about the provisions necessary for the special capabilities of ARC client-employees. Because they are versed in human factors analysis, they are able to

Many ARC Industries client-employee products are for direct sale. This employee operates a drill press on a woodworking project.

design processes to adapt the employees' skills to the tasks required by the customer. The production management teams estimate and monitor every subcontracted project. They also work with the sales force and customers to ensure that each project is properly organized for timely completion. For repeat customers, the production manager produces scheduling options that best fit the purchaser's recurring needs.

Production managers, all of whom are members of the American Production and Inventory Control Society (APICS), meet with the sales staff and production teams weekly to assess existing contracts and to schedule new jobs.

Each ARC Industries workshop is represented by a member of the sales staff. These staff members meet with area businesses to secure new subcontract work and to service existing accounts; they particularly target those industries that have packaging, assembly, salvage, and woodworking needs. Communication with present or potential customers is enhanced by ARC

Industries' fax and computer systems.

ARC Industries' Community Services Department fulfills service contracts with area businesses and agencies. This department offers transitional employment and skill development for its client-employees. Its largest accounts are in janitorial services, including office and carpet cleaning, restroom sanitation, and floor care, and in laundry services.

Some of central Ohio's largest businesses and agencies have found that contracting with ARC Industries means that they receive extremely cost-effective, high-quality services provided by a motivated, successful work force. Some of the agency's customers include Borden Home Wallcovering, Fruehauf Trucking, Business Telecom, The Limited, the State of Ohio, Friendship Village in Dublin, Cellular One, General Electric, School Book Fairs, Schottenstein Stores, Bob Evans Restaurants, and the Parent Child Resource Center.

ARC Industries has enjoyed consistent growth and expansion. Agency officials expect that growth to continue, as more candidates for employment enter the workshop system and as more businesses discover the value of the services available from ARC Industries' client-employees.

In the early 1990s, surveys indicated that more than 50 percent of the American work force received only minimal satisfaction from their employment. That's not true at ARC Industries. Empowered by the dignity of work, the agency's client-employees take satisfaction in the art of doing a job thoroughly and well, and their skill, dependability, and determination make them important assets to any employer interested in cost-containment and productivity.

This comprehensive program of job training, placement, and supervision is one of central Ohio's most admirable public-private alliances, a partnership in which everyone—employers, client- employees, the agency, and the community—wins.

RANCO INCORPORATED

Central Ohio has been the home and headquarters for Ranco Incorporated since it was founded in 1913. Tucked away in the Columbus suburb of Plain City, the international company has been manufacturing controls for more than 75 years.

Innovation came early in Ranco's history. The original company was named the Automatic Reclosing Circuit Breaker Company, after founder E.C. Raney's first invention. The circuit breaker corrected short circuits and shutdowns in coal mines, steel mills, interurban railways, and later, on many navy ships.

In the mid-1920s, when the old ice box was being replaced by mechanical refrigeration, Raney introduced the world's first inexpensive household refrigeration control. His invention helped the refrigeration industry grow by lowering the cost of refrigerators. In 1936, because Ranco controls were becoming so well known, the company name was changed to Ranco, and it continued to expand its product line in the ensuing years. The old Automatic Reclosing Circuit Breaker Company was sold.

Today Ranco, a division of British-based Siebe Plc, has strategically located operations throughout the world.

Ranco's 38,000-square-foot North America headquarters near Plain City, Ohio, was built in 1980.

Its companies include Ranco North America, which has a plant adjacent to Ranco's worldwide headquarters in Plain City. Other companies included in the international Ranco family are Paragon Electric Company, Ranco Controls Europe, Ranco Japan Limited, Gestra A.G., Barber Coleman Industrial Instruments, Aerospace and Power Controls, and Motors Divisions.

Ranco's record of achievement has earned the company a reputation for worldwide leadership in controls and control technology. At its 220,000-square-foot plant on 75 acres in Plain City, Ranco North America manufactures innovative, state-of-the-art controls for heat pumps, air conditioners, and refrigeration systems.

Its manufacturing facilities incorporate the latest processes in applied manufacturing technology, such as laser welding on electromechanical bellows and laser trimming on electronic controls. Thermostats are produced with automated assembly and brazing of temperature-sensing power elements. Thick film electronics technology is applied in many of Ranco's new hybrid and electronic products. Many key customers in different industries recognize the company's dedication to producing reliable controls by awarding Ranco contracts as a quality supplier and vendor.

Ranco North America is committed

In the automotive product manufacturing areas a "just-in-time" manufacturing philosophy is important to productivity.

to its future development by implementing just-in-time inventory management, computer integrated manufacturing, and statistical process control throughout its plants. Ranco ensures the long-term worldwide competitiveness of its products in the areas of cost, quality, and on-time delivery.

The controls Ranco North America manufactures serve four basic markets: Comfort, Commercial, Household, and Automotive.

• Comfort Products: Ranco is the world's leading supplier and producer of reversing valves, the heart of the heat pump system. It is also the major supplier of humidification, dehumidification, room and central air conditioning, space heater, and ventilating controls. New products reflect the transition from electromechanical to electronic controls. The Variable Speed Drive Compressor Controller reduces energy use by 25 to 35 percent by improving the system operation of heat pumps and precisely adjusting motor speed.

Another energy-saving product is the Electronic Demand Defrost control for heat pumps. This product is a microprocessor-based design and utilizes a thick film hybrid design using Ranco's latest manufacturing advances in circuit board testing and precise laser trim techniques. The Demand Defrost is the only control on the market approved by the Department of Energy for the 7 percent energy utilization credit.

• Commercial Products: For more than 40 years the company has been one

A Ranco design engineer works with a computer-aided design system, which assists in the continuous improvement of the design process.

of the world's major suppliers of commercial refrigeration controls. Commercial controls are used for food storage and display equipment, ice machines, vending machines, and drink dispensers in supermarkets, convenience stores, and restaurants. These controls incorporate technologies such as laser-welded bellows and computer calibration.

• Household Products: Ranco invented the first low-cost household refrigerator control, the first adaptable control, and the Short Kut concept in cold controls. The "K" series of temperature controls is used by home appliance and commercial equipment manufacturers in 68 countries. Other household products include range and oven controls, electronic motor speed controls, light dimmers, and fan speed controls.

• Automotive Products: A full line of electronic and electromechanical control products for automotive air conditioning is made at Ranco. The company is also the world's largest supplier of automotive water valves.

Even more important than its past accomplishments, however, is the promise of Ranco's future—a future made immeasurably brighter now that the company has become a member of the Siebe Group, one of the world's fastest growing multinational companies with dominant market positions internationally in key mechanical and electronic industries, including the controls industries.

Like Ranco, innovation has been important to Siebe from the start. Actually, the Siebe Group had its origins in the engineering genius of its founder, Augustus Siebe, an Austrian officer who migrated to England in 1816. He started his own business in 1819, developing and manufacturing his inventions. He is best known for his invention of the world's first underwater diving equipment.

Siebe's unquestioned commitment to research and development will ensure that the innovative approach followed by Ranco throughout its history will continue to meet the future needs of its customers. With annual sales of over $3 billion, Siebe's wide variety of resources makes it possible to build for the future with even greater assurance.

Ranco North America has been an integral part of and leading employer in central Ohio, continually investing in the improvement of its facilities. Ranco North America and its parent company are strong members of the community, active in community service and programs such as the United Way, Junior Achievement, and the chamber of commerce.

TOP: This candid photograph represents a typical work session of Ranco's highly skilled design engineers.

BOTTOM: Shipments made in the Ohio plant are distributed to customers throughout the world.

LIEBERT CORPORATION

With more than 500,000 systems installed and annual sales in excess of $500 million, Columbus-based Liebert Corporation is the world's leading manufacturer of support systems to protect computers and other sensitive electronics with similar support needs.

At Liebert success is attributed to many factors. One is clearly its people, guided by a charter founded on high-value products, responsiveness to customer need, and an overall "can-do" attitude.

Another factor is an important market phenomenon that has seen most businesses escalate the value of information networks to the point where they are now considered corporate assets. Today these assets are in the same league as facilities, equipment, and finances—as such, the information process demands comprehensive protection and support.

Liebert's primary business is the design, manufacture, distribution, and servicing of devices that support infor-

In 1990 Liebert associates celebrated the 25th anniversary of the company's founding.

mation resources. Primary products include precision air conditioning, developed by the company's founder, Ralph C. Liebert, as well as power conditioning and uninterruptible power supply (UPS) systems. Liebert also provides access security and site monitoring/management systems.

Liebert employs more than 4,000 associates and markets its products in 78 different countries. The sales efforts of its 150-plus offices are supported by the industry's most extensive customer service network.

The 25-year odyssey of Liebert Corporation has seen a small, family-owned business transformed into today's multinational industry leader.

Ralph C. Liebert, as a young mechanic in the late 1940s, founded Capitol Refrigeration Company in Columbus as a franchise for Carrier air conditioning systems. Capitol prospered, always exploring and expanding into new commercial enterprises, including custom cold storage rooms and pioneer efforts in the freeze-drying process.

A landmark enterprise was the development of a specialized environmental control system designed to meet the

A Liebert SiteScan system monitors and controls computer support equipment, including precision air conditioning and uninterruptible power supply systems, also made by Liebert.

unique cooling requirements of early computers. Conventional cooling systems were simply not capable of providing the specialized environment that enable computers to operate non-stop and at peak performance.

Working in his garage because there was no available space at Capitol, Ralph Liebert responded with a self-contained, modular system that guaranteed a computer-grade environment—constant, precisely controlled air temperature, cleanliness, and humidity.

With the help of International Business Machines, Liebert displayed his prototype at the 1965 World Computer Conference in Philadelphia. That prototype was sold directly from the show floor to General Motors, and Liebert returned to Columbus, his briefcase stuffed with orders that filled the first year's production capacity. Liebert Corporation was on its way.

Two years later a disastrous fire destroyed Liebert's building, equipment, and inventory—everything but the dream. Three weeks later, with solid support of suppliers, creditors, and the company's staff of eight associates, Ralph Liebert was back in business. During the next few years, customer acceptance for Liebert air conditioning grew rapidly.

In 1968, 38 associates helped to open a new headquarters plant and soon Liebert distinguished itself once again

by incorporating the industry's first solid state temperature and humidity controls. In this same period, substantial inroads were made into the international arena.

A 174,000-square-foot production facility in Columbus' north end was constructed in 1974.

Liebert broadened its product line significantly in 1978 as it prepared to enter a new market. Electrical power protection presented an ideal complement to the company's mission that promised comprehensive computer support. The first system incorporated a patented technology that used utility power as an energy source to "reconstruct" computer-grade power. Today that technology still dominates the power conditioning market.

During the next few years the manufacturing capacity was tripled, and a new facility opened in Delaware, Ohio. It was here that the company would satisfy the growing demand for Liebert power systems as well as house both the Research and Development Center

and the Heat Transfer Division.

Liebert Corporation funded growth with a public offering in 1981, and two years later strengthened its international position with the construction of a plant in Cork, Ireland.

During this time, Liebert further broadened its power systems product line with the acquisition of the Programmed Power Division from Franklin Electric. This move permitted immediate entrance into the largest and fastest growing segment of the power protection market—that of uninterruptible power supplies. These systems provide the capability for critical information systems to remain operational in the event of a total power outage.

Between 1979 and 1986 Liebert enjoyed an annual growth rate of nearly 30 percent, as sales leaped from $46 million to $290 million.

A new computer-based system offered total, centralized computer support management for an entire data center. The result was the emergence of a new market. For the first time customers had a single source for integrated computer support systems. This approach set Liebert apart from all of its competition.

In 1987 Liebert joined Emerson Electric Company. Most significant of all the milestones, this union added numerous power products, resources, and overall capabilities to solidify Liebert's leadership position.

Liebert remains successful as it continues to respond to the support requirements of the ever-changing

ABOVE: Ralph C. Liebert founded Capitol Refrigeration Co. in 1946. One of his many pioneering applications for cooling technology—precision air conditioning—led to the formation of the Liebert Corporation in 1965.

LEFT: Now a division of Emerson Electric Company, Liebert has manufacturing facilities in Columbus and Delaware, Ohio, as well as Santa Ana, California, Cork, Ireland, and Mexicali, Mexico.

technologies that drive more powerful information systems. The ability to anticipate customer need and keep pace with innovative, flexible, and creative solutions is the core of strategic planning efforts.

Today Liebert is beginning to grow in new ways. There is an increasing trend to serve markets outside of the traditional computer/computer room markets. Much of this new opportunity involves the critical needs of other sensitive electronics that are vital to such markets as industry, telecommunications, and medicine.

Liebert associates readily embrace the challenge to sustain growth as they are guided by the Liebert corporate philosophy, as originally penned by Ralph C. Liebert:

"No person or company could ever hope to realize full potential without goals that truly inspire, goals that transcend material considerations, pride in our work . . . integrity in our dealings . . . the fundamental human need to contribute.

"It is this clear sense of purpose that sustains us and permits us to serve our customers well."

COLUMBUS COL-WELD CORPORATION

From its beginnings in a two-car garage to its emergence as an internationally respected casting reclamation company, Columbus Col-Weld's story is one of careful, consistent growth.

Established in 1941, Columbus Col-Weld specialized in salvaging engine castings such as blocks and heads. Because of World War II, new castings were scarce. For founder William H. Stump, however, the problem presented an opportunity. He attended school in Indianapolis to learn salvage techniques, and after his training, the mechanically-minded Stump improved upon what he'd been taught and opened his own company at 162 North Fourth Street.

As knowledge of Stump's expertise spread, business flourished. Having made his reputation in rebuilding blocks and heads, Stump expanded his repertoire to include operations throughout the entire engine, slowly adding procedure after procedure.

Stump's four sons, Jon, Roger, Maynard, and Charles, brought into the business by their father long ago, continue

Saving engines, saving parts, saving money, saving time—that is the mission at Columbus Col-Weld.

as partners and managers. They describe Columbus Col-Weld as having transformed from a mechanical, "blacksmithing" company to a high-tech thermal-fusion reclamation business. Col-Weld's clients include corporations from Mexico to Zimbabwe. The company repairs castings ranging from tug boat power plants and industrial engines to submarine parts and piano frames—and does it well the first time. Company officials estimate Columbus Col-Weld's reject rate at less than three percent.

Columbus Col-Weld has benefited not only from its own reputation for quality but also from environmental concerns. Because of stringent Environmental Protection Agency regulations, many small foundries have closed, and the fewer the number of foundries producing new castings, the greater the demand for reclamation and rebuilding of present equipment. Sometimes, in fact, the company outperforms a sluggish economy, as clients decide to rebuild rather than buy new machines.

But Columbus Col-Weld doesn't restrict its environmental activities simply to gaining business from those affected by environmental rulings. The company takes proactive steps to

keep its own environment clean. During the 1990s, alkaline solutions used for cleaning will be replaced by salt baths, and an air scrubber will be installed. The company continually evaluates ways to reduce its volume of waste products.

Company officials also project that the 1990s will be a time of expansion. Columbus Col-Weld expects to add 20,000 square feet to its operations and additional members to its staff.

One of the company's growth areas will continue to be its affiliate, Engine Rebuilder's Supply. Originally created to supply parts to Columbus Col-Weld itself, this division now offers necessary parts and service to heavy-equipment customers in Ohio, West Virginia, Kentucky, Indiana, and Pennsylvania. This "one-stop shopping" concept means that customers who have repair and reclamation performed by Columbus Col-Weld can also purchase, on-site, the parts necessary to keep the rebuilt engine performing at peak efficiency.

Saving engines, saving parts, saving money, saving time—that's the mission at Columbus Col-Weld. This unique central Ohio company has fulfilled that mission for more than 50 years.

ASC COLAMCO

ASC Colamco is a major supplier of soft trim to the transportation industry, specializing in heavy truck interior. Its exclusive patented process for the bonding of fabric, vinyl, and leather trim is widely recognized as the quality leader in the soft trim industry.

ASC Colamco is headquartered at 1533 Alum Creek Drive in Columbus, Ohio. Columbus is also home to one of the company's four manufacturing facilities. The remaining manufacturing plants are located in Owosso, Michigan; Statesville, North Carolina; and Vancouver, Washington.

In 1987 ASC Incorporated, the leader in the production of specialty vehicles for nearly a quarter of a century, acquired Colamco Incorporated, a company founded in California in 1962 and a fixture in Columbus since 1968.

As the parent company based in Southgate, Michigan, ASC operates nearly 30 facilities in the United States and abroad, supplying parts, engineering, design, production services, along with total vehicle conversions to the worldwide transportation industry.

COLAMFORM™, a manufacturing process developed by ASC Colamco, highlights the company's pioneering ambition within the industry. COLAMFORM™ combines the original Colamco process of bonding together a surface, foam, and backing with three-dimensional molds for unique part configurations not available with other processes.

In response to its customers' needs for innovative and increasingly cost-effective products, ASC Colamco's product development activities have evolved from flat processed parts to three-dimensional components.

From concept to production, the company's experienced staff of engineers, draftsmen, and support personnel work together with ASC's resources to offer customers high-quality and cost-effective product development.

With the aid of advanced technology, which includes CAD, CAE, CAM, and CAPP capabilities that improve material yield and tooling accuracy, ASC Colamco's engineering and design departments can style, develop, and or-

ASC Colamco produces quality soft interior trim products for the heavy-duty truck industry and a wide variety of other products for such industries as marine, aircraft, medical, recreational vehicle, original equipment and aftermarket automotive, and home and office furniture.

chestrate an entire project, according to the customer's specifications. Computer-generated drawings assist in the development of tooling layouts. This process reduces leadtime and assures a uniform quality product.

ASC Colamco measures quality by its ability to meet, and even surpass, customer requirements, both specified and implied, in addition to a parallel commitment to cost efficiency. Continuous improvement is accomplished by approaching quality goals and objectives from a basic set of underlying operating principles.

Over the years ASC Colamco has developed a multitude of specialized products, including molded door panels, headliners, carpet and seat products, underhood acoustical and thermal insulation, acoustically insulated headliners, door panel inserts with integrally wrapped edges, and interior cabinetry and consoles.

Customers include many of the major automobile and truck manufacturers, including General Motors, Ford, Freight-

liner, Mack, Peterbilt, and Navistar.

ASC Colamco employs over 200 people at the Columbus plant and another 300 within the manufacturing network. Through the years each facility has helped to make ASC Colamco the innovator in soft trim manufacturing and the industry leader in setting quality standards for others to follow.

INLAND PRODUCTS INCORPORATED

Most businesses don't like to operate with a lot of fat, but one Columbus company is an exception. In fact, Inland Products Incorporated has thrived on it since the company was founded in 1867.

Inland Products is one of the oldest family-owned enterprises still in business in Columbus. Operated by the Baas family since its founding, Inland Products converts animal fat, meat, bones, and hides into products used daily by everyone, says Gary H. Baas, president and chief executive officer. It also is the sole remaining rendering operation in central Ohio.

About half of each animal slaughtered for human consumption ends up in the hands of a rendering plant, according to Baas. "For every 1,000-pound steer, we get 500 pounds," he says. "For every 220-pound pig, we get 110 pounds."

Renderers cook leftover animal fat, meat, and bones to produce tallow for soaps, protein for livestock feed, and oils for products ranging from automobile tires to lipstick. There are more than 200 uses in the chemical business for animal tallow.

Inland Products was founded by John B. Baas, the current president's grandfather, with two partners. At the time it was one of several rendering plants in the city.

The elder Baas, an immigrant from Holland, eventually bought out his partners and passed the business on to four sons. They, in turn, began expanding by buying the other rendering plants in the city and eventually throughout the region.

"In those days there was a rendering plant about every 25 or 30 miles because there were no freeways," Baas recalls. With the development of the highway system and the economies of scale achieved by processing at one plant, smaller companies have been going out of business.

"Our company has purchased 34 rendering plants in its history," Baas says. Most of those plants have been converted into collection points for Inland Products trucks. Inland currently operates seven terminals, or collection points, that supply three plants, located in Columbus, Gallipolis, Ohio,

and Pittsburgh.

Inland collects animal remains from packing houses, supermarkets, restaurants, and anywhere else it is generated. Once at a plant, the parts are cooked at about 280 degrees for about 45 minutes.

The tallow is strained and separated. For some customers Inland supplies tallow that meets very exacting specifications for specific uses—a process that allows Inland to charge more than the commodity price for its product.

Different animals produce fat of varying degrees of hardness. For example, beef fat produces the finest tallow because of its whiteness and is most likely to be used in fine soaps.

The bone and meat particles are squeezed through an extruder to separate the fat. The resulting product, about 50-percent protein, is further processed into animal feed.

Because animals can digest food containing a maximum of 27-percent protein, the product that Inland supplies can be cut almost in half with grain to make feed.

The process is more complicated than throwing everything in a vat. Inland's rendering plant is computer controlled with cooking times and temperatures determined electronically. "Once the parts are dropped into a hopper," says Baas, "it's never touched by

human hands."

Inland also recycles cooking oil used in fast-food restaurants. It, too, is cooked for sterilization and is filtered and purified. Recycled cooking oil is spritzed on animal feed as it is fed to livestock to enhance the flavor, increase the protein content slightly, and keep down the dust.

At one time Inland even owned its own animal food company after buying a competitor that operated a canned dog food line. Midwest Horsemeat Company slaughtered about 100 horses a day and supplied the feed to the Winchester Canning Company, in Canal Winchester, Ohio. Inland sold the oper-

ations after a short time, however.

Inland continues to be on the lookout for other rendering companies to buy, many of which are family owned, according to Baas. In 1990, 107 independent companies operated between 250 and 300 plants nationwide, and that does not include in-house plants operated by the large slaughterhouses.

Because of the worldwide demand for tallow and related products, Inland sells about 65 percent of its fine tallow overseas. European soap makers make more tallow-based soaps than U.S. companies, because tallow-based soap is gentler to skin. Inland's Pittsburgh plant is located on the Ohio River and routinely sends tallow by ship to foreign users.

Inland's foreign business is also developing in other ways. Inland-processed hides are sold to Italy, Spain, and other European countries that have fine leather industries. Hides are processed in a "pickling" vat for 18 hours in preparation for tanning. The 1,000 or so hides that Inland handles a day are then dried and packed for shipment overseas.

Inland officials are also working with foreign governments to either es-

tablish joint ventures or assist in the establishment of rendering plants. Baas and other company officers have been to the Soviet Union, where they are helping the Soviets learn how to process pigskins. The company also has had officials from Bolivia visit Columbus to learn more about basic rendering.

Until now the South American countries have had little need for rendering plants because they consume virtually the entire animal, says Baas, who noted that internal organs are eaten and bones are used for soups.

Establishing rendering plants in developing nations can increase the supply of protein available as feed, which in turn helps those nations' livestock industries. Rendering also helps them provide other basic commodities of their own, such as soaps and tallow.

After all, as Baas explains, "Virtually everything on an animal except the squeal is recyclable."

After nearly 125 years in business under the ownership of one family, Inland is looking forward to many more years of successful growth in its hometown, the Discovery City.

Inland Products currently operates three rendering plants, including this one in Columbus.

COLUMBUS STEEL DRUM COMPANY

The business of the Columbus Steel Drum Company is the manufacture and reconditioning of steel containers, but the missions of the company, according to senior officials, are controlled growth, total customer service, and environmental protection.

Columbus Steel Drum was incorporated in 1955 as a division of Franklin Steel Company. Both companies were founded by Sidney I. Blatt. Originally Columbus Steel Drum was in the reconditioning business only. The company received empty, used, open, and closed head drums; they chemically refurbished closed head drums and used a combination of thermal cleaning and steel shot blasting to cleanse and renew open head containers.

After becoming one of the largest single-site reconditioning facilities in the world, Columbus Steel Drum, as a complement to its primary business, opened a plant for the manufacture of new steel containers. This plant is one of the newest, most modern, and most up-to-date facilities in the United States. The drum company uses significant quantities of exterior and interior coatings for its containers. These are produced by Surface Research Corporation, a subsidiary Blatt established in 1959. Surface Research also produces such

compounds for other corporations that require chemical coatings.

In March 1985 Franklin Steel Company capitalized on its knowledge of the environmental issues surrounding industry by opening ChemServ Environmental Company. A fast-growing subsidiary, ChemServ's area of expertise is used by companies in a 500-mile radius of Columbus.

The numbers generated by Columbus Steel Drum's operations are impressive; the manufacturing company annually produces 500,000 new drums; the reconditioning company's contribution is 1.5 million drums per year. Its customer list is studded with the names of the major *Fortune* 500 companies.

All of the company's high-level production is done with an eye toward the environment, and Columbus Steel Drum management officials are proud of the corporation's environmental focus. They point out that a steel drum is a continuous resource and the only 100 percent recyclable semi-bulk industrial container

available in the world. The containers either can be reconditioned after use or, if reconditioning is inappropriate, returned to virgin steel.

By providing a facility that manufactures and ships new drums and then reconditions the used containers for resale, Columbus Steel Drum gives used drums a temporary home, thus reducing the temptation for users to scrap the drums or to dispose of them in ways that are ecologically unsound. Since these containers have at one time held nearly every imaginable chemical compound, keeping them gathered in a suitable lo-

RIGHT: An environmentally safe workplace and a continually modernized program keep Columbus Steel Drum on top.

BELOW: The company's 500 trailers can promptly deliver to the country's major markets.

cation is a considerable service to the country's environmental efforts.

As end-users become more and more sensitive to the public ramifications of container disposal, they respond favorably to Columbus Steel Drum's guarantee that something good will always happen to the containers that bear its customers' corporate names and logos. That is, the drums will either be reconditioned or recycled; they will not end up in landfills, rivers, fields, or illegal dumping grounds.

In addition to this guarantee, Columbus Steel Drum works closely with its customers to assist them in developing waste minimization programs.

For example, the company teaches client corporations how to empty a container of its entire contents. Officials estimate that if one inch of material were allowed to remain in each drum shipped, the resulting product waste would total nearly one billion dollars annually. Therefore, this educational program is referred to as "The Billion-Dollar Inch." By showing their customers how to "drip-dry" a container, Columbus Steel Drum saves its customers money and assures the most efficient use of materials.

But Columbus Steel Drum is involved with more than its customers. The company is an active partner in professional associations and in the community, as in the German Village Recycling Program and in its own Gahanna neighborhood, where the company provides college scholarships for Gahanna High School students.

Nationally the company is a leader in professional reconditioning associations that set standards for the industry. Of the four board chairmen of NABADA, two have come from Columbus Steel Drum, and the first was Sidney Blatt.

In 1989 Blatt was honored by the association with its prestigious Morris Hershson Award of Merit. The company also has been well represented in the Steel Shipping Container Institute, another highly respected professional association.

The corporation's concern for the environment, its customers, and the community is mirrored by its interest in its employees. A model reconditioning

ABOVE: Columbus Steel Drum's headquarters is located in the northeast part of the city in the Gahanna Industrial Park.

RIGHT: Columbus Steel Drum produces more than one million reconditioned drums annually.

facility, Columbus Steel Drum provides an environmentally safe workplace; a continual modernization program keeps the operation ahead of many others.

A number of programs also have been instituted to enhance employee productivity and morale. Quality circles were introduced in 1987, and upper-management Quality Control Teams are in place in both the reconditioning plant and the new container facility. A significant bonus program and a liberal vacation policy have been in effect for many years.

The company's Employee Assistance Program, including a drug and alcohol abuse component, also has been highly successful. As the reconditioning industry becomes more regulated and its products more sophisticated, there is a need for more professional-level employees; Columbus Steel Drum is meeting the challenge of finding such professionals.

Columbus Steel Drum looks forward confidently to continued growth in the 1990s. It expects to acquire smaller companies swamped by the ever-growing tide of governmental and environmental regulations. As more *Fortune* 500 companies employ sole-sourcing as a money-saving practice, the size and capabilities of Columbus Steel Drum make it possible for the company to compete effectively for

sole-source business.

The officers of Columbus Steel Drum find Columbus to be an ideal site for doing business. Columbus' central location means that the company's 500 trailers can be in most of the country's major markets quickly.

The company's headquarters is located in the city's northeast quadrant at Gahanna Industrial Park. Franklin Steel Company, the developer of the 200-acre park, expects that its presence will enhance the development of this area of Columbus and that Columbus Steel Drum will be a major part of this development. With its positive growth attitude and constant search for new and expanded markets, Columbus Steel Drum will continue to offer its vital services to the nation's industrial giants.

MEDEX, INC.

Entering the world of medical equipment manufacturing in the late 1950s was like piloting a ship in a stormy sea. The American public was demanding the best in quality care, yet the industry was pressed to curb rapidly escalating costs.

Buffeted by these conflicting pressures, hospitals adopted new policies and procedures that continue to be felt today. Many equipment suppliers faltered in the face of these changes and went under; others, such as Hilliard-based Medex Incorporated, with visionary sense and determination, rode out the storm and grew from the experience.

"A tremendous wave of change had overtaken the health care industry in those days," recalls Craig Waldbillig, founder, chairman, and chief executive officer of Medex. "Fortunately for us part of that change was the switch from reusable to disposable products and that created a niche for us."

Medex drew its name from the watchwords of the early 1960s, "medical expendables." From its modest beginnings in 1959, the company has become an international supplier of critical and acute-care products with

Today heart disease can be treated before heart attacks occur. Medex products are used in cardiac catheterization laboratories in procedures such as angioplasty.

annual sales approaching $75 million.

Medex's expanding lines of intravenous fluid and drug administration and invasive pressure monitoring products are used by hospitals and clinics in neonatal intensive care, cancer treatment, pain management, and other treatments.

"Ironically, the changes and continuing dynamics of the health care industry forced us to adopt certain disciplines that have become essential to our success," says Waldbillig. "These disciplines include vision and flexibility to anticipate market needs as well as cost consciousness and an ongoing commitment to improving product quality."

During its first decade Medex capitalized on hospitals' growing appetites for low-cost disposable products. Business grew steadily as the company concentrated on a relatively small product line, serving as a source of products for original equipment manufacturers. A vital link between Medex and end-users was missing, however, and product development suffered.

"It became apparent that we had lost touch with the market and that we had to do something to regain that contact," says Waldbillig. "We took what we thought was a bold step and established our own sales network and distribution channels. We found out almost immedi-

One example of Medex's innovation is their Hi-Flo Trauma™ set, used in trauma centers, emergency rooms, and other critical-care situations. The product delivers intravenous fluids 200 to 300 percent faster than a conventional IV set.

ately that it was the right thing to do."

The payoff was enormous. Armed with a stream of feedback from end-users, Medex enhanced its core line of fluid and drug administration products. By the mid-1970s the company was marketing 90 percent of its products directly to distributors and hospitals.

Market acceptance generated sustained sales gains, and Medex kept pace with demand. The company built and added on to its headquarters in Hilliard and purchased, equipped, and expanded its sub-assembly plant in Dublin. The acquisition of MedFusion Incorporated in Georgia and, later, Ivion Corporation in Colorado complemented its line of drug infusion products.

Medex also established an early presence in Europe through its subsidiaries—Medex Medical Incorporated in Rossendale, England, and Cardionova GmbH in Germany.

"Our timing was excellent," says Waldbillig. "Medex made its mark on the European economic landscape before many other U.S. companies reached for their maps. These inroads will pay great returns for the long term."

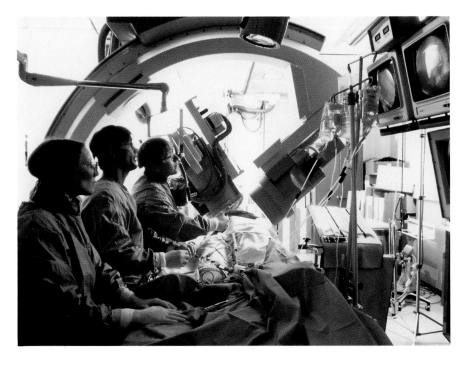

By 1990 combined operations filled a product pipeline that reached into more than 50 countries and included more than 400 items.

Phillip D. Messinger, president and chief operating officer, says Medex's current challenge is maintaining an entrepreneurial spirit while serving a rapidly expanding marketplace.

"We stay ahead in diverse markets by staying innovative and in touch," says Messinger, the company's former marketing director. "Our marketing and product development staffs work closely. They also get constant input from the sales representatives who maintain contact with physicians, clinicians, nurses, administrators, and others who use our products in the field."

Medex customers range from single institutions to large consortiums of hospitals leveraging volume for low prices. Medex shares the burden of mounting cost pressures and stays ahead of fierce competition by focusing on three main

Medex has a long-standing reputation for excellence. Members of the Medex quality control team examine all products to ensure that they meet the company's high standards.

RIGHT: Phillip D. Messinger, president and chief operating officer.

BELOW: Craig Waldbillig, chairman and chief executive officer.

product applications: fluid and drug administration, cardiac catheterization, and invasive pressure monitoring.

Medex's initial offerings, comprising the fluid and drug administration line, have become mainstays—"classics" requiring few changes even with the challenge of advancing technology. These products include plastic stopcocks, adapters, and tubing. In addition, a line of new technology pumps are produced and marketed by MedFusion and Ivion. Applications include anesthesiology, oncology, neonatal care, and pain management therapies—areas demanding precision and flexibility.

The company's catheterization devices meet the needs of the rapidly expanding cardiac care field and are being used to treat as well as diagnose patients. Angioplasty, an effective and efficient treatment to clear arteries and prevent heart attacks, is one example.

Invasive pressure monitoring devices produced by Medex assist in acute-care areas. A recent introduction is a closed monitoring system that combines pressure testing and blood gas sampling. The system protects clinicians and patients from contamination, prevents patient blood loss, and saves hospitals time and money.

Experience in the development and production of these product lines has been a key factor in Medex's ability to contain costs. The ability to deliver consistent quality is an equal concern, however.

"In the early days, quality control was much simpler when we were watching over a handful of products," recalls Waldbillig. "Today our quality control department is one of the most vital in the company. These professionals help establish guidelines for new products in all our plants and subsidiaries and

watch the international marketplace for new standards."

Waldbillig says that expansion in Europe and tremendous domestic growth have forced the company to build and formalize the quality function. Quality challenges are met head-on at monthly management meetings involving representatives of all facets of operations.

Investors have taken notice of Medex's frequent stock splits and annual cash dividends. The company's stock is traded over-the-counter on the NASDAQ National Market System.

On several occasions *Forbes* magazine has included Medex on its list of the best small companies in the country. After making the list for five consecutive years, Medex was put on the *Forbes* honor roll of small companies in 1986.

Medex's ability to identify and meet future challenges should continue to spur impressive growth for the company in a dynamic, global health care marketplace.

TECHNOLOGY ALLIANCE OF CENTRAL OHIO

Few businesspeople in central Ohio know better the importance of networking than the members of the Technology Alliance of Central Ohio (TACO).

This business development group was formed in 1982 as a way for executives of technology-oriented businesses to get together and share their experiences and thoughts about their industry. From its modest beginnings, it has become an organization in which executives can acquire a considerable amount of information concerning business opportunities, sources of capital for emerging technologies, legislation affecting their businesses, and technological developments in the field.

During its evolution, TACO has taken on a more formal structure, with the chief executive officers of the member companies meeting every other month for lunch. "We generally talk about how to do business, trying to promote better business techniques," says Lloyd Hackman, a former chairman of the group and chief executive officer of Ribbon Technology Corp., a Columbus-area specialty metals company that participates in the TACO organization.

On the alternate months, the CEOs bring along their support people, such as lawyers and research-and-development specialists, who make presentations concerning specific developments in various fields of interest.

"In those meetings we have presentations mostly on a given technology," Hackman says. "It helps the members get excited about what's going on."

The only fee involved is the cost of lunch, paid in advance for the year.

Hackman's company, Ribbon Technology, is proof that the TACO contacts are valuable. "I found out about the Edison program from a TACO meeting," Hackman says, referring to the state's Thomas Alva Edison program, which provides seed money for the development of new technology.

Gahanna-based Ribbon Technology has won two Edison program grants worth a total of $175,000. Ribtec, as the company is also known, was able to parlay those funds into obtaining a U.S. Department of Energy grant.

Hackman started Ribtec in 1972 by purchasing the license to some new metals processes from Battelle Memorial Institute. That process, called "melt extraction," produces materials with higher strength and improved corrosion resistance. Applications range from the

aerospace industry to miniature motors to concrete reinforcement. Melt extraction also allows for improved electrical and magnetic properties in some metals, which in turn allows motor manufacturers to make smaller motors, Hackman says. Some of those motors are finding their way into automobiles today.

"Our primary business over the years has been making steel fibers and reinforcing steel for concrete and industrial refractories," Hackman says.

Another TACO success story is Tracewell Enclosures, Inc., of Westerville. Established in 1972, Tracewell is a manufacturer and supplier of electronic packaging systems. It is one of the founding members of TACO.

Larry Tracewell, president and founder, says the company has become a supplier of VME, VXI, and custom system mainframes to major electronic and research organizations worldwide. Among the company's customers are Hughes Aircraft, NCR, Compuserve, Sandia National Laboratories and the research labs at Los Alamos, New Mexico, and the Argonne National Research Laboratory in Chicago.

Though Tracewell began as a company that only made enclosures for electrical systems, it now considers itself a systems integrater, Tracewell says. Its enclosures provide cardcages, back planes, and power and cooling for electronic equipment and monitor internal conditions. "After 19 years we are recognized as the innovator" in the industry, Tracewell says.

The company has kept a low profile in central Ohio because most of its business is in California and Boston. However, Tracewell noted that the company is well known in its field. Its products are sold through direct sales to its OEM base, and it has a private label agreement with a major manufacturer.

TACO member Optimum Technology, Inc., was started by President Josh M. Davda as a software development consultant. The company provides high-quality computer systems contract pro-

Tracewell Enclosures, Inc., is a manufacturer and supplier of electronic packaging systems.

A Ribbon Technology employee forms a direct cast steel strip using a process called "melt extraction," which produces materials with higher strength and improved corrosion resistance.

who is a native of India.

Industrial Ceramic Products Inc. is likely the oldest member of TACO, having been founded in 1936. The company, at 965 W. Fifth Avenue, manufactures pottery pins and refractory specialties used in the pottery-making business as well as goods used in the ceramic, foundry, steel, and heat-treating industries. Industrial Ceramic's products, made in a 40,000-square-foot facility, are shipped worldwide. Management and ownership today is by the second and third generations of the founding families: R.B. Oberst is president, R.C. Oberst is vice president, and H.S. Orth, Jr., is secretary-treasurer.

IRD Mechanalysis, Inc., based in Columbus at 6150 Huntley Road but with operations worldwide, has distinguished itself with the development of vibration monitoring equipment used in the predictive maintenance of machinery. IRD manufactures devices that monitor machinery health. By using standards established for each machine, IRD's devices can determine problems such as when a bearing is about to fail or when a shaft needs realignment by the change in the machine's vibrations. IRD instruments can be used continuously or intermittently and are manufactured as permanent or portable diagnostic tools.

The company, which was purchased by Dobson Park Industries of the United Kingdom in the late 1980s, has manufacturing facilities in Columbus, and the United Kingdom. Employment in Columbus has been a steady 250 people.

Some of the other members of TACO in the early 1990s include Danninger Medical Technology, a manufacturer of passive-motion therapy devices, implants, and special instruments for the spine; Medex, Inc., makers of disposable hospital products, pressure monitoring devices, and pumps; and Scientific Columbus, a manufacturer of electric power metering, monitoring, and control products.

gramming, digitized mapping, and high-volume data entry and word processing at costs 20 percent to 60 percent less than other local suppliers, Davda says. One of OTI's specialties is downsizing applications to run more cost-effective platforms. Some of the clients who have benefited from OTI's services include Honda, Borden, Columbia Gas, British Petroleum, and the state of Ohio. Clients served are located in Ohio as well as other states. Optimum Technology, formed in 1984 and based in Worthington, has also expanded to India with three joint ventures and an office in Calcutta, says Davda,

BETLIN MANUFACTURING

Betlin Manufacturing, located in Columbus, is in its 18th year of consistently providing high quality, custom uniforms for all athletes—males and females, little leaguers to professionals. Athletes wearing Betlin uniforms are just as likely to be seen at the neighborhood recreational center as they are on nationally broadcasted professional sporting events. The company has supplied uniforms for the Cleveland Browns, Cincinnati Reds, San Francisco Giants, and Philadelphia 76ers as well as teams involved in the Olympics and PanAm, Oceanic, and South Pacific games.

A positioning phrase often used by Mathew and Linda Levy, owners of the company, states: "If you can imagine it, we can create it." With the company's highly versatile customizing capabilities, teams can choose from an endless combination of styles, sizes, and trim packages. Their 1991 catalog displays more than 400 uniform combinations for baseball/softball, basketball, track, wrestling, football, volleyball, soccer, lacrosse, and hockey teams, as well as

apparel for cheerleading squads and coaches/officials, and all-purpose shorts and warm-ups. But the catalog just barely scratches the surface of Betlin's seemingly endless customizing capabilities. When taking into consideration the wide range of fabric and color selections, the 400 uniforms shown grow to more than 3 million uniform possibilities. This allows even the most particular teams to be able to find a uniform than satisfies their unique tastes.

All of the employees at Betlin pride themselves on the company's well-known reputation for quality. Examples of their quality are produced every day, in every uniform that is skillfully tailored, hand-sewn to the strictest standards, and pre-washed to ensure its color-fastness and true size.

Linda Levy calls their work force a "Little United Nations." At one time there were 12 nationalities represented throughout the manufacturing plant. Mathew Levy believes that the work force mirrors the fact that their products are sold worldwide, but he stresses that all of their uniforms are made in the U.S.A. and only from American-made materials. The company is also a strong

supporter of "Buy Ohio."

Customer service is one of those value-added areas to which the company is extremely dedicated. Starting with the initial contact and continuing through the selection process to the final decision and delivery, Betlin's customer service representatives are there to help. They know how important the uniforms are to each team and they make sure every customer is thoroughly satisfied with every aspect of Betlin's operation and the quality of the product delivered.

Betlin also knows that teams have tight deadlines which must be met. After all, what good are great-looking uniforms if they're not ready for the first game? The company's performance speaks for itself; since 1973 Betlin has had, and continues to maintain, the best on-time delivery record in the business.

The Betlin operation encompasses four expansive buildings, located on Marion Road, which house the hundreds of sewers as well as knitting machines and the computerized pattern drawing and cutting operations. The company actually fabricates many of its own materials, including a wide range of pinstripe fabrics.

By constantly creating new, fashionable designs as well as maintaining the classics, and by integrating new fabrics which enhance the athletes' looks and performance, Betlin is prepared for the future of sports apparel and will remain one of the industry's top suppliers of custom team uniforms.

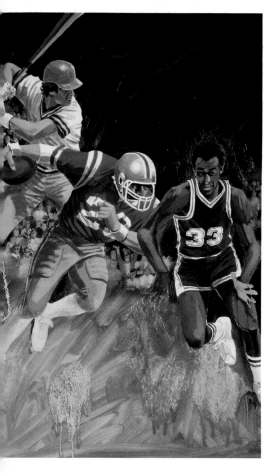

LEFT: Mathew and Linda Levy call Betlin Manufacturing a "one-stop shopping center for the athlete."

BELOW: From their base of operations on Marion Road, Betlin manufactures athletic uniforms in hundreds of styles, colors, and combinations.

LIQUI-BOX CORPORATION

Since its founding in 1961 by Samuel S. Davis, Liqui-Box has consistently met the challenge of introducing tomorrow's packaging products today. Liqui-Box, through continual pursuit of innovation and excellence, has become a leader in developing innovative packaging to contain liquid and other viscous products, ranging from milk to applesauce.

The key to its initial success stems back to the company's roots— The Corrugated Container Company, a Columbus-based corrugated box producer. The company was challenged by Borden, Inc., to develop a plastic lined box to replace the familiar five-gallon returnable metal milk can. Thus, the bag-in-box concept was developed for the dairy industry in the early 1960s. Once that concept was perfected, the company applied the same system to other products. From there, Liqui-Box has emerged as a leading supplier of an array of flexible packaging systems and blowmolded containers for the beverage, bottled water, dairy, processed foods, and wine markets. In recent years it has expanded into the detergents and commercial cleaning supplies market. This universal acceptance and popularity of its bag-in-box packaging and exceptional quality is one of the major reasons for its growth and success.

Liqui-Box Corporation's flexible bag-in-box packaging systems range in size from one gallon to 330 gallons and are available in both barrier and non-barrier structures. Another facet of the packaging industry, in which Liqui-Box is a major producer, is blowmolded dispensing containers. The Unglass® polycarbonate water cooler bottle is available in three-, five-, and six-gallon sizes. The blowmolded Handi-Tap® container is used for dispensing water, juices, and milk and is available in six-liter and 2.5- gallon sizes. Liqui-Box also produces a wide variety of complementary pouring and dispensing spouts

and fitments. Liqui-Box also markets state-of-the-art, fully automated, microprocessor controlled filling machinery for both product lines.

Liqui-Box has established a number of milestones in the packaging industry. In the soft drink industry, similar to the dairy, five-gallon bags replaced the stainless steel soft drink syrup transfer tanks found in fast food stores, institutions, and other commercial establishments. In the bottled water industry, Liqui-Box replaced the heavy, breakable glass bottle for water coolers with the Unglass®. Introduced to the packaging industry was the Orbiter 6000 filler, still recognized as the fastest bag-in-box filler in service today. The Modular One low-acid aseptic filler is the only one of its kind put into production in the United States. These are but a few accomplishments that have contributed to Liqui-Box's continual success, which has placed it in honorary standings by many reputable institutions such as *Forbes* magazine, which has ranked it as one of the 200 Best Small Companies in America year after year and

"The Best of the Best" for consistent growth and earning performance.

Presently, Liqui-Box employs approximately 800 employees throughout the continental United States and Europe. The publicly held company is headquartered in Worthington and operates 12 manufacturing facilities located throughout the United States and one in Luxembourg. It also serves additional markets around the world through foreign licensees, agents, and direct exports.

Liqui-Box Corporation, led by Samuel B. Davis, chairman and CEO, is committed to the continued excellence of its products, equipment, operations, and personnel. A strong corporate and civic commitment to the state of Ohio and specifically, the greater Columbus area, are also maintained through sponsorship of cultural and philanthropic interests such as the Columbus Museum of Art, the S.S. Davis Discovery Center, Columbus Zoo, Columbus Symphony Orchestra, and the United Way. These are all a part of the company's continuous improvement philosophy of "Excellence Is Our Only Goal."

GE SUPERABRASIVES

In this age of high technology, many companies maintain that they are on the cutting edge. Few, however, can support the claim with as much credibility as GE Superabrasives, a very special manufacturer based in Worthington.

GE Superabrasives makes diamonds, millions of carats of diamonds. In fact, about one-quarter of the world's total production of industrial diamond is manufactured at the plant on Huntley Road or at the GE facility in Dublin, Ireland.

The story of GE Superabrasives is one of creativity, ingenuity, perseverance, and technological excellence. Not only was there the breakthrough research that led to the first production of Man-Made™ diamonds in 1955, but there is also the ongoing innovation marked by the fabrication of more than 50 new products since then.

In 1951 General Electric assembled in Schenectady, New York, a group of nine men who were charged with doing the impossible: making diamonds. Many had tried before, and failed. The research trail is marked with the names of such men as J.B. Hannay, F.H.

World headquarters for GE Superabrasives is located in Worthington, a suburb of Columbus.

Moissan, W. Crookes, and C.A. Parsons. Yet each failed attempt made a contribution to the ultimate success at GE.

Armed with the knowledge from previous research and with devices developed by GE, the nine researchers, now known as the Diamond Team, began their quest. They believed that achieving and maintaining temperatures above 3,500 degrees at pressures approaching one million pounds per square inch—roughly equivalent to the earth's pressures at a depth of 160 miles—might be a fruitful approach.

Experiment followed experiment for days and weeks and months on end. In 1954 the breakthrough came in the laboratory, and on February 15, 1955, the first grayish-green and yellow crystals were unveiled for the public. Thirty-two months later the first Man-Made diamonds—known as Type A—were introduced commercially for tungsten carbide grinding applications.

This first commercial product launch in 1957 marked the real birth of the Diamond Products Section of GE, which later became the Specialty Materials Department, and ultimately GE Superabrasives.

When Type A Man-Made diamond came on the market, the diamond tool

Hal Bovenkerk is one of the "Diamond Team" of nine researchers who first unlocked the secret to the synthesis of diamond.

industry was firmly established around a single diamond source, namely the DeBeers Consolidated Mines cartel of Johannesburg, South Africa. One might have expected that GE's diamond would have been welcomed by tool makers as a leverage-producing second source.

The initial reaction was mixed, however. Not until GE's technical sales

team was able to convince the skeptics that Man-Made diamond was genuine and could outperform natural diamond did sales begin to grow.

Another important factor in gaining acceptance was that the Man-Made diamond process could be controlled and, in effect, tailored to different applications.

In 1958 came the Type B diamond, followed a year later by Type M diamond. In late 1959 these crystals were replaced by RVG® diamond, which was tailored even more specifically for resinoid and vitrified grinding wheels used primarily to grind carbide tools.

With the first diamond products, three major premises became manifest that have continued as basic business principles to this day:

• GE Superabrasives would focus on selling raw materials to tool makers. The company would not manufacture diamond tools to sell to end-users.

• GE diamond was to be a top-quality product, as good or better than any comparable diamond in the world.

• GE would continue to improve existing products whenever possible and to develop new products through progress in high-temperature/high-pressure technology.

Based on these principles, GE's diamond business thrived. Markets outside the U.S. were developed and an entire distribution system established to serve overseas customers. By 1968 more changes were warranted.

The Specialty Materials Department, the immediate predecessor to GE Superabrasives, became an independent business, with nearly 300 employees working in a plant in Detroit. It had become obvious, however, that the business had outgrown the plant, which could not be enlarged. A search for larger quarters was begun.

When GE settled on the former TRW plant on Huntley Road, it was because of the community's central location to major markets, there was room to expand on the site, and there was a suitable, established facility. By the end of 1968, the move had been made.

The new environment was obviously good for business. During the next 10 years sales doubled, doubled again, and

ABOVE: *Using enormous presses and applying the principles of high-temperature, high-pressure physics, diamond is manufactured.*

RIGHT: *MBS® diamond is used in cutting tools to process hard stone.*

redoubled yet again. New products kept coming. New applications were found, such as the automobile industry, oil well drilling, mining, and stone processing. New markets were penetrated at home and abroad.

Some of the unique new products had intriguing names: Borazon® cubic boron nitride, Compax® diamond blanks, and Stratapax® drill blanks. These and other products established GE Superabrasives as the world's preeminent producer of superabrasive products for grinding, cutting, drilling, sawing, polishing, and machining.

During the decade of the 1980s the business continued to flourish, and it finally acquired its present name. Additions were made to the Worthington facility where employment topped 1,000, making GE Superabrasives the largest employer in the Columbus suburb.

The plant in Ireland went on-line in 1984, and company sales and support technical staff can now be found from London to Tokyo. GE Superabrasives maintains two Application Development Centers overseas—in Dreieich-Dreieichenhain, West Germany, and

Gotenba, Japan—in addition to the center in Worthington.

Manufactured diamonds are made by competitors in at least 15 other countries, including the Soviet Union and the Peoples Republic of China, where there may be as many as 100 manufacturing plants. Nevertheless, the creator of the first Man-Made diamond is the dominant player in the worldwide market. About 70 percent of GE Superabrasives' total diamond production of more than 100 million carats per year is exported to over 1,500 customers in approximately 50 countries.

The business that had its genesis more than 40 years ago has indeed come a very long way. Even more important, perhaps, is that GE Superabrasives is strongly positioned with people and products to keep growing vigorously as it cuts its pioneering trail through the 1990s toward the next century.

FLXIBLE CORPORATION

In 1912 Hugo H. Young was operating a motorcycle sales agency in Mansfield, Ohio. He had an idea for a new type of motorcycle sidecar—one that would permit the third wheel to tilt and stay on the ground when the motorcycle leaned naturally while going around curves either to the right or the left. The sidecar was attached to the motorcycle with a "flexible" connection patented by Young.

A year later Young founded the Flexible Side Car Company in Loudonville, Ohio, to manufacture his vehicle. In 1914 the Flexible Side Car Company was incorporated for $25,000 with Young as its president. The popularity of Young's sidecar led the company to build its own factory.

In July 1919 the directors decided to change the name of the business to The Flxible Company, and increased capitalization to $500,000. It was then that the name Flxible—without the first "e"—was copyrighted, and it has been exclusive to Flxible ever since. At the same time the firm gained the distinction of being recognized as the "world's largest exclusive manufacturer of motorcycle sidecars."

In the early 1920s the sidecar market suddenly disappeared when Henry Ford established the price for a Ford Roadster at $360 less than the cost of a motorcycle and sidecar. The Flxible Company was forced to seek new products, prompting its entry into the bus, funeral car, and ambulance markets.

The first Flxible bus, a Studebaker 12-passenger sedan, was delivered to E.L. Harter in 1924. A second coach for Harter established an enviable record for long life and dependability, accumulating more than 275,000 miles. This same coach established a new record time during a trip from New York to Los Angeles.

In 1936 it was decided that Flxible would concentrate on intercity transit equipment. All of its resources were devoted to developing a coach that would be outstanding in this field.

Two years later a new Flxible model was put on the market. This coach, the 25-passenger Flxible Clipper, had an integral body/chassis design and was the forerunner of the company's line of streamlined intercity buses.

Groundwork for the shift of bus production from the Fageol Twin Coach Company in Kent, Ohio, to Flxible was laid in 1951, when the two companies cooperated in the production of 1,590 "convertibles" for Army Ordnance. Convertibles were coaches that could be changed to stretcher carriers to carry the wounded.

After studying the basic Twin Coach design, Flxible developed important modifications. This led to the first big city bus order for the firm—a 300-unit order from the Chicago Transit Author-

The first "e" was dropped in Flexible in 1919. At the time, the company was recognized as the "world's largest exclusive manufacturer of motorcycle sidecars."

ity, delivered in 1954.

The Flxible Two-Level Intercity Coach made its first appearance that same year. It offered new comfort for passengers with such advanced mechanical features as torsilastic springs, independent front-wheel suspension, air conditioning, and new type reclining seats.

In 1961 Flxible introduced a "New Look" transit coach, which was accepted as an industry standard for the next 18 years. The coach featured a rear-mounted Detroit Diesel engine, an enlarged, reflection-free windshield, double-bay passenger windows, and fluorescent lighting.

In more recent years of production, coaches were also equipped with wheelchair lifts and a kneeling feature that lowered the first step height. These additions were part of the company plan to make the "New Look" coach more accessible to elderly and handicapped patrons.

Flxible "New Look" coaches have logged millions of service miles in cities such as New York, Los Angeles, Chicago, and Cleveland. The final "New Look" coach produced was delivered to the city of Akron, Ohio, on October 31, 1978.

Flxible Corporation's headquarters has been a part of the Delaware, Ohio, landscape since 1974.

Rohr Industries of Chula Vista, California, acquired Flxible in 1970. Rohr Flxible pioneered development of a new transit coach design that evolved into the Model 870 ADB (Advanced Design Bus). The "870" was designed to meet federal performance, safety, and accessibility standards.

For logistical and supply reasons, the Rohr Flxible corporate headquarters and final assembly line operations were transferred to Delaware, Ohio, in 1974, but Flxible maintained various manufacturing operations in the Loudonville facility.

The association with Rohr lasted but eight years. It sold Flxible to Grumman Allied Industries Incorporated, a wholly owned subsidiary of Grumman Corporation. As a wholly owned subsidiary of Grumman Allied Industries, Flxible became known as Grumman Flxible Corporation.

In April 1978 the first 870 ADB rolled off the assembly line. It was the first of 134 units delivered to MARTA in Atlanta, Georgia. Grumman Flxible quickly accumulated an order backlog of more than 2,500 units from 28 transit systems.

In Flxible's 70th year—1983—Flxible was acquired from Grumman by General Automotive Corporation (GAC) of Ann Arbor, Michigan. Today Flxible is a wholly owned subsidiary of GAC.

It has established itself as the largest manufacturer of transit buses in the United States, operating in almost every major city as well as in smaller metropolitan areas. With nearly one million square feet of manufacturing space in Delaware and Loudonville and more than 1,200 employees, Flxible manufactures and markets the METRO model advanced design bus in 30-, 35-, and 40-foot lengths.

In addition to bus manufacturing, Flxible operates the most extensive transit service parts distribution system in the industry, maintaining parts distribution centers in Loudonville, Los Angeles, Newark, Dallas, Seattle, and Atlanta.

The Flxible METRO advanced design bus represents more than 78 years of transportation innovation and development. The term "advanced design" is best represented by the METRO's combination of low maintenance costs and excellent operational reliability, as well as maximum passenger safety, convenience, and comfort. Low operating and maintenance costs result from the METRO's optimum balance of proven components and advanced design technology.

Flxible is well positioned to maintain its technological leadership for the 1990s and beyond with its recent introduction of new "clean-air" METRO models powered by compressed natural gas, clean diesel, and methanol. These models, featuring the first transit bus in the United States designed from the ground up to run exclusively on natural gas, will significantly improve the nation's air quality. The first production model was delivered to the Columbia Gas Company in Columbus.

The Flxible Corporation is continuing the proud tradition it has established over the years—transportation innovation, high quality, cost-effective products, and outstanding customer service and parts support.

SCHULER INCORPORATED

Because of its central location and proximity to so many major manufacturing centers, Columbus is an attractive and important international center for foreign companies. From the capital city these companies can reach most of their major customers in less than two hours flying time.

Schuler Incorporated is one such company. This international group of businesses whose products set the world standard has had a presence in Columbus since 1978, four years after the German company began operations in the United States. Today Schuler's Columbus office is headquarters for its sales, service, engineering, and project management efforts for markets throughout the United States and Canada.

Schuler was founded in Goeppingen, Germany, near Stuttgart, in 1839 by Louis Schuler and the business continues today in the hands of his descen-

dants. L. Schuler GmbH has grown into one of the world's leading suppliers of state-of-the-art metal-forming machine tools.

Schuler metal-stamping presses are used in such diverse applications as the manufacture of coins at the U.S. Mint (and 40 other mints throughout the world), rotor and stator laminations for large motors and generators, auto body panels, near-net-shape parts formed from solid steel such as axle shafts and gears, and even sections of 0-gauge model railroad track. Schuler is a major press supplier to leading automakers in Europe,

Schuler Incorporated's Columbus offices at 2222 South Third Street with new high-assembly bay.

South America, and Asia, as well as to the American Big Three automakers—General Motors, Ford, and Chrysler.

The Schuler Group of companies employs about 3,500 people worldwide and has its main manufacturing facilities in Goeppingen, Germany, and Sao Paulo, Brazil. A joint venture between L. Schuler of Germany and Prensas Schuler of Brazil, Schuler Incorporated of Columbus is truly an international company.

In 1992 Schuler will deliver the world's largest transfer press to a U.S. stamping plant. This six-station press for auto body panels will be 112 feet long and 48 feet high, including 17 feet under the floor, and will weigh 3,750 tons, making it one of the largest machine tools ever built.

One of Schuler Incorporated's recent thrusts is in the area of rebuilding and retrofitting presses with quick die-change capability. This automation feature allows operators to change press dies in a matter of minutes instead of hours, significantly improving a manufacturer's flexibility and productivity. Among its customers in this area are General Motors, Ford, Chrysler, and Honda in the United States.

Though Schuler has had offices in the United States only a few years, a small part of its 150-year-plus history, the parent company has had U.S. customers for many years. Columbus now serves as an ideal central locale for the continued growth of international companies such as Schuler.

A Schuler tri-axis transfer press with six die stations, at the Volkswagen plant in Wolfsburg, Germany.

ELECTRIC POWER EQUIPMENT COMPANY

"Anything from a wall plug to a power plant."

The statement takes in a lot of territory in the electrical field, but then so does the Electric Power Equipment Company. For more than 70 years the downtown Columbus company has made the claim stick from coast to coast.

EPE also is a company that epitomizes the best of Columbus: a hometown spirit that springs from its deep roots in the community, a history of growth and progress unmatched in its field, and most important, a dedication to service.

The three founders of EPE—A.B. Weinfeld, president and general manager; H.R. Hartman, vice president and secretary; and F.B. McWilliams, treasurer—correctly perceived in 1920 the power of electricity. It would, they believed, allow the nation to flex its industrial muscle, its communities to mature, its businesses to flourish, and the American home to enjoy the many conveniences we have today. Their confidence in the magic current has been borne out time and again in the intervening years.

The founders also established princi-

Electric Power Equipment Company takes pride in its design and installation projects.

ples for the company which never have been breached: principles such as pride in workmanship, dedication to performance, and quality service.

"What we sell is service," says President James C. McAtee. "Electric Power Equipment gladly accepts the challenge of the ever-increasing demand for electricity, and it takes pride in knowing that any project associated with the use of electrical energy is within its scope of service."

Home base for EPE is 60 East Spring Street, within a block of where the company was founded at 51 E. Chestnut Street. Years ago, McAtee says, the company not only was an electrical contractor; it was also a provider of a wide assortment of electrical equipment, including the wire andpoles it sold to the telephone company. In fact, EPE even erected poles for the telephone company and strung the wire, too.

Today the company maintains a multimillion-dollar inventory in 57,300 square feet of warehouse space. Stored inside are transformers, reels of cable, splicing and termination kits, safety switches, line hardware, circuit breakers, and a wide variety of other basic materials to speed a project to completion.

In central Ohio alone EPE has

completed more than 40,000 jobs. Take the Anheuser-Busch brewery, for example. EPE electricians were there in 1968 when the Columbus brewery was built. Since then the company has successfully completed some 175 electrical projects at the brewery, a testament to EPE's dedicated service and performance.

There are many customers who have returned to EPE again and again: Lazarus, Owens-Illinois/NEG, The Ohio State University, and Port Columbus International Airport. EPE also has served Ross Laboratories since 1923.

EPE installed 24 separate power systems in this office-warehousing complex that contains more than 3.5 million square feet.

Municipal services include the Refuse- and Coal-fired Municipal Electric Plant, a 90-megawatt generating facility on which EPE served as the prime electrical contractor.

On a national scale, EPE has been the contractor on U.S. post offices in Washington, Detroit, and Chicago. Other clients across the country include J.C. Penney Co.; Sears, Roebuck & Co.; Nestles Corp.; and Eastman Kodak in Rochester, New York.

"Since 1920 we have been generating a current of service that has never stopped," says McAtee. "We take pride in every installation, using the best materials and mechanics available.

"There is no glory in tackling an assignment if there is no pride in the outcome, and to EPE pride is performance and performance is service."

TOLEDO SCALE

Toledo Scale is the nation's largest supplier of weighing equipment with sales and service available worldwide. Toledo manufactures scales and systems ranging from the familiar supermarket scales and wrapping equipment and high-precision laboratory scales to industrial counting/weighing applications and scales weighing airplanes and freight trains as well as everything in between. The slogan "Honest Weight" resulted from the company's efforts early in the century to encourage the enactment of Weights & Measures legislation throughout the nation—efforts that successfully led to equitable standards.

Since the company began in 1901, it has always taken quality seriously. Today, Toledo scales are still in use from the era of the First World War, still weighing accurately, testifying to their long-term reliability.

This performance over more than nine decades has helped establish the company as the nation's largest supplier of weighing equipment with a strong worldwide presence. Toledo Scale be-

RIGHT: Counting scales and bar code printers are used in many industries.

BELOW: Toledo Scale headquarters is located in the Columbus suburb of Worthington.

came "Weighmaster to the World" . . . including sporting events in which weight is a factor. Equipment and services are supplied to world-class sporting events such as Pan Am, Goodwill, and Olympic Games.

Scales for Olympic competitions have been supplied since the Lake Placid Winter Games in 1932. Since then, Toledo Scale has been appointed the Official Supplier for the Montreal, Lake Placid, Los Angeles, and Seoul Olympics. For the 1992 Olympics to be held in Barcelona, Spain, Toledo will again furnish scales and services. Aside from the Games themselves, Toledo Scale supplies equipment to training and medical centers to help athletes prepare for competition.

The games in Seoul, Korea, required more than 125 scales and printers to cer-

tify the weight of athletes, equipment, and food. As in previous Olympics Toledo technicians acted as Weighmasters and will again at the 25th Olympiad in Barcelona.

WORTHINGTON-BASED
Founded by Henry Theobald in 1901 in Toledo, Ohio, Toledo Scale is currently headquartered in the Columbus suburb of Worthington, Ohio. Almost half of the company's 1,500 employees in the U.S. are in the Columbus area with two additional operations also in Worthington; a heavy capacity plant in Columbus; and a systems plant in Westerville. In the U.S. additional manufacturing plants are located in New York, South Carolina, and Wisconsin.

Toledo Scale's Worthington plant is a prime example of World Class Manufacturing. It was named one of America's 12 Best Plants by *Industry Week* magazine.

INNOVATION
Finite element analysis and other CAD techniques are used to achieve maximum efficiency in materials with a high strength-to-weight ratio. Automated manufacturing eliminates human errors and provides constant quality. Robotic welders and many other modern manufacturing techniques assure consistent product quality.

No longer can a leading manufacturer count on products that simply increase output and provide higher productivity to maintain leadership. Leaders must be innovators. They must apply technology to solving problems in new ways. And Toledo Scale leads the way in the weighing industry with many innovations.

Toledo's Weigh-In-Motion (WIM) product line includes a high-speed heavy vehicle WIM system that weighs vehicles at highway speeds and provides the speed and profile of the truck. Of special interest in the Columbus area is a prototype WIM system that was installed in the northbound lane of I-270 about one mile north of Morse Road. This site was selected by the Ohio Department of Transportation (ODOT) and approved by Toledo Scale. The installation was completed and opened for traf-

ABOVE: *Stainless steel bench/portable scales, indicators, and programmable controllers are useful in wet, corrosive environments such as the food and chemical industries.*

RIGHT: *A Toledo Scale weigh-in-motion (WIM) system can measure the weight and the speed of a vehicle that is traveling at highway speeds.*

fic in December 1988.

WIM systems are used to sort out and identify overweight trucks, and to gather statistical data on truck traffic for highway planning. Toledo WIM systems measure the dynamic forces of axles (produced by truck in motion) and convert them into equivalent static weights. Highway engineers agree that these dynamic forces contribute to premature road and bridge deterioration. This premature deterioration prompts increased enforcement efforts which can result in enormous savings as they become more effective. Toledo's WIM system represents a real breakthrough in high-speed weigh-in-motion technology.

Another recent innovation that has done much to improve scale quality and reliability applies digital transducer technology to weighing. Exclusive DigiTOL® load cells are used in virtually all Toledo scales. It's the next generation beyond conventional load cells, and provides improved performance in everyday use. A microprocessor is built into the DigiTOL® cell which monitors the scale load "history" and automatically corrects for errors caused by creep, nonlinearity, and temperature changes.

Toledo Automation Weighing Systems meet the need for modern industry to acquire information which can be used by a controlling function to make a decision that directly affects profits.

Weighing systems innovations include instruments and accessories for batching/filling, hazardous area weighing, checkweighing, and data acquisition.

CONTINUING EDUCATION

Toledo maintains a Training Center in Worthington with modern training tools and full-time instructors. The continuing education of service technicians assure Toledo customers of fast and expert service that minimizes downtime and service costs. Continuing education of distributors and salespeople assures customers that they will be dealing with trained people who represent the latest technology, fully capable of solving their problems.

In addition, customer training programs are offered in the Training Center or on location to cover maintenance and troubleshooting of their scales and systems.

With more than 250 locations and well over 1,000 factory trained technicians scattered throughout the U.S., Toledo provides service nationwide.

Available too are Aftermarket Services from a dedicated Worthington facility to quickly provide everything a user needs to keep their scales operating properly. Same-day turnaround on parts orders, printed circuit board and load cell exchanges, and electronic scale repair is standard. Toledo Service Engineers are also available to provide professional engineering support on

large computer-based systems.

Pioneers in the use of mini-computers for complex weighing and control systems, the firm manufactures powerful and efficient weighing systems.

TOLEDO SCALE WORLDWIDE

Mettler-Toledo, Inc., known as Toledo Scale, is a subsidiary of Ciba-Geigy, headquartered in Switzerland, and a part of the Mettler-Toledo Worldwide group.

Around the world, more than 6,500 people work for Mettler-Toledo. In addition to seven dedicated facilities in the United States, additional production plants are located in Germany, Switzerland, Mexico, Canada, Australia, and the People's Republic of China, with sales companies throughout Europe, the Americas, and the Pacific Rim.

From their Worthington headquarters, International Operations manage the marketing of Toledo products in the Americas and the Pacific Rim. They believe the rapidly expanding global economy will make international operations even more important in the years ahead. The Mettler-Toledo Worldwide group markets Toledo products throughout the rest of the world.

People in business and industry and grocery shoppers everywhere are familiar with Toledo Scale. Whatever the product—from feathers to freight trains— the odds are high that Toledo scales have been measuring their "Honest Weight" values for nearly a century.

TS TRIM INDUSTRIES INCORPORATED

When it comes to producing a quality product, TS Trim Industries Incorporated takes a back seat to no one—except Honda. TTI, as the company is known in the industry, is a major manufacturer of seat coverings, door trim panels, headliners, and other interior trim parts for Civics and Accords made by Honda of America Manufacturing in Marysville and East Liberty, Ohio, as well as Honda of Canada Manufacturing.

The story of TTI is one of impressive growth, fostered by the high caliber of its work force, the efficiency and flexibility of its production system, and the excellence of its automotive products. Since its founding in the fall of 1986, TTI has become the largest private-industry employer in Canal Winchester and subsequently Athens, Ohio, where its two manufacturing facilities are located.

Corporate headquarters for TTI are at 59 Gender Road, Canal Winchester, in a factory once owned by the R.G. Barry Company, the slipper maker. A new life was given to the property when it was purchased by Tokyo Seat Company Ltd. of Japan and its equity partner in TTI, American Honda Motors. The 73,000-square-foot Canal Winchester factory on eight acres was totally renovated to TTI's specifications to create what is now a modern, 119,000-square-foot production facility. In addition, a second plant of 102,000 square feet has been built in Athens and has been in operation since 1988.

The factories are equipped with the newest, most innovative equipment. The Gerber fabric cutter, the automatic/stand-up sewing machines, and the presses used in the door lining assembly lines are all examples of the high technology that has been installed to ensure quality and efficiency on the production lines.

Although renovation was still in progress, the first door liner was produced on August 11, 1987, followed by the first trim cover in September and the first headliner in November. Today the Canal Winchester factory manufactures more than 1,400 sets of door liners, 1,100 sets of headliners, and 360 trim covers each day. All are shipped directly to Honda except the trim covers; they are sent to Bellemar Parts Industries near Bellefontaine, Ohio, where they are assembled on the seat frames before going to the two nearby Honda plants. At Canal Winchester TTI has a quality work force that has been drawn primarily from Columbus and the suburban/rural area just a few miles southeast of Ohio's capital city. Beginning with just a handful of associates in 1986, the number has grown to more than 500. To accommodate them and their workplace, the factory has been expanded twice, with further expansion

RIGHT & BELOW: TTI is a major manufacturer of seat coverings, door trim panels, headliners, and other interior trim parts.

projected on its 55 adjacent acres.

TTI's Athens plant began production in November 1988. There the dedicated work force, which has increased to more than 300 associates since, cuts and sews only trim covers, which are also shipped to Bellemar.

Just as any other manufacturing company, TTI pays the utmost attention to the quality of its products. Even after careful inspection during the manufacturing and assembly process, TTI's highly-skilled quality control associates utilize statistical techniques to assure customer satisfaction. Quality is measured in parts per million rather than percentages so commonly used in other companies (1000 ppm = .1 percent).

TTI is proud of its achievements in its industry and of its Ohio associates. It is confident of continued growth in the dynamic central Ohio business climate.

WORTHINGTON INDUSTRIES

Worthington Industries, headquartered in Columbus, is a leading manufacturer of metal and plastic products. From 25 manufacturing facilities in 10 states and Canada, the firm markets its products to a wide range of customers in the automotive, appliance, electrical, communication, construction, office equipment, machinery, and leisure time industries.

Founded by John H. McConnell, the chairman and chief executive officer, the company is a perfect example of the free enterprise system at work in America.

McConnell grew up in a small town in West Virginia where many of his relatives worked in the local steel mill. Unable to afford college after high school, he also became a steelworker. Following a stint in the Navy during World War II, he attended Michigan State University with the help of the G.I. Bill and graduated with a degree in business. He then returned to the steel industry as a sales representative covering the central Ohio territory.

During this period McConnell noted that the major steel mills were gearing their operations toward large-tonnage orders, while many steel users had a growing requirement for smaller, more specialized orders. He recognized a need and an opportunity for an intermediary, a processor, between the basic producers and the final users of steel.

In 1955, starting from the basement of a small apartment in Worthington, the company was founded to fill this specialized niche. To buy the steel for his first order, McConnell borrowed $600 from a bank, using his family's 1952 Oldsmobile as collateral. He then resold the steel for a small profit, marking the beginning of Worthington Industries.

In the company's first year of business, one piece of equipment and five employees produced sales of $342,000 and a net profit of $11,000. Today Worthington employs more than 6,000 people, sales are approaching one billion dollars, and the company is very profitable.

Worthington is the largest processor of flat-rolled steel in the United States. It also has expanded into several other businesses, such as the manufacture of low-pressure cylinders used to hold gases and metal grid systems for suspended ceilings. Worthington also makes injection-molded plastic parts and precision metal components for automobiles and appliances, and a variety of steel castings for rail cars and undercarriages for mass transit cars.

Worthington has always followed a rather simple philosophy based on the Golden Rule, "treating customers, employees, investors, and suppliers as the firm would like to be treated." Worthington is widely recognized for its innovative employee benefit and training programs. Its nonunion work force receives almost one-half of their compensation in the form of cash profit sharing. Paid quarterly, cash profit sharing offers each employee a stake in the success of the company by emphasizing bottom line performance. Team success takes precedence over individual honors.

As mentioned, Worthington's tie to Columbus goes back to its very beginning. Today more than 2,000 people are employed in the central Ohio area alone.

Much of the company's success is attributable to its people. The work ethic in Columbus and the surrounding area is one of the best in the country. Worthington Industries has only scratched the surface of its potential and is expected to grow rapidly in the years ahead. Columbus provides businesses like Worthington and its people a great place to grow.

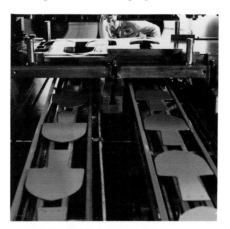

LEFT: The development of new products and capabilities is vital to Worthington's growth. For instance, it has expanded production of developed steel blanks, which can be formed by customers into finished products. Worthington blanks, such as those for shovel heads, are made of 100 percent usable material of assured quality and provide customers with significant cost savings.

BELOW: New tension slitters have been added to several of Worthington's steel-processing plants. These state-of-the-art lines can process wide, light-gauge coils as well as improve width tolerances and provide a tight wrap with virtually no surface defects.

HONDA OF AMERICA MANUFACTURING INCORPORATED

In the fall of 1990 the first Honda product completely designed, developed, and manufactured in the United States— the Honda Accord station wagon—rolled off the assembly line at the Honda of America Manufacturing (HAM) automobile plant at Marysville, Ohio, for shipment to customers in the United States, Japan, Canada, and Europe.

The debut of the Accord station wagon marked more than a decade of commitment, investment, and partnership between HAM, the State of Ohio, and central Ohio communities. It also reflected the growing capabilities of Honda associates and facilities in central Ohio as an important part of

ABOVE: The Honda Accord, manufactured in Honda's Marysville automobile plant, was the best-selling car in America in 1989 and 1990.

RIGHT: Honda's newest manufacturing facility, the East Liberty automobile plant, pioneered the use in the United States of water-borne paint for reduced emissions and a more environmentally friendly approach to automobile production.

Honda's international operations.

Although the business founded by Soichiro Honda in 1948 was small, its vision was international. From the beginning Honda forged a philosophy that commanded the young company to "maintain an international viewpoint" and manufacture products "of the highest efficiency yet at a reasonable price for worldwide customer satisfaction."

By 1991 Honda's investment in Ohio manufacturing totaled more than $2 billion as Honda of America Manu-

facturing grew to include two automobile plants and an engine plant in addition to the original motorcycle plant. With these four plants HAM created 10,000 jobs, becoming central Ohio's largest private employer.

As the first manufacturing facility built in the United States by Honda, the $35-million, 260,000-square-foot Marysville motorcycle plant began operations on September 10, 1979. The plant started with 64 associates who built the first motorcycle, a CR250® Elsinore motocross off-road machine.

In the next decade HAM associates built many of Honda's largest and most sophisticated motorcycles for customers in the United States and for export as well. The motorcycle for which HAM is best known is the Gold Wing, manufactured exclusively at the Marysville plant and exported to 15 countries, including Japan.

Demonstrating a commitment to continuous improvement, a $10-million renovation was completed at the motorcycle plant in 1987, making the facility among the most efficient and flexible in the world. With a total investment of $62 million, the plant employs about 380 associates who make 60,000 motorcycles and utility vehicles per year.

No sooner had the first motorcycle rolled off the assembly line in 1979 than the decision was made to construct an automobile plant next to the motorcycle facility. Ground was broken for the Marysville automobile plant in December 1980. Production began on November 1, 1982, with the Accord four-door sedan.

The success of HAM associates in building an automobile of quality equal to that produced in Japan led to an expansion of the Marysville automobile plant to 3.1 million square feet, increasing the company's investment to $962 million. Production of the Civic four-door sedan began in July 1986. HAM built its one-millionth car on April 8, 1988, as production reached a new high of 360,000 cars per year.

Earlier that year the efforts of HAM associates again made international headlines as the first export of U.S.-built Honda automobiles to Japan was shipped in March. That history-making car—the Accord two-door Coupe—is manufactured exclusively in Marysville. It became the top-selling U.S.-made car in Japan in its first year. By the end of 1989 the Honda Accord also had reached the top of the U.S. car sales list, becoming the best-selling car in the United States for the first time, a posi-

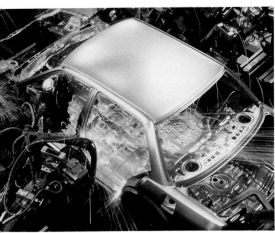

TOP LEFT: As part of its regular manufacturing duties, the Anna, Ohio, engine plant produces brake and suspension components for assembly in three different Honda auto plants in the United States and Canada.

LEFT: Honda's East Liberty automobile plant features a new generation of flexible spot-welding robot systems developed by Honda Engineering as well as the first use in the United States automobile industry of laser welding for mass production.

ABOVE: The Honda Gold Wing motorcycle, manufactured exclusively in Ohio since 1980, is shipped to customers in 15 countries.

tion it maintained into the 1990s.

Honda further increased its commitment to U.S. manufacturing by unveiling plans in March 1984 to construct an engine plant near the small town of Anna, Ohio. Originally designed to manufacture the four-cylinder Gold Wing motorcycle engine, the facility was soon expanded to include the Civic 1.5-liter four-cylinder engine, making HAM the first company to produce both motorcycle and automobile engines in the United States. The first GL1200 motorcycle engine was produced on July 22, 1985; the Civic engine production followed on September 23, 1986.

In 1987 a further expansion of the engine plant was started to allow full-scale production of Accord engines as well as drivetrains and suspension and brake components for both Civic and Accord models. With a total investment of $600 million, the engine plant supplies 500,000 engines and drivetrain components a year for HAM's three other manufacturing plants and the automobile plant at Honda of Canada Manufacturing. Unique to Honda, the engine plant embraces under one roof operations performed at seven Honda

plants in Japan.

When it began mass production in December 1989, the East Liberty automobile plant became known for its low emissions water-borne paint technology and environmentally friendly site development. Inside the plant, industry observers discovered a unique blend of modern Honda manufacturing methods (i.e., laser welding and advanced automation systems) with a comfortable working environment for HAM associates. In fact, more than 800 suggestions from Marysville automobile plant associates were implemented in the design of the 1.4-million-square-foot facility. The East Liberty automobile plant employs 1,800 associates with a production capacity of 150,000 cars per year.

On September 17, 1987, Honda an-

nounced its five-part strategy for establishing a self-reliant motor vehicle company in the United States with resources to compete in the world market. The main points of the strategy included the export of 70,000 HAM-built cars to Japan and other countries, increased U.S. research and development activities, an increase in domestic content to 75 percent, expansion of Honda's production engineering in the United States, and expansion of manufacturing capacity with the construction of a second U.S. automobile plant and further expansion of the Anna engine plant.

In 1990 some 20,000 cars were exported to Japan, South Korea, Taiwan, Israel, and Canada. A year later the Accord station wagon was exported to Europe. HAM's domestic supplier network grew to more than 240 original-equipment U.S. suppliers by 1991, bringing the domestic content of HAM-built cars to about 75 percent.

Honda's determination to be a leader in quality, an innovator in associate development, and a partner in the community has brought it to the forefront of American industry. By increasing its capabilities in the United States to meet and exceed customer expectations, Honda of America associates are building a solid future in the global motor vehicle industry.

EPRO INCORPORATED

The hand-manufacturing process might be too slow for some entrepreneurs, but not for Epro President Suzanne S. Edgar. Even with the increasing demand for the company's rustic product, she continues to produce tile by hand when mechanization would be the easier way to meet demand.

"Hand-made quality is what is so special about Epro's products," she says. "That's our competitive edge. I don't ever want to change that."

The national competition is narrow but stiff. Although there are more than 40 tile manufacturers in the marketplace, Epro has carved out an enviable niche. It is the largest producer of handmade tile in the United States, both in terms of sales revenue and the number of tiles produced annually.

The uniqueness of the product and Epro's ability to customize every order has caught the eye of numerous notables over the years. Among Epro's customers are Loretta Lynn, Henry Mancini, and Lee Iaccoca. Clint Eastwood came to

Epro for tile for his swimming pool. Paul Newman had peach-colored tile installed in his Jacuzzi.

A decade or so ago a sheik ordered cypress green Epro tile for the foyer of his home in Saudi Arabia. His foyer spread out over 7,600 square feet. It is one of the largest residential orders in the company's history.

The largest commercial order was one for some 350,000 tiles to cover about 80,000 square feet of a shopping mall in Lafayette, Louisiana. Another large project can be seen in Nashville, Tennessee, where visitors to the Opryland Hotel are greeted with Epro's Antiqua Washington Square tiles from its Heritage Collection.

The Heritage Collection is one of five in the company's product line, which also includes Gallery, Sandstone, A La Carte, and Chameleon. All are handcrafted, of course, but each offers a variety of colors and shapes. Names such as Windsor, Laredo, Regency, Washington Square, and Tavern all indicate a particular shape and size of tile for floors, walls, and countertops.

Edgar believes ceramic tile consumption is growing in the United States "because it is being used as a fashion

statement," particularly in the home, where 70 percent of the company's business lies. Epro's growth depends on its ability to spot the trends in styles and colors, but Edgar is confident that the company "is always going to be in the forefront of color first, then style."

The business of making ceramic tile begins in Ava, Ohio, where shale, plentiful in Ohio, is dug from company-owned pits. The shale is ground before it is shipped to Westerville, where it is mixed in a pugmill with water, color, and chemicals to make the clay stronger and fire harder.

After a vacuum pump sucks the air out of the clay, it is extruded into blocks, or slugs. These are put into plaster dies and ram pressed into flat tiles. After the clay is ram pressed for durability the clay is hand trimmed into its many shapes. It is during this process that Epro craftsmen occasionally place their "signature" on a floor tile with a thumbprint impression as they trim the tile. The thumbprint is a distinguishing mark found only in Epro floor products.

Each tile takes on a personality of its own for another reason. Because the dies are made of plaster, the dies wear each time they are used and create an ever-so-slight variation in the tile. Each die is good for about 3,000 impressions.

After the tile is hand trimmed it is placed in a dryer at 200 degrees for about eight hours. Then it is ready to be glazed or fired.

A thick coating of clear or colored glaze is applied to ensure durability and long-lasting beauty. The lighter tones and pastels are the most popular, Edgar says, but in recent years there has been a trend to more blues and greens. Some tiles also bear hand-painted herbal or floral motifs, adding splashes of color to a cream or white background.

In the final step the tiles are placed in a tunnel kiln that never gets a day off: It operates 24 hours a day, 7 days a week, 365 days a year. In the kiln the tiles are fired at 2,000 degrees for about 18 hours, hardening the surface to an indestructible finish that maintains its gloss and resists wear a variety of environments.

"In every step of the process you can see what makes this a very sound prod-

Epro's handmade tile adds to the charm of a Brewery District restaurant and cheese shop in Columbus.

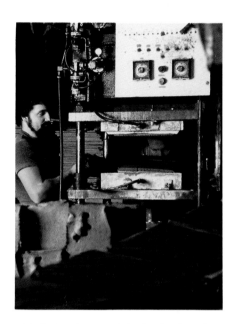

ABOVE: At its Westerville facility Epro's crafts-men make ceramic tile using natural clays dug from shale pits in southern Ohio.

RIGHT: Epro floor, wall, and counter tile is great for bathrooms, kitchens, family rooms, sunrooms, pool areas, and porches.

In this computer age of perfection, where products made by robots and other sophisticated machines are greatly admired for their uniformity, it is refreshing to discover a company that proudly boasts that no two of its tile are alike.

At its 40,000-square-foot Westerville plant, Epro Incorporated employees make ceramic tile the old-fashioned way—by hand. The end result is a product as unique as the techniques and materials employed in making it.

Edgar's father, Jerry Stilson, bought the firm in 1973 and more than doubled its capacity. At that time Edgar was in her junior year at Purdue University in the school of chemical engineering, but had to leave before her father died in 1977. She took over the company after his death and finished her degree in business from Otterdein.

Since then Epro has expanded the business several times over, "continuing to grow because we continue to bring unique, innovative products to the marketplace," Edgar says.

It is the attention to quality and detail—the hand-manufactured process, the customized service, and the creative colors and techniques—that has made Epro the nation's premier manufacturer of handcrafted ceramic tile. The dedication to excellence continues in the 1990s as Epro shows the way—the old-fashioned way.

Thousands of custom-made Epro tiles were used to create this beautiful mosaic fountain at the Missouri Botanical Garden in St. Louis.

uct," says Edgar. She adds, "Every order basically is custom made; that's one of the advantages of being a relatively small operation" with just 55 employees.

The business came from small beginnings. Epro was founded in March 1963 by A. Reif Blackburn, a ceramic engineer, and Harold Dawson, a mechanical engineer, with the idea of producing handmade tiles. Epro is actually an acronym for Earth Products or Engineered Products, either one of which the founders were ready to fall back on should the tile venture not pan out.

But it did. The first products were sold a year after the company's founding, and slowly Epro began to grow, first with unglazed products and then with glazed tiles in 1967.

MTM AMERICAS, INCORPORATED
PHARMACEUTICAL INTERMEDIATES DIVISION

Today's cost-conscious manufacturers are seeking opportunities to reduce raw material inventories, manage labor expenditures, shave production time while improving quality, and provide better customer service. In the pharmaceutical industry, a Columbus company has emerged to assist its clients in achieving all these goals.

The name, MTM Americas, Incorporated, is relatively new to the community, but its rich heritage began a generation ago at The Ohio State University. Since 1980 its home has been on 147 attractive acres at 1979 Atlas Street.

MTM Americas manufactures organic intermediates and finished products for the pharmaceutical industry. It is also the producer of fine organic chemicals for use in agriculture and general industry.

Much of the work MTM Americas performs is for industrial clients who are ready to take a new product from the research laboratory to commercial production. Chemists and chemical engineers at MTM Americas work together in customizing a production process to the customer's specifications for quantity, quality, and delivery. The chemists develop the synthetic method for producing the product; the chemical

The MTM Americas plant, located on 147 acres, was built in 1979.

engineers adapt it to the plant.

The creative and flexible capabilities of MTM Americas also allows clients to look upon MTM Americas as an extension of their own manufacturing facilities. Under a typical contract arrangement, for example, the client provides MTM Americas with the product specifications and manufacturing process. In a toll conversion, the client provides the production process, key raw materials, and specifications, while MTM Americas blends in its manufacturing expertise.

The original enterprise—Chemical Samples Company—was a blend between an OSU chemistry professor, Dr. Kenneth Greenlee, and his student, Vincent Wiley, who took a World War II research effort and turned it into a business in 1963. Chemical Samples built its reputation on supplying specialty organic chemicals and analytical standards for government, university, and industrial research laboratories.

In the early 1970s the company became Chemsampco, Incorporated, and developed considerable expertise in producing pheromones—chemical substances created to be sexually attractive to specific insects but disruptive to their reproductive cycles. Pheromones are an important biological alternative to insecticides in agriculture.

One of Chemsampco's prime customers was Albany International, a

Fine organic chemicals for agriculture and general industry are produced at MTM Americas' facility.

fibers company which acquired Chemsampco in June 1978. A major expansion was launched, including the construction in 1979 of the Atlas Street plant. When the facility opened in January 1980, David Wiley, Vincent's son, was plant manager, and it became the chemical division of AI.

Although in 1981 additional acres surrounding the plant were purchased for expansion, a year later AI decided to sell the division. It was acquired in 1983 by Essex Chemical Corporation and the name was changed once more to Orsynex, Incorporated.

The goal of Orsynex was to build a custom manufacturing business for pharmaceutical, agricultural, and special industrial contract sales, and once again the business was enlarged, along with the property.

Essex was acquired by Dow Chemical Company in late 1987, and in July 1989 Dow sold Orsynex to Biodor U.S. Holding. A year later the business had yet another name: MTM Americas. The new owner is MTM Plc, a large British chemical company.

As MTM Americas entered the decade of the 1990s, it was still growing in a community known for fostering creative enterprise. MTM Americas is proud of its role in the achievements of the Discovery City.

WORTHINGTON FOODS

As the world's largest producer of vegetable protein foods, Worthington Foods is well positioned to serve the growing market of health-conscious consumers who are taking greater interest in their dietary choices.

Once considered a niche marketer of specialty foods, the company is now catering to the eating preferences of Americans who seek to lower their intake of cholesterol, saturated fat, and calories.

Worthington Foods began operations in 1939 in a two-story frame house on the east edge of Worthington under the name Special Foods, Inc. The original concept of the company's founder, Dr. George T. Harding, Sr., was to provide vegetarian food products to meet the dietary and health needs of the Seventh-day Adventist Church, of which he was a member.

The fledgling company's first products—Proast and Numete—were peanut and wheat-based vegetarian foods developed in the kitchens of

Worthington Foods is the world's largest manufacturer and marketer of textured vegetable protein products.

nearby Harding Hospital. The company pioneered and patented the process of spinning filaments of soy protein into meat-like fibers.

During World War II another of the company's initial products, Choplets, was eagerly snapped up by the general consumer when meat was rationed. Immediately after the war, when the company adopted the name of its home community, it became the first U.S. company to produce frozen meat analogs. Today Worthington Foods is one of the world's largest producers of textured vegetable protein.

In the 1970s Worthington Foods introduced the concept of cholesterol-free meat substitutes into the nation's supermarkets under its popular Morningstar Farms label. Today this product line—including its Scramblers cholesterol-free egg product—is found in the frozen breakfast section of more than 90 percent of the grocery stores in the United States.

To meet the needs of its growing market, the company continues its aggressive development of foods low in saturated fat and cholesterol, products high in protein and fiber, and packaged goods offering the right combination of

Products from the Morningstar Farms line offer a delicious low-fat/low-cholesterol alternative to bacon, sausage, hamburger, and eggs.

superior nutritional quality, consumer convenience, and great taste.

Worthington Foods currently markets nearly 200 different healthy foods and beverages nationally under its four brand lines:

• The Morningstar Farms brand is the only full line of cholesterol-free products sold in U.S. supermarkets that provide lower-fat, lower-calorie alternatives to whole eggs and processed meats.

• The Worthington brand, available in specialty food stores, offers more than 50 meatless products that are generally accepted and used by vegetarians.

• The La Loma brand complements the Worthington product line by offering vegetarian consumers in the health and specialty food markets an even greater assortment of meat substitutes.

• The Natural Touch brand meets the needs of health food shoppers seeking meatless and other healthy products free of artificial additives, flavors, and colors.

With efforts to expand the availability and use of its products into restaurants and institutions— as well as international markets— Worthington Foods intends to maintain its industry-leading position with nutritionally aware consumers as it enters the next century with confidence and conviction.

BORDEN, INC.

Borden, Inc., which worldwide sells nearly $8 billion annually in food, packaging, nonfood consumer products, and industrial products maintains its administrative and four operating divisions headquarters in Columbus.

The company's presence in Ohio's capital began in 1929, when a milk and ice cream plant was purchased. Today more than 1,000 people work in the Borden building downtown and an additional 150 employees work in suburban Columbus in Borden's science and technology facility and corporate benefits office.

The company also has two manufacturing facilities in Columbus, employing almost 700 people: the Joyce Avenue ice cream plant, which replaced the old Columbus ice cream facility,

More than 1,000 Borden employees work at the company's 34-story administrative headquarters in downtown Columbus.

and Columbus Coated Fabrics, which makes wallcoverings. Worldwide the company employs more than 40,000 people and has 250 plants in more than 30 countries.

Borden ranks number one in the world in pasta, wallcoverings, adhesives, and vinyl foodwrap films; number one in U.S. dairy products; number two in salty snacks in North America; and number one or two (nationally or regionally) in 27 U.S. niche grocery products categories.

The company was founded in 1857 by Gail Borden, Jr., a man also recognized as the "Father of the Modern Dairy Industry." As an inventor, Borden developed a process for preserving milk by condensation in a vacuum. His product—condensed milk—led Borden into the dairy business.

A dramatic expansion of the firm began in 1928, with the purchase of more than 100 companies in just two years. Most were small regional dairies, but the acquisitions also included two large ice cream companies, several cheese producers, and Merrill-Soule, the premier manufacturer of whole milk powder. With the latter Borden acquired NoneSuch mincemeat—its first nonmilk food.

"Elsie the Cow" was introduced in the mid-1930s in medical journal ads as a cartoon spokescow for the purity and wholesomeness of Borden dairy products. "Elsie" has since become the most widely used food packaging symbol in the world and Borden's beloved ambassador of good will.

From these roots, Borden has achieved leadership positions in each of its six carefully chosen business areas:

Pasta: Borden's world leadership in pasta includes operations in the United States, Canada, Brazil, and Italy. Its flagship Creamette brand is the first and only full-line pasta sold nationally, supplemented by premium domestic and imported pastas, and by a coast-to-coast network of acquired regional brands and companies.

Snacks: Borden entered the salty snacks business in 1964 when it bought Wise Foods, a leading East Coast manufacturer. As in pasta, Borden assem-

Gail Borden, who founded the company in Burrville, Connecticut, on May 11, 1857, is recognized as the "father of the modern dairy industry."

bled a network of strong regional snack companies across North America and complements their locally popular brands by rolling out selected snack brands everywhere, including Krunchers! and Cottage Fries potato chips, Wise ready-to-eat popcorn, and Cheez Doodles corn puffs. Internationally Borden is the biggest maker of sweet baked snacks and specialty breads in West Germany, and has major salty snacks operations in Spain and the United Kingdom.

Niche Grocery: A total of 40 U.S. brands underlie Borden's leading category positions. Borden participates in just two categories that exceed the billion-dollar mark in annual retail industry sales and instead aims at leadership in small to mid-size categories, collectively amassing a large business while also providing stability and diversity. Among Borden's brands are such favorites as Eagle Brand sweetened condensed milk—Gail Borden's invention—Cracker Jack caramel popcorn and peanuts, ReaLemon reconstituted lemon juice, Wyler's bouillon, Cremora nondairy creamer, Classico pasta sauce, and Lite-line reduced calorie cheese. Many of the same products are sold in Canada, Europe, and the Far East.

• Dairy: Borden downsized its U.S. dairy business in late 1989, but remained the number-one U.S. producer.

ABOVE: "Elsie the Cow" was introduced as a company symbol in the 1930s and came to life at the Borden exhibit at the 1939 New York World's Fair.

RIGHT: Although it entered the pasta business in the United States as recently as 1979, Borden is today the largest producer of pasta in the world. Creamette is the company's flagship brand.

The company concentrates its fluid milk business regionally in the South and West, while maintaining ice cream operations there and throughout the East and Midwest as well.

• NonFood Consumer: Borden focuses on do-it-yourself products for home improvement. The company's top position in world wallcoverings includes major operations in the United States, Canada, and Europe. Side by side, Borden sells two of North America's best-known brands of consumer adhesives—the Elmer's

family and Krazy Glue.

• Films and Adhesives: In addition to its world leadership in adhesives for the forest products industry and vinyl foodwrap films, Borden has strong positions around the world in foundry and specialty phenolic resins and in specialty wood adhesives, and it produces high-technology coatings for fiber optics and other emerging, fast-growing end uses.

In 1989 Borden launched a plant expansion, modernization, and consolidation program to become a low-cost producer in each business by 1992, funded by a record level of capital expenditures. Part of the savings were slated for more aggressive advertising and market support for the company's new breadth of national and regional brands.

Borden's unique "SQP Program" focuses on Safety, Quality, and Performance. SQP created a partnership between managers and employees to improve performance at the plant level by enabling employees to participate directly in making changes for the better. Under the program, specific targets for safety, quality, and productivity perfor-

Borden's products are responsible for nearly $8 billion in annual sales throughout the world.

mance are set at each plant and shared with employees.

Employee teamwork is fundamental, and suggestions are solicited and acted on quickly. After tough safety and quality minimums are met, the dollar savings from productivity gains are shared with employees through awards of up to several hundred dollars per person.

Borden's approach to social responsibility includes:

• Equal employment opportunity: Borden has affirmative action hiring and promotion goals at each location as well as for the company as a whole.

• Minority purchasing initiatives: Borden was one of the first companies in the United States to voluntarily establish such a program.

• Charitable contributions: Grants from the Borden Foundation and direct corporate funds support health and human services organizations, civic programs, youth organizations, educational programs and institutions, the arts, and other cultural activities.

As Borden moves through the 1990s, it will maintain its emphasis on profitable growth, in the United States and internationally; on meeting its responsibilities to employees and shareholders; and on the commitment to customers—"If It's Borden, It's Got to Be Good!"

AKZO COATINGS, INCORPORATED

On a quiet residential street just a few minutes northeast of downtown Columbus is a company that few would know is one of the largest suppliers of quality industrial finishes in North America. Fewer still would suspect that it has been an important part of the Columbus business community for more than 100 years.

Of course the business wasn't always known as Akzo Coatings, Incorporated. Nor has it always been located on a 15-acre site at 1313 Windsor Avenue. But, it has a proud heritage for excellence that is recognized throughout the world.

Akzo is the top supplier of coil coatings in the United States. That may not mean much to most people, but coil coated products are all around us every day. They are as common at home, at school, and at our place of work as the light bulb.

That venetian blind in the office? It's probably made from coated steel coils. In fact, coil coating is a process created in the 1930s for the manufacture of venetian blinds. What followed were applications for refrigerators, washers and dryers and a host of other major and small appliances, as well as lunch boxes, file cabinets, pencil sharpeners, water heaters, and even entire buildings.

Akzo Coatings, Incorporated, is located at 1313 Windsor Avenue, just a few minutes northeast of downtown Columbus.

Building products is the largest application for high-quality coil coatings. The market includes building panel and roof applications for the agricultural, architectural, pre-engineered, and residential sectors. All of these are served by Akzo products.

The manufacturers of these many varied products buy coils of metal that have been coated to their specifications, thus eliminating the need to paint their products after they have been fabricated. As well as being both efficient and economical, coil coating is an environmentally friendly process as there are no emissions into the atmosphere.

Taking the process back another step, then, it is Akzo which provides the coil coaters with a wide variety of coatings, from long-lasting, sun-resistant products for outdoor use to flexible paint in decorator colors for a home freezer manufacturer.

The Akzo story begins in Columbus before the Model T and the Wright Brothers, on December 24, 1888. On that Christmas Eve Oliver Orr, Clarence Hanna, and John Abbott incorporated the Orr, Hanna and Abbott Company "for the purpose of manufacturing and selling paints, colors, varnishes, and painters' sundries, and dealing in the same." Clarence Hanna and his brother, James, who was named president of the new company, were former paint salesmen in Cleveland for the Sherwin-Williams Co.

The first office for Orr, Hanna and

Akzo is the country's top supplier of coil coatings.

Abbott was at 31 West Broad Street, across from what is now the Palace Theatre. Within two years of the company's founding, however, the Orr name was dropped and shortly thereafter, the Abbott name was gone, too. On June 25, 1899, the Hanna Paint Company was created by the brothers. It would be a half-century before the name was changed again.

It was, with only minor setbacks, the beginning of very prosperous years for the paint company. Just before the turn of the century Hanna Paint acquired a new plant at 111 East Long Street, the quality of its product became renowned, and Hanna's Green Seal brand of paints dominated a market that stretched into seven states beyond Ohio. Hanna salesmen were everywhere, it seemed, pitching exterior and interior paints for the home.

During this same period another Hanna brother, Walter, had been building the Columbus Varnish Company. It

ABOVE & RIGHT: Akzo's coil coatings have application for a wide range of products from large and small appliances to entire buildings.

billion worldwide. Hanna Chemical Coatings became a unit of Akzo Coatings, Inc., and one of 26 Akzo Coatings operations in North America, with headquarters in Louisville.

After a century under the Hanna name, the company has entered a new era with international ramifications. For example, the unique qualities of Akzo Coatings has led to a licensing agreement with the People's Republic of China for future manufacturing operations there.

made industrial finishes for "such manufactured items as automobiles, appliances, furniture, metal containers, and aircraft," according to the "Marketing Guide to the Paint Industry." Among its customers were the Columbus Buggy Works, Belmont Casket Company, and the Hanna Paint Company.

Between 1915 and 1930, however, the varnish company's business declined. Columbus Varnish was acquired by Hanna Paint on January 15, 1930, 13 months after Walter Hanna died, and operated under its own name as a wholly owned subsidiary. The date marked the entry of Hanna Paint into the industrial marketplace.

The company took a twisting road to the 1940s. James Hanna retired, Walter and Clarence were dead, as was Clarence's son, Robert, who had succeeded James as president. The firm's stock was sold to the Dean & Barry Company, but before World War II began Walter S. Hanna, Jr., bought back Hanna Paint and its subsidiary, Columbus Varnish. Once again the organization became the Hanna Paint Manufacturing Company.

World War II brought profound changes, not only at Hanna but throughout the entire paint industry. Wartime shortages of raw materials led to the development of synthetic substitutes and paint formulation became more a science than an art. After the war Hanna took advantage of its new discoveries to

become a major factor in the industrial coatings marketplace of the Midwest. For example, Hanna supplied almost 80 percent of the white enamel to the toothpaste tube industry.

In 1954 Hanna built one of the most modern coatings plants at its present site. Also constructed at the facility was a large development laboratory to explore ever-expanding coatings technology. Because of its increasing emphasis on industrial finishes, the firm's name was changed once again, in 1969, to Hanna Chemical Coatings Corporation.

In March 1985 Hanna became a subsidiary of Reliance Universal, Incorporated, a major paint manufacturer based in Louisville, Kentucky, and an operating company of Dallas-based Tyler Corp. Four years later Tyler sold its Reliance unit to Akzo N.V., a Dutch-based chemical company with sales of more than $9

Breakthrough products, which are still marketed under the Hanna brand name, include Trinar® protection for buildings and Ceram-A-Sil®, a fade-resistant coating. These products are what make Akzo Coatings the industry pacesetter.

Metal Construction News cited the Jacksonville, Florida, Landing as one of the top metal building and component projects of the 1980s. The roof panels for the waterside retail center were coated with terra cotta-colored Ceram-A-Sil® to resist fading in the sun. Hanna Trinar® finishes can be found on the roofs of the architecturally stunning Swan and Dolphin hotels at Disney World.

Akzo Coatings, its products a pinnacle of discovery, is proud to continue a tradition of more than 100 years in the Discovery City.

PHOTONIC INTEGRATION RESEARCH, INCORPORATED

A marriage of the research capabilities of Battelle Memorial Institute with the Nippon Telegraph and Telephone Corporation and the backing of Mitsubishi Corporation led to the creation in Columbus of Photonic Integration Research, Incorporated.

PIRI was established in July 1987 at Battelle's Columbus headquarters to develop for commercial use optical integrated circuit technology. Tadashi Miyashita, a Japanese trained physicist from Hokkaido, Japan, was elected to be the first president of the joint venture.

Optical integrated circuits are similar to fiber optical cables, only they do more, according to Miyashita, whose award-winning expertise is in optical-fiber technology. "Fiber optical cable transmits signals from point to point, like copper cable," he says. The devices that PIRI is developing split the message-carrying signals into different wavelengths. Each wavelength has a different capability.

For example, the spectrum of the wavelength known as the red band carries voice transmissions, while the blue band carries video, Miyashita says. Splitting and then merging these wavelengths allows more messages to be sent on one signal.

Applications are expected to be in computers, automobile sensing systems, telecommunications networks, aerospace, and defense applications.

Basic research on the project started in 1982 at Nippon Telegraph and Telephone's laboratories in Japan. Research was brought to Battelle because the institute has expertise in the field and because of its international reputation.

"The basic technology was developed by NTT and that technology was transferred to this company for commercialization in this country," Miyashita says.

Photonic Integration Research was capitalized with about $10 million. It employs about a dozen people who are developing prototype products, which Miyashita expects to be ready for commercial use in 1995.

Among the advantages of using fiber optical cables over copper wiring is that there is much less resistance to the electrical signal that carries the messages. Less resistance means that a weaker signal can be used to send the message.

Also, optical cables, which are made out of silica, have much higher volume capabilities than copper wires.

As the fledgling company entered the 1990s, it received four patents for the processes it has developed and more are forthcoming. "At this moment almost all development is in its infancy," Miyashita says.

NTT's commitment to this company is apparent from the resources it has dedicated to it. Besides transferring technology, patents, and capital to Photonic Integration Research, it has assigned Miyashita, one of its leading fiber experts, to the project.

Miyashita received the NTT President Award in 1978 for development of long-wavelength optical fiber systems and in 1982 for the Vapor-phase Axial Deposition fiber fabrication process. He also won the 1982 Imperial Invention Prize for the latter development.

Miyashita received his Ph.D. in optical-fiber technology from the Tokyo Institute of Technology in 1980. His bachelor's and master's degrees are in physics.

Before coming to the United States, Miyashita was head of the optoelectronic devices section at NTT's Ibaraki Electrical Communication Laboratory at Ibaraki-ken, Japan.

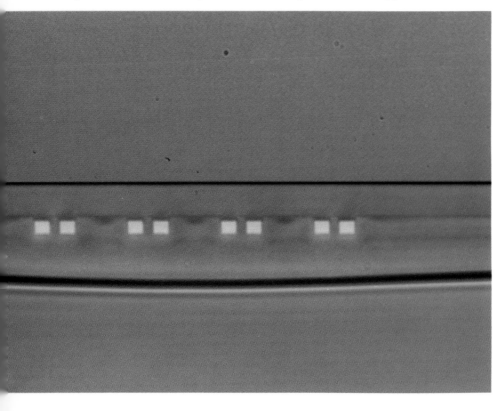

Photonic Integration Research is exploring optical integrated circuit technology for commercial use. This picture shows a cross section of etched waveguides after top cladding.

EDISON WELDING INSTITUTE

With Edison Welding Institute, Columbus is the heart of materials-joining technology—responding to a need required by nearly every manufacturer and process or utility plant in the United States.

Materials joining is present in every manufactured product. Manufacturers need to:

• Improve current welding techniques;

• Apply joining methods to new materials;

• Evaluate alternative welding processes;

• Prevent failure in structures and extend their lifespan.

The technologies involved include arc welding, laser beam processing, composite and plastics joining, explosive welding, micro-joining, welding automation, stress analysis, and nondestructive evaluation.

EWI offers the most complete materials-joining resource in the nation. Its assets are combined with the academic resources of The Ohio State University, which has America's only accredited university program for welding engineering, and with the allied materials capabilities of Battelle Memorial Institute, the world's largest private research and development organization. The three institutions are all within a few blocks of each other in Columbus.

A nonprofit, membership-based organization formed in 1984, EWI resulted from a cooperative effort of OSU, Battelle, The Welding Institute of the United Kingdom, and funding from Ohio's Thomas Edison program.

As a part of the Edison program, EWI converts research into practical applications and transfers needed technology to the production lines of member companies.

EWI technology transfer helps member companies shorten product introduction time, reduce manufacturing costs, and improve product quality and service life. Through projects, seminars, on-site specialized training, information retrieval, and telephone consulting and problem solving, EWI provides members with a competitive edge.

Six years after it was founded, EWI was serving more than 220 national and local firms embracing more than 700 affiliated organizations and operating plants. These companies are served by almost 100 professional staff members representing a wide range of technical backgrounds.

By 1990 EWI was experiencing an annual growth rate of more than 15 percent with the expectation to double in size within a few years. While its goal is to offer a complete range of materials-joining technology to companies of all sizes, it has a special interest in meeting the needs of Ohio's small and medium manufacturing firms.

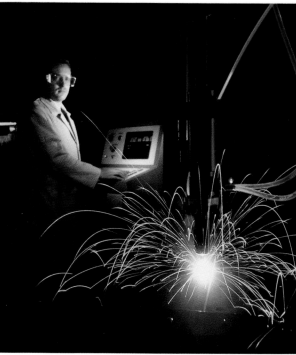

EWI uses new materials-joining technologies such as laser welding, cutting, and surface modification to help United States industry be more competitive.

Its technical work ranges from the application of technology on the shop floor or in the field to advancing the state of the art through its research efforts in Columbus and at other nationally prominent institutes and universities.

As a typical example of its practical application of technology, EWI engineers helped a major oil company save $3 million by analyzing and predicting the effect of microscopic cracks that could shorten the life of pressurized storage tanks.

In the area of advanced research, EWI developed a revolutionary technique to weld composite materials used on critical parts of advanced aircraft, technology that is eventually expected to be used in the automotive industry.

EWI is dedicated to improving U.S. manufacturing by advancing and applying materials-joining technology. EWI's goal is to enhance the bottom-line performance and competitiveness of its member companies through improved quality, increased productivity, reduced costs, and extended product life.

Servo-hydraulic test machines in the EWI engineering laboratory are used to analyze the mechanical behavior of various materials.

ANHEUSER-BUSCH, INCORPORATED

In the spring of 1966 the north side of Columbus was alive with cranes, bulldozers, torches, and cement mixers busily darting across more than 250 acres of land. For two years carpenters, engineers, construction workers, and architects worked to build the sixth brewery in the Anheuser-Busch network.

Since it opened in 1968 the Columbus brewery has played a vital role in helping Anheuser-Busch, Incorporated, maintain its position as the world's leading brewer. To keep pace with the company's rapid sales growth, Anheuser-Busch has expanded and modernized its Columbus brewery several times over the past 20 years. Shipping capacity at the plant is now 6.8 million barrels.

Beers brewed at the plant include Budweiser, Bud Light, Bud Dry, Michelob, Michelob Light, Michelob Dry, Busch, Busch Light, Natural Light, and King Cobra. Products produced here are distributed throughout Ohio, Michigan, Indiana, Kentucky, Pennsylvania, and West Virginia.

After completing a time-honored brewing process, Anheuser-Busch beers are distributed throughout Ohio by 27 independent wholesalers. Statewide Anheuser-Busch sold 44.1 million cases of beer in Ohio during 1989. This represented nearly 38 percent of all beer sales in the state, making Anheuser-Busch Ohio's leading brewer.

Anheuser-Busch wholesalers in Ohio employ 1,063 people with salaries and benefits totaling $46.4 million. These businesses contributed $17.8 million in federal, state, and local taxes. Additionally, their warehouses, truck fleets, and other properties represent a substantial investment. These wholesalers serve more than 20,000 retail accounts.

Growth in beer production and distribution at the Columbus brewery has also meant growth in the plant's most important resource—its work force. More than 1,000 people from Columbus and the surrounding communities are employed at the brewery, making it one of the largest private employers in the area.

Anheuser-Busch's presence in Ohio includes several diversified operations. Under the umbrella of Anheuser-Busch Companies, Incorporated, the corporation also operates four other facilities in the state: Metal Container Corporation and Busch Properties, Incorporated, in Columbus; Container Recovery Corporation in Marion; and Campbell Taggart, Incorporated, in Cincinnati, the corporation's baking subsidiary.

With an annual capacity of more than 1.9 billion cans, Metal Container's Columbus plant provides nearly all the can requirements of the Columbus brewery. The facility, at 350 McCormick Boulevard, employs more than 225 people.

Container Recovery Corporation, Anheuser-Busch's aluminum recycling company, operates a bottle sorting and recycling plant in Marion, Ohio. Formed in 1978 to provide a positive alternative to mandatory deposit legislation, Container Recovery Corporation is now the largest used-aluminum container recycler in the nation, employing 134 people

Anheuser-Busch has the most extensive and effective beer distribution system in the brewing industry.

LEFT: *Some things take time. The company still brews beer principally the way it has been brewing it for more than 100 years; it is a long, natural process taking up to 30 days or longer.*

ABOVE: *Anheuser-Busch recognizes the importance of employee relations for its continued success.*

RIGHT: *Because superior ingredients are essential in the brewing of truly great beers, Anheuser-Busch uses only the choicest imported and domestic hops.*

in the Marion plant alone.

Adjacent to the Columbus brewery is the Busch Corporate Center, an award-winning, 155-acre business/industrial park developed by Busch Properties, Incorporated. The development includes leased buildings, offices, warehouses, and light industry. Approximately 165 companies occupy the park.

All together Anheuser-Busch's Ohio operations have a sizable economic impact on the region. Annual wages and benefits for more than 1,700 employees top $69 million, state and local tax payments total $20.3 million, and $59 million is paid in federal excise taxes. In addition, the Columbus brewery and its employees purchase millions of dollars in goods and services from local suppliers each year.

The "ripple effect" of Anheuser-Busch activities and investments has

meant additional economic opportunities for all Ohioans. The company's commitment to quality and excellence is reflected not only in its products and economic impact, but also in its efforts on behalf of the communities it serves.

A recent national survey on charitable giving ranked Anheuser-Busch Companies among America's top 20 corporate contributors. In recent years the firm has contributed more than $500,000 to several groups and organizations in Ohio, including the Columbus Symphony, the Columbus Zoo, the Columbus Public Schools, and the Boys Club of Columbus.

Anheuser-Busch's community relations efforts also include involvement with minority communities in Ohio. The business funds scholarship programs, youth development organizations, athletic and cultural programs, civil rights efforts, and economic development efforts through business and banking relationships with minority-owned firms.

The company's brewery tours, including those at Columbus, hospitality centers, and Busch Garden parks exemplify how Anheuser-Busch practices the art of

making—and keeping—good friends.

Probably no promotion of Anheuser-Busch makes more friends for the company than the majestic Clydesdale horses. The unexcelled champion hitches tour the country, appearing at the Ohio State Fair and other fairs, festivals, rodeos, shopping centers, as well as appearing in nationally televised holiday parades. Each year they delight scores of millions of spectators in person and on television, serving as constant reminders of the quality and popularity of the King of Beers.

In times of community emergencies, such as the oil spill on the Monongahela River in Pittsburgh that caused a severe water shortage in 1988, Anheuser-Busch responds.

After the spill, Anheuser-Busch produced more than 260,000 cans of water at the Columbus brewery that was shipped to the affected area to help alleviate the shortage. As the spill made its way into the Ohio River, the Columbus brewery shipped another 288,000 cans of water to affected areas.

More than a century ago Adolphus Busch, founder of the Budweiser brand and industry innovator, coined the phrase, "Making Friends is Our Business." It is the foundation of the company's relations with consumers and communities, such as Columbus, and throughout the nation.

COMBIBLOC, INC.

Many consumers are not quite sure what aseptic packaging is. Yet the aseptic packaging process was voted the most significant food science innovation of the past 50 years by the Institute of Food Technologists—rated even more important than the development of the microwave oven.

Aseptic cartons and the systems used to package shelf-stable beverages and foods are the focus of Combibloc, Inc., at its 220,000-square-foot advanced manufacturing, research, and training facility at 4800 Roberts Road in Columbus' Westbelt area.

Aseptic packaging involves filling pre-sterilized cartons with a product that has been processed using ultra-high temperatures for short durations. Compared to traditional canning and bottling techniques, this innovative process maintains more of the natural nutrients, flavors, and textures of beverages and foods while ensuring product quality and safety. Aseptically processed products can remain "shelf-stable" for up to one year without refrigeration or preservatives.

Aseptic cartons were first used in

Combibloc, Inc., uses state-of-the-art manufacturing and printing equipment to produce aseptic cartons.

Europe in the 1960s to package milk. Combibloc, Inc., was established in 1983 to introduce the Combibloc aseptic packaging systems to the United States. The company is a wholly owned subsidiary of PKL Verpackungssysteme GmbH of Linnich, West Germany, which in turn is owned by the Swiss Industrial Group (SIG), a world leader in packaging machinery.

At its North American headquarters in Columbus, Combibloc develops, manufactures, and markets the aseptic cartons used on Combibloc filling machines made by PKL in Germany. The Combibloc aseptic package is a unique multilayer material that combines paperboard, plastic, and foil to form a carton that protects beverages and food from light and air, is lightweight and easy to use, and is both tamperproof and shatterproof.

Using sophisticated extrusion-lamination equipment, Combibloc manufactures the carton material, prints package graphics using rotogravure presses, and prepares the carton for customers by creasing it and forming the critical backseam.

These carton "sleeves" are shipped to food and beverage companies. The packaging process is completed on the Combibloc filler machine, which sterilizes the carton, fills it with a food or beverage, and tightly seals the contents.

Consumers may be most familiar with the aseptically packaged children's juice boxes. Two familiar food companies have purchased more than a billion cartons each from Combibloc: Del Monte Foods USA and Kraft General Foods. Popular brands packaged in Combibloc aseptic cartons include Minute Maid, Hi-C, Tang, Kool-Aid, Hawaiian Punch, and Tree Top.

Combibloc also has made significant investments in processing technology and skilled personnel at its Columbus site to expand the aseptic market into other beverages and foods such as soups, sauces, and gravies. To its growing customer base in the United States, Canada, and the Caribbean, Combibloc offers the

Aseptic packaging brought convenience and safety to the juice market.

most complete line of aseptic packaging sizes and configurations, including adult single-serve and family-size cartons.

Combibloc's packaging also makes environmental sense for three important reasons. First, aseptic cartons require less packaging material than other leading beverage containers, so they create less waste. For example, a single-serve product in an aseptic carton is 96 percent beverage and only 4 percent packaging by weight. The same serving in a glass bottle is 65 percent beverage and 35 percent packaging. Even a plastic bottle weighs twice as much as an aseptic carton.

Aseptic cartons also use far less energy to manufacture, ship, and store than other beverage containers. This is largely because the cartons don't need to be refrigerated, and their compact shape and light weight allows for more efficient shipping and storage. Aseptic cartons also can be recycled. In school and curbside demonstration recycling programs, drink boxes are collected with milk cartons and other polycoated paper packages. The packages are recycled into paper products such as tissues, napkins, and paper towels.

As Combibloc enters its second decade of packaging innovation, the company and its nearly 200 Columbus employees are proud of the contributions they are making to the future of food processing and to the community they call home.

EATON IDT INCORPORATED

Faced with a rapidly changing, computer-driven environment, industry today demands the latest technology in industrial automation systems. Eaton IDT Incorporated supports the companies that compete in this increasingly complex environment with a family of innovative industrial operator interfaces that meet the most challenging of applications.

Eaton IDT, which has its headquarters at 173 Heatherdown Drive in Westerville, was founded in 1975 as Industrial Data Terminals by a small group of industrial managers and engineers led by the company's president, Walter J. Doyle. They recognized the need for high-quality, easy-to-operate

color graphics systems for the production control marketplace.

In May 1989 IDT joined forces with Eaton Corporation, a worldwide manufacturer of engineered products serving automotive, industrial, commercial, and defense markets. IDT became a subsidiary within Eaton's Controls Group and then, in March 1990, the company's name was changed to Eaton IDT.

Today, with more than 150 employees, the company serves more than two-thirds of the *Fortune* 100 companies with a full line of industrial operator interfaces for computer integrated manufacturing (CIM) applications. These products complement Eaton's extensive line of pushbuttons, pilot devices, and other operator-interface devices sold under the Cutler-Hammer brand name.

Since its inception, Eaton IDT has recognized that user acceptance of factory automation technology is the key to CIM project success. Consequently, the company has emerged as the leader for the operator/machine interface (OMI) market by focusing on the real-time, interactive needs of the user.

A hallmark of Eaton IDT's success in industrial automation is the company's ability to focus on the industrial environment's interactive needs, which require lightning-quick, real-time information about each respective

manufacturing process in order for the user to make intelligent operating decisions and improve efficiency.

In metals and manufacturing, in pharmaceuticals and plastics, and in aerospace and automotive, Eaton IDT products, such as its FactoryMate® series of industrial personal computers, provide total information control on the plant floor. From the simplest of video control panels to the sophisticated, multi-tasking, industrial operator's console, Eaton IDT's fully integrated system capabilities furnish the continuous flow of critical operating information that is so essential to successful automation.

By constantly reinvesting in the company, Eaton IDT has continually expanded its engineering, production, marketing, and support services. As a result, it also is able to offer its customers the tools that allow these industrial manufacturers to achieve world-class quality and improved productivity. This keeps them competitive in their markets.

Eaton IDT is a success story to which the community can point with pride.

LEFT: An Eaton IDT PanelMate® Video Control Panel in use at Eaton's machining center at Eden Prairie, Minnesota.

BELOW: Eaton IDT's fully integrated industrial operator interfaces are designed to furnish a continuous flow of critical operating information so that the user can make quick, intelligent operating decisions and improve efficiency to achieve automation project success.

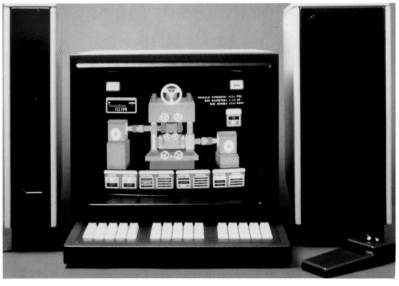

10 BUSINESS AND FINANCE

▲▲▲▲▲▲▲▲▲▲▲▲▲▲▲▲
367

Columbus' solid financial base has provided a dynamic environment for the economic growth and opportunity of both individuals and businesses in the community.

The Huntington National Bank, 368; Columbus Area Chamber of Commerce, 372; Household Bank, 373; BancOhio National Bank, 374; Online Computer Library Center (OCLA), 376; Grange Insurance Companies, 378; U.S. Check, 379; Battelle Memorial Institute, 380; Society Bank, 382; Nationwide Insurance, 384; Central Benefits Mutual Insurance Company, 388; Industrial Association of Central Ohio, 390; The Midland, 391; Banc One Corporation, 392; Chemical Abstracts Service, 394

Photo by Larry Hamill

THE HUNTINGTON NATIONAL BANK

Leadership by example, personal customer service, and community involvement are the guiding principles of The Huntington National Bank, a philosophy that has served Columbus well. Throughout its 125-year history The Huntington has been an integral part of Columbus' heritage, growing from a small, one-office bank to a multibillion-dollar regional holding company, Huntington Bancshares Incorporated. Huntington's traditional banking practices have helped maintain the financial stability of the community, while innovative products and investments in technology have revolutionized customer service. Its commitment to education has created opportunities for children to learn more about the world. The Huntington has returned to the community the support given to the bank by becoming actively involved in supporting the arts and community events. Every day, The Huntington carries out its principles through its business practices and leadership in the community.

The Huntington National Bank began as the P.W. Huntington & Company in 1866. Located in downtown Columbus on the northwest corner of Broad and High streets, Huntington & Company operated as an investment bank, offering commercial and correspondent banking services. In 1905 P.W. Huntington & Company was incorporated as The Huntington National Bank of Columbus and obtained a national charter that allowed the bank to offer additional services, such as checking accounts.

In 1966 Huntington Bancshares Incorporated, a holding company, was established to enable The Huntington to expand its services outside of Franklin County. By 1979 changes in

The Huntington furthered its commitment to Columbus by becoming the primary tenant of the 37-story Huntington Center at 41 South High Street in the mid-1980s. Located opposite the Statehouse, Huntington Center is the headquarters for many of the bank's consolidated operations. The building of red granite and bronze glass windows features four breathtaking atriums and a full-height glass wall that connects the center's two towers. Its construction added beauty and drama to the rapidly changing skyline of downtown Columbus.

ABOVE: The floor-to-ceiling glass wall at the front of the Huntington Center provides a spectacular view of the Statehouse and the downtown area.

RIGHT: By the turn of the century the bank's operations required more space than its current location could provide, and by 1925 the bank had relocated to 17 South High Street. The building boasted a three-story lobby whose dramatic ceiling featured a Tiffany mosaic and low-relief sculptures done in the style of the Italian Renaissance. The lobby ceiling is still the largest unsupported ceiling of its kind in existence.

Ohio law enabled all 15 of The Huntington's affiliate banks, including Huntington National of Columbus, to merge into one corporation: The Huntington National Bank. Since then, Huntington Bancshares has established several subsidiaries, including The Huntington National Bank, The Huntington Leasing Company, The Huntington Mortgage Company, The Huntington Trust Company, National Association, The Huntington National Life Insurance Company, and The Huntington Company.

The 1979 law changes also allowed the bank to expand into other Ohio communities. With the acquisition of the Union Commerce Corporation in Cleveland in 1982, The Huntington became the fourth-largest bank holding company in Ohio. In 1985 legislation was passed allowing the bank to grow beyond Ohio's borders. By 1986 the bank had become a major regional holding bank with the completion of four acquisitions: Commonwealth Trust Bancorp Incorporated in Covington, Kentucky; Central Bancorp Incorporated in Danville, Indiana; Wainwright Financial Corporation in Noblesville, Indiana; and Kasco Financial Corporation in Warren, Michigan. By 1990 Huntington Bancshares had a presence in 11 states, with a total of 281 offices.

As the bank enters the 1990s, it is

The Renaissance office design uses a glass-and-fabric paneling system to give Personal Banker office areas privacy while maintaining a feeling of openness. The Personal Banker's desk includes a work surface and rounded conference table end, enabling the banker and the customer to work side by side to discuss his or her financial needs.

Attention-getting product graphics placed throughout the banking office increase awareness of Huntington products. The graphics—reproductions of commissioned, Impressionistic-style oil paintings—illustrate situations where Huntington products or services can help a family or individual.

The Renaissance speed line is a long, narrow writing counter with artwork and text describing Huntington products and services. Brochures on related topics are positioned along the speed line.

meeting the challenges and opportunities created by deregulation, globalization, and computerization while holding fast to traditional values of personalized service and retail banking basics. It consistently has been the first to introduce innovative services and products that later have been used throughout the banking industry. Some of The Huntington's hallmark services include:

• Personal Banking Program. Established in 1986, the Personal Banking program assigns a Huntington employee to each retail customer to answer questions and provide services directly for that customer. The Huntington is the only bank in Ohio with such a program.

• Renaissance Project Office Design. The Renaissance Project, a physical manifestation of Personal Banking, was incorporated in 133 banking offices statewide in the early 1990s. The Renaissance office design concept transformed traditional banking offices into consumer-oriented retail centers to provide more personal service to customers and to showcase bank products and services through large, colorful posters and graphics. Key features of the Renaissance design include the office paneling system, Impressionistic-style graphics, and a "waitless" teller line.

• Huntington Customer Information System. Personal Banking was further enhanced in 1989 with the design of the bank's own computerized Customer Information System guided by computer-aided software engineering (CASE). Using computer terminals, Personal

Bankers in any banking office can access information immediately on all financial relationships a customer has with the bank. This allows Personal Bankers to tailor advice and services to each customer's financial situation. The Huntington was the first bank in Ohio to implement the CASE system.

• Image Processing System. In late 1989 the bank adopted Unisys Image Processing and Item-Processing Systems to streamline the processing of more than one million checks a day. The system produces digitized images that then can be captured, stored, and transmitted electronically to video display terminals or printers. The system enables the bank to read and sort 1,800 checks a minute or 25 million checks a month. Eventually customers will see the difference in their monthly statements, where as many as 18 check images can be reproduced on a single piece of 8- 1/2 by 11-inch paper, thus saving postage costs for the bank and simplifying record keeping for the customer.

• Telecommunication Device for the Deaf. Hearing-impaired Ohioans can bank by telephone using the bank's statewide, toll-free number for its Telecommunication Device for the Deaf (TDD). The Huntington was the first Ohio bank to provide this service statewide in 1989, giving customers an opportunity to bank from the convenience of their homes. This service is further evidence of The Huntington's commitment to Personal Banking.

The bank's dedication and leadership extends to its community involvement. The Huntington philosophy recognizes that active community involvement is a foundation of the company's success. From schools to bicycle tours to critically acclaimed art exhibits, The Huntington believes in giving back to the community the support and commitment it has received.

Children at the West Broad Elementary School, The Huntington's Adopt-A-School partner, participate in The Huntington's "Banking for Living" program. Once a month Huntington volunteers supervise students as they conduct basic banking services, such as account deposits for fellow students. Students learn about banking as well as good savings habits.

As part of the I KNOW I CAN program, the bank helps Columbus Public Schools students prepare for college by providing financial assistance to qualified students and parents about where and how to seek financial assistance. I KNOW I CAN, a program operated by The Columbus Foundation, encourages students to stay in school and prepare for a bright future through study and enrollment in the college of their choice.

The annual Tour of the Scioto River Valley (TOSRV) is one of the nation's best-known bicycle tours. Directed for more than 25 years by Huntington employee Charlie Pace, TOSRV annually attracts more than 6,000 entrants for the weekend event, going 210 miles round-trip from Columbus to Portsmouth, Ohio. The Huntington is an annual cosponsor of the event and Huntington employees serve as volunteers for the tour's operations.

The Huntington Challenge, the annual Ohio Squash Singles Championship, sponsored by The Huntington National Bank, has been a statewide competition for the past 35 years. Amateurs and professionals of all ages from around the state gather to compete in this prestigious three-day event.

Huntington IceScapes, first held in 1990, has become a successful Columbus winter tradition. This ice-sculpting demonstration and competition features the intricate and beautiful artistry of amateur and professional ice sculptors from throughout the region.

Community involvement for The Huntington also means support of the arts. In 1988 The Huntington took a leadership role in organizing and presenting the international "Son of Heaven: Imperial Arts of China" exhibition. This important and monumental exhibition permitted more than 670,000 viewers to see an unprecedented collection of artwork from the Forbidden City, much of which had never before been seen outside China.

The bank supports the Columbus Museum of Art through funding, loaning the museum pieces of The Huntington's private collection for display and promoting museum exhibitions. The "Treasures from the Jewish Museum" exhibition featured 57 art objects from the Jewish Museum in New York City, capturing the breadth of nearly 4,000 years of Jewish experience and reflecting the cultural diversity of Jewish communities around the world. The Huntington National Bank was instrumental in the organization and presentation of this exhibition and circulated information about it through radio and print advertising, public service announcements, promotional banners along downtown Columbus streets, and in 300,000 Huntington Bank customer statements.

As a continuing patron of the Columbus Symphony Orchestra, The Huntington has sponsored performances and has established an endowment for the Music Director's Chair in the name of Clair E. Fultz. A former chairman of Huntington Bancshares, Fultz's belief that the arts enrich individual lives as well as the life of the community serves as the guiding philosophy for The Huntington's involvement in supporting the fine and cultural arts.

"Trilogy: A Campaign for the Arts" benefited from the leadership shown by Huntington and other community leaders. The bank helped organize the campaign, which raised millions of dollars in private and corporate donations for the Columbus Symphony Orchestra, the Columbus Museum of Art, and the Columbus Association for the Performing Arts. The completion of Trilogy ensures the stability and continuity of the arts in the community as well as helps promote Columbus as a regional and national cultural arts center.

The Huntington continues to seek opportunities to serve all members of the community. It remains steadfast in the philosophy that corporate success is measured not only in assets, profits, and customer service, but also in the company's time, energy, and talent dedicated to furthering the growth of the community as a whole.

A Huntington volunteer supervises a West Broad Elementary School student as she helps a fellow student open an account.

The Huntington's long involvement with the Columbus Symphony Orchestra helps bring music and cultural enrichment to people of all ages.

Men and women from around the state come to Columbus to participate in the annual Huntington Challenge, Ohio Squash Singles Tournament, sponsored by Huntington National Bank.

COLUMBUS AREA CHAMBER OF COMMERCE

Christopher Columbus knew risk. He also knew the difference between taking an educated risk and being foolhardy.

While the romance of the Italian explorer's daring adventure has become legendary, Columbus was primarily a businessman. Years before he leased his fleet, hired his crew, and set sail, Columbus laid the groundwork for his trip by mapping out a business plan and negotiating financial backing from Queen Isabella. His resolve paid off with his discovery of the Americas--a new world rich with resources and opportunities that the community is still discovering.

As the Columbus Area Chamber of Commerce looks toward the next century, the continued economic growth and development of the region will depend on the courage of the community to explore uncharted waters, to take the educated risk necessary to discover the undiscovered potential of the region.

With the famed explorer in mind, the theme of ColumbusAmerica has been developed as the rallying call for growth and development in the area. The ColumbusAmerica Economic Development Campaign was initiated in 1990 by the chamber, the city, the county, the state, and almost 200 private business investors. The aim is to market the region as the best of America and American enterprise, and as an internationally oriented economic powerhouse for entrepreneurs and investors from throughout the world. The campaign goal is to generate 80,000 new jobs in the area by the end of 1995.

Columbus has no shortage of economic adventurers. One of the region's greatest marketing points is the entrepreneurial spirit of its people, from individuals born and bred in the region who turned small enterprises into multinational corporations, to those from other nations who built big businesses out of big ideas and hard work.

These modern-day risk takers and their small but developing successors make Columbus a city of achievers. More than two-thirds of the new jobs in this decade will be generated by small businesses. It is for this reason that a major part of the Chamber's resources are devoted to assisting small businesses to plan, seek financing, locate new local or international markets, manage growth, and retain the talent necessary to become big businesses.

As an indicator of growth in the community, one has to look no further than the downtown skyline or the region's suburban office and industrial developments that have steadily grown during the past decade. To ensure Columbus remains a dynamic, burgeoning city, chamber member businesses also work to assure the labor force remains strong and skillful, the city's economic base remains diverse as a buffer against fluctuations in the national economy, and business development remains a practical partnership among all segments of the community to provide new business with the best chance for success. These strong attributes have brought recognition to Columbus from throughout the nation and the world as a great place to do business.

The researcher in the lab, the businessperson starting out in a basement, and the retrained factory worker all possess the can-do spirit, the risk-taking initiative of Columbus. That spirit and drive make Columbus a celebration of discovery in America—ColumbusAmerica.

Columbus' burgeoning skyline is proof of the city's growth and dynamism. Photo by Don Olson

HOUSEHOLD BANK

Known as "America's Family Bank," Household Bank is dedicated to serving the needs of families and individuals.

As its first "de novo" market entry, Household selected Columbus in 1986. Up until then the bank had operated branches it had acquired in five other states: Maryland, Illinois, Kansas, Colorado, and California. So Ohio's capital city was the first market the bank entered by building new offices rather than by acquiring an established branch network.

The company wanted to test its full-service retail concept in a new, growth environment, and Columbus provided the ideal marketplace.

Prior to launching the "America's Family Bank" concept in Columbus in June 1987, Household first conducted extensive research on consumer attitudes toward banks and banking in general. Through this research Household found that most consumers were generally frustrated with their banking relationships.

The results showed that the major customer concerns centered around limited hours of operation, lack of respect and attention to individuals' needs as compared to the treatment of commercial customers, lack of service, high minimum-balance requirements, and high monthly fees tied to checking and savings accounts. In launching its Columbus market entry, Household was determined to make the difference for consumers in the central Ohio marketplace by creating a bank that offered them what they said they wanted.

The bank focused its resources on creating a new, high-tech, retail environment for delivering its innovative products, services, and conveniences. Household's focus was not on traditional banking, but on meeting specific consumer needs.

In order for its market entry to be successful, the bank had to ensure that its key points of differentiation were communicated not only through its advertising and promotional efforts, but also through its banking center "stores" and the talented pool of employees who would deliver the products and services consumers said they wanted in a bank.

In addition to offering this unique blend of products and services, Household Bank's offices also look different from most other banks. For instance, dominant exterior road and building signage provides maximum visibility in high-traffic areas. The interiors of the banks are arranged to provide an environment of warmth, friendliness, and convenience, with round tables for account managers to meet with customers, thus breaking the traditional barrier of "banker across the desk"; a stand-up desk at the front entry so that bank personnel can immediately meet and greet prospects and customers; and angled teller windows to pro-

The interior design of this typical Household banking center reflects the bank's innovation and warmth.

vide an environment of maximum privacy for customers to transact business.

Since 1987 Household Bank has grown from its four original offices to more than 20 serving the immediate Columbus area. The bank's extensive network of banking centers serve many surrounding communities as well. Yet despite its growth and success the purpose of Household Bank, "America's Family Bank," remains unchanged: to serve the banking needs of families and individuals with innovative products, added convenience, and unparalleled customer service.

Because Household believes that no customer is too small, it offers a special program for children— the Household Banker Bear® Savings Club.

BANCOHIO NATIONAL BANK

BancOhio National Bank, with headquarters in Columbus, is one of the oldest banks in Ohio, dedicated to delivering superior service to all of its business and individual customers in 27 central and southern Ohio counties.

As a member of National City Corporation, BancOhio is a major contributor to National City's standing as one of the nation's largest and most profitable bank holding companies.

Prior to its merger in 1984 with National City, BancOhio was Ohio's first statewide bank and the lead bank of BancOhio Corporation, Ohio's first bank holding company. It was formed in 1929 by Harry P. Wolfe and Robert F. Wolfe.

Since then BancOhio has taken a leading role in the communities it serves, making a major impact on Ohio's growth in many industries. The bank's blend of technical expertise, knowledge, responsiveness, and creativity has resulted in an ever-increasing portfolio of high-quality loans and loyal, satisfied customers.

Being located in the state capital has created special opportunities for BancOhio to become a service leader in providing financing expertise to the many local government agencies and municipalities. Its dedication to understanding a customer's business has also helped the bank to become a principal provider of financial services to central Ohio insurance companies.

BancOhio has earned a reputation as a leader in international banking, with extensive services and capabilities. In addition to handling international transactions for its domestic corporate customers, the bank has assisted overseas companies establish manufacturing subsidiaries in central Ohio. Many of these new companies have chosen BancOhio as their local Ohio bank.

BancOhio also is known for its specialists in construction and real estate lending, agribusiness lending, leasing, and vendor financing.

The bank has been a champion of small business growth in the state. Its efforts in assisting small businesses have resulted in a better understanding by public officials of the Small Business Administration's contribution, more participation by lenders in small

business financing, and more applications from potential borrowers.

BancOhio's investment in technology and product development has helped its corporate customers improve their cash flow through innovative cash management services.

Perhaps one of BancOhio's greatest strengths is the commitment of its employees to provide continuous, consistent, superior service to all its customers. BancOhio employees live daily by a pledge they helped compose, which reads in part: "In order to distinguish myself and differentiate BancOhio, it is my responsibility to deliver, with enthusiasm and pride, a superior level of

service each and every day: BancOhio Service." The pledge continues, promising accurate, responsive, courteous, anticipatory service.

BancOhio's service leadership is also evident in its "Red Carpet Line," a phone number customers can call to express their compliments, concerns, or ideas. Providing superior service is ingrained in the bank's culture, and to BancOhio's thousands of customers, "red carpet service" is synonymous

BancOhio National Bank Plaza, the imposing multi-towered headquarters for BancOhio National Bank, is located in the heart of downtown Columbus.

with "BancOhio Service."

Superior service doesn't stop when the customers leave the bank and the employees quit for the day. BancOhio is also a leader in its support of the many communities it serves.

The bank's charitable giving program reaches far into each of these communities, helping hundreds of thousands of people each year. With a charitable program exceeding one million dollars annually, BancOhio has built a tradition of philanthropy paralleled by only a few organizations in central Ohio.

BancOhio's annual gift to United Way and the generous individual gifts pledged by employees touch one in four residents of central Ohio. A gift from BancOhio to Children's Hospital helped fund a new research lab, and BancOhio's financial as well as volunteer leadership helped build a dormitory at Recreation Unlimited, a summer camp for handicapped children.

Whether it is helping finance a building for a meals on wheels program, a new exhibit at the Columbus Zoo, or a new gymnasium at a small college, BancOhio's service and financial leadership make an impact on the lives of thousands of Ohioans.

The bank's giving program also includes regular donations to the communities it serves outside Columbus. These donations help build technical colleges and hospitals, endow scholarships, fund scouting, 4-H, and Y programs for thousands of children, and support many other worthwhile projects.

In addition to its charitable giving, BancOhio also makes a significant impact on the quality of life in its communities through civic activities. A sponsor of the Columbus Arts Festival since 1989, the bank became a major corporate sponsor of the event as it entered the 1990s. The event attracts more than 500,000 visitors a year. Two million visitors are predicted for 1992.

For more than a decade BancOhio has treated thousands of people to a free concert by the Columbus Symphony Orchestra and sponsored a Holiday Celebration at COSI. The latter event draws more visitors to the Center

ABOVE: Rain or shine, hundreds of BancOhio employees are eager to walk or work at the annual United Negro College Fund/BancOhio Walk-a-thon. The bank-sponsored event is one of the largest UNCF fundraisers in the country.

RIGHT: BancOhio's devotion to delivering superior customer service often leads to simple, effective service enhancements, such as Express Teller lines for customers with single transactions.

of Science and Industry than at any other time of year.

Annually, hundreds of BancOhio employees join thousands of walkers from other companies in the United Negro College Fund/BancOhio Walk-a-thon. This event, one of the largest fundraisers for UNCF in the nation, has been a proud part of the bank's civic involvement almost since its inception.

The bank also annually recognizes volunteers who helped build the Columbus Martin Luther King Center for the Cultural and Performing Arts into a culturally and educationally powerful institution. The recognition is bestowed during the bank-sponsored annual anniversary celebration.

Recognizing the importance of education, BancOhio offers a matching gifts program, through which individual employees can donate up to $1,000 a year to their favorite colleges or universities. The bank then matches

these contributions.

Few institutions in central Ohio have the rich history of civic involvement by their employees that BancOhio does. BancOhio encourages employee involvement in civic activities and its employees are a mainstay of the central Ohio volunteer force.

Whether it's individual service in a banking office or service in the community, BancOhio is a proven service leader. Expect BancOhio service, and nothing less.

ONLINE COMPUTER LIBRARY CENTER (OCLC)

In 1967 the presidents of the colleges and universities in Ohio founded the Ohio College Library Center to develop a computerized system in which the libraries of Ohio academic institutions could share resources and reduce costs.

OCLC's first offices were in the Main Library on the campus of The Ohio State University, and its first computer room was housed in the OSU Research Center. It was from these Columbus roots that Frederick G. Kilgour, OCLC's first president, oversaw the growth of OCLC from a regional computer system for 54 Ohio colleges into an international network. OCLC is known today as OCLC Online Computer Library Center and serves more than 10,000 libraries of all types in the United States and 39 other countries.

A nonprofit membership organization, OCLC designs and markets computer systems and databases designed to increase availability of library re-

OCLC moved to its current facility at 6565 Frantz Road in Dublin in 1981.

sources and to reduce the rate of the rise in library costs. Its broad public purpose is to further access the world's information.

Since 1971 OCLC has operated an on-line computer system that has evolved into the world's foremost bibliographic network, handling on an average day more than 3 million transactions pertaining to the cataloging, locating, and lending of library materials. Users at more than 10,000 terminals are linked to OCLC's computers by a packet-switched telecommunications network of more than 300,000 miles of phone lines.

Central to OCLC's operations is the OCLC database, which contains more than 25 million records and more than 400 million location listings for library materials. The OCLC database enables libraries to reduce costs and increase the availability of library resources through a simple but powerful concept: Only one library needs to originally catalog a book or other item, and the other libraries in the network can use the same information for their needs.

When a library cannot find a record in the database for the item it wishes to catalog, it creates a new catalog record and adds it to the database for other member libraries to use.

The database grows by more than a million records a year, contributed by OCLC's member libraries. Many of these new records are for unique or rare items, and knowledge of their whereabouts increases the general availability of information for institutions in the entire network.

The database contains information similar to that found in a traditional card catalog—detailed descriptive information about the physical attributes (book, manuscript, map, sound recording, videotape, or journal, for example) and the content of individual items in library collections. Attached to the descriptive record for each item is a list of libraries that have it. Thus a patron in Columbus can effectively browse through the holdings of the 10,000 other libraries in the OCLC network.

Library patrons consult the database for general information about materials. Librarians use the database for some 60 technical services or processes, ranging from production of printed catalog cards to compact disc catalogs to microfiche to on-line reference systems.

The OCLC database is the world's largest on-line computerized catalog. It spans four millennia of recorded knowledge and includes works in some 340 languages. It contains information not only about books, but about journals, sound recordings, musical scores, audiovisual media, maps, archives and manuscripts, and computer programs and files.

OCLC currently operates two large on-line services—technical processing and reference—in support of its mission of furthering access to infor-

A librarian and a patron at Northwestern University in Evanston, Illinois, consult an OCLC terminal.

mation worldwide.

The technical processing service is designed primarily for use by professional librarians and library staffs. It is the latest version of the original system developed to support cataloging in Ohio libraries. These processes and products help libraries work together to reduce costs and improve services.

The more than 25 million records in the OCLC database provides support for local and regional computerized catalogs, for circulation, for reference, for interlibrary lending, and for printing customized catalogs and guides. Libraries catalog more than 22 million items annually on this service and transact more than 5 million interlibrary loans.

Introduced in 1990, OCLC's on-line reference service is designed for use by students, faculty, and researchers as well as by library professionals. It provides subject access and sophisticated searching techniques to a variety of information sources— from general databases such as OCLC's to specialized ones in education, business, law, science, and medicine.

Thanks to the OCLC database and OCLC's on-line services, scholars, researchers, and librarians now speak in terms of a "library without walls" and of being able to locate and gain access to materials more rapidly than ever before.

By the mid-1990s OCLC will have provided its member libraries with more than one billion dollars in computer services. But, as a nonprofit corporation with a broad public purpose, financial performance is only one, albeit a very important, measure of OCLC's accomplishments and directions. Through research and through collaboration with other institutions, OCLC has contributed to Columbus' growing reputation as a center for large databases and information services.

The OCLC Office of Research is devoted to solving problems related to library and information science. Researchers help libraries cope with the

ABOVE LEFT: Future generations of library users will have an increasing variety of electronic tools to help them find information.

ABOVE RIGHT: A library can ship its entire card catalog to OCLC, where the staff in this division will convert each card to computerized form.

radical and dramatic changes in the ways information is stored, distributed, and accessed. Research activities focus on enhancing use of the OCLC database, investing in the requirements of the library of the future, increasing productivity of library catalogers, digitizing library materials to preserve them for future use, and transforming paper publications into electronic documents for use in automated information retrieval systems.

OCLC also conducts research with other institutions and agencies. For example, Carnegie Mellon University and OCLC are working together to develop a prototype electronic research library. Through this new library, called Project Mercury, most of the necessary information needed for research would be accessed from a scholar's powerful personal computer.

As society crosses the threshold into what many call the "Information Age," OCLC is uniquely positioned to play an important role in bringing information in electronic form to people when and where they need it.

GRANGE INSURANCE COMPANIES

Grange Insurance Companies were first conceived in 1935, at an Ohio Grange picnic in Summit County. The idea stemmed from a discussion on beginning a new auto insurance company to provide lower rates to farmers because they drove less and had lower accident exposure than city dwellers.

Grange Insurance Companies have come a long way since that idea prompted the founding of the Grange Mutual Casualty Company. The organization now serves policy holders in five states, with a full line of auto, homeowner, commercial, and life insurance products.

During its early years the company was an integral part of the Ohio Grange organization. In 1945, however, it became an independent entity. Soon new coverages were added and operations expanded into urban areas. After just a few years Grange had become one of the leading Ohio based multi-line insurers.

Later Grange expanded outside Ohio and now offers insurance in Indiana, Kentucky, Tennessee, and Georgia. The company's growth was based on the original goal to "furnish safe, adequate, and economical auto insurance."

Innovative insurance coverages, multi-policy discounts, and constant attention to customer needs are examples of how that mission is carried out today.

The Grange group of companies now consists of the Grange Mutual Casualty Company, Grange Life Insurance Company, GM Premium Budget Inc., GrangeAmerica Corporation, Northview Insurance Agency Inc., and Trustgard Insurance Company, a subsidiary created to facilitate expansion into additional states.

The Grange Life Insurance Company, which began operations in 1968, has grown rapidly and already has nearly 3 billion dollars in force.

While holding to the philosophy that built a strong base, Grange today is dedicated to meeting the challenges of the 1990s and beyond. Included in this posture for action is Grange's strong interest in consumer education about the benefits of insurance. Grange feels the public would greatly benefit from a better understanding of how the insurance industry provides comprehensive insurance coverages at affordable premiums.

Under the leadership of J. Frederick Reid, chairman, president, and chief executive officer since 1983, Grange has embarked on a mission to plan the company's direction for the next 20 years.

"We recognize," Reid says, "that the next several decades will provide great challenges and great opportunities. We plan to be in a position to take advantage of these situations. Policyholders, employees, and agents, as well as those who are not our current customers, will benefit from Grange's preparation for the future."

To ensure Grange is ready, "Operation Focus"—an evolving plan—has been put in place. "Operation Focus" will analyze the companies as they are today, anticipate customer needs and wants, then develop products and the organization to meet these needs.

During this process Grange will continue its operations with increased emphasis on service to policyholders and

When Grange moved to its new headquarters, it used some of the old building's stained glass window to adorn the new lobby. The resulting artwork is representative of the company's commitment to using the best of the old while looking to the future.

Grange Insurance Company's headquarters is located at 650 South Front Street.

agents. "Our early studies," Reid explains, "show that competitive pricing will be essential in attracting policyholders, but outstanding service will keep customers on the books."

In meeting the challenges of the twenty-first century, Grange will continue to work with policyholders, agents, and employees as a partner in protection.

U.S. CHECK

U.S. Check is the banker's airline.

The company doesn't fly bankers. It does, however, fly billions of dollars worth of canceled checks every night. Why? Because time is money.

Moving checks quickly from bank to bank means interest that would have been lost while checks were in transit is recaptured, and that recapture may be worth several thousand dollars a day to U.S. Check customers. Banking officials appear to appreciate the company's specialized air courier network; U.S. Check has provided service to more than 250 banks and 200 commercial accounts.

Moving the nation's payment mechanism is big business. At the company's 75,000-square-foot hub in Columbus, U.S. Check maintains a fleet of approximately 30 Lear jets and 50 twin-engine piston planes. This armada flies more than 12,000 shipments per night through Columbus and smaller hubs in Charlotte, North Carolina; Teterboro, New Jersey; Des Moines, Iowa; and Denver, Colorado; which offer secondary sorting capabilities.

An operation of this magnitude requires the technical support provided by more than 50 flight technicians located in four maintenance bases throughout the United States. The service team is backed up with a $2-million in-house parts inventory to keep the fleet flying.

U.S. Check pilots receive recurrent training at the company's on-site flight training facility. Equipped with the latest flight simulators, the training school affords pilots the opportunity to "fly" their routes safely, on the ground, as they learn to anticipate and avoid potential problems in the air.

Ground service is critical, too, and U.S. Check employs a staff of more than 200 to sort, pick up, deliver, and route shipments throughout North America.

With aggressive, forward-looking management, U.S. Check has grown from a company that lost money its first quarter of operation in 1974 to a corporation that by early 1990 grossed in excess of $40 million per year.

Looking to expand its operations, U.S. Check entered the burgeoning

ABOVE: U.S. Check flies billions of dollars worth of cancelled checks every night.

RIGHT: U.S. Check employs a staff of more than 200 to sort, pick up, deliver, and route shipments throughout North America.

small-package delivery business. Utilizing the U.S. Check hubs, fleet, and support teams, the company created TIMEXPRESS. The service promises that a package that is picked up as late as 3:00 a.m. will be delivered by 9:00 a.m. the same day to any one of more than 100 cities throughout the United States. Company officials are quick to point out that because of the location of the hub in Columbus, local businesses can have packages picked up as late as 4:00 a.m. and still make the 9:00 a.m. same-day delivery deadline. This service also is available on weekends and holidays. Not every business has such time-critical transportation needs, but TIMEXPRESS has discovered that there are a substantial number who do, such as medical laboratories and hospitals, advertising agencies, and computer support businesses.

Columbusites can receive this service more economically than those in other cities, too. TIMEXPRESS management provides such a service for its Columbus neighbors, as it feels that the city's strategic location, uncrowded airport facilities, and pro-business philosophy have been instrumental in the company's rapid growth.

Careful development of niche markets, a commitment to complete customer satisfaction, and a 98 percent on-time delivery record make U.S. Check/TIMEXPRESS one of the city's entrepreneurial companies to watch in the 1990s.

BATTELLE MEMORIAL INSTITUTE

A secretary races to the nearby office copier to quickly produce 25 copies of a document for an important meeting. A supermarket shopper eases through the check-out lane—thanks to the use of a sophisticated product code. After completing the 18th hole, the weekend golfer notices that today's golf balls seem to be a bit more durable and cut-resistant.

Each of these "quality of life" improvements—the office copier, the consumer product code, and better golf ball coatings—are a result of the development of new, innovative technologies, and a major contributor to the development of these diverse technologies was Battelle, a global technology leader based in Columbus.

With a staff of 8,000 technologists, engineers, strategic business management consultants, and other specialists at 35 worldwide locations, Battelle puts technology to work for industry and government through the development, commercialization, and management of technology. At its major technology centers in the United States and Europe, Battelle solves problems, develops and improves products and processes, provides on-site technical assistance, identifies business opportunities, and brings a systems approach to integrate technology and satisfy client needs.

Founded in the 1920s by Columbus industrialist Gordon Battelle, the organization has maintained a keen "focus on the future" for more than six decades.

In its early years, Battelle was widely recognized for its leadership in industrial materials technology. With the coming of the postwar era, the organization's applied technology skills allowed it to enter rapidly expanding industrial and government markets.

During the postwar era, an independent inventor named Chester Carlson came to Battelle with a novel idea for a dry-copying process. Carlson, a New York patent attorney, had seen his idea rejected by more than 25 major companies. Working with Carlson and the Haloid Company of Rochester, New York, Battelle's technologists set out to help develop and commercialize the office copier.

By 1960 Carlson's idea had succeeded, Haloid became known as the Xerox Corporation, and Battelle received millions of dollars in royalties, which allowed it to significantly ex-

Battelle has developed high-tech lasers for a variety of health care, electronic, and defense needs. Here a technician is involved in laser shock processing.

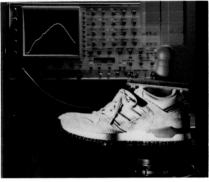

TOP: Information Dimensions, Inc., a Battelle computer subsidiary, offers a database management technology called BASIS to markets in the U.S. and Europe.

ABOVE: Battelle technologists evaluate a wide variety of new products. They recently completed a major project to test the "high tech" features of a new athletic shoe.

RIGHT: Battelle is at the leading edge in the research and development of biodegradable materials and environmentally compatible products.

pand its technology research and development activities.

Over the years Battelle's presence in Columbus has been a key link in the high technology synergism of central Ohio. With its close proximity to The Ohio State University, its collaboration

with city and state governments on a variety of key technology projects, and its ability to create commercial subsidiaries, Battelle has helped provide a foundation for central Ohio's continued economic growth.

Today Battelle's technologies stretch from the factory floor to cutting-edge information systems to new environmental technologies. Key markets are materials technology, manufacturing and product development, health and environment, information technology, electronic and optical sys-

tems, military systems and technology, energy, and transportation.

Annual revenues exceed $700 million and the organization's staff are involved in more than 5,000 projects for 1,600 industrial and government clients.

Leading-edge projects range from the development of environmentally compatible products and the evaluation of high-tech sports shoes to new laser technology and sensors for the European Space Lab. Battelle has also established an advanced materials research center to serve the special worldwide research and development needs of the Emerson Electric Company.

Battelle's increasing emphasis on the commercialization of technology is witnessed by the rapid development of Information Dimensions, Incorporated— a commercial database software subsidiary that within its first three years has reached more than $35 million in sales and 2,000 worldwide installations.

Battelle's commercial focus also has entered the environmental arena, where a subsidiary called Geosafe is providing a unique hazardous waste cleanup technology. In addition, a global partnership among Battelle, Mitsubishi Corporation, and Nippon Telegraph and Telephone is supplying state-of-the-art fiber optic devices to leading industries worldwide. In fact this venture, known as Photonic Integration Research, Inc., is establishing a new manufacturing facility in central Ohio for the production of these fiber optic devices.

As Battelle looks to the future, it sees an accelerated global economy with technology as a driving force. It believes the premium will be on people who can manage information and make decisions and that new technology and products will emerge with greater speed and flexibility. During the 1990s it envisions a business climate where global partnerships among industry will increase dramatically.

With its practical technologies, state-of-the-art equipment, highly skilled staff, and global presence, Battelle views the future as an exciting challenge and as a great opportunity to help advance the quality of life throughout the world.

SOCIETY BANK

Building excellence in our schools, improving race relations, revitalizing our neighborhoods, and helping entrepreneurs succeed are among the tough challenges we face in our community. As a corporate citizen, Society Bank attacks these issues head-on, always striving to find ways to make our communities stronger.

The bank has become a leader in the Columbus area as Society uses its resources to promote economic development and help Columbus businesses grow and prosper.

Society Bank's history in Columbus recalls Society Corporation's 140-year

Society Bank's headquarters at the corner of Broad and Third streets is a downtown Columbus landmark.

history in Ohio. The Society for Savings, forerunner of Society Corporation, began in a single room in a Cleveland office building in 1849. Society Bank's presence in Columbus began in 1972 in a single office at 88 East Broad Street.

Through prudent banking practices that resulted in high asset quality, attention to customer needs, and timely acquisitions, both Society Corporation and Society Bank grew. Today Society Bank's Columbus headquarters building at the original location is a downtown landmark.

Society's presence in Columbus took a quantum leap in 1976-1977 when it bought seven Borden Burger restaurants and converted them to branch offices. In 1979 it opened its 10th office, and a year later acquired American Bank of Central Ohio.

In 1981 Society bought Lancaster National Bank, and enjoyed further growth in 1984 with the acquisition of Scioto Bank. A short two years later it expanded to 20 offices when Franklin Bank became part of Society.

Toledo-based Trustcorp, Inc., with assets of $5.9 billion, had offices in Columbus, one of them in the same block of East Broad Street as Society Bank headquarters, when it announced its intent to become part of Society Corporation in June 1989. After the merger on January

5, 1990, Trustcorp's Columbus operations were integrated into Society Bank.

Most recently Society increased its presence in central Ohio by more than one-third when it bought the deposits and 13 offices of Dayton-based Citizens Federal Savings' central Ohio division.

Today Society Bank's presence in central Ohio comprises 29 offices, including those in Columbus, Chillicothe, Lancaster, and Washington Court House, and continues to enjoy an enviable reputation for its high asset quality. Moreover, its employees' involvement in, and concern for, the communities where they work and live have contributed greatly to the quality of life in Columbus.

Society is a success in Columbus because it works closely with many business owners to help them achieve their dreams. Together, Society bankers and the owners of these firms have written scores of success stories.

Society has been recognized by the Columbus Countywide Development Corporation, the U.S. Small Business Administration, and the Ohio Association of Certified Development Companies for its leadership in small business financing.

Society recently began offering a new program to educate businesses on how to obtain money to support, expand, or start a business. "How to Borrow Money" is

Society Bank continues to expand in the central Ohio area, focusing on quality and community commitment.

the first program of its kind in Ohio and evolved from Society's considerable experience in the small business loan market. The program consisted of a videotape and manual that helps to take the unknown out of the loan process.

Society's relationship with Columbus Neighborhood Housing Services has helped many individuals and families obtain affordable housing opportunities. As a primary lender to the organization, Society Bank has made available a significant amount of the funds borrowed by CNHS over the past several years, resulting in upgraded properties and the ability to provide low-cost housing in

ABOVE: Students explore the city during one of many field trips. Society employees volunteer at Beck Elementary School, opening new worlds for the grade-schoolers.

LEFT: Society Bank thinks of customers as part of the family, helping them to meet their financial goals.

valued neighborhoods.

Much of Society's success results from its commitment to local decision making. Lending decisions affecting the Columbus area are made by the Society bankers who know the central Ohio market best—those who live and work in Columbus and its surrounding communities—enabling the bank to respond to customers quicker.

Society is also a leader in electronic banking for corporations and consumers alike. On the corporate side, the chief financial officers of *Fortune* 500 companies and middle market firms enjoy the control and up-to-date information that Society's cash management services provide.

For consumers, access to more than 27,000 automated teller machines (ATMs) throughout the world through the Plus, Money Station, and Green Machine shared networks means they have ready access to their accounts 24 hours a day, seven days a week. In Ohio, more than 100 financial institutions belong to the Green Machine Network, owned by Society, and share 1,000 ATMs throughout the Midwest.

But Society is more than simply a provider of quality financial services. Its employees are involved in their communities through many different avenues.

One project, "adopting" Beck Elementary School in Columbus' inner city, has many involved employees. They

volunteer their time to help students at the school with one-on-one tutoring, establishing a "branch" where the children can save money, and hosting holiday parties and special school events.

Society Bank is also deeply involved in Operation Feed in Columbus, which provides more than 400,000 meals annually to those in need.

The employees of Society Bank take seriously their responsibilities to their customers and communities and have articulated a set of six shared values that reflect that commitment:

• Unwavering commitment to quality.

• Dedication to providing a consistently high rate of return to shareholders.

• Dedication to providing superior service to the customer.

• Active concern for the well-being of its communities.

• Emphasis on initiative and innovation.

• Commitment to the growth and well-being of employees.

Taken together, these values form a durable framework for ensuring a productive and enriching environment in which to conduct business. As long as Society employees adhere to them, Society will continue to grow and prosper with Columbus.

NATIONWIDE INSURANCE

The Nationwide Insurance enterprise provides financial service solutions for life's uncertainties. These solutions span a wide variety of insurance and other financial security services for individuals, families, businesses, and organizations.

Since Nationwide's beginning in 1926 as the Farm Bureau Mutual Automobile Insurance Company, Columbus has been its home. Says John E. Fisher, general chairman and chief executive officer: "We've grown up with Columbus. We seek always to make positive contributions to the city. We're both proud and thankful that this is our hometown."

Today Nationwide is at home on the northern edge of downtown in the 2.3-million-square-foot Nationwide Plaza complex. Other locations in the metropolitan area include a major regional office facility and the Nationwide Training Center, where thousands of employees and agents further their professional development each year.

Nationwide entered the 1990s as an organization of more than 80 companies with total assets exceeding $25 billion, and well over 40,000 employees and salespeople.

There are some 25 Nationwide regional offices and subsidiary and affiliate headquarters across the continental United States, as well as a major facility in Puerto Rico.

Nationwide also operates in the European community through a subsidiary group called Neckura, and lends financial strength to insurers around the world through reinsurance treaties in more than 40 countries.

Some 22 insurance companies in the Nationwide group now serve the holders of almost 11 million policies and certificates.

In 1926 the original auto insurance company was an answer to a consumer problem. Ohio farmers were paying the same rates for car insurance as city drivers who had more accidents. When existing insurers wouldn't help them

Nationwide's international headquarters, the towering One Nationwide Plaza, is a downtown Columbus landmark.

with lower, more equitable rates, they started Farm Bureau Mutual.

A leader of the founders was Murray D. Lincoln, who would head the organization for 38 years. He was also an early international spokesman for the cooperative movement. Through Lincoln and successive leaders, Nationwide's global cooperative ties have continued to strengthen over the years.

Today the parent Nationwide Mutual Insurance Company is the fourth-largest U.S. auto insurer. It is committed to providing a wide variety of quality insurance products and services at reasonable cost.

Nationwide has been a longtime and active advocate for auto and highway safety. This has recently included a heightened and outspoken commitment to efforts aimed at reducing alcohol-impaired driving.

Nationwide pioneered insurance incentives for auto seat belt use, and continues to support mandatory seat belt laws, air bags and passive restraints, highway construction safety features, youthful driver education, and tough enforcement of traffic laws.

Homeowners insurance is the principal product provided by Nationwide Mutual Fire Insurance Company. This company has grown, since its inception in 1934, to become the nation's fifth-largest writer of homeowners policies. A popular product is the high-quality Golden Blanket homeowners policy with its broad coverage. Protection for condominiums, tenant-occupied homes, mobile homes, and farm residences also is offered.

Another insurer, Nationwide General, is one of only a handful of companies making auto and homeowners policies available through employers and associations. This group approach offers an employee or member benefit that is competitively priced, with the convenience of payroll deduction plans as well as electronic funds transfer.

In 1980 Nationwide purchased Colo-nial Insurance Company of California to provide higher-risk auto and motorcycle insurance.

Nationwide services have included valuable, high-quality life insurance since the mid-1930s, and Nationwide Life Insurance Company is today an industry leader. This company's primary service thrust is competitive products delivered in a "user friendly" fashion. Supporting Nationwide agents in this delivery is aggressive effort to continually enhance service through state-of-the-art electronics and computer applications.

Full-service response to life's uncertainties extends to Nationwide's widely diversified annuities and related investment product services, to industry leadership in sales and administration of public employees' deferred compensation programs through PEBSCO—the subsidiary Public Employees Benefit Services Corporation—and to pension products provided through private pension administrators.

There is a special dedication to innovation in fixed annuities offered by Na-

ABOVE: Three Nationwide Plaza, completed in 1988, expanded the home office complex to help handle service needs into the 1990s.

tionwide agents and through brokers, along with single and flexible premium life products available through brokers.

A major affiliate, Nationwide Financial Services, offers a family of equity,

The Atrium at Nationwide Plaza is a focal point of beauty enjoyed by thousands of visitors and area workers year-round.

bond, and money market mutual funds with combined assets which have grown to more than one billion dollars since the 1950s when Nationwide was the first insurer to offer mutual funds.

In an increasingly challenging area of needs, Nationwide continues to offer a wide range of individual and group health and disability coverages. These high-quality products are cost-efficient, responsible in price and value, and designed to help bring escalating health care costs under better control.

Nationwide offers broad and varied business insurance programs. Enterprise insurers serve the full range of businesses, from the corner grocery to large industrial concerns, and a range of specialized risks. Nationwide is a

RIGHT: The Nationwide Training Center is on U.S. Route 23, three miles north of the Interstate 270 outerbelt.

BELOW: A meditation room in One Nationwide Plaza resulted from an employee suggestion when the tower was being built.

major provider of financial and insurance services to agribusiness.

Since 1985 the Nationwide group has included Wausau Insurance of Wausau, Wisconsin. Wausau has historically committed its people and resources to the needs of business.

Wausau pioneered managed health care in employee benefits. It is one of a very few property insurers capable of engineering highly protected risk (HPR) coverages with its professional fire protection consultants and a superior fire protection laboratory.

Wausau provides consistently exceptional service in such specialized areas

as claims management, underwriting expertise, and loss control consultation.

Nationwide and its companies can call forth the combined capabilities of a full range of interrelated service arms to take a thorough and encompassing approach to solving each client's needs.

For example, working closely with Wausau as well as other Nationwide entities is Gates McDonald, the nation's largest provider of unemployment and workers' compensation cost control services. Serving local and national employers, this company's personnel provide the expertise to optimize each client's cost control of risk and benefit programs.

Farmland Insurance of Des Moines, Iowa, in the Nationwide family since 1982, is a recognized leader in insurance and loss control for the cooperative and independent agribusiness marketplace. Farmland's history of specializing in agricultural risk management spans more than eight decades.

In another response to growing demand, Nationwide organized Scottsdale Insurance Company, which since 1982 has grown to be the second largest U.S. marketer of excess and surplus lines insurance.

There is diversification at Nationwide beyond the insurance and financial services. A valuable, interesting, and growing affiliate is Nationwide Communications, the owner and operator of radio and television stations and cable television systems around the country. This Nationwide broadcasting network reaches more than six million people weekly. The Columbus outlet of Nationwide Communications is WNCI (97.9 FM), broadcasting from Nationwide Plaza studios.

As citizens of Columbus, Nationwide and its employees are major contributors to the community through both financial support and extensive personal involvement.

Corporate payroll, real estate and equivalent taxes, contributions and grants to the United Way and other community causes, and purchases from local suppliers run into the millions of dollars annually. The enterprise generates cash flow through local banks well

into the billions of dollars.

Nationwide employees also make solid community contributions. They are known for their personal generosity to the United Way, and for helping feed the poor through the Franklin County Operation Feed campaign. Their blood-lending has ranked them first among all Ohio donor groups since 1977. Nationwide employees are active participants in civic, educational, cultural, charitable, church, and other citizenship activities. It is company tradition to encourage this volunteer spirit.

Another important corporate involvement finds Nationwide processing Medicare claims for nearly 2 million people in Ohio and West Virginia. This service is provided by the companies

Nationwide's Wausau Insurance affiliate is the largest employer in its hometown of Wausau, Wisconsin, and a national leader in business insurance service.

on a nonprofit, cost-only basis.

Attendant to the story of Nationwide growing with Columbus has been the outgrowing of home offices. From a single room at 199 East Gay Street for the first two years, there were home-office moves to 620-630 East Broad Street from 1928 to 1936, and then to 246 North High Street for four decades.

In 1978 One Nationwide Plaza was dedicated as the international headquarters of Nationwide. Its 40-story tower is a Columbus landmark. The high rise stimulated a massive building boom that revitalized Columbus' once-blighted north downtown, and Nationwide has had a leading role in the continuing renaissance in the area.

The Nationwide complex now includes Two Nationwide Plaza, an 18-story tenant office building completed in 1981, and the 27-story Three Nationwide Plaza, completed in 1988 as an essential home office expansion.

In 1989 The Atrium at Nationwide Plaza was completed and is a focal point of beauty in downtown Columbus. Inside are a tropical garden of thousands of exotic plantings, cascading waterfalls, peaceful pools, and a meandering stream.

The Atrium links Nationwide's headquarters complex with the 33-story office tower of the Ohio Bureau of Workers' Compensation and the Industrial Commission of Ohio. Three Nationwide Plaza, the state building, and

Two Nationwide Plaza, a companion structure to the company's headquarters, is an 18-story tenant office building.

The Atrium were planned, designed, and built in a coordinated venture, the largest that had ever been undertaken in the United States by government and private enterprise.

The Atrium and a walkway network connect the Plaza buildings and link them with nearby government buildings, hotels, parking garages, and the Greater Columbus Convention Center.

General chairman Fisher calls the Nationwide home office complex and surrounding neighborhood "a true human services center—a place for people and a place to help people. That's good for Columbus and good for us. We're excited about the future of Nationwide and our hometown," Fisher adds. "Nationwide has an enduring bond of progress with this great city that we fully intend to keep strengthening.

"We'll continue to emphasize—here in Columbus and everywhere our people work and serve—that 'Nationwide is on your side!'"

Illumination of the One and Three Nationwide Plaza buildings brightens the downtown Columbus skyline at night.

CENTRAL BENEFITS MUTUAL INSURANCE COMPANY

From a regional hospital service association to a multistate marketer of employee benefits through a national subsidiary, Central Benefits Mutual Insurance Company has, for 53 years, grown and matured along with the Columbus community where it makes its home.

Offices at 255 East Main Street—a cornerstone of Columbus' Downtown South district—are home base to Central Benefits Mutual and its wholly owned subsidiary, Central Benefits National Life Insurance Company, which is licensed in nearly half of the United States. There and at the regional offices of Central Benefits National throughout the Midwest approximately 500 associates work to maintain a tradition of service excellence: Quality products, rapid claims turnaround, and prompt, accurate handling of customer inquiries distinguish the company among its competitors in the industry.

Committed to a code centering on respect for the customer, these associates also carry a caring message into the central Ohio community through participation in civic and charitable events, including support of United Way in annual fund drives, and committee representation by Central Benefits management. An activities association conducts ongoing charity fundraisers, helps stock area food pantries through Operation Feed, adopts needy families during the holidays, and sponsors building improvements at a local nursing home.

Concern for the welfare of the central Ohio community also motivated the company's founder, Ralph Jordan. He formed the Columbus Hospital Service Association, a prepaid group hospitalization plan, in 1938 with money borrowed from his own life insurance policy. Jordan also devised an accounting system to aid area hospitals in improving their financial position in a struggling post-Depression economy. The prepayment plan he founded was one of many

emerging throughout the United States that would, from 1939, bear the Blue Cross name and symbol adopted by the American Hospital Association.

Known from 1939 to 1965 as Central Hospital Service Association, and from 1965 to 1986 as Blue Cross of Central Ohio (BCCO), the predecessor to Central Benefits Mutual had several homes in downtown Columbus: the LeVeque Tower (1938-1941); the Hartman Build-

ing on what is now Capital Square (1941-1955); and its own facility at 174 East Long Street (1955-1974). Its present offices in the historic Market Mohawk area were built in 1974.

During its first 45 years Central Benefits and its forerunners concentrated on a single insurance product—classic hospitalization—in a 29-county area of Ohio. But as the 1980s brought changing customer demands, competition

Offices at 255 East Main Street are home to both Central Benefits Mutual Insurance Company and its wholly owned national subsidiary, Central Benefits National Life Insurance Company.

with Blue Cross and Blue Shield Plans and commercial insurers, and the challenge to stem rising health care costs, the firm expanded and diversified. Through subsidiaries, BCCO added coverage for physicians' services, as well as life insurance, in 1985, the same year it published the nation's first health care buyers' guide.

In 1986 BCCO became Central Benefits Mutual Insurance Company and, a year later, formed its national subsidiary. It also built a network of independent agents and brokers to market its products.

First in the nation to implement a preadmission review program, Central Benefits continues to emphasize cost-effective health care in its benefit products and its INFORM cost management program. The company offers a broad selection of employee benefit products, including comprehensive major medical (CMM) products with a variety of options; managed care products; life and disability coverages; and flexible spending accounts.

From Ralph Jordan's resourcefulness to a host of cost-saving initiatives for the future, Central Benefits is proud of its history of innovation—and of the roots that link it to the equally proud traditions of Columbus.

INDUSTRIAL ASSOCIATION OF CENTRAL OHIO

The Industrial Association of Central Ohio (IACO) originated in 1942 during the onset of industrialization in the Midwest. IACO is a nonprofit incorporated organization serving the manufacturing and business community primarily in the central Ohio region. The membership is made up of regional companies from the broad spectrum of the central Ohio business community including manufacturing, electronics, construction, warehousing, food processing, and distributorships. IACO provides information and services to their executives and designated managers. Members work in concert to promote common interests and to advance the general welfare of the manufacturing and business community.

IACO is dedicated to identifying and meeting the needs of every member organization. To achieve this purpose, the association has the following objectives:

• To improve and advance the art of industrial business management.

• To collect and disseminate information and facts concerning management practices, industry, business conditions, and governmental regulations affecting industrial organizations.

• To improve the general industrial

BELOW: The Columbus area is filled with small- and medium-sized manufacturers who turn to the IACO for information concerning management practices, government relations, and the economic outlook.

RIGHT TOP: Many member companies of the Industrial Association of Central Ohio are active in industrial research.

RIGHT BOTTOM: The IACO staff works closely with the membership on a wide variety of subjects ranging from human resources to environmental regulations.

climate in central Ohio by developing relationships with community, legislative, and governmental bodies.

• To increase the ability of member organizations to effectively interact with employees, suppliers, and customers through education.

IACO keeps management informed about relevant legislation, the latest regulations from the Occupational Safety and Health Administration, the Environmental Protection Agency, and the Equal Employment Opportunity Commission, as well as other timely news through a twice-monthly newsletter, the *Communicator*.

Participating members also receive *Annual Wage and Salary Surveys*. These are comprehensive surveys of executive and professional salaries, and wages of nonexempt employees in central Ohio. Mini-surveys on current economic projections and legislative proposals are also provided. IACO conducts periodic mailings covering topics of special interest to management such as Consumer Price Index and Medical Cost Containment activities reports.

IACO's staff maintains a compre-

hensive library of video and audio cassette tapes, books, and technical and reference papers that are available for any member's use.

The association encourages active participation of its members with regularly scheduled meetings. These meetings are designed for specific company officers. For example, the Executive Round Table Discussion Group targets senior principal executive officers. Human resources and personnel directors meet in monthly council sessions, as do the plant engineers. Special meetings are held on such subjects as environmental regulations, occupational safety and health, equal opportunity, workers' compensation, and labor law.

Periodically IACO conducts seminars for all association members covering matters of current concern, such as "Substance Abuse in the WorkPlace" and "Hazard Communication" and "Communications Skills for Managers."

The world is rapidly changing into a global marketplace, and IACO is doing its part in keeping its members abreast of the times. As members' requirements change, IACO is determined to see that they receive the most up-to-date information and educational tools in a timely and cost-effective manner.

THE MIDLAND

Headquartered in Columbus since its conception, The Midland has been providing life insurance products and related financial services for close to 90 years. Currently the company's assets total nearly one billion dollars, and it has more than $20 billion of life insurance and annuities in force.

The Midland Mutual Life Insurance Company was founded in 1905 by 18 prominent Columbus men who were guided by a single philosophy: Create products and services that respond to people's needs, and at the same time develop a sound management system that promotes stability and growth.

The Midland's first president, William Oxley Thompson, was a nationally respected educator and president of The Ohio State University. Under his guidance The Midland offered the stability customers wanted in their insurer, with a high degree of innovation.

It was The Midland that pioneered

Backing the Buckeyes! The Midland is proud to support Ohio State University's athletic programs.

such industry breakthroughs as combining disability with life insurance in one policy. It was also The Midland that, shortly after World War I, when war clauses exempted insurance companies from having to pay for servicemen killed during the war, elected to honor these claims and pay death benefits to their survivors.

When the Great Depression hit a few years later, The Midland not only survived when many others failed, but it also met every one of its obligations.

During the 1950s Midland stockholders were faced with the threat of a hostile takeover of the business, but they voted to mutualize the company and thereby continue to honor the charter. It stated that business would be conducted, for all time, as a trust for the benefit of policyowners and that stockholders had no right to profits in excess of limits fixed in the charter.

The Midland was among the first to computerize the insurance business during the 1960s, in what became a prototype installation for IBM. To help consumers fight the rampant inflation and high interest rates of the late 1970s and early 1980s, The Midland introduced an inflation fighter policy that was tied to the Consumer Price Index and a universal life policy that offered flexible premiums and an adjustable death benefit.

The Midland was the first in the industry to introduce in the mid-1980s a

term life product with a five- and 10-year level premium guarantee; a 15-year level premium guarantee was added four years later. In 1990 the Midland began installing a state-of-the-art microcomputer network that will have a favorable impact on expenses for years to come.

The measure of financial stability in the life insurance industry is the rating system of the A.M. Best Company. The Midland has received Best's top rating every year since 1953. The Midland maintains a high-quality investment portfolio, and the delinquency rate on mortgages the company holds is one of the best in the industry.

The Midland is proud of its record and proud of its community involvement. As a patron of the arts, a supporter of education, and a loyal United Way contributor, The Midland is an active and eager corporate citizen.

A solid past is not enough to guarantee a solid future. That's why The Midland has equipped itself to effectively respond to the needs of an ever-changing marketplace with a company-wide product team/profit center concept, a multimillion-dollar, state-of-the-art computer system, and, most important, a commitment from its people to be the "best place to buy insurance."

The Midland building at 250 East Broad Street in downtown Columbus.

BANC ONE CORPORATION

Bank One, Columbus, NA, the lead bank of Banc One Corporation, has gained a national reputation for innovative banking service.

With assets of $30.3 billion by year-end 1990, the parent corporation is among the nation's 22nd largest banking organizations. In 1990 the "super regional" holding company ranked first among the 50 largest U.S. banks in return on average assets, a crucial measure of banking profitability.

The home office of Bank One, Columbus, NA, and headquarters for Banc One Corporation are at 100 East Broad Street, across from Ohio's state capitol.

The roots of Banc One go back to 1868, with the formation by F.C. Sessions, of Sessions & Company, a private banking firm in downtown Columbus. Following a series of bank mergers, in 1929 it became the City National Bank & Trust Co. of Columbus.

In 1968 City National and the Farmers Bank of Mansfield (Ohio) founded the parent corporation, which was at first known as First Banc Group of Ohio Inc. The bank remained City National until 1979, when the corporate name and those of its affiliates were changed to that which they are today.

Banc One chairman John B. McCoy, whose father, John G. McCoy, and grandfather, John H. McCoy, each served as chairman of City National, is committed to civic improvements in Columbus. For example, he served as the 1990-1991 chairman of Downtown Columbus, Inc., a planning agency comprised of members of the business community and government.

"Bank One has played a significant role in the development of downtown Columbus theater and special events," according to McCoy. For example, the bank underwrote the first production at Players Theatre's new home in the Vern Riffe Center for Government and the Arts and continues as a major underwriter and source of volunteers for Oktoberfest celebration in historic German Village.

Bank One also focuses on the education and training of disadvantaged youth. Major contributions are made to Columbus Public Schools' "I Know I Can"

Foundation, and Bank One scholarships are a staple of youth programs at Ballet Met and at Martin Luther King Jr. Center.

With the opening of the Pickerington banking center and acquisition of four offices of Equitable Savings in Delaware, Sunbury, and Lancaster during 1990, Bank One began the 1990s with 45 banking locations serving residences and businesses in a six-county, central Ohio region.

Bank One has gained a national reputation of being an innovator in the delivery of financial services. In 1950 the bank was the first in the country to introduce drive-in banking. By 1966 it was the first to offer VISA (formerly

BankAmericard) credit cards outside of California.

Bank One's Sawmill Financial Marketplace, opened in the late 1980s, offers a supermarket of financial services, seven days a week, in a unique customer-oriented environment. "The Marketplace is now a prototype for financial service centers of the 1990s," says Michael J. McMennamin, chairman of Bank One, Columbus, NA.

To better serve the customer of the

The home office of Bank One, Columbus, NA, and the headquarters of Banc One Corporation are located in downtown Columbus at 100 East Broad Street.

1990s, Bank One has developed such services as the Blue Max Account and Bank at Work. Bank One also has been expanding its service to small business through a Business Loan Center.

In January 1990 the corporation made an initial investment in Bank One, Texas, NA, which, at that time, had assets in excess of $13 billion. As of mid-1991 Banc One operated 51 banking organizations with 745 offices in Illinois, Indiana, Kentucky, Michigan, Ohio, Wisconsin, and Texas.

Banc One Chairman McCoy explains, "Wherever our bank affiliation opportunities lead us during the 1990s, the heart of Bank One remains in its hometown of Columbus."

BANC ONE CAPITAL CORPORATION

Banc One Capital Corporation is an investment banking firm that provides customers in the private and public sectors with investment banking services. It was established in 1981 as Meuse, Rinker, Chapman, Endres & Brooks and became affiliated with Banc One Corporation in the second half of 1990.

"The affiliation complements and strengthens our efforts in meeting the challenges of even more sophisticated investment banking needs of the 1990s

Bank One's Sawmill Financial Marketplace is a unique facility offering investment, travel, and home real estate services in addition to traditional banking services.

Ronald D. Brooks, vice chairman in charge of sales and trading (left), and Sandra Edgar, trading assistant, price a transaction in the trading room of Banc One Capital Corporation.

and beyond," says David R. Meuse, chairman of Banc One Capital.

As a private investment banking firm Meuse Rinker specialized in identifying and developing new financial concepts and translating them into viable solutions. Rapid growth of the corporation during the 1980s is attributed to deliberately seeking clients with involved financial problems, often attended by significant regulatory difficulties and complex tax problems.

"The determination to accept the challenge of resolving the difficult has equipped our organization with a highly developed capacity to design innovative solutions to client problems," Meuse explains.

Banc One Capital's Corporate Finance activities include business sales, including mergers and acquisitions, management buyouts, private placement of debt, merchant banking, and general advisory work for corporate debt and equity restructuring. These services are offered primarily for middle-market companies with annual sales of $10 million to $250 million.

Asset Securitization enables the corporation to broaden a customer's borrowing base and lower its cost of capital by ex-

panding its effective lending base through the securities markets.

In the area of Public Finance, Banc One Capital is an active participant in the area of tax-exempt securities, with concentration on housing, health care, industrial development, and public finance issues. It provides complete packages for the primary market sale of a new debt issue, including origination services, underwriting, and distribution.

The mission of the corporation is to redefine banking for the middle-market companies. This is accomplished by combining the financial technology and sales culture of Banc One Capital with the relationship banking and analytical abilities available through Bank One affiliate banks. Additional objectives are to create change and to establish a new standard of customer service in middle-market banking.

Looking to the future, Meuse believes that, "With our energy and innovative approach to investment banking, we look to serving an even greater number of Banc One Capital customers throughout the 1990s."

CHEMICAL ABSTRACTS SERVICE

There are no chemicals at Chemical Abstracts Service. No laboratories, no Bunsen burners, no glass vials, no beakers, no maze of tubes.

But among the more than 1,500 employees of the Columbus-based service, many are chemists, as well as biologists, physicists, engineers, computer specialists, and a host of other professionals working to make the latest information from chemical research accessible to users throughout the world.

The task of reviewing and refining some 12,000 scientific and technical journals from 150 nations, as well as thousands of public and private papers, is given to the CAS document analysts. In addition to being specialists in various scientific disciplines, many are bilingual or multilingual, fluent in everything from Afrikaans or Azerbaijani to Macedonian and Vietnamese. Their product is a concise English summary of the research for publication by CAS.

Today about 10,000 of these summaries are published each week, or more than 500,000 annually. Each has been carefully and completely indexed so that a medical researcher wondering if a particular chemical has proven to be effective against tumors, or an industrial chemist interested in a new process for manufacturing a particular chemical compound, can be led to the pertinent journal articles and patents.

Each weekly issue of the publication *Chemical Abstracts* contains more than 10,000 condensations. Nearly 4,000 pages of abstracts are published every month, and every five years CAS compiles the semiannual indexes into a massive collective index of its chemical publications. In 1992 this gargantuan undertaking will encompass 210,000 pages in 120 volumes.

This is a long way from the genesis of CAS more than 84 years ago. American chemists, dissatisfied with the coverage of American chemical literature in European abstract journals, advocated a national journal that would recognize their accomplishments. They realized their dream in January 1907, when the American Chemical Society first published *Chemical Abstracts* as a non-profit editorial enterprise.

The first editor was William A. Noyes, Sr., chief chemist for the Bureau of Standards in Washington, D.C. He was succeeded by Austin M. Patterson, which was fortunate for Columbus. Because the former chemical editor of *Webster's Dictionary* lived in Xenia, Ohio, the society agreed in 1909 to move the editorial office to the campus of The Ohio State University, which had invited the move.

There were four members of the staff at that time, working in one 15- by 30-foot room. Together they published 15,459 abstracts that year.

In 1914 Patterson resigned due to poor health and was succeeded briefly by John J. Miller, who also resigned that same year. Evan J. Crane, who had been on the staff since 1911, was named editor in 1915. He remained at the helm for the next 43 years and became the first director of Chemical Abstracts Service when the growing editorial organization was renamed and elevated to the status of a division of the American Chemical Society in 1956.

The years Crane served were both critical and formative years for CAS as it strived for "complete coverage" of the world's chemical literature. Two world wars made the collecting of data particularly difficult.

During World War II, for instance, European papers were sent to CAS in Columbus through Italy and Siberia. Many documents on microfilm were smuggled into Switzerland and routed through Moscow, including all-important German patents.

Following the war, chemical literature from throughout the world began to pour into Columbus. By the mid-1950s

about three-quarters of the publications abstracted for *Chemical Abstracts* came from outside the United States.

As the volume of chemical information grew so did expenses, and the American Chemical Society determined that if CAS was to continue to be self-supporting, subscription policies had to be changed. Today CAS pays its own way, including a share of the society's general and administrative expenses, and contributes toward maintaining CAS's general reserve fund.

When Crane, a Columbus native, retired in 1958, his successor as director was Dale B. Baker, a chemical engineer who had come to CAS from Du Pont in 1946. He, in turn, was succeeded in 1986 by Ronald L. Wigington, an electrical engineer who had been deputy executive director for Washington operations of the American Chemical Society.

During the 1960s and 1970s CAS advanced into the modern era, introducing the world's first computer-produced periodical, *Chemical Titles*, a weekly that lists newly published articles relating to chemistry. Other periodicals that have been added include *CA Selects*, *CA Section Groupings*, *Chemical In-*

ABOVE: The 1,500 chemists, biologists, physicists, engineers, computer specialists, and other professionals at Chemical Abstract Service work to make the latest information from chemical research accessible to users throughout the world.

LEFT: CAS document analysts create abstracts and precise index entries for CA issues.

CAS is located in two large buildings just north of the OSU campus.

dustry Notes, and *CAS Biotech Updates*.

In 1965 CAS moved into its own large building just north of the OSU campus. A second structure of almost equal size was added in 1973.

Also in 1965, CAS established the Chemical Registry System, a collection of information on chemical substances reported in the world's scientific literature. Since 1965 the CAS Chemical Registry System has recorded information on more than 11 million chemical substances, including organic compounds, coordination compounds, polymers, alloys, mixtures, and minerals. Each week, information on over 10,000 additional substances is added to the system.

Today the CAS Chemical Registry System has become the international standard for chemical substance identification and reporting. Scientists and information specialists from Australia to Zaire can use their computers to access the Registry System in the CAS Registry File.

In the last half of the 1960s CAS set out to build a highly automated pro-cessing system that would produce printed abstracts and indexes more efficiently and economically, and at the same time create a machine-readable database that could provide the basis for new forms of information services.

This was largely achieved by the mid-1970s. Automated processing opened new doors for publishing, locating, and retrieving chemical information. Major emphasis was placed on expanding the direct delivery of information through on-line computer services, providing answers in seconds that could take hours or even days of page turning to discover through printed abstracts and indexes.

While CAS began as an American information service, today it is global in terms of the primary sources it covers, the databases it creates, the audiences it serves, and the reach of its printed and electronic services. To better serve the worldwide scientific community, CAS works closely with scientific and technical organizations in Europe and Japan in operating an international online computer network for scientific and technical information—STN International.

Through STN International, scientific information searchers in most of the world can conveniently access the CAS databases and more than 100 other scientific and technical computer files via connections to the nearest of three service centers—Columbus, Tokyo, or Karlsruhe, Germany. All computers in the STN network operate on Messenger software developed by CAS for the network.

In 1990 CAS offered the Materials Property Data Network on STN International, providing on-line access to worldwide sources of numeric data on materials property research and engineering.

CAS has changed greatly over the years, but one thing has remained the same—a total commitment to providing the most comprehensive and accurate secondary information on chemical science and technology in the most useful and convenient form to support the continuing progress of scientific research and development.

11 PROFESSIONS
▲▲▲▲▲▲▲▲▲▲▲▲▲▲▲▲▲
397

Columbus' professional community brings a wealth of ability and insight to the area.

Brubaker/Brandt, 398; Myers-NBD Incorporated, 400; Jones, Day, Reavis & Pogue, 401; R.D. Zande & Associates, Limited, 402; Zande Environmental Service, Inc., 403; Burgess & Niple Limited, 404; Ernst & Young, 406; Emens, Hurd, Kegler & Ritter Co.,L.P.A., 408; Moody/Nolan Ltd., Incorporated, 410; M-E Engineering, Inc., 411; Squire, Sanders & Dempsey, 412; Porter, Wright, Morris & Arthur, 414; KPMG Peat Marwick, 415; Arthur Andersen, 416

Photo by Jim Baron

BRUBAKER/BRANDT INCORPORATED

Brubaker/Brandt Incorporated, a national architectural and planning firm based in Columbus, is known for the clients it keeps . . . and keeps . . . and keeps.

For more than three decades Brubaker/Brandt has served local, state, and national clients who have turned to the firm more than once because of its unique ability to tailor highly complex projects and fulfill specialized needs. Brubaker/Brandt also is widely recognized for its beautifully proportioned and functional designs that create elegant environments of lasting beauty.

The professional team approach Brubaker/Brandt has practiced for more than 30 years has proven highly successful, as evidenced in part by its many award-winning projects. Clients, too, appreciate the pulling together of the firm's management skills and the talent of its architects, planners, program analysts, and interior specialists. All contribute to the successful completion of superior projects—on time and within budget.

The fundamental philosophy of Brubaker/Brandt is to maintain an orga-

nizational staff of highly qualified professionals with the client's needs foremost in their minds. They are cost-conscious, design-oriented specialists who work well in the multidisciplinary environment nurtured by partners Roger W. Lott and Kurt G. Howard, and by the firm's founding principals, Leland F. Brubaker and Kent H. Brandt, both distinguished alumni of architecture at The Ohio State University who have been in partnership since 1957.

This extensive and varied talent has produced an abundance of projects just as extensive and varied. Office buildings, high-tech centers, performing arts theaters, sports arenas, hospitals, and suburban multi-family communities— such diverse projects as these are a part of the work of Brubaker/Brandt at its national headquarters, 4640 Executive Drive, Columbus, Ohio.

Borden, Monsanto, General Electric, Banc One, Nationwide Insurance, Mutual of New York, Ohio Bell, Greyhound, Ross Laboratories, and JC Penney Insurance are but a few of the major corporations nationwide that have sought Brubaker/Brandt's services. In

The Rhodes State Office Tower is located across Broad Street from the capitol (right). Photo by Balthazar Korab Studios

Columbus the firm has designed headquarters facilities for the Online Computer Library Center (OCLC), Chemical Abstracts Service, Worthington Industries, Ohio Bell Telephone, Motorists Mutual Insurance Company, the Columbus Board of Realtors, and the Tuberculosis Society.

Public sector projects include the 42-story Rhodes State Office Tower, the Federal Office Building, and the Central Safety Building in downtown Columbus, as well as Port Columbus International Airport. And institutions of higher learning—The Ohio State University, Denison University, Baldwin-Wallace College, Wright State University, Kenyon College, Ohio University, Muskingum College, Wooster College, and Edison Community College in Fort Myers, Florida—have put Brubaker/ Brandt to the test in designing academic, recreational, and cultural facilities for them.

The Performing Arts Center at Edison Community College is a perfect example of the Brubaker/Brandt team philosophy. The firm assembled nationally recognized experts in theatrical and acoustical technology to work on the center with Brubaker/Brandt architects

An artist's rendering of the Central Safety Building, Columbus. Photo by Art Associates, Inc.

and engineers. By gathering together experts from all the required disciplines and placing them under one management, the client was assured of a single, unified source of creativity, productivity, and responsibility.

In the 1970s and 1980s the firm developed a strong reputation for the design and execution of high-technology and computer-related facilities. This was due not only to the number of projects it undertook, but also to the range of projects and the solutions it found to complex design considerations.

At the headquarters of OCLC in the Columbus suburb of Dublin, high technology was interfaced with high security. OCLC operates 24 hours a day to provide on-line computerized referencing for libraries throughout the world. In addition, more than one million library cards are printed, processed, and mailed from OCLC every week. Reliability and security were key design considerations.

Brubaker/Brandt fashioned a plan incorporating three separate stacked computer rooms, linked vertically, with more than 43,000 square feet of raised computer floor. Major building systems are protected by computer monitoring, and on-line banks of batteries are ready to supply fail-safe power until emergency generators could start up. Key access points throughout the four-story facility are centrally monitored and controlled by a magnetic, computerized card-reader system.

Two other examples of high-tech facilities that required Brubaker/Brandt's special skills are the Banc One Computer Center on a 59-acre site in

LEFT: Edison Community College Performing Arts Center, Fort Myers, Florida. Photo by Courtesy of Edison Community College

ABOVE: Headquarters for Online Computer Library Center in Dublin. Photo by Balthazar Korab Studios

RIGHT: Port Columbus International Airport. Photo by Chroma Studios

Westerville, Ohio, which had needs similar to OCLC because of security and extensive computer operations, and the Learning and Communications Center for General Electric at its Transportation Systems Business Operations headquarters in Erie, Pennsylvania. This unique facility, which is part of GE's "Factory of the Future," includes advanced computerized, audio-visual training areas, one of which allows a diesel locomotive to be brought into the building for hands-on training. The Agronomy, Natural Resources and Plant Pathology Building at OSU is one of more than 60 projects for educational institutions completed by Brubaker/Brandt. It contains 43 flexible teaching and research laboratories, a greenhouse, an auditorium serving the university at large, special support areas, and offices for the three departments in the building.

Another unique expression of Brubaker/Brandt's diverse talents is seen

at the General Electric Lighting Institute in Cleveland. GE asked Brubaker/Brandt to not only completely restore the classical beauty and function of their world-famous lighting institute (already on the National Register), but at the same time to join with national lighting consultants to provide magnificent spaces for demonstrating advanced lighting products and techniques.

Although the architectural and planning firm has been successfully serving its clients since 1957, Brubaker/Brandt is still on the cutting edge of its profession. With its talented team and forward-looking approach, Brubaker/Brandt is dedicated to playing an active role in the development of the challenging world of tomorrow.

MYERS-NBD INCORPORATED

Making a contribution in business and in the community is an attitude that Myers-NBD Incorporated believes important to its success and to the growth of Columbus and central Ohio. This concern for more than just bricks and mortar may be the reason that some of its clients have been with the design firm for more than 40 years.

The company's management also believes in giving back to the community. Most of the management serve on local boards, from the Arthritis Foundation to the Columbus Zoo.

They also give to their industry. Bob Myers and Bob Nichols are both past presidents of the Builders Exchange. They, along with others, remain involved with the American Institute of Architects, the Construction Specifications Institute, the International Facility Management Association, and many other professional and civic organizations.

The success of Myers-NBD is due to the highly qualified professional staff of registered architects and support personnel. They work together to form a creative and administrative nucleus of a professional design team.

The Daimler Building, at 1500 Lake Shore Drive, is one of numerous office buildings Myers-NBD has designed.

The principals, registered to practice in more than a dozen states, are also members of the National Council of Architectural Registration Board. Their broad-based experiences have provided the exposure and opportunity to solve many complex problems related to human activity and environment. This experience has also helped Myers-NBD to resolve difficult budgetary problems and become familiar with a wide range of special systems, products, and equipment.

The client list of Myers-NBD ranges from A to Z, aviation projects to the zoo. The aviation projects include all of Lane Aviation, Executive Jet Aviation, and several projects for Port Columbus International Airport. Zoo projects include master plans as well as exhibits for the animals of Asia, South America, and Africa and for reptiles of the world.

Other endeavors include financial

LEFT: Myers-NBD has been involved in several projects at the Columbus Zoo including the design for the pachyderm facility.

ABOVE: Lane Aviation, a fixed-based operator at Port Columbus International Airport, is one of the aviation clients Myers-NBD has served.

facilities for Banc One Corp., headquarters and parking for Grange Mutual Insurance Co., motels for Country Hearth Inns in several states, all the buildings for Franklin University, and several buildings for The Ohio State University and Otterbein College. The firm undertook seven schools for Westerville and completed the entire $44-million project within 30 months.

Myers-NBD has also been involved in libraries, computer centers, supermarkets, stores in several states for Big Bear and Hart's, and shopping centers including Worthington Square. There have also been numerous office buildings and industrial facilities built, such as those for The Nippert Co.

The professional background gained through these varied experiences has enabled the firm to aid its clients in an experienced and economical manner toward solving their project needs.

"Columbus and central Ohio certainly have been good to us," says Robert H. Myers, president of Myers-NBD. "We are proud to be a part of such a dynamic area.

"The reasons for the success of continued growth in central Ohio are many, but I believe success is the result of good people, and central Ohio has good people."

JONES, DAY, REAVIS & POGUE

Jones, Day, Reavis & Pogue is one of the largest law firms in the world, with more than 1,200 lawyers and offices in 20 major cities, including Columbus.

With origins that trace back to the late nineteenth century, Jones, Day always has had its head office in Ohio. The globalization of business generally, as well as the diverse needs of its clients, which presently include about one-half of the *Fortune* 500 companies, have caused Jones, Day to expand geographically to a total of 11 domestic offices and nine offices abroad.

Jones, Day's Columbus office opened in January 1980 with a complement of five lawyers. By the beginning of the next decade, it had some 60 lawyers on three floors in the Huntington Center, which is opposite the statehouse. Like the capital city in which it is located, the Columbus office is young, confident, and growing.

The office offers a full range of legal services to public and private corporations, as well as other business organizations and individuals.

The litigation practice and personnel are a particular strength. With an active and diverse docket of matters in both state and federal courts, as well as before a variety of governmental agencies, the Columbus litigation practice includes products liability, hostile tender offer, environmental, health and safety, labor, First Amendment, and general litigation matters.

The corporate practice comprises a broad range of highly sophisticated general corporate, securities, and business matters. These include negotiated acquisitions and dispositions, hostile takeovers, public securities offerings and private placements, leveraged buyouts, bank acquisitions, commercial lending, and general business law, representing a wide variety of public and closely held corporate clients.

A particularly active specialty of the Columbus office involves sophisticated nationwide credit card and consumer fi-

nance matters and regulatory work for a variety of financial institutions throughout the country.

The tax practice includes deferred compensation, personal planning, tax-driven financing, and ruling and controversy matters. A noteworthy strength of the tax practice is in the area of state and local tax matters.

Other practice areas include a broad range of international, health care, and real estate matters, legislative counseling, and an extensive administrative law practice before a variety of governmental agencies.

The Columbus office and its lawyers have assumed an active and visible role in the dynamic life of the city and its suburbs. In addition to serving on several corporate boards and as trustees for numerous arts organizations, a number of the lawyers are actively involved in assisting various social, health, and human service organizations throughout the community.

Jones, Day is considered to be among the most prominent general corporate law firms in the United States and abroad. Notwithstanding the diversity of its practice and geographic locations, the firm is structured, managed, and operated as a single, fully-integrated partnership committed to excellence in the practice of law.

Jones, Day has an advanced technology system capable of linking all of its

offices around the world and around the clock. Sophisticated interoffice computer technology is one of the firm's most important assets and places Jones, Day in a position of leadership in the legal profession. These systems, coupled with the firm's commitment to excellence, enable Jones, Day to draw upon the experience of its lawyers worldwide in dealing with its clients' legal problems in a manner which is both efficient and cost effective.

As international boundaries change and become redefined, the practice of law grows increasingly complex. With its international network of offices and a structure that assures the highest quality of legal service, Jones, Day is uniquely positioned to respond to the diverse and multifaceted needs of today's business clients.

Senior members of the firm, such as Robert Duncan (center), work closely with their younger associates to ensure continued excellence in the practice of law.

The Jones, Day Columbus office, which was established in 1980, is today located on three floors of the Huntington Center in the heart of the city's downtown.

R.D. ZANDE & ASSOCIATES, LIMITED

R.D. Zande & Associates, Limited, has been an integral part of the growth of Columbus since the firm's inception as a civil engineering firm in 1968.

Primary in the Zande business philosophy was the commitment to create a listening environment and to establish a partnership with the client. With an unparalleled dedication to service, the company established a tradition for combining engineering expertise, experience, and creativity to design long-term solutions for the client's unique project requirements, solutions that resolve today's problems and anticipate tomorrow's needs.

In serving both governmental jurisdictions and the private sector, Zande has made a significant contribution to Columbus in providing engineering excellence for a large variety of projects, some of which are familiar landmarks of Columbus. Others are in the unseen background of the Columbus infrastructure.

Examples of Zande projects include: Port Columbus International Airport, Interstate 670, Westbelt Business Park, Hayden Run Bridge, Crosswoods Center, Franklin County Landfill, Golfview

R.D. Zande & Associates, Limited, offers one-source engineering capabilities from design to construction administration for the least complex job to a multidiscipline project.

Woods, Villages at Hayden Run, and Ballymead at Dublin.

Zande offers a full complement of services in its multi-discipline approach to meeting engineering needs. Services include the following:

• Transportation and Structural Division: Complex bridge and major highway design; transportation studies; pavement analysis and design and structural inspection; airport planning and airport runway, taxiway, and ramp design; bikeway studies and design.

• Private Development Division: Annexations; feasibility studies/site research; land planning; zoning assistance; residential developments; industrial/commercial complexes.

• Environmental Division: Wastewater collection and treatment systems; water treatment, storage, and distribution systems; industrial pretreatment; solid and hazardous waste management; permit assistance; environmental assessments and hydrogeological services.

In addition to the three major divisions, Zande maintains a field survey department and a construction services department. Both departments provide services to Zande in-house projects as well as independent clients.

From inception throughout the continuous expansion of services, the firm's objectives have remained constant:

R.D. Zande provides specialized site/land development design services for a wide variety of projects.

• To establish effective communication with clients so that Zande professionals develop engineering solutions that meet the client's specific needs.

• To provide high quality and cost-effective engineering solutions that continually demonstrate the integrity of the product, service, and engineering excellence.

• To create and maintain a work environment that challenges Zande employees and provides an environment for professional growth.

Consistent with the business philosophy, the Zande staff is committed to providing the Columbus community with more than engineering excellence. Community involvement and contributions range from Junior Achievement, United Way, Red Cross Donor Drive, and St. Stephen's Community House to active participation in the Columbus Area Chamber of Commerce, Development Committee for Greater Columbus, and a variety of professional organizations.

In addition to the Columbus offices of Zande and Zande Environmental Service, Inc., offices are maintained in Cincinnati and Orlando, Florida.

ZANDE ENVIRONMENTAL SERVICE, INC.

Equipped with state-of-the-art specialized instrumentation, the Zande laboratory provides accurate and timely evaluations that adhere to U.S. EPA methods and procedures.

Zande Environmental Service, Inc., provides a broad range of environmental analytical testing services to industry; local, state, and federal governments; private institutions; professional clients; and individuals.

Richard D. Zande, chief executive officer of the parent company, R.D. Zande & Associates, Limited, founded Zande Environmental Service in 1988 to meet the growing need for analytical evaluation services for water, air, soil, sediment, and hazardous waste.

Today Zande Environmental Service is recognized as one of the most sophisticated analytical labs in the Midwest and has been certified by the Environmental Protection Agency. Its comprehensive in-house capabilities allow Zande Environmental Service to execute a wide range of analytical analyses, from the least complex to the highly sophisticated.

Equipped with state-of-the-art instrumentation, from complete Finnigan and VG GC/MS systems to a Leeman ICP spectrometer, the company's laboratory provides full in-house environmental analyses, ranging from conventional organic and inorganic compounds to specialized organic analyses such as those indicating pesticides/herbicides, PCBs, and volatile and semivolatile organic compounds.

Producing quality data which meets the needs of the client on a timely basis is the paramount objective of Zande Environmental Service. To assure the highest standards of quality, the staff of scientists, chemists, and technicians strictly adhere to all analytical methods and procedures established by the EPA. All lab operations are performed in accordance with a stringent quality assurance program.

Analytical results are only meaningful if proper sampling procedures are utilized. Uncompromised analytical results are accomplished by using appropriate field sampling techniques and procedures, and by developing field sampling manuals and methodologies. The Zande field personnel are thoroughly trained in a variety of sampling technologies and utilize state-of-the-art sampling equipment.

These field service capabilities include: sampling soil/sediment, surface water, leachate, and asbestos; groundwater monitoring; waste characterization; measurement of organic vapors, dusts, and mists; 24-hour composite sampling; and industrial pretreatment sampling.

The divisions of R.D. Zande & Associates benefit from the support provided by Zande Environmental Service and, in turn, ZES profits from the engineering expertise provided by the parent company. Combining engineering expertise with analytical and scientific capabilities provides a much needed interdisciplinary approach to solving today's diverse environmental challenges.

Zande Environmental Service shares the business philosophy of its parent company and emphasizes both the quality of service provided and the responsive manner in which the service is provided. The lab is firmly dedicated to understanding and being responsive to the clients' changing needs, and, as it has done since its inception, it will continue to expand its services as legislation and events impact environmental concerns and requirements.

Zande Environmental Service provides on-site testing and field sampling as an additional service to clients.

BURGESS & NIPLE, LIMITED

When Philip Burgess left his home state of Massachusetts soon after graduating from the Massachusetts Institute of Technology, he could not have imagined the impact his engineering work would have on Columbus and Ohio.

In 1912 Burgess teamed with Chester A. Niple to form Burgess & Niple, a consulting engineering firm specializing in water testing and treatment, sewage treatment, drainage systems, streets, and bridges. Among B&N's first ventures were an innovative water plant in Niles, Ohio, featuring sand filters for purification, and major street improvements in the communities of Grandview and Marble Cliff.

From its early days as a small business to its present status as a large, multidisciplinary engineering and architectural firm, B&N has enjoyed a reputation for integrity, professionalism, and quality of service.

Burgess & Niple, Limited, is a limited partnership association with headquarters at 5085 Reed Road in northwest Columbus. It also has district offices in Akron, Cincinnati, and Painesville, Ohio; Crestview Hills, Kentucky; Park-

ersburg, West Virginia; and Payson and Phoenix, Arizona. B&N employs more than 500 people in these eight offices, more than 300 of whom are located in Columbus.

While B&N continues to work extensively in the fields of water and wastewater treatment and highway design, it has developed a strong practice in bridge design and inspection, environmental audits, geotechnical services, solid and hazardous waste management, land development, utility design and rate analysis, and architecture.

Its nationally recognized team of bridge inspection engineers and technicians pioneered the use of rock climbing techniques to access large bridges. Since 1980 more than 1,600 bridges have been inspected in Ohio, Kentucky, West Virginia, Arizona, Oregon, and Idaho, 130 of which have incorporated this state-of-the-art technique.

In the area of bridge design, B&N has been involved in nearly 100 prominent projects, including designs for two new bridges across the Ohio River and the new Broad Street Bridge over the Scioto River in downtown Columbus. For this landmark project, B&N teamed with one of the world's most respected bridge design experts from Germany and with urban design architects from Philadelphia, Pennsylvania. Features of

On average, Burgess & Niple laboratory personnel analyze more than 10,000 samples per year in an in-house facility that began as an engineering support service in 1912.

this unique bridge include portal sculptures, wide plazas, sidewalks, and a riverwalk that further encourages downtown activities along the riverfront.

Other prominent local bridges include the twin bridges carrying I-270 across the Scioto River in northwest Franklin County. Highway projects in central Ohio have been equally visible. B&N planned much of the I-71 freeway between Columbus and Cincinnati and major portions of I-670 and I-270 Columbus outerbelt. The firm also designed the $13-million improvements to a one-mile corridor of High Street in downtown Columbus. Assisted by another design firm, the project included bus lanes, vehicle lanes, sidewalks, curbs, lighting, transit shelters, streetscape features, and utility relocations.

More than 30 architects at B&N provide a diverse range of design services. These include design and/or renovation of facilities for primary and secondary education, offices, warehouses, medical and long-term health care, prison industries, and laboratories.

In Ohio B&N is the lead architect for development of the $110-million Perry Community Education Village, a unique community-oriented facility on a 150-acre campus in northeast Ohio. Another innovative architectural project involved the design of a combination elementary-middle school facility in Solon, Ohio, with an associate architectural firm. Master plans have been prepared for such major institutions as

A 31,000-square-foot expansion of Burgess & Niple's corporate headquarters on Reed Road in northwest Columbus was completed in May 1990.

West Virginia University and Morehead State University.

The firm's most prominent local architectural project involved the design, with an associate firm, of the $17-million Bioscience/Parks Hall Research Laboratory addition at The Ohio State University.

Other architectural designs include physics and chemistry laboratories at Bowling Green State University, renovation of the Ohio Departments Building, a new Franklin County Sheriff's Department Communications facility, a warehouse for Highlights for Children, and a manufacturing facility for Newman Technologies, Inc., in Mansfield.

Since 1987 the legal ramifications of the way land was used in the past have heightened the need for environmental audits. Since that time B&N has completed more than 100 environmental audits of real estate parcels to determine their condition relative to past waste treatment, solid and hazardous waste management practices, the presence of contaminated materials, and potential remediation costs.

In 1988 the firm completed conceptual design and reviewed detailed design plans for the $103-million hydroelectric plant on the Ohio River at New Martinsville, West Virginia. This is the largest such facility in the United States to be licensed as an independent, non-utility hydro project under the Public Utility Regulatory Policies Act of 1978.

The firm was also responsible for the design of Hoover Reservoir, the main water supply for greater Columbus. The reservoir, eight miles long and 1.5 miles wide, was formed by the 2,500-foot-long, 112-foot-high Hoover Dam.

Maintaining a strong commitment to the roots of its operation, in 1989 B&N expanded its corporate headquarters on Reed Road in Columbus. Designed by its architectural staff, the 30,000-square-foot expansion mirrored an existing 29,000-square-foot facility. Prior to this expansion a 7,100-square-foot addition in 1988 provided space for an expanded environmental laboratory and storage facility.

Strong local support of the arts was a prelude to B&N's 75th anniversary cel-

ebration in 1987. During that year the firm donated a sculpture to the Columbus Museum of Art, sponsored an employee arts and crafts fair, and cosponsored a sculpture at Inniswood Botanical Garden and Nature Preserve.

Burgess & Niple initiated a bridge inspection program in 1969. Its nationally recognized team of bridge inspection engineers and technicians pioneered the use of rock climbing techniques to access large bridges.

When it is completed in mid-1993, the 120,000-square-foot, $17.6-million BioScience/Parks Hall addition at The Ohio State University will house research laboratories, a biological sciences/ pharmacy library, and a chemical instrumentation center to service the campus. Design assistance was provided by Perkins & Will.

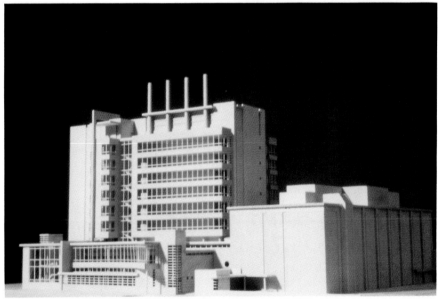

In addition B&N supported the Columbus Association of the Performing Arts by sponsoring various events in CAPA's Signature Series.

In recognition of its support of the arts during its diamond jubilee, the firm received the Greater Columbus Arts Council's Business/Arts Partnership Award for large businesses.

Although most of its work comes from clients in the public sector, Burgess & Niple's impressive private sector clients include such names as American Cyanamid Company, American Electric Power Company, Battelle Columbus Laboratories, BP America (SOHIO), Coca-Cola USA, E.I. duPont de

Nemours Company, Inc., Ford Motor Company, General Motors Corporation, General Electric Company, Honda of America, Mfg., Inc., Highlights for Children, The Hoover Company, LTV Steel Company, Liebert Corporation, Owens-Illinois, PPG Industries, The Procter & Gamble Company, Whirlpool Corporation, and Worthington Industries.

As the firm plans another 30,000-square-foot expansion of its headquarters, its diversity, reputation, and expertise continue to have a substantial impact in central Ohio and the Midwest. It seems certain to continue its strong presence through the 1990s and into the next century.

ERNST & YOUNG

Ernst & Young is the leading U.S. and worldwide integrated professional services firm.

As the practice leader in key markets and industries around the world, the firm provides a broad range of professional services that include auditing *Fortune* 500 companies and small businesses, providing tax advice on mergers and acquisitions and business valuations, helping clients with business solutions and strategic planning, and selecting, designing, and implementing software. The firm integrates this wide array of highly specialized services to enable its professionals to provide clients of all sizes with solutions to their business problems.

Ernst & Young has more publicly held clients than any other firm in the United States and leads in service to many industry segments. It is a major force in the communications, extractive, financial services, health care, insurance, manufacturing, retail, transportation, and wholesale industries.

Specialization in these and other industries is the key. The Ernst & Young specialization strategy is one which provides leadership to the industry and which is in step with the increasing complexity of business. The successes the firm has achieved in the manufacturing/high technology, health care, and entrepreneurial services areas are good examples of the initiative Ernst & Young is taking in industry and market segments.

The firm's Entrepreneurial Services Group annually sponsors the Entrepreneur of the Year Award to recognize superior achievement by successful, growing companies. This strong connection to privately and publicly owned and emerging companies demonstrates the firm's leadership and dedication to helping young companies succeed. To honor the winners further, the firm has created the Institute of American Entrepreneurs, an archive of entrepreneurial experience located at the University of North Carolina at Chapel Hill.

Ernst & Young's publication programs in specialized industries and in the fields of professional accounting standards, taxation, retirement plan-

ABOVE: Ernst & Young has served Worthington Industries, one of the largest and most successful industrial companies in the nation, for more than 25 years. John Krulcik (center), controller of the Columbus steel division of Worthington, examines coils of steel at the company's processing plant, with Ernst & Young advisers Steve Starbuck (left) and Randy Anstine (right).

RIGHT: Lisa Wineland (left) and Steve Starbuck (center) of Ernst & Young listen to a manager of a Bob Evans Farms Family Restaurant.

ning, and business planning are unmatched by any other firm. The "Ernst & Young Tax Guide" annually makes best-seller lists.

To complement the industry specialization framework, the firm has programs which enable its professionals to keep abreast of hardware and application advances and help companies deal with technological change. The firm's Navigator Systems Series represents a comprehensive, integrated approach to systems planning and building through Computer-Aided System Engineering (CASE) technology. The approach of Navigator is to plan, build, and maintain information systems by bringing

users, developers, and information technology together.

On an international basis, Ernst & Young has a balanced practice, with strength in North America, Asia and the Pacific Rim, and Europe. The firm's in-depth involvement in the European business community gives it an advantage in advising companies preparing for business relations with the united European market. In addition, the firm is moving rapidly to capitalize on opportunities in China, the

Jim Blankmeyer (right), founder and chief executive officer of MetoKote Corporation, and Dean Miller, Ernst & Young audit manager, view a product called Coated at the corporation's Lima plant. MetoKote, an Ernst & Young client, has grown to one of the nation's most successful primary coating companies.

Soviet Union, and the Eastern Bloc countries. The firm has staff throughout Eastern Europe and has cooperative or joint venture agreements in the USSR and Poland.

The Columbus office, which was started in the 1920s, exemplifies the firm's U.S. practice and has strong service capabilities in the manufacturing, financial services, health care and long-term care, insurance, education, and retail industries. In addition to being one of the largest professional service firms in Columbus, Ernst & Young is in the forefront of many important segments of the central Ohio community.

Members of the firm serve on more than 90 boards of Columbus charitable, civic, arts, and professional organizations. They serve as financial advisers to a dozen United Way agencies and are volunteers in Big Brothers/Big Sisters as well as for numerous fund-raising efforts. The firm backs its community volunteers with leadership contributions to those organizations. This participation demonstrates the firm's philosophy of active participation in the community, of sharing and

giving back to the community.

Ernst & Young is the firm which resulted from the merger of Arthur Young and Ernst & Whinney. This complex international merger was completed with remarkable precision, making the combination a model for the consolidation of any two huge international organizations. From the first day of the merger, the combined firm was operating under one financial and management information system, and all of the U.S. offices were fully integrated and functioning as one unit. In addition, a worldwide audit method was developed and implemented.

This worldwide audit approach permitted Ernst & Young to obtain economies of scale by developing uniform audit automation tools and training materials which are critical in a global economy. The audit approach recognizes that small businesses are a large part of Ernst & Young's practice and provides practical guidance in streamlining the risk assessment process and minimizing documentation.

A look at the backgrounds and personalities of the men who founded the two predecessor firms, Arthur Young and Alvin C. Ernst, shows how this

combination came together so easily.

Arthur Young opened an accounting office in Chicago in 1894, and A.C. Ernst began his practice in Cleveland in 1903. Both men were strong leaders and had a deep appreciation for the value of accounting. For them, quality in public accounting services was a preoccupation.

Young was an experienced businessman, and he got along well with top businessmen because he understood what motivated them. Ernst was a visionary who understood what accounting could do for business. The lives of these accomplished and distinguished professionals ended only 40 days apart in 1948.

Ernst & Young has almost 100 years of tradition in providing timely, cost-effective, quality services to its clients. That tradition will be enhanced by its present professionals, those future leaders who serve the firm and its community.

Barry Gowdy (right), Ernst & Young audit senior, meets with one of more than 100 pilots who fly every night for U.S. Check. The company provides air transportation services for financial institutions and is based in Columbus along with its affiliate TIMEXPRESS.

EMENS, HURD, KEGLER & RITTER CO., L.P.A.

Columbus, as one might expect of a state capital, has many law firms. One is unique.

Emens, Hurd, Kegler & Ritter is the Ohio member of the State Capital Law Firm Group, a national group of law firms that provides businesses, professionals, and institutions throughout the nation with a centralized source of information about lawmaking and regulation in every state. Forty-nine other law firms—one in each state and each with extensive practice in its state capital—comprise the group.

At a time when businesses are active in more than one state and lawmaking is being emphasized at the state level, Emens, Hurd, Kegler & Ritter is ideally situated. Its attractive, three-floor headquarters is located in the heart of downtown at 65 East State Street, directly across the street from the Capitol. It is also adjacent to the historic Ohio Theatre, the Hyatt on Capitol Square, and the Columbus City Center shopping mall.

As a capital city law firm, Emens, Hurd, Kegler & Ritter has a strong commitment to interact with state and

Emens, Hurd, Kegler & Ritter's boardroom is often used for client meetings and meetings of its attorneys.

The firm's extensive law library enhances its ability to serve its clients.

federal governments and an active governmental relations practice area. Attorneys of the firm have held high elective or appointive offices, such as Ohio attorney general, lieutenant governor, attorney for the National Labor Relations Board, attorney for the Internal Revenue Service Office of Chief Counsel, member of the Ohio House of Representatives, and various assistant Ohio attorney general positions and state boards.

Being the Ohio member of the State Capital Law Firm Group is a critical direct link to the leading attorneys and law firms in every state capital.

Professional excellence is what clients have come to expect from Emens, Hurd, Kegler & Ritter. The firm has been fortunate in attracting attorneys with diverse academic and personal backgrounds to better interrelate with clients and understand their objectives. Emens, Hurd, Kegler & Ritter's broad-based practice and experience enhances its ability to serve individuals and small businesses as well as multifaceted national and international corporations.

One of the busiest areas of practice is business and corporate law. Many of the firm's attorneys concentrate on matters related to the organization, merger, reorganization, acquisition, or liquidation of corporations, partnerships, and other business entities.

Emens, Hurd, Kegler & Ritter has been particularly active in helping to organize businesses in many Midwestern industries. It is able to bring to the table advice concerning both large and small business structures, including advice on patents, trademarks, and copyrights. For example, Drug Emporium, a multimillion-dollar, publicly held discount drugstore chain based in Columbus, has always relied on the expertise of Emens, Hurd, Kegler & Ritter. The firm also has represented Patrick Racing International since this three-time Indianapolis 500 winning auto racing team was formed in 1968.

Emens, Hurd, Kegler & Ritter's litigation area is well known for its aggressive and successful representation of businesses and individuals involved in litigation and dispute resolution. The firm's trial attorneys practice extensively, with cases involving nearly every aspect of litigation, in federal and state courts and arbitration tribunals, as well as at appellate levels of state and federal judiciaries both in Ohio and elsewhere throughout the country.

Another increasingly important practice area involves financial institutions. Emens, Hurd, Kegler & Ritter has developed and implemented a practice area to deal exclusively with the regulatory, lending, and other activities of banking and thrift clients, as well as those involved with credit unions, production credit associations, and federal land bank associations.

A significant practice area that now requires an increasing amount of attention is that of environmental, energy, and natural resources law. Since the firm was founded in 1964, its environmental, energy, and natural resources law practice has become one of the largest in the Midwest. The firm has helped clients resolve many environmental issues associated with industrial energy and development projects.

Other major areas of practice include:

• Creditor's rights and bankruptcy, including all facets on behalf of the creditors. Attorneys have acted throughout the United States as counsel to a number of banks, other secured parties, and creditors in proceedings involving real estate, oil and gas, insurance, steel, and retail companies.

• Construction law, representing general contractors, subcontractors, owners, architects, and lending construction associations.

• Health care, providing services that address the complex issues that challenge companies and individual practitioners.

• Insurance law, including formation of companies, advising, and obtaining approvals and permits.

• International business law, representing clients engaged in business abroad, as well as foreign companies with business interests in the United States.

• Labor and employee relations, representing management in addressing the myriad of restrictions on the

workplace and employee rights. The attorneys in this area also advise in workers' compensation and occupational safety issues.

• Personal planning of estates, trusts, and probate, all of which require the careful, personal, and confidential approach emphasized by the firm.

• Public utilities law, dealing with clients in regulated and unregulated businesses concerning gas, electric, telecommunication, water, and sewer services at the local, state, and federal levels.

• Real estate, actively involved in addressing commercial, industrial, and residential real estate, development and construction transactions requiring sophisticated legal services.

• Securities, which advises many clients of federal and state securities laws covering all aspects of public and private financing of business activities and corporate formation and reorganizations.

• Small business, which assists the expanding and diverse entrepreneurial economy in central Ohio.

• Taxation, both of businesses and individuals, by local, state, and federal entities, all of which demands scrutiny by attorneys familiar with all aspects of tax law.

• Women and minority business, which demands experienced legal representation to focus on the distinct needs and opportunities of these clients.

Clients of Emens, Hurd, Kegler & Ritter are greeted in the firm's reception area.

Through all its practice areas and individual attorneys, Emens, Hurd, Kegler & Ritter thus serves its stated purpose: "To provide the highest quality legal services in a timely manner with dedication to the needs of its valued clients."

The view looking north from the firm's offices at the state capitol.

MOODY/NOLAN LTD., INCORPORATED

The 1980s, the years that established Columbus as the growth center of Ohio, were also years of dramatic growth for Moody/Nolan Ltd., Incorporated, an architectural and engineering firm that opened its doors in 1982.

From its earliest days the two founders, Curtis J. Moody and Howard E. Nolan, planned for growth through their experience, expertise, and employees. Both Moody, the architect, and Nolan, the engineer, had been associated with other firms before each became president and principal of their own firms: Moody & Associates, Architects and Planners, and Howard E.

Nolan, Engineers and Planners.

Moody/Nolan is involved in a wide variety of building types indicative of the firm's creative process and innovative capabilities. The spectrum of projects includes the Biocontainment and Plant Inspection facility at The Ohio State University to serve Ameri-Flora '92, participation in the renovation of the state capitol, and work for the Southerly Wastewater Treatment Plant in Columbus, for which the firm designed and installed the automatic instrumentation and control systems.

The firm's activities have also spread beyond central Ohio, but Moody/Nolan completed two major projects in Columbus in the last decade that are outstanding examples of the firm's client-service philosophy, attention to detail, and cost-responsive design imperative.

The first was the Martin Luther King, Jr., Center for the Performing Arts. Moody/Nolan was commissioned by the Community Arts Project Group to design the renovation of the former Pythian Theater into an arts center. Moody/Nolan recognized that a performing arts center needed other features to assure success: improved traffic access, parking, an adjacent park area for outdoor events and gatherings, and additional support space for the original facility.

First the theater building was completely renovated, providing an updated theater as well as a ballroom with a kitchen and offices. The theater building was joined with the adjacent Garfield School, creating needed rehearsal and office space, as well as the Elijah Pierce Art Gallery. The total project was enhanced by the development of a boulevard, access to a major highway, and two new parking lots.

Subsequently the King Center won no less than six design awards for

TOP: The expansion of Port Columbus International Airport included the concourse and operations levels for USAir.

LEFT: The firm received six design awards for its renovation of the Pythian Theater for the Martin Luther King, Jr., Center for the Performing Arts.

Moody/Nolan principals stand on the steps of the firm's headquarters (from left): Paul F. Pryor, Curtis J. Moody, Howard E. Nolan, and Robert K. Larrimer.

Moody/Nolan, including the prestigious James B. Recchie Design Award of the Columbus Landmark Foundation.

The second major project for the firm was the expansion of Port Columbus International Airport. This project for the City of Columbus provided a new two-level concourse, including six gates for full-sized aircraft and one gate providing passenger loading to commuter aircraft.

In addition, the existing terminal was renovated for expansion of the ticketing lobby and the baggage claim areas. The project also included tenant work for USAir on both concourse and operations levels including airline ticket offices, passenger waiting rooms, and crew areas.

Expansion of Port Columbus defined a new "Gateway to the City," contributing to the city's image as a center of culture and commerce.

Moody/Nolan is excited about the future of Columbus and Ohio in the 1990s, confident that the well-laid plans of today will provide increased opportunities and recognition in the years to come.

M-E ENGINEERING, INC.

The people of M-E Engineering, Inc., are proud of their reputation for providing quality engineering services. The firm's tradition of "managed innovation" has brought to it and to the city considerable national recognition through a number of award-winning projects. Through The Limited World Headquarters, the Whetstone Branch Library, and numerous other award-winning and landmark projects in which the firm has participated, the people of M-E clearly demonstrate their right to this reputation for quality.

Michael Wren, the firm's founder and chief executive officer, came to Ohio from London, England, in 1968. At the time, the United States was experiencing a shortage of qualified engineers and Wren was recruited, as were many European engineers, to help fill the gap. That same year he visited Columbus for the first time. Aware that the future would require a new center of commerce in the Midwest, he recognized immediately the potential offered by this dynamic city. A year later Wren made the Columbus area his permanent home.

M-E was founded in 1973 as a simple partnership offering engineering services in the mechanical and electrical disciplines. The firm has steadily grown in both size and scope of services. M-E now consists of more than 140 professionals and support staff who provide design and documentation of building, mechanical, electrical and structural systems as well as civil site development and land surveys.

The professionals of M-E Engineering, Inc., are licensed and working in more than 30 states and have completed projects in several foreign countries. Their sole base of operations, however, remains in Columbus.

The firm's relationship with Columbus has not been one-sided. Wren and the other members of M-E are active in numerous civic and cultural activities. Their fund-raising efforts in behalf of the Columbus Museum of Art are well known. The firm has donated professional services to help create space for charitable organizations, including the Columbus Foundation, and a facility

for training mentally retarded citizens to work in "mainstream" jobs. Furthermore, M-E's vision of excellence encompasses its industry. The firm endowed a scholarship for outstanding students in the graduate architect program at The Ohio State University.

M-E has its offices on two floors of the landmark Brewery District Office Building at 500 South Front Street, on the south side of downtown. M-E provided all engineering services for the building. The unique design, which employs structural members to create a particular facade feature, is but one example of M-E's ability to respond with "managed innovation" to its

clients' most unusual requests or requirements of design.

Wren and the people of M-E believe that the opportunities offered by the Columbus market are just beginning to be realized and that the possibilities are greater than ever.

The firm's tradition of growth and quality will carry it forward far into the future, and M-E Engineering, Inc., will set the standard for excellence in engineering everywhere its work takes it.

The 500 Building at 500 S. Front Street is headquarters for M-E Engineering and a landmark in the city's historic Brewery District.

SQUIRE, SANDERS & DEMPSEY

Founded more than 100 years ago, Squire, Sanders & Dempsey is today one of the largest firms in the United States, with offices in Columbus, Cleveland, Phoenix, Miami, Jacksonville, New York, Washington, D.C., and Brussels, Belgium.

The firm's growth and the development of its unusually diversified general practice is the result of its commitment to retaining its position as a market leader by satisfying its clients with the most efficient and cost-effective legal services. The office's location in Ohio's capital city offers the firm unique opportunities in which to serve its clients.

This century of national and international expansion is mirrored in the Columbus office, promoting the growth of the office from three attorneys in 1978 to more than 80 attorneys and 90 staff members as it entered the 1990s.

In 1988 Squire, Sanders & Dempsey

combined practices with Murphey, Young & Smith, a Columbus firm with roots dating back 80 years. This combination expanded Squire, Sanders & Dempsey's presence in the business community.

With almost 400 attorneys firmwide, Squire, Sanders & Dempsey represents business entities of all sizes, financial institutions, public bodies and utilities, nonprofit corporations, and individual clients on a wide variety of civil matters.

The practice of the Columbus office, located in the Huntington Center in the heart of the city's business and financial district, is divided into five broad areas: business law, public law, litigation, environmental law, and labor law.

A significant amount of the work performed in Columbus is on behalf of clients in central, southern, and southeastern Ohio, with the balance focused on national and international

client needs. Clients of the Columbus office include architects and engineers, banks, charitable and cultural organizations, construction companies, federal agencies, foundations, businesses—from emerging entrepreneurships to *Fortune* 500 companies—health care institutions, real estate developers, school boards, state and local governments, stock brokerage firms, underwriters, and individual clients.

Within the business law practice, Squire, Sanders & Dempsey represents a diverse group of clients. Representative work includes estate, tax, and business planning; mergers, tender offers, and leveraged buyout and privatization transactions; legislative counseling;

Squire, Sanders & Dempsey serves as legal counsel for state agencies and commissions, particularly in the financial arena. Courtesy, the Ohio Division of Travel and Tourism.

health care joint venture and medical equipment syndications; and matters relating to foreign investment in the United States.

One of the areas in which the Columbus office offers significant experience is serving the needs of the small- to mid-size business client, from start-up through all phases of business development.

According to *The Bond Buyer*, the municipal bond industry's newsletter, Squire, Sanders & Dempsey has consistently ranked among the top national firms in the number of issues in which it participates. The bond issue for the Riffe Center for Government and the Arts exemplifies this area of practice.

The Columbus office plays a major role in the firm's public law practice and advises local, regional, and state governments on community development, finance, and land use/zoning. It serves as bond counsel to the State of Ohio and many of its agencies, and to villages, towns, cities, school districts, and special authorities in financing municipal and redevelopment projects.

A growing segment of the firm's business is its legislative services practice. Attorneys specializing in this area provide counseling, technical analysis, monitoring, and drafting of legislation. Counseling on state regulatory agency matters is also available.

In the litigation practice arena, Squire, Sanders & Dempsey boasts several of Columbus' leading trial lawyers complemented by a diverse group of litigators experienced in local, state, and federal courts. The litigation group handles corporate and commercial disputes; securities matters; products liability and medical cases; directors' and officers' liability; shareholder issues, and First Amendment cases.

Squire, Sanders & Dempsey is one of the nation's leading environmental law firms, and the Columbus office is involved with a full range of environmental issues, including negotiating with government agencies; representing clients in administrative rule-making; and advising clients on compliance wih federal and state environmental statutes regarding air, water, Superfund, solid

and hazardous waste, asbestos, and hazard communication.

For example, the firm represented Ottawa County in its sewer project, including solving problems with its EPA grant, providing legislative work resulting in a change of statute, defense of litigation regarding the contract, and facilitating project financing. With the combined talents of the firm's public law, litigation, legislative and environmental law practices, this project demonstrates the experience Squire, Sanders & Dempsey will provide.

The firm's labor practice is conducted by one of the largest groups of private practice labor lawyers in Ohio. The Columbus office is involved in negotiations, labor arbitrations, workers' compensation, discrimination, civil rights, and wrongful discharge actions, as well as pension plans, ERISA matters, and union avoidance procedures.

Squire, Sanders & Dempsey has increased its visibility in health care practice, particularly in managed care contracts, third-party reimbursement, labor matters, medical staff proceedings, and Certificate of Need applications. The Columbus office offers health care clients the resources of a national firm combined with the knowledge of local conditions so necessary to health care decision makers.

In 1990 Squire, Sanders & Dempsey

Squire, Sanders & Dempsey is committed to the Columbus community, including a major role in the exciting "America's Celebration of Discovery," where Columbus will be the international and national focus of America's quincentennial.

expanded the firm's international practice through the addition of two experts in eastern European law. Simultaneously the firm asserted its commitment to establishing a working presence in Prague, Czechoslovakia. The continually changing face of eastern Europe bears witness to the wisdom of this decision; the continent offers exciting opportunities for client services.

Squire, Sanders & Dempsey, however, is more than its legal business. Active in the community, the Columbus office is represented on the boards of The Ohio State University, Thurber House, the Columbus Museum of Art, the Columbus Area Chamber of Commerce, the Columbus Urban League, and a wide variety of other community organizations and agencies.

The firm is a major supporter of AmeriFlora '92, the international floral exhibition that serves as the centerpiece of the city's 1992 Quincentennial celebration. This commitment reflects Squire, Sanders & Dempsey's pledge to be not only a national law firm, but also a partner in the betterment of its communities.

PORTER, WRIGHT, MORRIS & ARTHUR

The history of Porter, Wright, Morris & Arthur and its predecessor law firms has been marked by a strong commitment to both the legal profession and the communities in which it maintains offices. Nowhere is that more evident than in Columbus, home to a partnership that predates the Civil War but is as forward-looking as the twenty-first century.

The founding fathers were Richard A. Harrison, an Englishman who graduated from Cincinnati Law School in 1846, and William A. Rodgers, already a judge in London, Ohio. That partnership, and those of others who were to join them later, flourished in postbellum Columbus and ingrained a tradition for excellence that continues today. It also established the largest Columbus law firm and one of the largest in the state.

Harrison, who was to serve in the Ohio House and Senate and then the United States House of Representatives, demonstrated a dedication to the law that is evident among those who followed through various successions and mergers.

The partnership of Porter, Wright, Morris & Arthur was formed through a

The law firm's atrium viewed from the 28th-floor reception area.

1977 merger of two of Columbus' leading law firms: Porter, Stanley, Platt & Arthur and Wright, Harlor, Morris & Arnold. Those two distinguished firms had deep Ohio roots, flavorful histories, and the same spirit of dedication to the profession.

It goes without saying that the firm is proud of its heritage. In a rapidly changing world, many companies that became clients in the early 1900s are still represented by the firm. Among them are the Central Union Telephone Company (Ohio Bell), Southern Ohio Electric Company, Columbus Railway Power and Light Company (American Electric Power), Huntington Bancshares, Midland Mutual Insurance Company, and Jeffrey Manufacturing Company (The Jeffrey Company).

Today the firm's practice encompasses an interesting, diverse client group, ranging from multinational and national public companies to privately held companies in many industries, and federal, state, and local government entities.

Porter Wright is committed to building upon the foundation established by its founding fathers through strict ad-

Conference rooms overlook the five-story atrium.

herence to one principle: excellence in the quality of its legal services to clients. With this philosophy as its base, the firm has grown dramatically in recent years to meet the needs of its clientele and has opened additional offices in Cincinnati, Cleveland, and Dayton, Ohio; Washington, D.C.; and Naples, Florida.

Serving the legal profession as well as the community is a responsibility firm members do not take lightly. Four have served as president of the Ohio State Bar Association, while others have been elected to lead the American Bar Association, the Columbus and Dayton bar associations, the Defense Research Institute, and the American Judicature Society, as well as to chair various committees and sections of federal, state, and local bar organizations.

Community involvement has included service as directors and officers of a wide number of educational and cultural institutions, charitable organizations, and special events related to the arts, sports, and other civic endeavors.

KPMG PEAT MARWICK

KPMG Peat Marwick is an international accounting, tax, and consulting firm with 90 years of experience and a reputation for excellence.

The company has more than 800 offices in 123 countries, employing 75,000 people worldwide. Nearly 20,000 of them work in 139 offices in the United States.

Peat Marwick has been a part of Columbus since the early 1950s, and has grown into one of the more successful offices within the firm. Its office of approximately 150 people is dedicated to the highest levels of quality service and responsiveness to client needs.

The words "quality service" are more than just buzz words at Peat Marwick. It is the only international accounting firm with a formal Quality Service Program designed to qualitatively measure client satisfaction.

The Columbus office also formed a Quality Service Council to generate ideas and stimulate enthusiasm internally so clients receive the services they need in the most responsive manner possible. To this end, the organization is designed

The international practice of KPMG Peat Marwick is one of the area's largest, serving companies with interests in both inbound and outbound investment.

to deliver services in a timely, cost-effective, and efficient manner through a network of specialized industry groups and professional practice departments.

The office's industry practices have allowed it to tailor the delivery of its services to meet the needs of its clients. In Columbus, it serves the following specialized industries:

- Insurance
- International and local manufacturing
- Middle market
- Mutual funds/broker-dealers
- Government
- High technology
- Agribusiness
- Retail/Merchandising
- Real Estate/Construction
- Nonprofit

Peat Marwick's largest specialized industry segment, both at the local and national levels, is the financial services industry. This includes services to insurance companies, commercial banks, thrifts, mutual funds, and broker-dealers.

In the Columbus office, the insurance industry is the crown jewel of its practice. The office provides professional services to more insurance companies locally than any other firm, and

The Columbus office Quality Service Council at KPMG Peat Marwick meets regularly to discuss ways to improve service to clients.

its professionals are considered experts in this area.

The office also has a dominant international manufacturing practice. Its clients include some of the largest international manufacturers in central Ohio as well as a variety of local manufacturing companies.

Services to these industrial clients include inventory systems development, assistance with U.S. Customs and Foreign Trade Zone matters, compensation and employee benefits consulting, third-party verification of contract cost systems, and traditional tax and auditing services.

Finally, another integral part of the client base in central Ohio is what the firm calls "middle market" companies. These owner-managed enterprises employ six out of every 10 working people in the United States, and Peat Marwick is proud of its reputation as a trusted adviser to these indispensable local businesses.

Middle market services focus on obtaining funds for growth, maximizing profits through the development of long- and short-term business plans, minimizing taxes through diligent tax planning, developing compensation and employee benefit programs, performing executive searches, and assisting in computer hardware and software selection.

The evolution of KPMG Peat Marwick, as evidenced by the growth of its Columbus office, has been monumental. It also reflects the company's dedication to fulfilling the highest expectations of the Columbus community.

ARTHUR ANDERSEN

From the start of the firm in 1913, founder Arthur Andersen was known as a maverick in the accounting profession. He was the first to organize client service teams by industry, the first to establish formal training programs, and the first to hire inexperienced college graduates directly into the profession. Those maverick traits have pervaded the firm's innovative, aggressive culture and personified the tens of thousands of professionals around the world.

The trust Andersen built with his clients established the firm's reputation for quality and integrity. Today Arthur Andersen provides audit, tax, financial consulting, and business advisory services through a unique network of offices in more than 50 countries. Every office upholds Andersen's original vision by providing state-of-the-art services while maintaining the timeless standards of honesty, thoroughness, and assurance of quality.

Since 1968 Arthur Andersen's Columbus office has served the needs of businesses and individuals throughout central and southern Ohio. The Columbus office has long claimed a reputation for serving the needs of both large public and privately held corporations as well as small and emerging private enterprises.

Local expertise in such industries as regulated utilities and telecommunications is complemented by a diverse client base of private companies in the construction, distribution, manufacturing, and retail industries. The firm's commitment to private enterprise is best illustrated in its "Discovery" program, which annually recognizes central Ohio's 100 largest private companies for the significant contribution these businesses make to the Columbus economy.

Partners (from left) Ed Onderko, Carl Nelson, Tim Cooper, Tim Michaels, and Mike Gagel.

ANDERSEN CONSULTING

In this decade of fierce and nimble competition, more businesses must rely on the power of information technology not only to compute, but also to compete.

Back in 1954 Andersen Consulting brought together the experimental world of computer technology with the pragmatic world of business administration. The firm designed and installed the first computer application of a business function, an automated payroll system for General Electric. Today Andersen Consulting serves thousands of clients throughout the world, empowering organizations to effectively apply information technology to their business advantage.

With over 200 professionals in Columbus, Andersen Consulting serves many of central Ohio's leading businesses. The firm's vast resources and comprehensive approach to business integration provide executives with assistance in strategic business planning, computer systems design, systems integration, facilities management, software products, and organizational and change management services. This "seamless" approach to business and information consulting services compels executives around the world to entrust Andersen Consulting with "mission critical" initiatives designed to derive the optimum benefit from today's technology.

Andersen Consulting helps its clients achieve a competitive advantage by working with management to rethink and reshape their businesses. Today's competitive environment calls for a total business perspective, synchronized at every stage. Properly executed, management combines business strategy, technology operations, and people into one successful formula. At the same time, the organization eliminates activities which add cost but contribute no value to end products. The resulting benefits can be enormous— better quality, higher profitability, competitive pricing, shorter lead times, and greater responsiveness to customers.

Andersen Consulting's Columbus office is one of nearly 200 locations worldwide, but its commitment to the local community runs deep. Andersen Consulting actively supports many cultural and civic organizations in central Ohio, and it recruits a majority of its professional staff from area colleges and universities. The

Andersen Consulting's nine partners include: (standing, from left) Craig Miller/associate partner, Bill Storts, and John Rife; (seated, from left) Steve Louis/associate partner, Chuck Pisciotta, Eric Leininger, and Vance Hughes; and (not pictured) Joe Ratterman and Chuck Winslow.

Columbus office is part of a network of over 25,000 people, working together to ensure that each client receives the highest quality service from the best-trained strategic business and information technology consultants in the world.

Photo by Jim Baron

Photo by Jim Baron

12 ▼ BUILDING GREATER COLUMBUS

▲▲▲▲▲▲▲▲▲▲▲▲▲▲

419

Developers, contractors, and real estate professionals work to shape the Columbus of tommorrow.

Borror Corporation, 420; Turner Construction Company, 424; HER Realtors, 426; Continental Real Estate, 428; King, Thompson/Holzer-Wollam, Realtors, 430; Gioffre Construction Incorporated, 431; Capital Fire Protection Co., 432; The Galbreath Company, 433

Photo by Mike Steinberg

BORROR CORPORATION

As you discover Columbus, you will find a thriving city, a city whose growth has brought it great strength and diversity. In many respects, the Borror Corporation reflects the city in which it is based.

It is a growing, thriving company, with a diverse group of divisions that gives it strength born of balance, regardless of changing economic conditions. The Borror Corporation is involved in homebuilding, apartments and condominiums, automotive parts remanufacturing, advertising and public relations, and lumber and building supplies.

The history of the multifaceted corporation is as varied as the company itself. In 1952 Don Borror went into business as a building contractor. The first home he built was a modest ranch house along a quiet street in Upper Arlington, a Columbus suburb.

Even Borror could not have predicted the growth that would follow. Over the next three decades he went on to form

RIGHT: (From left) Don Borror, Doug Borror, and David Borror are all involved in the company.

BELOW: Borror corporate headquarters is located in Dublin, Ohio.

a Borror family of companies that developed a large part of northwest Columbus, the most prolific quadrant of a fast-growing city.

As business boomed, so did Don Borror's impact on the Columbus community. His varied activities for a better community included serving on the Columbus Area Chamber of Commerce board of directors, acting as a trustee of the Pontifical College Josephinum, sitting on the board of the Capital South Urban and Redevelopment Corporation, and serving as president of the Columbus Clippers of baseball's International League.

In 1984 Beasley Industries, a 45-year-old, publicly held company with a variety of divisions, merged with the Borror family businesses to form the Borror Corporation. The new company's new divisional portfolio included Dominion Homes, builders of single-family homes; The Borror Company, which specializes in multifamily apartments and condominiums; Beasley

Motor Rebuilders, an authorized Ford engine remanufacturer; Noble Motor Rebuilders (later renamed Borror Automotive Remanufacturing), an engine rebuilder and supplier of engines to distributors and dealers along the East Coast and Mid-Atlantic states; and Linden Lumber and Building Supplies in Columbus.

To centralize the new Borror companies, corporate headquarters was built in 1987 on Frantz Road in Dublin. Integrated into its surroundings by beautifully landscaped grounds and a pond, the three-story structure is designed to be both efficient and attractive.

Today's diversified Borror Corporation remains a family affair. Don Borror continues as chairman, offering years of experience and knowledge of the community. A graduate of The Ohio State University Law School, he brought the company to its present position as a well-balanced and financially secure organization.

Both of his sons hold senior positions in the company. Doug Borror is the guiding force behind the company's expansion. As president, he manages all corporate divisions and day-to-day operations. David Borror lends legal expertise critical to the management

of each division within the corporation as general counsel.

From the corporate headquarters, the Borror family manages several hundred dedicated employees in jobs that span 13 states. With an extensive background in land development, complemented by solid construction and manufacturing businesses, the Borror family has combined its talents to build a multidivisional, balanced company.

At the heart of the corporation is Dominion Homes, a leader in the construction of high-quality single family housing. Located in fine neighborhoods throughout the Columbus area, Dominion Homes come in a variety of modern floor plans that are constantly updated. This design emphasis recently brought the division national recognition when, in 1990, Dominion Homes made *Better Homes and Gardens'* annual "best home coast-to-coast" list.

Dominion has a product diversity that is unique in the industry. The company's market niche was originally inexpensive homes for the first-time buyer. In the late 1980s Dominion gradually moved up-market, offering homes that appeal to both entry-level buyers and those buying their second house.

In 1990 Dominion began a new marketing program. Called "The Best Building Experience," the program is designed to give the consumer a positive feeling about homebuilding by providing a level of quality, value, and service unsurpassed in the industry.

"The Best Building Experience" involves providing all the advantages of custom building at a cost affordable to the target market. For example, like a custom builder, Dominion Homes are stick-built on-site to provide a solid framework that matches the foundation perfectly. The level of options and color choices

make the customer feel as if the home was custom-designed just for them. Building sites are always in the most desirable locations, with fine neighborhoods close to shopping, parks, and schools.

Serving the customer before, during, and after the sale is part of the experience. A two-step process prior to move-in is designed to provide information. Dominion's pre-build conference is a review by the salesperson of every step of the building process, so the buyer knows what to expect.

Just prior to closing, the construction supervisor overseeing an individual home walks through with the buyer during the pre-settlement meeting, making sure that the interworkings of the house, as well as warranty information, are explained. After move-in, Dominion offers the protection of a comprehensive warranty program and a maintenance department recognized as the finest in the Columbus area.

The success of Dominion Homes prompted the Borror Corporation to launch Tradition Homes in 1989. An upscale line of homes, Tradition Homes

TOP: Dominion Homes is committed to giving "the best building experience" by providing an unsurpassed level of quality, value, and service to the neighborhoods they construct.

ABOVE: Karric Place Shopping Center was developed by the Borror Corporation.

effectively takes advantage of the large market niche between Dominion and the custom builder.

An innovative approach to American classic homes, Tradition Homes merge classic architectural features from the great homes of the past with floor plans designed to enhance modern life-styles. These floor plans combine truly traditional form with the twist of modern functions. Familiar features like spacious rooms, cathedral ceilings, well-placed windows, and touches of marble are combined with modern features such as garden baths within master suites, and open-and-airy great rooms with balcony overlooks.

Tradition Homes also provide a level of luxury expected within the target market. Many Tradition kitchens offer oak cabinets, bevel-edged countertops, Jenn-Aire grills, and bay windows. In the bathrooms there are whirlpools and brass bath fixtures. The living rooms feature cathedral ceilings, and the dens have six-panel doors.

The Tradition Homes customer enjoys the same "best building experience" as the Dominion home buyer, benefiting from a prebuild conference, pre-settlement meeting, comprehensive warranty, and responsive maintenance.

From the beginning the Tradition Homes concept was well received. During Tradition's first year of operation in 1990, sales were higher than expected, exceeding projections by 30 percent.

Underneath the Tradition Homes umbrella is TreeTops Condominiums. An upscale condominium community of 88 units, TreeTops is located in a wooded area just south of Muirfield Village, site of the prestigious Memorial Tournament hosted by Columbus native Jack Nicklaus.

Like Tradition Homes, TreeTops Condominiums offer modern floor plans designed for today's life-styles. Available as townhouse or garden condominiums, each is designed to provide a quiet and low-maintenance environment for customers. TreeTops offers such design features as cathedral ceil-

ings and fireplaces and exterior finishes of cedar and brick in soft earth-tones.

Perhaps the most outstanding feature of TreeTops condominiums is its wooded setting. Its architecture is designed to take full advantage of this location, as each window has a view of the mature pine forest that surrounds it. TreeTops owners are also treated to such quiet recreational features as a bike path, a park, and a pond on the property.

In an uncertain condominium

marketplace, TreeTops offers a solid property investment with its wooded location and outstanding design.

The success of the homebuilding divisions has been repeated by Borror Corporation's other divisions.

For example, the Borror Corporation has taken advantage of Columbus' seemingly endless demand for apartments, condominiums, and shopping centers. The multifamily housing/commercial division has been an integral part of the area's building boom in this market, having developed, built, or managed more than $100-million worth of property.

Borror Corporation's successful approach to this marketplace was built on extensive research, which made it possible to accurately anticipate population shifts and changing life-styles. The research also made it possible for the company to selectively invest in high-quality residential rental real estate at the lowest possible cost.

Using research as a base, the Borrors attractively packaged the properties, built them with the same commitment

LEFT: Six-panel doors open into a Tradition bedroom.

BELOW: Many Tradition kitchens offer oak cabinets, bevel-edged countertops, and all of the most modern features.

to quality found in the homebuilding divisions, and located them in the most desirable high-growth areas of central Ohio.

The names of Borror Corporation's rental and condominium properties are immediately recognizable to Columbus residents. Some of the more prominent ones include Ramblewood, Karric Place, Springburne, Silvertree, Stone-brooke, Edinborough Commons, Woodrun Place, and The Enclave.

RIGHT and BELOW: Tradition family rooms and living rooms are open and spacious with classic architectural features.

Linden Building Supplies is a perfect complement to the Borror Corporation's extensive involvement in building single-family homes, multifamily units, and shopping centers. In business since 1912, Linden sells lumber and building supplies to area builders and contractors, and is one of the largest distributors of quality lumber and building products in central Ohio. It offers the Borror Corporation a high-quality internal source of lumber and building supplies, as well as a profit center from sales to both individual and commercial customers.

Borror Corporation's automotive re-manufacturing division is made up of two highly profitable plants that are the "elder statesmen" in their corporate lineup.

Beasley Motor Re-builders of Altoona, Pennsylvania, is an authorized remanufacturer of Ford engines. In business since World War II, the plant holds territorial contracts with the Ford Motor Company of Detroit, Michigan, a relationship it has enjoyed since 1941. The contracts give Beasley exclusive rights to service a five-state area that includes Pennsylvania, West Virginia, Ohio, New York, and Maryland.

Borror Automotive Re-manufacturing of Easton, Maryland, is a virtual twin of Beasley. Another business that got its start during wartime, this facility rebuilds and supplies engines to independent distributors and dealers in a 10-state market area including Maine, Rhode Island, Connecticut, New Hampshire, Massachusetts, Delaware, Maryland, Pennsylvania, Ohio, and West Virginia.

These plants produce thousands of remanufactured engines each year for use by automotive equipment distributors and dealers. With sales in excess of $10 million annually, they play an important role in Borror Corporation's continuing financial growth.

Together, the divisions that make up the Borror Corporation paint a picture of a strong, diverse company. Looking back over the decades, Borror Corporation's unique past sets the tone for today's Columbus life-style. Looking toward the turn of the century, the company's future looks to be solid because of its unique stability.

As you discover Columbus, you will find a vibrant city. An area of uncommon growth. A place that has managed its growth by diversifying itself into a position of great strength that other cities of its size and location can only envy.

The Borror Corporation proudly reflects the city it calls home.

Borror Corporation's automotive remanufacturing division is responsible for the Beasley Ford plant in Altoona, Pennsylvania.

TURNER CONSTRUCTION COMPANY

ABOVE: The Columbus skyline shows off six Turner projects: (from left) AEP Corporate Head-quarters, the Bureau of Worker's Compensation office building, Nationwide III office building, Nationwide Insurance Company Corporate Headquarters, the Hyatt Regency Hotel, and The Ohio Center Convention Center.

RIGHT: The Banc One Corporation office build-ing, located in the John G. McCoy Center in Westerville, Ohio, is one of 5,000 buildings erected by Turner Construction Company.

It would not be an exaggeration to say that Turner Construction Company has helped change the face of Columbus as well as the nation.

Look around downtown Columbus: Banc One, Ohio Bell, Borden, Nation-wide I and III, Motorists Mutual, Rhodes State Office Tower, American Electric Power, Ohio Center, the Ohio Bureau of Workmen's Compensation and Industrial Commission, two ho-tels—the Hyatt Regency Columbus and the Hyatt on Capitol Square—and the 65 East State Street office building. All these landmarks were built with Turner on the job. And more Turner-adminis-tered face-lifts for the heart of Ohio's spirited capital city are on the way, such as the Greater Columbus Convention Center and the 42-story Capital Tower.

The scope of Turner's activities in Columbus has been much broader than just high-rise buildings, however. Its projects have included suburban hospi-tals, educational institutions, banks, of-fices, retail establishments, and public buildings.

For instance, Turner was engaged

for the expansion of the Columbus Metropolitan Library's main downtown branch, the renovation of the Old Post Office Building into law offices for Bricker and Eckler on South Third Street, and the construction of the edu-cation building at Children's Hospital and the new Worthington High School.

A challenge for the company's Special Projects Division—a separate group created to handle projects under $3 million—was to complete the 115,000-square-foot Jacobson's depart-ment store in time for the opening of Columbus City Center. At the same time, Turner was working on five addi-tional stores at the downtown mall: Gucci, Brooks Brothers, Milano Fur and Leather, Page Boy Maternity, and Huntington National Bank.

These are all big projects from the New York-based construction company that has had a Turner Construction office in Columbus since 1965. But there are many smaller projects, too, such as the McDonald's restaurant on Bethel Road, and the renovations of classic older cam-pus buildings at Otterbein College and Ohio Wesleyan University.

However, it all adds up. Since its founding in 1902, Turner has erected more than 5,000 buildings totaling ap-proximately 600 million square feet. Many of these bear names all would recognize: the United Nations Secre-tariat and Lincoln Center for the Per-forming Arts in New York, the John F. Kennedy Memorial Library in Boston, and the towering headquarters for Owens-Illinois in Toledo, U.S. Steel in

Pittsburgh, and International Business Machines in New York.

These magnificent achievements were possible because of the visionary thinking of a young Swarthmore College engineering graduate, Henry C. Turner. He took his sheepskin and put it to work in ways that changed the construction industry forever.

Turner gained his first professional experience working with the little-known Ransome system of construction. It used steel bar reinforced concrete—a novel idea at the turn of the century. Turner became convinced this was a faster, less expensive way to build than the wood frame and masonry methods commonly in use at the time.

With DeForrest H. Dixon, Turner raised $25,000, obtained rights to the Ransome system, and founded Turner Construction Company on May 6, 1902. Although not an immediate success, an early milestone for the company was the contract for the stairways for New York's first subway stations. Their strength and ease of construction gained the company much-needed attention.

The big break came in 1904 when manufacturer Robert Gair was convinced to use reinforced concrete for his eight-story industrial building in Brooklyn, New York. When load and fire tests proved the technology's safety, many similar contracts followed. The young firm was on its way.

Turner's emphasis on concrete technology was the company's hallmark throughout its early years, and research to improve building methods continued long after the general acceptance of reinforced concrete. "Turner for Concrete" became the slogan as the company's speed and the quality of workmanship won numerous contracts, including some large government orders during World War I.

Following the war, Turner Construction continued to rack up "firsts." In 1919 it won its first international contract, a fish-freezing plant in Newfoundland, Canada. A year later Turner entered Ohio, opening an office in Cleveland. The nation's first high-rise office building, a 16-story job, was built in Buffalo, New York, in 1921,

and the company's first hotel project, the San Juan Hotel, was undertaken in Orlando, Florida, in 1922, in addition to the famed horseshoe-shaped Municipal Stadium at the University of Pennsylvania.

In 1927, the year Turner celebrated its 25th anniversary, Charles A. Lindbergh flew solo across the Atlantic. The construction company was flying high, too, but then came the Great Depression and projects dried up.

In the late thirties Turner participated in the construction of numerous naval air bases in the Pacific—Hawaii, Midway, Guam, Wake Island, and others. By 1941, the year founder Henry Turner retired as president, defense work constituted 81 percent of Turner's income.

After the war the company joined up with many large developers, including J.W. Galbreath & Co., a name with strong ties to Columbus. This sturdy and long relationship, which led to the opening of Turner's Columbus office in 1965, helped establish Turner's repu-

tation as a builder of high-quality office towers that altered skylines in cities from Boston and New York to Los Angeles and San Francisco.

Turner Construction, which went public on the American Stock Exchange in 1969, was reorganized 15 years later and became The Turner Corporation. Turner Construction is today one of several subsidiaries.

Turner credits its more than 25 years of success in Columbus to the expertise and dedication of its professional staff and the skills of the local tradespeople, who have not lost the traditional Midwestern work ethic and pride in workmanship.

While the company glances back at its accomplishments with pride and satisfaction, it also looks forward each day with confidence in its role in shaping Columbus' future growth.

Turner renovated the Old Post Office Building into law offices for Bricker and Eckler.

HER REALTORS

"The Helpful People." That's HER Realtors' positioning statement, and helpfulness in many forms is the single most important ingredient in the company's amazing growth and success.

Founded in 1956 by Harley E. Rouda, HER has grown from a one-man business to become central Ohio's largest real estate company. With 23 neighborhood offices, nine franchised offices, a team of more than 500 associates, and annual sales in excess of $525 million at the beginning of the 1990s, HER Realtors is certainly one

Columbus company that is in touch with its community, its customers, and its employees.

Though HER Realtors boasts Commercial/Investment, Property Management, Corporate Services, and Appraisal divisions, the company was built on the belief that home ownership is part of the American Dream, and that providing help and understanding to clients pursuing that dream would result in a profitable business. The company is first and foremost residential-oriented, and its most successful activities revolve

around home and family concerns.

HER, for example, knows how important a school system is to any family relocating to central Ohio, moving within the area, or leaving for another state. To answer a family's school questions, HER provides School Match, a unique, innovative, and exclusive service.

The School Match database is chock full of information about all public and more than 14,000 private and parochial schools in the United States, as well as American-accredited international schools in more than 60 countries. The relocating family answers a series of questions to develop a profile of its desired school system; from these facts a comparative report is generated in two formats. First, the report gives the name and location of up to 15 school systems that match the family's requirements and a detailed presentation about each school. If the family wants to find a school situation as much like their present one as possible, the report can also offer a "twin" of the current school system in the new location.

The "Herley Bear" safety program is another way HER demonstrates its involvement both with families and the community. Herley Bear is HER's red and white life-size mascot, whose purpose is to promote safety among central Ohio kindergartners and early grade school children. Consistently booked throughout the school year, the program is a presentation given by an HER associate who is accompanied by Herley Bear.

After listening to the presentation, each child is given a safety-oriented coloring book, a Herley sticker, and a Safety Certificate. The children are then asked to contribute their own safety tips and to meet Herley personally. "Born" in 1985, Herley had met more than 185,000 people by the age of six, and had been the star attraction to thousands more at many area events, including community celebrations, parades, and festivals.

Families like good food, and HER's

Harley E. Rouda founded HER Realtors, central Ohio's largest real estate company.

HER's "Herley Bear" program promotes safety among central Ohio kindergartners and early grade school children.

cookbook program has also been a major success. The annual cookbooks, first published in 1974, became a company signature. In fact, a Realtor in another state once called Columbus' information operator, asked for the "cookbook Realtor," and was put through to the HER administrative offices immediately. More than one million books— the one-millionth was presented to Nancy Reagan—have been distributed, and they have now become treasured collectors' items.

But HER didn't become the area's largest Realtor through school programs and cookbooks. The company made its mark by anticipating market trends and training its associates to take advantage of those conditions. HER management feels that "The Helpful People" motto

should apply internally as well; they believe that their management mission is to help and support their sales staff and to create an atmosphere of success.

To carry out this mission, the company has developed an associate training program that is one of the most comprehensive in the United States. The two-week program is led by the company's full-time training director. There are also follow-up sessions held in the individual offices. Advanced education is part of the package, and if market conditions require additional training, courses are developed. For instance, in the early 1980s, when financing became a major issue, the company designed a course called "100 Ways to Finance a Home." The course is still referred to when financing becomes a factor.

In addition to the educational program, HER is proud of its marketing support materials. It feels that its specially designed presentation kit makes

a professional statement that assists the average listing agent to become superb and the excellent listing agent to excel beyond his or her expectations.

In the 1990s HER is preparing itself to take advantage of opportunities in the return to downtown living, the need for alternative housing among the aging population, continued suburban expansions, and the possible construction of a second outerbelt. The company also foresees the necessity for greater specialization within the HER organization.

In addition, management predicts that homeowners will continue the trend toward remodeling their present homes rather than searching for new houses. Though it would seem that those who make their living from the turnover of housing might be alarmed at such a prospect, the management of HER is unruffled. They see the remodeling boom as good for business. In their opinion, remodeling simply upgrades available housing stock and enhances the value of entire neighborhoods.

When Harley Rouda opened his doors in 1956, he never expected to become central Ohio's leading Realtor, but Columbus, with its diversified economy, exceptional public-private cooperation, and lack of natural barriers, made growth possible, both for HER and for Rouda personally. In 1991 Rouda served as president of the 800,000-member National Association of Realtors, having previously served as regional vice president for Ohio and Michigan, as president of both the Ohio Association of Realtors and the Columbus Board of Realtors.

By following Rouda's philosophy of "consistently doing every job just a little bit better," HER Realtors expects to add more "helpful people" to its ranks, more satisfied homeowners to its clientele, and more chapters to its exciting success story.

CONTINENTAL REAL ESTATE

Continental Real Estate Companies are a logical outgrowth of the company's original business, Continental Office Furniture & Supply Corporation. Based on their knowledge of the needs of their office furniture and supply customers, Continental Real Estate began in 1973 to design and construct functional, attractive facilities for specific corporate clients.

Initial projects included only offices and office warehouses for companies with home offices and branches in Columbus. In 1978 Continental developed Brooksedge Corporate Center in Westerville, Ohio at Interstate 270. Encompassing more than one million square feet, Brooksedge utilizes the flexspace concept. Flexspace continues to be a practical solution to the business environment by allowing sales and service to work together in a space that combines flexibility and aesthetics. The single story building provides ceiling heights that make storage, light assembly, and loading dock access feasible and yet offers the proper amenities of first class office space.

In the early 1980s, with the addition of Larry Lehring, Continental Real Estate began developing retail centers throughout Ohio. The company combines outstanding retail locations with a market need for quality retail goods and services. This retail concept is most fully realized in the Dublin Village Center.

A project of the Drexel Development

BELOW: Brooksedge Corporate Center exceeds one million square feet.

Corporation (a partnership of Continental Office Interests and the Don M. Casto Organization), the Dublin Village Center was built at a major intersection (Sawmill and I-270) of Ohio's fastest growing community (Dublin) that had not yet realized a corresponding growth in entertainment services or home products. Thus, the Dublin Village Center became the nation's first "theme" shopping center offering convenient, one-stop shopping for all of its customers' home needs, from drugs and sundries to hardware; from furniture to linens; from kitchenware to flowers; from car-

RIGHT: With a variety of quality merchandise to choose from, customers at the Dublin Village Center can find everything they need for their homes.

BELOW: During the mid-1980s Continental Real Estate developed reliable, cost-efficient medical office space for hospital campuses such as St. Ann's Hospital.

peting to stereo equipment; from paint to home fitness apparatus. Dublin Village Center presents a dramatic, unified appearance featuring sand-mold bricks detailed with polished and matte copper, a green tile roof that sets the complex apart from other structures, beautiful landscaping, and attractive signage. An unparalleled success, 96 percent of the first phase of Dublin Village Center's space was leased two months before the opening.

Another successful area for Continental Real Estate has been in identifying market niches. Being a specialty developer and recognizing the demand for medical services now and in the future, Continental created solid, functionally designed and cost-effective medical office space adjacent to or part of a hospital campus, completing projects since the mid-1980s for Mount Carmel East, Health One, and St. Ann's Hospital.

In 1989 Jack Lucks, an orginal Continental Real Estate Companies partner, formed Hallmark Communities Ltd. for

ABOVE LEFT: The Residence at Turnberry is a luxurious, multifamily residential community.

ABOVE: Management Horizons Division Price Waterhouse is one of three new corporate facilities.

LEFT: The Rax Restaurants corporate headquarters is one of several clients that has had expert renovations done by Continental Real Estate.

the purpose of developing exciting mixed-use, multifamily condominium and apartment communities in central Ohio. The first completed project is Pickerington's The Residence at Turnberry, an upscale, multifamily residential community, and The Shoppes at Turnberry, a 55,000-square-foot retail center, featuring a stone and cedar setting for small and medium-size tenants. Additional projects of Hallmark are underway in Gahanna (Christopher Wren), Grove City, Westerville, and the Short North.

The 1990s have already seen banks slow to finance speculative developments. Continental has been able to maintain its varied projects through the boom and bust cycles that plague the building industry in two ways. First, by providing equity to supplement bank debt on all of its new projects. In 1990

Larry Ritter joined the company to start an equity capital business to accelerate the company's ability to raise equity on a continuing basis. Secondly, by keeping its focus on the customer, the company has always been conservative in its approach, not building until a tenant is identified and his needs thoroughly assessed. Designing buildings for specific corporate users began more than a decade ago and led to the creation of exciting corporate facilities, exemplified by the headquarters of Shelly Berman Communicators, the American Ceramic Society, and Management Horizons.

In addition, the company has a history of offering meticulous, thorough, award-winning renovations of existing structures which have both economic and aesthetic benefits. Some of the building renovations include the archi-

tectural offices of Richard Trott and Partners at 77 Nationwide Boulevard (1981), the Rax corporate headquarters (1984), the State of Ohio Student Loan Commission at 309 S. Fourth (1987), the old SCOA building at 35 N. Fourth St. (1989), and, most recently, the Empire Building, the 1925 downtown landmark located at the corner of Fourth and Broad streets.

Continental Real Estate Companies have developed and currently manage more than 3 million square feet of fine office, multipurpose, and retail space in central Ohio. The company's success is built upon listening to the needs of customers and tenants and solving their problems through extensive planning; solid, functional design; and cost-effective, high quality construction.

Continental believes that downtown is the place to do business, having moved both its headquarters and the office furniture division to the downtown area. Because the company expects that pent-up demand for office space will be released within the decade, it is poised to create high-quality downtown buildings. Continental believes in the city's future—and in its own.

KING THOMPSON/HOLZER-WOLLAM, REALTORS

A legacy that includes the development of one of central Ohio's finest communities and a long-term dedication to the residential real estate business are among the highlights of King Thompson/Holzer-Wollam, Realtors.

King Thompson/Holzer-Wollam was established September 1, 1988, with the merger of two well-known companies—King Thompson Realtors and Holzer, Wollam, White & Strait Realtors. The union resulted in the oldest real estate company in Columbus and the second largest based on business volume.

Reflecting the roots of the two companies that formed King Thompson/Holzer-Wollam, the emphasis is on the sale of residential properties, but not in quite the same manner it was once done. In the beginning—that was 1912—Henry Wollam rented a horse and buggy to show homes to prospective buyers near Fifth Avenue and High Street.

Two years later, in 1914, King Thompson and his brother, Ben, began purchasing land and laying out neighborhoods northwest of that intersection in what later became the Columbus suburb of Upper Arlington. The idea of buying a large tract of land and controlling most aspects of its development was new at the time, leading Upper Arlington to become one of the first planned communities in the state.

The two real estate companies prospered over the years through their dedication to residential real estate. In fact, Wollam took the bold step in 1918 of moving his downtown Columbus office to the Upper Arlington suburbs to better serve his customers.

After 25 years in the business, Wollam passed his company on to his son, Emerson C. Wollam, who in 1969 merged his firm with the enterprising young broker by the name of Max Holzer. The firm of Holzer-Wollam became well known in the central Ohio real estate business.

Meanwhile, King Thompson built its reputation on handling homes primarily in Upper Arlington—the town that the realty firm built—under the direction of George "Rocky" Frost.

ABOVE: King Thompson/Holzer-Wollam is committed to providing the finest real estate service available.

RIGHT: King Thompson, founder of King Thompson Realtors.

In the 1980s the company merged with the Patrick M. Grabill & Company Realtors in the growing Dublin area and also acquired the Bexley company of Larry Wade Realtors.

King Thompson/Holzer-Wollam maintains a sales force of more than 300 full-time associates who work out of nine neighborhood offices and the corporate headquarters. Patrick M. Grabill is president and CEO, Michael Huntley serves as executive vice president, and George Frost and Max Holzer serve in an advisory capacity as cochairmen of the firm's Board of Directors.

Numerous additional acquisitions and mergers have expanded the company's coverage to all of Columbus. King Thompson/Holzer-Wollam is planning its newest office for Gahanna in early 1992.

King Thompson/Holzer-Wollam's dedication to residential real estate is evident in its affiliation with Homequity, the largest international relocation network, and in its continuing education and training program for its associates. Considered one of the best in central Ohio, it is attended by all associates to provide clients with the best personal service from people who not only know their neighborhoods, but also know their industry.

The company also has a long history of community and professional service. The first school in Upper Arlington convened classes in King Thompson's basement. That commitment continues to the current leadership, as firm president Patrick Grabill assumes the presidency of the Columbus Board of Realtors in 1992.

Today, King Thompson/Holzer-Wollam is recognized throughout the industry for their integrity, innovation, and commitment to providing the finest real estate service available.

GIOFFRE CONSTRUCTION INCORPORATED

"Columbus is where we began, and it's where we are going to be in the 1990s. We are going to grow with Columbus."

The speaker with the hometown convictions is Tony Gioffre, president of Gioffre Construction, Incorporated. He and John Gioffre, his brother and company vice president, look to the future of the community where they grew up. Together they saw the opportunities that Columbus and the central Ohio area had to offer two young men with a strong work ethic, and they seized those opportunities to build a business that has left its mark on the metropolis.

Tony and John Gioffre are first-generation Americans; their parents were born in Italy. After John graduated from The Ohio State University and Tony completed a tour of duty in the United States Navy, they entered the home construction and the concrete business. In 1977 they established Gioffre Brothers Construction Company which specialized in building six-figure custom homes in the Columbus area. That same year, Gioffre Brothers Concrete Company was formed to serve not only the internal needs of their custom home division, but also the needs of other local constuction companies.

The 125,000-square-foot Sawmill Road Center project was part of Gioffre Construction's expansion during the 1980s.

"We began with one employee, $1,500, and a commitment to a product we could be proud of," recalls John.

Today Gioffre Construction, Inc., is a multimillion-dollar company with more than 30 employees.

In 1980 the two companies were merged into one—Gioffre Construction, Inc. As the nation was entering a recession and the interest rates rose, dampening the home construction market, the Gioffres shifted their energy to the flourishing commercial market primarily on the northern perimeter of the city. In doing so, they caught one of the biggest construction booms in the history of Columbus.

At the outset Gioffre Construction, Inc., built more than 100,000 square feet of medical and professional office condominiums, as well as warehousing, retail centers, and a variety of other properties for companies large and small. Although the company has grown considerably, the brothers continue to give each project their personal attention.

Among the company's projects during the 1980s expansion were the Columbus Medical Center and Arthritis Center at 1211 Dublin Road; warehousing and a trailer operations center for Fruehauf Corporation at 1525 Georgesville Road; a 125,000-square-foot retail center for Toys 'R' Us and Glick's Furniture Store; and two Unfin-

ished Wood Furniture Stores at 5936 Scarborough Boulevard and at 3505 West Dublin-Granville Road.

Toys 'R' Us has continued to show its faith in Gioffre Construction, Inc., with nearly a half-dozen more stores, including a 45,000-square-foot retail center in Clarksburg, West Virginia. These projects served as a catalyst for Gioffre's territorial expansion into Pennsylvania, Kentucky, and Indiana, as well as West Virginia.

In the 1990s Gioffre Construction, Inc., completed the renovation of Worthington High School, the corporate headquarters and grand salon for Charles Penzone Hair Designers, and the Marriott Residence Inn on Frantz Road in Dublin.

In addition to their corporate clients, the Gioffres are particularly proud of their complete renovation of the Salvation Army's Greenwood Lake Camp in Delaware. The facility was originally built on 80 beautiful acres in 1912 and serves as home to some 250 youngsters each summer.

"What we want to say is 'Thanks, Columbus,'" says Tony. "We truly appreciate and recognize the opportunity we have had as two individuals to create a business from scratch, to nurture it, and to reach the level of success that we enjoy today. It has been a rewarding experience."

CAPITAL FIRE PROTECTION CO.

Most people do not give a lot of thought to fire safety; they expect the safeguards to be in place. So do the 80 or so owners of Capital Fire Protection Co.

Since 1963 employee-owned Capital Fire Protection has been designing and installing automatic sprinkler systems that fire departments and insurance companies recognize as the most effective means of combating fire.

Founded in the basement of the Hilltop-area home of the late Harold E. Recob, the company has become the largest independent in-house fire protection contractor in the state, with an-

office building. The installation was the first high-rise, retro-fit sprinkler system in Columbus and Franklin County.

Although sprinkler systems represent the lion's share of the business, Capital Fire Protection has been on the leading edge each time new fire suppression systems were developed, such as carbon dioxide for paint spray areas, Halon 1301 for computer rooms, foam systems for airports, and a variety of dry chemicals for different installations. The company also sells and services fire extinguishers, fire alarms, and smoke detectors.

It is this wide-ranging expertise that

ABOVE and LEFT: The Nationwide Insurance data processing center, just north of Columbus, is protected by a sophisticated preaction sprinkler system installed by Capital Fire Protection.

TOP: Capital Fire Protection installed Halon 1301 and an automatic preaction sprinkler system for Banc One's John B. McCoy Computer Center in Westerville.

nual sales of more than $6 million—30 times the value of sales during its first year of business.

The work of Capital Fire Protection is not readily apparent—that's the whole idea—but its lifesaving systems are found in more than 1,100 of the city's largest private and public institutions, such as Columbus City Center; and the headquarters offices and operations of Borden Incorporated, Banc One Corporation, EBCO Manufacturing Company, the Nationwide Insurance Companies; and the McDonnell-Douglas plant adjacent to Port Columbus. In 1981 the company installed an automatic sprinkler system for Motorist Mutual Insurance Company in its 21-story

led Capital Fire Protection to one of its most interesting and challenging contracts. The Air Force needed a fire protection system in its two ammunition handling and reloading rooms in the Aircraft Survivability Research Facility at Wright-Patterson Air Force Base in Dayton, Ohio. In these rooms both domestic and foreign ammunition is handled and stored.

Due to the extreme likelihood of explosions in the event of a fire in this facility and the possible loss of life, an ultra-high-speed, automatic deluge system was designed. Tests determined that to suppress an explosion in the highly hazardous areas of the facility, water in adequate quantities had to be

applied to the problem area within 50 milliseconds—.05 seconds.

In response to these stringent demands, Capital Fire Protection developed a system to utilize a high-speed deluge valve that decides within 7 milliseconds whether to open and flood the room with water. The system is linked to ultraviolet detectors that immediately discern the very first light from an explosion or fire but are insensitive to sunlight and normal artificial lighting.

Since 1966 the company has expanded five times at its 24,000-square-foot Valleyview Drive headquarters, most recently with an addition of 8,000 square feet. It also has a full-service office in Canton, Ohio.

THE GALBREATH COMPANY

John W. Galbreath was once honored with the prestigious Horatio Alger Award—and for good reason. After struggling through the Depression years, Galbreath, at age 32, launched a small business that became a thriving international development company now known as The Galbreath Company.

Today, under the leadership of Galbreath's son, Daniel M. Galbreath, the firm is the nation's third-largest real estate development company. The company's operations span the globe, with more than 40 million square feet developed internationally. Along the way, the Galbreaths have helped reshape the Columbus skyline and contributed significantly to urbanscapes, from New York City to Hong Kong.

Starting The Galbreath Company with a belief in Columbus and the American system, John Galbreath helped Ohio workers realize their dreams of owning their own homes in the 1930s and 1940s. Joined by Dan in the 1950s and 1960s, the Galbreaths rehabilitated and built residential communities throughout America.

Once the company was established in residential real estate, high-rise office buildings and corporate headquarters were the next major challenges. The Galbreaths developed, arranged financing, managed, and leased high-rise office buildings with mixed-used developments across the United States. Joined by corporate partners, the Galbreaths built corporate headquarters for such giants as USX Corporation (formerly U.S. Steel) and Mellon Bank in Pittsburgh; Goldman Sachs, Mobil Oil, and Merrill Lynch in New York; Del Monte in San Francisco; and Montgomery Ward in Chicago.

The company has also built high-rise buildings in other gateway cities, including Los Angeles, Boston, Washington, D.C., and Denver. The company also manages 45 million square feet of office space nationwide and 8.5 million square feet in Columbus.

Adding to the skylines of Ohio, the Galbreaths developed Erieview Plaza, Ohio Bell headquarters, and One Cleveland Center in Cleveland; the Westin Hotel and Star Bank, Fifth Third Center, and the Dubois Tower in Cincinnati; Mead Corporation headquarters in Dayton; Owens-Illinois and Owens-Corning Fiberglas headquarters; and Seagate in Toledo.

Reaching across the oceans to Hong Kong in the 1970s, the company built Mei Foo Sun Chuen—99 20-story apartment buildings built on 40 acres of land—and Tsuen Wan's Riviera Garden, a condominium community of 23 35-story high-rise towers.

John and Dan Galbreath also emerged as community leaders and builders of their own hometown. Corporate headquarters were built in downtown Columbus for American Electric Power Co., Banc One Corp., Borden Inc., Columbia Gas Systems, and Nationwide Insurance Companies. The Galbreath Company helped develop the Rhodes State Office Tower, the Ohio Center, the Hyatt Regency Columbus, the Hyatt on Capitol Square, and Capitol Square Plaza. Under construction in 1991 were the State of Ohio Workers' Compensation complex and the City of Columbus Public Safety Building, as well as the long-awaited Greater Columbus Convention Center downtown.

In 1991 the Wolfe-Galbreath Interests initiated development on Capitol Tower, a 42-story high rise that will anchor the east side of State House Square.

Dan Galbreath is also involved in the renovation of the Ohio State House Capitol grounds.

The Galbreath family has had a great interest in sports as well. At Darby Dan Farms in Columbus and Lexington, Kentucky, the family raises thoroughbred horses. Counted among their victories are the Kentucky Derby

The Galbreath Company has built high-rise buildings in cities all over the country and, indeed, all over the world.

and the English Derby. In fact, John Galbreath is the only man to have bred and owned race horses that were derby winners on both sides of the Atlantic.

The family's championship tradition also extends to major league baseball. While owned by the Galbreaths, the Pittsburgh Pirates won the World Series three times.

Established as a major national developer during the 1980s, The Galbreath Company began the decade of the 1990s with 8.5 million square feet under construction. The firm stands ready to meet the development challenges of Columbus and the world in the 1990s and on into the twenty-first century.

13 QUALITY OF LIFE

▲▲▲▲▲▲▲▲▲▲▲▲

435

Medical, educational, and recreational facilities draw people to Columbus and contribute to the quality of life of Columbus area residents.

The Ohio State University Hospitals, 436; Arthur G. James Cancer Hospital, 438; Riverside Methodist Hospitals, 440; Grant Medical Center, 442; Otterbein College, 444; Capital University, 445; Center of Science and Industry (COSI), 446; Saint Anthony Medical Center, 447; Ohio Dominican College, 448; Ohio Wesleyan University, 449; Mount Carmel Health Center, 450; Children's Hospital, 452; Franklin University, 454; Columbus Zoo, 456; Columbus College of Art and Design, 457; Columbus State Community College, 458; Greater Columbus Convention Center, 460

Photo by Larry Hamill

THE OHIO STATE UNIVERSITY HOSPITALS

The Ohio State University Hospitals is a modern, 963-bed health care facility that brings international recognition to itself and the community through dedicated patient care, education, and research.

Its 750 staff physicians and 4,000 staff members provide the 5 million residents of central and southern Ohio with a matchless blend of medical expertise and intensive caring service that flourishes in the outstanding academic environment of Ohio State and its College of Medicine.

The support of talented research scientists and the availability of sophisticated technologies enable University Hospitals to fulfill its mandate to advance medical knowledge and to share this knowledge with practitioners throughout the state and nation.

Patients at University Hospitals are the first to benefit from innovative therapies, newly developed medications, and advanced medical technologies.

For patients debilitated by heart disease, University Hospitals has a proven record of leadership in cardiac care. Ohio State cardiologists were among the first in the nation to perform cardiac catheterization and to create a laboratory for diagnosing electrical problems

of the heart. This led to University Hospitals' national prominence in the evaluation of pacemakers.

As a result of continuing research, University Hospitals today offers cardiac patients the most advanced diagnostic services. It nurtures as well the latest drug and surgical therapies, including the implantation of heart assist devices, artificial hearts, and human donor hearts.

The heart transplant program was the first in Ohio to use a totally implantable artificial heart.

Organ transplantation has offered a new chance for life for numerous central Ohio residents. Liver transplantations are among the most difficult of solid organ transplants, yet University Hospitals surgeons, who performed the state's first liver transplant in 1984,

RIGHT: University Hospitals provides comprehensive heart care service, including a highly successful transplant program.

BELOW: University Hospitals' SKYMED aeromedical helicopter program provides rapid transportation and specialized care around the clock for patients with life-threatening injuries or illnesses.

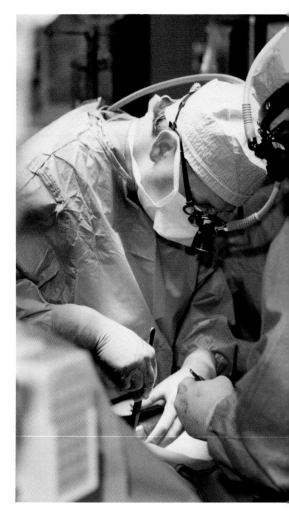

continue to post a high success rate.

One of the nation's largest kidney transplant programs also calls University Hospitals home, and pancreas transplants, which offer the only cure for diabetes, are among the facility's many significant medical achievements.

It is worth noting that about once every 24 hours a heart, kidney, pancreas, liver, or cornea transplant takes place at the University Hospitals. The pioneering surgeons also perform multiple organ transplants, such as pancreas-kidney and liver-kidney transplants, which vastly improve the opportunities for seriously ill people to enjoy healthier life-styles.

This dedicated service to the community has gained national recognition for distinguished research in transplant surgical techniques and anti-rejection medications, such as cyclosporine.

University Hospitals delivers a full range of health services for women. For

RIGHT: University Hospitals is part of an internationally recognized medical center providing patients with a highly trained and caring staff, the expertise of world-renowned physicians, and the latest technology to diagnose and treat illnesses and injuries.

BELOW: University Hospitals offers central Ohio's most complete range of obstetric and gynecologic services. The women's health program includes a variety of maternity care and childbirth options along with specialized programs to deal with high-risk pregnancy and infertility.

pregnant women, University Hospitals provides comprehensive obstetric services, including state-of-the-art care for those who are considered high risk.

The hospital serves as the perinatal referral center for all of central and southeastern Ohio. Aided by modern technologies, physicians in the Department of Obstetrics and Gynecology offer pre-pregnancy evaluations and counseling, monitoring of fetal development, and detection and intervention for signs of premature labor. Through the University Hospitals' progressive, 37-bed neonatal intensive care unit, premature and ill newborns receive the best medical expertise available.

For those who have difficulty conceiving, the most advanced therapies for infertility are provided at the University Hospitals' in vitro fertilization center—the first in the Midwest.

Among the prevention services are breast cancer screenings, offered both on-site and by the University Hospitals' Mobile Mammography Unit, as well as screenings for uterine cancer and osteoporosis.

University Hospitals is renowned for its care of people who have suffered physical disabilities as a result of injury, disease, or age. Computer-enhanced imaging devices allow physicians to pinpoint the causes of physical disabilities and determine the most appropriate rehabilitative services.

These services, at the 72-bed Dodd Hall, are aimed at giving patients a positive start toward a more productive life, including physical, occupational, and speech therapy and a full-service driver education program for handicapped individuals. Specialized pro-

grams, such as the computerized gait laboratory to analyze walking patterns, are available for those with neuromuscular disorders, such as multiple sclerosis and muscular dystrophy, and for those with chronic pain.

The William H. Davis Medical Research Center is dedicated to research and treatment of disorders affecting arthritic and elderly patients. The center's geriatric program, based on the complete needs of the patient, spans dietary assistance, rehabilitation therapy, and a complete range of medical services.

Advancements in the understanding of mental disorders are prompting University Hospitals to continue the expansion of its psychiatric services. Diagnostic tools such as electroencephalographic imaging to map the brain's electrical activity allow physicians to pinpoint problems and determine appropriate treatment.

University Hospitals was the first in central Ohio to dedicate a psychiatric unit solely to the care of children ages 12 and under. Treatments include occupational and recreational therapy, remedial education, and counseling.

SKYMED, the University Hospitals' aeromedical helicopter program, provides rapid transportation and specialized care 24 hours a day for patients with life-threatening injuries or illnesses.

University Hospitals provides the only adult burn intensive care unit in central Ohio, along with highly specialized intensive care units for newborn, medical, surgical, neurosurgical, and coronary acute care patients.

University Hospitals' mission is to take its knowledge of healing and caring to the people. MedOHIO Centers and other primary care facilities are equipped and staffed to care for the daily medical needs of today's families. Similar outreach programs, such as on-site health screenings and free ASK-A-NURSE health information services, allow University Hospitals to bring advanced technologies and medical expertise closer to home.

The dedication of The Ohio State University Hospitals to bringing the latest in medicine to the Discovery City and the broader community it serves positions the institution well for the century ahead.

ARTHUR G. JAMES CANCER HOSPITAL

M.D. Anderson, Houston. Memorial Sloan-Kettering, New York City. Roswell Park, Buffalo, New York. For Americans whose lives have been touched by cancer—and 3 out of 4 families will be struck by the disease—the names of these hospitals hold special hope. Until 1990 they were among only a handful of hospitals in the nation dedicated exclusively to the treatment of cancer.

Today the Midwest has such a hospital of its own: the $61-million Arthur G. James Cancer Hospital and Research Institute in Columbus.

Despite the tremendous advances in the diagnosis and treatment of cancer during the past decade, with cure rates for certain forms of cancer as high as 90 percent or more, the national average cure rate for all cancer cases is still only about 50 percent.

Specialized cancer hospitals like the new James Cancer Hospital offer important advantages for more difficult cases. Costly, advanced equipment such as the sophisticated radiation therapy systems installed in a large specially-shielded area at the James Cancer Hospital are simply out of reach for general hospitals where only a few patients will use them. But with approximately 4,800 in-patient cases coming to the 160-bed facility each year, as well as up to 100,000 out-patients, the investment becomes reasonable.

In addition, the exceptional resources of such cancer hospitals, combined with the opportunity to work on the most challenging cases, tend to draw the most talented oncologists in the field, and, along with them, the most experienced and skilled specialized nursing and support staff.

But even among the exclusive handful of specialized cancer hospitals, the James Cancer Hospital is unique.

According to Dr. Arthur G. James, the professor emeritus of surgical oncology at Ohio State and past president of the American Cancer Society for whom the facility is named, the original concept behind this institution is somewhat different from the others.

"From the time I joined the staff at Ohio State in 1948, I could see the po-

tential for a major cancer research and patient care facility," he explains. "Until now, medical research has been physically segregated from medical practice, and that tends to slow down the interactions between them, prolonging the time it takes for new treatments and protocols to reach actual patients. This facility, with two floors of research laboratories right in the building, is designed to speed up the process as much as possible."

The cancer hospital, located in The Ohio State University Hospitals complex, has been designated by the National Cancer Institute as a Compre-

The 12-story, $61-million Arthur G. James Cancer Hospital and Research Center is at the hub of The Ohio State University Hospitals complex.

hensive Cancer Center since 1976, and the source of several important new discoveries and testing programs.

"Bringing all patient care and many of the research programs under one roof opens up many new avenues of opportunity for our researchers and physicians and their patients," says Dr. David Schuller, director of the institution. "In addition, we are in close touch with some 177 related research projects

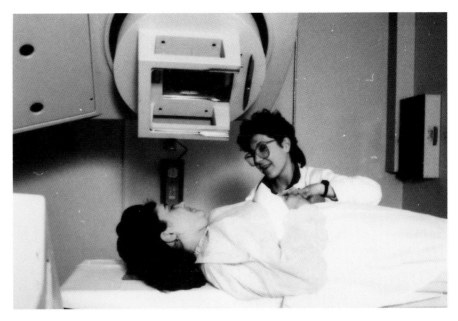

ABOVE: The ground floor radiology unit has its own cyclotron. The hospital offers the most advanced technology for diagnosis and treatment.

LEFT: Dr. Arthur G. James, professor emeritus of surgical oncology at The Ohio State University, was the first to propose the unique research and treatment center for OSU.

under way in 11 academic departments throughout the university, any of which may result in improved chances for recovery for our patients in the future."

Dr. Schuller cites as an example the original work of Dr. Bertha Bouroncle, who retired in May 1990. Her identification of the rare hairy-cell leukemia in 1958 was the beginning of a long, arduous effort to find effective, safe treatment for this disease. Today the final stages of research on a new drug, dioxycoformycin, or DCF, that may prove to be a major anticancer agent for this and other forms of cancer, are in progress at the James Cancer Hospi-

tal, one of only eight institutions in the nation awarded contracts by the National Cancer Institute for this kind of testing.

There are many other unique features in the James Cancer Hospital, including the rigid control of air quality throughout the building (maintained by a triple-level air-cleaning system) and other specialized systems to provide a near-sterile environment to protect patients.

The architecture of the hospital itself is not sterile in feel: lots of curves, natural wood surfaces, and even irregu-

larly-shaped patient rooms create a welcoming, comfortable atmosphere.

According to Administrator of Nursing Nancy Davis, the environment is designed as part of the treatment. "People recover better when they feel comfortable and secure. Everything in this building was designed with that principal in mind."

The extra-specialized 24-bed bone marrow transplant unit is a striking example of the principle in practice. The greatest risk to bone-marrow transplant patients—whose natural immune systems must be destroyed before the transplant can take place—is from infection during the preparatory stages of treatment. In other hospitals, patients are kept isolated in plastic "bubble domes," which keep them completely bedridden for many weeks. At the James Cancer Hospital, the atmosphere of the bubble has been created in the entire patient room, with an ultra-purified curtain of air that is invisible, but just as effective. As a result, patients feel far more free and "normal."

What effect does this have on recovery? "It is immeasurable," states Dr. Peter Tutschka, director of the bone-marrow transplant unit and a key adviser on its design. "For patients at standard risk, we are achieving recovery rates in the 80 percent range, where the national average is nearer 55 percent. Much of that is due to our innovative use of drugs in place of radiation treatments, but the atmosphere enhances the process very much."

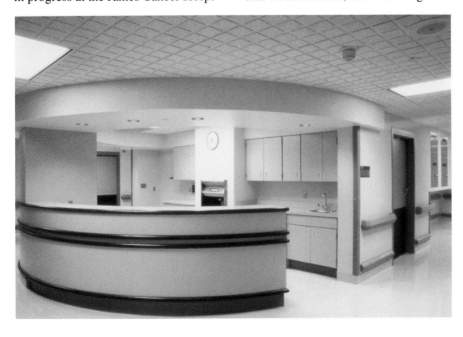

LEFT: A round, centralized nursing station is part of the hospital's design, created to look warm and inviting while allowing for maximum efficiency in patient care.

RIVERSIDE METHODIST HOSPITALS

Riverside Methodist Hospitals is celebrating a century of providing health care to central Ohioans. From its beginnings in a 15-room house in Columbus' Short North area, Riverside has evolved into a 1,063-bed major medical center at 3535 Olentangy River Road. Recent national health care publications recognize Riverside as one of the top 10 most successful hospitals in America in providing quality, first-class service.

By delivering the ultimate in family-centered patient care, Riverside aims to "create a new national model for health care." According to Erie Chapman, J.D., president and chief executive officer, Riverside is working toward achieving the ideal in thousands of ways. Physicians, nurses, management teams, health care professionals, and employees at every level are networked into an innovative and extensive service orientation program.

"For all its growth," Chapman stresses, "Riverside has not lost sight of the value of the individual. Here, primary care is indeed primary, but we also have the ability to offer the specialized services of a tertiary facility."

Chapman, who came to Riverside in 1983, initiated and engineered Riverside's "total-commitment-to-service" philosophy. He also serves as president of U.S. Health Corp., Ohio's largest multi-hospital system.

The corporation oversees the operation of Riverside, its flagship hospital, along with Grant Medical Center and four other hospitals in Ohio. In a 1990 survey by *Modern Healthcare* magazine, U.S. Health was the third-largest non-Catholic religious affiliated system in the country.

Ron Zemke, author of *The Service Edge*, cited Riverside as one of the nation's three health care service leaders along with the Mayo Clinic and Beth Israel Hospital in Boston. Riverside's pro-

gressive, "customer first" credo incorporates special touches to meet a patient's personal as well as medical needs. From patient advocates who keep families continuously and fully informed, to a nurse-at-the-entrance emergency room, valet parking, room service, and more fashionable (and modest) patient gowns, patient consideration is foremost.

Riverside also extends its philosophy of quality service to its employees. They have access to an on-campus, state-of-the-art child care center as well as a time-saving employee convenience center offering grocery delivery, dry cleaning, and videotape rental services.

"Life Choices with Erie Chapman," America's Emmy award-winning weekly health show, offers the public current health information. It also has become the core of Riverside's communication effort. The half-hour television program, seen in markets throughout the country, has an hour-long, local, live radio call-in counterpart. Produced

With 1,063 beds, Riverside Methodist Hospitals is the largest private medical center in Ohio. The facility on Olentangy River Road will take on a different look by 1993 with the addition of a nine-story critical care tower.

by a team of health care and television professionals, "Life Choices" fulfills the public's need for health care information from health care experts together with inspiring stories.

Hospice at Riverside and the Elizabeth Blackwell Center at Riverside are prime examples of Riverside's community outreach.

Hospice at Riverside provides a continuum of care for patients and their families, including home care, day care, and inpatient services. The Kobacker House, one of the nation's few freestanding hospice facilities, opened in 1989.

Offering central Ohio's first and most comprehensive health program for women, the Elizabeth Blackwell Center opened in 1985 to provide education, support, and innovative access to women-centered health care. The center recently was the topic of a feature in Tom Peters' national newsletter, "On Achieving Excellence." For its unique shared management system he termed the center "a feminine model of leadership."

Riverside public services include a Cancer Call information line, Physician Referral line, specialized support groups, a community re-entry program for neurologically handicapped people,

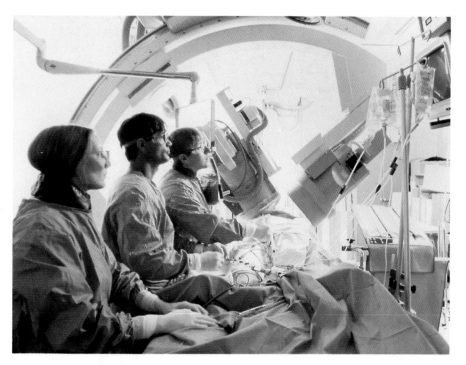

Riverside provides its employees with numerous on-site services that help make busy life-styles more convenient, such as a child care center as well as a grocery store, dry cleaning facility, and videotape rental service.

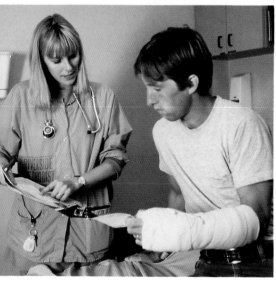

ABOVE: The Riverside Heart Institute of Ohio, where this patient is being diagnosed by heart catheterization, is one of the hospital's most outstanding health care services. The institute is foremost in the state for this medical procedure and second in the region for the number of open heart surgeries performed at one institution.

LEFT: Patient care is of primary importance at Riverside. Ron Zemke, author of The Service Edge, *cites Riverside beside the Mayo Clinic in Rochester, Minn., and Beth Israel Hospital in Boston as one of the nation's three health care service leaders.*

HotelCare for out-of-town family members of patients, a library, and "Healthy Choices," a joint community nutritional service campaign in selected central Ohio Kroger stores.

Riverside's commitment to public health is also evidenced through its funding and staffing of many medical assistance programs, community education classes, public health forums, and screenings throughout the community.

Founded in 1892 as Protestant Hospital, Riverside's church ties were formed in 1922 when the name was changed to White Cross Hospital.

Riverside is affiliated with the West Ohio Conference of the United Methodist Church. By 1961, White Cross transformed to "Riverside" when it moved to the present Olentangy River Road site. Riverside has grown in tandem with the increasing central Ohio population, and progress continues.

• Scheduled for completion in 1992 is a $75-million nine-story addition which will help address the community's critical care bed shortage.

• In May 1990 Riverside broke ground for central Ohio's first freestanding comprehensive Ambulatory Care Center for outpatient medical treatment.

• January 1991 marked the opening of Riverside's freestanding adolescent alcohol and drug dependency center offering unique inpatient and extensive outpatient services.

Several hospitals within a hospital, Riverside incorporates:

• The Elizabeth Blackwell Hospital, central Ohio's leading birth center which focuses on maternity, gynecological and women's health care.

• The Wesley Health Center, which provides alcohol, drug dependency, and psychiatric services.

• The Riverside Heart Institute of Ohio, the state's leader in coronary angioplasty procedures and one of the largest open heart surgery centers in the area.

• The Riverside Regional Cancer Institute, including several clinics in outlying communities to better serve Ohio residents.

Riverside is a recognized health care leader providing additional high quality services in the area of alcohol and drug dependency, diabetes, gerontology, neuroscience, psychiatry, reconstructive services, renal-urology, critical care, emergency, pulmonary, and outpatient services.

More than 850 outstanding physicians compose the medical staff, representing nearly every specialty. At Riverside health care professionals work with state-of-the-art technology to continue the tradition of innovation.

GRANT MEDICAL CENTER

In the heart of growing downtown Columbus, the dedicated employees and medical staff at Grant Medical Center provide quality health care to the people of central Ohio.

In the past few years Columbus has seen tremendous growth. Grant has grown as well by adding new services and employing a staff of more than 2,400.

Since 1900 Grant has served central and southern Ohio with the most modern medical equipment and treatment. According to Bill Wilkins, president and chief executive officer, "Our location, and the ease of travel around the metropolitan area, has meant Grant has established itself as a primary health care provider for central Ohio."

Grant's mission statement reads: "Grant Medical Center, in partnership with our medical staff, is committed to the best possible quality of life for those we serve. We will provide exemplary health care by delivering superior service for the physical, spiritual, and emotional needs of our patients and families."

Grant provides a wide range of diagnostic, treatment, rehabilitative, and preventive services. A designated Level One trauma center, Grant sees more than 30,000 patients a year in its Emergency Care Center. A modern facility that includes an urgent care center and experienced staff makes Grant the hospital of choice for emergency care.

Many of those treated in Grant's Emergency Care Center are brought to the hospital by LifeFlight, Grant's emergency aeromedical transport service. With one helicopter based in

Columbus and another in Wellston, Ohio, LifeFlight can make the lifesaving difference for patients throughout the state.

Patients needing specialized eye, ear, nose, or throat treatment receive the most advanced care from Grant Eye and Ear Hospital. This hospital performs advanced ophthalmic procedures and is ranked among the top eye care centers in the country.

Hundreds of joint replacement patients travel from all over the Midwest to the Grant Joint Implant Center. Specialized surgeons provide the latest surgical techniques, including laser-read, computer-assisted, and custom-made hip replacements.

The Grant Laser Center maintains a national reputation as one of the country's leaders in laser treatment and research. The hospital features more than 20 laser systems for treating patients on an inpatient and outpatient basis. Many new laser procedures and techniques are tested and developed at Grant.

Grant also serves as home to the Ohio Digestive Disease Institute, an inpatient and outpatient treatment center specializing in all forms of digestive disease. The institute prides itself on a multidisciplinary team providing a full range of treatment and diagnostic options, many of which are not available at other facilities.

Expectant parents in central Ohio are benefiting from Grant's maternal child

Located in the heart of downtown Columbus, 640-bed Grant Medical Center continues to grow as a leading health care provider to the area.

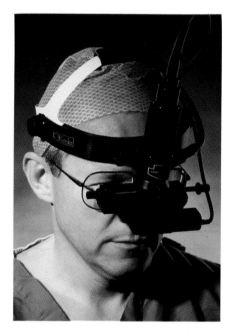

Physicians and surgeons at Grant's Eye and Ear Hospital use state-of-the-art technology to treat a full range of eye, ear, nose, and throat disorders.

unit featuring private birthing suites and home-like postpartum rooms. It is comforting for parents to know that Grant also features one of the area's finest newborn intensive care units for the treatment of ill or premature infants.

Women who visit Grant receive specialized care by experienced gynecologists. For women who require special procedures, Grant has facilities for mammography and breast care, as well as services for complete gynecological care.

The Elizabeth Blackwell Center at Grant affords women a variety of educational, health, and wellness program-

Grant Medical Center's LifeFlight, Columbus' premier emergency aeromedical transport service, provides lifesaving care throughout central and southern Ohio.

ming and special events throughout the Columbus community.

A leader in sports medicine, Grant offers state-of-the-art diagnostic and rehabilitative equipment through SportsMedicine Grant. The hospital's 25,000-square-foot fitness center is committed to helping individuals achieve more healthful life-styles. Open to the public, the fitness center provides fitness programs for a variety of individuals, including downtown workers, policemen, firefighters, and cardiac rehabilitation patients.

Grant's two family practice centers located in the eastern and southern Columbus suburbs provide comprehensive care for central Ohio families. They also serve as teaching facilities for the physicians in Grant's family medicine residency program.

Downtown businesses also benefit from Grant's convenient location with the Corporate Emergency Services program. The program offers a wide range of services for employees of member companies, including fast emergency care, information for supervisors, and benefits assistance. As an added service, free cab service to and from Grant is offered for most ill or injured employees.

Grant's closed-circuit television station provides a variety of informative programming for patients in the hospital. These educational videos cover topics ranging from child care to preparing for surgery to segments from "Life Choices with Erie Chapman," a

half-hour television program featuring a variety of health care subjects.

Grant is an experienced leader offering additional high-quality services in the areas of oncology, cardiology, peripheral vascular and psychiatric services, neurology, gastroenterology, and endocrinology. A skilled nursing facility affords patients a comfortable place to recuperate following their discharge from acute care beds. Grant's outpatient unit provides a variety of services for patients who require only minor procedures.

Employees at Grant also recognize the importance of patient care and satisfaction. Nurses at Grant can earn financial rewards for attaining proficiency

at different levels of their nursing specialty. Employees receive a comprehensive benefits package, and they are given many opportunities for career growth and advancement.

Grant Hospital opened its doors in July 1900 in downtown Columbus with 50 beds and a medical staff of 30 leading physicians, surgeons, and specialists. By 1904 Grant, with 100 beds, was the largest private hospital in the country.

The hospital's founder was Dr. James Fairchild Baldwin, a Columbus surgeon who studied leading facilities in the United States and Europe prior to opening Grant Hospital and the Nursing School. In 1985 Grant Hospital had expanded and changed its name to Grant Medical Center, becoming one of the most technologically and physically modern facilities in the area. In 1989 Grant became affiliated with the U.S. Health Corporation, one of the largest multihospital systems of its kind in the country.

Maternity services at Grant Medical Center include family birthing and private postpartum suites, a newborn intensive care nursery, and a staff experienced in the care of both mother and infant.

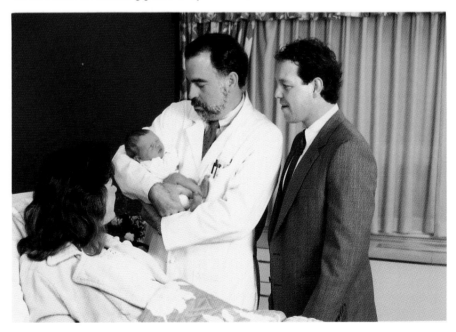

OTTERBEIN COLLEGE

Otterbein College is well positioned to enter the future while building on its past.

Founded in 1847 by the United Brethren Church on just eight acres of land with two buildings and 81 students, the college has grown to a 70-acre, 25-building campus with nearly 2,500 students. Approximately 80 percent of the student body is from Ohio.

Otterbein was the first college in North America to open its doors to women without limitations. It was the second to admit black students. Accepting change and adapting to it has always been a part of the institution's basic philosophy. Consequently, Otterbein has emerged as a significant educational force in central Ohio.

The college balances a solid liberal arts education with the practicality of career training. Because of this dual position, in recent years Otterbein has been cited by a *U.S. News and World Report* poll as one of the top 10 comprehensive colleges in the nation.

President C. Brent DeVore points out how Otterbein has avoided great pendulum swings throughout its history and has held to its traditional beliefs.

Thus, students are assured of "a sufficient blend of breadth and depth across their programs of study," DeVore says, as well as "a commitment to continuity and change, to values and excellence."

Otterbein firmly believes the liberal arts are the best foundation for any career choice. A series of required courses, called Integrative Studies, provides perspectives on human nature from various disciplines, such as the natural and social sciences, the arts, literature, religion, and philosophy. The Integrative Studies program is nationally recognized for its excellence.

Learning is a lifelong process not limited to the young. Therefore, the college created its Continuing Studies program, a wide range of undergraduate and graduate courses to meet the needs of adult students. Day, evening, weekend, and self-paced courses are available to adults who wish to pursue college work on a part-time basis while maintaining family and career commitments.

The relationship between student and teacher is of prime importance. Besides being professionally competent, faculty members act as role models and mentors, and the student-to-faculty ratio is 14 to 1.

At Otterbein the opportunities beyond the classroom are endless, ranging from a variety of extracurricular activities such as social, performance, cultural, and communication involvements

Otterbein's tree-lined, suburban campus is just minutes from the state capital of Columbus.

to college government and intercollegiate athletics and recreation.

Otterbein's "Cardinals" play in the NCAA Division III in both men's and women's sports, including football, baseball, basketball, soccer, volleyball, softball, track and field, and tennis.

Now on the brink of a new century, the college has laid the groundwork for its strategic plan—Otterbein 2000. Outlined in the plan are the college's mission and specific goals for academics, enrollment, facilities, campus environment, and finances.

Old and new have always blended well at Otterbein. The historic buildings and charming brick streets provide a pleasant mix of styles on campus. While offering the advantages of a small, friendly campus, Otterbein is neighbor to Ohio's capital city of Columbus. As a result, Otterbein students experience the best of two worlds.

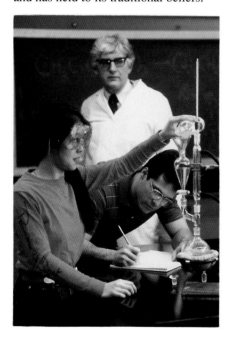

ABOVE: Thirty-five major courses of study are available to Otterbein students.

RIGHT: Founded in 1847, Otterbein has been ranked among the top 10 comprehensive colleges in the nation.

CAPITAL UNIVERSITY

For more than 100 years, Capital University has continuously responded to the changing educational needs of a growing central Ohio, while joining in partnership with many sectors of the community to offer a full palette of educational, cultural, and social opportunities to its students. Founded by the Lutheran church, Capital is recognized as an outstanding coeducational university. Today it provides a value-based liberal arts education, coupled with professional training, for approximately 3,200 students each year.

Capital has three undergraduate colleges and two graduate schools. Capital's College of Arts and Sciences offers more than 30 majors. Students enrolled in the university's Conservatory of Music benefit from such innovative programs as jazz studies and music industry. Capital students can also earn a bachelor's degree in nursing through the School of Nursing.

At the graduate level, a master of business administration degree is offered. In addition to the juris doctor de-

Chartered in 1850, Capital University is the oldest four-year comprehensive institution in central Ohio. It offers three undergraduate colleges and two graduate schools.

A variety of events on Capital's campus gives students and the Columbus community an opportunity to enjoy theatrical and musical performances, lectures, art exhibits, and athletic events.

gree, Capital's Law and Graduate Center offers three master degree programs.

Recognizing that many highly motivated adults are excluded from traditional programs by the time constraints of family and job, Capital also offers an Adult Degree Program (ADP) with centers in Columbus, Cleveland, and Dayton.

"The dynamics of this city are clearly leading Columbus toward recognition as the 'Education City of the Twenty-first Century,'" notes Josiah H. Blackmore, president of Capital University. "We're proud of the contributions we're making toward this movement."

One example is Capital's expertise in the area of dispute resolution. This process involves using a third party mediator to facilitate negotiations between two disputing parties as an alternative to violence, self-help, or litigation. Capital first gained prominence in this field in 1971, when several members of the university's law school established the Columbus Night Prosecutor Program as the first court-affiliated mediation program in the United States. Recently, Capital shared its knowledge with Jamaica, marking the first time that a university-sponsored mediation program has been

brought to a Third World country.

Capital University is also the only school in the country which offers a semester of undergraduate study at the Zoltán Koldály Pedagogical Institute of Music in Kecskemét, Hungary.

Closer to home, partnerships with Columbus corporations and businesses provide internships for Capital students. The School of Nursing also offers a cooperative education program—one of only two such state-approved programs in Ohio.

Accomplishments such as these are indicative of why Capital has repeatedly earned recognition as one of the top 15 regional colleges and universities in the Midwest by *U.S. News & World Report*. In addition, the university has been recognized as a "best buy" by both *Barron's 300: Best Buys in College Education* and by Edward B. Fiske, education editor of *The New York Times*.

"Our role in higher education is as relevant today as when we were chartered by the State of Ohio in 1850," says Blackmore. "Our past history of success gives us the foundation we need to move into the twenty-first century, addressing the needs of traditional undergraduate students as well as graduate students and adult learners."

OHIO'S CENTER OF SCIENCE & INDUSTRY (COSI)

Ohio's Center Of Science & Industry, or COSI®, has been landing space capsules at doorsteps, bringing the stars down from the heavens into reach, and, since 1964, offering more than 9 million visitors unmatched opportunities for discovery about themselves and the world around them.

Hundreds of dazzling, interactive exhibits, programs, and demonstrations entice and amaze visitors. From the team members and volunteers to the exhibits and demonstrations, excitement abounds at COSI, and the wonderment of discovery is everywhere. The opportunities for exploring the marvels of science are as limitless as the borders of the imagination, springing up at every turn at COSI.

ABOVE: COSI demonstrations, like this Rat Basketball game, are fun for visitors of all ages.

LEFT: A young visitor to COSI gets a real charge out of the electrostatic generator.

Permanent exhibits that COSI visitors of all ages have come to know and love include the Foucault Pendulum, the coal mine, the electrostatic generator, and the Street of Yesteryear.

Other exhibit areas, such as KIDSPACE®, were designed for a special age group. First opened in 1984, KIDSPACE was developed by COSI with generous local support and with the help of national experts who were interested in the needs of very young children. KIDSPACE is for kids under 48 inches tall and COSI's new FAMILIESPACE is for families of all shapes and sizes. They're areas of hands-on science activities for youngsters and their favorite grown-ups to explore together. KIDSPACE has been acclaimed as the premier science area in the country for young children. COSI has helped develop similar KIDSPACEs for science museums in Dallas and Lubbock, Texas, and in Atlanta, Georgia.

Aside from state-of-the-art exhibits like KIDSPACE, COSI is also known for outstanding programs and workshops such as COSI On Wheels, Summer Workshops, and the Young Experimental Scientist program.

One program that began 20 years ago and is still going strong today is Camp-In®. It is the largest informal science education program for women in the nation. COSI's renowned Camp-In program serves predominantly girls aged 6 to 16 with hands-on, minds-on science over a period of about 19 hours. Since 1972 more than 550,000 girls have participated in the program.

COSI is one of only 22 science-technology centers in the world and the only facility that is 97 percent privately funded. Nearly 25 percent of COSI's visitors are from Franklin County, 50 percent are from the rest of Ohio, and nearly 25 percent are visitors from outside the state.

COSI is in the midst of creating Ohio's twenty-first century science-technology center, targeted for completion by the end of 1994. Exciting new exhibits of a whole new scale are being created for the new 300,000-square-foot flagship facility in Columbus, to be supported by regional centers across Ohio; potentially, the first is to be located at Portside in Toledo.

Exhibits like MISSION TO MARS™, now traveling the country, will capture visitors' imaginations and demonstrate the need for strong math and science skills in space exploration.

Planet Ocean exhibitions and programs will create a twenty-first-century aquarium designed from the visitor's point of view, offering experiences in marine biology, oceanography, and sea exploration.

Science of Sports®, a major national traveling exhibit designed by COSI and seen by more than 9 million people in 21 museums nationally, will return to its home.

Science centers, particularly COSI, are places where kids of all ages come to dream, and take small steps into extraordinary worlds. So embark upon a journey into the past, present, and future at COSI, Ohio's Center Of Science & Industry.

SAINT ANTHONY MEDICAL CENTER

Saint Anthony Medical Center is at the forefront of many new surgical procedures ranging from cosmetic and laparoscopic technology to vascular techniques and neurosciences.

Proud of its history and confident in its future, Saint Anthony Medical Center is celebrating its second century of providing visionary health care in central Ohio.

Located at 1492 East Broad Street between downtown Columbus and Bexley, Saint Anthony is a 404-bed acute-care hospital centered in a neighborhood undergoing rebirth and revitalization.

Revitalization abounds at and around Saint Anthony. The hospital was honored with the City Beautiful Award for its landscaping program. Across the street, Franklin Park is the site of AmeriFlora '92, an international floral exhibition. To its north, Interstate 670 has opened, linking downtown with Port Columbus, making Saint Anthony one of the most accessible hospitals in the city.

A HISTORY OF CARING

Founded and operated by the Franciscan Sisters of the Poor, Saint Anthony maintains its mission of providing quality, state-of-the-art health care to those in need.

That need first manifested itself in Columbus in 1862, when five Franciscan sisters used an abandoned house on Rich Street to treat soldiers wounded in the Battle of Shiloh during the Civil War. Three years later they established the nation's first teaching hospital, St. Francis

BELOW: A patient room at Saint Anthony Medical Center.

RIGHT: Saint Anthony Medical Center, located between downtown Columbus and Bexley, is the focal point of a neighborhood undergoing renewal and growth.

Hospital, on the corner of Sixth and Town streets. St. Francis was the prototype for similar institutions around the county and the precursor of The Ohio State University College of Medicine.

Originally Saint Anthony was built in 1890 to relieve overcrowding at St. Francis Hospital. Its first patients were those requiring long-term care. It became an acute-care facility with state-of-the-art surgery, laboratory, radiology, emergency room, and additional services necessary to a medical-surgical hospital.

The original hospital building was replaced in 1969 with a modern, 18-story cylindrical tower which houses both patient rooms and physicians' offices.

In 1974 Saint Anthony pioneered the treatment of substance abuse with the establishment of Talbot Hall, a 60-bed unit devoted exclusively to the treatment of drug and alcohol addiction. Four years later adolescent care was added, the first of its kind in Ohio.

SPECIALIZED SERVICES

Today Saint Anthony's major areas of specialization include not only substance abuse treatment, but also oncology and the treatment of circulatory disorders. Each year, more than 1,200 surgical procedures are performed on diseased veins and arteries at the Saint Anthony Center for Circulatory Disorders.

The Saint Anthony Regional Oncology Center offers comprehensive cancer care including radiation therapy, and inpatient and outpatient chemotherapy in one convenient location. More than 150 patients receive personalized

cancer care each week at the center.

Other burgeoning specialties at Saint Anthony Medical Center include cardiology, gastroenterology, cosmetic surgery, and neurosciences, which includes a sleep disorders laboratory and headache clinic. Saint Anthony also houses a full-service endoscopy suite and a diagnostic cardiac catheterization lab.

Additionally, abnormalities of the brain, spinal cord, and neurological system are diagnosed and treated at Saint Anthony with a wide range of procedures including laser surgery.

The hospital is responding to the ever-changing health care environment by broadening its range of outpatient services. These services include minor surgery, diagnostic and therapeutic radiology, laparoscopy, and occupational medicine.

Now in its second century, Saint Anthony continues to steer the same dedicated course set by its founders. In an era of rapid change and high technology, Saint Anthony continues to provide quality, cost-effective health care with unparalleled dignity and compassion.

OHIO DOMINICAN COLLEGE

"Veritas"—"truth"—is a motto that Ohio Dominican College has carried proudly during almost a century of service. To contemplate truth and to share with others the fruits of this contemplation is a tradition that guides the institution's educational mission.

At Ohio Dominican students discover that truth is the basis of human freedom and the source of human effectiveness. It is found in all cultures and traditions and throughout the arts and sciences.

Although Ohio Dominican is a Catholic college, it offers students of many faiths opportunities to seek learning and truth in their own way. The college has a goal to "enable" students by providing them with the knowledge and skills that will serve them in both their personal and professional lives.

Ohio Dominican is only a few minutes from downtown Columbus. The intimate, tree-lined campus that fosters friendships is dominated by the spire atop Erskine Hall, the largest of the college's learning centers. Providing contrast to the traditional are the nearby Spangler Library and the athletic center, which exhibit decidedly modern architecture and reflect the dynamic and forward-looking approach of the institution. The college is sponsored by the Dominican Sisters of Saint Mary of the Springs. It was chartered in 1911 as the College of St. Mary of the Springs, but

RIGHT: Ohio Dominican's campus is presided over by the spire atop Erskine Hall.

Ohio Dominican students profit from the college's outstanding faculty and from the individualized attention afforded by small classes.

The college's goal is to provide students with the knowledge and skills that will serve them in their personal and professional lives.

in 1968 the name was changed to Ohio Dominican.

As a liberal arts institution, the college specializes in individual academic development that is based on an outstanding faculty. This learning environment is enhanced by small classes. The average class size is 20 students and the student to faculty ratio is 15:1.

More than 1,300 students are enrolled at Ohio Dominican. While most

come from Ohio, several different states and over 20 foreign countries are represented on campus. The college provides two dormitories for resident students.

Accredited by the North Central Association of Colleges and Secondary Schools and Ohio's Department of Education, Ohio Dominican offers more than 40 majors and programs leading to bachelor degrees, associate degrees, and certificates.

For adults determined to obtain the degree they have always wanted, Ohio Dominican offers the Weekend College for the "No hassle tassel." The Academic Development Center assists beginning or returning students over the "hassle" with free individual instruction in study and language skills, as well as providing workshops on time management, essay writing, test taking, and the preparation of research papers.

As an added incentive to return to school, Ohio Dominican reduces the tuition fee by 50 percent on all courses for adults over 60 and provides financial aid counseling for those seeking assistance.

Degrees in business administration, criminal justice, cross disciplinary studies, health administration, and social science are available at the Weekend College following the successful completion of 124 semester hours. Associate degrees and certificate programs also are available at the Weekend College in such diverse areas of study as library science, theology, and gerontology.

For nearly a century Ohio Dominican College has created for its students and faculty a stimulating, rewarding, and friendly Christian environment for intellectual and personal achievement. That environment has been key to the proud role the college and its graduates have played in the growth of the Columbus community.

OHIO WESLEYAN UNIVERSITY

The stately University Hall on Ohio Wesleyan's beautifully wooded campus serves as the backdrop for an outdoor classroom session.

Founded by Methodists in 1842, Ohio Wesleyan University will celebrate its sesquicentennial in 1992, having emerged as one of the premier liberal arts institutions in the country.

Since his 1984 inauguration as the university's 13th president, David Warren has guided Ohio Wesleyan through a remarkable resurgence—in the size and academic quality of the student body, the strength and potential of university fund-raising efforts, the scope and commitment of student community service, and the vitality of teaching and learning in and out of the classroom.

U.S. News & World Report ranked Ohio Wesleyan number one among the Midwest's 136 regional liberal arts colleges. The university has been among the top 20 undergraduate liberal arts institutions in producing graduates who go on to earn a Ph.D. Another survey placed Ohio Wesleyan 15th among similar colleges in producing future U.S. business leaders.

Exceptional academics are a hallmark of the university. Uncommon offerings include the National Colloquium, the Center for Economics and Business, the Arneson Institute for Practical Politics, professional programs in the arts, the Riverside School of Nursing, and involvement in an eight-college consortium promoting science research and education. The development of a first-rate Honors Program has had a stunning effect on the campus. Small honors classes, tutorials with senior faculty, and extensive research opportunities have attracted top honor students, while elevating the quality of academic life generally. In the last six years, as enrollment has increased by almost 600 students, the average SAT scores of incoming freshmen rose by 145 points.

At the heart of academic life are the faculty: exceptional scholars dedicated to teaching undergraduates. Faculty research fields range from long-term memory, acid rain, the effects of laser light on the eye, and gender roles to all manner of creative endeavors. However diverse their scholarly interests, they share a common commitment to the classroom. As one professor put it, "Here we are teachers, first and foremost."

The university's 2,000 students come from 41 states, 40 countries, and many ethnic, religious, economic, and racial backgrounds. Diversity also characterizes campus life: The student community supports more than 100 clubs, an energetic Greek system involving about half the students, and 21 varsity sports. In fact Ohio Wesleyan has one of the most successful Division III athletic programs in the country.

Nearly 75 percent of all students participate in community service, from Habitat for Humanity to fund-raising, food drives, and Big Pal/Little Pal.

Approaching its 150th anniversary, Ohio Wesleyan has embarked on a $50-million capital campaign to fund a new campus center, a fine arts complex, renovations in most academic and residential buildings, and increased student scholarship support.

In President Warren's words, "This campaign is predicated on a single powerful concept: that Ohio Wesleyan will become the premier college of our kind in the nation. Our aim is high, but no higher than the standards we have set for our students, our faculty, our academic programs, and our facilities."

Ohio Wesleyan is a community of teachers and students working together toward three goals: imparting knowledge, developing the capabilities of the students, and placing education in the context of values.

MOUNT CARMEL HEALTH

"The first wealth is health," wrote Ralph Waldo Emerson, and for more than a century Mount Carmel Health has enhanced the richness of human life through a holistic approach to health care, providing people with the resources and direct care that empower them to gain knowledge and control over their well-being.

A leading central Ohio health care provider with a strong heritage of quality and caring, Mount Carmel Health comprises Mount Carmel Medical Center, a 523-bed teaching hospital west of downtown Columbus, and Mount Carmel East Hospital, a 292-bed suburban community hospital. Providing a full range of general and specialized care, Mount Carmel Health's family of 700 physicians, 3,500 health professionals, and 700 volunteers grew from a small founding group of the mid-nineteenth century's leading physicians and spiritual pioneers.

In 1866 *Harper's* magazine wrote of Columbus that no western city of its size "has a larger or sounder financial responsibility, and none whose citizens have more public spirit or enthusiastic enterprise."

Columbus residents also possessed strong charitable instincts. For example, a shining event of 1866 was a ball that raised more than $1,000 for a home for elderly women. Other local groups that year dedicated themselves to caring for the poor, supporting education, and providing shelter for homeless women. With a similar commitment to serving the elderly, the poor, and the underserved, Columbus' first hospital—known as the Hawkes Hospital of Mount Carmel—was begun.

Construction started in 1865 on a four-story brick hospital with 18 private rooms, an operating room, an amphitheater, and two wards. Doctors W.B. Hawkes and John Hamilton, both board members of the Columbus Medical College, planned and raised funds to build the much-needed facility.

Dr. Hamilton sought out the Sisters of the Holy Cross to manage the new hospital. The Catholic order, founded in France just 20 years earlier, had a strong commitment to health care, caring for

By the year 2000, we will care for 500,000 lives annually, each treated as a whole person capable of making choices about his or her own health.

Vision for the Year 2000
Mount Carmel Health

The glass cupola atop Mount Carmel Medical Center.

INSET: Mount Carmel Health, circa 1910.

wounded Confederate and Union soldiers during the Civil War and staffing the Navy's first hospital ship.

Surrounded by bare walls, the sisters worked quickly and diligently to collect the basics—furniture, food, and medical and surgical supplies. True to form, the people of Columbus gave fruit, vegetables, equipment, and other necessities. Buggies, cows, horses, and money

were gratefully accepted, as were free water and gasoline from the city.

The hospital immediately earned a reputation for excellent nursing care, a pleasant and hygienic environment, and a highly talented medical staff. This public confidence and positive perception continue today, as Mount Carmel has remained true to its mission of quality and service.

After a tragic flood in 1913, Mount Carmel returned Columbus' charity. When the Olentangy and Scioto rivers overflowed, Mount Carmel, situated on a high point of land, was an island in the muddy water. The staff provided food, clothing, shelter, and care for the homeless. City residents nicknamed Mount Carmel "The Ark" during the crisis. To safeguard the area, Mount Carmel led an effort to erect a flood-wall that still stands today.

As the twenty-first century approaches, Mount Carmel is spearheading approval and construction of a new, stronger floodwall for the benefit of the city's near west side.

In addition, Mount Carmel Health is

• Hospice allows those with a life-limiting illness to receive care in their homes among family and familiar surroundings, thus improving the quality of life.

• Outreach, with its mobile medical clinic, travels to community centers and homeless shelters to provide much-needed care to the underserved.

• Mount Carmel Connection transports the elderly and the poor to Mount Carmel and its physicians' offices for care.

ABOVE: Mount Carmel's Advanced Treatment and Bionics Institute (ATBI) quickly brings the newest, most effective technologies to patients who might otherwise wait years for access to them. Pictured here is a laser system used in cancer research and treatment.

LEFT: Mount Carmel's caring approach to health care touches the lives of more than a quarter of a million patients every year.

a charter member of the Franklinton Housing Partnership, providing both financial and management staff assistance in support of the community's efforts to rehabilitate and stabilize housing in the Franklinton area. Committed to ensuring affordable housing for low and moderate-income families in the Franklinton neighborhood, the program includes offering low-interest loans and grants, energy audits and conservation, paint projects, workshops, and individual consultation.

Mount Carmel's community commitment extends far beyond the Franklinton neighborhood. Here are a few examples:

• A home care program enables patients to leave the hospital sooner and continue their recuperation at home, thanks to the assistance of visiting nurses, therapists, and home health aides.

• Golden LifeStyles offers a wide array of services, discounts, educational programs, and enrichment opportunities for senior citizens.

• A Family Practice Center provides Mount Carmel's brand of high-quality office-level medical care.

Mount Carmel's reputation has resulted in a steady demand for growth and technology. Bricks and mortar are ever rising on both hospitals' campuses to meet the community's need for services and to accommodate the latest medical advances. Mount Carmel's administration and medical staff have worked together to bring central Ohioans the most innovative diagnostic and treatment procedures available.

As a result, Mount Carmel often is the first hospital to provide a new treatment or diagnostic procedure in the area or in the entire state.

This commitment to state-of-the-art care has culminated in the development of Mount Carmel's Advanced Treatment and Bionics Institute (ATBI) to identify new and innovative treatments and technologies and to coordinate their acquisition and cost-effective use. The institute concentrates not only on medical devices but also on new drug developments and obtaining investigational study grants.

Mount Carmel has established a clear vision of its work into the next century. Within this vision is a commitment to leading the development of new health care financing methods; increasing the geographic availability of care in specialized areas such as women's and family health, cancer treatment, and cardiovascular care; and strengthening cost controls while continuing to aggressively assimilate new technologies.

At the beginning of the next century, Mount Carmel will touch 500,000 lives each year, relying on state-of-the-art technology and a history rich in purpose and quality. Service, performance, initiative, respect, innovation, and teamwork—these are the elements of Mount Carmel's spirit of life.

CHILDREN'S HOSPITAL

The Patient Tower is the heart of the Children's Hospital campus, which is located just southeast of downtown Columbus.

Imagine a place where kids are king and nearly 3,600 caring adults work around-the-clock to serve them. A place where color-coded walls and halls are adorned with the friendly visages of wild and domestic animals. A place frequented by clowns, magicians, singers, and actors who team with child life specialists and an outstanding staff of health care professionals to make a youngster's stay happy and healthful.

You've just envisioned Children's Hospital in Columbus, a sprawling facility that has evolved through a century of growth into one of the nation's most progressive and sophisticated pediatric health care centers. Children's Hospital personnel know kids are not miniature adults, that they have special needs and require special treatment, both medically and emotionally. That is why Children's staff members are committed to giving kids exactly what they need every day.

It is a commitment handed down from a group of concerned citizens who founded the hospital in 1892 after feeling the need for an institution dedicated to giving children the best available medical attention, regardless of their

parents' ability to pay. The facility was operated for half a century as a small community hospital serving mainly nonpaying patients and depending almost entirely on local support and volunteer medical services.

It was during this period that a

unique and enduring relationship began between Children's Hospital and Columbus. The two have grown together, mutually dependent on and supportive of each other. Central Ohio has responded generously and enthusiastically to the hospital's needs, enabling Children's to continually expand facilities, programs, and services to maintain that margin of excellence the community has come to expect.

The original hospital, built with $12,000 in donated funds, was at the corner of Miller and Fair avenues on the city's east side. It had a nine-bed capacity that was later increased to 25. The first hospital built on the present-day campus was opened in 1924 on Stone Street across from Livingston Park, just southeast of downtown Columbus. This five-story, 75-bed structure was made possible through $517,000 in community contributions.

The Stone Street facility still stands, but it has been extended and built

Babies with a variety of major problems receive the best care available in the hospital's newborn intensive care unit.

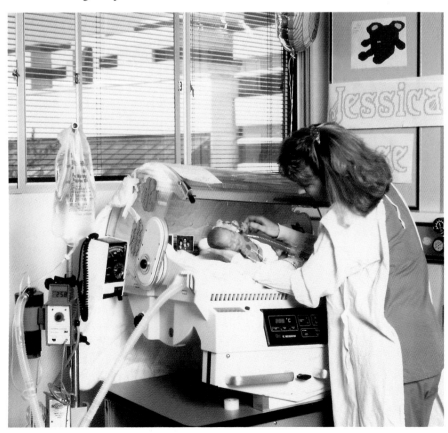

around through the decades as the hospital's modern complex has taken shape. Today the hospital is a 313-bed facility that annually treats more than 270,000 patients ranging in age from newborns to 21. More recent additions include a six-story patient care tower and a two-story Surgical Addition with nine state-of-the-art operating rooms, a 20-bed recovery room, and a 25-bed Outpatient Surgery unit.

Anchoring the hospital complex to the west is The Wexner Institute for Pediatric Research, a five-story, 122,000-square-foot facility built in 1987 that enables Children's researchers to probe medical mysteries and further enhance the lives of youngsters.

They study the entire spectrum of childhood problems, from societal concerns—substance abuse, violence, and environmental hazards—to the hidden secrets of human cells and their components. They conduct nutritional studies with implications for patients now in Children's and for whole populations of hungry children. They study viruses and the body's responses to them. They search for suspected communication passageways between the immune system and the brain.

Since 1916 Children's has been affiliated with The Ohio State University's College of Medicine. Today it serves as the site for the College of Medicine's

Department of Pediatrics. As the pediatric education center for much of Ohio, the hospital trains 1,800 full-time medical, nursing, and allied health students annually, with community outreach programs providing various types of pediatric training for several thousand other persons each year.

This degree of activity fostered the need for a six-story, 130,000-square-foot education building, the complex's newest addition. Included in this state-of-the-art facility is extensive conference and teaching space, a laboratory for teaching high-technology skills, faculty and staff offices, medical and patient/family libraries, classrooms, and the latest computer-based systems.

Being at the forefront of pediatric education and research supports and enhances excellence in patient care.

Among Children's several specialty areas are a 25-bed newborn intensive care unit, 20-bed newborn developmental unit, 12-bed surgical/infant intensive care unit, 16-bed pediatric intensive care unit, 38-bed infectious diseases unit, 20-bed hematology/oncology unit, 13-bed burn/trauma unit, 19-bed neurosurgery unit, 10-bed inpatient rehabilitation unit, 19-bed pulmonary unit, and 20-bed cardiac unit.

Children's provides emergency transport via mobile intensive care units. The hospital's emergency room, the most active in central Ohio, treats more than 6,600 patients annually. Children's also has a major child abuse identification, treatment, and prevention program, a childhood epilepsy center, and liver and kidney transplantation programs.

Children's has 27 specialty outpa-

tient programs with services ranging from health assessment and medical diagnostic to specialized care, including eye, dental, tumor, allergy, and myelomeningocele clinics. The hospital provides the largest outpatient mental health system in central Ohio for children, adolescents, and families through four neighborhood locations of the Children's Hospital Guidance Centers.

The Central Ohio Poison Center, a certified regional facility housed at Children's, receives more than 35,000 calls each year from people throughout central and southern Ohio who need instant assessment of poison and chemical emergencies or who request prevention information. The center is staffed around-the-clock by registered pharmacists and nurses who are certified as poison information specialists by the American Association of Poison Control Centers. Four physician toxicologists are also available to offer advice.

To help ease a child's (as well as parents') fears about an impending visit to the hospital, Children's sponsors weekly pre-admission orientation parties for the entire family. In addition, the hospital has a large staff of child life specialists, professionals not usually found in general hospitals. They plan developmental, educational, and therapeutic activities for children of all ages. These activities help foster a child's normal growth and development during hospitalization through playroom activity, special events, and psychological preparation for medical and surgical procedures.

The hospital's physical expansion through the past several decades reflects not only central Ohio's growth but spectacular advances in techniques for saving and improving young lives.

As Children's enters its second century, it looks confidently forward to continued research that will generate more medical breakthroughs, to educating future generations of care givers, and, of course, to the provision of ever-improving patient care. Life is exciting in the hospital the community built for its children—a hospital that has proved to be a lasting investment in the community's future.

FRANKLIN UNIVERSITY

Sitting amidst the excitement of City Center and the historic Grant/Washington Discovery District in downtown Columbus is Franklin University, a university which, for almost 90 years, has provided working adults with a "learn while you earn" education.

Franklin University is committed to developing innovative programs, providing flexible scheduling, emphasizing practical and applied teaching methods, and maintaining a responsive attitude toward the needs of its students and the business community.

The university is also committed to teaching excellence, an accessible faculty, and small class size. Experienced professionals who make teaching their career serve as full-time faculty members.

The part-time faculty includes men and women who combine the requisite education with a desire to share their practical experience in successful careers such as certified public accountants, business executives, attorneys, engineering technologists, scientists, and government officials.

Accredited by the North Central Association of Colleges and Schools, Franklin offers a variety of majors in fields such as business management, accounting, banking, finance, commu-

nications, computer science, engineering technology, public administration, nursing, and real estate.

A student-centered philosophy best characterizes the university. Its commitment to an open admissions policy means that anyone with a high school diploma or GED equivalency may pursue an education at Franklin. Its two colleges—the College of Business and Technology and the College of Arts and Sciences—offer educational programs designed to provide students with up-to-date professional and technical skills as well as opportunities for personal growth and professional development.

Franklin's mission is to provide student-centered, community-responsive education for personal and career development. As an institution of higher

learning, it seeks to develop its students' creativity and independence of thought so they will be able to face challenges with confidence.

Franklin University was formed under sponsorship of the Young Men's Christian Association in 1902. Classes were held at the YMCA on East Long Street. In 1964 Franklin separated from the association, and in 1969 the university moved to its present Grant Avenue site.

The university has made its mark in higher education in Columbus. For example, in 1902 Franklin became the first institution to establish a night school program so working adults could easily get a college degree. In 1978 Franklin was first to present college classes on cable television and to establish on-site classes in industry. In 1983 the institu-

RIGHT: Franklin University's accessible, centralized location within a thriving business community offers an ideal setting for its students.

BELOW: The Franklin University Bunte Gallery is committed to increasing awareness and support of the arts in Columbus.

tion implemented the nation's first undergraduate degree program in employee assistance counseling.

Today Franklin University is the largest independent institution in central Ohio and boasts an enrollment of more than 4,000 students. It is financed by tuition and fees paid by the students, along with corporate and private gifts. In any given trimester, students may range in age from 17 to 75, with an average age of 28.

More than 85 percent of the students work either full or part-time, in positions relevant to their studies at Franklin. Almost 90 percent of the university's 21,000 alumni live or work in central Ohio.

Franklin's Center for Applied and Professional Education (C.A.P.E.) is yet another link between the university and

ABOVE: *Known as Columbus' downtown urban university, Franklin has been serving the central Ohio community for nearly nine decades.*

LEFT: *Acquired in 1987, Franklin's South Hall houses laboratories, classrooms, and administrative offices.*

the central Ohio community. C.A.P.E. was designed to help individuals and organizations in the midst of a changing and increasingly competitive workplace fulfill their potential, both professionally and personally.

C.A.P.E. offers a wide range of short-term courses, seminars, workshops, forums, and conferences. Additional services include an extensive computer education system called the Computer Learning Center, designed for companies and individuals to develop essential computer literacy skills and expertise. The Real Estate Institute prepares participants for their licensing exams. An AutoCAD Training Center, the only one of its kind in central Ohio,

assists businesses and their employees with design training.

Franklin's library is considered the best business library in central Ohio. Its computerized circulation system and on-line union catalog allows the user to search both the university's collection and that of the Columbus Metropolitan Library from Franklin's library, from the public library's main or branch locations, or from a home computer with a modem.

An up-to-the-minute collection of business references, including an extensive tax information center available to the public, makes the Franklin library a significant and valuable resource for both the university's community and the community at large.

As a major showcase for local and regional artists, the Bunte Gallery on campus provides a stimulating, aesthetically rich setting for students and a broad audience of viewers from central Ohio. Six highly acclaimed exhibitions are presented each year.

The gallery's overriding commit-

ment to the community is characterized by the goals which it has established for its operation: to increase awareness and support for the arts in the community, to provide local and regional artists with space in which to exhibit and promote their works, and to act as an arts education resource in the downtown community.

Through the leadership and creativity of Dr. Paul J. Otte, president of Franklin University as it entered the 1990s, the institution now more than ever offers its students and the business community the kinds of programs and skills that are needed today.

"Franklin University provides the kind of educational environment where people can learn, create, think, and prepare themselves to shape the future," said Otte. "As a center of learning in the center of Columbus, Franklin prepares its students for the challenges of tomorrow by providing them with an education that will serve them a lifetime."

Behind every successful institution lies a committed board. Franklin's trustees have recruited and retained some of the city's most influential leaders. Through their generous support, commitment, and belief in Franklin, the university has made great progress during the twentieth century. This leadership of today bodes well for the Franklin of tomorrow.

COLUMBUS ZOO

It is fitting that the Discovery City is the home of the Columbus Zoo, where new worlds are discovered and explored every day of the year.

It was at the Columbus Zoo that the world discovered that gorillas really could reproduce in captivity. The world's first captive-born gorilla was Colo, who was born at the zoo December 22, 1956. Since then her family has grown to four generations, creating the foundation for one of the largest lowland gorilla collections in the nation.

Founded in 1927 when the *Columbus Dispatch* donated reindeer purchased for a city Christmas celebration,

ABOVE: Colo, the world's first gorilla born in captivity, treats her grandson, JJ, to a piggyback ride. Photo by Nancy Staley

ABOVE RIGHT: Many of the zoo's animals are placed in habitats resembling their natural environments. Photo by Rick Prebeg

the 92-acre zoo today houses more than 5,000 animal specimens from six continents in a park-like setting. An adjacent 266-acre golf course, bought for the zoo in 1989, will lead to the development of the third-largest municipally owned zoo in the nation.

In recent years keepers, architects, and grounds keepers have brought the outstanding collection out from behind bars and into naturalistic habitats. The most dramatic example of this effort is the North American complex where bobcat, cougar, bears, wolves, moose, and eagles live "in the wild" while bison and pronghorn antelope roam a nearby hillside.

Enthralled visitors discover lions, tigers, and elephants, of course, but also koalas from "down under," a rare species of chimpanzee called bonobo, one of the nation's largest collections of breeding cheetahs, and, in the Reptile Building, a collection of turtles

and snakes considered among the nation's finest.

Even Christopher Columbus didn't find the wide variety of marine and freshwater specimens on display, including shark, Lake Victoria cichlids, five species of lungfish, and loggerhead sea turtles, whose young are fostered at the zoo for release in the wild.

Youngsters discover the joy of touching at the Children's Zoo Petting Barn, where barnyard animals hold sway. At Paw Prints Park and Theatre, children become involved in an interactive educational experience that makes learning about nature fun.

A high level of community and corporate support has enabled the zoo to bring an "around the world" experience to more than one million visitors annually. The Columbus Zoo is a dynamic tribute to dedication to the welfare of wildlife and belief in the future.

LEFT: More than one million visitors a year enjoy the parklike setting of the zoo. Photo by Nancy Staley

BELOW: Youngsters really grab hold of fun at the Children's Zoo Petting Barn.

COLUMBUS COLLEGE OF ART AND DESIGN

There are no shortcuts in art and aesthetics, only time and work. Progress follows tenacity.

As we approach the twenty-first century, the challenges and opportunities facing the professional artist and designer grow ever more complex. In order for students to best prepare to meet these challenges, a private college of art must provide a broad-based, disciplined education with a strong emphasis on fundamentals, encouraging quality development.

Founded in 1879, the Columbus College of Art and Design is an internationally recognized leader in the

V-Hall is one of the many areas on campus to view student work.

study of the visual arts. Where some colleges simply talk about a strong foundation program, CCAD delivers with a 112-year history of excellence. With its unique and sequential development, the freshman year at CCAD is an intensive program where all areas of exploration enfold a clear approach in art and aesthetics.

The institution offers the Bachelor of Fine Arts degree after the successful completion of this program of study. Major areas of study are offered in the divisions of Fine Arts, Advertising Design, Illustration, Retail Advertising, Industrial Design, Interior Design, and

ABOVE AND BELOW: These two works are representative of the many styles of painting and drawing taught at the Columbus College of Art and Design.

Photography. An art therapy minor is available within any division. Specific directions also are available in fashion design, fashion illustration, packaging, glassblowing, video, computer graphics, and computer animation.

Approximately 40 states and 30 foreign countries are represented at the college. With a total enrollment of nearly 1,600 students, CCAD is proud to be able to point to the growth of its enrollment and the expansion of its curriculum as it enters the decade of the 1990s.

CCAD is one of the select few art colleges in the country to have an internship program with Walt Disney Studios, which further acknowledges the quality and strength of the CCAD program and the caliber of its students.

CCAD graduates have been, or are, employed in professional art and design positions in companies throughout the world, including at the Smithsonian Institution in Washington, D.C., the National Aeronautics and Space Agency, and at such major corporate institutions as Hallmark Cards, the Cleveland Clinic, Xerox Corporation, General Motors Corporation, Gibson Greeting Card Company, Westinghouse Corporation, ABC Television, American Greetings, and Hewlett Packard, to name just a few.

CCAD students consistently dominate national art competitions, winning top honors in illustration, package design, and poster design contests, among others.

With an 11-building campus in downtown Columbus, CCAD students are within walking distance of museums, theaters, shopping, and recreational attractions.

Each year CCAD conducts a national scholarship competition, awarding nearly 130 scholarships to graduating high school seniors. The scholarship awards are based on talent and require the submission of a portfolio of original student artwork.

The Columbus College of Art and Design is accredited by the Commissions of Institutions of Higher Education of the North Central Association of Colleges and Schools and by the National Association of Schools of Art and Design. In addition, CCAD is approved by the National Association of Foreign Student Affairs.

COLUMBUS STATE COMMUNITY COLLEGE

Since 1963 Columbus State Community College has been an active contributor to the dynamic growth of Columbus and central Ohio. That year, in response to requests from local business and industry, the Columbus Area Technician School was created through the foresight of the Columbus (Ohio) Board of Education. The new school was housed in the basement of the former Central High School, with an initial enrollment of 67 students.

To accommodate the growth in enrollment that was experienced during the first two years of operation, the board of education purchased the Columbus Aquinas Parochial High School property in 1965, and moved the school to a permanent campus. The facility at Spring Street and Cleveland Avenue is where the first class of 39 students graduated, and is currently a part of the college's main campus.

On May 25, 1965, the Ohio Board of Regents gave approval to a proposal from the Columbus Board of Education to create the Columbus Technical Institute, a two-year state technical college. The charter was effective July 1, 1967, and this authorized C.T.I. to award two-year associate degrees in 11 technical programs of study or technologies.

During the next five years C.T.I. added evening classes and additional technical degree programs, and experienced growth in enrollment. In 1973 the college was accredited by the North Central Association of Colleges and Schools. Many of the college's degree programs are also accredited by professional associations, organizations, and agencies. From 1967 to 1987 C.T.I. continued to add additional degree programs and soon grew to be Ohio's largest two-year state technical college.

C.T.I. was rechartered by the Ohio Board of Regents as Columbus State Community College in July 1987 and

ABOVE: The main campus of Columbus State is on 60 acres of land near the heart of downtown Columbus. The college also maintains a number of off-campus suburban centers.

LEFT: A statue of Christopher Columbus presides over Columbus State's main campus, located in the heart of downtown Columbus.

was authorized to award transfer degree programs. The associate of arts and associate of science transfer degree programs enable students to complete the first two years of a bachelor's degree and transfer these credits to The Ohio State University and many other four-year colleges and universities.

In addition to these transfer programs, Columbus State offers more

than 35 two-year technical degree programs. These career-oriented associate degree programs are offered in a variety of different career areas within the major fields of business, health, public service, and engineering technologies. Within these technical areas, a number of short-term certificate programs and individual "career-builder" courses also are available.

These programs have been developed in response to local employment needs and were designed with input from professionals in each field who serve on the college's advisory committees. These committees constantly review each program and recommend changes to ensure that they reflect the emerging employment needs of tomorrow.

With more than 13,000 students from different backgrounds and age groups, Columbus State accommodates

ABOVE: The transfer degree programs at Columbus State enable students to transfer credits to four-year colleges and universities.

RIGHT: Many programs of study were designed with the aid of professionals in the field who serve on the college's advisory committees.

the needs of a diverse student population by offering classes during the day, at night, and on weekends. About 80 percent of Columbus State's students are employed, so they can find classes to fit their busy schedules.

Columbus State is committed to helping students succeed personally as well as academically. The college offers a variety of support programs such as counseling, handicapped student services, transfer assistance, and placement and career services. The college's educational resources center, bookstore, exercise facility, and cafeteria provide additional services for students.

Since there's more to college life than classroom studies, the Student Ac-

tivities Department promotes varsity and intramural sports and many recreational, cultural, and social activities to enrich a student's college experience.

Columbus State is a public college with an open admissions policy, providing each individual with the maximum opportunity to learn and develop. If an

individual can benefit from the educational opportunities available at Columbus State, he or she is welcome as a student.

Senior citizens can enroll in credit courses, tuition-free, through the college's "Good as Gold Program," and telecourses are offered on campus and through local television stations.

Columbus State also has a Business and Industry Training Division that provides hundreds of custom-designed training programs, workshops, and seminars to meet the training needs of local employers. These programs are offered either on campus or at the employers' places of business.

The main campus of Columbus State comprises 60 acres near the heart of downtown Columbus. The campus includes 11 modern buildings, including the highly regarded Educational Resources Center and the solar heated and cooled Franklin Hall. The main campus is also easily accessible to the handicapped.

In addition to the main campus, the college has a facility at Bolton Field Airport, which houses Columbus State's Aviation Maintenance Technology, and a number of off-campus centers operated throughout central Ohio. Entry-level classes are offered at these suburban centers, which are convenient for individuals who want to attend classes close to home or near work.

As a state college, Columbus State is able to maintain its tuition and fees at the lowest possible level. An education at the college is affordable, providing access to a segment of the community who otherwise would not have the opportunity for higher education.

The future for the college is promising. With the cooperation and support of the entire community, Columbus State Community College will continue to meet the educational needs of the community it serves.

GREATER COLUMBUS CONVENTION CENTER

The best word to describe the Greater Columbus Convention Center, scheduled to open in 1992, is "spacious." The convention center's 28.7-acre North High Street site will be the home of a grand structure of approximately 580,000 gross square feet, with the building's footprint covering 10 acres.

Almost half of the area will be occupied by an enormous exhibit hall. The size of 4 football fields, this hall can be divided into two separate areas. Adjacent will be meeting room space totaling 81,000 square feet, including 57 separate rooms with a 25,000-square-foot ballroom.

An enclosed, on-grade connector joins the convention center with Battelle Hall, hotels, specialty shops, and parking to form a major entrance to the complex. Battelle Hall, located in the Ohio Center, has 6,000 retractable seats and 90,000 square feet of exhibit space.

The total project budget of $93.9 million is being financed by a countywide hotel/motel user tax and will be owned by the Franklin County Convention Facilities Authority.

The convention center's innovative design arose from a national competition. The creative team of a local architect, the late Richard Trott, and New York-based Peter Eisenman imaginatively combined the old with the new, using an image of lines as connectors: the railroad lines of the last century, the super highways of today, and the fiberoptics for information exchange in the future.

The design reflects High Street's architectural tradition of narrow structures with articulated facades. The center, with its 11 separate facades, bridges the high-rise buildings of downtown with the surrounding North Market and Short North communities. In addition, with its plazas, public spaces, and sidewalk cafe, the center will revitalize the pedestrian life along High Street.

A major concourse and prefunction area extends north and south through

ABOVE: Blending into the architecture of North High Street was an important design consideration for the 29-acre Greater Columbus Convention Center.

LEFT: The convention center's main exhibit hall and 57 other meeting rooms will be connected with nearby hotels, retail shops, and parking.

the entire width of the convention center. Main entrances with access roads for cars, taxis, and buses are on the north at Goodale Boulevard and on the south at Ohio Center Way. Four additional entrances are on High Street.

Each section of the exhibit hall has its own concourse, entry, service area, concession stands, restrooms, and support areas. The exhibit space is serviced by 24 loading docks, two oversized drive-through doors, and an adjacent staging area for trucks.

Meeting rooms are clustered across the concourse from the exhibit halls. Each meeting room cluster is centered on a skylighted atrium. The meeting and banquet space is fully carpeted and includes acoustical wall treatment;

individual room control of temperature, sound, and lighting; and a centrally located recording room. The ballroom, at the south end of the concourse and with its own entrance off High Street, is serviced by a full-service banquet kitchen.

Additional design plans call for a laser light system, allowing for both dramatic light shows and special programs. Other special features of the center include restrooms adjustable for varying male/female population, a registration area with movable walls, and total accessibility for individuals with disabilities.

The convention center site, four blocks from the historic state capitol, will have easy access to I-670, the primary expressway route from downtown to Port Columbus International Airport just 10 minutes away. Parking for 7,000 cars is available within a two-block area, including more than 2,100 spaces on site.

Photo by Larry Hamill

14 MARKETPLACE

▲▲▲▲▲▲▲▲▲▲▲▲▲▲▲▲▲

463

Columbus' retail establishments, service industries, and accommodations are enjoyed by both residents and visitors.

Ricart Ford Incorporated, 464; White Castle System, Incorporated, 466; McGlaughlin Oil Company, 468; Stouffer Dublin Hotel, 470; The Limited Incorporated, 472; Wendy's International, Inc., 473; Executive Office Place, 474; Temporary Corporate Housing, Inc., 476; Kroger Company, 478; Continental Office Furniture & Supply Corporation, 480; Chemlawn Inc., 482; Columbus Marriott North, 484; Mid-American Waste Systems, 485; The Butler Company, 486; Frigidaire Company, 488; Columbus City Center, 489; Big Bear Stores Company, 490; Headquarters Companies, 492; Long's College Book Store, 494; Fiesta Salons Incorporated, 496

Photo by James Blank

RICART FORD INCORPORATED

J.D. Power describes Ricart Automotive as the world's largest automobile complex. Fred Ricart says it isn't an auto dealership at all. And his perception is the key to their success.

"We think of it as the Disneyland of the automotive business. We operate in the same way as successful *businesses*, not just successful *automobile* businesses. We like to think beyond our own industry." There is a difference. In building the complex, Fred steered clear of much of the industry's accepted methods, drawing instead from other businesses and in many cases inventing the methods and procedures for his operation.

The results are nothing short of staggering. The 75-acre Ricart complex has its own system of roads lined with $31 million in new car, truck, and mini-van inventory. Many visitors think they have just arrived at a Detroit assembly plant as cartoons of Fred direct them through the 118 different models from Ford, Mitsubishi, Isuzu, Mazda, Nissan, Chrysler's Jeep-Eagle, as well as the world's largest used-car department.

In the last year alone, 23,674 cars were sold, prepped, and put on the road by the 500-plus employees of Ricart Automotive.

Not surprisingly, Ford is the flagship of the operation, which has led the nation in retail Ford sales for five years running. In the last two years Ricart Ford has led all makes and models in total new and used sales.

But how did it all happen? What turned a dealership, founded in 1953 and selling 300-400 cars a year, into the world's largest? The move to the top began in 1975, nine years after the dealership moved to its current location at Route 33 east and South Hamilton Road, when Fred Ricart assumed the reins.

Fred's background in biochemistry and research with Case Western Reserve and three years as a research sci-

RIGHT: Publications across the country have featured Ricart and its innovative approaches to the automobile business.

BELOW: Many visitors to the the world's largest automobile dealership's 75 acres think they've stepped into a Detroit assembly plant.

entist form the foundation of his "cause and effect" approach to business. The organization's central focus is people. "When people are treated honestly, with respect and appreciation, anything is possible," maintains Ricart.

For customers, it means a sincere effort to find the specific vehicle they really want and can afford. "We don't have to talk customers into anything. With 75 acres of vehicles the odds are excellent that we have exactly what the customer wants right here. Our volume also means we can make less on each car than other dealers. Together, that's the secret of the Ricart deal," says Fred. "It takes the pressure out of the buying process, and our customers really appreciate that. When a customer is treated properly, things are as smooth as squeezing toothpaste out of a tube. Handle them poorly, and it's like trying to put toothpaste back in the tube. At best, it's messy. Usually it's impossible."

For employees, this people orientation has created a family atmosphere in the dealership. "We

AUTOMOTIVE INDUSTRY

INSIDE REPORT

Ricarts deal their way to the top

ABOVE: Visitors to the Ricart complex are greeted by a larger-than-life caricature of Fred that guides them through the Ricart road system.

LEFT: The combination of marketing and management skills shared by the Ricart brothers has made Ricart Automotive number one in the world.

stress teamwork and professionalism. We're not big on titles around here. We are big on smiles and encouragement. And we don't hesitate to pat people on the back or the wallet for a job well done," says Fred.

Even the scientifically based innovations in systems and procedures that have been instituted are geared to people. Specially designed computer software monitors everything from up-to-the-minute buying trends to the service center's daily activities. Psychologically designed showrooms and procedures create an anxiety-free atmosphere for customers. "Our whole technological focus is directed toward systems that allow our people to do their jobs better, and our customers to receive better service," maintains Fred. "Profit is a mirage. People and customer service are the keys. If you take care of customers, the sales and profits take care of themselves." According to the Ricarts, many businesses are more elocution than execution: "We don't just talk about how we want things to be here. We make them happen."

Fred is also quick to credit his brother Rhett, co-owner of Ricart Automotive, with a large portion of their success. Rhett's business and administrative skills are a perfect complement to Fred's marketing and advertising strengths. Rhett is the company motivator.

"I don't open mail here. I don't write letters here. I don't read trade journals here. I do all that at home. We have the best people in the business, and I like to be here, letting them know that we appreciate what they're doing and cheering them on," says Rhett.

Everyone in central Ohio knows the public persona of the Ricart complex. It's Fred, and his fun, often outrageous, commercials. He writes the 50 commercials he produces each year himself, with an assist from his wife Lynne and their five children. And he records many of his song parody commercials at his own home studio. His friendly style and good-natured humor attract a lot of attention on the airwaves, but he insists that advertising is not the key to sales: "Advertising reflects what you really are. It doesn't make you what you are. If we really weren't offering better deals and world-class service, the word would get out and no amount of advertising, no amount of creativity could overcome it."

The Ricarts also believe they have a responsibility to do the right thing for the community that has so dramatically patronized their business. Together they are involved in more than 30 organizations, though Fred's closest attention goes to his work in the war on drugs. His BioPower Program for children has been acclaimed as uniquely effective by drug education scholars. And his "Scared Stiff" program in conjunction with the Franklin County Sheriff's Department has had a hand in the marked reduction in teenage highway fatalities in participating schools around central Ohio.

Community, corporation, and customers: they are the Ricart's people-driven "three C's" and are the core of what they are as individuals and successful businessmen.

The BioPower educational model has been praised by educational experts as uniquely effective.

WHITE CASTLE SYSTEM, INCORPORATED

There are many wonderful tales about White Castle hamburgers and the loyal customers who have gone to incredible lengths to obtain them.

One true story involved a White Castle-starved fan who had waited for years for a White Castle restaurant to open near him. When one finally did, he waited for 12 hours outside the door just so he could be the first customer. He bought 1,500 hamburgers for himself and his coworkers.

Another concerned the brother of a woman who had moved to a distant city without a White Castle location. To satisfy her craving for the hamburgers, he periodically flew his private plane over her house to drop off large carry-out orders of White Castle hamburgers to her.

There are hundreds more of such "Castlerific" true stories about this unique quick service restaurant chain and the millions of hamburgers they've served over the years. In Columbus, Ohio, White Castle restaurants date back to 1929, but the company was actually founded in Wichita, Kansas, in 1921 by Walter Anderson and E.W. "Billy" Ingram, Sr. Their brief partnership was formed when Anderson, who had a trio of hamburger stands, wanted to open a fourth on property owned by a dentist. The dentist refused to grant Anderson a lease unless Ingram, then in real estate and insurance, was a backer.

Thus the White Castle System of Eating Houses Corporation was founded on $700 in borrowed capital that was paid back in 90 days. The transaction established for the firm the principle of little or no debt that served it well during the Depression years. "He who owes no money," said Ingram, "cannot go broke."

The name White Castle was selected because it signified purity and cleanliness as well as strength, stability, and permanence. The name was right on target, as today the White Castle System is the nation's oldest privately owned and operated hamburger chain.

The first White Castle restaurant in Wichita under the Anderson-Ingram partnership was an unusual-looking cement block building with only five stools where customers could get a

ABOVE: All White Castle restaurants, such as this one in Cincinnati, are family-held, privately owned.

LEFT: White Castle products include the unique 2-inch-square, 100 percent U.S. beef, steam-grilled hamburgers, french fries, and soft drinks.

White Castle hamburger for five cents. But already the building featured the now-famous tower, battlements, and architectural style inspired by Chicago's landmark Water Tower.

From the beginning, the White Castle System designed and erected its own buildings and most of the fixtures. In 1928 the modern, all-metal structure was introduced, employing for the first time porcelain enamel as an architectural mix. Six years later the Porcelain Steel Buildings (PSB) Company was established in Columbus to manufacture all the buildings and fixtures for the restaurant chain.

With restaurants in several states, Ingram began looking to move his office to a more centralized location.

After Anderson left in 1933 to try his hand at the aviation industry, Ingram moved his headquarters to Ohio's capital city in 1934.

As the business grew, so did the fame of the little square hamburger with five evenly spaced holes. Unlike ordinary hamburgers, White Castle hamburgers are steam-grilled on a bed of onions, without cooking oils or grease. The meat and onions are placed between soft buns, which are produced at company-owned bakeries in Evendale, Ohio, Carteret, New Jersey, and Rensselaer, Indiana.

These three bakeries annually bake nearly 496 million buns for White Castle restaurants in Ohio and as far west as Kansas City. The Evendale facility alone, just outside of Cincinnati, produces more than 224 million buns.

The company has been responsible for many innovations, not the least of which are the griddles on which the hamburgers are steam-grilled. After some 60 years of development, the griddles are now made of cast alu-

Wichita No. 4 was the beginning of the White Castle System and the first building under the partnership of Walt Anderson and E.W. Ingram. The white cement block restaurant had five stools, a stand-up window, and the now-famous tower and battlements.

minum, designed so they can be removed and easily cleaned.

Another innovation, which dates back to the early 1930s, is the idea of selling hamburgers by the "sack." In order to keep the hamburgers intact for the customers as well as to retain as much of the heat as possible, White Castle developed individual heat-resistant cartons for its hamburgers, an idea that only much later caught on at other quick service restaurant hamburger chains.

The PSB Company has been an innovative leader of products developed for outside clients and customers. During World War II, for instance, it manufactured parts for amphibious trucks and radio antennas.

In more recent years, PSB has been manufacturing its own Prizelawn line of lawn spreaders as well as private-label spreaders for a number of companies. The firm also fabricates and paints parts for other businesses in widely diverse fields such as the automotive, appliance, air conditioning, construction, and communications industries. PSB also has a powder paint facility in Dayton.

In 1987 White Castle Distributing, Incorporated, began mass producing and distributing a new frozen microwaveable hamburger and cheeseburger product line

from its one-of-a-kind "hamburger factory" in Louisville, Kentucky. It is the only frozen microwaveable hamburger line sold in supermarkets by a major quick service restaurant chain.

The product is recognized as a leader in the frozen microwaveable category wherever it's sold. Though not yet national, White Castle's frozen packaged goods retail markets are expanding sizably each year.

Founder Ingram was succeeded by his son, E.W. Ingram, Jr., in 1966 and by his grandson, E.W. Ingram III, in 1979. Bill Ingram III prefers "a deliberately moderate but steady expansion... rather than leaping the continent in a single bound." With more than 250 restaurants in the United States, the White Castle System is undertaking restaurant franchise licensing agreements in the Pacific Rim and the Caribbean as well.

As an employer, the White Castle System offers a benefit plan which is one of the most comprehensive in the quick service restaurant industry. All full- and part-time employees receive annual cash bonuses based on sales as well as profit sharing and retirement benefits. Full-time employees enjoy life and health insurance benefits as well.

The founder's philosophy that "we have no right to expect loyalty except from those to whom we are loyal" continues to be practiced by his successors.

The philanthropic activities of the White Castle System, Inc., and the Ingram family are channeled through three conduits: corporate contributions; the Edgar W. Ingram-White Castle Fund, an advised fund of the Columbus Foundation; and the Ingram-White Castle Foundation. The latter offers support for agencies and institutions concerned with quality of life, especially education.

TOP RIGHT: E.W. "Bill" Ingram III, grandson of the founder, serves as president and chief executive officer of White Castle System, Inc.

ABOVE RIGHT: E.W. Ingram, Jr., is chairman of the board of White Castle System, Inc.

RIGHT: E.W. "Billy" Ingram, was a co-founder of White Castle System, Inc., in 1921 in Wichita, Kansas.

McGLAUGHLIN OIL COMPANY

Before Ray Kroc ever met the McDonald brothers to create the first of the national hamburger chains, before R. Davis Thomas' daughter Wendy was even born, or before anyone had ever heard of something called quick lube shops, William McGlaughlin and his father started a company that would eventually affect both types of business.

The company that was founded in 1947 was, logically enough, the McGlaughlin Oil Company, which has its offices at 3750 East Livingston Avenue. The company's business interests range from supplying the fast food industry with lubricants to ensure that milkshake machines run smoothly and efficiently to one of the nation's first chains of quick automobile lubrication facilities as well as a regional Pennzoil distributorship.

The basis of the company was a product called Chainlube, developed by the elder McGlaughlin, also named William. He was described as the consummate tinkerer by his son. "He just liked to fool around with stuff like that," McGlaughlin says.

The "stuff" in this case was Chainlube, a light lubricant that came in a spray can. The attributes of the product made it just right for the lubrication of bicycle, motorcycle, and chainsaw chains. The product was such a success that it put the McGlaughlins in the lubrication business.

McGlaughlin's father also developed a product called Petrol-Gel, a sanitary petroleum jelly used in the dairy industry worldwide. Walk into any fast food restaurant and chances are you will find a tube of Petrol-Gel near the milkshake machine, McGlaughlin says.

One of the characteristics of Petrol-Gel is that it is sanitary. The mineral oil-based lubricant can be used in dairy product dispensing machines to lubricate moving parts without the fear of contamination. Petrol-Gel is "absolutely tasteless and odorless," according to the tube, and each ingredient is approved by the U.S. Food and Drug Administration. It is also popular with bakers, meat and poultry packers, beverage and fruit juice canners, and other food related businesses.

Today McGlaughlin Oil contracts out the production of Petrol-Gel but still markets it from its Columbus offices. "I am sure there are a few tubes over there in Moscow," McGlaughlin says, referring to the McDonald's that opened in the Soviet Union's capital in 1990.

With the success of Chainlube—no longer made by the company—and Petro-Gel, McGlaughlin Oil expanded in 1962 into the motor oil business when it obtained a Pennzoil distributorship for central Ohio, supplying retail stores and bulk users.

Almost 20 years later, the company took a natural leap forward when it pioneered the quick automotive lubrication business in Ohio. McGlaughlin established the FASLUBE chain, a series of fast oil-change centers.

FASLUBE was the first 10-minute oil-change business in Ohio and among the first in the Midwest, McGlaughlin says. The fast lubrication concept started on the West Coast and moved east during the 1970s. "When we got started we were kind of in the infancy of it," he adds.

McGlaughlin emphasizes that all of the FASLUBE centers are company owned, not run by franchisees as are some of the competitors' chains. McGlaughlin says he did not want to become a franchisee when he started the business and is not interested in franchising the FASLUBE concept to others. "There's too much red tape," he says.

McGlaughlin says the idea for the centers came out of a Pennzoil distributors meeting he attended in 1978. At the time more motorists were beginning to use self-service gasoline stations, McGlaughlin recalls. People accustomed to having a gas station attendant check their oil and change it were running out of places to go, he says.

He opened the first FASLUBE at Livingston Avenue and Courtright Road in 1980 and added 11 more during the next eight years.

"We have more or less the Columbus area covered," McGlaughlin says. While he would like to add more, he doubts he will because of the scarcity of labor.

The business makes perfect sense for McGlaughlin Oil because of the synergies, he adds. "Being a Pennzoil distributor, it sounded like a good place to move motor oil. That's our objective."

McGlaughlin says that the fast lube centers appeal to a broad range of customers. "We could have a Cadillac come in and the worst looking car in the world come in right after that."

FASLUBE services a lot of commercial vehicles, such as trucks owned by plumbers and electricians, because the fast service allows the tradesmen to return to work quickly. Also the drivers can keep an eye on their expensive equipment and tools while their trucks are being serviced, according to McGlaughlin.

A FASLUBE shop averages about 48 customers a day and business is growing. "I think it's getting up to 25 to 30 percent of the people in the U.S. are going to these operations," says McGlaughlin.

Because of the volume of business it does, FASLUBE also is in the recycled oil business. Motor oil does not wear out, but does get dirty from the combustion process that occurs in internal combustion engines. Oil recyclers buy used motor oil from companies such as FASLUBE. McGlaughlin estimates that FASLUBE recycles 3,500 gallons of used motor oil a week.

Once the fast lubrication industry was established, it entered a period of price-cutting. Some of the national chains cut prices to the point that, combined with a labor shortage, it made expansion difficult. "Like any business, you get into a situation where somebody is thinking 'If he can make money at it, I can too,'" McGlaughlin explains.

Because of those factors he expects FASLUBE to remain a central Ohio business and his company's employment to continue at its 1990 level of approximately 85 people.

Though McGlaughlin Oil has expanded into the fast lube business its oil distribution business is still the heart of the company, McGlaughlin says. The company services between 300 and 400 commercial accounts, including car dealers and retailers for motor oil, and factories and machine shops for industrial oils, hydraulic fluids, and cutting lubricants.

The McGlaughlin Oil Company established the FASLUBE chain, the first 10-minute oil change business in Ohio and among the first in the Midwest.

STOUFFER DUBLIN HOTEL

Situated in a beautifully landscaped 130-acre park in the northwestern suburb of Columbus, Stouffer Dublin Hotel offers easy access to many of the city's recreational, cultural, and business destinations.

Though the hotel was established in a serene and peaceful business park environment, its I-270 location means that travelers are only minutes away from Port Columbus International, The Ohio State University, the Columbus Zoo, Wyandote Lake Amusement Park, and, of course, the Jack Nicklaus-designed Muirfield Village Golf Club, site of the Memorial Tournament.

A full-service facility that has been designated an American Automobile Association four-diamond hotel, Stouffer Dublin Hotel meets the needs of both business and recreational travelers and provides a pleasant atmosphere for meetings, conventions, and social events.

In 1990 the second phase of a $2.4-million renovation was completed. Designed to appeal to the business traveler, 138 rooms feature new carpeting, wall vinyl, draperies, custom-designed furniture, remote control televisions, two telephones, and in-room refreshment centers. New carpeting was installed in all meeting rooms and the prefunction areas.

All spacious and handsome guest rooms and suites are designed to offer a comfortable setting for doing paperwork or for relaxing. Each features individual temperature control and remote control television with complimentary HBO, CNN, and ESPN; pay movie channels are also available. With their wake-up calls, guests receive a complimentary newspaper and coffee.

Other guest services include a gift shop, professional valet and complimentary shoe shines, and complimentary coffee and breakfast breads in the lobby each weekday morning. Nonsmoking rooms are available, and care has been taken to make the hotel completely accessible to the physically challenged.

Long noted for the quality of its food, the hotel's Village Grill offers American cuisine and country cooking for breakfast, lunch, and dinner. GWTs features generous cocktails, delicious lunches, entertainment, dancing, and a library lounge for meeting with friends or business colleagues.

Stouffer's Sunday brunch is known throughout central Ohio for its sumptuous array of mouth-watering selections, including waffles and omelets made to order, specialties of the day, smoked salmon, steamship round of beef, and

TOP: Stouffer Dublin Hotel is situated on a beautifully landscaped 130-acre park.

ABOVE: At Stouffer Dublin Hotel the emphasis is on service.

an abundance of fresh breads, salads, fruits, pastries, and beverages. Of course, room service is available 24 hours a day.

But there's more to a hotel stay than eating and sleeping. At Stouffer Dublin Hotel guests can enjoy a skylit indoor pool, exercise room, and sauna. The park-like setting for the hotel entices cyclists, walkers, and joggers. Golf, tennis, and extensive athletic club facilities are available nearby for a nominal fee. Columbus, Ohio's largest city, also offers a variety of cultural, sports, and entertainment opportunities.

For meeting- and convention-goers, the hotel has a selection of 10 different rooms. The John Sells Ballroom can be divided into five separate meeting rooms or opened completely to accommodate groups up to 650. The Metro Club is a popular setting for private parties, banquets, and social gatherings. In addition, there are four conference suites for smaller functions. Complimentary blackboards and public address systems are furnished on request. Other audio/visual equipment is available on a rental basis.

Beyond its amenities, however, Stouffer Dublin Hotel emphasizes service. While others will use the 1990s to develop their service quality programs, exemplary service expectations have been part of the Stouffer business philosophy from the beginning.

Stouffer Hotels and Resorts recognize that employees are the key link between the guest and the hotel; consequently, for many years hotel management has empowered line employees to make decisions regarding guest concerns. The hotel's Participate and Report program, which was implemented in 1990, encourages employees to record specific types of interactions with guests and results in a quick tracking of trends, both positive and negative, so that appropriate actions can be taken immediately, either to correct a situation or to recognize outstanding accomplishments.

Hotel employees have been extremely supportive of this program. It provides them with a realization of their importance to the organization and offers them an opportunity to effect change within their hotel.

To complement employee input, Stouffer solicits comments from guests, too. From these comments, the hotel's Guest Satisfaction Index is tabulated. Both employees and management are aware of the hotel's Guest Satisfaction ranking and work hard to keep it high.

Systemwide, Stouffer has eliminated certain telephone surcharges, instituted a new policy of free fax receipt and a modest flat rate for fax transmission, and installed a front-desk "hot line" to hotel general managers. Not surprisingly, this emphasis on quality resulted in Stouffer Hotels and Resorts being ranked among the top five luxury hotel chains in the country in the September 1990 *MDUL Consumer Reports*. A very high percentage of repeat business testifies that the Dublin hotel has learned the quality lesson.

Luxury. Quality. Full Service. The management of Stouffer Dublin Hotel believes that these attributes will continue to enhance its market position,

ABOVE: Guests can enjoy a skylit indoor pool (shown here) as well as an exercise room and sauna.

LEFT: Newly remodeled guest rooms feature new carpeting, wall vinyl, draperies, custom-designed furniture, remote control televisions, two telephones, and in-room refreshment centers.

even in the face of competition from lower-priced chains targeted directly at the business traveler, Stouffer's primary customer.

Stouffer Dublin Hotel is convinced that even in times of corporate downsizing and belt-tightening, there will always be a significant number of business travelers who require not only a place to rest, but also an elegant atmosphere in which to meet and entertain business associates. It recognizes business travel can be stress-producing and exhausting, and will continue to offer a favorable guest/staff ratio in order to give customers the amenities that relieve such stress.

Stouffer's concern with quality requires that the company follow a course of controlled growth rather than attempt to dominate every market. Careful targeting of priority markets, combined with excellent site selection, will result in a larger, but no less responsive, chain of hotels and resorts.

By continuing to reflect the values of its parent company as well as those of the growing Columbus metropolitan area, the Stouffer Dublin Hotel looks to thriving in the decade and century ahead.

THE LIMITED INCORPORATED

The Limited Incorporated is one of central Ohio's most notable success stories. It also is a story of a company that has changed the face of retailing through vision and verve.

The Limited was founded by Leslie H. Wexner in 1963 in Columbus, Ohio, with a single store and first-year sales of $160,000. Today the company is the largest retailer of women's apparel in the world, with close to 4,000 stores and more than $6 billion in projected 1991 sales.

The Limited's unparalleled climb to the top in an incredibly competitive and rapidly changing industry has been based on the company's understanding of its customers. At The Limited, the company's mission begins and ends with the customer. Management believes customers know what they want; the retailer's job is to provide the goods and services the customer demands, rather than trying to dictate what the company thinks they should want.

By listening to its customers, The Limited once again has confirmed that "retail is detail"—that shopping is a

total experience, comprising hundreds of details, all of which must be managed for the customer's benefit. Success in retailing is more than offering merchandise; there also is the meticulous attention to ambience, presentation, and service. The Limited has proven its commitment to providing its customers with the best of all these elements in each of its nearly 4,000 stores.

Even with a 5-million-square-foot distribution operation in Columbus that is second to none, how can a conglomerate the size of The Limited maintain the agility to make the rapid changes the marketplace requires? According to Wexner, it can't, and that's why each of The Limited's retail businesses—Limited Stores, Lerner New York, Lane Bryant, Express, Victoria's Secret, Structure, Limited Too, Abercrombie & Fitch, Henri Bendel, Cacique, Victoria's Secret

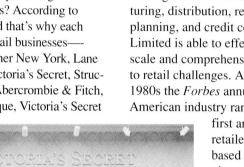

Bath Shops, Bath & Body Works, and Penhaligon's, and catalog businesses for Victoria's Secret, Lane Bryant Direct, Roaman's, and Lerner Direct—operates as an entrepreneurial entity. By "thinking small," maintaining independent management teams, and keeping in close touch with customers, each division anticipates and interprets trends, moving much more quickly into the market than many other retailers.

The Limited's concern with qualitative results has translated into impressive quantitative outcomes as well. Through the utilization of its manufacturing, distribution, real estate, store planning, and credit companies, The Limited is able to effect economies of scale and comprehensive approaches to retail challenges. At the end of the 1980s the *Forbes* annual report on American industry ranked The Limited first among specialty retailers surveyed, based on return on equity, earnings per share, and sales growth.

During the next decade, Wexner expects The Limited to continue its expansion through corporate financial stability and strength, to test and to invest in new approaches to retailing, and to maintain the freshness of the retail environment through the remodeling of existing stores, all with a view to creating twenty-first-century systems.

Effectively debt-free entering the 1990s, the company expects to achieve $10 billion in sales by the middle of the decade and improve its current industry-leading after-tax margin of 7.6 percent. By maintaining its entrepreneurial focus and bold, innovative merchandising, The Limited looks to that plateau and to continuing as central Ohio's success paradigm.

"Our only limitation is ourselves," Wexner says.

Victoria's Secret's world headquarters, Columbus (right), and Structure, Columbus City Center (below).

WENDY'S INTERNATIONAL, INC.

When R. David Thomas decided to create a chain of restaurants in Columbus specializing in hamburgers, common sense made the experts shake their heads.

When he said he was going to fix hamburgers from fresh beef, hot off the grill, with each customer's choice of toppings, there probably was some laughter from those who knew the business.

The experts said the country already was saturated with hamburger chains; another would have a tough time even surviving, no less thriving. Furthermore, giving the customers what they wanted just didn't make good economic sense.

Thomas went ahead against all the good advice. He opened his first Wendy's restaurant in downtown Columbus in 1969 just a few blocks from the statehouse. And the rest is history.

Sales that were less than $300,000 in 1970 jumped over the one-billion-dollar mark in 1980, over $2 billion in 1984, and over $3 billion in 1989.

Today Thomas is the senior chairman of a hamburger empire that is noted for its variety and quality of products. It's a company that promotes nutrition in an industry that's sharply criticized for lacking any.

Wendy's trademark, a redheaded and freckle-faced little girl in pigtails, is seen in some 3,800 restaurants across the nation—more than 70 in central Ohio alone—and in several dozen foreign countries.

The company is named after Thomas' daughter, Melinda Lou, who had been nicknamed "Wendy" by her brother and sisters.

Thomas calls himself a "hamburger cook," and says he had hamburgers on his mind for some time. "Since I was 12 years old, that's what I liked to eat. I started my own restaurants because I didn't like the way the other guys were making them."

It didn't take long for Thomas to turn into an enterprising restaurateur. In 1962, with experience as an Army cook and short-order cook behind him, Thomas advanced to a larger challenge—saving four failing Kentucky Fried Chicken restaurants in Columbus. This success earned him $1.5 million in

seed money for his Wendy's venture when he sold the units back to KFC in 1968.

Wendy's success came somewhat as a surprise to Thomas, who had hoped for moderate prosperity in preparing for others what he enjoyed himself: "hot 'n juicy" hamburgers.

Wendy's advertising over the years has been memorable. The first national television campaign, "Hot 'n Juicy," won a Clio Award. In 1984 "Where's the Beef?" swept three-Clios and registered the highest consumer-awareness levels in advertising industry history. Thomas, who had appeared in some commercials in the early 1980s, returned as company spokesman in 1989.

Giving something back to the community always has been the foundation of Thomas' philosophy. He practices what he preaches. He has supported hospitals and the performing arts, athletic and scholarship programs, the

United Negro College Fund, and research into childhood disease. He has close ties to Ohio State Cancer Research Hospital, Recreation Unlimited, and the Charity Newsies. He has bought the top steer at the Ohio State Fair, and ballet slippers for *The Nutcracker*.

Orphaned as an infant and with his adoptive foster mother dying when he was five, Thomas spent his childhood moving from state to state while his adoptive father sought work. Thomas now works to help find loving homes

TOP: R. David Thomas, the senior chairman of Wendy's International, founded the hamburger restaurant chain.

ABOVE: Since the first restaurant opened on November 15, 1969, at 257 East Broad Street, just a few blocks from the state capitol, the Columbus community embraced Wendy's.

LEFT: Thomas has been active as a national spokesperson for the White House initiative on adoption.

for children by serving as a national spokesperson for the White House initiative on adoption.

"Some people see my early life as full of adversity, but it created a drive in me," Thomas says. That drive, which he hopes to instill in Wendy's 120,000 employees systemwide, is a large part of the company's formula for success in the 1990s.

EXECUTIVE OFFICE PLACE

Gail and Frank Fabish are the owners of Executive Office Place.

"Every small business wants a big office image," according to Frank Fabish, and he provides it.

Fabish, together with his wife Gail, are owners of Executive Office Place, a Columbus-based chain of attractive office suites that offers clients a business environment comparable to any found in a major corporate setting. In fact, it is often better for a start-up business that requires a proper, prestigious—and affordable—address.

Executive Office Place has three suburban locations in the Columbus metropolitan area with a total of nearly 115 offices for lease. The locations, all within 15 minutes of downtown, are: 438 East Wilson Bridge Road, Worthington; 1654 East Broad Street; and 1335 Dublin Road. A fourth location is planned to open in Dublin in 1992.

From the moment one enters any Executive Office Place, there is the feeling of professionalism. Plush, pastel-colored carpet, complemented by the art-decorated walls, the plantings in the reception area, and the soft, indirect lighting working together with the setting gives visitors confidence in the establishment. They are hardly aware that this is a place multiple businesses call home.

Clients of Executive Office Place come in all sizes and shapes. Many, of course, are the small, one-person businesses watching pennies at the outset. Their requirements are for the minimum office space of about 10 feet by 12 feet as well as a minimum amount of office services.

What Fabish finds exciting is seeing these start-up businesses flourish, often moving two and three times into expanding office space. For Fabish each

RIGHT: Each Executive Office Place is elegantly and professionally furbished.

BELOW: Each location offers a fully equipped conference room where audio/visual presentations can be made.

Gail and Frank Fabish are the owners of Executive Office Place.

such move confirms that he is providing the right environment to nurture growth in a city that parallels his endeavors.

"At Executive Office Place," Fabish says, "the entrepreneur can concentrate on growing the business" without the concerns for office furniture, secretarial help, maintenance, insurance, or security. "The money spent here on rent and all the services we provide will be less than hiring just one person for a year," he says.

He estimated traditional office space and service of comparable quality would cost $45,000 annually, or about $30,000 more than at an Executive Office Place address. "Not only do you save that money, but you also eliminate the burden of hiring, supervising, and maintaining your own personnel and office

equipment needed for traditional office space," Fabish notes.

The multitude of services is what attracts larger businesses to Executive Office Place, too, such as *Fortune* 500 companies requiring a first-class address for a presence in Columbus, or a federal government agency that perhaps requires office space in a particular area of the city for an extended period of time.

Starting from the front door, basic services include 24-hour access, although at most locations there is key access only after 6 p.m. There is a receptionist, of course, who also takes calls for clients during regular business hours, and adds a very important individual touch. Each call answered is personalized with the name of the client.

The conference room at every location, where audio/visual presentations can be made, is available to clients not only where they have an office but at any Executive Office Place around the city. For example, a client leasing space at the Dublin Road location but needing a conference room nearer the airport can arrange the meeting at the East Broad Street location.

Incoming mail is sorted and delivered to each office every business day. Parking is never a problem for clients

and visitors. Janitorial services are provided five nights a week. A kitchenette area is equipped with a microwave oven and a refrigerator, and the coffee pot always is on for clients and guests.

Perhaps what is most important, however, is the availability to office equipment that makes each job that much more professional and easier. Need a letter to be typed and mailed to a list of 300, or an order to be placed immediately to the West Coast by facsimile? Every Executive Office Place

is equipped to handle word processing, desktop publishing, photocopying, facsimile transmissions, copying, and a variety of other tasks.

Additional services that are available include messenger and courier service, catering, notary public, report binding, purchasing of individual office supplies, and reservations for hotels, automobiles, and airlines.

Most of these services are on a pay-as-you-go basis, and clients are conveniently billed once a month for the services used.

Executive Office Place is a member of the Executive Suite Network and Global Office Network with over 400 locations nationwide. That means a Columbus client can obtain the same services, and even an office for a day or two on a space-available basis, in cities throughout the country.

"Office suites such as those we provide are an extremely attractive option for a wide range of businesses," Fabish says. With three Executive Office Place locations in the Columbus metropolitan area, "we intend to play a meaningful role in the business growth of the community in the 1990s," he says.

Executive Office Place has three suburban locations in the Columbus metropolitan area, including these at 438 East Wilson Bridge Road in Worthington (ABOVE) and at 1654 East Broad Street.

TEMPORARY CORPORATE HOUSING, INC.

"I'm being spoiled, and I love every minute of it!"

That is how one corporate resident recently described living in an apartment provided by Temporary Corporate Housing. TCH, with headquarters at 1515 Bethel Road in Columbus, fills a specialized need for many of today's businesses. It provides temporary living quarters for individuals whose work brings them to Columbus on a less-than-permanent basis.

More and more corporations are finding that TCH is an excellent and cost-effective housing alternative for management and other personnel who must work away from their home base for short periods of time. Anyone who has traveled extensively knows that being forced to spend off-hours confined to a single hotel or motel room, eating a steady diet of restaurant food, is not a desirable way to live. For employees sent to a strange city, away from family and friends, such living accommodations can result in distractions that lower productivity and even affect the person's capacity to perform.

"What we do," says Lynda Clutchey, senior vice president of TCH, "is make that old cliche about 'your home away

from home' a true reality." It was Lynda's father, Max W. Holzer, who developed the original concept almost 20 years ago. A realtor by profession, he would occasionally rent apartments as temporary living quarters for individuals forced to vacate their old home before they could move into a new one. Families with children found this to be far more desirable than staying in a hotel or motel.

"My father got the idea for offering the service to corporations," Clutchey says, "from a group of auditors who were temporarily in town on business. They were unhappy with the confinement of a hotel room and tired of eating in restaurants. So he rented them apartments on a no-lease basis."

The idea of no lease and no deposit continues to be the policy at TCH. Apartment units can be rented for as

short a period as one day, and for as long as the client desires. While the apartments offer more space and amenities than hotel rooms, the cost is often less—a fact that appeals to companies seeking to hold down costs. Rates are determined both by the size and location of the facility and the length of

time it is to be used. Apartments needed for 30 days or longer generally can be rented at the lowest rates.

Each TCH resident enjoys a fully furnished living room, kitchen, and a minimum of one bedroom and one full bath. With individuals of all ages more conscious of diet and the importance of good eating habits, many TCH clients appreciate the availability of a kitchen. The opportunity to prepare favorite dishes, as well as breakfasts and late-night snacks, can help to lessen boredom and those yearnings for "back home."

Whatever is needed to assure the client a comfortable and pleasant stay, TCH makes every effort to provide it. The apartments are equipped with everything from color television to sheets, blankets, and bath linens. Kitchens have dishes, cutlery, and cookware. Actually, clients move into a facility that is virtually a fully stocked home that includes a private telephone line. Residents wanting such special items as a VCR, exercycle, or word processor can obtain it from the TCH "general store."

Before they arrive, clients are provided with a list of the items they will find at the residence, and they can specify additional furnishings and home equipment they may wish to have. Residents can choose an apartment either near their work or, if a permanent move is in the works, in the area where they may ultimately want to live. Virtually every request can be met, whether for a garage, fireplace, or athletic club facilities. Clients can even stipulate their preferences regarding the availability of transportation, shopping, and opportunities for recreation.

For those who may wish to bring along the family, TCH can provide appropriate accommodations—and often at less cost than putting up the family in a hotel. For family visits the service will supply extra beds, linens, and other necessary items. Daily housekeeping services eliminate the need for clients to concern themselves with such duties. Each resident is given a single phone number to call should utilities or equipment not function properly.

"Our top priority," Clutchey emphasizes, "is the complete satisfaction of the individual. And we want the corporation that's picking up the tab to rest easy as well." She explains that this includes taking responsibility for seeing that the firm's people receive keys to their units, together with a welcoming packet of information with location maps, emergency telephone numbers, and the location of cleaning, shopping, hair salons, medical facilities, and other important services. A TCH account representative will arrange billing to meet the needs of the corporation.

Each year, a growing number of major companies are opting for the one-call service of TCH to fill their temporary housing needs. Among them are firms with executives who make regular visits to Columbus and those bringing in important guests and customers or new executives who lack permanent housing. Some companies are

making the services of TCH an integral part of planning for seminars and training sessions. As more businesses develop international markets for their products and services, they are finding that TCH housing accommodations are often appreciated by foreign visitors who have special living or eating re-

quirements or want a warmer and more relaxed atmosphere than a hotel can provide.

The success of its Columbus operation has prompted TCH to establish offices in Cleveland, Cincinnati, and Pittsburgh. Plans are under way to expand into other markets as well. As one of the founders of the National Interim Housing Network, TCH is helping to carry the concept of temporary apartment housing into cities across the nation where it does not now exist.

One thing is certain. TCH will never stop trying to "spoil" its residents. "We're constantly seeking to improve upon the services that we offer," says Clutchey. "Setting high standards and exceeding them has been the key to our past success, and will attract more firms to use our services as we build for the future."

KROGER COMPANY

Down on Cincinnati's Pearl Street in the 1880s, "rich aromas from the bake shops mingled with the odors of horses, dogs and swine in the streets," penned Kroger historian George Laycock. "The neighborhood was noisy with the sounds of animals, the rumble of street-cars and the screech of steamboat whis-tles along the nearby waterfront."

There, in the midst of merchant mayhem, young Barney H. Kroger set up shop. To be noticed in the crowd, he painted the front of his small grocery store bright red, stuck a sign on the front that practically shouted that here was the Great Western Tea Company, and opened his doors for business on July 1, 1883.

The establishment B.H. Kroger and his early partner, B.A. Branagan,

founded on a shoestring that hot sum-mer's day has made considerable progress since, as he would have ex-pected. It is unlikely, though, that he ever envisioned his enterprise would lead to one of the nation's largest and most innovative grocery chains.

Today it's supermarkets and conve-nience stores for the Kroger Company, which it operates under a variety of names. In addition to Kroger, its su-permarkets are known as King Soop-ers, City Market, Fry's, Dillon Food Stores, Circle Super, Gerbes, and M&M Markets, and its convenience stores are recognized by customers as Turkey Hill Minit Market, Tom Thumb, Kwik Shop, Quik Stop, Loaf 'N Jug, and Mini Mart.

Within the Kroger organization, B.H. Kroger's credo, "Be particu-lar. Never sell anything you would not want yourself," finds its expression in stores designed around the needs of modern consumers.

The "superstores" average approximately 30,600 square feet and offer a selection of specialty departments sur-rounding a traditional grocery store core. The "combina-tion" food and drug stores, averaging 50,300 square feet, provide the majority of the company's food sales and

profits. Each also produces substantial revenue from additional sales in the nontraditional departments, such as flo-ral shops, cosmetic and fragrance coun-ters, and video rental areas.

Within these facilities the company contends with the many complex issues surrounding the production and distri-bution of food. With the growth of the environmental movement, Americans are becoming increasingly particular about what they eat and how it is pro-duced. There are concerns about pesti-cides, preservatives, and packaging, and health controversies surrounding the importance of food in the preven-tion of various diseases. Consumers have demanded greater accountability from those entrusted with supplying the nation's food.

Kroger has consistently held that as the food purchaser's agent, the com-pany has a responsibility to provide wholesome products at fair prices, and that the safety of food products is best assured by buying only from the most experienced growers and manufactur-ers. In areas in which the company has direct control, such as the manufacture of its own products and the mainte-nance of its stores, it assumes responsi-bility for high standards of cleanliness and sanitation.

In addition, Kroger has one of the country's most comprehensive food safety programs, encompassing food-handling training, a voluntary fish and seafood inspection plan, outside laboratory testing for pesticide residue, and a toll-free meat and seafood infor-mation line.

Kroger is also a corporate leader in the nation's recycling effort. As the decade progresses, the company will make a major commitment to the envi-ronment by continuing to expand on-site recycling facilities until all Kroger stores are involved.

The company recognizes that if re-cycling is arduous or time-consuming, customers are less likely to participate

TOP: B.H. Kroger, 1918

LEFT: Kroger is one of the nation's largest and most innovative grocery chains.

Kroger actively participates in many fund-raisers and activities that benefit the community.

in solid waste reduction programs. By making it easy and convenient to recycle, the company hopes to encourage those who already do so and to motivate consumers who haven't yet joined the recycling movement. Kroger thus will play a major part in alleviating pressure on the Columbus area's landfills.

Like many other businesses, Kroger considers its employees to be its most important asset. Kroger employees own more than one-third of the company's outstanding shares. Their buy-in gives them a real interest in the company's success, creates a bond between individual incentives and corporate goals, and builds awareness of the importance of customer service in generating both goodwill and profits.

Incentives tied to store, division, or overall corporate results, and employee recognition programs that honor both group and individual contributions to the community, enhance productivity and promote team unity. In 1990 employees of the Dublin Kroger store won the company's prestigious B.H. Kroger Employee Group Award for Community Service for their work with Youth in Action. The individual B.H. Kroger Award had been won previously by a Columbus employee for his activities among the homeless and destitute of his community.

Corporate responsibility doesn't end with Kroger employees. The company has a nationwide reputation for participation in community activities. For many years Kroger has been committed to combating domestic hunger, through support of local hunger initiatives and Second Harvest, a national food bank organization. In Columbus the portion of the corporate mission regarding hunger is manifested in the company's leadership in Operation Feed, one of the nation's most successful community food bank drives. The corporation has donated several tons of food items to Operation Feed over the life of the program.

Kroger is also proud of its involve-

ment with the Columbus Zoo. A longtime corporate sponsor of a variety of activities and concerts at the zoo, Kroger in 1991 underwrote the "Australian Walkabout," an exciting exhibit of Australian wildlife, including kangaroos and wallabies. The highlight of the exhibit was the debut of the zoo's newest Australian acquisition, the koala bears. The Walkabout also featured performances and displays that showcased Australian life and culture.

Kroger promotes the arts, including annual sponsorship of BalletMet's *Nutcracker* holiday performances and support for the area's exciting Jazz Arts Group.

Children are important to Kroger; Easter Seals, The March of Dimes, and other children's charities have benefited from Kroger's dedication to the community's smallest citizens.

Kroger is a corporate leader in the nation's recycling effort. On-site, 24-hour recycling centers make it easy and convenient.

Though Barney Kroger would certainly be astonished at the size and scope of the stores that bear his name today, he would no doubt be pleased that his admonition to "be particular" is still guiding his company.

CONTINENTAL OFFICE FURNITURE & SUPPLY CORPORATION

The associates of Continental Office Furniture and Supply Corporation subscribe to four basic tenets:
- The company must have a focus and all associates must be committed in that direction;
- It must routinely exceed the customer's expectations;
- All associates must be challenged and rewarded for their productivity to foster career opportunities; and
- The community must benefit from the organization's presence.

Continental's management believes if these conditions are fulfilled, the bottom line will take care of itself.

Founded in 1941 as an office supply and offset printing company, Continental has developed into a regional corporation, with additional locations in Cleveland, Dayton, and Indianapolis. The company has developed from internal growth and from careful acquisition, resulting in an organization with three divisions: office furniture, office products, and architectural floors.

Continental recently reemphasized its commitment to Columbus when the corporation moved its corporate offices, including furniture and flooring show-

rooms, downtown in support of the community's concerted effort to create a dynamic center-city environment. Continental saw the move as a way to make it easier for its officers and associates to become more involved in civic and human services projects. The company encourages all of its associates to

take part in programs that make things better for the community.

THREE DIVISIONS

Continental Office Furniture sells both freestanding pieces and furniture landscape systems. The Office Furniture Division markets to the private busi-

ABOVE: Customer service center

LEFT: Bountiful stock of office products

ness sector as well as the public sector, working closely with architects and designers.

In early 1991 the furniture division added a clearance center targeted to the occasional buyer looking for an excellent value. Its stock is comprised of budget furniture lines and clearance items from the contract furniture operation.

The second of the corporation's divisions, Continental Office Products, offers a full line of office supply items. Under its Paperhouse label, it sells bulk paper supplies to schools and government entities.

This division's marketing approach is to demonstrate the value of its "stockless inventory system." To advance this concept fully, the company maintains an inventory of 5,000 items in the Columbus warehouse. Fill rates of 99

ABOVE: Corporate offices—Banc One

percent are common, and delivery is guaranteed within 24 hours. To complete the circuit, the customer is furnished management reports that detail utilization by department.

Finally the Architectural Floors Division furnishes and installs carpet, resilient flooring, raised floors, and ceramic and marble products. In addition to the customer base of the furniture division, Architectural Floors markets to construction managers and general contractors.

QUALITY ASSURANCE

Quality is paramount. The company is involved in an ongoing quality assurance program, and its associates are pivotal to the success of this endeavor. Quality improvement teams throughout the organization create new ideas for increasing customer satisfaction.

A key ingredient of quality assurance is training. The company's training coordinator provides opportunities for associates to learn about their own jobs and the tasks that other Continental associates perform. Continental's orientation program, attended by all new personnel from vice presidents to drivers, is the entry point for the organization's continuing education process. From this program and others Continental will enhance synergy among its three divisions and make the corporation a more rewarding place for its associates to pursue their own career paths.

LOOKING AHEAD

With the wide array of office necessities at its disposal, Continental constantly searches for new ways to satisfy its customers. Not content simply to sell furniture and supplies, the company keeps ahead of industry trends and assists customers with the choice of products, providing the research necessary to help them make the best decisions concerning the office environment.

In the 1970s and 1980s the "open office" concept was the driving force in office design. During the 1990s, however, businesses will be required to modify such plans. The company predicts a greater emphasis on office customizing, as employers become more attuned to the requirements and preferences of individual employees. Continental expects to be on the leading edge of this trend. By the end of 1990 the company was already consulting with psychologists and chief executive officers concerning the concept of "officing," which concerns itself with productivity advantages and worker retention values of an office setting that responds to the needs of its inhabitants. This kind of innovation and value-added marketing is one of the ways Continental exceeds its customers' expectations.

As the decade unfolds, Continental will concentrate more on the "aftermarket," that is, working with facility managers on their incremental needs, such as reconfiguration or redecorating projects involving reupholstering or repainting furniture, reflooring, adding wall panels, or similar services not involving the sale of new products.

Like many other local businesses, Continental's management has nothing but praise for Columbus as an advantageous place to begin a regional network. Its central location as well as the presence of state government and The Ohio State University are all mentioned as positive factors for business development. Continental represents another group of individuals committed to the success of the Columbus community.

Creative and productive environments

CHEMLAWN INC.

ChemLawn began as the seed of an idea—nurtured with hard work, dedication, perseverance, and vision—that took root and grew into a company recognized as the pioneer and undisputed market leader of the multibillion-dollar lawn care industry.

In the late 1940s in Troy, Ohio, the father-son team of Paul and Dick Duke established the Duke Garden Center and eventually added a sod farm. Each year, garden center customers would buy the dry, bagged, do-it-yourself products to spread over their lawns, often with spotty results.

With their strong agricultural and horticultural backgrounds, the Dukes knew there was more to turf care than spreading fertilizer every spring. Research they had been conducting on their own sod farm since the early 1960s showed them that liquid applications of selected materials four times a year produced beautiful turf. Applying products in liquid solution, a technique common in agriculture, was then unusual in lawn care.

Ever a dreamer and tinkerer, Dick Duke envisioned a service that would professionally apply lawn care formulations regularly throughout the year. At the sod farm he worked on delivery methods and equipment. At the garden center he studied his customers. He spent at least four years honing his plan.

In 1968 the Dukes offered their customers a new service that would apply liquid solutions of lawn fertilizer and pest control products—results guaranteed. The first year the 400 customers who signed up soon saw healthy, rich, green expanses of grass across their suburban landscape. The service was termed a success, and in January 1969 ChemLawn Corporation was created.

To finance their venture the Dukes sold their garden center and sod farm, raising $40,000 to outfit a pair of gleaming white trucks. By June, with less than a dozen employees, the new company expanded to Columbus, using an old house as its first warehouse. That year ChemLawn rang up $225,000 in sales in Troy, Dayton, and Columbus.

There was not enough profit to finance expansion, however, so in 1970

Dick Duke took his new company public, offering common stock at five dollars per share. The Dukes quickly sold 30,000 shares to 4,000 customers.

The $150,000 raised allowed ChemLawn to expand to five additional markets and post one million dollars in sales by the end of the year. Within five years, the company reported $15.2 million in sales, and two decades later charted more than $390 million in sales.

Dick Duke's death in 1977 rocked ChemLawn, but he left a strong legacy that was carried on by the men and women he had selected to run his growing company. Duke had built ChemLawn on a philosophical foundation that he would later describe in a letter:

". . . (a) small group of ordinary folks accepted an idea and created a business. The central theme of the idea involved the elevation of the worth and dignity of individual human beings; the conviction that ordinary people could join together, with conviction, dedication and sound purpose, to achieve extra-ordinary success. Success would be measured in many ways, not necessarily attached to size or profit. Success achieved or measured by conventional

ABOVE: ChemLawn's first branch office in Columbus.

TOP: The ChemLawn Center today. ChemLawn also has an engineering center and a research and development center/clinical laboratory in the Columbus area.

business standards or practices could be the exact opposite of the success we sought.

"In many respects, we latched onto a dream, loaded with idealism, and the dream became a fascinating reality."

In 1987 ChemLawn was acquired by Ecolab Inc. of St. Paul, Minnesota. Ecolab, with sales of more than one billion dollars worldwide, is a leading developer and marketer of premium cleaning, sanitizing, and maintenance products and services for the hospitality, institutional, and residential markets.

From ChemLawn's Columbus headquarters today, the company directs services throughout the United States and Canada. The contemporary stone-and-glass ChemLawn Center, designed by Columbus architects Trott & Bean and dedicated in 1982, sits on a 28-acre campus, overlooking an expanse of manicured grass peppered with trees and shrubs. Its centerpiece is a large pond that has become a popular way station for migrating flocks of ducks and geese.

Seven miles north is ChemLawn's Research and Development Center and Clinical Laboratory. At R&D, scientists in various areas of agronomic and horticultural specialties evaluate traditional

is staffed by registered medical technicians.

Just west of Powell, Ohio, ChemLawn maintains a Distribution and Engineering Center. One of the earliest achievements of equipment research was the patented "ChemLawn Gun," which is almost universally used to apply liquid products efficiently to lawns.

The core of ChemLawn's business remains lawn care, but the company expanded its services in 1977 to include tree and shrub care, pruning and mulching, and a commercial division. It provides lawn, tree, and shrub care services to large commercial accounts, such as multifamily housing complexes, motels, retail stores, and schools.

PestFree by ChemLawn concentrates on residential indoor pest control in selected markets located primarily in the South and in Columbus.

Although the major share of ChemLawn is company-owned and -operated, ChemLawn has offered franchise opportunities since 1977. Franchise operations are located across North America in markets with

populations of less than 250,000.

Any description of ChemLawn would be incomplete if it did not include the company's extraordinary behind-the-scenes commitment to the environment. Stemming from its earliest years, and demonstrated by its research practices, product selection, facility design and construction, and employee training, ChemLawn's mission has included taking responsibility for environmental quality. The men and women who are ChemLawn take pride in the fact that healthy lawns, trees, and shrubs are part of the solution to the ecological problems that captured headlines in the late 1980s.

Caring has been the basis for ChemLawn's customer service philosophy since the company was conceived by Dick Duke more than 20 years ago. From the beginning, the visionary Duke instilled in his compatriots the idea that taking care of people came first.

Even today, to complement its unparalleled expertise, caring enough to do the right things right—for the customer, for the employee, for the neighbor, and for the environment—sets ChemLawn apart from its multitude of competitors. It's a philosophy that will carry the company well into the twenty-first century.

ABOVE: ChemLawn people serve people. A tree and shrub care specialist shares his observations with his customers.

RIGHT: A lawn care specialist runs an inspection to determine the best course of treatment.

and alternative landscape care products, application methods, equipment, timing, and techniques to keep ChemLawn on the leading edge of landscape care. ChemLawn's research efforts also extend to sites in Georgia, Florida, and California.

The Clinical Lab, an integral component of ChemLawn's comprehensive health and safety program, monitors ChemLawn employees who work with landscape care products and provides similar services to outside companies. Established in 1977, the lab is equipped with advanced automated laboratory equipment and

COLUMBUS MARRIOTT NORTH

With its Busch Corporate Center address, the Columbus Marriott North is favorably located to serve central Ohio's bustling business community. It is 10 miles north of the historic state capitol, the magnificent City Center mall in the heart of downtown, the Ohio Center, and the soon-to-be-completed Columbus Convention Center complex. Closer still are the active and assorted shops of the popular French Market.

Port Columbus International Airport is a quick 12 miles away along the nearby I-270 outerbelt. Also just a few minutes from the Marriott North is the famed Columbus Zoo, the campus of The Ohio State University, and "the course that Jack built," Muirfield Village Golf Club in Dublin, which was designed by Columbus native and golf's player of the century, Jack Nicklaus.

As a result of this central location, the 300-room hotel has proven to be ideal for local and regional meetings as well as for the individual business and vacation traveler.

There is a feeling of spaciousness once inside the Marriott North. Just off the lobby is the popular Panache Restaurant, where dining is an elegant, yet casual, experience. Any palate would be pleased and any hunger satisfied with selections from the restaurant's varied and extensive breakfast, lunch, and dinner menus.

Adjacent to the restaurant is Panache Lounge, a warm and inviting spot to relax after a busy day. This multilevel lounge includes two bars and three lighted dance floors where patrons can dance the night away.

All the guest rooms have been designed with modern comfort in mind. Each is equipped with individual climate control, color television with HBO, CNN, and ESPN channel services, in-room movies, an AM/FM radio, and a telephone message light.

Marriott North's six luxury suites offer individual decor for that very special occasion. Parlor rooms—efficient and attractive meeting quarters during the day—can convert to handsome guest rooms at night.

The Concierge Level is the ultimate in exclusive travel accommodations. Twenty-six rooms are located on the ninth floor. This deluxe level includes its own lounge and concierge attendant.

Complementing the various types of accommodations are numerous amenities. There is complimentary van service to the airport, for example, and valet, laundry, and room service. There is also an indoor/outdoor pool for year-round enjoyment, a hydrotherapy pool, a sauna, an outdoor jogging track, and an indoor electronic game room. Tennis, racquetball, and golf are available nearby.

The meeting facilities at the Marriott North are highlighted by a 7,500-square-foot, unobstructed grand ballroom with convenient access for exhibitors. Divisible into four sections, each with a separate banquet entrance, the ballroom can accommodate up to 1,000 people for meetings and seat 650 people for banquets.

The hotel also offers for groups of up to 80 six conference salons, each with views of either the landscaped interior courtyard or the attractive mini-lake. When two salons are combined, a meeting room of more than 1,100 square feet is created for banquets, exhibits, conferences, and receptions.

Corporate travel managers have voted Marriott the "easiest hotel to work with to arrange meetings" as well as the "best value" in hotel facilities. At the same time, Meeting Planners International has named Marriott the "best supplier" of meeting facilities. The convenient Columbus Marriott North proudly upholds this reputation.

Panache, located just off the lobby of the Columbus Marriott North, offers a wide variety of dishes in an atmosphere of casual elegance.

MID-AMERICAN WASTE SYSTEMS

ABOVE: Christopher White is Mid-American Waste System's president and chief executive officer.

LEFT: Valley Landfill, located near Pittsburgh, is a state-of-the-art landfill featuring an engineered clay base, a double synthetic liner, a methane extraction system, and a leachate collection system—all designed to meet Mid-American's commitment to the environment.

Canal Winchester-based Mid-American Waste Systems Incorporated has grown from its founding in the latter part of 1985 to one of America's top solid waste disposal companies. With operations that serve the Chicago area, Fort Wayne, Columbus, Pittsburgh, Philadelphia, and other major markets throughout the country, Mid-American is well positioned to take advantage of its niche in the solid waste disposal field.

Wall Street recognized this in May 1990 when Mid-American went public with one of Columbus' largest initial public offerings, raising more than $80 million. The offering was sold out almost immediately with investors from coast-to-coast and in major markets throughout the world, including London, Paris, and Geneva, snapping up the stock.

Why all the interest?

"We believe it's because we take a different approach to the marketplace than any of our competitors," says Christopher White, president, chief executive officer, and a founder of Mid-American. "The response to our company has been tremendous, and I believe it's because we have filled a need for a customer-driven solid waste company.

"Right from the beginning I realized that you couldn't run a solid waste company on a 'business as usual' basis. Not in times like these," says White.

To be successful, the company believes that it will have to continue to address the four major areas of emphasis that have contributed to its success thus far. These are protecting the environment, providing outstanding service, contributing to the communities in which it serves, and operating on a high ethical standard.

Mid-American has one of the strongest records in the nation among solid waste disposal firms for environmental management. The company's staff includes engineers and hydrogeologists whose sole job is to make sure that the environment is well taken care of.

Wherever the company has trash-hauling operations, the trucks are always well-maintained, late-model vehicles driven by uniformed drivers who have been grounded in the company's rigid standard of customer service.

The company also strives to contribute substantially as a solid corporate citizen to each community in which it serves. The company provides free landfill space to municipalities and

counties for litter prevention programs. The company has also contributed in other ways to communities by supporting the arts, education, and other worthwhile endeavors.

Mid-American has also made a strong commitment to ethical standards that will not be compromised. The company employees are instructed to operate "by the book" in all dealings with business, government, and the public. Any deviation from those ethical standards is met with dismissal.

As a company involved in landfill operation and management, waste hauling, recycling, and other facets of the nonhazardous solid waste disposal industry, Mid-American is poised to take advantage of the many opportunities that exist in the market today. Cities and counties all over the nation are turning to companies like Mid-American for answers to their solid waste disposal problems. With the technical expertise and the commitment to excellence, Mid-American stands ready to answer the need for quality environmental services well into the coming century.

THE BUTLER COMPANY

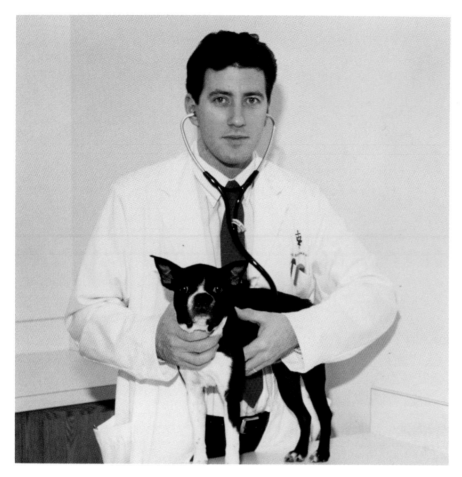

The Butler Company is a privately held corporation which distributes pharmaceuticals, biologicals, medical supplies, instruments, equipment, and specialized pet foods exclusively to the veterinary profession.

It is the largest privately owned veterinary supply distributor in the United States. In 1988 the company celebrated 35 years in business and surpassed $100 million in sales. Serving more than 14,000 veterinary practices, Butler distributes products to the veterinary profession for approximately 250 manufacturers.

Columbus is the birthplace of Butler. Founder William A. Butler opened shop in 1953 in a storefront building south of The Ohio State University. Using his many years of experience in the human and veterinary marketplace, and with the help of the university's College of Veterinary Medicine as well as local veterinary practitioners, he formed a strong foundation upon which he could build.

Carrying a broad line of products to serve the veterinarian's every need, the "one stop shopping concept" has been the slogan for Butler's more than 90 sales representatives for many years.

The first sales territories were in Ohio and were serviced from the Columbus headquarters at 1497 North High Street. Through the next two decades, the company expanded in several ways. Service branches and sales territories were added, and a Butler-label line of generic veterinary pharmaceuticals was created, putting the Butler name in every customer's pharmacy.

In the early 1970s the company was purchased by Narco Scientific Industries of Fort Washington, Pennsylvania. Butler was acquired yet again in 1975, this time by Stephen A. Ritt, a successful Philadelphia businessman. Under Ritt's leadership Butler experienced tremendous sales growth both from its existing markets and through key expansion moves.

Management and operations were restructured to put the company into closer proximity to its customers and the dynamics of the marketplace. A new sales compensation program was initiated, employee incentives were instituted on all levels of the company, training programs were upgraded, and in-house data processing was begun. Throughout this transition of ownership and period of growth, the corporate office never left its roots: Butler's headquarters remained in Columbus.

After the death of his father in 1986, Stephen A. Ritt, Jr., took the reins of the firm and continued steering it toward the vision of a national company with branches from coast to coast.

ABOVE: The Butler Company has served the veterinary profession for more than 35 years.

BELOW: The Butler Company's convention display.

As the 1990s began, Butler had 20 service branches, including operations as far west as Dallas and from Wisconsin to Massachusetts to Florida. The largest concentration of both branches and employees remains in Ohio, and especially in Columbus.

Butler continues to be recognized as one of the top 100 private companies in central Ohio. The annual "Discovery Award," presented by the Columbus office of Arthur Andersen & Company, started in 1989 and included The Butler Company (ranked 26th). Since that first year the company has moved up in the rankings, demonstrating its commit-

ABOVE: A variety of products distributed by The Butler Company.

LEFT: A Butler Company truck makes a delivery to the Columbus Veterinary Emergency Service.

ment to growth, as well as its commitment to remain headquartered in the Columbus area.

The company's mission statement also clearly defines that commitment: "We are responsible to each other, to our customers and vendors, and to the communities in which we live and work. We have an inherent responsibility to be a good neighbor and a good citizen."

Butler employees have donated blood for their local Red Cross chapters, and the company sponsors an annual fund-raising competition to raise money for animal-related charities, such as Pilot Dogs Inc. in Columbus. The competition pits all of Butler's offices and branches against each other, and the company provides a match for funds raised.

Butler prides itself in being an important link in the professional side of the animal health industry, which has sales in excess of $1.5 billion annually and is growing.

Butler works closely with the many state and national veterinary associations, including the Ohio Veterinary Medical Association. Sponsorship of meetings, seminars, and special events are ongoing. The company has sponsored and provided educational programs for veterinarians and their technicians that are recognized by the state associations as qualifying the veterinarians for continuing education credit.

Several support awards have been received from state associations, and on a national scale from the American Veterinary Medical Association. This type of support for the veterinary industry has been a major factor in the excellent relationship Butler has with its customers, and therefore the success of the company as a whole.

The future of Butler is promising. There is a commitment to continue expansion while still providing customers with value-added services, such as next-day delivery throughout the com-

pany's marketing area. The company will continue to sponsor seminars and continuing education programs, as well as support the industry associations and teaching institutions.

There also is a commitment to reward excellence within employee ranks, and to promote from within whenever possible. Butler remains dedicated to supporting the communities where the company employees live and work. These commitments—to the customers, the industry, the employees, and the communities—are what made The Butler Company what it is today, and what will help it to remain the leader in the veterinary health care distribution industry in the future.

Butler's business philosophy is to be responsive to the needs of the veterinary profession and to enhance the product line with value-added services that are meaningful and deliverable to its customers. Butler's vision is to deliver those products and services to veterinarians from coast to coast.

From its start on High Street in Columbus to its present location in Dublin, The Butler Company has come a long way. With the teamwork and dedication of its employees to fulfill the visions, the dreams of the future will not be dreams for long.

FRIGIDAIRE COMPANY

The nation's third-largest manufacturer and marketer of major appliances, Frigidaire Company has its headquarters just outside of Columbus in Dublin, Ohio. The company is a division of Stockholm, Sweden-based A.B. Electrolux, the world's leader in the manufacturing, sales, and service of major appliances.

Corporate management, sales, marketing, consumer service, distribution, and administrative divisions, as well as the National Order Center, all are under one roof at the national headquarters.

A significant addition to Frigidaire Company's wealth of international resources is its dynamic Industrial Design Center. Located in Hilliard, Ohio, the Design Center—one of only four A.B. Electrolux facilities in the world—sets the pace for the styling and design of the company's products. Its mission is to execute concepts and design products by utilizing its unique global perspective.

Also based in Hilliard is the company's Integrated Manufacturing System Group. This group deals with advanced technology and manufacturing techniques for national and international applications throughout the company's production facilities.

Frigidaire Company manufactures

BELOW: A designer at Frigidaire's Hilliard, Ohio, Industrial Design Center works on the future form and function of major appliances.

National headquarters for Frigidaire Company, whose brands include Frigidaire, White-Westinghouse, Tappan, Gibson, and Kelvinator brand appliances, is located in Dublin, Ohio.

and markets a full line of major appliances, including refrigerators, food freezers, washers, dryers, electric and gas ranges, microwave ovens, dishwashers, disposers, room air conditioners, and dehumidifiers. The company's brand names have become synonymous with quality and value: Frigidaire, Gibson, Kelvinator, Tappan, and White-Westinghouse.

Frigidaire has earned an extremely strong reputation with consumers as a high-end major appliance line that offers exciting convenience features and upscale styling. Its image and performance make it a leader in the appliance industry.

A value-oriented line for the more experienced, mature consumer, Gibson utilizes independent distributors to supply its dealer network, rather than the factory-direct process used with other brands.

Another value-oriented line is Kelvinator,

which offers consumers a wide range of full-featured products that make performance affordable.

With its successful line of gas and electric ranges, Tappan maintains its reputation for precision cooking machines. Tappan introduced the first microwave oven for home use in 1955.

White-Westinghouse is known for its line of value-oriented features and styling. White Westinghouse is the "smarter choice" of many consumers.

The company also manufactures private-label major appliances for nationally respected retailers, such as Sears and Montgomery Ward.

While the company's resources make it the most technologically advanced manufacturer in the industry, its people make it an integral part of each and every community in which it operates. In central Ohio, Frigidaire Company people support vital programs like the American Red Cross, Project Feed, and the United Way through many employee-directed activities.

The company is strongly committed to the development and well-being of its own people as well. Its dedication to employee fitness is evidenced by its on-site fitness center and the Recreational Wellness Committee, a group which plans and conducts numerous activities to benefit employee health and social development.

COLUMBUS CITY CENTER

You can hear the sounds of the city—the vibrant, urgent, exciting sounds of a city on the grow.

But to feel the city's pulse, to sense its heart and soul, step inside Columbus City Center. It is truly the city's center; the place where Columbus focuses its vision of what a city can be.

More than a shopping experience, Columbus City Center immerses the visitor in the rhythm and beat of downtown life in the 1990s.

From the moment it opened its doors in August 1989, City Center became a showcase of America's urban renaissance. Since then some 40,000 people a day have discovered that renaissance in the extraordinary mix of shops, stores, and restaurants right in the heart of Ohio's largest city.

The center's 140 retail outlets cover 18 acres and 1.4 million square feet, all under one roof and all designed with the ease and convenience of the shopper in mind. The three levels of shopping space provide a place, and a pace, to suit everyone's style. Whether you're a shopper on a mission, just shopping for ideas, or simply browsing away a break during a busy day, you'll find what you're looking for at City Center.

While the escalators and glass-enclosed elevators whisk you through a bright and airy expanse of adventure, you can plan your next stop and spot your next shop. From the fabulous variety of department stores such as Marshall Field's, Jacobson's, and Lazarus, to the unique offerings of scores of specialty stores, the possibilities are limited only by the imagination.

And imagination is at the heart of City Center. The Grand Court, a dramatic three-level performing arts area where musical and artistic entertainment offers a pleasant interlude during the day, is a place where the city itself seems to pause to reflect on all that is good about life in Columbus.

City Center also offers conveniences to absorb the urban energy of Columbus. Parking for nearly 5,000 cars is directly connected to City Center; space for thousands more is within a four-block area. Pedestrian walkways connect to two major office buildings, the Hyatt on Capitol Square, and the Ohio Theatre. The state capitol is a block away.

The center's central location in the heart of downtown means it is within a 25-minute drive of nearly a million people; nearly 3.5 million are less than a two-hour drive away. About 80 percent of the shoppers come from the seven-county central Ohio area. During its first year, City Center attracted an average of 40,000 visitors daily, far exceeding projections.

"City Center offers the most exciting retailing between New York and Chicago," according to the center's developer, The Taubman Company.

The city has also reaped rewards from the project. The 2,500 jobs that have been created bring in nearly one million dollars annually in tax revenues.

Whether it's a first visit or a part of a regular routine, a step into Columbus City Center is a step into the center of excitement.

BIG BEAR STORES COMPANY

Today's modern Big Bear supermarkets average 50,000 square feet in size and provide many full-service specialty shops under one roof.

In 1934, as the nation began to recover from the Depression, an innovation in food retailing was introduced to Columbus when Wayne E. Brown opened the first self-service super-market in central Ohio.

Brown leased a 70,000-square-foot building on Lane Avenue near The Ohio State University campus that had failed as a dance hall and roller rink.

The name Big Bear was chosen because Brown felt it was catchy and easy for people, especially children, to remember.

More than 200,000 people visited the store during the first three days it was open and were amazed by the huge variety and low prices. Advertised specials such as coffee for 18 cents a pound, butter for 25.5 cents a pound, and ham for 10 cents a pound were bargains, even in 1934.

Big Bear was an instant success with consumers, who liked the opportunity to select their own items and the conve-nience of one-stop shopping. A reputa-tion for quality fruits, vegetables, and the finest meats was quickly estab-lished and endures to this day.

Self-service allowed Big Bear cus-tomers to choose what they wanted and become responsible for their own pur-chases. Displays changed from a few cans stacked in the window of a small, drab building to interior mass merchan-dising displays of a variety of products. Modern self-service refrigeration units meant that the customer could see and select the best buys in fresh meats and dairy products. Grocery carts sup-plied by the supermarket replaced hand-held baskets and bags carried in by customers. People could save time and money by shopping less frequently and buying more goods at one time.

Children enjoyed going to the store with their parents because a trained bear was caged near the entrance and did tricks for those who stopped to watch. Employees took turns washing the tame mascot in the nearby Olen-tangy River. After a few years, the bear was donated to the Columbus Zoo.

ABOVE: Big Bear and its 13,000 employees have maintained a reputation for quality and good corporate citizenship.

RIGHT: Specialty shops within each Big Bear in-clude a bakery, a delicatessen, a fresh seafood department, a cheese shop, and, of course, a butcher shop.

Since most people in Columbus re-lied on streetcars for transportation and the Lane Avenue store was nearly a mile from High Street, a free bus ran every 20 minutes from the store to the trolley stop.

By February 1935 the second Big Bear store opened at 2030 East Main Street in an old piano factory. The shelving in this store was made out of old piano crates.

Departments in the two stores in-cluded a restaurant, flower shop, bakery, soda fountain, pharmacy, appliances, and a shoe repair service. Together the stores provided a parking area for 3,000 cars in an era when few people could afford to drive.

By 1939 the company had four stores open and two under construction. Brown realized that he needed to sell a huge volume to defray the costs of of-fering such a wide variety at low prices. He used many unique promotions, such as auctions and contests to bring cus-tomers to the store. Big Bear was one of the first companies to use radio adver-tising as a major part of a promotional program. From the beginning, Big Bear's promotions have all been aimed at the same goal: giving customers the highest quality at the lowest price.

Expansion slowed during the war years, but the company again began growing in the late 1940s and 1950s. In 1947 the warehouse was opened at its present location at 770 West Goodale Boulevard. There were 11 Big Bear stores at that time and plans were an-nounced to open 10 new stores by the end of 1949.

Big Bear is responsible for many innovations in the supermarket business. They were the first to introduce motorized counters controlled by the cashier. Unique store layouts, placing perishable departments in the center of the store with low fixtures and a pleasing decor, brought international attention to the Columbus chain. The layout of the Graceland store quickly became the industry standard. A leader in technology, Big Bear implemented use of the new IBM 305 Ramac accounting machine in the supermarkets.

In 1948 the company began to move into new fields of business. Brown met with several other supermarket operators to form Topco Associates, Inc., the company that produces private label products under the Food Club, Top Frost, Mega, and other labels.

The predecessor of Harts Discount Department Stores supplied general merchandise and drugs to Big Bear's

In 1947 Harts opened department stores in the basements of four Big Bear supermarkets. Seven years later the grocery chain acquired Harts and began running them in the same quality manner as their original stores.

home center departments. In 1947 Harts opened department stores in the basements of four Big Bear supermarkets. Seven years later Big Bear acquired Harts, and in 1963 Harts opened its first department store in Bridgeport, Ohio.

Harts are full-line self-service stores with more than 30 major departments, including men's, women's, and children's apparel, auto accessories, health and beauty aids, prescription drugs, cosmetics, electronics, jewelry, sporting goods, toys, home furnishings, and housewares.

Quality together with everyday low prices on national brands is emphasized.

Big Bear also operates the Betty Brown Bakery at 1550 North High Street to produce fresh bread and baked goods for all store locations. In 1990 Big Bear added a 535,000-square-foot, state-of-the-art grocery warehouse to its Goodale complex.

Today's modern Big Bear supermarket averages 50,000 square feet and provides many full-service specialty shops under one roof: a bakery, a delicatessen, a fresh seafood department, a butcher shop, and a cheese shop, along with a large selection of produce, groceries, and frozen food.

At the checkout counters, customers discover another of Big Bear's technical innovations: the Vision System. The interactive video monitor offers customers the opportunity to select instant rebates, coupons, recipes, and community service messages. Every dollar the customer spends at Big Bear earns points in the Vision Value Club which can later be redeemed for free merchandise. The Vision System provides customers with state-of-the-art financial service, as well. Consumers can pay for their groceries using electronic checking or a store-issued credit card. By 1992 Big Bear plans to have the Vision System available in every supermarket they operate.

Big Bear and its 13,000 employees have maintained a reputation for quality in all operational aspects, including catering. The company operates a unique catering facility in Powell, Ohio, that was originally a working farm owned by Brown. Big Bear Farms

The first Big Bear store was opened in 1934 in an old roller rink on Lane Avenue across from The Ohio State University.

handles hundreds of wedding receptions, business meetings, luncheons, picnics, and barbecues annually.

The company has always been an active supporter of local community organizations and sponsors many worthwhile events. Each summer, Picnic With the Pops, an outdoor concert series with the Columbus Symphony Orchestra, generates tremendous revenues for the musical organization.

In the fall, Big Bear, along with two other Columbus corporations, presents the Holiday Parade benefiting Charity Newsies. Through the year, Big Bear is involved with many organizations, large and small, including the Boy Scouts, Recreation Unlimited, Children's Hospital, United Way, Mid-Ohio Food Bank, Columbus Police Athletic League, Big Brothers/Big Sisters, Columbus Clippers, The Ohio State University, March of Dimes, YMCA, Ohio Historical Foundation, and Columbus USA Weekend.

For three years Big Bear has worked to improve education in all of its marketing areas by placing over $4-million worth of free Apple computer equipment in schools through the highly successful Apples for the Students program.

The company believes in being a good corporate citizen by returning something to each community in which it does business.

Big Bear Stores Company operates 62 supermarkets, 23 Harts Discount Department Stores, and 7 Big Bear Plus combination stores in central and southern Ohio and northern West Virginia.

The corporate philosophy of meeting the needs of the customer continues the tradition begun by Wayne Brown and Big Bear more than a half-century ago.

HEADQUARTERS COMPANIES

It wasn't so very long ago that if you wanted to open an office there was no option but to spend a lot of time finding the right space, negotiating a lease, buying furniture, hiring secretarial help, and getting telephones installed. Even after the office opened, the time-consuming duties of managing the office took attention away from the most important thing—running the business.

The proliferation of executive office suites throughout the country in recent years indicates that some people in business don't want to be burdened with all that an independent office entails. Jane Booras, executive director of Executive Suite Network, a Dallas-based trade association for owners and operators of executive suite businesses, estimates that there are 4,000 companies in the United States operating 175,000 executive offices totaling 50 million square feet. According to Booras, the future for executive suites is promising, in part because it's such an economical and simple way for companies to expand to other markets.

RIGHT: HQ conference rooms are designed for relaxed and productive meetings.

BELOW: HQ offers an elegantly appointed lobby area that makes clients and their guests feel welcome.

The three Headquarters Companies locations in Columbus—downtown at Capital Square, in Dublin, and in Worthington—are part of a network of executive offices throughout the United States and in Europe. The HQ network began with one executive center in San Francisco in 1977 and was sold as a multi-unit chain seven years later to United Technologies Corporation.

In 1985 United sold HQ to existing franchise owners who continue to run it as a franchised system today.

Calvin W. Hunter, president of the Cleveland-based franchise that owns the locations there and in the Columbus metropolitan area, believes HQ has many advantages for the business owner in quick need of office space.

"We offer virtually an instant office,

complete with telephones, furniture, secretarial help, and state-of-the-art technology. Clients look as if they are well-established the first day they open for business," Hunter says. "We also accommodate expansion in additional office space as the client's business grows."

Hunter's company has been recognized for its rapid growth, popping up on the Weatherhead 100 list as one of the fastest growing companies in northeastern Ohio. The list is published annually by *Crain's Cleveland Business*, a weekly business newspaper.

"We grow because we enable our clients to grow," says Hunter. "We don't sell offices; we sell productivity."

In today's competitive environment, productivity depends largely upon being able to effectively use the latest in business support services. In addition to the

Attractive offices with the client's choice of furnishings make HQ desirable to business executives.

features that have become fixtures in offices today, such as fax, copying, and word processing machines, HQ also offers many high-tech support services that most small-business owners would not be able to afford.

One such service is a computer-based information system that provides the telephone operator in each HQ office with complete information about the client company the instant the telephone rings. The client receives a hard copy of the messages for returning calls and for file history. Messages are available 24 hours a day.

Another efficiency is realized in the sharing of the workload between HQ offices. With computers able to communicate from office to office, if one center is overloaded with word processing, the work can be shared with another center. It enables HQ to provide the high-tech office services of the 1990s without increasing the cost. With this service, as with all services at HQ, clients only pay for those services they actually use, so it's cost-efficient for large and small clients alike.

Booras estimates that a company can "operate at approximately 40 percent to 50 percent of the cost of equipping and staffing a conventional office." In addition, lease arrangements are often much more flexible than with a typical office lease.

HQ offers a variety of programs that fit each client's particular needs. The full-time office plan provides a private office with a liberal monthly allotment of support services. The business identity plan serves the needs of a client who doesn't need an office full time but does need a corporate setting for intermittent use, the identity with a prestigious business address, and the availability of staff and services in a central location. In either case, a well-appointed conference room, equipped with a video recorder for client use, is made available.

For HQ clients who are frequently on the road, the HQ system offers an additional advantage—an office away from home. With almost 100 HQ centers in most major metropolitan areas of the United States and in London and Brussels, a brief phone call reserves an office for meetings with clients or simply a quiet place to get work done and make telephone calls.

The three HQ locations in Columbus meet somewhat different needs. A 47-office Capitol Square office is especially sought after by lobbyists because it is located directly across State Street from the state capitol. It is also a favorite office location for associations, lawyers, and businesses that share a need to be near the center of commerce and finance in central Ohio. In addition, the office is adjacent to the Hyatt on Capitol Square and to the Columbus City Center shopping mall with its more than 100 stores and restaurants.

The Worthington office, located at 100 East Wilson Bridge Road, is used by many business professionals who value ready access to the Interstate 270 outerbelt and the Worthington area. This facility has 47 office suites.

HQ acquired Dublin Office Suites at 4900 Blazer Memorial Parkway in 1990. With 62 office suites totaling 15,000 square feet, it serves one of the fastest-growing areas of greater Columbus.

The expansion of HQ is a direct result of the growth of the Columbus metropolitan area and a reflection of the entrepreneurial spirit of the community as it enters the final decade of the twentieth century.

BELOW: A computer-based information system assists telephone operators and provides clients with a hard copy of messages.

LONG'S COLLEGE BOOK STORE

Textbooks and supplies were on the first floor of the 7,500-square-foot structure; the family's apartment and meeting rooms were on the second floor. Dr. Long recalls that it was a bustling place during his childhood.

By 1928 it was time to expand once again. Long leased the basement and the third-floor dance hall of the adjacent Hennick building, and a large

LEFT: The two-story Long's Book Store, located at 15th and High streets, was built in 1909. This photograph was taken 10 years later.

BELOW: One of the first neon signs in Columbus went up on Long's in the 1930s. It was still there in 1990 when this photograph was taken.

On the campus of The Ohio State University there are many traditions, but just across High Street from the university there is another tradition that is just as enduring as any on campus—Long's College Book Store.

At the beginning of the quarter each year thousands of OSU students find their way to Long's in search of the books that they need for classes. At the end of the quarter many of the books are purchased back, only to be sold once again to more knowledge-seeking collegians. Some textbooks turn over as many as three times in a year.

A goodly number of Columbus' most successful citizens—physicians, bankers, lawyers, retailers, corporate executives, developers, and stock brokers, among others—prowled the stacks of books at Long's as students. What they found there surely played a role in their subsequent success. The legendary Buckeye football coach, Woody Hayes, would have said so. According to Dr. Frank C. Long, Jr., the scholarly Hayes "was always perusing through history and military books."

Dr. Long is not the founder of the store bearing his name. He was born in December 1909 in the family's apartment over the business his father, Frank C. Long, founded while still a student on the OSU campus.

At the turn of the century Long was majoring in agriculture when he acquired from a classmate a student-run book agency located in the basement of University Hall. Attracted by the book business, Long abandoned agriculture upon graduating in 1902, borrowed $500 from his father, and founded his first off-campus business in space he shared with Kiler's Drug Store at 11th and High streets, which was then the main entrance to the university. With a memory that befitted his surname, Long knew which students had textbooks to sell and who wanted to buy them. The business grew, and within three years Long was able to purchase his own property, at 15th and High streets, where the bookstore has been ever since.

A handsome, two-story brick building, which still stands, was built on the site and opened for business in 1909.

house behind the first building was later acquired for storage.

More and more books found their way to Long's, as did more and more customers. Today sales are handled quickly and efficiently by computer, but prior to the 1960s each customer required personal attention. It became Long's policy to hire only OSU students who needed the financial assistance to attend school. It is a policy Dr. Long has continued.

Long's not only provided its service to OSU students and professors, the service also was extended to schools throughout the land. The founder realized that the constant ebb and flow of people and textbooks on the campus of Ohio State was occurring on every campus, so he began buying and selling books at many institutions. Long thus pioneered the concept of interschool exchanges, and he was a charter member of the National Association of College Bookstores.

Long's also dealt with book wholesalers on an international scale. At one time representatives of the bookstore visited American colleges and universities two or three times a year in search of used texts. Bookstores and libraries associated with institutions of higher learning throughout the land, as well as overseas, knew to come to Long's wholesale division first for used books.

RIGHT: Dr. Frank C. Long, Jr., son of the founder, has overseen the purchase and sale of millions of textbooks since he began working at the store upon the death of his father in 1956.

BELOW: The bookstore's present management team: (from left) Dr. Frank C. Long, Jr., president; James C. Clucus, general manager; and Joseph Casagrande, chief financial officer.

Andrew Carnegie himself would have been impressed with the sheer number of volumes, which easily topped 3 million after World War II. The wholesale operation was expanding, requiring the construction in 1948 of a four-story, concrete building to cope with the millions of weighty tomes.

A massive catalog—some remember it being larger than the Sears Roebuck catalog, although that is not true—was published regularly by Long's. It often listed more than 20,000 titles in the 100 pages or so. Circulation to other bookstores and libraries was more than 100,000 copies. At its peak Long's published some 50 specialized catalogs of books of an educational and general nature.

As the volumes continued to grow in number, Long's also became the headquarters of rare and out-of-print books desired by libraries and researchers everywhere. Dr. Long's brother, Robert, advanced the rare book business. Upon his death in 1953, however, the specialty division was discontinued. Ohio State acquired many of the rare volumes; the remainder were sold to collectors.

Publishing was another enterprise. A number of Ohio State professors had their own texts published by the famous bookseller.

Founder Frank C. Long was personally involved in the daily operations virtually up until the day of his death in 1956. At the time Dr. Long, who graduated from the Ohio State College of Medicine in 1936, was practicing family medicine in Point Pleasant, West Virginia. With the passing of his father, however, Dr. Long returned to Columbus to assume management of the business.

While some operations, such as rare books and catalogs, were scaled back or eliminated, Dr. Long expanded the business in other areas. More consumables—nonbook items such as clothing, supplies, greeting cards, teacher resource material, and Buckeye paraphanelia—were added. He also introduced the largest commercial art department in central Ohio.

In 1990 Dr. Long estimated there were "more than 15,000 titles and 500,000 volumes" at the store. Only about half are used, however; the rest are in the general fiction and nonfiction departments that were introduced in 1931. Dr. Long recognizes that it is becoming more difficult to acquire used texts as habits change and the competition becomes keener. No longer is it possible for one entrepreneur to dominate the marketplace as Long's once did.

As his father was before him, Dr. Long has been active in OSU affairs. He is, for example, a trustee of the University Community Business Association. He has also established an endowment fund in his father's name at the Arthur G. James Cancer Hospital and Research Center.

Long's and the Long family represent an enduring tradition at Ohio State and in the Columbus community.

FIESTA SALONS INCORPORATED

Fiesta Hair and Tanning Salons is the Midwest's largest salon chain with more than 255 locations in Ohio, Michigan, Indiana, Kentucky, and West Virginia.

Founded in 1973 with just two Columbus salons, Fiesta today has gross sales of more than $37 million annually. Each salon is company-owned because Fiesta's management believes corporate ownership allows for greater standardization of services and the observance of a company-wide policy to provide outstanding customer service.

Based on its premise that "Great hair doesn't have to be expensive," Fiesta offers quality service at affordable prices. Costs to consumers are held down by a no frills approach to beauty.

"No frills" doesn't translate to "cut-rate," however. Fiesta salons are maintained as neat, clean, bright, functional, attractive operations, and the company sports an upscale corporate identity program. Designed not to be elitist, the salons are frequently located in WalMart, K Mart, and Kroger shopping centers—family-centered locations where mom, dad, and the children can all feel comfortable and relaxed.

Clayton Jones, chairman of the board of Fiesta, attributes the company's success to its "stick-to-the-knitting" philosophy. The company knows what its business is and it focuses on

that business, rather than on unrelated diversification efforts.

"We have held true to our original concept," says Jones. "That concept was to provide our customers with convenience and quality at affordable prices." Salons are open seven days a week and accept no appointments, both innovations in which Fiesta was an industry pioneer.

Customers want more than just convenience, however; they want style. They want to know that their stylist keeps current with the latest looks and styling techniques. Fiesta, therefore, has a corporate design team that provides ongoing training to more than 1,800 stylists, keeping them up-to-the-minute on new trends and styling tips.

By listening to its customers, Fiesta learned what additional services were most desirable and added those to its repertoire. In response to customer demand, Fiesta offers the latest in tanning technology in all its locations. Thousands of customers use the Wolff tanning beds on a weekly basis, making Fiesta, with nearly 500 beds in operation, number one in tanning in the United States.

As Fiesta looks to the future, Jones predicts an increase in the number of males taking advantage of the company's services. In addition, he expects still greater retail activity in salons. As more products are made available exclusively through salons, and as beauticians become more knowledgeable about the results customers can achieve by using these new products, hair stylists will be able to prescribe a variety of solutions to hair and beauty problems. Jones and his wife, Phyllis, Fiesta cofounder and vice president of operations at the company's 23,000-square-foot headquarters at 6363 Fiesta Drive, are pleased that the 1990s find the company in the ranks of the top 10 hair styling chains in the world.

Back in 1973, the "experts" in the beauty business predicted that there was no way Fiesta could make a go of offering no appointment service every day of the week at its low prices. Many of those experts are now out of business, Jones notes, while Fiesta continues to offer its unique services to a rapidly growing list of steady customers.

Fiesta corporate headquarters is located near Linworth.

PATRONS

The following individuals, companies, and organizations have made a valuable commitment to the quality of this publication. Windsor Publications and The Columbus Area Chamber of Commerce gratefully acknowledge their participation in *Columbus: The Discovery City.*

Access Energy*
Adria Laboratories*
Akzo Coatings, Incorporated*
American Electric Power/Columbus Southern
    Power Company*
American Telephone & Telegraph*
Anheuser-Busch, Incorporated*
ARC Industries, Incorporated*
Arthur Anderson*
Arthur G. James Cancer Hospital*
ASC Colamco*
BancOhio National Bank*
Banc One Corporation*
Battelle Memorial Institute*
Betlin Manufacturing*
Big Bear Stores Company*
Borden, Inc.*
Borror Corporation*
Brubaker/Brandt Incorporated*
Burgess & Niple Limited*
Business First of Columbus*
The Butler Company*
Capital University*
Capitol Fire Protection Co.*
Central Aluminum Company
Central Benefits Mutual Insurance Company*
Central Ohio Transit Authority (COTA)*
Chemical Abstracts Service*
Chemlawn Inc.*
Children's Hospital*
Columbus City Center*
Columbus College of Art and Design*
Columbus Col-Weld Corporation*
Columbus Gas Co.*
Columbus Marriott North*
Columbus State Community College*
Columbus Steel Drum Company*
Columbus Zoo*
Combibloc, Inc.*
Continental Office Furniture & Supply

Corporation*
Continental Real Estate*
Crane Plastics*
Daifuku U.S.A. Inc.*
Eaton IDT Incorporated*
EBCO® Manufacturing Company*
Edison Welding Institute*
Electric Power Equipment Company*
Embassy Suites Hotel
Emens, Hurd, Kegler & Ritter Co., L.P.A.*
Epro Incorporated*
Ernst & Young*
Executive Office Place*
Fiesta Salons Incorporated*
Flxible Corporation*
Frigidaire Company*
Franklin University*
The Galbreath Company*
GE Superabrasives*
Gioffre Construction Incorporated*
Grange Insurance Companies*
Grant Medical Center*
Greater Columbus Convention Center*
Harvard Industries, Inc.
Headquarters Companies*
HER Realtors*
Honda of America Manufacturing Incorporated*
Household Bank*
The Huntington National Bank*
Industrial Association of Central Ohio*
Inland Products Incorporated*
Jeffrey Division, Dresser Industries*
Jones, Day, Reavis & Pogue*
Kal Kan Foods Incorporated*
Karlshamns USA Inc.*
King Thompson/Holzer-Wollam, Realtors*
KPMG Peat Marwick*
Kroger Company*
Lake Shore Cryotronics, Incorporated*
Lennox Industries*
Liebert Corporation*
The Limited Incorporated*
Liqui-Box Corporation*
Long's College Book Store*
McGlaughlin Oil Company*
Medex, Inc.*
M-E Engineering, Inc.*
Mid-American Waste Systems*
The Midland*
Moody/Nolan Ltd., Incorporated*

Mount Carmel Health*
MTM Americas, Incorporated/Pharmaceutical
    Intermediates Division*
Myers-NBD Incorporated*
Nationwide Insurance*
Ohio Bell Telephone Company*
Ohio Dominican College*
Ohio's Center of Science and Industry (COSI)*
The Ohio State University Hospitals*
Ohio Wesleyan University*
Online Computer Library Center (OCLC)*
Otterbein College*
Photonic Integration Research, Incorporated*
Porter, Wright, Morris & Arthur*
Rage Corporation*
Ranco Incorporated*
R.D. Zande & Associates, Limited*
Ricart Ford Incorporated*
Riverside Methodist Hospitals*
Saint Anthony Medical Center*
Schuler Incorporated*
Society Bank*
Squire, Sanders & Dempsey*
Stouffer Dublin Hotel*
Superior Die, Tool & Machine Company*
Technology Alliance of Central Ohio*
Temporary Corporate Housing, Inc.*
Toledo Scale*
TOMASCO mulciber, Inc.*
TS Trim Industries Incorporated*
Turner Construction Company*
U.S. Check*
WBNS-TV*
Wendy's International, Inc.*
White Castle System, Incorporated*
Worthington Industries*
Worthington Foods*
WSNY/WVKO*
Zande Environmental Service, Inc.*

*Participants in Part Two, "Columbus' Enterprises." The stories of these companies and organizations appear in chapters 8 through 14, beginning on page 277.

CHAMBERS OF COMMERCE—GREATER COLUMBUS AREA

On behalf of the Columbus Area Chamber of Commerce, we wish to acknowledge and express sincere appreciation for the support for this book from the surrounding area chambers of commerce. *Columbus: The Discovery City* could not have been such a tremendous success without their contribution.

—Jonathan L. York
President
Columbus Area Chamber of Commerce

Bexley Chamber of Commerce
Bexley, OH 43209

Canal Winchester Chamber of Commerce
Canal Winchester, OH 43110

Chillicothe-Ross Chamber of Commerce
Chillicothe, OH 45601

Circleville Pickaway Chamber of Commerce
Circleville, OH 43113

Delaware Area Chamber of Commerce
Delaware, OH 43015

Dublin Chamber of Commerce
Dublin, OH 43017

Gahanna Chamber of Commerce
Gahanna, OH 43230

Grandview/Marble Cliff Area Chamber of
Commerce
Columbus, OH 43212

Grove City Chamber of Commerce
Grove City, OH 43123

Groveport Chamber of Commerce
Canal Winchester, OH 43110

Hilliard Area Chamber of Commerce
Hilliard, OH 43026

Lancaster-Fairfield County Chamber of
Commerce
Lancaster, OH 43130

London Area Chamber of Commerce
London, OH 43140

Marion Chamber of Commerce
Marion, OH 43302

Marysville Area Chamber of Commerce
Marysville, OH 43040

Mid Ohio Regional Planning Commission
Columbus, OH 43215

Mt. Vernon Area Development Foundation
Mt. Vernon, OH 43050

Newark Area Chamber of Commerce
Newark, OH 43055

Ohio Chamber of Commerce
Columbus, OH 43215-3181

Pataskala Area Chamber of Commerce
Pataskala, OH 43062

Pickerington Chamber of Commerce
Pickerington, OH 43147

Plain City Area Chamber of Commerce
Plain City, OH 43064

Reynoldsburg Chamber of Commerce
Reynoldsburg, OH 43068

Upper Arlington Area Chamber of Commerce
Upper Arlington, OH 43221

Washington Court House Area Chamber of
Commerce
Washington Court House, 43160-2227

Westerville Area Chamber of Commerce
Westerville, OH 43081

Whitehall Business Association
Whitehall, OH 43213

Worthington Area Chamber of Commerce
Worthington, OH 43085

Zanesville Area Chamber of Commerce
Zanesville, OH 43701

BIBLIOGRAPHY

Barrett, Richard E. *Columbus and Central Ohio Historian*. Nos. 1, 2, and 3. Orton Publications, 1985.

Battelle. *Putting Technology to Work: Annual report of Battelle Memorial Institute.*

-----. *Science Serving Human Needs: The Story of Battelle Memorial Institute.*

Campen, Richard N. *German Village Portrait*. West Summit Press, 1978.

Chemical Abstracts Service. *CAS Report*. Vol. 12.

Columbus Association for the Performing Arts. *60th Anniversary of the Ohio Theatre.*

"Columbus Mayors: A Bicentennial Presentation." Reprinted from the *Columbus Citizen-Journal*, 1976.

Garrett, Betty, and Edward R. Lentz. *Columbus: America's Crossroads*. Continental Heritage Press Inc., 1980.

Goulder, Grace. *This is Ohio*. The World Publishing Company, n.d.

Landstrom, Bjorn. *Columbus*. Macmillan, 1967.

Lee, Alfred Emory. *History of the City of Columbus*. 2 vols. Munsell and Company, 1892.

Lincoln, Murray D., and David Karp. *Vice President in Charge of Revolution*. McGraw-Hill Book Company, 1960.

Martin, William T. *History of Franklin County.* Follett, Foster & Co., 1858

The Ohio State University. Office of Communications and Development. *Ohio State Quest.*

Stockwell, Rachel N. *The Columbus College of Art & Design: First Hundred Years 1879-1979.* CCAD Alumni Association, n.d.

Studer, Jacob H. *Columbus, Ohio: History, Resources and Progress*. Jacob H. Studer, 1873.

Thomas, Robert, publisher. *Columbus Unforgettables*. 1983.

-----. *More Columbus Unforgettables*. 1986.

Tibbets, Paul W., Harry Franken, and Clair Stebbins. *The Tibbets Story*. Stein and Day, 1978.

Ware, Jane. *An Ohio State Profile: A Year in the Life of America's Biggest Campus*. Morrow, 1980.

INDEX

COLUMBUS' ENTERPRISES INDEX

Access Energy, 282-283
Adria Laboratories, 312-313
Akzo Coatings, Incorporated, 358-359
American Electric Power/Columbus Southern Power Company, 284-285
American Telephone & Telegraph, 292-293
Anheuser-Busch, Incorporated, 362-363
ARC Industries, Incorporated, 322-323
Arthur Anderson, 416
Arthur G. James Cancer Hospital, 438-439
ASC Colamco, 329
BancOhio National Bank, 374-375
Banc One Corporation, 392-393
Battelle Memorial Institute, 380-381
Betlin Manufacturing, 338
Big Bear Stores Company, 490-491
Borden, Inc., 356-357
Borror Corporation, 420-423
Brubaker/Brandt Incorporated, 398-399
Burgess & Niple Limited, 404-405
Business First of Columbus, 296
Butler Company, The, 486-487
Capital University, 445
Capitol Fire Protection Co., 432
Central Benefits Mutual Insurance Company, 388-389
Central Ohio Transit Authority (COTA), 290-291
Chemical Abstracts Service, 394-395
Chemlawn Inc., 482-483
Children's Hospital, 452-453
Columbus Area Chamber of Commerce, 372
Columbus City Center, 489
Columbus College of Art and Design, 457
Columbus Col-Weld Corporation, 328
Columbus Gas Co., 288-289
Columbus Marriott North, 484
Columbus State Community College, 458-459
Columbus Steel Drum Company, 332-333
Columbus Zoo, 456
Combibloc, Inc., 364
Continental Office Furniture & Supply Corporation, 480-481
Continental Real Estate, 428-429
Crane Plastics, 320
Daifuku U.S.A. Inc., 315
Eaton IDT Incorporated, 365
EBCO® Manufacturing Company, 306-307
Edison Welding Institute, 361
Electric Power Equipment Company, 345
Emens, Hurd, Kegler & Ritter Co., L.P.A., 408-409
Epro Incorporated, 352-353
Ernst & Young, 406-407
Executive Office Place, 474-475
Fiesta Salons Incorporated, 496
Flxible Corporation, 342-343
Franklin University, 454-455
Frigidaire Company, 488
Galbreath Company, The, 433
GE Superabrasives, 340-341
Gioffre Construction Incorporated, 431
Grange Insurance Companies, 378
Grant Medical Center, 442-443
Greater Columbus Convention Center, 460
Headquarters Companies, 492-493
HER Realtors, 426-427

Honda of America Manufacturing Incorporated, 350-351
Household Bank, 373
Huntington National Bank, The, 368-371
Industrial Association of Central Ohio, 390
Inland Products Incorporated, 330-331
Jeffrey Division, Dresser Industries, 316-317
Jones, Day, Reavis & Pogue, 401
Kal Kan Foods Incorporated, 300-303
Karlshamns USA Inc., 310-311
King Thompson/Holzer-Wollam, Realtors, 430
KPMG Peat Marwick, 415
Kroger Company, 478-479
Lake Shore Cryotronics, Incorporated, 308-309
Lennox Industries, 321
Liebert Corporation, 326-327
Limited Incorporated, The, 472
Liqui-Box Corporation, 339
Long's College Book Store, 494-495
McGlaughlin Oil Company, 468-469
Medex, Inc., 334-335
M-E Engineering, Inc., 411
Mid-American Waste Systems, 485
Midland, The, 391
Moody/Nolan Ltd., Incorporated, 410
Mount Carmel Health, 450-451
MTM Americas, Incorporated/Pharmaceutical Intermediates Division, 354
Myers-NBD Incorporated, 400
Nationwide Insurance, 384-387
Ohio Bell Telephone Company, 278-281
Ohio Dominican College, 448
Ohio's Center of Science and Industry (COSI), 446
Ohio State University Hospitals, The, 436-437
Ohio Wesleyan University, 449
Online Computer Library Center (OCLC), 376-377
Otterbein College, 444
Photonic Integration Research, Incorporated, 360
Porter, Wright, Morris & Arthur, 414
Rage Corporation, 318-319
Ranco Incorporated, 324-325
R.D. Zande & Associates, Limited, 402
Ricart Ford Incorporated, 464-465
Riverside Methodist Hospitals, 440-441
Saint Anthony Medical Center, 447
Schuler Incorporated, 344
Society Bank, 382-383
Squire, Sanders & Dempsey, 412-413
Stouffer Dublin Hotel, 470-471
Superior Die, Tool & Machine Company, 304-305
Technology Alliance of Central Ohio, 336-337
Temporary Corporate Housing, Inc., 476-477
Toledo Scale, 346-347
TOMASCO mulciber, Inc., 314
TS Trim Industries Incorporated, 348
Turner Construction Company, 424-425
U.S. Check, 379
WBNS-TV, 294-295
Wendy's International, Inc., 473
White Castle System, Incoporated, 466-467
Worthington Foods, 355
Worthington Industries, 349
WSNY/WVKO, 286-287
Zande Environmental Service, Inc., 403

GENERAL INDEX
Italics indicate illustrations

AccuRay Corporation, 64
Actors Summer Theatre, 155
"Adopt-A-School" program, 109-110
Air National Guard, 21, 41
Air transportation, 174, 176-178, 180-184, 186-189, 192
Airway Limited, 177
AIU Building, 40, 71, 75, 80
Alfieri, Edoardo, 22
Allen, Nimrod Booker, 214
Alloys of Iron Research, 51
Alum Creek, *262-263*
Alum Creek Dam, 271
American Cancer Society, 56
American Chemical Society, 59
American Electric Power, 75
American Express office, *32*
American HealthMark, 133
American Institute of Architects, Columbus chapter, 180
American Insurance Union Citadel, 40, 71, 75, 80
American Machine & Foundry, 57
AMF, 57
Amusement parks, 34, 42-43
Anheuser-Busch, *88-89,* 194, 240
Aquinas High School, 23, 115
Arcetri Observatory, 55
Arch Park, 199, 200
Arches, 34, *34*
Armstrong, Jeremiah, 18, 20
Armstrong, John, 20
Armstrong, William, 20
Army Air Corps, 41
Army National Guard, 186
Arthur G. James Cancer Hospital And Research Institute, *54,* 55-56, 127
Atomic Energy Commission, 51
AT&T Bell Laboratories, 46, *46,* 47, 48, *50*
August Wagner Brewery, 223
Autech Corporation, 65
Avery, F.E., 57
Aviation Hall of Fame, 125

Baccaloni, Salvatore, 22-23
Backyards-by-Candlelight, 222
Baker, Dale B., 63
BalletMet, 142, 147, 148
Baltimore and Ohio Railroad, 200
BancOhio National Bank, 68, 84, *98*
Bank One of Columbus, NA, *96,* 98, 101
Barack, Nick, 240
Barnhard, Ernest S., 124
BASISplus, 48
Battelle Auditorium, 147
Battelle-Darby Creek Metro Park, 259, 261, *261*
Battelle, Gordon, 48, 51, 52
Battelle Memorial Institute, *44-45,* 46, 48, *48, 49,* 51-52, *52, 53,* 55, 57
Baxter, Warner, 212
Beggs Building, 68, 84
Beightler Armory, 99
Bell Laboratories, 46, *46,* 47, 48, *50,*
Bellows, George Wesley, 120, 125, 162, 212
Bendele, Pat, 186

Bendele, Ron, 186
Benva, Louis, 188
Berliner, Lou, 240, 243
Beulah Park, 233, 269
Bexley, 21, 32, 99, 110, 112, 167, 235, *236,* 265
Bexley High School, 218
B.F. Goodrich Company, 64
Big Bear stores, 57, 95
Big City Diner, 101
Big Darby Creek, 261
Bijou Theater, 156
Bionics and Transplants exhibit, 167
Blacklick Woods, *110,* 256, *258,* 259, 261, *263;* Golf course, 261
Blendon Woods Metro Park, 256, *257,* 261
Blue Angels, 189
Bob Evans Farms Restaurants, 92
Bolton Field Airport, 118, 184, 187, *187,* 194
Bolton, Francis A. "Jack," 178, 184, 187
Booth, Lucy Adelaid, 56
Borden Building, 78, 84
Brass Band of Columbus, 153
Brewery District, 32, 78, 223, *231*
Brickell, John, 18, *18*
Bricker & Eckler, 217
Bricker, John W., 23, 217
Bridgman, Bill, 188
Brown Fruit Farm, 256
Brown, Wayne E., 95
Brownfield, C. William, 198
Bryan, William Jennings, 34
Buckeye Dinner Theatre, 155
Buckeye International, Inc., 90
Buckeye Lake, 34, 43, 271
Buckeye Lake Yacht Club, 43
Buckeye Union Insurance, 85
Bucklew, Phil H., 212
Bureau of Standards, 59, 63
Burkhart, Emerson, 162
Burnham, Daniel, 198
Burns, Ken, 30
Businessmen's Athletic Club, 271
Byrd Polar Research Center, 55

Camp Bushnell, 21, 32
Camp Chase, 21, *28,* 29
Camp Jackson, 21, 28
Campbell Mound, 18, *19*
Canal Winchester, 233
Caniff, Milton, 125
Cannon, Jack, 208
Capital Club, 271
Capital Law School, 113
Capital Music Center, 233
Capital, selection of, 24-25
Capital University, 110, *112,* 119, 124-125, 155, 162
Capitol Square, 68
Capitol Square Office Tower, 68, *71,* 78, 84, *97*
Capitol Tower, 68, 84
Caplan, Benjamin B., 214
Carlson, Chester, 51, 57
Caruso, Enrico, 34
CAS ONLINE Registry File, 59
Cassady, Howard "Hopalong," 208, 264
Casto, Sr., Don M., 92, 93, 95, 177
Catholic Migration And Refugee Resettlement Office, 225
CBS, Inc., 124
Cedarwood school, 107
Celehar, Jane, 171

Cellar, Bernie, 256
Center for Operative Laparoscopy, 138
CenterStage Theatre, 153
Central Benefits Mutual Insurance, 85
Central High School, 40, 115, 208, 269
Central Ohio Area Agency on Aging, 240, 245
Central Ohio Psychiatric Hospital, 99, 138
Central Ohio Railroad, 200
Central Ohio Rowing Association, 245
Central Skyport, 182
Cessna Citations, 183
Chadeayne, Robert Osborne, 212, 214
Chamber of Commerce, 101, 109,198
Chase, Salmon P., 26, 27, 28
Chemical Abstracts, 59, 63
Chemical Abstracts Service, 46, 58, 59, 59, 63, 144
Chesapeake And Ohio Railroad, 200
Chestnut Ridge, 259
Children's Hospital, 36, 133, 135, 138
Chillicothe, 24
Christopher Columbus Award, 64
Circle S Farm, 260
Circleville, 189, 194, 218
Citizens Trust and Savings Bank, 98
City Center, 94, 95
City Hall, 22, 23, 40, 142, 208, 212
City National Bank, 95, 98
Civilian Pilot Training Program, 188
Civil War, 21, 28-29, 32, 199
Clear Fork, 271
Cleveland Browns, 208
Cleveland, Columbus, & Cincinnati Railroad, 199, 200
Cleveland Indians, 124
Clintonville, 231
College Hill, 123
College of St. Mary of the Springs, 115, 117
Colonel Crawford Inn, 31, 166
Columbia Gas of Ohio Building, 78, 84
Columbus Aircraft Division, 180
Columbus Area Chamber of Commerce, 101, 109, 198
Columbus Area Technician School, 115, 118
Columbus Art School, 120
Columbus Arts Festival, 214, 215, 216, 217
Columbus Association for the Performing Arts, 142, 144
Columbus Automobile Club, 34
Columbus Barracks Recruit Depot, 21
Columbus Board of Education, 21, 115
Columbus Board of Trade, 101, 198, 199
Columbus Boys' Academy, 155
Columbus Buggy Company, 85
Columbus, Christopher, 16-17, 22-23, 24, 115
Columbus City Attorney's Office, 113
Columbus City Council, 155
Columbus Civic Center, 40
Columbus Clippers, 268-269, 269, 270
Columbus College of Art and Design, 119, 120-121, 121, 125
Columbus Community Hospital, 133
Columbus Country Club, 271
Columbus Day Parade, 22, 23
"Columbus Discovery" Award, 106, 109
Columbus Dispatch, 43, 68, 147, 240, 243
Columbus Driving Park, 34
Columbus Federation of Musicians, 155
Columbus, Ferdinand, 22
Columbus and Franklin County Metropolitan Park District, 252
Columbus General Depot, 41

Columbus Hall of Fame, 208, 212, 214, 217-218
Columbus Health Department, 138
Columbus Horizon basketball team, 270
Columbus Jets, 208
Columbus Marathon, 264, 264
Columbus Metropolitan Area Community Action Organization,154
Columbus Museum of Art, 158, 160-161, 162
Columbus Mutual Life Insurance, 85
Columbus Park of Roses, 243, 248-249
Columbus Project, 55
Columbus Public School System, 101, 106, 107, 109, 110, 154
Columbus Quartermaster Reserve Depot, 21
Columbus Railway Power and Light Company, 42
Columbus Recreation and Parks Department, 23, 149, 155, 164, 171, 235, 243, 245, 252
Columbus Safety Building, 75
Columbus and Southern Ohio Electric Company, 42, 199
Columbus Southern Power Company, 42
Columbus State Community College, 22, 23, 115, 118, 118, 187
Columbus Street Railway Company, 42, 43
Columbus Symphony Orchestra, 59, 142, 144, 145
Columbus Technical Committee for Flight Operations, 188-189
Columbus Technical Institute, 115
Columbus Union Station, 198-199, 200
Columbus & Xenia Railroad, 199, 200
Columbus Zoo, 43, 95, 245, 250, 250-251
Combibloc, Inc., 78
ComCare, 46
"Come to Columbus And Discover America" slogan, 41
Comin' Home African American Community Festival, 231
Commercial Bank, 98
Community Arts Project Board of Trustees, 155
Community Internship Program, 109
CompuServe, 46
Conrail Buckeye Yards, 200, 202-203, 204
Conservatory of Music, 110, 113
Consolidated Freightways, Inc., 197, 197
Contemporary American Theatre Company, 155
Continent Shopping Center, 158
Continental Basketball Association, 270
Convair 880, 182
Conversant 1 Voice System, 46
Cooper, Harold M., 269
Cooper Stadium, 269
Corrigan, Douglas "Wrong Way," 180
Council of Independent Colleges, 115
Crane, Evan J., 63
Cray X-MP/24 supercomputer, 55, 55
Crystal Ballroom, 43
Cultural Arts Center, 154-155, 164, 165, 240
Curtiss Aero Industries, 174, 176
Curtiss-Wright Corporation, 41, 87, 178, 188
Custom Coach Corporation, 90

Dallas and East Dallas, 157
Darby Creek Drive, 261

Darby Dan Farm, 95, 233
Daughters of the Confederacy, 21, 29
Davidson, John, 124
Davis Discovery Center Shedd Theatre, 171
Dayton, 194, 199, 204
Defense Construction Supply Center, 21, 41
Defense Logistics Agency, 21, 48
Delaware, 138, 194, 269
Delaware County Fairgrounds, 269
Denison University, 123, 124, 155
Denison, William W., 123
Dennison, Jr., William, 28
Department of Defense, 186
Department of Human Services, 225
Depression, Great, 40, 51, 63
"Deshler Corner," 71
Deshler Hotel, 71
Designs of Wood, 186
Developmental Center, 99
Devonshire school, 107
DeVry Employment Activity Network, 120
DeVry, Herman, 119
DeVry Institute of Technology, 119-120, 120
Disney studios, 124
Dispatch Printing Company, 68
Doctors Hospital, 138
Dodd Hall, 127
Dodge, Mel, 240
Don Scott Field, 99, 184, 190-191, 192, 194
Doo Dah parade, 223
Dorsey, Herbert G., 124
Douglas, James "Buster," 210
Douglas school, 107, 108
Dreamland Theatre and Nickelodeon, 167
Droste, Paul, 153
Dublin, 192, 208, 233, 235, 267
Dublin Arts Council, 20
Durst, Gerald, 22
Dusenbury, Joseph, 42, 43
Dusenbury, Will, 42, 43
Earhart, Amelia, 177, 180
Early Music in Columbus concerts, 150-151
East High School, 208, 218
Eastern Airlines, 36, 184, 212
Eastland Career Center, 118
Eastmoor High School, 208
Ebco Manufacturing Company, 188
Edward S. Thomas Nature Trail, 256
88 East Broad Street Building, 84
83rd Army Reserve Command of Ohio, 21
Eisele, Donn, 23
Eisenhower, Dwight D., 22, 123, 127
Eisenman, Peter, 158
Eisner, Michael, 124
Elderly Nutrition Program, 245
Elijah Pierce Gallery of Fine Art, 154, 165
Elizabeth Blackwell Center and Hospital, 127
Elliott Hall, 123
Employment, 80, 99, 101
EmUrgent Care Center, 127
Engineering Experiment Station, 56
Erieview Tower, 95
Eubanks, Ray, 147, 149, 153
"Evenings with Authors," 165, 166
Executive Jet Aviation, 172-173, 182-183
Fairbanks, Charles, 124
Fairground Coliseum, 270
Family Practice Center, 127
Farm Bureau Mutual Automobile Insurance Company, 80

Farmers Insurance Group, 78
Fawcett, Sherwood, 51
Federal Express, 184
Ferdinand, King, 16-17
Ferguson, Maynard, 147
Ferrara, Franco, 144
Fetch, Frank, 217, 218, 222
Fidelity & Guaranty Underwriters, 85
Fifth-Third bank, 98, 100
Fisher, John E., 85
Flemming, Arthur, 123
Flood of 1913, 36, 40
Florida Marine Research Facility, 51
Flytown, 231
Foeller's Drug Store, 46
Foos, Joseph, 24
Ford Foundation, 113
Ford, Gerald, 106
Ford Tri-Motor, 177, 180
Foreign trade zone, 186
Fort Hayes, 21, 29, 41, 41, 106
Foster AirData Systems, 64-65
Foster, B.F., 29
Foster, George Barclay, 64-65
Foster Technology Corporation, 64, 65
Franciscan Sisters of the Poor, 132
Franklin Commons, 243
Franklin County Board of Alcohol, Drug Abuse, and Mental Health Services, 138
Franklin County Courthouse, 18
Franklin County Fair, 233
Franklin County Hall of Justice, 75, 78
Franklin County Health Department, 138
Franklin County Probate Court, 252
Franklin County Tower, 75, 79, 84
Franklin Park Conservatory, 119, 243, 244
Franklin University, 65, 118-119, 225
Franklinton, 20, 24, 25, 36, 231
Frasch Hall, 119
Frasch, Joseph F., 119
Frontiers International, 214

Gahanna, 194, 233
Gahanna Community Theatre, 155
Galbreath Company, 68, 95, 96
Galbreath, Daniel M., 95
Galbreath, John W., 95, 214, 233
Gallery Hop, 162, 162, 222-223, 228
Gallery Players, 155
Gallo, Oreste Paul, 22, 23
Garfield Annex, 153
Garfield School, 154, 165
Garfield School Artists Co-op, 240
Gambrinus, King, 223
G.D. Ritzy's, 92
"Geology Ramble," 261
German Village, 92, 155, 218, 222, 223, 230, 264
German Village Oktoberfest, 222, 226-227
Gessaman, Myron B., 198
Gillars, Mildred Elizabeth, 124
Gillespie, Edward A., 174, 176, 180-181
Gillette, Horace W., 51
Gladstone immersion school, 109
Goal Systems International, 46, 48
Golden Hobby Shop, 240, 245
Goodale, Lincoln, 20
Goodale Park, 20, 21, 28, 231
Gooding, Floyd, 43
Gowdy, Horace "Hank," 208
Graczyk, Ed, 142, 153, 154
Grandparents Living Theatre, 171
Grange Mutual Casualty Company, 85

Grant Hospital Fitness Center, 271
Grant Medical Center, 127, 130, 135; Life
    Flight, 130, *134*
Grant, Ulysses S., 28
Granville, 123, 124, 194, 204
Granville College, 123
Great Southern Hotel, 142
Greenlawn Cemetery, 29, 36
"Green Line" streetcar, 43
Green Meadows Country Inn, 71
Griffin, Archie, 208, 266
Griggs Reservoir, 245, 271
Grimm, Harold, 124
Griswold's Photograph Rooms, *32*
Grocers Association, 43
Grove City, 186, 194, 233, 269
Groveport, 233
Guidos Pizzeria, 156

Haas, Margo, 171
Haelein, Elmer, 43
Haelein, Leo, 43
Hagglunds Denison Corporation, 78
Hall of Honor, 189
Hallock II, S.N., 166
Haloid Company, 51, 57
Hanby, Benjamin R., 124
Hanford Laboratory, 51
Hanna, Jack, 250
Hard Shot Cafe, 156
Harding Hospital, 138
Harley, Charles "Chic," 208
Harmon, Judson, 124
Harrison, William Henry, 24
Harts Family Centers, 95
Haunted House, The, 157
Haus and Garten Tour, 222
Hayes Hall, 123
Hayes, Lucy Webb, 123, 124
Hayes, Rutherford B., 21, 28, 123, 124
Hayes, W.W. "Woody," 208, 264
Heart Institute of Ohio, *127*
Heaton, Leonard, 124
Heinzerling Foundation, 138
Heinzerling, Otto Carl, 138
Helmick, Robert, 20
Hennicks, 36
Hideaway Bar, 43
Highbanks Metro Park, 252, *252*, 256, 261
Higher Education Council of Columbus,
    110
Highway Patrol Academy, 99
Hilliard, 194, 200, 233
Hilltop district, 36, 99
Himont USA, Inc., 78
Historic Hilltop Bean Dinner, 231
Hitler, Adolf, 40, 63, 125, 266
Hoge, James, 20
Hoge Memorial Presbyterian Church, 20
Holbrook, Hall, 124
Holcombe, Alan R. "Bud," 189
Hollander, Jack M., 56
Holliday, F.C., 29
Hollingsworth, H.S., 57
Honda of America, 46, 78, 87, *87*, 90, 194
Horvath, Les, 264
Hoskins, George W., 189
Hostetter, Carol, *136*
Howard, Arnett, *151*
Hughes, Howard, 180
Human Services Department, 231, 232
Huntington Center, *3*, 26, 68, 84
Huntington, Peletiah Webster, 98, 100
Huntington Plaza, 101

Hyatt Regency, 68, *71, 72-73,* 157

IBM, 48, 57
Incorporation, 25
Indians, 18, 20
Indianola Park, 34, 42
Information Dimensions, 46, 48
Inniswood, 256, *256*
Institute for Advanced Pelviscopic
    Surgery, 138
Insurance industry, 41, 80, 85
International business, 78, 80, 90
International Gateway, 179, 182
Isabella, Queen, *16-17*
Italian Village, 223

Jackson, Kenneth E., 57
Jackson, Richard, 194
Jacobson's, 98
James A. Rhodes State Office Tower, 68,
    69, 84, 99
James, Arthur G., 56
Janis, Elsie Bierbower, 36, 212
Janowicz, Vic, 266
Japanese Garden And Tea House, 42
Jazz Arts Group of Columbus, 147, *149*,
    153
Jeffers, Dean, 71
Jefferson Academy of Music, 65
Jesse Owens Track & Field Classic, 266,
    267
Jessing, Joseph, 22, 121, 123
John and Dorothy Galbreath Pavilion, 142
Johnston, James, 24
Joy Mill, 42
Jump, A. Gordon, 124
Juvenile Detention Center, 75

Kenwood immersion school, 109
Kerr, John, 24
Keys, C.M., 176
Kids Fest, *240-241*
Kincheloe, Ivan, 188
King, Martin Luther, Jr., 155
King Tut's, 156
Knauss, William H., 21
Kobacker House, 127
Korean War, 21, 178, 180, 189, 212
Kroger, 57

La Scala Opera, 144
Lake Breeze Hotel, 43
Lally, Letty, 46
Lamb, Thomas White, 142
Lancaster-Winchester Pike, 259
Lane Aviation Corporation, 167, 182
Lane Bryant Division, 95
Lane, Foster A., 167, 182, 192
Lassiter, O.F. "Dick," 182-183
Lausche, Frank, 23
Lawrence, Mary, 22
Lazarus, Simon, 92
Leatherlips, 20
LeMay, Curtis Emerson, 41, 125, 186,
    208, 212
Leo Yassenoff Jewish Center, 155
Leppert's Lodge, 43
LeVeque, Katherine S., 144
LeVeque, Leslie L., 43, 57
LeVeque Tower, 40, *66-67*, 68, 71, *74*, 78,
    84, 142
Levier, Tony, 188

Lexington, 270
Leyshon, Mike, 199
Life Flight helicopter, 130, *134*
Life Science Theater, 167
Limited, The, *88*, 95, 158, *185*, 225
Lincoln, Abraham, 27, 28, 29, 32, 199;
    funeral, *29*
Lincoln, Murray D., 80, 85, 231, 233
Lincoln Theatre, 155
Lincoln Village, 231, 233
Lindbergh, Charles, 176, 177, 180, 189
Lindbergh, Mary Ellen, 189
Linden, 188
Little Brown Jug Race, 269
Little Theatre Off Broadway, 155
"Live New Breed," 153
Lloyd, William B., 26
Lockbourne, 233
Lockbourne Air Force Base, 21, 41, 184
Loews and United Artists Ohio Theatre,
    142
London Industries, 90
Lost City of Atlantis, 156
Lou Berliner Sports complex, 240, *243*
Luna, Armando, *148*
Lustron Corporation, 87
Lutheran Church, 110

McCall, Robert T., 120, 125
McConnell, John, 90
McCracken, Donald W., 189
McCusker, Don, 189
McDonald, 95
McDonnell Douglas, *86, 87,* 178
McDowell, James, 20
McDowell, Lucy, 20
McFall, John, 147
McIntosh, Ladd, 153
McKinley, William, 212
McKinsey & Company, 57
McLaughlin, Alexander, 24
McPherson Chemical Laboratory, 63
McPherson, William 63
Mad River Mountain, 271
Madden, John, 90
Manhattan Project, 51
Mansfield, 270
Mansion House Hotel, 123
Marble Cliff, 235
Market Exchange Branch, 98
Marshall Field's, 95
Martin Luther King Jr. Center for the Per-
    forming and Cultural Arts, 142, 153,
    154, 155, 165, 240
Martin Luther King Jr. Institute for the
    Arts, 154, 155
Martin Luther King Jr. Memorial Tribute
    Committee, 155
Martin, William, 26
Marysville, 78, 87, 194
Masonic Lodge, 31
Matesich, Mary Andrew, 115
Matthews, Jr., Tom, 101
Medex facility, *60*
Mei Foo Sun Chuen building, 95
Memorial Hall, 34, 166
Memorial Tournament, 192, 208, 210,
    267, 269
Meroy Hospital, 133
Mershon Auditorium, 158
Metro Parks, 252, 256, 259, 261
Metropolitan Statistical Area, 80, 87, 101
Meyer, Armin H., 124
Miami University, 218

Mid-Ohio Sports Car Course, 270
Mid-West International Band and Orches-
    tra Clinic, 153
Midland Building, 78, *78*, 84
Midland Mutual Life Insurance Company,
    85
Migration And Refugees Service of the
    United States Catholic Conference,
    224
Military installations, 21, 29, 184, 186-187
Miller, B. Lee, 188-189, *189*
Miller, Bonnie, 188
Miller, Marge, 188
Miller's Flying School, 188
Minerva Park, 34, 42, 43
Minority Business Development Center,
    101
"Miracle Mile," 92, 93
Mobil Building, 95
Mock, Jerrie, 184
Mohler, Chris, *163*
Monaghan, George, *158*
Montgomery Ward Plaza, 95
Moddy, Tom, 124, 194
Morgan, John Hunt, 29
Morse Ronel, 95
Motorist Building, 78, 84
Motorists Mutual Insurance Company, 85
Mound Builders, 18
Mount Carmel Medical Center, 127, *131*
Muirfield Golf Course, 192, 208, 210, 233,
    267, 269, 271
Muirfield Village, 233
Municipal Court Building, 75, 78
"Music in the Air" concerts, *149, 243*

National Academy of Art, 120
National Air And Space Museum, 120,
    125, 184
National Historic Landmark, 142
National Hotel, 26
National Limited, 199
National Recovery Act (NRA), 40, 41
National Register of Historic Places, 31,
    142, 198, 222
National Zoo, 184
Nationwide II, 75, *76*, 84
Nationwide III, 75, 84
Nationwide Complex, 71, 75
Nationwide Insurance, 71, 80, 85
Naval Air Test Center, 189
Navy Blue Angels, 189
Neal, Jeanette, 21
Neal, Robert, 21
Neil Armstrong Air & Space Museum, 31
Neil House, 26
Nelson, Ricky, 157
Nestle Dairy Systems, 78
New Albany, 188, 194, 233
New Deal, 41
New Horizons, 138
New Rome, 233
Nguyen family, 224-225
"Nickel Days," 43
Nicklaus, Jack, 208, *211*, 267, 269, 271
Nissen Chemical Industry Company Ltd.,
    90
Norfolk and Western Railroad, 200
North American Aviation, 87, 174, 178,
    180, 181, 188, 189
North American Brass Band Association,
    153
North Area Mental Health Emergency Ser-
    vices, 138

North High Street Lanes, 57
North Linden, 231
North Side Business Association, 43
Noyes, Sr., William A., 63

Obetz, 233
Oceana Naval Air Station, 187
Office of Strategic Services, 63
O. Henry, 34
Ohio Agricultural Research and Development Center, 56, 113
Ohio Agriculture and Mechanical College, 32, *33*, 113. *See also* Ohio State University
Ohio Air National Guard, 186
Ohio Bell Building, 84
Ohio Board of Regents, 115
Ohio Bureau of Workers Compensation, 75
Ohio Center, 71, 157
Ohio City, 99
Ohio Department of Administrative Services, 99
Ohio Department of Aging, 245
Ohio Department of Agriculture, 99
Ohio Department of Highway Safety, 99
Ohio Department of Natural Resources, 65
Ohio Department of Taxation, 225
Ohio Department of Transportation, 99, 192
Ohio Dominican College, 115, *117*
Ohio Expositions Center, 92, 99, 165, 271, 273
Ohio Farm Bureau Federation, 80
Ohio General Assembly, 30, 55, 218
Ohio Historic Preservation Office, 31
Ohio Historical Society, 30-31, 36, 165, 198
Ohio History of Flight Museum, 167, 182
Ohio Hospital Association, The, 34
Ohio Industrial Commission, 75
Ohio Institute of Technology, 120
Ohio Kidney and Gall Stone Center, 127
Ohio National Bank, 95, 98
Ohio Penitentiary, 29, 32, 34
Ohio's Center of Science and Industry (COSI), 34, 166-167, *170*
Ohio Stadium, 208, 266
Ohio State Fair, 271, *272-273*; boxing championship,208
Ohio State House, *3*, 22, *24*, 25-26, *27*, 28, 29, 30, 68, *71*, 99, *99*
Ohio State Journal, 26
Ohio State University, The, 32, *33*, 36, 40, 41, 42, 46, 51, 55, *55*, 56, *56*, 59, 63, 65, 99, 101, 113, *113*, 114, *114*, 125, 127, 144, 147, 153, 154, 155, 158, 171, 184, 186, 192, 208, 210, 212, 225, 261; Golf Club, 271; Research Foundation, 56; sports, 264, *265*, 266, 269
Ohio Supercomputer Center, 55
Ohio Technical College, 120
Ohio Theatre, *140-141*, 142, *143*, 144
Ohio Trust Company, 98
Ohio University, 138, 218
Ohio Village, 30-31, *30-31*, 165-166, *168-169*
Ohio Waisenfreund, 121
Ohio Wesleyan University, 123, 126, 127, 155; Telescope, *62*
Ohio Youth Commission, 208
Oktoberfest, 222, *226-227*
Old Blind School, 99

O'Leary, Michael, 57
Olentangy-Lower Scioto Bikeway, 270
Olentangy Park, 34, 42-43
Olentangy Park Theatre, 42
Olentangy River, 42, 99, 194, 252
Olentangy Villa, 42
Olentangy Village, 43
Olesen, Douglas E., 51, 55
Olympics, 40, 124, 125, 208, 266, 267
Onassis, Aristotle, 189
One Columbus Tower, *66-67*, 71, *75*, 84
160th Air Refueling Group, 186-187
One Nationwide Plaza, 71, 84
One Riverside Plaza, 75, 84
Online Computer Library Center, Inc., 46, 48
Opera/Columbus, 144
Operation Desert Storm, 21, 186-187
O'Shaughnessy Dam, 271
Osteopathic Medical College, 138
OSU Ice Rink, 269
Otterbein College, 115, *116-117*, 124, 155, 261
Outerbelt, 194, *196*, 197, 252, 269
Owens, Jesse, 40, 125, *125*

Pacific Northwest Laboratories, 51
Page, Jerry, 208
Palace Theatre, 71, 142, 144
Palais de Versailles, 142
Pallone, Dave, 156-157
Pallone, Jed, 156-157
Paramount Pictures, 124
Parkview Amusement Company, 43
Patriots Point Naval and Maritime Museum, 189
Patterson, Austin M., 63
Paul Laurence Dunbar Cultural Arts Center, 154-155
Paul, Ronald S., 51
PDQ Aviation, *179*, 182
Peale, Norman Vincent, 124
Pearce, James, 189
Pearl Alley, 222
Pelzer Brothers, 22
Penney, J.C., 92, 95
Pennsylvania and B&O Railroad, 176
Pennsylvania Railroad, 174, 176, 180, 200
Pennsylvania Station, 177, 180
Peoples Development Company, 231, 233
Peppe, Mike, 266
Perkins, Susan Yvonne, 218, *222*
PGA Memorial Tournament, 208, 210, 267, 269
Pham, Hoang Tam, 225
Pham, Hoang Thy, 225
Pharoah's Valley of the Nile, 156
Physicians Insurance Company of Ohio, 85
Piambino, Gianeario, 23
Pickerington Ponds, 259
"Picnic with the Pops" series, 59, 144, *149*
Pier Ballroom, 43
Pierce, Elijah, 162, 165, 212, 24
Players Theatre Columbus, *143*, 153, *154*, 171
Plaza Restaurant, *157*
Polaris Centers of Commerce, 235
Pontifical College Josephinum, 22, 110, 121, *121,122*, 123, 124
Port Columbus International Airport, 23, 41, 86, 87, 167, *172-173*, 174, *175*, *176*, 176-178, *177, 178, 179*, 180, 181, *181*, 182-184, 187, 188, 189, 233

Port Columbus Naval Air Station, 41
Porter, William Sydney, 34
Portsmouth, 271
Post Office building, 217
Pottenger, Frances M., 124
Powell, 225
Prairie Township, 231
Preservation Pool Hall, 156
Pro Musica Chamber Orchestra, 147
Professional Football Hall of Fame, 208
Prohibition, 36
P.W. Huntington And Company, 98, *100*
Pythian Theatre, 154, 155

Rahal, Bobby, 270
Railroads, 198-200, 204
Rax Restaurants, Inc., 92
Raydata Corporation, 64
Reality Theatre, 155
Red Roof Inns, Inc., 217
Red, White, And Boom celebration, *213*
Reilly, Joy, 171
Reliance Electric Company, 65
Representatives Hall, 25
Reserve Naval Mobile Construction Battalion Twenty, 187
Reynoldsburg, 89, 95, 99, 184, 233
Rhodes, James A., 217-218
Rickenbacker Air Force Base, 21, 41
Rickenbacker Air/Industrial Park, 184, *184*, 186-187,194
Rickenbacker Air National Guard Base, 41, 184
Rickenbacker, Edward Vernon, 21, 32, *36*, 184, 208, 212
Rickenbacker Port Authority, 184
Rickey, Branch, 123, 124
Riffe Center for Government and the Arts, 68, *70*, 84,99, 142, *143*, 147, 153, *153*, 171
Rifee, Jr., Vern, 153
"Right From The Start" project, 106
Ringside Cafe, 162
Riverfront Amphitheatre, *149*, 155
Riverside Methodist Hospitals, 127, *127*
Riverside Neurological Rehabilitation Center, 127
Riverside Regional Cancer Institute, 127
RNAV equipment, 64
Robinson, Jackie, 123, 124
Rockwell International Corporation, 87, 178, 181, 188
Roman Catholic Diocese of Columbus, 106-107
Roman, Walter, 65
Ronald McDonald House, 138
Roosevelt, Theodore, 124
Rosenthal Stock Company, 43
Rosie O' Grady's, 156
Rosser, Ronald E., 212
Russell, Timothy, 147
Russell, William E., 144, 147
Ryan, Paul, 57
Ryan Stormscope, 57

Saigon Police Force, 224
Saint Ann's hospital, 133
St. Anthony Medical Center, 130, *132*, 133
Saint Anthony Mercy Hospital, 133
Saint-Gaudens, Augustus, 22
St. John Arena, 266, *266*
St. John, Lynn W., 266
St. Louis Exposition, 42

Saint Michael School, 224
St. Patrick's Church, 32
Sanese, Maggie, 30, 31
Sanda Maria, 23
Sarsaparilla Rock Concerts, 157
Save the Ohio Theatre Committee, 142
Scaggs, Ricky, 157
Schafer, Laurel Lea, 218
Schiller, Johann Christoph Friedrich von, 222
Schiller Park, 32, *155*, 222, 223
Schrock Lake, 256
Schuller Company, 225
Schumacher Gallery, 162
Schweibert, Ernest, 124-125
Scioto Country Club, 271
Scioto Downs, 194, 269, *269*
Scioto Park, 20 .
Scioto River, *6-7*, 20, 23, 24, 36, 78, 99, 194, *213*, *218-219*, *220-221*, *246-247*, *248*, 271, *271*
Scioto River Road, 20
Scioto Superfest, *218-219*, *220-221*
Scott, Don, 192
Scott, Larry R., 197
Screamin' Willies, 156-157
SeaBees, 187
Seattle Research Center, 51
Sensenbrenner, M.E. "Jack," 23, 41, 199, 217, 218
Sensenbrenner Park, 13, 198, *198*, 200, *200*
Sessions And Company, 98
Sharon Woods Metro Park, *4-5*, 194, 252,*254-255*, 256, 261
Shawnee Hills, *237*
Shedd Theatre, 171
Shepard, Minerva, 43
Shepardson College, 123
Sheridan, Philip P., 28
Sherman, William T., 28
Short North, 155, 162, *162*, 222-223, *228*, 264
Shuck, John, 124
Siciliani, Alessandro, 144
Siciliani, Francesco, 144
Sir Laffalot's, 157
Sisters Chicken & Biscuits, 92
Skelton, Red, 106
S. Lazarus' Sons & Company, *33*
Slate Run Metro Park And Historical Farm, 259, *259*
Small Business Innovator Award, 64
Smith, George C., 198
Smithsonian Institution, 120, 184
Snapps, 92
SnoPake, 57
Snow Trails, 271
Snyder, Larry, 266
Society Bank, 98
Solani, Alfred, 23
South High School, 41, 186
South Side, 32
Southern Theatre, 142, *142*
Spanish-American War, 21, 32
Species Survival Plans, 250
Spirit of Columbus, 184
Spirit of St. Louis train, 199
Spring Hollow Outdoor Education Center, 261
S.S. Davis Youth Complex for the Performing Arts, *155*, 240
SSP Programs, 250
Standard Oil, 57
Stanley, Sylvester, 199

Stanton, Edwin, 28
Stanton, Frank, 124
Starling, Lyne, 20, *20,* 24
Starling, Sarah, 20
Stassen, Harold, 22
State Auto Mutual Insurance, 85
State Bank of Ohio, 98
State Highway Patrol, 99, 192
State House, *3,* 22, *24,* 25-26, *27,* 28, 29,
    30, 68, *71,* 99, *99*
State House Square, 68
State Office Tower, 40, 99, 101
State Office Tower II, 68
Stearn, Max, 43
Steel industry, *87,* 90
Strategic Air Command, 21, 41, 125, 186,
    212
Studio Theatres, 153
Success IMPACT, 109
Sullivant Avenue Airport, 178, 183, 188
Sullivant, Lucas, 20
Sumitomo Corporation of America, 90
Syracuse University, 180

TACAN, 64
Tactical Air Command, 186
"Technology Corridor," 64
Thatcher, Rick, 57
"These Are My Jewels" statue, 28
Third Street School, 106
Thomas, B.D., 51
Thomas, R. David, 90, 92
Thomas, Wendy, 90, 92
Thoreau Lake, 256, 257
30lst Bombardment Wing, 21
Three Nationwide Plaza, 75, 84
Three R Technologies, Inc., 65
Thurber, James Grover, 32, 165, 166, *212,*
    223; Thurber home, *166,* 212
Thurston, Howard, 212
Tibbets, Paul W., 183
Town & Country Shopping Center, 92, *93*
Townley, Mary Catherine Campbell, 218
Tracy, Spencer, 188
Trans World Airlines, *174,* 176
Transcontinental Air Transport, Inc., 174,
    176, 177
Travolta, John, 156
Trott, Dick, 158
Truculent Turtle, 183-184
Trueman, James R., 217
True-Sports Auto Racing team, 217
Truman, Bess, 199
Truman, Harry S, 184, 199
Turner, Robert M., 42
Turner, Roscoe, 180
Two Nationwide Plaza, 75, *76,* 84
Tyson, Mike, *210*

Underwater Sound Laboratories, 64
Union Arch, 198, *198,* 199, 200, *200*
Union Depot Arcade, 198-199
Union Depot Company, 199
Union Station, 29, 198-199, 200
United Methodist Church, 115
United States Courthouse, *25,* 26
United States Department of Agriculture,
    245
United States Department of the Interior,
    31, 198
United States Navy Flight School, 174,
    180
United States Navy Test Pilot School, 174,
    180
United States Treasury Department, 48
Universal Guaranty Life, 85
Universal Product Code, 48, 57
University Hospitals, 56, 127
Upham Hall, 127
Upper Arlington, 192, 194, 235, *238-239,*
    265
Upper Arlington High School, 208, 210
Urban League, 214
Urban Renewal Department, 222
USAir, *176,* 178

Valley Dale, 36
Veterans Memorial Building, 166
Victoria's Secret stores, 95
Victorian Village, 223, 264
Vietnam Mutual Assistance Association,
    225
Vietnam War, 21, 178, 186, 214, 224
Villa Milano Party Center, 155
Villages At Rocky Fork, 233
Virginia Military District, 20
Vo family, 225
Vorys, John, 23

Wagons-Lit Travel USA, 78
Walden Waterfowl Refuge, 256, 257
Washington Institute of Foreign Affairs,
    124
Waterford Tower, 78, 84
Watkins Ronel, 197
Webb, Lucy, 123, 124
Weekend College, 115
Weigel Hall, 144, 147, 158
Wendy's International, Inc., *90,* 92
Wenzell, Sr., Richard M., 189
West High School, 212
Western Airways, 177
Western Reserve, 28
Westerville, 115, 117, 133, 233, 256, 261
Westerville Civic Symphony, 115
Westerville Family Practice Center, *136*
Westerville Music And Arts Festival, 115
Westgate Park, 231

Wexner Center for the Arts, 142, 158, *159*
Wexner Institute for Pediatric Research,
    135, 138
Wexner, Leslie H., 89, 95, 158
Whetstone Park, *248-249*
Whingway Pooshies ("Big Cat"), 18
White Castle Systems, Inc., 90, 92
White, George, 22
Whitehall, 233

W.H. Mullins Company, 22
Wilberforce College, 212
William E. Clapp Laboratories, 51
William Green building, 75, 84, 99
Williams, Clyde E., 51
Williams, Joe, 147
Willis, Bill, 208
Wilson, Nancy, 212
Wilson, Phillip, 106
Wolf, Lawrence, 182
Wolfe Brothers Shoe Company, 214, 217
Wolfe, Harry Preston, 98, 214, 217
Wolfe, Robert Frederick, 98, 214, 217
World Columbian Exposition, 22
World War I, 21, 36, 199, 208, 212
World War II, 21, 29, 40-41, 51, 63, 86,
    87, 120, 124, 125,178, 184, 186, 188-
    189, 192, 199, 200, 208, 212
Worthington, 24, 194, *206-207,* 224, 233,
    252
Worthington Community Theatre, 155
Worthington Industries, Inc., *87,* 90, 192
Worthington Square, *93*
Worthington, Thomas, 26
WPA projects, 40
WRFD Radio station, 71
Wyandot Lake Amusement And Water
    Park, 43
Wyandotte Building, 34, *35,* 71, *73,* 84,
    198
Wyandotte Office Building Company, 71
Wyandotte Savings & Loan Company, 71
Xerox Corporation, 51, 57

Yeager, Chuck, 188
YMCA, *32,* 119
Young Ladies Institute, 123
Youth Theatre Columbus, 153

Zanesville, 24, 194
Zengara, Liz, *148*
Zimmer, Bob, 23
Zivili dance troupe, *152*
Zoltan Kodaly Pecdagogical Institute of
    Music, 113
Zoo Park, 43